THE POP CULTURE ZONE

Writing Critically About Popular Culture

SECOND EDITION

THE POP CULTURE ZONE

Writing Critically About Popular Culture

Allison D. Smith • Trixie G. Smith

SECOND EDITION

CENGAGE
Learning®

Australia • Brazil • Japan • Korea • Mexico • Singapore • Spain • United Kingdom • United States

CENGAGE
Learning®

The Pop Culture Zone: Writing Critically About Popular Culture, Second Edition
Allison D. Smith, Trixie G. Smith

Product Director: Monica Eckman

Product Manager: Kate Derrick

Content Developer: Laurie Dobson

Content Coordinator: Danielle Warchol

Media Developer: Cara Douglass-Graff

Marketing Manager: Lydia LeStar

Content Project Manager: Dan Saabye

Art Director: Marissa Falco

Manufacturing Planner: Betsy Donaghey

Rights Acquisition Specialist: Ann Hoffman

Production Service: S4 Carlisle

Text Designer: Riezebos Holzbaur Group

Cover Designer: Roycroft Design

For product information and technology assistance, contact us at **Cengage Learning Customer & Sales Support, 1-800-354-9706**

For permission to use material from this text or product, submit all requests online at **www.cengage.com/permissions**. Further permissions questions can be emailed to **permissionrequest@cengage.com**.

Library of Congress Control Number: 2013937751

ISBN-13: 978-0-840-02843-3

ISBN-10: 0-840-02843-1

Cengage Learning
200 First Stamford Place, 4th Floor
Stamford, CT 06902
USA

Cengage Learning is a leading provider of customized learning solutions with office locations around the globe, including Singapore, the United Kingdom, Australia, Mexico, Brazil and Japan. Locate your local office at **international.cengage.com/region**.

Cengage Learning products are represented in Canada by Nelson Education, Ltd.

For your course and learning solutions, visit **www.cengage.com**.

Purchase any of our products at your local college store or at our preferred online store **www.cengagebrain.com**.

Instructors: Please visit **login.cengage.com** and log in to access instructor-specific resources.

Printed in the United States of America
1 2 3 4 5 6 7 17 16 15 14 13

CONTENTS

*indicates new reading

CHAPTER 4
reading in the pop culture zone 69

*indicates new reading

CHAPTER 5
researching in the pop culture zone 87

PART II
THE CONTENT ZONE

....

CHAPTER 6
writing about advertisements 115

*indicates new reading

*indicates new reading

CHAPTER 9
writing about music 329

*indicates new reading

CHAPTER 10
writing about television 407

*indicates new reading

RHETORICAL CONTENTS

*indicates new reading

SYNTHESIS

VISUAL

*indicates new reading

THEMATIC CONTENTS

*indicates new reading

*indicates new reading

EDUCATION

*indicates new reading

ENVIRONMENT/LOCATION

FAITH

GENDER AND SEXUALITY

*indicates new reading

GOVERNMENT/POLITICS

HEALTH/PSYCHOLOGY

HUMOR/SATIRE

*indicates new reading

IDENTITY

*indicates new reading

TECHNOLOGY/SCIENCE

*indicates new reading

PREFACE

WHY WE WROTE *THE POP CULTURE ZONE: WRITING CRITICALLY ABOUT POPULAR CULTURE*

As writing program administrators for a large freshman composition program, our own search for a first-year composition (FYC) textbook that utilized pop culture for its content proved frustrating. Although we found textbooks that included cultural or pop cultural readings, most did not include the focus on writing that we wanted for our first-year students or our new instructors or teaching assistants. We needed a textbook that used pop culture as a starting point—a point where teachers could meet their students, reflect on personal preferences, and review different aspects of pop culture together, and use all of this as a transition to the critical analysis and writing that we wanted our freshmen to do.

The Pop Culture Zone: Writing Critically About Popular Culture, second edition, focuses on pop culture because it is something that first-year college students know and can get passionate about. Pop culture is the bridge between their lives and the critical reading, thinking, and writing that are part of freshman composition. *The Pop Culture Zone* focuses on the relationship students have with pop culture and how this relationship can help them become more critical readers and writers. As Ernest Morrell, professor of education at Teacher's College, Columbia University, and subject of the Chapter 1 essay about how important popular culture is to achieving literacy, confirms, "What a teacher can do is capitalize on the special knowledge that her students do have to build bridges to the curriculum, and to the literacies students need."

ABOUT THE SECOND EDITION OF *THE POP CULTURE ZONE*

Often, FYC classes or their textbooks are so focused on questioning or mastering the content in a reader that the primary goal of improving writing is weakened or lost entirely. The overriding purpose of an FYC class is to improve student writing, and the textbooks, readings, and assignments used in such a course should all be aimed at reaching this goal. The reading selections and writing assignments in *The Pop Culture Zone* are included to get students thinking critically as they read, respond, analyze, and criticize the pop culture of today and yesterday. We use decades to organize the reading selections and to show readers that pop culture is not just what is happening now, but also includes the current connections we make to popular media of the past. The book's primary focus is getting students to think more critically about the pop culture world around them and to write critically about their thoughts and reactions.

The Contact Zone

We use pop culture as a contact zone where students can engage with pop culture elements, readings, and their classmates. The pop culture zone approach is influenced by Mary Louise Pratt's theoretical model of the contact zone, a place where students are encouraged to make choices, disagree with readings, and argue with their peers and others about interpretations and the importance of pop culture. *The Pop Culture Zone* meets students where they are and then asks them to do what they already do when they choose to watch a particular television show or read multiple books in the same pop literature series—critique, review, and then present supporting evidence. Students tell personal stories and explain their reactions, analyzing not only the pop culture element but also themselves and others as they do so.

Persuasion

Bringing pop culture into the composition classroom allows students not only to learn the discourse of academia: It also allows them to use the familiar forms of persuasion that are often already present in student discourse as the bridge to the critical reasoning and writing that occur in a college writing course. Students learn to listen to viewpoints that differ from their own, summarize their views effectively, compare and contrast, and present their ideas in a way that creates a continuing conversation of ideas.

The Reading Zone

Our text provides sections called The Reading Zone, where students meet ideas through reading and connect those ideas to their own culture, and *Contemplations* and *Collaborations in The Pop Culture Zone*, where students connect their ideas with others inside and outside the class through cooperative and collaborative discussions and writing assignments. These zones are needed to decode texts, connect the author culture to the student culture, and provide opportunities for discussion that lead to collaborative and/or individual writing. The readings used can trigger warm reflections or heated debates on issues related to student lives and their identities, including topics related to power, gender, sexuality, race, and culture. Students and instructors can also bring their own theories and methods of analysis to the various texts and genres of writing. *The Pop Culture Zone* uses an approach that focuses more on a critical analysis of the self in relation to popular culture rather than just an analysis of pop culture or culture itself. This critical analysis provides the pedagogical apparatus for students to write review, reflection or response, analysis, and synthesis essays.

NEW TO THIS EDITION

Thirty-seven New Readings. In Chapter 8, Writing About Social Networks, students can compare Facebook and MySpace while examining the role of online games. The ever-popular *Glee* makes two appearances (in Chapter 9, Writing About Music, and Chapter 10, Writing About Television) as we consider its role in the popularity of school choirs as well as the portrayal of gay teens on TV. In Chapter 10, students can also read about a range of programming from *Hoarders*, to *SNL*, to the popularity of black sitcoms in the 1980s and 1990s. New reviews include Michael Jackson (Chapter 9), venues for up-and-coming country artists (Chapter 9), and Amazon sales strategies for Kindles (Chapter 6, Writing About Advertisements). Other new readings include "Stupid Girls" by Pink (Chapter 9), a look at advertising through A&E's *Mad Men*, (Chapter 6), and a comparison of the two *Star Wars* trilogies (Chapter 7, Writing About Film).

Readings of Varying Lengths. We have introduced essays of varying lengths, as well as styles, throughout each chapter to accommodate different reading requirements and assignments, and to illustrate the possibilities for student writing.

New Reading Chapter. To help students read more complex works, a new critical reading chapter has been added: Chapter 4, Reading in The Pop Culture Zone. This new chapter includes sections and strategies on helping students to become more critical readers, including advice on how to annotate reading selections effectively, summarize important information, and analyze reading selections. A highlight of the new chapter is a section on analyzing visuals with strategies on how to analyze design, content, context, audience, and purpose.

Multimodal Composition. *The Pop Culture Zone*, second edition, includes both visual essays and multimodal writing assignments for each chapter, from list essays to mapping to blogs. In addition, the new Chapter 4, Reading in The Pop Culture Zone, includes a section on analyzing visuals.

Revised Chapter 8. The most popular readings and topics from the previous Chapter 6, Writing About Groups, Spaces, and Places, and Chapter 9, Writing About Sports and Leisure, are paired with new readings on social networks to create a new chapter—Writing About Social Networks—which allows students and instructors to think more strategically about the role of networks in forming and/or claiming identities in and through popular culture.

Stump Your Instructor. The last question in each chapter-opening quiz is now a write-your-own "Stump Your Teacher" question to allow for more instructor–student engagement.

Decades Readings. The decades have now been combined in the following way: the 1970s and 1980s, the 1990s and 2000s, and the 2010s.

New Images. More than 30 new images have been added throughout.

New Thematic TOC Topic. A new topic, Gender and Sexuality, has been added to the Thematic TOC

Briefer Text. The second edition has been edited to allow for more efficient classroom use.

FEATURES OF THE BOOK

The Parts

The Pop Culture Zone is divided into two main parts: Part I: Introduction to Writing About Popular Culture, and Part II: The Content Zone. As the opener for Part I, Chapter 1, The Pop Culture Zone, gives an overview of the text's features. Chapter 2, Defining Popular Culture, introduces students to the broad scope of popular culture. Chapter 3, Writing in The Pop Culture Zone, provides a strong writing apparatus, the equivalent of which is normally not found in other popular culture readers. Newly added to the book, Chapter 4, Reading in The Pop Culture Zone, focuses on strategies to help students be more critical readers, including advice on how to annotate reading selections effectively, summarize important information, and analyze reading selections. A highlight of the new chapter is a section on analyzing visuals with strategies on how to analyze design, content, context, audience, and purpose. Part I concludes with Chapter 5, Researching in The Pop Culture Zone, an overview of researching strategies and documentation styles, especially in connection to popular culture.

Part II consists of five content chapters devoted to a variety of media or themes encountered in popular culture, including advertisements, film, social networking, music, and television. The revised Chapter 8, Writing About Social Networking, allows students to see how their world and worldview are affected by the social networks, including those based in technology, to which they belong. As experienced teachers, we recognize that other experienced instructors may not find it necessary to use the writing or research chapters in their courses, but new teachers may appreciate the support these chapters provide. Experienced teachers can also expand and modify these chapters to use with their beginning writers.

The Chapters

Each chapter begins with a trivia quiz to get students thinking and talking about the pop culture unit coming up. These informal quizzes are provided as conversation starters to the chapter. Newly added is the *Stump Your Instructor* question that students will collaborate on and then engage with popular culture with their instructor. Following the quiz, each content chapter provides a description of what writing in this field or this medium looks like, why people write about it or may want to, and then discusses how to write about this medium or theme, including presentations of related content and techniques. For example, the chapter on film introduces students to concepts and terms such as "mise-en-scène," "cinematography," and "character." This introductory section in each chapter also includes a sample annotated essay, which calls attention to writing and analysis techniques, followed by about ten other readings, including a student essay, organized into three sections: the 1970 and 1980s, the 1990 and 2000s, and the 2010s.

The reading selections in each chapter are preceded by *Engaging with Topics*, prereading questions designed to stimulate student thinking and conversation before reading the selections. *The Reading Zone*, a collection of essay selections, follows the prereading questions. Each of the individual essays is preceded by *Considering Ideas*— questions that can be used for journaling, blogging, or in-class writing. Each is followed by *Decoding the Text* and *Connecting to Your Culture* questions, which ask students to analyze the text and then connect the ideas from the reading selection to their own lives. At the end of The Reading Zone, questions given in the sections entitled *Contemplation in The Pop Culture Zone* and *Collaboration in The Pop Culture Zone* are used to stimulate critical thinking and subsequent discussion and writing. These chapters close with several wide-ranging essay ideas in the section *Start Writing About* (the pop culture element).

Range of Readings

We include a wide range of selected readings in each chapter gathered from a variety of disciplines, including student essays, online film or music reviews, newspaper articles and blogs, and more sophisticated analysis and synthesis essays from academic journals. Each chapter includes student and professional writers and also includes examples of review, reflection or response, analysis, and synthesis essays. The readings were selected to encompass multiple viewpoints and perspectives: liberal and conservative, biased and unbiased, pro and con. This second edition includes essays of varying lengths and styles throughout each chapter to accommodate different reading requirements and assignments and to illustrate the possibilities for student writing.

The Case Studies

In content chapters, some readings are grouped together in case studies, which provide a variety of perspectives on smaller topics related to the same overall theme. Having your students read the essays as a case study encourages them to investigate complex, multifaceted issues and to share their thoughts with others in class and in writing.

Student Writers *Are* Writers

In an effort to empower and encourage students, we treat student writers in our text equally to professional writers by providing the same apparatus for both student and professional readings. Student essays are sometimes annotated as samples or offered as regular reading selections.

Visuals

Because pop culture often includes visual rather than just written text, we include more than eighty-five photos and visuals throughout our text. In Chapter 4, Reading in The Pop Culture Zone, a new section includes guidance for students in how to analyze visuals. Some reading selections are primarily visual essays, including the four-color case study of Coca-Cola images in the advertising chapter (see the color insert). In addition, we also offer visual essays as alternative assignments for students to create.

Assistance in the Writing and Research Process

The Pop Culture Zone, second edition, includes a writing instruction apparatus both in Chapter 3, Writing in The Pop Culture Zone, and also at the beginning of each content chapter. This assistance is often missing from pop culture readers, and we are excited to present such a strong writing apparatus in a pop culture reader. *The Pop Culture Zone* also includes a sample annotated essay for each content area—a feature unique to this market—to help students see what makes for good organization or good detail when pop culture is the subject. In Chapter 5, Researching in The Pop Culture Zone, we provide guidelines for connecting research around specific pop culture media and themes—another feature unique to this market. The book itself uses MLA documentation throughout; however, both MLA and APA documentation styles are introduced, including many examples of popular culture documentation often left out of basic overviews.

Test Your Pop Culture IQ

As a form of metacognitive blueprinting, we provide a short pop culture quiz at the beginning of each chapter to remind students how much they do (or do not) know about the content area. The quizzes are an amusing way to jump-start students' critical thinking, help them make connections to pop culture, and create the cognitive dissonance that can lead to active engagement and learning. Not meant to be graded, the trivia quizzes may be used by students and teachers as a fun way to start discussing the medium or theme. Additional ideas for using the quizzes are available in the online Instructor's Manual.

Grappling with Ideas

Each chapter includes *Grappling with Ideas* boxes that ask students to think critically about their own experiences with either the pop culture element or their culture. Teachers and students can use these questions as triggers for student discussion, journal writing, blogging, or other low-risk class assignments.

Alternative Tables of Contents

We recognize that teachers sometimes want to take an alternative approach when using pop culture reading selections, so we provide both a rhetorical and a thematic table of contents at the front of the text to help you plan possible alternative teaching units using themes or rhetorical strategies. Since some of the writing assignments ask for particular genres, such as reviews or analysis essays, using the rhetorical table of contents, in particular, is a quick way to share examples with students.

ANCILLARIES

Online Instructor's Manual

Especially useful for new teachers, the online Instructor's Manual (IM) provides insights into how to use particular essays and general pop culture topics effectively as content. The IM also provides reading questions, alternative prewriting and discussion topics, and additional writing assignments. A bibliography of resources on teaching pop culture, writing, and the contact zone is also provided. The Instructor's Manual can be found on the password-protected companion site. The second edition has been revised by Holly Hamby.

Teaching in The Pop Culture Zone: Using Popular Culture in the Composition Classroom, edited by Allison D. Smith, Trixie G. Smith, and Rebecca Bobbitt

A Cengage Learning professional development textbook that offers insights and strategies about using pop culture in the writing classroom is also available. The edited volume includes essays by instructors, who share details of their most effective class ideas and writing assignments.

ACKNOWLEDGMENTS

From all of us, we say thank you to the people who helped us at various times throughout this second edition writing project. We cannot say enough, but many thanks to all of you: Dianna Baldwin, Andy Coomes, Matt Cox, English 6560/7560 students, English 6570/7570 students, Mark Francisco, Darlene Fults, the Graduate College at MTSU, Emily James, Beth Keller, Daisy Levy, Madhu Narayan, Tom Strawman, Agapi Theodorou, Holly Tipton Hamby, Brad Walker, Shari Wolke, Shayna Wood, The Writing Center at MSU. We also want to thank Stacia Watkins for her contribution to the first edition of this book.

We also give our utmost thanks to all those who assisted us in the editorial, permissions, production, and marketing process: Kate Derrick, product manager; Leslie Taggart, senior content developer; Laurie Dobson, content developer; Dan Saabye, content project manager; Lydia Lestar, market development manager; Marissa Falco, art director; Danielle Warchol, content coordinator; Ann Hoffman, rights acquisition specialist; Susan Buschhorn, permissions project manager, PreMediaGlobal; Kristine Janssens, text permissions project manager, Cenveo.

First, thank you to Trixie for her support and patience as we progressed through the writing and revision of this book. It took many emails, meetings, trips, discussions, and jokes to get to the final product, and I could not think of anyone else with whom I would have wanted to work on this pop culture project. An additional thank-you to Emily, Shayna, and Agapi for the time they each spent as my assistant—you all are first-rate support. Laurie Dobson, you helped keep us to deadline but also knew when we needed more time; thanks for your insight and never-ending support and patience. Each year, forty or so teaching assistants show me new ways to teach and new pop culture to investigate—thanks to all of them for keeping me up to speed. In fact, this book took flight as a project in my English 6560/7560 and 6570/7570 courses, and I thank all those freshman students and graduate teaching assistants who helped with the brainstorming. Also, thanks to Tom Strawman, and the Graduate College at MTSU for support both financially and academically; this kind of teaching scholarship cannot happen without administrators who understand the need for it. I also give kudos to Julie Myatt Barger, Jenny Rowan, Patricia Baines, Wes Houp, Caty Chapman, Laura Dubek, and Kristi Serrano; sharing administrative duties with you helped me do other things, so thanks for giving me that extra time each day. On the home front, I thank my family and friends for always being supportive of my need to do some writing or grading or watching films and television (for this book or not). I give special thanks to Lynne Murphy, one of my first academic writing partners, for always giving good advice and support. And finally, my part of this book is dedicated to my mother, Mary Anne Smith, who always encouraged me and my interests in reading, writing, and education.

—Allison

First and foremost, I would like to thank my coauthor, Allison, for the time, energy, and laughs that went into this project; I'm especially grateful for her willingness to think creatively and brainstorm new ideas, as well as to share books and DVDs. Likewise, I'm thankful for the invaluable help from a number of research assistants at both MTSU and MSU who helped locate articles and images, create and test quizzes and questions, and track down sources—Dianna Baldwin, Becky Bobbitt, Matt Cox, Beth Keller, Daisy Levy, Madhu Narayan, and Shari Wolke. There were also a number of students, TAs, and writing center consultants who willingly shared experiences, assignments, feedback, writings, and their love of pop culture to help make this text a reality; thank you. Likewise, thanks to my faculty writing group at MSU—Janice, Eva, Manuel, and Wen, and to the administrative staff at The Writing Center at MSU—Dianna Baldwin, Judy Easterbrook, and Cathy Vaughn; keeping the center running smoothly allowed me time to research, write, and edit. Finally, thanks to my friends and family members who have always believed in me and have always given their support for my various endeavors, most especially Mom and Jerry, Dad and Annie, Melanie, Teresa and family, and my niece Tabitha who was even willing to clean house and wash clothes during her summer vacation so I could attend one more book meeting, as well as watch endless episodes of *The Gilmore Girls* or Harry Potter movies.

—Trixie

And finally, thank you and much appreciation to our reviewers. Your insights and comments helped us refine both the readings and the framework, and we truly appreciate your time in assisting us with this project.

James Burns, *University of Delaware*

Pamela Childers, *The McCallie School*

Nicolette Constantino, *Tallahassee Community College*

Earnest Cox, *University of Arkansas at Little Rock*

Anthony Edgington, *University of Toledo*

William Etter, *Irvine Valley College*

Gareth Euridge, *Tallahassee Community College*

Africa Fine, *Palm Beach Community College*

Katheryn Giglio, *University of Central Florida*

Stephanie Harper, *Nashville Christian School*

Kevin Haworth, *Ohio University*

1

the pop culture zone

"When I say essay, I mean, essay. I do not mean a single word repeated a thousand times."

—From *The Breakfast Club*

UNIVERSAL/THE KOBAL COLLECTION/PICTURE DESK

1. Match the film title to the decade it was released in theaters.

1.	*Easy A*	a.	1990s
2.	*The Breakfast Club*	b.	2010s
3.	*Mean Girls*	c.	1980s
4.	*Scream*	d.	1970s
5.	*Grease*	e.	2000s

2. Match the fictional president to the actor who plays him or her.

1.	President Abraham Lincoln in *Abraham Lincoln: Vampire Hunter*	a.	Stephen Colbert
2.	President Hathaway in *Monsters vs. Aliens*	b.	Martin Sheen
3.	President Josiah "Jed" Bartlet in *The West Wing*	c.	Harry Shearer
4.	President Arnold Schwarzenegger in *The Simpsons Movie*	d.	Mel Brooks
5.	President Skroob in *Space Balls*	e.	Benjamin Walker

3. Place these children's educational series in order of when they began.

a. *Wishbone*
b. *Reading Rainbow*
c. *Sesame Street*
d. *The Magic School Bus*
e. *Schoolhouse Rock!*

DIMENSION FILMS/THE KOBAL COLLECTION

4. In which song do hordes of students chant the mantra, "We don't need no education/We don't need no thought control"?

a. "Jeremy," Pearl Jam
b. "School," New Edition
c. "Centerfold," the J. Geils Band
d. "Another Brick in the Wall," Pink Floyd
e. "School's Out," Alice Cooper

5. Which of these films is not based on a sketch from a television series?

a. *Wayne's World*
b. *Borat*
c. *The Simpsons*
d. *The Blues Brothers*
e. *Legally Blonde*

6. Which of these television series was first a film?

a. *Gilmore Girls*

b. *Saved by the Bell*

c. *Friday Night Lights*

d. *Veronica Mars*

e. *Beverly Hills, 90210*

LFI/PHOTOSHOT

7. In what year did companies begin advertising products in school systems via *Channel One News*?

a. 1988

b. 1990

c. 2001

d. 1997

e. 1982

8. Which actor played a teenager in *Even Stevens* and *Disturbia* and was also the voice for a penguin in *Surf's Up?*

a. Channing Tatum

b. Chad Michael Murray

c. Shia LaBeouf

d. Topher Grace

e. Ben Savage

9. Which of these TV series does not focus on teens in and out of school?

a. *Fame*

b. *Dawson's Creek*

c. *Degrassi High*

d. *The Vampire Diaries*

e. *Arrested Development*

10. **Stump Your Instructor:** In small groups, write a question here about education and pop culture (in advertising, films, music, social media, or television). Give your instructor five choices for answers.

a.

b.

c.

d.

e.

ANSWERS

1) 1. b. 2010s 2. c. 1980s 3. e. 2000s 4. a. 1990s 5. d. 1970s **2)** 1. e. Benjamin Walker 2. a. Stephen Colbert 3. b. Martin Sheen 4. c. Harry Shearer 5. d. Mel Brooks **3)** c. *Sesame Street* (1969) e. *Schoolhouse Rock!* (1973) b. *The Magic School Bus* (1983) d. *Reading Rainbow* (1994) a. *Wishbone* (1995) **4)** d. "Another Brick in the Wall," Pink Floyd **5)** e. *Legally Blonde* **6)** c. *Friday Night Lights* **7)** b. 1990 **8)** c. Shia LaBeouf **9)** e. *Arrested Development*

> "All objects, all phases of culture are alive. They have voices. They speak of their history and interrelatedness. And they are all talking at once!"
>
> —*Camille Paglia*
>
> "Like other secret lovers, many speak mockingly of popular culture to conceal their passion for it."
>
> —*Mason Cooley*

WHY WRITE ABOUT POP CULTURE?

Pop culture is your culture. It is what you watch, read, listen to, take part in, and enjoy each and every day of your life. Pop culture is *Glee* and *The Walking Dead, Hunger Games* and *A Game of Thrones, Bridesmaids* and *Bad Teacher*. It is Adele and Bruno Mars, Facebook and Grand Theft Auto, fandom sites about NASCAR, Harry Potter, and *Star Wars*. You can even make money exhibiting your knowledge of pop culture at local trivia contests held across the country. Pop culture crosses time and also changes with time since pop culture icons can disappear as quickly as they become popular, return with a wave of nostalgia, or stay around for decades. Pop culture is a powerful part of all our lives. You are an expert when it comes to your own pop culture; you know what appeals to you and what does not, and you know why. Because critical thinking and writing both rely on the writer's interest in and knowledge about the topic, pop culture is a surprisingly interesting and uncomplicated way to begin the journey of thinking, reading, and writing critically. Pop culture itself is the content that you will read about, observe, grapple with, discuss, and write about. In the pop culture zone, the term *content* is often synonymous with *text*, which refers to the different types of pop culture available for studying. Be sure to read Chapter 2 to help you figure out what pop culture means to you.

LUCASFILM/20TH CENTURY FOX/THE KOBAL COLLECTION/PICTURE DESK

The reading and writing assignments in *The Pop Culture Zone* revolve around how you read, respond to, analyze, and criticize pop culture, using what is familiar to you as a bridge to the writing you do in an academic setting. The questions related to the reading selections and the writing assignments ask you not only to critique pop culture but also to analyze and describe the relationship you and others around you have with it. Your knowledge of and familiarity with pop culture are at the center of everything you read and write about in *The Pop Culture Zone*, and this is why writing about pop culture can help you begin or expand your critical thinking, reading, and writing.

WHAT IS THE POP CULTURE ZONE?

The pop culture zone is where you can meet with other students in class or writers of the essays in the book to investigate, discuss, and sometimes argue about your personal responses to pop culture in a critical way. The pop culture zone approach is influenced by the contact zone theoretical model presented first by Professor Mary Louise Pratt in her talk at a Modern Language Association conference and published in *Profession* in 1991. The title of her talk, "Arts of the Contact Zone," refers to those places where students and instructors are free to "meet, clash, and grapple with each other, often in contexts of highly asymmetrical relations of power." (A highly asymmetrical relationship is one in which a person has more power due to social status or socioeconomic level.) Pratt proposes the contact zone model to emphasize the idea that members within any community are not always the same in their thinking or actions.

The Pop Culture Zone takes this model and applies it to the writing classroom, assuming that all students in the class community are enlightened and knowledgeable about the topic in question—pop culture—and that all members of the class can feel free to discuss, argue, and clash with others about their views in the pop culture zone. However, we are not trying to take away or change the enjoyment you have in your own pop culture choices, and we expect that you are also free to express your ideas in what Pratt calls the "safe house," a place where you can meet with others who share your opinions and experiences. Sometimes, you will find this safe house in collaborative projects or in the writing you do in class, but most often, you will find it where you have always found it, with your friends or others who enjoy and make the same pop culture choices you do.

WHAT ARE SOME OF THE BOOK'S SPECIAL FEATURES?

Test Your Pop Culture IQ

Each chapter begins with a trivia quiz that provides an opening to the contents of the chapter. Getting all the answers correct is not the goal; using the quizzes as a conversational starting point is. See how many of these pop culture questions you know, and compare your answers with your classmates or test your friends. There's even space with the Stump-Your-Instructor item for you to develop your own question(s) based on your interests in the content of the chapter. Once the conversation gets around to pop culture, see how many people become interested in what you are doing in your writing course.

Grappling with Ideas

Throughout the book, you will find Grappling with Ideas boxes that ask you to think more deeply about the information in that portion of the book or in a section that follows. Your instructor may ask you to answer these questions in a journal, a blog, or some other type of informal writing. Use these questions as a way to reflect on your own thoughts and opinions before you encounter the thoughts and opinions of your classmates, your instructor, or the essay authors in this book.

GRAPPLING
with Ideas

Be sure to take the pop culture IQ trivia quiz at the beginning of this chapter.

- How well did you do on the quiz?

- What answer(s) surprised you the most? The least? Why?

- What other television programs, films, songs, or advertising campaigns have focused on the educational experience?

GRAPPLING
with Ideas

Think about and share some of your favorite pop culture "texts."

- What types of advertisements make you want to purchase a product? Why?

- What are three of your favorite films? Why do you think these are your favorites?

- What are some of the groups or networks—formal or informal—that can call you a member? Where or how do these groups meet? Is there any special language you share with these groups?

- What are some of your favorite songs? Do these songs have anything in common?

- What kinds of television programs do you enjoy the most? Has your taste changed over your lifetime? If so, in what way?

Annotated Sample Essays

We provide annotated sample essays in each chapter to highlight features that combine to create interesting and effective writing. Many of these samples are written by students who use their personal interest in pop culture to help them create essays that fit into the chapter topic. Read these essays, check out the features that are highlighted, and use the essays as examples of how to write about pop culture.

The Reading Zone

The Reading Zone in each chapter is a place—a contact zone—where you meet new ideas through the readings and the reactions these readings generate in you and your classmates. The reading selections in The Reading Zone provide topics that you can investigate, discuss, or argue with; these selections also provide models for writing review, reflection or response, analysis, and synthesis essays—the types of essays that are later asked for in the writing assignment sections of the chapters.

Sometimes it is easier to be critical about the things that are not so close to us. *The Pop Culture Zone* is not focused on you picking apart the things you like; it also allows some distance for those who want or need it by looking at pop culture in other time periods. In addition, to appeal to all students and to show that pop culture is not just something that is happening now, but also can be what happened in an earlier time, the essay selections are organized into the last five decades. The chapters, which are organized into the 1970s–1980s, 1990s–2000s, and 2010s, include essays about pop culture items during that time period and/or essays that were written during that time. Being able to see how pop culture affected others will help you investigate how it may be affecting you as well. Since some pop culture icons never go out of style—Michael Jackson or Elvis, for instance—and some go out and come back over and over again—like Madonna or Paul McCartney—being able to place your pop culture in the overall continuum sometimes helps you take a backseat look at what is driving the pop culture of your time.

The Reading Zone is not a place where one idea, one analysis, or one argument is expected to be the only one. At the beginning of The Reading Zone, you are invited to see how much you know about the coming topics with the Engaging with Topics questions. Before you read the essays, you can share your ideas in Considering Ideas questions, which are provided to get you thinking about the topics and sharing your prereading ideas about the specific essay topics as you write in journals or blogs or have conversations with your classmates. After you read, you are asked to analyze the readings in Decoding the Text questions and to analyze and share reactions to readings in the Connecting to Your Culture questions. Throughout The Reading Zone section, you are invited to share your own pop culture favorites, as you contemplate and react to the pop culture mentioned in the reading selections.

After you and others grapple with, share, and possibly argue about your reactions and analyses of the readings and how they relate to your own culture, you are invited to connect the chapter readings or unite with your classmates in the Contemplations in The Pop Culture Zone sections. Here you investigate how the pop culture medium or type affects you personally, and you look for connections across readings in the chapter or across chapters or topics throughout the book. Possibly, you can figure out what topic you may be interested in writing about for your next essay. You can then use the Collaborations in The Pop Culture Zone questions to share your ideas with your classmates, looking for things you have or do not have in common and considering topics in preparation for writing. The Collaborations questions can also help you expand on your knowledge about class topics by helping you investigate websites, conduct interviews, or discuss class topics with your friends, family, or colleagues.

Writing and Research Advice

Each content chapter is set up using the same format for both reading selections and the questions that follow. Beginning with a Why Write About section, each chapter discusses the importance of reading and writing critically about the pop culture in question and then gives guidance in preparing to write and the types of essays that could be written. Although there are many ways to write about pop culture, *The Pop Culture Zone* focuses on four types of essays that are useful for evaluating and writing about pop culture: reviews or review essays, reflection or response essays, analysis essays, and synthesis essays.

MICHAEL OCHS ARCHIVES/GETTY IMAGES

Reviews or Review Essays

We all find it easy to applaud or criticize songs or films or websites; however, detailing out why we like or do not like something is a much tougher task. The Reading Zone selections and the questions that precede and follow them can help you begin to think about the structure or influence pop culture has on you; they can also help you critically analyze which parts of a film or song are leading you to your opinions or arguments. Each chapter describes how to write reviews or review essays specifically about the pop culture media or item in question.

In general, a review, such as a song or film review, is an evaluation that describes whether you find something interesting or of value for yourself or others. Like the reviews found in newspapers or on websites, reviews are usually rather short because they focus on the evaluation of one song or film or other piece of pop culture. You may be asked to review the same item as your classmates, or you may be allowed to choose your own item from pop culture to review. Either way, reviews usually follow a somewhat conventional format, giving a short synopsis or description first and then a judgment or evaluation that is supported with details from the piece or relevant material from outside the piece. Each chapter has a set of key questions to help you write reviews or the longer review essays, which can focus on multiple items or ask you to delve a bit more deeply into the history of a pop culture time period or style.

Reflection or Response Essays

When we react to pop culture, we are not only reacting to the item or experience in front of us or around us, but we are also reacting to how that item or experience fits in with other experiences we have had. Writing reflection or response essays allows you to write critically about pop culture but from your own personal viewpoint; in other words, you examine your reaction, asking yourself key questions that are given in each chapter, and then write critically about your response or reflection to the pop culture being studied. Since pop culture helps you reflect on your life, your choices, and your opinions, reflection and response essays usually use the pop culture item or experience as a starting point, not as the focus of the entire essay.

Analysis Essays

An analysis essay may be the essay you are more likely to associate with academic writing. When you write an analysis essay, you are presenting an analytical argument or an in-depth discussion about a pop culture item or experience and then supporting your position with details drawn from the pop culture item or experience. For instance, you may suggest that certain types of games appeal to a particular gender due to the way genders are socialized in the United States. You would offer your opinion, most likely your thesis, and then support it with details drawn from the game and possibly from outside sources if your essay assignment requires research. Being analytical and critical is at the center of writing a strong analysis essay. Analysis requires more than just a description of pop culture; it needs you to have strong opinions or arguments that are supported by observations you have made about the pop culture item and possibly the observations of others that you have gathered through research.

Synthesis Essays

Pop culture does not occur in a vacuum, and this means that sometimes you have multiple ways of evaluating and writing about pop culture. A synthesis essay is often the best choice for writing about pop culture. Synthesis essays allow you to bring narration often associated with reflection and response essays into the more analytical writing you might want to do. If you have a very strong argument or opinion that can be supported not only by your own personal experiences but also by outside research or sources, you may want to consider writing a synthesis essay. Different instructors and classes focus on different types of rhetorical strategies, so be sure to look over your assignment carefully to determine which type of essay or type(s) of rhetorical strategies might work best for organizing and writing about the topic of your choice. If you use a mixture of essay strategies, you can look at the key questions in each chapter for review, reflection and response, and analysis to help you make confident and effective choices.

Reading, Writing and Research Processes

Writing, analyzing, and researching advice is offered throughout the content chapters and is also available in Chapter 3, Writing in The Pop Culture Zone, Chapter 4, Reading in The Pop Culture Zone, and Chapter 5, Researching in The Pop Culture Zone. Because writers craft their essays in many different ways, these chapters give you an overview of various predrafting and composing strategies, as well as strategies on helping students to be more critical readers, including advice on how to effectively annotate reading selections, summarize important information, and analyze reading selections. Writers are usually quite familiar with the pop culture that surrounds them but may not be that familiar with their own writing strategies and processes. Chapters 3 and 4 also allow you to investigate your usual writing and reading process and try out strategies that you may not normally use. In addition, a highlight of the new reading chapter is a section on analyzing visuals with strategies on how to analyze design, content, context, audience, and purpose.

Not all students using *The Pop Culture Zone* will be asked to do outside research about their essay topics; however, if you are asked to research or decide that it is needed to strengthen your essay, Chapter 5 introduces some general research strategies, along with some particular to researching about the areas of pop culture presented in this book. You can also find tips on using Internet search engines and library portals, documenting sources, and avoiding plagiarism.

FINDING IDEAS FOR YOUR ESSAYS

At the end of each content chapter, *The Pop Culture Zone* offers a Start Writing About section that offers various suggestions for essay topics separated into review, reflection or response, analysis, and synthesis essays. You may find the topic you want to write about in these offerings, or you might want to return to other questions offered throughout each chapter to help you narrow down your topic. For instance, look for essay topics in the Grappling with Ideas blocks throughout the chapter or the Considering Ideas questions before each reading selection. You might also look back again at the questions asked in the Connecting to Your Culture at the end of each reading or the Contemplations or Collaborations you discussed or wrote about at the end of each chapter. Just remember, pop culture is yours, and the topic you choose to write about should be something that interests you and inspires you to write the best essay you can.

THE READING ZONE

CONSIDERING IDEAS

1. What is your own definition for essay writing?
2. How is essay writing different from other types of writing?
3. Do you write anything that you might not be asked to share at school?
4. Do you read outside of school? If so, what are some of the things you read? Why do they appeal to you?

AUTHOR BIO

Art Peterson *is a senior editor and writer for the* National Writing Project, *which is a group that works to improve writing and learning in our nation's schools. You can read more essays by him at* http://www.nwp.org/cs/public/print/nwp_au/3.

THE SUBJECT

Ernest Morrell *is a professor of English Education at Teachers College, Columbia University, and director of the Institute for Urban and Minority Education. His research, writing, and lecturing interests include examining the intersections between urban adolescent literacies and the literacies of the educational system. He teaches courses in literacy theory and research, critical pedagogy, urban education, and activist methodologies. You can read more about him at* http://www.ernestmorrell.com/bio. *Be sure to watch his interview at* http://www.nwp.org/cs/public/print/resource/3495.

ERNEST MORRELL LINKS LITERACY
TO POP CULTURE

Ernest Morrell had a revelation when, in 1994, after finishing his teacher training under the tutelage of the Bay Area Writing Project at the University of California, Berkeley, he took a job teaching high school in Oakland, California. He realized "that academic records don't tell the whole story, that we need to broaden our definition of intellectual activity.

"I'd see a kid considered close to a nonreader walking around with a backpack full of books, or a girl who seldom wrote in class dashing off poems in her personal journal," he explains. Students were learning and making meaning in ways that weren't necessarily recognized in the classroom.

His work in Oakland fortified his interest in popular culture as a road to literacy and led to the publication of his seminal work, *Literacy and Popular Culture*.

POP CULTURE AS RESEARCH TOOL

Morrell, who has just taken a position as director of the Institute for Urban and Minority Education at Teachers College, Columbia University, will be the keynote speaker at the 2011 NWP Urban Sites Network Conference, April 29–30, in Boston. He'll be speaking on how popular culture can advance literacy and act as a bridge to the communities that urban educators serve.

Community outreach is nothing new to Morrell. During his just-completed tenure as an associate professor at the UCLA Graduate School of Education, he worked with high school teens as director of the Council of Youth Research, where he introduced them to college-level research techniques as they investigated issues of concern to them.

For example, students have been researching the changes since the 2000 filing of *Williams v. California*, a class-action suit that alleged the state and other agencies had failed to provide equitable access to learning materials, a safe and secure campus, and qualified teachers. The young researchers are visiting, observing, and surveying conditions at various schools in the Los Angeles area. They'll present their findings to city officials in August.

On other occasions, Morrell has plugged his young researchers into using popular culture as a learning tool. One year students interviewed and surveyed students, teachers, and families about the influence of hip hop.

They asked students, "What impact, if any, does hip hop music have on the way you see the world?" And they asked teachers questions such as, "How do you define culture? According to your definition does hip hop constitute a culture?"

POPULAR CULTURE AND ACADEMIC STANDARDS

But Morrell's focus is not just on connecting to teen culture. He is very much dedicated to fostering academic standards, and committed to the classic learning and curriculum that underscore these objectives. That's why in his book he demonstrates how he links *The Godfather* trilogy with *The Odyssey*, and the themes of T. S. Eliot's "Love Song of J. Alfred Prufrock" with "The Message" by hip hop musician Grandmaster Flash.

"Hip hop texts are rich in imagery and metaphor and can be used to teach irony, tone, diction, and point of view. Hip hop text can also be analyzed for theme, motif, plot, and character development," he says.

Aware that many, even most, teachers are not experts on teen popular culture, Morrell advises them to pay attention to everything that is going on around them.

"Teachers should be alert to hallway conversations," he says, in order to be attuned to what is going on with teen culture.

"What a teacher can do is capitalize on the special knowledge that her students do have to build bridges to the curriculum, and to the literacies students need," he says.

This advice is an understanding that Morrell wants to transmit to the university students he works with. One of them, Cliff Lee, a Bay Area Writing Project teacher-consultant and a UCLA PhD candidate working with Morrell, says, "He has made me aware of the funds of knowledge students bring with them. Working with him, my view of literacy in student learning has been constantly evolving."

STUDENTS AS PRODUCERS OF POPULAR CULTURE

In an interview with Morrell, Lee asked how his thinking about popular culture and teaching popular culture has changed since the publication of *Linking Literature and Popular Culture* in 2004. Morrell responded that in fact "a lot has stayed the same." Popular culture still has centrality among teens, and the tenets he advanced in the book are still of value.

But in the last ten years students have become producers as well as consumers of popular culture. "If I were to do the book again, I'd put much more emphasis on production," rather than consumption alone.

That's why the high school students that Morrell works with are no strangers to blogs, Facebook, video production, and Twitter. All of these formats, says Morrell, are about writing.

A writer himself of poems, plays, novels, and academic books, Morrell often asks the young people with whom he works how they would like to change their world. Many answers come back, and the key tool he promotes to advance all of these goals is always the same: learn how to write.

"Words are power, freedom, the source of revolution—personal and societal. Words define meaning. Words influence thought," he says. Morrell advances an idea of socially engaged writing that is not merely a comment on the world, but rather is a means for changing the world for the better.

At the upcoming Urban Sites Network meeting he will invite teachers, using the content of popular culture and the tools of the new media, to join him in this quest.

Source: *Ernest Morrell Links Literacy to Pop Culture, by Art Peterson. 2/28/2011. Found at http://www.nwp.org/cs/public/print/resource/3495.*

DECODING THE TEXT

1. In his essay, how does Peterson describe Morrell's realization that school literacy does not include all possible literacies?

2. Why does Morrell describe pop culture as a learning tool?

3. How does Peterson divide his essay? In what way does this division help the reader process different facets of Peterson's description of Morrell?

CONNECTING TO YOUR CULTURE

1. Think of one aspect of popular culture that you enjoy. What impact does this pop culture have on how you view the world?

2. How do you and your peers produce pop culture?

3. Morrell suggests that by learning to write, students can change the world. Do you agree? Why or why not?

2

defining popular culture

Tracy Jordan: So what's your religion, Liz Lemon?

Liz Lemon: I pretty much do whatever Oprah tells me to do.

—From *30 Rock*

1. **The Pop Culture Zone:** Who was the most frequent female celebrity guest on *The Oprah Winfrey Show*?

a. Celine Dion
b. Gayle King
c. Rosie O'Donnell
d. Angelina Jolie

2. **Defining Pop Culture:** Who boasted to *The Source* in 1994, "I AM Hip-Hop"?

a. Tupac
b. L. L. Cool J
c. Ice-T
d. Dr. Dre

3. **Writing About Pop Culture:** What founder of *Ms. Magazine* claimed, "I don't like to write. I like to have written"?

a. Jane Fonda
b. Debbie Stoller
c. Gloria Steinem
d. Betty Friedan

4. **Reading About Pop Culture:** Which of the following television shows have comic book spin-offs?

a. *The Simpsons*
b. *Buffy the Vampire Slayer*
c. *Star Trek*
d. All of the above

REUTERS/LANDOV

5. **Researching Pop Culture:** Who said that he did not sample Queen and David Bowie's "Under Pressure" in a 1990 song because Queen and Bowie's version was "Ding, ding, ding, dingy, ding, ding" and his was "Ding, ding, ding, ding, dingy, ding, ding"?

a. Snow
b. Vanilla Ice
c. Eminem
d. Marky Mark

6. **Advertisements:** Which television advertisement was voted best of all time by *TV Guide*?

a. "Hare Jordan" Nike (1992)
b. "1984" Apple Computers (1984)
c. "Where's the beef?" Wendy's (1984)
d. "Brilliant!" Guinness (2003)

7. **Film:** How many film versions of *Romeo and Juliet* have been produced?

a. Two
b. Six
c. Ten
d. More than ten

8. **Social Networking:** In March 2006, the Hells Angels Motorcycle Club sued which group for copyright infringement?

a. The Rolling Stones
b. The Los Angeles Police Department
c. The Walt Disney Company
d. The American Motorcyclist Association

9. **Music:** What television show's theme song has these lyrics? "Won't you be my neighbor?"

a. *The Simpsons*
b. *Mr. Rogers' Neighborhood*
c. *Sesame Street*
d. *The Rugrats*

10. **Television:** Which of these animated series is a spin-off?

a. *Daria*
b. *King of the Hill*
c. *Beavis and Butthead*
d. All of the above

MTV/THE KOBAL COLLECTION

In their 2004 hit "1985," Bowling for Soup sings about a mother who is still living in the pop culture of her teens and the teenage children who are embarrassed by their mother's inability to adapt to contemporary pop culture "'Cause she's still preoccupied with 19, 19, 1985" (look up the full lyrics online). Like these teens, many people think that popular culture is only what is happening right now immediately around them; however, popular culture bridges generations, decades, and levels of significance. It is the Afro from the 1970s, Madonna singing "Like a Virgin" from the 1980s, the box office returns of *The Titanic* in the 1990s, our nation's reaction to the collapse of the World Trade Center in the 2000s, and the social and political power of Twitter in the 2010s. Popular culture stretches across time to influence and create our language, our interests, our activities, our environment, our beliefs, our opinions, and our identities.

Popular culture became an academic subject in 1967 when Ray B. Browne first conceived the idea for *The Journal of Popular Culture*, and its initiation into the university environment continues today. Popular culture has been defined in many different ways by those who study it. Basically, though, popular culture includes any product (Katy Perry shatter nail polish), social network (snowboarders), environment (Radio City Music Hall), idea (the creation of a character in a role-playing game), or event (the Super Bowl) that is widely known or received by many people. More often than not, the general population accepts this piece of popular culture. At a deeper and sometimes controversial level, popular culture includes the cultural patterns within a population, such as those items and ideas that appeal more commonly to the working class or the majority culture. Examples may be as varied as the use of grassroots politics and web campaigning to reach a broader audience in presidential elections or the requirement for women to wear head scarves in certain cultures. Finally, although those who study popular culture in academia would probably not agree, popular culture is often considered "low culture" compared to what is sometimes called "high art" or "high culture." Low culture is Lil' Kim; high culture is Josh Groban. Low culture is *The Jerry Springer Show*; *Mad Men* is the high art of TV. Low culture is NASCAR; high culture is lacrosse. If popular culture is considered the opposite of high culture, then that suggests that a traditional opera such as *La Boheme* is a more valid means of cultural expression than a rock opera such as *Jesus Christ Superstar* or that *Miss Saigon* is a more authentic theater production than *Seussical the Musical*. These definitions—some very broad and others narrower—are obviously controversial because of the biases for or against popular culture that they suggest.

Like some scholars, you might think that the term *popular culture* is a contradiction. To many of us, "culture" often means the most impressive or important contributions to a civilization, such as the construction of the Sears Tower or the composition of George Gershwin's *Rhapsody in Blue*. On the other hand, "popular" often refers to something that is common, ordinary, or generally accepted among the masses, such as "Mother" tattoos and Laffy Taffy candy. Owing to this discrepancy, early scholars of popular culture used the term *mass culture*, though this term is not generally used today because it is considered insulting, as it seems to refer to people as groups or masses of unthinking participants or users of nonelite culture. Just as artifacts of high culture are produced for an audience's pleasure, appreciation, and education, so, too, is popular culture.

TRENDS AND HISTORY

In fact, many aspects of high art were once a part of popular culture. The most common example is the writing of William Shakespeare. When writing in the sixteenth century, Shakespeare was a popular poet and playwright enjoyed by both commoners and royalty. Because they were so well liked, Shakespeare's company of players became the King's Men, who both wrote and performed for King James I. Shakespeare, however, was not considered a poet of high stature in the Renaissance, as was Philip Sidney or Edmund Spenser, who was granted a high political position because of his popularity. Of course, today, Shakespeare is considered a part of the literary canon taught to all and a representative of high culture.

Other areas of popular culture may also make the switch from what is considered low culture to high culture. For example, fusion cuisine, the combination of traditional culinary products (such as grits, collard greens, and country ham in the South) with gourmet techniques and ingredients (such as caviar and crème fraiche or techniques such as sushi rolling or the use of organic farming), has become increasingly popular. Whereas grits were once considered a food of the common person because of economics and availability, now they are being incorporated into foods served in upscale restaurants that may be inaccessible to the original consumers because of location, reputation, or cost.

The opposite of this trend may occur as well when elements of high culture modify their presentation or composition to appeal to a wider audience. For example, Cirque du Soleil attempted to break into popular culture through its run on Bravo network, its new theatrical production in Las Vegas, and its incorporation of music from The Beatles in the production *Love*.

CONVENTION + INVENTION = POPULAR CULTURE

Because popular culture is a combination of the likes and needs of millions of consumers, each specific aspect of it can be considered. A variety of questions can be asked, such as why a product or event was created, who produced it, who its target audience is, what similarities or differences it has with other major cultural artifacts, and why this specific combination of attributes is successful. Typically, a popular culture event or artifact is composed of conventional elements and an element of invention to make it new. For example, *The Flintstones* was a combination of the successful television show *The Honeymooners* and Hanna-Barbera children's cartoons.

GRAPPLING with Ideas

- Is there such a thing as high culture? If so, what is it?

- Are blockbuster films treated differently in academic circles from indie films?

- Does this film example also translate to advertising? Television shows?

- Can consumers give value to a text, whether it is a television series, a film, or a social media network?

- Is there inherent value in a television series or a film without fans to watch it or in a game without fans to play it?

WHAT/WHO DEFINES AMERICAN POPULAR CULTURE?

American popular culture is defined by consumers—those who watch *El Mariachi*, purchase MP3s of Martina McBride, wear Maurice Malone fashions, go to the Monster Jam Truck Rally, and eat at McDonald's. These consumers are often discriminating, which explains why every song is not a hit, every film is not a blockbuster, and some television series do not even stay on the air until midseason. However, American popular culture is also defined by the corporations that back the production and dissemination of a certain product, advertisement, or event. To explain further, if Interscope Records spends millions to produce No Doubt's first new album in a decade, *Push and Shove*, the company will more than likely demand a return on its investment. The band will be expected to tour, appear on *American Idol* or *The X Factor*, be interviewed for *Spin* or *Rolling Stone*, and behave in such a way that they will become "news." The hype around a new album is not inconsequential; it is the way that a band's future studio work is decided. Many sophomore albums, a band's second effort, are promoted heavily by both the record company and the band because of the rarity of matching the success of a first hit recording. Likewise for comeback albums. "Selling out" is also a concern of many sophomore efforts because fans often turn on a band that spends more time promoting itself than making music.

The benefit of corporate promotion is that it creates a national popular culture, which can unite teenagers in southern California with those in upstate New York through their common interests. Fortunately, though,

GRAPPLING
with Ideas

- Our population is expanding, so our popular culture is as well. However, many people look back to the past and regret this expansion of the popular. Were there really "good ol' days" when life was easier?

- Should the popularity of a book, an advertisement, or a video game make it important for study? Why or why not?

- Is popularity often viewed as a negative aspect of a film or television series? Can this opinion be justified?

GRAPPLING
with Ideas

- What role do American subcultures play within your everyday life?

- Think about your own interests: your favorite film, your appointment television series (the one you make sure to watch weekly), the magazines you subscribe to, and the songs you listened to on the way to class. Do your interests fit into the definition of popular culture? Subculture? Folk culture?

- What about your parents' interests? Your grandparents'?

many consumers are becoming more aware that they are seen only as potential consumers and are vulnerable to corporate, political, and even personal marketing strategies through their access to Facebook, television channels, and sporting events. Corporate promotion of popular culture raises valid concerns about censorship. If one CEO is deciding what music will be played on thousands of radio stations, television soundtracks, and advertisements, then millions of other songs and artists are censored by not having the opportunity to be played or to gain an audience. The Internet, with its ability to reach millions of potential consumers, can assist in combatting the limitations of corporate promotion.

WHAT/WHO DEFINES AMERICAN POPULAR CULTURE STUDIES?

The study of popular culture is defined by both the scholars of the field and the members of the associations who contribute to the scholarship. The Popular Culture Association (PCA) in conjunction with the American Culture Association (ACA) includes people who enjoy the study of relevant areas of popular culture such as film, television, music, and gaming, and less studied areas of academia like motorcycling, food culture, and the tarot. Both organizations also sponsor resources and publications in the field, the most well-known being *The Journal of Popular Culture*, as well as an annual conference where members and nonmembers gather to present their most recent research in the field.

Regional branches of PCA/ACA also provide insight into the field with their annual conferences and publications. The PCA/ACA has thousands of members internationally, and because of this, the area of study has become increasingly relevant in a number of academic fields. For example, the largest of these regional organizations, the Popular Culture Association of the South (PCAS), produces the journal *Studies in Popular Culture*. Many online journals have also contributed to popular culture studies, such as *Americana: The Journal of American Popular Culture*, *Images: A Journal of Film and Popular Culture*, and more specialized journals, including *Slayage: The Online International Journal of Buffy Studies*. Any of these publications are appropriate sources for research into popular culture or appropriate models for learning to write about popular culture for an academic audience.

THE POPULAR CULTURE DIVIDE

Popular culture is a branch of cultural studies. According to scholar John Storey, cultural studies is more broadly defined as the study of a "particular way of life, either of a people, a period or a group" (Storey 2). American popular culture is obviously a part of American culture; however, there is much more included in cultural studies than what is popular. For example, religious hymns, opera, underground rap, and classical music are not always a part of popular culture, though these boundaries can be blurred. These cultural ideas and artifacts can be divided into various categories.

Counterculture or subculture, folk culture, and high culture are not typically considered a part of popular culture, though their study often bleeds into the field. Counterculture or subculture is the cultural development, advancement, or achievement that can take place outside popular culture but also often crosses over into popular culture. Typically, this includes movements such as the rise of rap in the 1970s, the increased marketing of independent films in the 1980s, or the grunge fashion trends of the 1990s. For example, Latin pop music is rooted in Latin American folk cultures and subcultures that are centuries old. However, artists such as Los Lobos, Gloria Estefan, and the Barrio Boyzz helped to popularize Latin pop music in the American music scene. Then, in the late 1990s, the American Music Awards added a category for Favorite Latin Artist, and in 2000, the Latin Grammy Awards were broadcast internationally, signifying the fame of Pitbull, Jennifer Lopez, and Shakira for a broader and younger audience. Remnants of what was once only a part of Latin American culture can now be seen, and have been seen, on television screens, in movie theaters, and on iPods across the United States.

Folk culture is the lifestyles, artifacts, and traditions—typically determined by locale—of a specific group of people. This culture is usually passed down orally and varies greatly by region. Folk culture can, as it is passed from generation to generation, grow in both its appeal and its appreciation. Bluegrass music and quilt making are good examples of how folk traditions can bleed over into popular culture.

Classical music, art, and literature are often considered branches of high culture. As discussed previously, this distinction should not be seen as a hierarchy. The terms *high* and *low* come from traditional definitions and have nothing to do with the legitimacy of the subjects. However, the difference in these cultures is often determined by money and history. High culture most often merges with popular culture through the use of allusions or references to commonly known works, such as a reference to biblical passages in *The Da Vinci Code*. Almost every cultural artifact can be viewed through the lens of popular culture because anything that is available to the public eye is popular culture.

POPULAR CULTURE IS ACADEMIC

Popular culture consumers and participants are valuable to academia because their choices create culture, which impacts and influences future fields of study. Some scholars of popular culture view its study as their social responsibility; to understand a culture, the commonly known, enjoyed, and consumed artifacts, ideas, and events must be studied for their relevance. Others study the influence and impact of popular culture on individuals, on families, and on social institutions such as religion, capitalist structures, and academia itself. Still, many scholars view popular culture as a distraction from more important responsibilities of citizenship and study it from a more critical vantage point; however, since the study of popular culture is relatively new, its own influence and impact are difficult to determine even though the influence of popular culture and popular culture studies on academia is undeniable.

The field of popular culture also contributes to many forms of art or media, which are often seen as academic. Film, music, television production, and advertising are major contributors to the art world. These forms of expression

GRAPPLING
with Ideas

Popular culture researcher Ray B. Browne writes, "Society is dominated by the hard sell of reality, both on campus and off. Popular culture studies urge us to reach out into the world around us and do a more effective job for the introduction and understanding of everyday culture. Those students who best understand and participate in their everyday cultures develop into the most useful citizens. The world should not be artificially divided into everyday and 'intellectual' life. Both mix and coextend and are part and parcel of each other" (*Popular* 4).

- Should you separate your academic interests from your cultural interests? What advantages might that give you? What disadvantages might that cause?

- How does popular culture apply to your major area of interest or study?

have surpassed art exhibitions and performances in their appeal and availability. Even visual art exhibits show the influence of popular culture and pop art. One example of this is how photographer David LaChapelle's work has been featured everywhere from Burger King commercials to the cover of *Rolling Stone* to the VH1 fashion awards to small galleries in the Chelsea neighborhood of Manhattan. Another example is how filmmaker Spike Lee's work can be seen on Nike commercials, HBO documentaries, feature-length films, and music videos, or you can shop the H&M clothing collection inspired by the film *The Girl with the Dragon Tattoo*.

GRAPPLING with Ideas

Cultural critic John Storey argues, "Our dominant view . . . in discussions of globalization and popular culture is to see it as the reduction of the world to an American 'global village' . . . in which everyone speaks English with an American accent, wears Levi jeans and Wrangler shirts, drinks Coca-Cola, eats at McDonald's, surfs the net on a computer overflowing with Microsoft software, listens to rock or country music, watches a mixture of MTV and CNN news broadcasts, Hollywood movies and reruns of *Dallas*, and then discusses the prophetically named World Series, while drinking a bottle of Budweiser or Miller and smoking Marlboro cigarettes" (*An Introduction* 153).

- Is there one representative American culture?

- Are cultures determined nationally or within divisions of race, gender, sexual orientation, and class?

- Is a culture's success driven only by economic expansion? Is America the only country that exports culture?

POPULAR CULTURE IN ACADEMICS

Popular culture is most often studied in the field of liberal arts. As cultural studies become more popular, many universities are developing separate coursework in the field; however, most commonly, popular culture and cultural studies are currently incorporated into several departments: English, communications, music, fine arts, history, philosophy, women's studies, film, and folklore. Each of these departments may use a different approach to the field of study and may only study a portion of the field. For example, in English, pop culture—even that which is not printed—is studied as a text. A film, song, or dachshund race is analyzed in the same way as a novel, poem, or short story. English scholars look for both the internal and external meanings of the "text." Take the characters of the popular novel, later turned into a popular film, *The Great Gatsby*, for example. Scholars may look at the actual subject matter, such as Jay Gatsby's relationship with Daisy, or how the cultural context surrounding the text relates to the subject matter, such as how extramarital affairs were accepted in "The Jazz Age." They may also delve into how actions in the text represent a commonplace example, such as Nick's caution in dealing with Jay and Daisy's relationship. In addition, English scholars often explore how other texts from the time period treat the subject matter—this is referred to as the intertextuality. In this case, they may look at how other works from the 1920s handle extramarital affairs. And, finally, they may look at the purpose F. Scott Fitzgerald had in writing about this particular relationship. Just as with studying literature as text, all of these internal or external investigations can be applied to the texts of pop culture.

Business colleges may also investigate popular culture. Economics and business departments often offer courses on the big business of popular culture. Blockbuster films, top forty albums, and the Clio Award winners for the best television commercial advertising campaigns often generate large amounts of money for both American and international corporations. These patterns of income are important for study and are important for students to use as models of successful business practices, especially for students in marketing programs. The representation of the business world in popular culture is important for student discussion, as well as the use of popular culture by professors to keep classroom material relevant and contemporary. Students interested in these fields may also study the spread of popular culture through the technology of the Information Age.

Basic and applied sciences, with departments such as anthropology, sociology, psychology, health, and geography, use popular culture to update their models, research, and class investigations. Some would argue that popular culture cannot be studied without some application of these methodologies. Audience studies, regional diversity of what is popular, and the study of what is significant in our (and historical) times all add to the importance of clinical studies in popular culture.

The value of popular culture in education is increasingly understood and accepted. As professors and teachers realize the attraction and relevance of using popular culture to reach their students, more areas of popular culture are being used as classroom resources. Not only can students learn from popular culture, but professors and teachers may use popular culture to bridge the gap between their students' frames of reference and their own. This textbook is an example of how popular culture can increase classroom discussion and debate without requiring extensive knowledge of the subject.

YOUR PLACE IN POPULAR CULTURE/POPULAR CULTURE'S PLACE IN YOU

You are a participant in popular culture. The television shows you watch, the movies you rent, the games you play, the music you listen to on the radio, the online communities you belong to, and the magazines you read are all choices that impact popular culture and that impact you. You are probably more familiar with all of these than the last book you read in high school or the history of traditions in your hometown. Popular culture can be explored on many different levels, but to truly understand or appreciate an artifact of popular culture, you must do more than memorize facts or trivia. Through this exploration, you may find common ground with your friends or family who enjoy television shows, films, or music that you currently do not watch or listen to. Popular culture is aptly named for its wide appeal; however, as you are impacted by popular culture, popular culture is also formed by your choices. Corporations and individuals who produce popular culture need to understand you— your likes and dislikes—to understand how to produce goods that will interest you, goods on which you will spend hard-earned money. Even when you were in grade school, your disposable income was of great interest to these producers. You are a valued consumer and have been considered one since you were a child.

You are also an outsider of popular culture. Think about the following list of words from pop culture with definitions recently added to dictionaries: Bollywood, bromance, crackberry, crunk, d'oh, dead presidents, dumpster diving, DVR, fanboy, fist-bump, Frankenfood, ginormous, gray literature, headbanger, java jacket, LOL, longneck, man cave, McJob, mouse potato, muggle, podcasting,

KEY TIPS

To Becoming a Critical Reader or Reviewer

- Question everything; nothing should be taken at face value:
  - What topics are being addressed?
  - Who produced this text?
  - Who is the intended audience? How do you know?
  - How is this audience addressed?
  - Does the text have a single author? A corporate authorship?
  - What do you know about the author(s)?

- Be honest with yourself and your judgments; if you do (or do not) enjoy a text, ask why.

- Find connections in the content. What does the text remind you of? Are there allusions to other texts in or out of popular culture?

- Conquer confusion; "I don't know" isn't an answer, but it may lead to interesting questions.

- Do not let the message manipulate you; again, constantly questioning is the answer!

- Find evidence to support your judgments; always back yourself up with facts from the text.

- Do not depend on those who are paid to make judgments—be an independent thinker. Often, media outlets that review a film are owned by the same company that produced the film. Are their judgments always going to be critical and valid?

sexting, soul patch, spoiler, straightedge, supersize, telenova, tweet, webisode, wiki. How many can you define? Do you know where each word originated? It is impossible for any individual to be familiar with all popular films, songs, advertisements, social networks, or television shows. Although you may be an expert in any one or two of these areas, it would take a great deal of time and devotion to keep up with all popular culture as it is currently produced, marketed, and consumed. For example, to familiarize yourself with the back catalogs of advertising alone would take years of careful research and study. Therefore, many areas of popular culture are left to be explored. Perhaps your study of this textbook could lead you to a film, music artist, or television show—that is new or new to you—to spark a pursuit in an area of popular culture that you were previously unaware of. Talking to those who were born or who grew up in a different time than you may also help you find artifacts of past popularity to discuss and explore. Although it is nice to have a background of popular culture interests as your frame of reference, to apply your prior knowledge about pop culture to an unfamiliar subject might encourage critical thinking and an adaptation of these new thinking, reading, and writing skills throughout your college career.

CRITICAL READING AND VIEWING OF POPULAR CULTURE

All popular culture can be considered a text, just as it can be valued for the meanings inherent in its materiality. A film, an advertisement, or a sporting event may all be mainly visual texts, whereas most music and radio advertising is an auditory artifact. Even a network or group can be considered a text by looking at its history, traditions, and agendas. To analyze popular culture as an academic or cultural text, remember a few tips. Do not take anything you read or view at face value. Often, in popular culture, the main argument of a text or artifact may be hard to identify; it may be hidden beneath comedy, new trends, or interesting characters. However, this does not mean that the argument is any less important. It is significant to determine what is being conveyed to a mass audience, whether consciously or subconsciously, and to examine how American culture is being portrayed.

In *The Pop Culture Zone*, popular culture is connected to composition because of its controversy, its relationship to you—the reader—and its significance in society. While composing your thoughts about texts within popular culture, use your frame of reference and your new experiences with these texts by asking the Grappling with Ideas questions and considering their answers.

RESEEING POPULAR CULTURE

The Pop Culture Zone uses the contact zone theoretical model to help you think critically about the impact and influences of pop culture. By using this model, we ask for personal reflection and analysis from you, your classmates, and your instructor to engage in discussion about how American popular culture impacts you. See Chapter 1, The Pop Culture Zone, for more information on how this approach can help you as you progress through your academic career.

Popular culture is reviewed and analyzed in a variety of resources, from magazines to online journals to satires, such as *Saturday Night Live*, *In Living Color*, and *MadTV*. Television series and magazines are often in the unique position of both responding to popular culture and creating popular culture at the same time. For this reason, critical thinking, reading, and viewing are incredibly important, and research may be required to find where a trend began, how cultural critics are responding to a text, or to get basic facts about a text's production. The Internet is typically the most effective way to research contemporary popular culture, although more and more print texts are being published and produced to help with your study. Internet research, once considered an ineffective method of investigation, is now essential to keep up to date with current cultural texts. It is important, though, for you to make sure that the information you find on the Internet is from a reputable source. Pay close attention to the guidelines in Chapter 5 for more information.

AREAS OF STUDY FROM THE POPULAR CULTURE ASSOCIATION/AMERICAN CULTURE ASSOCIATION

The following list from the Popular Culture Association/American Culture Association demonstrates the variety of subject areas that are considered American popular culture. Take a minute to peruse these subject areas and think about your major interests within popular culture. This list may help you when brainstorming for essay topics. For more help in prewriting activities, see Chapter 3.

ACADEMIC CULTURE

Academics ACA
Collegiate Culture: Higher Ed & Pedagogy PCA
Language Attitudes & Popular Linguistics PCA
Popular Culture & Education/Teaching & History PCA
Popular Culture, Rhetoric & Composition PCA
Technical Communication PCA
Two-Year Colleges PCA

BUSINESS & PROFESSIONAL CULTURE

Business/Corporate Culture PCA
Professional Placement PCA
Technical Communication PCA

ENTERTAINMENT & TRAVEL CULTURE

Automobile Culture PCA
Celebrity Culture PCA
Circuses & Circus Culture PCA
Festivals & Faires PCA
Travel and Tourism PCA
World's Fairs & Expositions PCA

ETHNIC STUDIES & CULTURE

African-American Culture PCA
American Indian Lit. & Cultures ACA
Asian Popular Culture PCA
Black Music Culture PCA/ACA
Caribbean & Latin American Literature & Culture PCA
Chicana/o Culture: Literature, Film, Theory PCA

FILM, TELEVISION, & RADIO CULTURE

Adaptation (Film, TV, Lit. & Electronic Gaming) ACA
Adolescence in Film & Television ACA
Children's Television PCA
Documentary PCA

Film & History PCA
Film Adaptation PCA
Film and Media Studies PCA
Film PCA
Humanities & Popular Cultures PCA/ACA
Musicals, Stage & Film PCA
Radio PCA
Shakespeare on Film and Television PCA
Slapstick Comedy/Early TV PCA
Soap Opera PCA
Television PCA
The Vampire in Literature, Culture & Film PCA/ACA
Westerns & the West PCA

GENDER CULTURE

Cultural Conflict & Women PCA/ACA
Gay & Lesbian Studies PCA/ACA
Gender & Media Studies PCA
Gender Studies PCA
Masculinities ACA
Masculinities PCA
Men/Men's Studies PCA
Sports PCA/ACA
Women's Lives & Literature PCA
Women's Studies ACA

GEOGRAPHIC CULTURE

Appalachian Studies ACA
Border Culture (Political, Cultural, Geographical) PCA/ACA
Geography PCA
Midwest Culture ACA
New England Studies ACA
Vietnam PCA
Westerns & the West PCA
World Popular Culture PCA

(continued)

HISTORIC & FOLK CULTURE

Appalachian Studies ACA
Baby-Boomer Culture PCA/ACA
Cemeteries & Gravemarkers ACA
Civil War & Reconstruction PCA/ACA
Film & History PCA
Festivals & Faires PCA
Folklore PCA
Medieval Popular Culture PCA
Popular Culture in the Age of Theodore
    Roosevelt PCA
Popular History in American Culture PCA
Postcolonial Studies ACA
The Sixties PCA
Sports PCA/ACA
World Popular Culture PCA

HUMOR CULTURE

Comedy and Humor ACA
Slapstick Comedy/Early TV PCA
Sports PCA/ACA

INTERNATIONAL CULTURE

Asian Popular Culture PCA
British Popular Culture PCA
Caribbean & Latin American Literature &
    Culture PCA
European Literature & Culture (excl. UK
    and Germany) PCA
German Literature and Culture PCA
World Popular Culture PCA

LITERATURE & LITERARY CULTURE

Adaptation (Film, TV, Lit. & Electronic Gaming) ACA
American Literature PCA
Arthurian Legends PCA
Biographies PCA
Children's Lit. & Culture PCA
Contemporary American Prison Writing PCA
Creative Fiction Writing PCA
Detective & Mystery Fiction PCA/ACA
Dime Novels/Pulps/Juvenile Series Books PCA
Eros, Pornography & Popular Culture PCA
Gothic Literature PCA
Heinlein Studies PCA
Horror (Fiction, Film) PCA
Humanities & Popular Cultures PCA/ACA
Jack London's Life & Works PCA
Literature & Society ACA
Literature & Visual Arts PCA
Literature and Politics ACA

Literature and Science ACA
Madness in Literature PCA
Medieval Popular Culture PCA
Motorcycling Culture and Myth PCA/ACA
Non-Fiction Writing PCA
Poetry Studies PCA
Poetry, Creative PCA
Popular American Authors PCA/ACA
Romance PCA
Science Fiction/Fantasy PCA
Sea Literature PCA/ACA
Shakespeare & the Elizabethan Age in Popular
    Culture PCA
Southern Creative Writing (reflects Southern
    Culture & Tradition) PCA
Southern Literature and Culture PCA
Sports PCA/ACA
Stephen King PCA/ACA
The Vampire in Literature, Culture, & Film PCA/ACA
Women's Lives & Literature PCA

MATERIAL CULTURE

Automobile Culture PCA
Collecting & Collectibles PCA
Fashion, Appearance, & Consumer ID PCA/ACA
Food in Popular Culture PCA
Libraries, Archives, & Popular Culture Research PCA
Material Culture ACA
Motorcycling Culture and Myth PCA/ACA
Senior Culture: Seniors and Aging PCA

MEDIA CULTURE

Advertising PCA
Gender & Media Studies PCA
Journalism & Media Culture ACA
Journalism PCA
Media Bias & Distortion PCA
Film and Media Studies PCA

MUSIC CULTURE

Black Music Culture PCA/ACA
Hip Hop Culture (Black Music Culture) PCA/ACA
Music PCA
Music ACA
Musicals, Stage & Film PCA
Rock, Film & Contemp. Arts ACA

PHYSICAL & HEALTH CULTURE

The Body and Physical Difference PCA
Fashion, Appearance & Consumer Identity PCA/ACA
Fat Studies PCA

Health & Disease in Popular Culture PCA
Senior Culture: Seniors and Aging PCA
Sports PCA/ACA

POLITICS, LAW, & POLITICAL CULTURE

Literature and Politics ACA
Motorcycling Culture and Myth PCA/ACA
Politics in a Mediated World ACA
Politics, Law & Popular Culture PCA

RELIGION & RELIGIOUS CULTURE

Culture & Religion PCA
Jewish Studies PCA

SOCIAL ISSUES & CULTURE

Animal Culture PCA
Collective Behavior: Panics, Fads & Hostile
   Outbursts PCA
Ecology and Culture ACA
Protest Issues & Actions PCA
Senior Culture: Seniors and Aging PCA

TECHNOLOGY CULTURE

Adaptation (Film, TV, Lit. & Elec. Gaming) ACA
Automobile Culture PCA
Digital Games PCA
Electronic Communication & Culture PCA

Internet Culture PCA
Technical Communication PCA

THEORY, MYTH, & CULTURAL BELIEFS

Conspiracy Theory/Claims for the Paranormal PCA
Memory & Representation PCA
Mythology in Contemporary Culture PCA
Philosophy and Popular Culture PCA

VISUAL CULTURE & THE ARTS

American Art & Architecture ACA
Comic Art & Comics PCA
Dance Culture PCA/ACA
Eros, Pornography & Popular Culture PCA
Humanities & Popular Cultures PCA/ACA
Literature & Visual Arts PCA
Musicals, Stage & Film PCA
Popular Art, Architecture & Design PCA
Tarot PCA
Theatre PCA/ACA
Visual Culture PCA/ACA

WAR & CULTURE

Civil War & Reconstruction PCA/ACA
Vietnam PCA
World War I & II PCA

The following reading is a sample essay on a general topic in popular culture: Oprah's influence on almost every subject in this text from the obvious, television, to music artists, popular literature, film, fashion, politics, and social networks. This essay should encourage you to practice your critical thinking and reading skills while preparing for the more specific readings in the following chapters.

READING SELECTION:
DEFINING POPULAR CULTURE

CONSIDERING IDEAS

1. How does television's popularity and easy access affect other areas of popular culture, such as social networking, film, and music?

2. Does Oprah Winfrey's gold thumb signify a positive or a negative attribute of American culture?

3. In 2011, Winfrey retired her daily show after twenty-five years on air. Do you think someone else will take her place in popularity or influence?

AUTHOR BIO

PopEater claims to have the most up-to-date news about celebrities, entertainment, movies, and music, as well as the hottest celebrity photos. This blog/news site started as an online feature from AOL Television *but is now part of* The Huffington Post *news site.*

THE OPRAH EFFECT

Her Endorsement Goldmine

As Oprah Winfrey rides into the final countdown of her hit talk show, businesses and entrepreneurs alike will probably pull out all the stops to get Winfrey to utter their brand name on air . . . even if it's just once. It's no secret that anything Oprah chats about on her show goes from rags to riches in a matter of minutes. We admire her "popular girl" power to influence her audience to buy the products she endorses. It's difficult to say if any other celebrity will take her reigning ability to shill an unknown product and make it a must-have item. Let's take a look at Winfrey's Midas touch. Her show reaches about 44 million people a week, so you can understand why people want Oprah to plug their products. But time might be running out for people hoping to strike gold with an Oprah stamp of approval. In a statement released Thursday, her company announced that the *Oprah* show will end as its 25th season draws to a close on September 9, 2011. "I love this show. This show has been my life. And I know when it's time to say goodbye. . . . Twenty-five years feels right in my bones and feels right in my spirit," Winfrey said.

THE OPRAH EFFECT

1. **Neti Pot**. When Dr. Oz first introduced Americans to the Neti Pot, a natural remedy for sinus pain and congestion, they flew off drugstore shelves. Now, Oprah says she can't go anywhere without hers.

2. **Oprah's Book Club.** The proof is in the pudding. If Oprah puts a book into her elite club, usually it turns into a New York Times' best seller. *The Bluest Eye*, *Middlesex* and *Love in the Time of Cholera*, are just a few books Winfrey has promoted through the club—helping authors reach a wider audience.

   And don't mess with Oprah either. The now infamous incident of James Frey's memoir, *A Million Little Pieces*, a 2005 selection, has been outed from her club after she found out the author had fabricated most of the novel. The controversy resulted in Frey and publisher Nan Talese being confronted and publicly shamed by Winfrey on live television during her show.

3. **Charities & Philanthropic Involvement**. From education in Africa to reconstruction in New Orleans, Oprah has raised awareness about major world issues (and spent millions of dollars of her own money to promote these causes). Earlier this year, Oprah featured an impromptu segment with the human rights organization Invisible Children, which focuses on telling the stories of war-affected children in east Africa. The group's segment made their grassroots project into a worldwide name—even gaining the attention of celebrities like Rachel Bilson, Miley Cyrus, and Pete Wentz.

4. **Barack Obama.** In her first public endorsement, Winfrey gave Barack Obama's presidential campaign her seal of approval, which a University of Maryland study found may have netted him one million votes. During the election campaign, she even snubbed Sarah Palin by not inviting her to be on her show. (But that changed this week when she invited Palin to chat about her memoir *Going Rogue*.)

5. **Thermage**. Few Americans had heard of a beauty treatment called Thermage until Oprah began discussing it on her talk show. Billed as a procedure to tighten skin, Thermage uses a radio-wave emitting machine to heat and expand collagen beneath the skin's surface. Oprah called Thermage a "lunchtime face-lift" that requires no recovery time. When it was first showcased in 2003, sales reps were selling the machines over the phone to doctors for about $30,000!

6. **We Take The Cake**. In 2003, Lori Karmel bought a floundering mail order business which later became We Take the Cake. The business only turned a $19 profit in 2004. But the company was pulled from the brink of bankruptcy after becoming one of Oprah's Favorite Things. Ten thousand cakes were sold after the show and today it is a million-dollar business.

7. **Spanx**. In 2000, Oprah chose Spanx shape wear as one of her "Favorite Things." The Atlanta-based clothing company quickly sold $50,000 worth of products in just three months.

8. **Music Impact**. When the Black Eyed Peas performed on this year's *The Oprah Winfrey Show* season opener, the band's album sales jumped 29 percent. And when Whitney Houston gave a two-part interview to Oprah, her album sales shot up 77 percent.

9. **Celebrity Superstars**. Being on Oprah's buddy list can help you, too. Dr. Oz and Rachael Ray can thank Oprah for her continued support of their careers, giving them time on her show to introduce new products, shows and books. (And hey—Dr. Oz even got his own TV show after working alongside Oprah.)

10. **LAFCO**. Jon Bresler and Vincent LaRouche of LAFCO pitched their European bath and body products to Oprah's "Favorite Things" show for seven years—even though they already had celebrity clients including David Bowie and Penelope Cruz. After being featured on Oprah's show 2007, sales peaked at more than a million dollars in just 30 days.

Source: *"The Oprah Effect: Her Endorsement Goldmine" located @ http://www.popeater.com/2009/11/20/the-oprah-effect-endorsements-books/ © 2012 AOL Inc. Used with permission.*

DECODING THE TEXT

1. What is the author's purpose in describing Winfrey's "popular girl" power? What powers are described?

2. Does the author make a judgment on whether Winfrey's influence is positive or negative?

3. What does the author mean when stating, "And don't mess with Oprah either"?

CONNECTING TO YOUR CULTURE

1. Has the end of *The Oprah Winfrey Show* affected her influence or power? Why or why not?

2. Has Winfrey ever impacted your purchases? Have you read a book from her book club, subscribed to her magazine, or bought one of her "favorite things"?

3. If so, why did you make the choice to purchase the goods? If not, why are you exempt from her endorsements?

4. How does product placement affect your other purchasing decisions? How does it affect the decisions of your family and friends?

3

writing in the pop culture zone

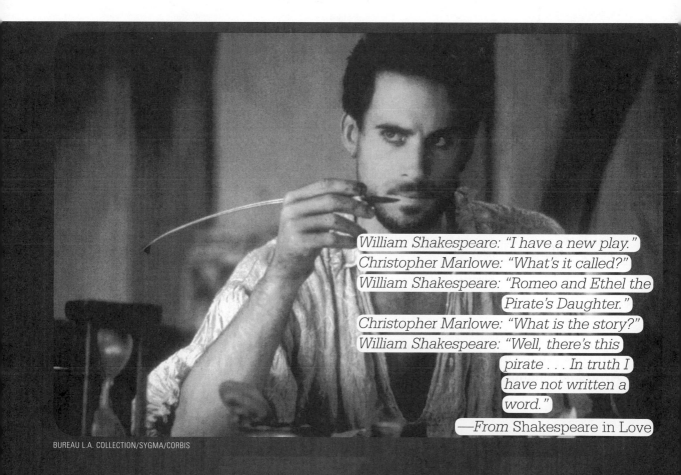

William Shakespeare: "I have a new play."
Christopher Marlowe: "What's it called?"
William Shakespeare: "Romeo and Ethel the
    Pirate's Daughter."
Christopher Marlowe: "What is the story?"
William Shakespeare: "Well, there's this
    pirate . . . In truth I
    have not written a
    word."
    —From Shakespeare in Love

1. E. B. White, the author of *Charlotte's Web,* cowrote what popular writing guide used often in writing classes?

a. *Fun with Style*

b. *The Writer's Guide*

c. *The Elements of Style*

d. *A Fun Guide to Writing*

2. Which of the following movies based on Stephen King books does not include a main character who is a writer?

a. *Misery*

b. *The Shawshank Redemption*

c. *The Shining*

d. *Secret Window*

e. *Salem's Lot*

3. Match the TV character writer with the appropriate television show.

1. Ray Barone   a. *Sex and the City*
2. Jessica Fletcher   b. *Everybody Loves Raymond*
3. Rob Petrie   c. *30 Rock*
4. Carrie Bradshaw   d. *Murder, She Wrote*
5. Liz Lemon   e. *The Dick Van Dyke Show*

4. Who has received the most Academy Award nominations for writing?

a. Oliver Stone

b. Woody Allen

c. Billy Wilder

d. Ben Affleck

COLUMBIA PICTURES/COURTESY EVERETT COLLECTION

5. Match these writers with their publications.

1. Lois Lane   a. *Blush*
2. Nina Van Horn   b. *The Yale Daily News*
3. Peter Parker   c. *The Daily Planet*
4. Rory Gilmore   d. *The Daily Bugle*

6. What pseudonym does best-selling romance novelist Nora Roberts use when she's writing sci-fi suspense?

a. Anne Rice

b. J. D. Robb

c. Elizabeth Lowell

d. Sherrilyn Kenyon

7. For what film did Ben Affleck win his first screenwriting Academy Award?

a. *Argo*

b. *Gone, Baby, Gone*

c. *Shakespeare in Love*

d. *Good Will Hunting*

8. Match these musicians with their autobiographies.

1. Joan Jett
2. Frank Sinatra
3. I Would Die 4 U
4. Kurt Cobain

a. *All the Way*
b. *Heavier Than Heaven*
c. *Bad Reputation*
d. *Prince*

---

9. In October 2012, Facebook had how many users?

a. around fifty million
b. around one hundred million
c. around five hundred million
d. around one billion

10. **Stump Your Instructor:** In small groups, write a question here about writing or writers in pop culture. Give your instructor five choices for answers.

a.
b.
c.
d.
e.

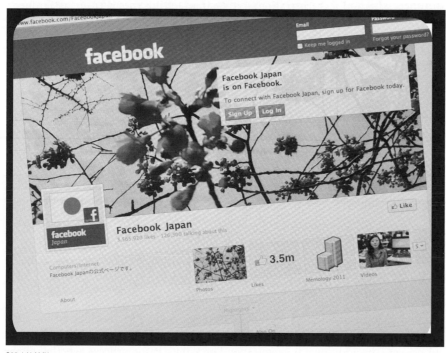

Q28 / ALAMY

People write for all kinds of reasons. Students, like you, write for class assignments—essays, lab reports, test answers, class notes—but also to send e-mails to friends, post entries on Facebook, and make lists for the grocery store. You may write notes for your child to take to school, letters to the editor of the local newspaper, and annotations in your Bible on Sunday mornings. In your work life, you may find yourself writing memos to your employees, presentations for potential clients, reports for your boss, and remarks on drafts for fellow team members. Of course, you may also write to document your daily activities in a blog or journal, to compose original poetry, or to record amusing anecdotes. Whatever your reasons for writing, you are more likely to achieve your purposes and communicate your message if your writing is easy to read and clearly addresses your intended audience and purpose.

Of course, clear and concise writing does not happen by accident. It is a process that takes work. The same is true for writing about pop culture, the kind of writing you are asked to compose in this textbook. Although writing about pop culture is a good way to explore your own thoughts and feelings about the various media around you, it does not necessarily come naturally or effortlessly. However, the purpose of this chapter, as well as all of the hints and guidelines in the other chapters, is to help the process move more smoothly for you and to help you come up with more interesting ideas for your writing.

Writing about pop culture can serve a variety of diverse purposes and audiences and can utilize many different formats: Reviewing, responding or reflecting, analyzing, and synthesizing are just a few of the possibilities. In the freshman composition class, this writing might be completed in class or out of class. When you learn more about and practice the recursive or overlapping steps of the writing process, all of these types of assignments can become more successful and less frustrating. Rather than letting your writing assignment sit on your desk or in your bag for days or weeks as the deadline looms closer and closer, you can take control of both your time and assignment and appreciate the composing process along the way. Follow all of the hints given, and you will be able to turn in a text that is more thoughtful and most likely better composed than those written at the last minute.

There are several key steps to becoming a successful writer who clearly communicates a purpose or answers the problem that has been posed. In this chapter, you will find explanations of these key steps in the writing process. Of course, writing is a messy endeavor, circular in nature, and sometimes never-ending. The following steps are presented in a linear format, an approach to writing that is often not seen in real writing since you often revise as you plan and draft or go back to brainstorming when you get stuck as you write. However, these steps should help you begin to evaluate your current writing process and improve it in some way.

- **Brainstorming:** This is what you can do to find an interesting and comfortable topic, propose a problem to be solved, or create a persuasive argument, as well as figure out how to support what to say about the topic, problem, or argument.

- **Planning and Drafting:** In this step, you organize and create your first draft.

- **Revising:** At this stage, you write additional drafts, rethink or resee your thesis, and improve content, organization, support, and word choice.

- **Editing:** In this step, you double-check grammar and mechanics and proofread.

Attempt all of the various revision and editing steps or tips given in this chapter for your first out-of-class essay, and then adopt the ones that most improve your writing for the quicker in-class essays and for later out-of-class assignments in all of your classes. The additional time you spend on your writing process, whether alone or with your peers, should help your writing be more successful. Taking control of your writing and your writing process is an important step in becoming a skilled writer, and the guidelines in this section will help you get on the right track.

WHAT IS WRITING?

In its most basic definition, writing is a process that allows you to communicate thoughts to an audience by managing symbols—usually words and images. Your writing can serve a variety of purposes and achieve a number of different goals. For example:

Writing supports

- insight, giving you an outlet for your internal discussion.
- discovery, offering a visual space to prepare your ideas for public view.
- creative expression, allowing you to construct and compose thoughts.

Writing communicates

- thoughts to yourself and to others in a formal as well as an informal setting.
- imagination, making it visible to others.
- identity, as choice of words, punctuation, and mode of writing unite to reveal facets of your individuality.

Writing manages

- ideas, for clarification.
- symbols, enabling you to manipulate alphabetic characters to create words and meaning.
- language, allowing you to gain power and authority by learning how to control language so that it concisely conveys your message.
- people, by guiding, stimulating, exciting, and placating human beings.

Many people do not consider themselves actors, yet we do, in fact, act every day. Just as an actor's performance is shaped by an audience, our behavior changes depending on the setting or the audience. When in an informal setting, we might perform in a manner not considered appropriate in a more formal setting.

Likewise, most people do not consider themselves writers; however, each day, our lives may include such informal writing tasks as composing a text or writing in a personal journal or blog or the more formal writing required for an office memo, a résumé, or an essay for school. Similar to an individual's performance as an actor, a writer also must consider such issues as setting and audience when shaping a performance on the page or on the computer screen.

Shaping a Written Performance

While many factors ultimately determine the final performance for an actor or the final product for a writer, several factors are crucial to both. The *rhetorical triangle* (see Figure 3.1), sometimes called the *communication triangle*, illustrates these key factors to consider when shaping a written performance.

Writer: Although it may seem obvious, the writer is the person who writes. The writer explores, explains, and/or expresses his or her knowledge of a subject in writing, which leads the writer to ask, "What do I, as the writer, know about this subject?"

Subject: A writer thinks about the subject of the text and what information about or connected to that subject the audience, or reader, needs to know, which leads the writer to ask, "What about this subject do I want my reader to know?"

GRAPPLING with Ideas

- When you hear the words *writing* or *writer*, what image(s) come to mind?

- Can you think of writers you have seen in the movies or on TV? Do these images mesh with your own idea of what it means to be a writer?

- Do you consider yourself a writer?

- What role does writing play in your life?

- What kinds of writing do you do?

Reader: A writer also thinks about his or her reader or audience—the person or people being addressed through the text. Considering the audience leads the writer to ask, "Who is my reader (or audience), and what do they want to know or need to read?"

Context: A writer also considers the context of everyday life when shaping an effective message for the audience. Considering the context leads the writer to ask, "What are the moral, political, economic, geographic, historical, and generation issues that come into play?"

Message: The message is the product of the writer's consideration of the answers to the preceding questions; in other words, the message is the writer's main idea or thesis and is the result of considering what the writer knows about the subject and the reader.

GRAPPLING
with Ideas

- Reminisce about a first experience in your life: your first day of high school or college, your first crush, your first award, your first kiss, your first day of driving all by yourself.

- Where were you? Who was around? How did it feel physically? Emotionally?

- Now record this same experience in a letter to a friend or a family member. How does your language change? Your content? The details?

Consider how you convey knowledge to the reader. For example, think about how you set up a personal page on Facebook, and then think about the different ways you set up your own personal blog on Blogger or how you might write in a personal journal that is on paper. With Facebook, you are publishing your information, but you can still control who sees it by limiting your friends list. Consequently, you could be writing for a limited audience of friends. With most blogs, however, anyone can access your space and read what you have written. So while you may treat your blog as a personal journal, you are always aware that you are writing for a large, public audience. In both examples, the writer is the subject of the text, but the distinct differences in purpose and audience result in a much more personal, and possibly informal, tone in Facebook writing than in blog writing. Of course, both of these are probably less formal than an essay you would write for a class.

Think about your own writing habits. How might the writing describing your experiences in a personal journal or in an e-mail to a friend differ from the writing you might use to compose a cover letter to a potential employer or a personal narrative written for an essay assignment? Again, in both situations, the writer is the subject, but each has a clearly different purpose and audience.

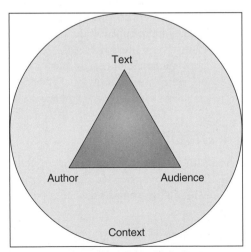

FIGURE 3.1 The Rhetorical Triangle.

WHAT IS BRAINSTORMING?

We write best when we write about topics we are interested in and are familiar with. Finding these topics and what you want to write about them through brainstorming is the first key step to improving your writing process. You can come up with ideas for essays in many ways, which include responding to and questioning the world around you and the model essays in this textbook. If, however, you are stuck and cannot find a topic, brainstorming, as part of your prewriting, can help narrow down general ideas into a focused topic and then help you decide what to use as supporting detail. You may already have your own style of prewriting; however, experiment with different methods to find what best suits your style.

Freewriting

Freewriting is a no-holds-barred type of brainstorming. When you freewrite, begin by allotting yourself a specific amount of time, such as ten to fifteen minutes. This technique is more constructive when you already have an idea for your topic. However, freewriting can be used to generate ideas for topics. Begin by simply writing. Write whatever comes into your mind. Do not be concerned with punctuation, grammar, or complete sentences. Use symbols or question marks in place of words that you cannot come up with automatically. If you cannot think of anything to write, simply jot down the phrase "I don't know" until you begin writing other words. Remember, this does not have to make sense to anyone else. Freewriting should be as stress-free as possible.

EXAMPLE

Topic: Freewrite for seven minutes about the picture you brought in today, a peer or family picture that triggers memories associated with being part of a group or association. (Harper, "Freewrite")

> Me and Lyndsey—my favorite pic. My first pic of us was when she was born. In this picture she is 13. We were at homecoming. Her sister and brothers also went. It was at the U of Mobile. I can't believe how much those kids ate. The boys liked the air toys and the fishing for those really small prizes. Too much money. L and I got our faces painted, but the boys didn't. I don't know why. Lyndsey's face—she got a cherry painted on it. I didn't know why. But then someone in the crowd told us it looked just like the Pac-Man game. No wonder then. The '80s was the theme of homecoming. The T shirt for homecoming also had a pacman on it. I ended up buying Lyndsey a T shirt anyway with the pac-man because she was cold and she kept on bugging me about buying one so she could get warm. My face has a flower. I think it was orange, but the picture doesn't look like it. I love this picture. We look at our face art, we smile at each other. It's a great picture because it shows love. Our face art wasn't the point of the picture. It was the love. And the smiles. L gave me the picture in a great frame for Christmas. I'm pretty sure that she sees the picture and thinks of me and that time and the smiles and the love. Think think think. It's a great sign—it's small—but it's great. Our relationship is important to both of us. We have a close one. I can't think of a time when we weren't close. We talk on the phone—Cingular is great. She calls me about tests and boys and her parents and her sister and her brothers and her parents, and I'm glad we have cell phones or I'd miss a lot of the great conversations we've had. It's me she wants to stay with every summer. We have a great relationship. We have been together for a lot of things—a lot of things important to her and me. Her first bra fittings, her 8th grade dress, my trips home . . . I've always tried to be there for her. I was even in the delivery room when my sister delivered her. My sister wasn't breathing. I was worried about the baby and her getting some/ enough oxygen. My sister cracked me up when she said, "The baby can come out and get its own damn oxygen." She did come out and became my best friend. And I'm hoping that I am. . . .

Once your time is up, sit back, and look at what you have written. Separate out the promising phrases, organize these ideas, and then expand them. Go back and read your paragraph again, <u>underlining</u> potential topics and subtopics.

Looping

Looping is a variation of freewriting. It can be a more constructive brainstorming exercise for those who need a little more focus than freewriting provides. This technique works best when you already have a general topic in mind. For example, if you have been assigned to write on the general topic of "war and the media," you could take out several sheets of paper and begin to freewrite as defined earlier. When time is up, read over what you have written and try to pinpoint a central idea that has emerged from what you have written. Perhaps it is the idea that you liked best for whatever reason or an idea that stands out to you. Put this thought or idea in one sentence below the freewriting; this is called your "center of gravity" statement and completes loop number one.

To begin loop number two, begin freewriting from the previous center of gravity statement. Freewrite for another ten minutes. Upon completion of this freewriting session, you will once again assess what you have written and extract a compelling or important idea that emerged from your writing. Write this main idea below your freewriting; this is your second center of gravity statement. You can now begin freewriting from the second center of gravity statement.

EXAMPLE

Loop Number 1

> **Is the media biased? Liberal? Conservative? Patriotic? Anti-American?** <u>Whatever it is we all question it during times of war.</u> While some newspapers receive praise for accurate, timely, honest reporting, others are seen as bad, evil, villains. Unfortunately, these labels have less to do with the media than with those reading or seeing the messages offered.

Loop Number 2

> Whatever it is we all question it during times of war. While Americans choose media outlets for a variety of reasons, few willingly watch, read, or listen to media that offer opinions, stories, or programming contrary to their personal views. During the height of the Vietnam War, network news outlets aired graphic taped footage of the death and destruction of war. <u>However, while the violence displayed might be the same, viewers maintained that only network "A" or network "B" presented it without bias.</u>

You can continue this looping process until you are satisfied and comfortable with the topic you have generated.

Journaling

Sometimes, instructors will lead you toward a topic or problem by assigning journals—handwritten in class, on a personal blog, or through a class discussion board. These are informal writings that allow you to take a vague idea and write about it. These journals allow you to follow an idea or a hunch without worrying about penalty; you can think of these journals as a more controlled version of freewriting. Once you complete a journal entry or a Grappling with Ideas section, you can set it aside for a time and come back to it later when you are rested and ready to approach the topic once again. You may even have new ideas or a different take than you initially had.

Example—Writing Case Study, Draft 1

Journal Assignment: Pick a character from Se7en. List major ethical decisions that he or she makes in the movie. (Tipton, "Journal")

Ethical Decisions

Erin Halcott
Feb. 26

Good to have a few quotes to help support ideas.

Mills

• gets cliff notes • gets coffee for Somerset on 1st day • makes fun of every crime and crime scene • apologizes to Tracy when he cusses in front of her • is upset when he can't remember the name of his friend who was shot • gets caught up in emotion • acts on emotion • knocks camera away • impatient to work • dismisses John Doe as a lunatic • kicks in Doe's door • pays a homeless lady to be a "witness" • even though he doesn't agree with what Somerset had to say, he thanks him for his advice • goes with Doe to get confession • calls John Doe a freak • fiercely questions and argues with Doe • keeps referring to Doe as a P. O. S. • becomes #7 – wrath • has a flash of Tracy • kills Doe

career over family • selfish • decided to move into the city eventhough he knew Tracy didn't want to • shot the criminal who killed his friend

Somerset

• tries to get Mills off the case b/c of "integrity of the scene" ① *shows he REALLY cares – careful* • wanted to finish a case before retirement • didn't want the Doe case • didn't think it should be Mills' first case • called the 1st crime scene the "obesity murder scene" not "fat boy case" • respects the victims • integrity • takes the time to really research • creates reading list to help Mills • always carries a switch blade • divorces himself from emotion in crimes • meets Tracy to talk • tells Tracy that if she chooses not to keep the baby, she should never tell Mills about the pregnancy

Marginal notes (left and top):

Look up seven deadly sins. for extra research maybe

Inferno by Dante

start @ Wikipedia... look @ recommended books

• kills Tracy - the only victim to not commit a sin

• smacked Doe when Doe told Mills about the pregnancy

wikipedia 7 deadly sins

trying to Google protect Mills

research detective maybe

Main notes:

• a long time ago, convinced his girlfriend not to keep his baby • knows he made the right decision but wishes he chose the other option • tells Tracy that if she keeps the baby to spoil it every chance she gets • tells Mills not to dismiss Doe as a lunatic • pays $50 for a secret, illegal library list • doesn't kick in Doe's door • throws the metronome • throws switchblade at target • decides to retire AFTER case is closed • goes with Doe to get confession to "finish it" • shows restraint with Doe in the car • leaves Mills with Doe and goes to stop the white van • tells Mills not to shoot Doe • tells Mills that if he shoots Doe, Doe wins • tells cop to accommodate Mills with anything he needs • seems to have new respect for Mills

Tracy   cite imdb & movie! (crime drama)

• calls Mills at work to invite Somerset to dinner • tries to get Somerset and Mills to see each other as David and William • stays in city and doesn't tell Mills she is miserable • doesn't want to be a burden • calls Somerset sounding upset, wanting to talk in the morning • doesn't tell Mills about her pregnancy

John Doe

• kills innocent strangers • takes on non-identity • patient with killings • beats but doesn't kill Mills • calls the apartment to declare admiration • turns himself in • calm • will take Mills $ Somerset to last 2 scenes • or will plead insanity • delusions of grandeur • knows just how to rouse Mills • wants to be shot for his sin of envy, #6

Using this journal entry, you can revisit the topic after possibly utilizing other brainstorming exercises or even after discussion with your instructor and other classmates; you can see notes on this journal entry from the instructor and classmates. To get you thinking and to jump-start your writing ideas, *The Pop Culture Zone* has numerous journal ideas scattered throughout, including the Grappling with Ideas and Considering Ideas sections.

Clustering or Mapping

Another technique you can use for brainstorming is clustering, sometimes referred to as mapping. You can cluster in many different ways.

- Start with possible topic ideas and then cluster them by drawing circles around them and organizing them into clusters.
- Start with a clustering grid and then fill in the circles with ideas.
- You can also find free clustering and mapping programs online to help you.

Whatever way you decide to cluster, start by putting your general topic in the middle of a blank page. If you want to use the first clustering method,

- Jot down possible subtopics and details all around the central circle.
- After you have written down as many subtopics or details as you can, locate the more general subtopics, circle them, and attach these circles to the middle circle that holds the general topic.

- After this, find details that will support the subtopics, circle them, and attach these circles to the subtopic circles.
- When you have circled enough subtopics and details to start outlining or writing your paper, erase or cross out all the extra or unconnected information.

If you want to try the second clustering method,

- Write your general topic in the middle of a blank page and draw lines from this circle to five or six circles (these will hold your subtopics).
- Then, draw lines from the subtopic circles to three or four other circles (these will be your supporting details).

If you use an online clustering or mapping program, follow the instructions given, but be sure to start with the general topic.

Regardless of the clustering method you choose, you should allot between ten and twenty minutes for this brainstorming process. What you end up with might look something like the cluster/map on the next page that uses the movie *Fight Club* as the general topic.

Cubing

Yet another way to generate ideas is cubing. Imagine a cube with six sides, or use a die from a game set you have around your home or dorm room. Next, imagine the following questions or methods of interrogation, written on each side of the cube, or in the alternative, use the numbers of the actual die to help you choose from the numbered questions below. Here are the questions to visualize on your cube or to match the numbers on the die you roll.

1. **Describe it:** What does the subject look like? Sound like? Engage all five senses if possible.
2. **Compare and contrast it:** What is the subject similar to? What is it different from? How so?
3. **Free-associate with it:** What does the subject remind you of? Any particular memories?
4. **Analyze it:** How does it work? What is its significance?
5. **Argue for or against it:** What advantages and disadvantages does it have?
6. **Apply it:** What are the uses of your subject? What can you do with it?

Write whatever comes to your mind for ten minutes or so. When you have finished cubing, take the topics and subtopics you have generated and organize them by clustering or outlining them. (More on outlining on page 44.)

Listing

Another way to brainstorm is to simply jot down any ideas or questions that pop into your head for about ten minutes. After you have finished your list, look for connections between ideas, or look for one main idea that encompasses several small ones. Here is an example for the general topic of television.

EXAMPLE

Entertaining	Usually Thirty- Or Sixty-Minute Programs
Informative	Media
Corrupting	Listen
Poisoning	Corporate Sponsorship
News	Music Television
Comedy	Home Shopping
Drama	"Boob Tube"

Sports	Game Shows
Educational	Remote Control
Biased	Mind-Numbing
Commercials	Weight Gain
People Magazine	Possible Contributor To "Dumbing Down" Of Society?

After examining the list, do you make any connections? Does anything stand out that you might want to write about? If so, try clustering or outlining the idea to see if it can be developed further; you may then want to freewrite about the idea.

Interviewing and Discussing

Sometimes, we have an idea that is unclear in our minds; however, once we begin talking about this topic with others, our idea becomes clearer, or the other person may be able to offer a perspective that you had not thought about before. Think about your subject or topic while a classmate or friend asks you questions about the subject—questions that would naturally come up in conversation. Also, your "interviewer" might ask you what are termed "journalism questions," such as

Who?	Who believes X? Who is involved?
When?	When did it happen? When did you change?
Why?	Why did X do Y? Why is this interesting?
What?	What happened? What did you do?
Where?	Where did it happen? Where were you?
How?	How did you become involved? How is it interesting?

Make sure you listen to what you are saying as you are being "interviewed." Consider jotting down some notes as you answer or audio-taping the interview. Was there a particular part of the subject that you were most interested in talking about? If so, why? You may find that you have discussed your way into an interesting topic. However, this may not have given you all of the information you need for an effective essay. If you are still without a clear subject by the end of the interview session, ask your classmates or friends questions. If they had to write an essay based on the information you had just discussed, what would they write about? Why?

If you end up using quotations from the person you have interviewed in your final essay, be sure to follow the appropriate documentation method to cite where you got this information. You can find the information for documenting interviews in Chapter 5.

Questioning

Sometimes, no one is available to interview you. If this type of brainstorming works best for you, try questioning yourself about the subject. Think of your favorite attorney on television or in books—How would he or she cross-examine a witness? Model your cross-examination of yourself in this manner; ask yourself a lot of questions about your subject. However, here is a list of five categories to help you start narrowing your subject.

- **Definition:** How does the dictionary define the word or subject? How does the majority define it? How do your friends or family members define it? What is its history? Where did it come from? Give some examples.
- **Compare and contrast:** What is it similar to? What is it different from? Think also along the lines of similar terms (synonyms) and opposites (antonyms).

- **Relationship:** What are its causes and effects? What subjects are connected to this one?
- **Circumstance:** Is it possible or impossible? When has it happened before? Are there any ways to prevent it?
- **Testimony:** What do people say about it? What has been written about it? Have you had any experience with it? Has any relevant research been done on the subject?

Outlining

Outlining can help you brainstorm for subtopics, or it can be used as a method for organizing the material that other invention techniques have helped you generate. Either way, the value of the outline is its ability to help you plan, see logical connections between your ideas, and see obvious places to add new ideas and details.

An informal outline can be just a map of paragraphs that you plan to use. For example, here is a short, informal outline for the topic "women in music videos."

> Body paragraphs, topic one: discussion of female pop stars
>
> Body paragraphs, topic two: discussion of women in rap videos

EXAMPLE

  I. Female pop stars
      A. Lady Gaga
      B. Beyoncé
          a. Destiny's Child
          b. Solo career
      C. Fergie
          a. Black Eyed Peas
          b. Solo career
      D. Gwen Stefani
          a. No Doubt
          b. Solo career
  II. Rap videos
      A. Female rappers
          a. Missy Elliott
          b. Lil' Kim
          c. Eve
          d. Salt-N-Pepa
          e. Mary J. Blige
          f. Angel Haze
      B. Backup dancers/singers for male rappers

Note that this is not a formal outline, which would have strictly parallel parts and might be expressed in complete sentences. Follow the outline form you find most useful or that has been assigned. An informal or working outline helps you get to the drafting stage, but it should not restrict you from changing subtopics or details to make your essay topic stronger.

You can also see by looking at this outline that you may have more information than you need for one paper. You could choose to focus on just female pop stars and develop it a bit more, perhaps adding other artists like Britney Spears, Rihanna, or Kelly Clarkson. This brief outline also points out the possibility of looking at women who used to front various bands or groups and then broke out on their own. You could choose to focus on just female rappers, possibly even adding others like Queen Latifah and MC Lyte. You would have to do more brainstorming if you wanted to write about women in the videos of male rappers.

Brainstorming, no matter which technique you use, is just the beginning of your writing process. These invention strategies can help you discover what you want to say and how you are going to support or illustrate your ideas. Of course, they do not necessarily tell you how to say it; writing or drafting is the next stage, when you take your ideas and put them into the desired form for your audience and purpose. As you write, you will also find yourself continuing to freewrite, make lists, ask questions, and use other prewriting techniques to expand your ideas or come up with additional supports because writing is a recursive and messy process that rarely happens in linear form.

WHAT IS DRAFTING?

Drafting is taking the ideas that you have generated through brainstorming and outlining and constructing a rough draft or perhaps two or three different rough drafts. As you write, go back to the rhetorical triangle (see Figure 3.1) and think about your audience, purpose, and subject. Who are you writing to? What language and style are appropriate for this audience? What is the context of the essay? What is the topic of your essay? What is the purpose of your essay? Are you reviewing a new CD? Narrating your personal reaction to a film? Analyzing an advertisement for gender bias? Comparing and contrasting two different places where you like to hang out? What question are you answering or what problem are you solving? As you consider audience and purpose, consider what format will help you reach your readers. Also think about what approach will make you most believable or credible to your audience. At times, your format or genre may be assigned, but if you have a choice, consider alternatives to the traditional essay. Letters, memos, PowerPoint presentations, websites, songs, videos, liner notes, or reviews for newspapers and magazines can be just as valid as the academic essay.

No matter what format you choose, your text will need to have a central idea or topic, otherwise known as the *thesis* or *thesis statement*. Your thesis can be explicit or implied, but either way, it answers the question, "so what?" Why should a reader be interested in your review, narrative, or analysis? What is the point of what you are writing? Your thesis can also serve as an organizing device because in your text you will want to include examples, anecdotes, details, descriptions, illustrations, pictures, and other forms of evidence that support your thesis and make your essay interesting and convincing for your reader. You may also include outside support or references to the media you are discussing. When you use other texts in your paper, you will want to make sure you document your materials in your essay and with a Works Cited page to validate your sources and your credibility and to avoid plagiarism (read more about plagiarism as well as how to create a Works Cited page in Chapter 5).

When composing your draft(s), you will also want to keep in mind the three main parts of most essays: the introduction, the body, and the conclusion.

INTRODUCTION

Although you may not actually write your introduction first (yes, it is okay to write your introduction last), at some point you will want to include an introduction that gets your readers' attention and makes them want to read more. In fact, the introduction generally has three main purposes: to capture your readers' attention, to give them background information, and to give them an idea of what is to come. This preview may come from the thesis or from a more general overview if your thesis will be located elsewhere in the essay. For example, an essay may build up to the main idea; in that case, the thesis will be closer to the end of the essay. In some essays, the thesis is even implied, so while the writer has a clear point and uses it to guide his or her writing, the thesis might not show up as a specific sentence in the essay.

Keep in mind that introduction does not necessarily mean introductory paragraph. Your introduction may require more than one paragraph to adequately interest and inform your reader. A longer introduction will also push your thesis further into the paper and not necessarily at the end of the first paragraph, as you may have done in the past.

BODY

The body of the essay will be the longest and most important part of your text because it is here that you will use many of the ideas generated in prewriting, as well as those that come to you as you begin to write, rewrite, and revise. It is also in the body paragraphs that you will support or illustrate your thesis. As you decide how to organize your body paragraphs, go back to the rhetorical triangle and consider your subject, audience, context, and purpose; likewise, consider the conventions of the genre you have been assigned or the format you have chosen for your essay. For instance, are you composing a traditional essay, writing a letter, or creating a website? In *The Pop Culture Zone*, you will be asked to write in four different broad genres: a review or review essay, a personal reflection or response essay, an analysis essay, or a synthesis essay, which utilizes at least two different rhetorical strategies or genres. These strategies can be presented in a variety of ways: traditional essays, letters, brochures, websites, and visual essays, just to name a few. See Chapter 1 for more information about the four types of essays used in *The Pop Culture Zone*, as well as writing instructions in each of The Content Zone chapters.

CONCLUSION

Finally, you will need a conclusion that indicates you have come to the end of your essay but that still leaves your reader with something to think about and possibly reflect on. The conclusion is a place to reinforce your key ideas, pull all of your points together, and leave your reader wanting more. It is a time to point out the significance and effectiveness of your thesis and how you have proven or illustrated it. The conclusion is also where you can call your reader to action or ask for a response—watch this movie, check out this television program, learn more about this group of people, or avoid this badly written book.

Now, let us go back to one of our earlier brainstorming activities and turn it into a rough draft that is ready for peer commenting and then revision.

Example—Writing Case Study, Draft 2

Assignment: For this essay, you will engage with a film that deliberates an ethical dilemma. This will require you to consider the complexity of the film's characters and the quandaries that they face and require you to go beyond the movie, the characters, and the circumstances as just pure entertainment. Your essay will be an investigation, analysis, and evaluation of the ethical issues in Se7en. This means you will analyze and evaluate one, several, or all characters in the film and the ethical choices they make. (Tipton, "Ethical")

Erin Halcott
English 1020-028
Prof. Tipton
March 02, 2013

Somerset's Ethical Decisions

Consider combining the first two sentences (to condense).

In 1995, David Fincher directed a movie called *Se7en* (imdb). It follows mainly two detective, David Mills (Brad Pitt) and William Somerset (Morgan Freeman) on a hunt to catch a serial killer, John Doe (Kevin Spacey) (*Se7ve*). Detective Mills, unlike Somerset, is harsh and impatient. Somerset's decisions show that he is a calm, collective, and calculating individual.

What is your thesis? Are you comparing Somerset's ethics with Mills's ethics? I take from your title that you're going to focus on Somerset.

Throughout the movie, Somerset really takes his time to research before he makes decisions. He is the kind of person who wants to know everything before he acts. Unlike Milss, Somerset does not get caught up in the moment and make rash decision. He takes his time to collect all he knows.

Can you provide any scenes from the film as evidence for these assertions?

Somerset also seems to have respect John doe's victims. At the first crime scene, all of the associates make fun of the victim by labeling the crime scene "the fat boy scene." Somerset takes a higher road and calls it the "obesity murder scene." Instead of making light of the victim and scene, Somerset shows his maturity by dealing with the crimes professionally.

Great examples here of Somerset's ethics!

He also shows great restraint when he, Mills, and John Doe are in the car on the way to the "last two murder scenes." As Mills fiercely questions and mocks Doe, Somerset asks questions respectively. Detective Mills passes Doe off as a crazy lunatic, but Somerset sees differently. He has more respect for Doe. He sees him as more than a crazy lunatic.

Somerset seems to have a certain respect for Doe, and instead of mocking him, he tries to understand him and why he did the things he did. Instead of wasting his time irritating Doe, he uses his time to learn all he can about him.

Good use of your own ethical system here to analyze the characters' ethics.

All of Somerset's decisions make a lot of sense to me. By knowing all the information before hand, you avoid making decisions in the heat of the moment that you might regret later on. Take, for example, when Mills and Somerset go to John Doe's apartment. Mills is ready to kick in the door, but Somerset warns him otherwise. Somerset thought about how they found the apartment in the first place and knew that they could get in serious trouble. Mills, on the other hand, kicks in the door anyway, deciding to worry about it later.

It seems as though this essay focuses mostly on Somerset, but there is enough of Mills in there for me to think that you also want to analyze his actions. Do you intend to further analyze Mills's ethical decisions? Consider expanding your essay's reach.

Detective Somerset choose to learn as much about the murders as possible before acting. By knowing everything, he was able to make sound judgement and was guaranteed to not regret any rash actions. As Somerset sarcastically told Mills, "It's impressive to see a man feeding off his emotions," (imdb).

Reprinted with the permission of the author.

SOREL, PETER /NEW LINE / THE KOBAL COLLECTION

WHAT IS REVISING?

When you draft, you get your ideas out on the paper or the screen. But this is not the end of the process; it is really just the beginning. Once you have a rough draft, you are ready to start rereading and rewriting—you are ready for revision. *Revision* literally means to resee or look at again, and this is what you do when you revise your writing. Many writers confuse revision and editing, but they are really two different parts of the writing process, even when writers and instructors try to group them together or refer to the two processes with one label such as rewriting, revision, redrafting, editing, or proofreading. However, revision is one of the creative parts of the writing process rather than a time to correct your grammar or spelling—that is for the editing process.

Revision is what writing specialists consider the **global** process of redrafting. Global characteristics of writing focus on overall issues, such as content, thesis, organization, word choice, and word use. When you edit, you focus on what writing specialists call **local** issues of writing, such as grammar, sentence variety, mechanics, spelling, and formatting.

Often, writers try to revise and edit at the same time; however, this is not a good idea. The focused attention to minute parts of words and sentences when editing often distracts a writer from thoroughly developing ideas. Thus, instructors and skilled writers recommend that all writers try to separate revision and editing into two activities. In many freshman composition classes, instructors purposely divide revision from editing by using separate peer workshop days and by giving different grades or grade percentages for these activities as part of an overall paper grade.

Why Revise?

When writers revise, they often discover and develop new or better ideas through the revision process. Revision is changing the paper, ideally for the better. Most professional or skilled writers view revision as a necessary part of their writing because it is useful for generating new ideas, focusing and reorganizing ideas, and polishing the overall paper. As mentioned earlier, a draft is a work in progress, and it is a good idea to write multiple drafts for each essay to write the best paper and get the best grade possible. In Chapter 2, we discuss several strategies for critically reading and viewing popular culture; these same strategies can be applied to your own essays and to the writings of your peers.

You can add, delete, and substitute material during the revision process. For example, if a point is unclear, you can add details to clarify your point, delete ambiguous words or phrases, or substitute new examples that have more clarity. Sometimes, you will find it necessary to cut material you like but that does not fit your point, or you will find that you have gone in a different direction and need to start over. Do not feel bad—this is just part of the drafting and revising process. When you revise, you focus on content, organization, and word choice, global issues that can be found at all of the different levels of your essay. The next few sections will help you revise on all of these levels: the overall essay, paragraphs, sentences, and words. It is best to divide these levels of revision and to work on them separately because a good revision plan includes investigation of all these levels.

Revising at the Essay Level

When you revise at the essay level, focus on large-scale changes that will improve the overall essay. Here is a list of essay-level concerns to consider each time you write and revise an essay.

- **Look first at the central idea of the essay.** If all sentences in the essay do not support this main idea, consider revising the main idea or revising the support in the essay. Although it is not necessary to have an explicit or stated thesis statement, it is a good idea to include one in a college essay, so you have a clearly defined central idea that will help you write the essay and help guide your reader through it.

- **Make sure that you have an audience in mind when writing and revising the essay.** If a reader cannot see himself or herself as the audience or you cannot envision the audience, then pay more attention to the audience of the essay when you revise.

- **Check the introduction and the rest of the essay for your underlying purpose in writing the essay.** If any of the support given throughout the essay does not support your purpose, you can cut what does not fit and add the support that is missing.

- **Review the overall organization of the essay.** Does each body paragraph support the central idea of the essay? Are the paragraphs ordered in a way that will make sense to the reader?

- **Check the balance inside the essay.** Are any of the supporting paragraphs out of balance with the rest of the essay? If so, check whether or not large paragraphs can be split or short paragraphs can be reorganized together.

- **Make sure that your essay flows well.** Use transitional words such as *however*, *next*, or *finally* and phrases such as *in comparison* or *on the other hand* between body paragraphs, so your reader will not get confused when you change topics.

- **Review your central idea if it is an argument, making sure that you have addressed counterarguments at some point in the essay.** You will lose some of your credibility with your reader if you do not acknowledge what others have to say about your topic, especially those who disagree. Showing that you know and can even counter the opposing arguments will make your argument that much stronger.

- **Be sure to use an interesting title that will encourage your reader to take the time to read your essay.** The title is your first chance to gain your reader's attention, so make it catchy as well as informative.

Revising at the Paragraph Level

After revising on the essay level, you will want to check whether the paragraphs in your essay are effective. Here is a list of paragraph-level concerns to consider each time you write and revise an essay.

- **Reread the introductory paragraph(s).** Does it include an effective lead-in to the central idea? Will the introductory material capture your readers' interest? Perhaps an interesting anecdote, vivid description of the pop culture topic, or a set of startling statistics will capture your readers' attention. Be sure to stay away from overused introductory strategies, such as providing a dictionary definition or general statements like *today's society*.

- **Focus on topic sentences or main ideas.** Can you put into one sentence what each paragraph says? Do you have one sentence within each paragraph that gives a good indication of the central idea of the paragraph? Does the supporting evidence work with this topic or main idea?

- **Add more examples and details to weakly developed paragraphs.** Stay away from only giving generalizations. For example, instead of writing, "Comic book sales are on the rise," write, "In 2012, comic book sales in North America topped $474.6 million," and cite the source of the information.

- **Check summarized, paraphrased, or quoted material that you use for support**. Make sure you have accurately represented your source materials and that you have acknowledged your sources. See Chapter 5 for more information about citing sources.

- **Check for coherence within body paragraphs, making sure all of the pieces of the paragraph fit together and make sense.** If you provide multiple supporting sentences, use transitions to join them together. Review and perhaps rewrite the introduction and conclusion.

- **Reread your concluding paragraph(s).** In addition to reinforcing key ideas from the body of the essay, try to end in a way that makes your reader want to read more. Make a prediction or invite a response from your readers, but be careful not to introduce new information. You can also call attention to the significance of your argument or what the reader should do with the information provided.

Revising at the Sentence Level

Writers often check sentences for grammar and punctuation errors and forget to check for sentence-level changes that would clarify content or organization. Here are some sentence-level strategies to use when you revise your essays.

- **Check sentences for clarity.** Does each sentence make sense? Check for ambiguity. For instance, a sentence such as "Filming crews can be fun" has multiple meanings and needs clarification. Changing this sentence to "The crews who shoot films for a living often have a great sense of humor and fun" or "I like to film people while they're working" will clear up the ambiguity.

- **Try not to use long introductory phrases or clauses.** These usually distract the reader from what you are trying to emphasize in the sentence. A sentence such as "Before I got to work and had to fix the copy machine and spilled my Starbucks Caramel Macchiato on my new shirt, I won tickets to the Sheryl Crow concert" has a long unnecessary introductory clause that de-emphasizes the main point of the sentence.

- **Use sentence-combining techniques to provide more sentence variety in the essay.** Readers get bored reading the same structure over and over again. Balancing short, simple sentences with compound or complex sentences usually works best. Refer to the next section on editing for more information on how to do this.

Revising at the Word Level

Choosing your words well helps your reader understand the central point more easily. Not only will revising word-level problems improve the content of your essay, but it will also improve the way the paper flows. Here are some word-level strategies you can use when revising your essay.

- **Look for wordiness.** Cut empty phrases, such as *there are, it is, I feel that, I know that, you will understand that, I think, in today's society*.

- **Use concrete nouns for subjects and avoid overusing pronouns, especially at the beginning of sentences.** For example, instead of generalizing about all films, let your reader know that you are referring to horror films based on Stephen King novels.

- **Ask your instructor about his or her policy on using first person (I, me, my) and second person (you, your, yours).** Some instructors prefer that students write only in third person, which can give a paper a more objective tone, while others may ask students to consider which approach is most appropriate for a given format, topic, or audience.

- **Be sure to use you appropriately if you use it.** *You* can only be used if the reader is actually the *you* referent, or the person you are talking to. For example, when writing directions, the writer is talking directly to the reader and often directly addresses the reader.

- **Change passive verbs to active ones, unless the passive form serves a specific purpose in your essay.** Passive verbs, which use a form of the verb *to be*, conceal who did what or who is responsible for the action in the sentence. Look at this sentence for example: "Women are portrayed in negative ways in some rap music." This passive form, "are portrayed," does not tell the readers who is portraying women in this negative way; it doesn't tell us who is responsible for this negativity. If you rewrite it with an active verb, you will have to name the actor, or the person responsible. The new sentence might say, "T. I. often portrays women in negative ways through his song lyrics." In a few instances you might actually want to conceal the responsible party or divert blame for something; in this case you might consciously choose to use the passive voice. For example, "The payment for the birthday party was delayed."

- **Use the literary present tense.** When you write an essay that reviews, reflects on, responds to, or analyzes literature, music, film, or television, use the literary present tense. For example, when describing a scene that you are reflecting on, write "Homer Simpson grins smugly and then leaves the barber shop" instead of "Homer Simpson grinned smugly and then left the barber shop." However, if you are writing a research paper focused on a historical event, past tense is more appropriate.

- **Read aloud for unnecessary repetition.** Replace overused words with synonyms, but be careful that you clearly understand how to use words you borrow from a thesaurus.

- **Check the tone of your essay since word choice plays a role in creating the overall tone.** If your instructor asks you to use academic tone, do not use contractions such as *can't* or *won't* or conversational-type word choices, such as, "Well, I then went to the bus stop on the corner and then got on the bus and then took it downtown."

- **Review transition use throughout the essay.** Pay particular attention to using transitions between body paragraphs and within body paragraphs when switching from one supporting point to another.

Revision Helpers

The person most invested in helping you revise is **you**. Be sure to include enough time for a thorough revision in your writing process, and focus on the essay, paragraph, sentence, and word levels one at a time.

Next, find someone else who is in your class or who is taking a writing class with the same instructor because this person is the most familiar with your assignments. You can also ask your roommate, friend, work colleague, or family member to help you revise; however, these revisers will probably need instruction in what revision really is. It will not help you if they focus on editing when you need to be focusing on revision. In addition, be careful not to have anyone rewrite your words or write sections of your paper. Your revisers need to make suggestions, but you are the only one who can put those suggestions on paper because having someone else rewrite your words is a type of plagiarism.

The best way to find people to help you revise is to participate fully in your class peer revision workshop. Finish a rough draft of your paper and revise it thoroughly yourself. Then, bring this revised draft to your class revision workshop. Incorporate any changes that your peer reviewer suggests if the change improves your paper. If your school has a writing center, the writing assistants, tutors, or consultants there can also help with revision. Again, be sure to incorporate those suggestions that you feel will improve your essay.

PEER REVIEWERS:
QUESTIONS YOU CAN ASK

(Check lists and examples throughout this chapter for further explanations.)

1. Is there a title? Is it interesting? If you answered "no" to either of these questions, suggest a title to the writer after you read the entire essay.

2. Does the introductory material work well as an attention-getter for you as a reader?

3. How well does the writer keep his or her audience in mind? What does the writer's purpose seem to be? How could it be clarified?

4. Read the beginning of the essay and then pause. What is the main idea of the entire essay? Is there a clear and well-written thesis? Underline it. Provide information on how to make the thesis and/or the introduction better or more effective.

5. Read only the topic sentences of the body paragraphs in order. Do they give a general outline of the paragraphs on their own? Does each paragraph have a topic sentence that relates directly to the thesis or main point?

6. Look at each of the body paragraphs individually now. Does each paragraph have enough support/specific detail? Does each paragraph support the topic sentence given at the beginning of the paragraph?

7. Does the writer use transitions to move the reader from one idea to another (between body paragraphs and within body paragraphs)?

8. Should the writer expand on any points? Go to the essay and mark three places with an X where you think the writer needs to provide more developed and effective details to support the main idea. Next to these, offer suggestions to help the writer revise for more effective support.

9. Look at the word level now. Are there word-choice problems?

10. What do you like best about the entire essay?

Peer revision, whether it is inside or outside class, gives you a chance to hear from an immediate audience rather than from an instructor. This midstep allows you to improve your paper without negatively impacting your grade, and when you exchange papers with someone else, it is usually a win-win situation. Getting immediate feedback is also a plus since using this strategy will help you develop your essay more before it gets turned in for evaluation.

Working with other writers can also help boost your confidence about an essay. If your peer reader enjoys your essay and gives you good advice, you feel better about the essay and, in turn, will probably work harder on it. In addition, peer workshops allow you to see firsthand that other writers also struggle with the same things you do; most first drafts are less than excellent essays, and you will feel better about your own in-process essay by being aware of this. Peer revision, most importantly, gets you into the habit of working collaboratively, something you will do in other classes and in the workplace after you leave the freshman writing classroom.

When you ask for revision help, you often need to give feedback in return on your peer's work. Sometimes, it is difficult for students to participate in peer revision; it takes time to feel comfortable incorporating this step into the writing process. Here are some effective strategies when participating in peer revision.

- **Work to get over your shyness about sharing your work with others.** Understand that all writers are in the same boat when it comes to sharing their work; it is difficult to let others see a work in progress, but sharing your writing and receiving feedback improve your writing.

- **Be an interested reader and give good comments and critiques.** As you respond to your peers' writing, you will also be modeling for them the kinds of responses you want to receive about your own writing. The comments "That's good" or "I like it" are not really very helpful when revising.

- **Use peer revision forms to help you give advice: one provided by your instructor, or the one in the box on page 53.** Answer all the questions on the forms with full answers that will help the writer revise later when you are not present.

- **Never apologize for your first draft.** Do the best you can in your rough draft and your revised draft, and then turn the essay over to your peer reviewer.

- **Throw your ego out the window.** Peer reviewers are helping you improve your writing and your grade; if they were not available and the essay went directly to the instructor for grading, your grade would probably be lower.

- **Focus on global concerns only.** Save any comments on grammar, mechanics, spelling, and formatting for the editing review or workshop.

- **Pick and choose what you want to use from your peer reviewer's comments.** You might not want to change everything mentioned; however, be sure to consider everything your peer reviewer suggests. Sometimes, others can see what we cannot see ourselves, and they can help us get out of an ineffective writing rut.

You can also ask your instructor for revision help during office hours. You can make the most of such a conference if you have specific questions ready when you go. Make a list of things that you found difficult to revise when you did your thorough revision or questions that came up as you rewrote. Some instructors allow students to submit papers electronically for revision help; however, before you do this, check with your instructor about his or her policy. Most instructors like to have you and your paper present when they discuss possible global changes to the paper.

When to Stop Revising

Nearly all good writing is revised often and in a thoughtful manner, so taking time and making a substantial effort are important if you want to improve your writing and your writing grades. Most competent writers can become excellent writers if they take the time to revise their writing significantly before turning it in for evaluation. Multiple drafts are important because each time you draft, you have the opportunity to learn something new, clarify an idea for your readers, or make your language more accessible and interesting. Plus, doing significant revision that is separate from significant editing improves all writing; even professional writers do it.

Although an essay is never really finished, it may be ready to turn in when

- It follows all instructions in the writing assignment.

- It says what you want it to say in the most effective way.

- It looks right on the page—it follows your assignment guidelines as well as the expectations for the chosen format or genre.

- It has content and a central theme that are fully developed.

- It is well organized.

- It has effective word choice.

- It has been edited well.

Revising in a Timed Writing Situation

In-class writing sometimes does not allow time for massive revision; however, you can and should build time into any writing assignment for revision. If given an in-class essay, break the time allowed into short blocks that resemble the parts of the process for an out-of-class essay. If you have sixty minutes, use five to ten minutes to brainstorm and outline, thirty to forty minutes to write the first draft, five to ten minutes to revise for global concerns, and five to ten minutes to edit for local concerns. If you are writing on a computer, print a copy of the paper, if possible, to revise and edit offline. Then, add changes, correct spelling and typos, and print your final draft. Even in a tight writing situation, it pays to always make time for revision and editing.

Example—Writing Case Study, Draft 3

This draft shows a combination of comments made by peer reviewers and the instructor.

10 STEPS
WAYS TO REVISE

1. Put aside your rough or first draft for a time before you start your revision.
2. Print your draft and read it slowly, making notes as you go.
3. Revise on the essay level.
4. Revise on the paragraph level.
5. Revise on the sentence level.
6. Revise on the word level.
7. Ask someone to read your essay for revision purposes only. It is best to find someone who understands the difference between revision and editing and who will comment only on global concerns.
8. Incorporate changes from 7.
9. Participate in a peer-revision workshop in class if available.
10. Incorporate changes from 9 and then begin the editing stage.

Halcott

Erin Halcott
English 1020-028
Prof. Tipton
March 9, 2013

Crossing Ethical Lines

I like the new title! Have you expanded your essay topic then?

The movie *Se7en*, directed by David Fincher in 1995, follows mainly two detectives, David Mills, played by Brad Pitt, and William Somerset, played by Morgan Freeman, who are on a hunt to catch a serial killer, John Doe, who is played by Kevin Spacey (imdb). Although the movie mainly focuses on the murders themselves, there is an emphasis on several ethical dilemmas. Each of the three main characters,

Good work on combining this into one sentence. Could it still be condensed a little more?

Somerset, Mills, and Doe, struggle with their own ethical decisions. The biggest thing all three of them struggle with is deciding what is considered ethical for them in their minds. What is ethical for Somerset is not ethical for Mills or Doe and vice versa any way. Many times, it is hard for each of hem to decide what is ethical and what is not. We too, are a lot like the characters. We have a hard time deciding what is ok and what is considered wrong. We struggle with holding ourselves to the same standards as we hold other people.

Detective Somerset is a man who lives by the book. He plays by the rules and never steps out of line. He thinks about every move before he makes it and every word before he says it. So it's not too surprising that he rarely fights to act within his own ethical system. His beliefs tell him that breaking into an apartment is wrong, but when Detective Mills kicks in the door, Somerset walks in with no hesitation. As long as Somerset didn't break his ethics physically, he is ok with whatever happens and easily walks into that apartment.

Somerset also believes that murder is wrong. He took his job as an investigator to keep people safe, not to harm anyone. In the last scene of the movie, as Mills is being driven away in the police car for shooting and killing John Doe, Somerset is talking to a near-by policeman. He tells him to make sure that they really take care of Mills and give him anything he needs. To me, that shows that even though Somerset knows murder is wrong, he does not look down on Mills for killing John Doe. I think he understands why Mills acted unethically and let Doe get the best of him. Even though Somerset believes that murder is wrong, he does not judge Mills for killing John Doe. He doesn't extend his ethical beliefs to those around him.

Detective Mills is very different than Somerset. Mills doesn't worry about the consequences of his actions. He acts first and worries about it later. He knows that breaking into the apartment is wrong, so he gets around it by paying off a homeless woman to tell the police man that Mills and Somerset should search the apartment. He sneaked around his ethics and ended up doing what he knew he wanted to do anyway.

In the climax of the movie, Mills faces the biggest ethical struggle of the whole movie when he is deciding whether or not to kill John Doe. You can easily see on his face the internal struggle he is going through. He obviously believes that murder is wrong, but he also obviously believes in revenge. He can't just turn his head when he finds out that Doe has just killed his wife, Tracy, but he knows that the only way to get even is to kill him. So he fights with himself. Does he kill Doe and show his true wrath, or does he let Doe live, and never avenge Tracy's murder? You can easily see that he know murder is wrong, otherwise, he would have just killed Doe right away. Instead, he goes back and forth with himself. Can he break his own ethics? Yes. In the end, Mills has a flash of Tracy and kills Doe. It was the only way Mills could make things right in his mind.

John Doe's ethics are so askew, but in his mind, he is perfectly sane. He believes that what he is doing is fine, because he does not see his actions as murder. He sees himself as teaching a lesson to society. He is preaching. The only sin he sees himself committing is envy. He is able to overlook his own sin of murder, but he does not overlook his victims' sins. We see his victims as innocent civilians, but Doe sees them as filthy sinners, and he believes that by killing the sinners, he is doing a good thing. His ethics tell him that he is ridding the world of evil.

As crazy as it may sound, I see a lot of us in John Doe. It is so easy for us to point out everyone else's sin and flaws but go around as if we are totally innocent. We walk around all day making judgements about the people we encounter but never stop to think that we are no better. Say, for example, that you're in class. You hear two girls talking behind you about one of their friends. They call her various names, say more bad things about her, and you begin to think, "They are so mean to be saying those things." But wait- haven't you talked bad about somebody behind their back? Of Cource you have! Everybody has. But it doesn't matter. It is so much easier to focus on the flaws of others thatn it tis to examine ourselves and our own ethics.

Everyone has their own set of ethics, and at some point, everyone has broken their own code of ethics. Just as Somerset disregards the fact that Mills killed Doe, just as Mills finally crossed his line and killed Doe, and just as Doe himself ignores his own crime, so have we crossed our own lines. So next time you feel yourself beginning to hate John Doe, just remember how similar we really are.

Works Cited

The Internet Movie Database. 2007. *Web. 3 March 2008.*

Se7en. Dir. David Fincher. 1995. Film.

Reprinted with the permission of the author.

WHAT IS EDITING?

Editing is usually one of the last steps in the writing process. As you learned in the last section, many students make the mistake of focusing on error correction and proofreading before taking the time to develop, clarify, and organize ideas fully through drafting and revision. Although the parts of the writing process are not finite and oftentimes do overlap, editing is a separate activity designed to address local writing issues, such as grammar, sentence variety, mechanics, spelling, and formatting. Resources such as dictionaries and grammar handbooks, whether in print or online, may help at this stage. In fact, if you do not understand any of the concepts in the editing lists that follow, check with a handbook, your instructor, or a tutor at your local writing center.

When to Edit

Editing should begin after you feel confident about the choices you have made in content, organization, and style. You might compare editing and proofreading to washing, waxing, and polishing your car—it would be absurd to take the time to do these things to a vehicle that does not run! Drafting and revising ensure that your writing is first fine-tuned; then, you edit to make it shine on the surface.

Different Levels of Editing

- Paragraphs
- Sentences
- Words
- Proofreading

— Punctuation
— Spelling
— Capitalization and italics
— Formatting (this can also be considered the essay level)

Paragraph-Level Editing

Think of paragraphs as larger forms of punctuation that broaden the connections shown by traditional punctuation marks, such as commas, semicolons, periods, and question marks. Paragraph indentations and lengths provide readers with visual guidance to relationships and connections between major ideas.

When you begin editing at the paragraph level, consider the following:

1. **What does each paragraph say (main idea) and do (introduce, provide proof or support, give an example, illustrate, connect, conclude)?**
   - Did you begin a new paragraph for each new idea?
   - Is the order of the paragraphs logical?
   - Look at what the paragraphs do, like introducing new material and providing support for the main idea, and then question the usefulness or purpose of each.

2. **Are sentences within paragraphs unified and consistent?** Check for
   - Unrelated ideas within the paragraph; paragraphs should focus on one main idea at a time.
   - Illogical sequences and series, such as when a car blows up before it crashes into the eighteen-wheeler in a TV show or film.
   - Mixed metaphors and/or confusing comparisons, for example, "A leopard can't change his stripes" (Bozell).
   - Mismatched subjects and verbs, for example, *butter reads* or *books believe*.
   - Transitional words or phrases.

Sentence-Level Editing

Using a mixture of sentence types makes your writing more interesting and does not distract readers, unlike when you use the same sentence type repeatedly. There are four main sentence patterns from which you can choose, including simple sentences, compound sentences, complex sentences, and compound-complex sentences. Punctuation marks relate directly to the kind of sentence you use and indicate pauses, relationships, and connections within and between sentences. Be sure to proofread for punctuation when you use a variety of sentences.

A *simple sentence* is made up of a subject–main verb combination: "*The Godfather* is my favorite film." The subject can be conjoined, as in "*The Godfather* and *Carlito's Way* are my two favorite films," or the verb can be combined, as in "Al Pacino stars in both and steals the films." Simple sentences may have many optional elements, such as prepositional phrases ("In the first film, Pacino plays Michael Corleone") or adverbials ("Pacino plays his character effectively").

A *compound sentence* combines at least two simple sentences. The new sentence can be joined with a semicolon ("Julia Roberts is Vivian Ward; Richard Gere is Edward Lewis") or with a comma and coordinator ("Julia Roberts is Vivian Ward, and Richard Gere is Edward Lewis"). If the two sentences are closely related, and the right side of the sentence gives more specific information about the left side, a colon can be used to coordinate both sentences together ("Julia Roberts has played many interesting parts: she was a hooker in *Pretty Woman,* a fairy in *Peter Pan,* and a spider in *Charlotte's Web*").

A *complex sentence* is made up of a simple sentence plus one or more subordinate clauses. Complex sentences can use subordinators (such as *after, although, as, because, before, if, since, when, where*) to join two or more sentences together: "After I saw *The Godfather*, I realized that Al Pacino was a great actor." They can also be joined with relative pronouns (such as *that, who, whom, which, what*): "Julia Roberts, who starred in *Pretty Woman*, had her breakout role in *Mystic Pizza*."

A *compound-complex sentence* is made up of two or more simple sentences (this is the compound part) and one or more subordinate clauses (this is the complex part): "Julia Roberts, who is in *Ocean's Eleven* and *Ocean's Twelve*, and Al Pacino, who is in *Ocean's Thirteen*, never made a film together; however, Julia Roberts and George Clooney have made several together."

When you begin editing on the sentence level, ask yourself

1. **Are the connections between ideas communicated effectively through your sentence construction and variety?** Check for

   - **Short, choppy sentences,** especially a group of simple sentences that all begin with a subject: "I enjoyed *The Simpsons Movie*. Homer was unusually funny. The audience laughed a lot."

   - **Excessively long, hard-to-follow sentences:** "Drawn into the Pygmalion-like story of Vivian and Edward and suspending a firm grasp of reality for two hours, the audience, taken away from their everyday humdrum lives, enjoys *Pretty Woman* as a modern-day fairy tale about a modern-day relationship between a businessman and a prostitute and their adventures inside and outside an expensive hotel located in Beverly Hills."

   - **Unclear emphasis due to faulty or excessive subordination:** "Julia Roberts, who had an early role on *Crime Story* (1987) and who also had her breakout role in *Mystic Pizza* (1988), and Al Pacino, who had an early role on *N.Y.P.D.* (1968) and who also had his breakout role in *The Panic in Needle Park* (1971), had surprisingly similar arcs to their careers."

2. **Are individual sentence structures clear and easy to follow?** Check for

   - **Misplaced or unclear descriptions:** "Although she has been nominated for an Oscar three times, Julia Roberts only has won one." (**Corrected:** "Although she has been nominated for an Oscar three times, Julia Roberts has won only one.")

   - **Modifiers (such as verb phrases, adjectives, or adverbs) that have no referent in the sentence:** "Nominated for an Oscar for *Les Misérables*, the audience was excited to see Russell Crowe at the Academy Awards." (**Corrected:** "Nominated for an Oscar for *Les Misérables*, Russell Crowe attended the Academy Awards.")

   - **Modifiers that are too far from the words they modify:** "The audience enjoyed the three songs from the film *Enchanted* that were nominated for Oscars." (**Corrected:** "The audience enjoyed the three *Enchanted* songs that were nominated for Oscars.")

3. **Are ideas balanced through the use of parallel elements?** Check for

   - **Lists that do not have parallel parts of speech,** such as all nouns or all verbs: "I enjoy adventure films, action television shows, and watching NASCAR." (**Corrected:** "I enjoy adventure films, action television shows, and NASCAR.")

   - **Phrases and clauses that do not have the same grammatical structures,** such as all prepositional phrases or subordinate clauses within one sentence or a list within a paragraph: "The Academy Awards usually broadcast when I am on vacation or how I like to see award shows." (**Corrected:** "The Academy Awards usually broadcast when I am on vacation or when I am working on a paper for school.")

4. **Are there any sudden shifts in grammatical structures, tone, or style?** Check for

   - **Inconsistent use of verb tense;** be sure to write all present tense or all past tense unless there is a reason for the shift: "Ferris Bueller plays a tape of his mother's voice when the principal called." (**Corrected:** "Ferris Bueller plays a tape of his mother's voice when the principal calls.")

- **Inconsistency or lack of agreement in person and number;** be sure to put plural nouns (antecedents) with plural pronouns, or singular verbs with singular nouns: "Every princess in Disney films has their prince charming." (**Corrected:** "Every princess in Disney films has her prince charming.")

- **A tone or style that is not unified;** in a formal essay, for example, maintain the formal tone throughout the whole essay: "When visiting the Florida Keys, tourists often get trashed at local bars." (**Corrected:** "When visiting the Florida Keys, tourists often stay up late drinking at local bars.")

5. **Are sentences concise, free of deadweight or unnecessary words?** Check for

- **Placeholders like *there, it, this,* and *these,*** which often serve no purpose in the sentence: "There is another movie that also shows King's love of abused authors." (**Corrected:** "*Misery* also shows King's love of abused authors.")

- **Excessive use of forms of the verb "to be";** replace with strong, specific verbs: "In *Misery,* Kathy Bates is wonderful, and James Caan is remarkable." (**Corrected:** "In *Misery,* Kathy Bates superbly depicts obsessed fan Annie Wilkes, and James Caan remarkably portrays vulnerable author Paul Sheldon.")

- **Overuse of passive verb forms,** such as "is hit" or "has been improved"; replace with strong, specific active verbs: "George Michael's song 'Faith' was improved by Limp Bizkit when the vocals were changed to be more aggressive and the music speed was made faster." (**Corrected:** "Limp Bizkit improved on George Michael's version of 'Faith' by making the vocals more aggressive and speeding up the music.")

- **Lengthy phrases that can be replaced with one or two words** such as "because" rather than "for the purpose of": "Harry Potter fights Voldemort repeatedly for the purpose of saving the world due to him being the hero." (**Corrected:** "Harry Potter fights Voldemort repeatedly because Harry portrays the hero.")

Word-Level Editing

When you edit for word choice, ask yourself

1. **Are any words vague?** Check for

- **General nouns** and replace with specific or concrete nouns such as *Dell PC* instead of *computer* or *30 Rock* instead of *a sitcom.*

- **General verbs** and replace with specific, active verbs, such as *argues* instead of *says* or *sprinted* instead of *ran.*

10 STEPS
WAYS TO EDIT

1. Set the work aside for a time after revising.

2. Participate in editing workshops if available in your classes.

3. Use your resources: previous papers, the Writing Center, and your instructor.

4. Know your problem areas.

5. Read aloud, to yourself or to another person, to avoid self-correcting or thinking you have written the correct form because your mind automatically puts in the correct form when you read to yourself.

6. Read backward, starting with the last sentence, to ensure a focus on editing, not revision.

7. Learn tricks, such as acronyms like FANBOYS (coordinating conjunctions: for, and, nor, but, or, yet, so) and THINTIC (conjunctive adverbs: therefore, however, indeed, nevertheless, thus, in fact, consequently), to help you remember rules or common lists.

8. Use your tools. Keep your dictionary, thesaurus, grammar handbook, class notes, and handouts nearby when editing.

9. Have someone else read your work for proofreading errors, clarity, and sensitivity to audience.

10. Know that you will always have to edit your writing or work. You cannot depend on others to do it for you.

- **General adjectives or modifiers,** where more specific words can be used to give a more concrete image: "The nice tones of Tori Amos's voice on her *American Doll Posse* album are beautiful and nice." (**Corrected:** "The lovely honeyed tones of Tori Amos's voice on her *American Doll Posse* album juxtaposed with the political undertones create a powerful statement.")

2. **Are any words or phrases overused?** Check for
   - **Repeated words at beginnings of sentences:** "The Marlboro Man appears in many types of advertisements. He appears in billboards. He appears in magazines. The Marlboro Man also used to appear on television commercials." (**Corrected:** "The Marlboro man appears in many types of advertisements, including billboards, magazine ads, and television commercials.")
   - **Use of clichés:** "In her song 'Bitch,' Meredith Brooks hit the nail on the head about female stereotypical roles." (**Corrected:** "In her song 'Bitch,' Meredith Brooks sings truthfully about female stereotypical roles.")

3. **Has redundancy been cut?** Check for
   - **Unnecessary words:** "In Stephen King's novel *Salem's Lot*, Ben and his friends fight and kill bloodsucking vampires who bite the necks of victims." (**Corrected:** "In Stephen King's novel *Salem's Lot*, Ben and his friends kill vampires.")

4. **Does the vocabulary reflect sensitivity to audience, purpose, and context?** Check for
   - **The use of stereotypes:** "The audience for chick flicks is always crying into their Kleenexes." (**Corrected:** "*The Holiday* with Cameron Diaz and Kate Winslet made me cry.")
   - **Biased language** based on gender, race, ethnicity, sexuality, religious affiliation, age, or social class: "In *Death Proof*, stuntman Mike (Kurt Russell) whimpers like a little girl when he is shot." (**Corrected:** "In Tarantino's *Death Proof*, stuntman Mike [Kurt Russell] cries out in pain when he is shot.")
   - **Connotations associated with words.** When using a thesaurus, make sure you understand how the word is used and the nuances of meaning associated with the word in various contexts or cultures. Consider the difference in meaning for these two sentences: "In *Working Girl*, Tess McGill ruthlessly works her way to the top." versus "In *Working Girl*, Tess McGill ambitiously works her way to the top."
   - **Jargon,** making sure technical words are defined or explained. For example, in an episode from *Buffy the Vampire Slayer*, the older, highly educated Giles says, "There is a fringe theory held by a few folklorists that some regional stories have actual very literal antecedents." Oz, the teenage werewolf, summarizes this same idea without jargon when he says, "Fairy tales are real."

5. **Does your tone (attitude toward the subject) engage your readers or alienate them?** Check for
   - **A hostile tone:** "*The Dark Knight Rises* is a horrible movie that sucks eggs, and all the actors could not act their way out of a paper bag." (**Corrected:** "The slack-jawed and unrealistic acting in *The Dark Knight Rises* is disappointing.")
   - **Assumptions about the readers or their beliefs:** "No one could possibly blame Erica Bain (Jodie Foster) for becoming a vigilante in *The Brave One*." (**Corrected:** "Many people can understand and condone the actions taken by Erica Bain [Jodie Foster] in *The Brave One*.")
   - **The use of *you*,** which should only be used when speaking directly to the reader: "When you see *The Cabin in the Woods*, you'll be really surprised." (**Corrected:** "*The Cabin in the Woods* surprises its audiences.")

Proofreading: Punctuation

When you edit for punctuation, ask yourself

1. **Do sentences have the correct closing punctuation?** For example, do statements end with periods and questions end with question marks?

2. **Are commas, semicolons, dashes, apostrophes, and other internal punctuation marks used correctly?** Use a handbook if needed to check the rules; likewise, refer to previous explanations of commas splices and fused sentences.

3. **Are quotations correctly introduced, punctuated, and carefully cited? Are quotation marks turned the right way—toward the quoted material?** Refer to Chapter 5 for additional guidelines about incorporating direct quotes.

4. **Are in-text citations correctly punctuated?** Refer to Chapter 5 for additional guidelines about punctuating in-text citations.

Proofreading: Spelling

When you edit for spelling, ask yourself

1. **Are all words spelled correctly?** Remember that spell-checkers are not always foolproof! Check for commonly confused words, such as *their/they're/there*.

2. **Have you used the correct forms?** Double-check any abbreviations, contractions, or possessive nouns.

3. **Have you used hyphens correctly?** Double-check any hyphenated adjectives.

Proofreading: Capitalization and Italics

When you edit for capitalization and italics, ask yourself

1. **Are words capitalized appropriately?**

2. **Are quotations capitalized correctly?**

3. **Are proper names and titles distinguished with appropriate capitalization and punctuation?**

4. **Are titles punctuated correctly with italics or quotation marks?** (See Chapter 5 on researching and documenting for some of these guidelines.)

Proofreading: Formatting

Formatting correctly shows that you care about the presentation of all your hard work. However, looks can be deceiving, and a paper that looks good can still contain serious errors. Computers have made it much easier to produce a professional-looking document, but editing is still essential. When you edit for formatting, ask yourself

1. **Have you followed all of your instructor's directions about formatting?**

2. **Are the margins correct?**

3. **Is the spacing correct between words, sentences, and paragraphs?**

4. **Is the assignment block present and correct? Does it contain all of the required information in the correct order and form?**

5. **Do you have a title that is centered and spaced correctly—and not underlined, italicized, bolded, in quotation marks, or in a different font?**

6. **Do you have a header with your name and page numbers?**

7. **Does your paper follow the citation guidelines required: Modern Language Association, American Psychological Association, or something else?**

PEER EDITORS:
NOTES ON WORKING TOGETHER

Paragraphs

1. On a separate sheet of paper, write a sentence summarizing what each paragraph says and does.

2. Mark any places within paragraphs where sentences lack consistency in thought, language, or style.

Sentences

1. Mark any places where sentences are unclear, incorrectly constructed, or indirect.

2. Note any unnecessary repetition in sentence lengths and structures.

3. Underline any agreement errors or illogical shifts—subjects-verbs, pronouns-antecedents, verb tense, or point of view.

Words

1. Circle or bold any words that are unclear, vague, or unnecessary. Suggest two replacements for each.

2. Mark any places where words and tone do not reflect sensitivity to audience, context, or purpose. Explain these responses to the writer.

3. Circle or bold any words that are repetitive, overused, or clichéd. Suggest a replacement for each.

Proofreading

1. Place square brackets around any missing or misused commas, semicolons, colons, dashes, apostrophes, quotations marks, or end punctuation marks.

2. Underline any misspelled words or incorrect/confused forms.

3. Place square brackets around any missing or misused capitalization and/or italics.

4. Note any places in the paper where the formatting fails to follow the instructor's directions.

Example—Writing Case Study, Draft 4

This is a final edited draft of the essay. Notice that the instructor and peer suggestions from the last draft have been considered, and the commas and spelling errors have been cleaned up. The citations in the Works Cited are also more complete. The author of this essay is ready to turn it in, but notice from the questions and suggestions in the annotations that the author could still revise at least one more time to make the paper stronger.

Halcott 1

Erin Halcott
English 1020-028
Prof. Tipton
March 9, 2013

Crossing Ethical Lines

Excellent expansion and revision of your introductory paragraph. Your thesis is clearer.

The movie *Se7en*, directed by David Fincher in 1995, follows two detectives,

David Mills, played by Brad Pitt, and William Somerset, played by Morgan Freeman,

who are on a hunt to catch a serial killer, John Doe, who is played by Kevin Spacey (imdb). Although the movie mainly focuses on the murders themselves, there is an emphasis on several ethical dilemmas. Each of the three main characters, Somerset, Mills, and Doe, struggles with his own ethical decisions. To me, ethics is what is believed to be right and wrong for each person. Different people in society have different ethics. The biggest thing all three main characters struggle with is deciding what is considered ethical for them in their minds. What is ethical for Somerset is not ethical for Mills or Doe and vice versa. Many times, it is hard for each of them to decide what is ethical and what is not. We, too, are a lot like Somerset, Mills, and John Doe. We struggle with deciding what is right and what is wrong, and we also struggle with holding ourselves to the same standards as we hold other people.

Detective Somerset is a man with very strong ethics. He lives by the book, plays by the rules, and never steps out of line. He thinks about every move before he makes it and every word before he says it. Instead of getting caught up in the emotions of every crime scene, Somerset really takes his time to research everything so that he knows all he can before he makes any decisions. He doesn't mind spending the extra time to prepare. During late nights, he is found in the library looking up everything he can about the seven deadly sins, so that maybe he can understand John Doe that much better. So it's not too surprising that he rarely fights to act within his own ethical system. About halfway through the movie, though, Somerset begins to cross the line of his own ethics. His beliefs tell him that breaking into an apartment is wrong, but when Detective Mills kicks in the door, Somerset walks in with no hesitation. As long as Somerset didn't break his ethics physically, he is OK with whatever happens and easily walks into that apartment.

You used more examples from the film here—great!

Somerset also believes that murder is wrong. He took his job as an investigator to keep people safe, not to harm anyone. In the last scene of the movie, as Mills is being driven away in the police car for shooting and killing John Doe, Somerset is talking to a nearby policeman. He tells him to make sure that they really take care of Mills and give him anything he needs. To me, that shows that even though Somerset knows murder is wrong, he does not look down on Mills for killing John Doe. I think he understands why Mills acted unethically and let Doe get the best of him. Even though Somerset believes that murder is wrong, he does not judge Mills. He doesn't extend his ethical beliefs to those around him. Somerset understands that what is right for him may not be right for everyone. On the other hand, Detective Mills is very different than Somerset.

Mills doesn't worry about the consequences of his actions. He acts first and worries about it later. I believe his disposition has a lot to do with his youth. Mills is much younger than Somerset. He thinks he knows everything, and he is just ready to get out into the field and work. He really doesn't want to spend the time to research. He would rather be out working and believes that he can make his decisions when faced with the problem. He doesn't believe he needs a set plan. He knows that breaking into an apartment is wrong, so he gets around it by paying off a homeless woman to tell the policeman that Mills and Somerset should search the apartment. He sneaked around his ethics and ended up doing what he knew he wanted to do anyway.

You've clarified your analysis of Mills, which is good. But it still seems to need evidence from the film to support your argument.

In the climax of the movie, Mills faces the biggest ethical struggle of the whole movie when he is deciding whether or not to kill John Doe. He just learned that Doe killed his wife out of envy. Doe also tells Mills that his wife was pregnant, a fact that Mills didn't know. Can you imagine what must have been going through his mind? You can easily see on his face the internal struggle he is going through. He obviously believes that murder is wrong, but he also obviously believes in revenge. He can't just turn his head when he finds out that Doe has just killed his wife, Tracy, but he knows that the only way to get even is to kill him. So he fights with himself. Does he kill Doe and show his true wrath, or does he let Doe live, and never truly avenge Tracy's murder? You can easily see that he knows murder is wrong, otherwise, he would have just killed Doe right away. Instead, he goes back and forth with himself. As an investigator, his job is to help people, and he has a hard time deciding whether or not to uphold his job's ideals. John Doe killed his wife. She is all he had in the city. Could he turn from the job he is so passionate about and avenge Tracy's death? Can he break his own ethics? Yes. In the end, Mills has a flash of Tracy and kills Doe. It was the only way Mills could make things right in his mind.

John Doe's ethics are so askew, but in his mind, he is perfectly sane. He believes that what he is doing is fine, because he does not see his actions as murder. He sees himself as teaching a lesson to society. He is preaching. He doesn't see his victims as victims of murder. Instead, he only sees the sin that they have committed. To him, they are nothing more than sinners. God gave him the mission of getting rid of sin in the world, and his victims are nothing more than a job he is completing. They mean nothing. He doesn't see that he is committing murder. Instead, he is doing a great work for God. The only sin he sees himself committing is envy. He is able to overlook his own sin of murder, but he does not overlook his victims' sins. We see his victims as innocent civilians, but Doe sees them as filthy sinners, and he believes that by killing the sinners, he is doing a good thing. He believes that God told him to do it, so that makes it OK. His ethics tell him that he is ridding the world of evil, just as God told him to do. In his mind, he is doing nothing wrong. He is completely blind to his own sin.

Very good analysis of Doe! Could you use any scenes or lines from the film to help illustrate Doe's ethical beliefs?

As crazy as it may sound, I see a lot of society in John Doe. It is so easy for people in society today to point out everyone else's sins and flaws but go around as if they are totally innocent. They walk around all day making judgments about the people they encounter but never stop to think that they are no better. By only focusing on everyone else's flaws, somehow society forgets about its own. They get so caught up in everyone else's business that they never have to worry about their own ethics. It's the same with John Doe. He gets so caught up worrying about what everybody else is doing that he completely disregards the fact that he has killed six people. By only worrying about what other people are doing wrong, society has become blind to its own ethics. It needs to stop being a John Doe and begin being itself again.

Good job revising here. You've expanded your analysis of ethics in general and interwoven Doe's decisions into this part of your argument. You've used a much more formal tone here than in your last draft, but this suits the rest of your paper much better.

Everyone has their own ethics, and at some point, everyone has broken their own code of ethics. Just as Somerset disregards the fact that Mills killed Doe, just as Mills finally crossed his line, and just as Doe himself ignores his own crime, so have we crossed our own lines. When people think that they are so much better than John Doe, they should remember how similar they really are.

It is easy to see that each main character has a unique set of ethics. Somerset's ethics tell him to take his time and really absorb all the information he can. Mills, on the other hand, believes that his job is better done in the field instead of from behind a book. He is very eager to go out to the crime scenes without knowing very much about them at all. Finally, John Doe has his own unique set of ethics too. While the society doesn't understand why he did the things he did, the murders made perfect sense to John Doe. It's because of his ethical system that he was able to commit six murders with a sound mind.

The point is, what is right for one person may not be right for all people. As long as no harm is done, I believe that every person is entitled to their own set of beliefs. Society should quit worrying about others' shortcomings and begin worrying about their own. The book of Matthew, chapter seven, verse three of the *New International Version of the Bible* says it perfectly when it states, "Why do you look at the speck of sawdust in your brother's eye and pay no attention to the plank in your own eye?"

Good summary of your arguments. Interesting use of a Bible quote in your conclusion, given the nature of Doe's ethical beliefs.

Works Cited

The Internet Movie Database. 2007. Web. 27 Feb. 2007.

New International Version Bible. Anaheim: Foundation, 1997. Print.

Se7en. Dir. David Fincher. 1995. DVR.

Reprinted with the permission of the author.

4

reading in the pop culture zone

"You cannot open a book without learning something"

—Confucius

1. Which of these films was not a book first?

a. *Argo*
b. *Skyfall*
c. *Life of Pi*
d. *Silver Linings Playbook*
e. *The Hunger Games*

---

2. What is the average length of a print bestseller?

a. 200 pages
b. 275 pages
c. 300 pages
d. 375 pages
e. 400 pages

---

3. Which of these television shows' main purpose is not helping kids to read better?

a. *Busy Town*
b. *Reading Rainbow*
c. *Wishbone*
d. *Between the Lions*
e. *Super Why*

COLUMBIA PICTURES/COURTESY EVERETT COLLECTION

4. Which one of the following magazines is not usually read by children in varying K-12 grade levels?

a. *Appleseeds*
b. *Weekly Reader*
c. *Noteworthy Artists*
d. *Highlights*
e. *Time for Kids*

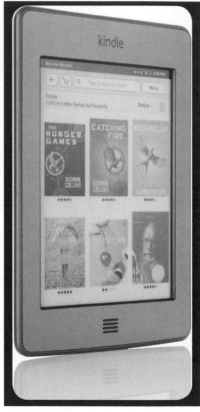

COLUMBIA PICTURES/COURTESY EVERETT COLLECTION

5. What was the most literate city in the United States in 2013?

a. Seattle, WA
b. Los Angeles, CA
c. Washington, DC
d. New York City, NY
e. Boston, MA

6. How many copies of *Harry Potter and the Deathly Hallows* sold within the first 24 hours it was available?

a. ½ million
b. 5 million
c. 10 million
d. 15 million
e. 20 million

Q28 / ALAMY

7. What percentage of those who read e-books also read print books?

a. 80 percent
b. 60 percent
c. 40 percent
d. 20 percent
e. 10 percent

8. Which U.S. city has an average of more branch libraries, volumes held in libraries, and number of checked-out books per person than any other U.S. city?

a. Cleveland, OH
b. Detroit, MI
c. Chicago, IL
d. Pittsburgh, PA
e. New York, NY

9. Which of the following has the least influence on reading fluency?

a. household income
b. parent(s) who read
c. an e-reader in the house
d. a large print book collection in the house
e. a large e-book collection available to the reader

10. **Stump Your Instructor:** In small groups, write a question here about reading and pop culture (in advertising, films, music, social media, or television). Give your instructor five choices for answers.

a.
b.
c.
d.
e.

Reading is an important part of the writing process in most college courses. You come into college with an ability to read, think analytically about what you have read, and then use this exploration to find a topic or argument to write about. As a college student, you add on to this previous knowledge, so you can learn to read and think more critically about all the topics you encounter within your writing courses and the courses that you take across the entire curriculum. Reading more frequently will improve your reading ability, but what might not be obvious is that reading more also improves your writing ability because you get to experience new vocabulary, a range of sentence variety, and different text structures. Reading also provides you with more chances to experience other people's opinions or other cultures. And, finally, reading in a writing course provides you with sources that can be used to support your own opinions. Reading is a process, just as writing is a process, as was seen in Chapter 3. In this chapter, you will be introduced to what makes up the reading process and to a variety of strategies that will help you read more effectively and critically, thus improving your vocabulary, analytical skills, and writing skills.

HOW TO READ EFFECTIVELY

In the thinking, reading, and writing prompts for *The Pop Culture Zone*, we focus on both pleasure and scholarly reading. Remember, however, that when you read popular culture texts, you read more than words alone. You also read the audio, video, textual, and contextual components that surround or are linked to the words in a print text such as an ad, or you read these components in a different manner as you look at and think about texts that are in the form of films, music, social networks, and television shows. You will learn about both these types of reading: literacy (for the printed word) and visual literacy (for images). Even though many of the readings in this text and the topics they explore could be read for pleasure, the reading that is described in this chapter is the scholarly reading you do as you prepare to write reviews, reflection/response essays, analytical essays, or synthesis essays.

Thinking Critically About Reading Selections

To be an effective scholarly reader, you must be an analytical or critical reader. By asking detailed questions about the reading, whether it is an ad or a source that you find to support your argument, you take the first step toward critically reading by engaging with the text in a serious way. A critical reader asks why a reading is assigned, why the author presents the argument in a certain way, or why the text is convincing.

The Purpose of an Assigned Reading

If your instructor assigns only a few readings in a chapter or all of them, use the following questions to understand and appreciate why your instructor chose these readings for your class. This is one of the ways you can gauge how much time you may want to spend on a reading.

- How does this reading fit with the objectives or theme(s) of the course (which may be described on the course syllabus or on the course or department website)?
- How does this reading fit with the objectives or themes of the writing unit you are currently studying?
- Is the reading an introduction to the unit or a critical part of an assignment that will follow?

How Much Time to Devote to an Assigned Reading

Before you read an assigned reading, reflect on exactly how your instructor wants you to read, process, and analyze the reading. The time you take and the effort you make on an assigned reading should be in direct proportion to how much you need to take from the reading. Some readings, as mentioned above, will be used as an introduction to a theme or unit and may not have to be read as deeply or critically as readings to which you will be directly responding. Whatever media you use to do your reading (in a printed book; on a Kindle, Nook, or iPad; in an audio file), the following questions will help you appreciate the significance of the reading within the context of the unit, thus helping determine how much time and effort to spend on the reading.

- Was the reading assigned as an introduction to the unit theme?

- Was the reading assigned for your entertainment?

- Was the reading assigned so you would come to terms with a certain idea?

- Was the reading assigned for you to find or highlight important detail(s)?

- Was the reading assigned so you could answer a specific question?

- Was the reading assigned to be evaluated in a particular way?

- Was the reading assigned as a model for something you will compose?

- Was the reading assigned to apply its concepts to a piece of popular culture?

HOW TO BE AN ACTIVE READER

Just reading or even re-reading a text is not being an active reader. You need to engage critically with the reading and use active reading strategies to improve your comprehension, retention, and recall. Divide your reading process into three separate stages: prereading, reading, and postreading. By doing this, you will process the reading in at least three different ways, which will immediately help you to better comprehend the reading and also retain or recall the material for assignments related to the reading.

Active readers

- give themselves enough time to go through the entire reading process.

- understand the purpose for a reading.

- activate their background knowledge on the reading topic.

- consult their instructor or an online source if they lack background knowledge on the topic.

- preview the reading.

- ask questions before reading.

- visualize what they are reading.

- read aloud sentences or sections that are difficult to process.

- identify and define unfamiliar terms.

- underline and highlight key ideas.

- write notes in the margins.

- take notes outside the text.
- use graphic organizers or create outlines to help process the material.
- re-read the material.
- ask questions after reading.
- freewrite or journal write after they read.
- talk to others about what they have read.

PREREADING AND PREVIEWING

Before you read, it is important to activate your background or prior knowledge about the topic. What you bring to the text will help you better understand the reading. For readings in this text, be sure to look at and answer the Considering Ideas questions before you start your reading. These questions were designed to help you focus on prior knowledge you may have about the reading topic. Also, read the author biography closely, noting where the author has been published and whether writing is his or her profession. Next, examine the title closely. Is there an indication of the purpose of the essay? Is there a sign that the author will be on one side or another of an issue? Does anything point to who the original audience was for the essay?

If the reading is not from this text, look at any other materials that are offered at the beginning of the reading. If an article or essay has a summary or abstract at the beginning of the reading, be sure to read it and highlight the topic and any arguments that are presented. If you are reading a book, look at the table of contents, preface, and any other introductory material that the author included. Sometimes, what you learn about the author or the text before you start reading can help you understand why the author takes a stand or makes an argument.

Draft a list of questions you have about the topic or reading before you begin reading. Then skim or scan the reading, looking for headings and subheadings; charts, tables, and graphs; and bulleted lists. What types of support or evidence does the author use? What does this tell you about the type of essay or the topic? Next, read the introductory paragraph(s), searching for a thesis or argument. If you can find this before you begin reading in earnest, be sure that you have enough background knowledge to continue on. If not, consider doing some informal online research just to become familiar with the general topic. Create a **K-W-L (Know-Want to Know-Learned) table** to help you discover what you know about the topic before you begin your reading. (See Figure 4.1.)

What I **K**now	What I **W**ant to Know	What I **L**earned

FIGURE 4.1 K-W-L Table Template.

Checklist for Previewing or Prereading a Text

✓ Activate background knowledge.
✓ Read introductory material, such as table of contents, preface, author biography, prereading questions.
✓ Examine the title closely.
✓ Look for an abstract or summary.
✓ Create a list of questions about the topic.
✓ Skim or scan the reading, looking for headings, subheadings, charts, tables, graphs, and lists.

- ✓ Read the essay or article introduction.
- ✓ Highlight the thesis or main argument(s).
- ✓ Create a K-W-L table.

READING (FOR CONTENT)

Being a critical reader involves taking the steps necessary to summarize, review, and study the reading, whether it is an assigned reading from this text or another reading (a handout, article, book chapter, or book) that you are using to learn more about a topic or to support your arguments in an essay.

Critical readers

- are intellectually independent.
- are knowledgeable about how arguments are formed.
- are skeptical and do not take anything at face value.
- look for possible author bias in what they are reading.
- read between the lines.
- ask questions.
- scrutinize concepts and assumptions presented in a text.
- base their decisions on evidence.
- manage their time effectively, only reading when they can focus clearly and carefully.

Strategies to Read Critically

If you have used an approach that focuses on reading as a process, you will be prepared to think critically about a text as you begin reading. Reading critically can be done in a variety of ways; as a reader, you choose to do what works best for you. First, design a plan that puts you in control of the time you spend on reading. For example, an efficient plan for you may be reading for about thirty to forty-five minutes, reviewing what you have just read for about five minutes, and then taking a short five-minute break away from the material. When you take a break from reading, stop at a natural break in the text, so you can organize your notes one section at a time.

Annotating Reading Selections

Be sure to highlight or circle new terms and underline their definitions if provided in the text. If the term is not defined, immediately look it up and note the definition near the term. Use a graphic organizer or a notebook to record new terms associated with the reading. This will provide you the vocabulary later on to respond to the reading in a discussion, a journal or blog entry, or an assigned essay. In addition to marking new terminology, annotate the text by drawing attention to main ideas, important points, or supporting evidence. Use highlights, underlines, circles, asterisks, or other markings. Do not overdo the annotations; marking items excessively will not help when you want to go back and find items.

Checklist for Annotating a Text

- ✓ Highlight or underline the main thesis or argument.
- ✓ Circle new terms, and use a graphic organizer or your notebook to keep track of them and their definitions.

✓ Draw attention in the text to main ideas, important points, or supporting evidence.

✓ Emphasize or highlight only those points that you will need for your discussion, journal or blog entries, or essay.

✓ Provide a short review in your notebook or by using a graphic organizer for each section of the text or whenever you take a break from reading.

✓ Use information management software to take notes, add tags to highlight related ideas, and then organize your notes into folders. (See examples in table below.)

Information Management or Note-Taking Software		
AllMyNotes Organizer	Memonic	SilverNote
AudioNote-Notepad	Microsoft OneNote	Tiddly-Wiki
BasKet Note Pads	MyInfo	Tomboy
Catch Notes	MyNotex	TreeDBNotes
CintaNotes	Notee	WikidPad
Evernote	Okular	Windows Journal
Gnote	PDF Studio	XLnotes
Jarnal	Personal Knowbase	Xournal
KeepNote	Qiqqa	Zim
Keeppy	SilverNote	Zotero
KeyNote	Personal Knowbase	
KNote	Qiqqa	

Reviewing Reading Selections

When you take a break from reading, reach the end of a section, or finish reading the entire text, review what you have read. Creating a graphic organizer or table such as the one that follows with which to organize your notes is a good idea. An example is provided here, but you can also add other questions or points that you would like to cover or information for which your instructor has asked you to search. You can also find other types of graphic organizers online by searching for "graphic organizers for reading."

Graphic Organizer	
What is the overall topic?	
What is the thesis, topic sentence, or main problem discussed?	
What conclusion does the author reach?	
How does the author support the conclusion reached?	
Is the conclusion based on fact?	
What are some of the terms the author uses to discuss the topic?	
Does the author use an appeal to logic or emotion in his or her arguments or supporting evidence?	

FIGURE 4.2 Sample Graphic Organizer.

You can also create your own questions by using any of these **self-questioning stems**, filling in the blanks in the questions with something appropriate for the reading selection.

Self-Questioning Stems

Explain how/how often _____

Explain when _____

Explain where _____

Explain why _____

How are _____ and _____ similar or different?

How does _____ affect _____?

How does _____ cause _____?

How does this reading relate to _____ that we have read before?

How does _____ work?

How would you use _____?

What are some solutions to the problem of _____?

What are the strengths of _____?

What are the weaknesses of _____?

What do I already know about _____?

What is a good example of _____?

What is the best _____? Why?

What is the difference between _____ and _____?

What is the meaning of _____?

What would happen if _____?

Why is _____ important?

POSTREADING

When you finish reading an entire reading selection, review the annotations that you have added to the text and the notes that you have taken as you read. Select particularly challenging sections again, and augment the notes that you have taken as you read. After you have collected as much information as you can from the reading, use the **shrinking outline method** by drafting an outline of the information you have collected so far and then making the information more concise by removing repeated or unimportant information. Then, read through your notes one more time, and create a summary or abstract for everything you have collected. This summary, if it is of a reading selection for class, is what you want to read right before class starts. This will serve as a reminder of the important information you will want to bring to a class discussion. If you are creating the summary for a source you will be using for a researched essay, this is the time to use the steps that are described in Chapter 5.

Your instructor may also give you study questions, or you can design study questions on your own, within discussion groups, or outside of class with classmates. Also check if any questions are included at the end of a section in a textbook or on a website associated with the text, and answer these completely in your notebook or in your notes management software. Always bring your text and reading notes to class. As your instructor lectures or leads a discussion on the reading or the topic of the reading, highlight any facts, figures, or supporting information that your instructor asks questions about or covers again in class. For this step, be sure to use a highlighting system that is different from ones you have used for previous steps. You will want to find this information quickly because by covering it in class, your instructor has signaled that this information is important enough to emphasize in both the reading and in your notes.

After a class that covers the reading material, return to your notebook, graphic organizers, or notes management software, and expand your notes once more or explain any difficult concepts in more detail. You will then be able to access this information when you start a writing assignment related to the readings.

Strategies to Summarize Effectively

For readings that are difficult due to content or form, use special strategies in addition to those described earlier to process the material. Try creating a **flowchart** that details how ideas or sections relate to each other; flowcharts start with an idea at the top or left and then break down the idea into smaller components as the chart flows downward or to the right. The sample provided here (see Figure 4.3) is one you can use with a reading selection that introduces a term or concept and then immediately gives examples or definitions.

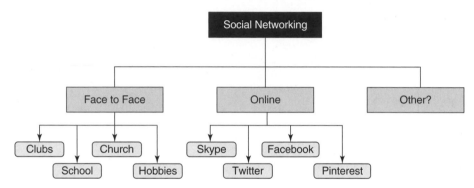

FIGURE 4.3 Flowchart.

You can also create a **concept map**, which is similar to the clustering mentioned in Chapter 3 in the section about brainstorming. However, when you create a concept map for a reading selection, you fill the circles in with terms and ideas from the reading, and then you draw arrows to indicate how the terms or ideas are related. The concept map is much more fluid than the flowchart because you create it as you read and then continue to fill it out as you review the reading and your notes. How you configure the concept map will be dependent on how much information is in the reading selection or how much information you decide is important.

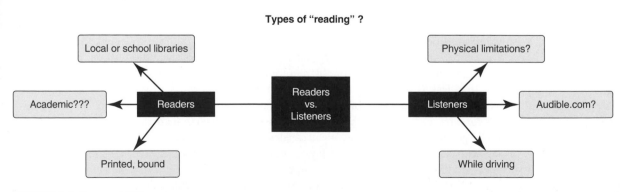

FIGURE 4.4 Concept Map.

Also consider using the detailed **SQ3R (Survey-Question-Read-Recite-Review) method** you might have been introduced to in high school (see Figure 4.5). In an article in *Psychological Science* published in 2008, scientists reviewed over 65 years of research on this type of study method and found that this method (including all of its varieties, such as the SQ4R or PQRST methods) is very successful for college-level readers. In fact, if you review the methods presented earlier, the prereading, reading, and postreading strategies fit into the SQ3R pattern. You may, however, want to build your own model after reading this chapter, including only those strategies that work consistently for you. Included here is a brief breakdown of the most common methods of this kind.

S ⟶ SURVEY
Q ⟶ QUESTION
3R ⟶ READ, RECITE, REVIEW

S ⟶ SURVEY
Q ⟶ QUESTION
4R ⟶ READ, RECITE, RELATE, REVIEW

P ⟶ PREVIEW
Q ⟶ QUESTION
R ⟶ READ
S ⟶ SELF-RECITE
T ⟶ TEST

FIGURE 4.5 SQ3R.

Checklist for Postreading Strategies

✓ Review the annotations you have added to the text.

✓ Add more explanation to challenging sections.

✓ Use the shrinking outline method to narrow down to the most important information.

✓ Create a summary or abstract for what you have read.

✓ Answer study questions from your instructor.

✓ Design study questions on your own, in discussion groups, and with classmates outside of class.

✓ Check for study questions or other types of questions at the end of the reading.

✓ Search for a website associated with the text.

✓ Consider using notes management software, or update what you have done while actively reading.

✓ Bring your text, assigned readings, or reading notes to class, and highlight anything your instructor covers in class.

✓ Review all your notes after class, expanding anything that needs more details.

✓ Create a flowchart to confirm main ideas and how ideas relate to each other.

✓ Create a concept map as you read, and expand it after you review your notes.

✓ Use a study method such as SQ3R.

READING AND ANALYZING VISUALS

Reading about popular culture includes reading the visuals that are present in books and essays, in advertisements, on social networking sites, and with music, films, and television shows. What would a Kindle ad be without an image of a Kindle? What would Pinterest be without images? Being visually literate is an essential part of being a critical reader and thinker. Although visual literacy is a relatively new addition to academic books or chapters about reading, the profusion of computers and other technology used in higher education, the workforce, and everyday life means that we all must be able to communicate not only through the written word (literacy) but also through images (visual literacy). Like with the written word, to comprehend visuals, you need to comprehend the images and then analyze them and the arguments they present. But to do this, you need to use active reading strategies to read the image and then do many of the same prereading and postreading activities presented earlier with regard to print text.

Your instructor may ask you to analyze something with visuals; this is sometimes called a visual rhetoric analysis essay or a rhetorical analysis essay. Some questions other than the ones used for word-based texts can be asked when you read and analyze visuals or visual rhetoric. Investigating who created the visual text, for whom the visual text was intended, and what the purpose the creator had in mind for the visual text are good places to begin your analysis. Here are some questions that may help you with your exploration.

- Who created the text?
- What other texts has this person created?
- Is the author an individual or does this person represent a company or a larger organization?
- What visual effect is the creator aiming for?
  - What does the creator use to give this effect?
- Who is the intended audience?
- Are you a member of the intended audience?
  - If so, how does the visual affect you?
  - If not, how do you think the visual will affect the intended audience?
- Does the creator seem to hold any assumptions about the intended audience?
  - If so, what assumptions?
  - How do you know?
- Why was the visual created?
  - What is its purpose?
- Does the visual achieve its purpose?

You can use any or all of the above questions to analyze advertisements and brochures, social networking websites, films, television shows, music, or anything that includes a visual component. Asking even more questions about the content, context, design, and your overall impression will allow you to discover just how effective a visual text is.

- What is the first thing you noticed about the visual text?
  - Why do you think you noticed this first?
  - Do you believe that this was intended by the creator of the piece? If so, why?
  - What effect does the first thing you notice have on you?

- What is the subject of the visual?
- How effective is the visual in presenting the subject?
- What form does the visual take?
- How are the parts of the visual arranged?
- Where is the visual presented or published?
- If the visual is placed along or around words, how is it placed?
  - Is there an obvious reason for this placement?
- Is the visual paired with words?
  - If so, how is the visual connected to/with the words?
  - Do they work together well?
  - Would the words alone or the visual alone be as effective in sending the intended message?
  - What font(s) are used for the words?
  - How does the font affect the visual?
- Does the visual use color?
  - If so, what colors are used?
  - Why do you think the creator chose those colors, the particular shades, and the particular brightness?
  - Does the choice of color(s) add to or detract from the image(s) (and words)?
- Are any of the visuals repeated, disjointed, or unclear?
  - Do you believe this is intended? If so, why?

GRAPPLING
with Ideas

Examine the image of Julia Roberts that is on the opening of this chapter. On your own or with a small group of your classmates, use the visual rhetoric questions from this section and analyze the visual.

SAMPLE VISUAL/RHETORICAL ANALYSIS ESSAY

Michael Kimble
Rhetorical Analysis
ENGL 1010-088
Professor Clint Bryan
27 November 2013

Symbolic Importance of Vader's Suit

Sith lord Darth Vader is one of the best-known and iconic fictional villains to ever be seen on film. His legacy is one that consumed and inspired fans of all ages and generations. George Lucas created Darth Vader in *Star Wars* (1977) so that the audience could instantaneously grasp that this character was a villain. He wanted to portray him as something that represents all that is evil and unjust. Before Vader even speaks, the audience is able to accept that this being is undoubtedly evil. It may be because it's natural for humans to not immediately impose trust into people when we can't see their face, or it could be the dark and ominous tone of the *Imperial March* that supports Vader's strut, but the association is there for most.

Over the years, *Star Wars* has still mesmerized its audience. *The Phantom Menace* (1999) was one of the longest awaited films ever and despite its disappointment, is still one of the highest grossing movies of all time. The entire franchise is known around the globe and is considered by many as the greatest trilogy (episodes IV-VI) of all time. This wouldn't have been the case if Lucas's portrayal of his characters weren't so deep and symbolic. Today, Vader's mask has made its way into our culture as a sign of a villain from a classic saga. It is worn on Halloween and decorates rooms by supporters of the series, but is what we think of when we see this mask the same thing that George Lucas thought of when he created it? Vader's mask has more meaning to it than just invoking fear in the audience. The mask and suit play a large part in a subliminal portrayal of good versus evil.

Being all black, Vader's suit is an icon and explanation of the dark side, which is a collective of evil that wish to rule the galaxy and destroy all that don't support or benefit their own selfish desires. The other side of the force, referred to as the lighter side, seeks to stop the dark side from ruling and destroying everything in its path. In Western literature light/dark and black/white have long been a symbol of good versus evil. Obi-Wan describes Darth Vader by saying, "He's more machine now than man, twisted and evil" (*Return of the Jedi*). Vader's suit is his own in that it has a respirator that breathes for him, special contributions to his fake arm, and shielded eye-holes which we later learn is to cover his face and prevent any exposure to his skin.

The appearance of the suit is faceless and lacks any emotion, which helps portray him as machine, thus taking away all outward signs of his humanity. His low and forceful voice is the only sign that a human is hidden somewhere under his cloak. The suit even makes a noise similar to that of a stereotypical machine sound when it breathes for him. Beyond the light/dark battle is one between man and machine, which is very common in science fiction. With all of Vader's machine-like sounds, limbs, and looks, he is shown to be less human.

Vader's suit also represents his isolation from the outside world. He was an eager and talented young Jedi that the Republic never really recognized or allowed to branch out. Because of this, he felt like an outsider. The Empire (dark side) attracts outcasts who feel as if they are only out for themselves. Other Sith lords wore robes that represented their involvement in the dark side, which could be taken off at any time. Vader's fate and life were dressed in the balance of the suit that ultimately wore him. In order for him to leave the dark side and defeat the evil imposed in him and those surrounding him, he would have to embrace his death as well, which he did. Vader's suit is shown to be a metaphor for whatever holds us back from doing what is right, and represents all we have to lose in doing so. It is symbolic of the disguise we wear in our lives to cover up the person underneath.

Works Cited

Star Wars Episode VI: Return of the Jedi. Dir. George Lucas. Lucas Films, 1983. Film.

Reprinted with the permission of the author.

THE READING ZONE

CONSIDERING IDEAS

1. Do you ever "read" a book by listening to it? If so, where do you do this reading?
2. What do you think the difference is between reading the print version of a book and listening to the same book?

AUTHOR BIO

Kristi Jemtegaard is the Youth Services Coordinator for the Arlington Public Library system in Arlington, VA. She has taught courses on children's and young adult literature at Catholic University of America and the University of Virginia and has served on both the Newbery and Caldecott Award Committees for the American Library Association. She is a regular reviewer of children's literature and audio productions for national publications such as The Washington Post and Booklist.

READERS VERSUS LISTENERS

Reading a Book Versus "Reading" an Audiobook

Kristi Jemtegaard

As members of a book-discussion group that includes audiobooks in its final list of recommended titles, the audiophiles among us occasionally find ourselves at odds with the bibliophiles over the quality of a title. Inevitably questions arise: Is it fair to judge a book by the audio version? Do you have to read a book first and form a judgment about its quality before moving on to the secondary experience of listening? Because there are no clear-cut answers, we happily and endlessly debate the issue.

Years ago when we had a text-oriented audience, and when audiobooks lagged years behind the print versions, I would have had a different answer. When reading the book first was the only real option, the tendency to judge the audiobook by the print version was a logical model. Today, however, the answer is less clear. Library patrons are coming at books in many different ways, and audiobooks do not serve the same function they once did. As my library's long reserve list for Kate DiCamillo's *Because of Winn Dixie* attests, many kids see the movie first and then seek out the book. For these youngsters, the book is a secondary experience.

True, the book and audiobook versions are joined more closely than the movie and book combination because audios use the same words. Many readers still reach for an audiobook as a way to reexperience something they have enjoyed in print. While listening, they may pick up on the humor they missed in their rush to find out what happened next, or they may fall in love with the descriptive prose that their eyes slid over the first time around. That's the art of the audiobook—to provide a genuinely new sensory experience. At its best, it expands the experience of the book by adding a fourth dimension to plot, character, and setting—the dimension of sound.

One of the most frequent additions to audio is music, often used to introduce the title or to add drama. Carefully chosen music can set the stage for what is to come. Another aspect of audios is the ability to establish character through the reader's voice. In the hands of a skilled narrator, the characters' personalities come to life. Ensemble casts can also underscore significant contrasts and relationships, and the cast can alter the pace, underscore dramatic highs and lows, and create a sense of spontaneity.

Audio also allows listeners to tackle difficult words, which can be real stumbling blocks for readers. Susan Cooper's fantasy *The Grey King* takes place in Wales. Words such as *Clwy* and *tyre* (not to mention the tongue twisters *cwpanaid* and *diolch*) are enough to halt even hardy readers in their tracks; less able ones may desist altogether. Yet in the capable hands of narrator Richard Mitchley, the words and phrases are both lilting and understandable. Titles that feature characters from other locales or take place in other countries can also benefit from audio. Julia Alvarez's *Before We Were Free,* in which Anita de la Torre and her family flee the Dominican Republic, and Narinder Dhami's *Bindi Babes,* featuring two Anglo-Asian sisters, are two examples in which narration establishes both place and ethnicity.

Increasingly, there is another type of audience—one that comes to the audiobook first. For them, the audiobook is the primary experience, and if they choose to read the book, they do so because of the unique capabilities the printed page affords, including the ability to flip back and forth between chapters, peruse illustrations, and even daydream.

In the end, it's not a question of whether listening or reading is the better choice or which one should be done first. When listening, we can rightfully focus on how well the narrator matches the material, how pitch and cadence enrich the text, and other audio-specific aspects of the production. When reading, we instinctively think in terms of plot, character development, setting, theme, genre, and style. But whether we read or listen, it comes down to quality. Can a spectacular narrator enhance a mediocre book? Of course. Can a magnificent book mask a run-of-the-mill performance? No doubt. Audiobooks must be faithful and true interpretations of the written texts, and like books, they need to stand on their own merits. As readers, listeners, and evaluators, it is up to us to maintain open minds, embrace the experience, and make judgments. It is fine to savor, even to prefer, the voice we hear in our own heads as we read, but confining ourselves to our own voice means a more narrow experience of literature. We may be able to read a musical score, but how much more glorious it is to hear it sung.

Source: *"Soundings: Readers vs. Listeners" by Kristi Jemtegaard from* Booklist, *April 1, 2003, Vol. 101, Issue 15, p. 1399. Used with permission from the American Library Association.*

DECODING THE TEXT

1. What are some of the ways the author makes the comparison between readers and listeners?

2. Is the essay biased or even-handed? Explain your answer with examples.

3. According to the author, what are some of the benefits that you can receive when you listen to a book?

CONNECTING TO YOUR CULTURE

1. Do you read for fun? If so, do you ever listen to books for fun as well? What types of recreational books do you believe would be better to listen to than others?

2. Do you believe you would be more likely to listen to books for fun or to books for your classes? What are the benefits of both? What are the drawbacks?

5

researching in the pop culture zone

Giles: Um, I've not found any creature as yet that strikes terror in a vampire's heart.

Buffy: Try looking under things that can turn their heads all the way around.

Giles: Nothing human can do that.

Buffy: No, nothing human. There are some insects that can. Whatever she is, I'm gonna be ready for her.

Giles: What are you going to do?

Buffy: My homework. Where are the books on bugs?

—From *Buffy the Vampire Slayer,* "Teacher's Pet," Season 1

1. All of the following movies have a form of plagiarism. Match the movie title to the plagiarist.

1. *A Murder of Crows*
2. *Bring It On*
3. *Secret Window*
4. *Good Will Hunting*

a. Lindsay Sloan as Big Red
b. Scott William Winters as Clark
c. Cuba Gooding Jr. as Larson Russell
d. Johnny Depp as Mort Rainey

COLUMBIA TRISTAR / THE KOBAL COLLECTION

2. Which of the following bands or artists did not use the drum introduction from Led Zeppelin's "When the Levee Breaks" in their own songs?

a. Beastie Boys
b. Tone-Loc
c. Mike Oldfield
d. Erasure

3. Match the following forensic scientists with the cities where they conduct their research.

1. D. B. Russell
2. Megan Hunt
3. Kay Scarpetta
4. R. Quincy

a. Los Angeles, CA
b. Las Vegas, NV
c. Richmond, VA
d. Philadelphia, PA

4. Many modern movies are retellings or paraphrases of classic novels and plays. Match the modern film title with the classic work.

1. *Clueless*
2. *Ten Things I Hate About You*
3. *Scrooged*
4. *She's the Man*

a. *A Christmas Carol*
b. *Twelfth Night*
c. *Emma*
d. *The Taming of the Shrew*

5. Name the authors of the classic works in the previous question.

6. Many rap songs use samples of music (lyrics and/or melodies) from songs recorded by other artists. Match the following rap songs with the original artists the samples were taken from.

1. "Pretty Woman"
2. "You Can't Touch This"
3. "If"
4. "Fergalicious"

a. Diana Ross and the Supremes
b. Salt-N-Pepa
c. Roy Orbison
d. Rick James

7. In the previous question, which group's use of sampling sparked a debate over the legality of the practice?

8. Which of the following television shows does not require research as a key element of the plot?

a. *NCIS*
b. *Sherlock*
c. *Cougar Town*
d. *Person of Interest*

9. Name the character names or actor names for the librarians in the following films and television shows.

a. *The Mummy*
b. *Buffy the Vampire Slayer*
c. *The Librarian: Quest for the Spear*

WARNER BROS TV / THE KOBAL COLLECTION

10. **Stump Your Instructor:** In small groups, write a question here about research and pop culture (in advertising, films, music, social media, or television). Give your instructor five choices for answers.

a.
b.
c.
d.
e.

ANSWERS

1) 1. c. Cuba Gooding Jr. as Larson Russell 2. a. Lindsay Sloan as Big Red 3. d. Johnny Depp as Mort Rainey 4. b. Scott William Winters as Clark **2)** b. Tone-Loc **3)** 1. b. Las Vegas, NV 2. d. Philadelphia, PA 3. c. Richmond, VA 4. a. Los Angeles, CA **4)** 1. c. Roy Orbison 2. d. *The Taming of the Shrew* 3. a. *A Christmas Carol* 4. b. *Twelfth Night* **5)** a. Charles Dickens b. William Shakespeare c. Jane Austen d. William Shakespeare **6)** 1. c. Roy Orbison 2. d. Rick James 3. a. Diana Ross and the Supremes 4. b. Salt-N-Pepa **7)** 2 Live Crew's "Pretty Woman" **8)** c. *Cougar Town* **9)** a. *The Mummy*—Evelyn Carnahan (Rachel Weisz) b. *Buffy the Vampire Slayer* (television series)—Rupert Giles (Anthony Head) c. *The Librarian: Quest for the Spear*—Flynn Carsen (Noah Wyle) **10)** Your answers

89

YOU AND THE RESEARCH PROCESS

When writing about pop culture, you may rely on your own personal knowledge, evaluations, experiences, and reactions. In addition, you may draw upon primary and secondary research to give background information, to illustrate or back up what you have to say, to support your conclusions, or to provide various reactions and points of view. Primary research includes the actual show, book, group, or event you are writing about as well as data you collect yourself, perhaps through surveys or interviews. Secondary sources include all of the material related to your topic—for example, a *Rolling Stone* review of the film you intend to analyze, an argumentative essay in *Time* online about the subculture you are studying, and a sportscaster's commentary about the game you just watched. When you use information from any source in your writing, you need to verify that the information is accurate and trustworthy and then document the source, usually parenthetically (inside the essay) and in a Works Cited page at the end of the essay. Using source information without documentation is one type of plagiarism and a quick way to receive an F on an assignment and suffer other ramifications. Consequently, this section provides information about how to

- Find reliable source material, particularly when working with pop culture topics.
- Summarize, paraphrase, and/or properly quote source material.
- Document source material using Modern Language Association (MLA) or American Psychological Association (APA) guidelines.

Your instructors may have specific requirements for the number and type of sources you may use, so always check with them or consult your assignment sheet.

GRAPPLING with Ideas

- Where do you start when you need to research something? Do you visit the library? Turn to the Internet? Talk with a friend? Make lists? Search randomly?

- How does research change when the topic is pop culture? How is it the same as any other research process?

- What types of pop culture research have you done in the past, whether for school projects or personal interest? What types of sources did you use?

KNOWING YOUR RESOURCES ON CAMPUS

Researching an idea takes time; most projects will require many hours of research before you even begin writing and perhaps even more research after you begin the writing process. Random researching will sometimes turn up information about your chosen topic but more often results in wasted effort. On the other hand, a purposeful search will usually yield more useful results. Once you have a topic, you must know where to find information for your project. This involves first knowing what resources are available on your campus. Most campuses have a central library; others may also have specialized libraries devoted to particular topics, times periods, or media—for example, a music library or a law library. Likewise, many campuses now have database or online subscriptions that can be accessed from computers anywhere on or off campus. Do not forget your local city, county, or state libraries; they may also have materials you can use and databases you can access. When conducting research on pop culture, it is especially important to know where to look because many primary and secondary resources in the field may be found outside the traditional venues and sources you have used in the past. For example, you may visit the archives at the local television station or talk to people on Facebook when conducting your research.

RESEARCHING A TOPIC: SECONDARY RESOURCES

Once you have determined a general topic through the use of brainstorming techniques (see Chapter 3 for an explanation of various approaches to brainstorming), you can begin looking up materials to help you expand your points, support your ideas if you need more information, or narrow your ideas if you have too much information. If you are unfamiliar with the topic, then it is always a good idea to consult a basic reference such as an encyclopedia or dictionary to get some general knowledge of your subject. However, you should note that such general works, although useful for helping you get started or narrow down your topic (this includes Wikipedia), may not be appropriate as a final source for your project, especially when writing analysis and synthesis essays. You should find out what your instructor allows.

Suppose, for example, you have been asked to analyze the television program you just viewed, and your assignment sheet asks you, or even requires you, to use outside sources. You might begin by looking up the director or creator in a biographical dictionary, or you might research the genre in an encyclopedia or a reference book such as *The Television Genre Book*; both of these secondary sources will help you get started. In addition, you might look up published reviews for the show or even the episode; the viewing statistics for the show; interviews with the cast, director, or creator; or reviews and critiques of previous works by the same people. This information might lead you to write about how the creator develops his or her characters or how the director films certain types of shots. You may even want to narrow your topic still further to one particular character. Following are some places to start with your research.

The Reference Section

The reference section of your brick-and-mortar library, as well as its online resources, is often a good place to start for background information and for help narrowing your topic and understanding research terms. Check your library for the following resources.

ENCYCLOPEDIAS

Encyclopedias are a good resource for getting general information about a topic. They often include lists of works on a topic, which can cut down research time. Examples of general encyclopedias include *Compton's Encyclopedia*, *Encyclopaedia Britannica*, and *World Book Encyclopedia*; many of these can be found in print and online. When researching pop culture, you may also want to look at encyclopedias about specific topics such as music, art, or business—for example, *The Encyclopedia of Popular Music* or the *African Music Encyclopedia*. A useful online tool to get you started is Wikipedia. *Caution:* Because Wikipedia entries can be written and edited by anyone, including you, it should not be considered a valid source to use in your paper, but it can provide general definitions and a direction to get you started.

DICTIONARIES

In addition to dictionaries of the English language, libraries often have dictionaries for numerous other languages. Libraries also have specialized dictionaries with topics such as slang, aphorisms (short, pithy statements expressing a general truth such as "Believe nothing you hear, and only half of what you see" by Mark Twain), slogans, clichés, and other phrases. You might use one of these when you want to better understand the lyrics to a popular song or the dialogue in your favorite television show. One well-known example of this type of dictionary is *Bartlett's Familiar Quotations* (http://www.bartleby.com/reference). Many of these dictionaries can be found online as well, either through library subscriptions or free to the general public.

HISTORICAL DICTIONARIES

Historical dictionaries document not only a word's meaning but also how its meaning has changed over time. The most comprehensive English historical dictionary is *The Oxford English Dictionary* (often called the *OED*), which is now available online as well as in hard copy at many libraries. The *OED* would be useful if you wanted to trace the use of a word being adopted by a particular group of people or a subculture or a word newly coined by the news media.

BIOGRAPHICAL DICTIONARIES

Biographical dictionaries contain short biographies of various individuals who have some characteristic in common. For instance, *The Dictionary of American Biography* contains short biographies of famous American artists, authors, scientists, and others. The library and various online databases have numerous *Who's Whos* and still others that are extremely specialized—for example, *Grove's Dictionary of Music and Musicians* and *The Dictionary of Victorian Painters*.

SCIENTIFIC ABSTRACTS

The Reference Section contains numerous abstracts of various scientific experiments, articles, and observations. *Chemical Abstracts* is one such work. Perhaps you want to know how violence in films affects young teens; you can look at studies in psychology, sociology, nursing, and anthropology, just to name a few areas.

Internet Sources

Often, the quickest way to find information on many topics is to use the Internet; however, the Internet has advantages and disadvantages for writing academic essays. Although an hour surfing the web can yield a great deal of information, not all of it is accurate or from a reliable source. Many companies put misleading information into their meta tags or indexes, which are used by search engines such as Google or Bing, so their site will appear more often in basic searches and thus increase traffic to their site. More traffic means more advertising dollars.

Government websites (.gov sites) usually contain reliable information. If a website is sponsored by a university (.edu), journal, well-known organization (.org or .net), or other established corporate entity (.com), then information from these sites is probably usable. Websites sponsored by individuals (these can also be .com, .edu, .net, or .org) can be useful ways of gathering information, but for the most part, unless the individual is an

CARS Checklist

You can use the CARS checklist to help you establish the validity of a website. These questions are not guarantees, but they will help you eliminate unauthoritative websites.

- **Credibility:** Is the information from a trustworthy source? What are the author's credentials? Is there evidence of quality control? Is the author a known or respected authority? Is there organizational support for this work? Can the author be contacted through this website?

- **Accuracy:** Is the information up to date, factual, detailed, exact, and comprehensive? Do the links work? Are there obvious grammatical or spelling errors?

- **Reasonableness:** Is the account fair, balanced, objective, and reasoned? Are there any conflicts of interest? Is it free of fallacies or slanted tone? Who is the site's intended audience?

- **Support:** Are supporting sources listed? Is there contact information? Is corroboration or a bibliography available? Are all claims supported and is documentation supplied?

acknowledged authority in the field, these sites are considered unreliable or at least biased. Always look at who created the site and for what purpose, as well as what the author's credentials are. Many universities, for example, provide server space for their faculty and students to use in any way they see fit, which means the information could be one sided or even inaccurate. It is always a good idea to verify information by using multiple sources.

Listed next are some resources to get you started. You should also look at the sources that have been approved (and probably linked to) by your own librarians; many of these sources are available online through subscriptions, so check out what your local libraries have to help your research.

ARTS

Dance Heritage Coalition — http://www.danceheritage.org

The Getty Online — http://www.getty.edu
(info about art, artists, and architects)

BUSINESS

Consumer.gov — http://www.consumer.gov

Consumer World — http://www.consumerworld.org

GENERAL

Commercial Portals

GovSpot — http://www.govspot.com

LibrarySpot — http://libraryspot.com

The Library of Congress — http://loc.gov
(check for their spoken word audio,
music, and video titles free to download)

New York Public Library — http://www.nypl.org

Publications.com — http://www.publications/factbook/index.html

U.S. Census Bureau — http://www.census.gov/
(maintained by the U.S. Census Bureau,
the guide to government resources on the web)

The World Factbook — https://www.cia.gov/library/publications/the-world-factbook/
(maintained by the CIA)

HEALTH/NUTRITION

Health Resources and Services Administration — http://www.hrsa.gov/

National Library of Medicine — http://www.nlm.nih.gov/

USDA Food and Nutrition Information Center — http://fnic.nal.usda.gov

LITERATURE

Books in Print, Book Review Index, and *Book Review Digest* — http://www.booksinprint.com/default.ashx
(for short reviews, periodicals that contain book reviews)

MOVIES

Internet Movie Database — http://www.imdb.com
(for basic information about film producers, characters, actors, and release dates, but be aware that this site is maintained by self-proclaimed "movie fans" and is supported by commercial sponsors)

Movie Review Query Engine — http://www.mrqe.com
(this site collects and indexes published reviews, but it also provides space for users to post their own reviews, so pay attention to the various sources on this site and their reliability)

Music

Oxford Music Online, home for *Grove Dictionary of Music and Musicians*
or *Grove Music Online*   http://www.oxfordmusiconline.com
(these are usually subscription sites, so check your library's holdings)

Periodicals

Ulrich's Periodical Directory, LexisNexis, and InfoTrac College Edition
(for many newspapers and magazines, you can also go directly to their sites; some will require a personal login, and others may require a subscription for full access)

Science/Technology

National Science Foundation—Statistics   http://www.nsf.gov/statistics/

National Science Resources Center   http://www.nsrconline.org/

Wired   http://www.wired.com

Quick Search Example

A popular general database available in most libraries is Academic OneFile, previously known as InfoTrac, which contains access to a variety of online databases. These databases are similar in the way they are searched and are much like other commercial or subscription databases. Following is a brief guide for a basic search in Academic OneFile, which is often a good starting place for research about popular culture because it indexes numerous magazines and newspapers, as well as more academic journals and even videos, blogs, and images.

Notice that the start page in Figure 5.1 is set up for a basic search and that it defaults to the *keyword* search. Keywords are words and short phrases that indicate the subject matter of the article; they can be chosen by the author or by the indexers. You can also search by subject terms, which are broader categories used by Academic

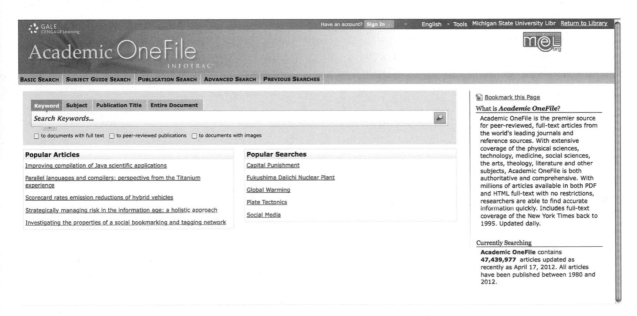

FIGURE 5.1 Basic search in Academic OneFile

OneFile for organizing materials; in addition, you can search for words that appear anywhere in a document. Searching the entire document is not very useful unless your research question lends itself to such a search—for example, if you are trying to determine how many different authors make reference to Harry Potter. Another search option to be aware of is the advanced search, which allows you to narrow your search using more than one keyword and/or putting in the author's name or the publication name. It also lets you put in date parameters or search for articles of a certain type, such as full text, peer reviewed, or multimedia.

Now, suppose you want to know more about college football. Where would you start your search? You can put the word *football* into your basic search and see what you get (Figure 5.2).

According to the search on this particular day, the keyword *football* gets 12,069 hits in Academic Journals, 66,712 in Magazines, 35,6320 in Newspapers, 6,702 in Images, as well as a number of other hits in various resources indexed for Academic OneFile. This large number of resources is not very useful, so you may want to narrow your search. On the left-hand column, you can see the subject terms that are linked to the keyword *football*; these are narrower categories already set up by the database. As you go down the list, you will see that *college football* is one of the database's categories. Click this link, and you will get a New Results page using the more specific term (Figure 5.3).

As you can see, the subject term takes us to more specific articles about college football. We have also clicked the tab on the left for Magazines to show that this option gives you more choices but is set up the same way. We now have 454 articles, which is more manageable, but we can also narrow again if we choose—perhaps you want to focus on the NCAA or on players specifically. Now you can read through the abstracts to see which articles might be of use to you or which ones catch your attention. When you find articles you want to hold on to, you can mark them by clicking the mark box next to the title of the article; a check mark should appear when an essay is marked. When you have marked all of the essays you are interested in, you can go to the top-right menu and choose how you want to share/save your resources (see Figure 5.4). Across the top you will find the menu options for starting a new search.

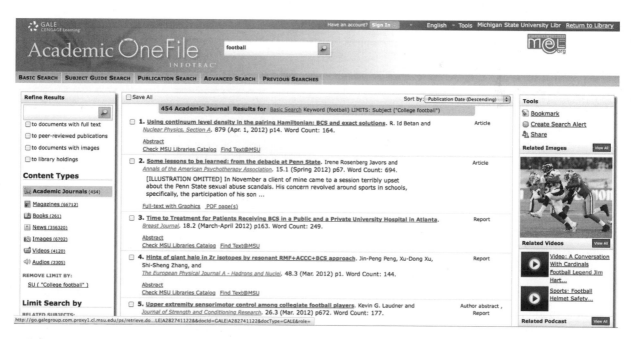

FIGURE 5.2 Search for *football* in Academic OneFile

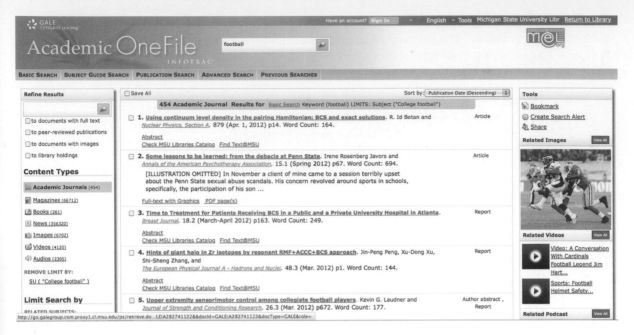

FIGURE 5.3 Search for *college football* in Academic OneFile

FIGURE 5.4 Bookmark and share options in Academic OneFile

Not all databases work in the same way, but they do share many similarities. All have a Help or Getting Started option, where you can learn about the basics of searching with that particular index or search engine. The Help menu will usually tell you what kinds of searches you can do, what kinds of search limits or Boolean logic you can use (for example, AND, OR, NOT), and how to retrieve the resources you have found. Some also have lists of subject or index terms as well as lists of periodicals and other sources indexed in the database. It is usually worth your time to look at the Help section and learn how to conduct a useful search instead of just scrolling through pages of resources or settling for the first few articles that appear, which may or may not be relevant for your project. Also, do not forget to use your local librarian as a resource. Most college libraries and some local libraries have librarians who specialize in helping patrons locate research sources.

RESEARCHING A TOPIC: PRIMARY RESOURCES AND RESEARCH

As mentioned previously, the film, book, advertisement, group, television show, or other artifact is your primary resource. It is the primary object of study and research and will need to be read, viewed, and analyzed multiple times (see next section for an example of how this is done). The secondary sources help you think about this primary source and analyze it.

In addition, when writing about pop culture, you may also find it useful to conduct your own primary research. For example, to write about a particular subculture or network, you may want to talk to members of the group through interviews or surveys, even comparing the stories of different research participants. Interviews may happen face to face, but they have also become quite common online; similarly, a number of programs such as SurveyMonkey or KwikSurvey are available to make online surveying easy. Likewise, you can observe a music concert or live performance at the stadium or theater to note how the performers and audience act, the language or behaviors they use, and how they dress or represent themselves. You can also study the documents of a particular group or network, such as brochures, websites, letters, music lyrics, liner notes, or movie scripts, for insight into how artifacts were developed, revised, and eventually used. As with secondary research, you will want to keep accurate records of who you talk to, when you talk to them, and when you conduct observations, as well as precise records of what is said.

One tool you may find useful is the double-entry notebook or log. The idea is to take your interview and observation notes on one side or half of the page while leaving space to go back and comment on or respond to your entries on the other side. The first entry represents the language of your research participants, notes on your observations, or maps of the places you visit. The second entry represents your personal thoughts about what you have recorded, including questions, your readings of the text, the messages presented by the research participants or space, your conclusions about what you are seeing and hearing, and your working thesis.

Remember, all sources must be listed on a Works Cited page, so you should write down the information (that is, web addresses, authors' names, where you found the source, and the date of publication) for your in-text citations and the bibliography. Note files, whether in the form of notecards or digital information, can be an effective way to collect citation information that you may need to use later. Always know where you found your information and how to get back to it. Also, be sure to record names and dates of interviews for your Works Cited.

ANALYZING AND USING RESEARCH MATERIALS

It is important to analyze your sources and decide which books, articles, or sites have the most reliable information about your topic. In most cases, entire books are not devoted to narrow topics such as those found in a first-year composition essay; therefore, use the indexes or table of contents to locate topics within books. Abstracts of journal articles will usually give necessary information for determining the value of the source. Internet sources that come from a guided search often are useful sources. If the website has a lot of information, it can be helpful to break this down into notes about various aspects of your topic.

GRAPPLING with Ideas

- Have you ever completed a survey? How were you recruited for this research? Did you complete it online or with pen and paper? How did your answers help the researcher with her or his research? What was the topic?

- Have you ever participated in a focus group? How were you recruited for this research? Who else was there? How was the group run? Did you feel free to share your thoughts on the topic? How did you help the researcher by being in the group?

Now you can read or view the materials in the order of their value, starting with the most useful. You will probably want to take notes, making sure to include bibliographic information (see the sections for MLA or APA citation guidelines). Be sure to follow your instructor's guidelines for recording notes and turning in note files (whether on cards, papers, or electronic files), as well as the documentation style necessary for the class, assignment, or discipline you are working in. As you read and take notes, think about the most useful way to organize your annotations, using some system that works for you and your writing project: chronological order, points in your argument, or sources. Once your notes are categorized and organized, you may be ready to start writing.

When writing about pop culture, your most important source is the movie, song, television show, artwork, novel, group, location, event, website, or advertisement that you are writing about. Many writers find it useful to read and analyze this primary source multiple times throughout the brainstorming, researching, and writing process. For example, if you were writing about an episode of *Buffy the Vampire Slayer*, perhaps "Teacher's Pet," the episode quoted at the beginning of this chapter, you would want to watch the episode numerous times. Each time you watch it, you should take notes about important details. Perhaps you can ask some questions about what is happening in the episode: Why do Buffy and Willow think the biology teacher is a predator? Or you can ask why characters act in particular ways: This is the first of Xander's demon love interests; does this episode foreshadow other crushes or relationships in later episodes? As you watch, you will find it useful to record important quotations or pieces of dialogue that support your argument points. Once you have a working thesis and perhaps an outline or web of your analysis, you might find yourself watching the episode again to test your ideas or to look for additional support. After finishing a draft of the paper, it would be a good idea to watch the episode one more time just to make sure you have not missed any important details or misrepresented anything. You would also want to properly document this source within your text and your Works Cited because, as mentioned previously, documentation is important for avoiding plagiarism.

TIPS FOR AVOIDING PLAGIARISM

1. **Know what plagiarism is.** Although definitions of plagiarism vary slightly, they all usually contain the same basic ideas. Plagiarism occurs when a student tries to present another's words or ideas as his or her own, using them in some parts of the paper or for the entire paper. The most common types of plagiarism occur from Internet use: Either the student cuts and pastes from one or more documents/websites, or the student purchases the entire paper from a website that sells documents.

   Although the Internet has become the most common source of plagiarism, plagiarism can also occur when a student incorrectly uses print sources in part or in their entirety. Additionally, a student who copies a paper topic, point, or wording from a peer, a parent, or some other source is generally subject to the same consequences as a student who plagiarizes from an Internet or print source. Be sure to check your school's rules about what constitutes plagiarism. You might be surprised at how some actions—such as turning the same paper in for two different assignments in two different classes—can also be considered plagiarism or academic dishonesty.

2. **Decide in advance that all of your work will be your own.** A paper that is weak, a late paper (if accepted by the instructor), or a zero on the assignment is better than the consequences of plagiarism.

3. **Give yourself sufficient time to write the paper,** so you do not become desperate and resort to plagiarism.

4. **Learn to properly document your sources.** If you are unclear about citing sources, consult your instructor, your textbook, your school writing center, or a librarian at the reference desk. If you do not take the initiative to ensure that your source material is documented correctly, you have *intentionally* plagiarized.

5. **Take careful notes as you research.**

    a. Make photocopies of your sources and write down all of the bibliographic information, including the URL and date of access if researching online.

    b. If you take notes instead of making photocopies, write down the information in direct quotes and give the necessary information, such as page numbers, as well as the bibliographic information.

    c. Save paraphrasing and summarizing for the actual writing process. Do not paraphrase or summarize in the note-taking stage of research; otherwise, you may inadvertently plagiarize later on.

6. **Use your own words and sentence structure to write a paraphrase;** pretend that you are explaining the material to someone else. However, be careful: The intent of the original passage must remain the same, which means that you do not distort the author's meaning with your own opinions. Also, a paraphrase should be approximately the same length as the original.

Example of Paraphrasing

- **Original Quote:** "Most teachers believe that violence occurs in hallways or under staircases, in the lunchroom or cafeteria, or in unattended classrooms. Students concur that most acts of violence occur in these places, but add the gym and locker room as prime sites" (Futrell and Powell).

- **Paraphrase:** According to a study by Futrell and Powell, both teachers and students agree that violence occurs in places within the school where there are many students and where there is not as much adult supervision, such as empty classrooms, the hallway, the gym, and the cafeteria.

7. **Summarize your material.** Like a paraphrase, a summary puts the original passage into your own words and sentence structure without changing the meaning. Since a summary shortens the original passage and focuses on its main points, partial quotations may be used along with your own words to highlight the most important information.

Examples of Summarizing

- **Original Quote:** "America's children are exposed to a steady diet of verbal and physical violence that begins early and continues throughout their lives. . . . Most of what children watch, including cartoons, is unsupervised and much of it is filled with scene after scene of unadulterated sex and violence. All too often children who behave violently are themselves victims of an overdose of violence" (Futrell and Powell).

- **Summary Without Quotes:** Too much television watching exposes children in the United States to violence, which may be a factor in their own violent behavior (Futrell and Powell).

- **Summary with Partial Quote:** Too much television watching makes children in the United States "victims of an overdose of violence," which may contribute to their own violence (Futrell and Powell).

8. **Ask for help.** Take your essay and the copies of your sources to your instructor or your school writing center if you have one. Ask for help with double-checking whether or not you have properly used and cited your sources within the essay as well as in the Works Cited.

DOCUMENTATION

As you take courses in a variety of fields or disciplines, you will encounter and use a number of different documentation styles. This range of styles exists to govern the research, writing, and documentation of various genres and disciplines. For example, in a psychology, business, or nursing class, you might be asked to use APA style; these rules have been set up by the American Psychological Association. In an engineering or math class, you might be asked to use the Institute of Electrical and Electronics Engineers (IEEE) style, or your biology instructor might ask for the Council of Science Editors (CSE) style. A journalism instructor will want you to follow *The Chicago Manual of Style* for a magazine article and the Associated Press (AP) guidelines for a newspaper article, which often does not include a Works Cited or References page.

In most English classes, you will be asked to use MLA style; consequently, many writing classes also use MLA. All of these documentation styles are designed to inform your reader about what the field finds important about source materials, including a record of the original research you have conducted with both primary and secondary sources.

MLA GUIDELINES

The Modern Language Association (MLA) offers specific guidelines for formatting texts and for crediting sources used in your research. MLA style uses a type of cross-referencing that includes in-text, or parenthetical, citations and a separate Works Cited page. In this section, you will find a general overview of MLA style rules, especially as they apply to common pop culture resources. For more specific questions, you should consult the most recent edition of *The MLA Handbook for Writers of Research Papers* or the MLA section of your grammar or writing text. Citing correctly is a skill you are expected to have as an academic writer.

Citing Sources in Your Text

When you make reference to someone else's idea, either through paraphrasing, summarizing, or quoting, you should

- Give the author's name (or the title of the work) and the page (or paragraph) number of the work in a parenthetical citation.
- Provide full citation information for the source in your Works Cited.

Remember that paraphrasing and summarizing involve putting a source's information into your own words and sentence structures, whereas quoting is copying the author's words and structures exactly as written or spoken.

Parenthetical Citations

MLA style uses an author–page method of citation. This means that the author's last name and the page number(s) from which the quotation or paraphrase was taken should appear in the text. The author's name may appear either in the sentence itself or in parentheses following the quotation or paraphrase, and the page numbers always appear in parentheses. The period goes after the parentheses, and you need a space, and only a space, between the author's

In *Listening to the World: Cultural Issues in Academic Writing,* Helen Fox explains to a teacher upset about plagiarism, "This student [from Korea] comes from a system where the relationship between the student and the authority of teachers and texts is very different from what it is here. . . . In our culture, children are trained to think of themselves as separate individuals from the time they are born. . . . But in most cultures, children have grown up much more connected to other human beings, so it's hard for them to feel convinced that it is all that important to delineate whose ideas are whose" (123–24).

- What is your response to Fox?

- What have you been taught, at home or at school, about referencing famous people, quoting aphorisms, or developing original ideas and arguments?

- Why is plagiarism such an important issue for Western academics?

last name and the page number of the source. Also notice that the quotation mark goes before the parentheses and has no ending punctuation mark inside the quotation itself.

EXAMPLE: AUTHOR'S NAME IN TEXT

Yu claims that Tiger Woods's move from amateur to professional in 1996 "said much about the current situation of race, ethnicity, and capitalism in the United States" (197).

Hague and Lavery have explained this concept in detail (2).

EXAMPLE: AUTHOR'S NAME IN REFERENCE

"The strange career of Tiger Woods said much about the current situation of race, ethnicity, and capitalism in the United States" (Yu 197).

This concept has already been explained in detail (Hague and Lavery 2).

When quoting verse, such as poetry or song lyrics, use a slash (/) to indicate line breaks and put the line numbers in your parenthetical citation rather than a page number.

EXAMPLE: QUOTING TWO LINES OF A SONG IN THE TEXT

Many children's songs have remained a part of popular culture for years as they keep being handed down. I'm sure you know these lyrics: "Twinkle, twinkle, little star/How I wonder what you are."

If the work you are making reference to has no author, use an abbreviated version of the work's title or the name that begins the entry in the Works Cited.

EXAMPLE: NO AUTHOR GIVEN

In a leaflet passed out at a number of gay pride parades in the '90s, a group of anonymous homosexuals argue that being "queer is not about a right to privacy; it is about the freedom to be public, to just be who we are" ("Queers Read This" 138).

At times, you may have to use an indirect quotation—a quotation you found in another source that was quoting from the original source. Use "qtd. in" to indicate the source.

EXAMPLE: INDIRECT QUOTATION

Eco says that parody "must never be afraid of going too far" (qtd. in Hague and Lavery 1).

Your parenthetical citation should give enough information to identify the source that was used for the material as the source in your Works Cited. If you have two or more authors with the same last name, you may need to use first initials or first names as well—for example (R. Wells 354). If you use more than one work from the same author, you may need to include a shortened title for the particular work from which you are quoting—for example (Morrison *Bluest Eye* 58).

Long or Block Quotations

Sometimes, you will want to use long quotations. If your quotation is longer than four typed lines, omit the quotation marks and start the quotation on a new line. This block quote should be indented one inch (ten spaces or two tabs) from the left margin throughout, should extend to the right margin, and should maintain double spacing. With a block quote, your period will come at the end of the quotation, before the parenthetical citation. If you are quoting poetry, song lyrics, or dialogue from movies, television shows, or plays, you will use a block quote for more than three lines and should maintain the original line breaks.

EXAMPLE: BLOCK QUOTE OF PROSE

In "A New Vision of Masculinity," Thompson calls for a change in the socialization of young boys:

> In his first few years, most of a boy's learning about masculinity comes from the influences of parents, siblings, and images of masculinity such as those found on television. Massive efforts will be needed to make changes here. But at older ages, school curriculum and the school environment provide powerful reinforcing images of traditional masculinity. This reinforcement occurs through a variety of channels, including curriculum content, role modeling, and extracurricular activities, especially competitive sports. (209)

EXAMPLE: BLOCK QUOTE OF POETRY OR MUSIC

The chorus of "Take Me Out to the Ball Game" has become a staple of both local and national sporting events:

> Take me out to the ball game,
> Take me out with the crowd.
> Buy me some peanuts and cracker jack,
> I don't care if I never get back,
> Let me root, root, root for the home team,
> If they don't win it's a shame.
> For it's one, two, three strikes, you're out,
> At the old ball game. (1–8)

Citing Online Sources

Online sources, particularly websites, often lack specific page numbers. If the author has not assigned clear page numbers to the text, do not assign page numbers to online material yourself because page numbers for a website, which are assigned if you print the material, can differ among computers; what appears on page 3 of one printout may appear on page 5 of another. If the creator or author of the source numbers the paragraphs of the source, you can use paragraph numbers in the parenthetical citation as follows: (par. 1). Only cite by paragraph number if the author of the source numbers the paragraphs. Do not assign numbers to the paragraphs yourself.

There is a difference between a parenthetical citation for a print source and an online source. In the citation for the online source, there is a comma between the author's last name and the paragraph number, if numbers are given by the author.

EXAMPLE: AUTHOR IN PARENTHETICAL CITATION

"We miss *Buffy the Vampire Slayer*. We really do. The kicks. The quips. And Willow. Wonderful, wonderful Willow" (Jensen).

Adding or Omitting Words in Quotations

If you find it necessary to add a word or words in a quotation, you should put square brackets around the words to indicate that they are not part of the original text. However, be sure that the words do not change the original meaning of the text.

EXAMPLE: ADDING WORDS TO A QUOTATION

In "Code 2.0," Lawrence Lessig describes the advent of Second Life: "[It is a] virtual world in the sense that the objects and people are rendered by computers. [It has been] built by its residents [Second Life users] in the sense that Second Life merely provided a platform upon which its residents built the Second Life world" (108).

If you find it necessary to omit a word or words in a quotation, you should use points of ellipsis—three periods in a row with spaces in between—to indicate the deleted words. If information is deleted between sentences, use four periods (the final period of the first sentence and the points of ellipsis).

EXAMPLE: OMITTING WORDS IN A QUOTATION

Lessig writes, "On any given day, 15 percent of Second Life residents are editing the scripts that make Second Life run. . . . Residents acquired land in that world, and began building structures" (108).

PREPARING YOUR WORKS CITED

The Works Cited should appear at the end of your essay. It provides readers with the necessary information to locate and read any sources you cite in your text. Each source you use in your essay *must* appear in your Works Cited; likewise, each source in your Works Cited *must* have been cited in the text of your essay. Remember: Make sure your header (containing your last name and page number) appears on your Works Cited page as well as in your essay.

> **GRAPPLING with Ideas**
>
> - What experiences have you had with creating Works Cited in the past?
>
> - What particular challenges does the use of pop culture create when conducting and citing research? How can these be overcome?
>
> - Why is it important to include an accurate Works Cited? What's the difference between a Works Cited and a For Further Reading?

Basic Guidelines for Works Cited

- Begin your Works Cited on a separate page at the end of your essay. The Works Cited page has one-inch margins on all sides and a header with your last name and the page number one-half inch from the top, just like all the other pages of your essay.

- This page should be titled Works Cited, which is centered at the top (with *no* italics, quotation marks, or underlining).

- Make the first line of each entry flush left with the margin. Subsequent lines in each entry should be indented one-half inch. This pattern is called a *hanging indent*. You can use your word processing software to set up an appropriate hanging indent.

- Maintain double spacing throughout your Works Cited with no extra spaces between entries.

- Alphabetize the Works Cited by the first major word in each entry (usually the author's last name). Do not use articles for determining alphabetical order.

Basic Guidelines for Citations

- Author's names are inverted (last name first, e.g., Presley, Elvis). If a work has more than one author, invert the first name only, follow it with a comma, then continue listing the rest of the authors (e.g., Lennon, John, and Paul McCartney).

- If you have cited more than one work by the same author, order the works alphabetically by title, and use three hyphens in place of the author's name for every entry after the first.

- If a cited work does not have a known author, alphabetize by the title of the work, and use a shortened version of the title in the parenthetical in-text citation.

- Capitalize each word in the titles of essays, books, films, and other works. This rule does not apply to articles, short prepositions, or conjunctions unless one of these is the first word of the title or subtitle (e.g., *Race, Class and Gender: An Anthology*).

- Italicize the titles of books, journals, magazines, newspapers, films, television shows, and album or game titles.

- Place quotation marks around the titles of articles or essays in journals, magazines, newspapers, and web pages, as well as short stories, book chapters, poems, songs, and individual episodes of a television series.

- For works with more than one edition, give the edition number and the abbreviation ed. directly after the title of the work (e.g., *Feminist Frontiers*. 5th ed.).

- For numbers with more than two digits, use only the last two digits of the number in the second half of the page range (e.g., if you refer to a magazine article that appeared on pages 150 through 175, list the page numbers on your Works Cited citation as 150–75; 201 through 209 would be listed as 201–09).

- When giving the place of publication, give the city and the state unless the city is well-known such as New York or Chicago.

- MLA no longer uses URLs in citations. Give database names (e.g., Gale PowerSearch or LexisNexis) when applicable. You should also give the date of access for online sources. If your instructor requests URLs, place in angled brackets (e.g., <http://www.newyorktimes.com>).

- For each citation on your Works Cited list, you should include a description of the medium for the source you have accessed (e.g., Print, Web, Advertisement, etc.)

BASIC MLA FORMS FOR ALL MEDIA

1. ADVERTISEMENTS

Name of Product, Company, or Institution. Descriptive label (Advertisement). Publisher date. page numbers, if applicable. Medium of Publication.

Sony. Advertisement. *People* 30 Dec. 2002: 42–43. Print.

America Online. Advertisement. NBC. 14 Feb. 2003. Web.

NOTE: This same format is used for documenting such items as product labels, billboards, rebate/refund forms, and posters.

2. ANTHOLOGY OR COLLECTION

Editor's Name(s), ed. *Title of Book*. Place of Publication: Publisher, date. Medium of Publication.

Hague, Angela, and David Lavery, eds. *Teleparody: Predicting/Preventing the TV Discourse of Tomorrow*. London: Wallflower P, 2002. Print.

3. ANTHOLOGY: WORK WITHIN

Author's Name. "Title of Work." *Title of Anthology*. Ed. Editor's Name(s). Place of Publication: Publisher, date. Pages. Medium of Publication.

Yu, Henry. "How Tiger Woods Lost His Stripes: Post-Nationalist American Studies as a History of Race, Migration, and the Commodification of Culture." *Popular Culture: A Reader*. Ed. Raiford Guins and Omayra Zaaragoza Cruz. London: Sage, 2005. 197–209. Print.

4. ARTICLE IN A SCHOLARLY JOURNAL WITH CONTINUOUS PAGINATION

Author's Name. "Title of Article." *Journal Title* vol.issue number (year of publication): pages. Medium of publication.

Robinson, Bobbie. "Playing Like the Boys: Patricia Cornwell Writes Men." *The Journal of Popular Culture* 39.1 (2006): 95–108. Print.

5. ARTICLE IN A SCHOLARLY JOURNAL THAT PAGINATES EACH ISSUE SEPARATELY

Author's Name. "Title of Article." *Journal Title* vol.issue (date of publication): pages. Medium of publication.

Silbergleid, Robin. "'The Truth We Both Know': Readerly Desire and Heteronarrative in *The X-Files*." *Studies in Popular Culture* 25.3 (Apr. 2003): 49–62. Print.

6. BOOKS (INCLUDES BROCHURES AND PAMPHLETS)

Author's Name. *Title of Book*. Place of Publication: Publisher, date of publication. Medium of publication.

Gonzalves, Theodore S. *The Day the Dancers Stayed: Performing in the Filipino/American Diaspora*. Philadelphia: Temple UP, 2010. Print.

Strauss, William, and Neil Howe. *Millennials and the Pop Culture*. Great Falls, VA: LifeCourse, 2006. Print.

King, Stephen. *Dreamcatcher: A Novel.* New York: Scribner, 2001. Print.

—-. *Misery.* New York: Viking, 1987. Print.

7. COMIC OR COMIC STRIP

Artist's Name. "Comic or Comic Strip Title, if any." Label Comic or Comic strip. *Publication Title* date: page number. Medium of Publication.

NOTE: If this title might be confused with another paper, additional identifying information may be added such as city, state, or associated paper or press.

Byrnes, P. Cartoon. *The New Yorker* 27 Nov. 2006: 131. Print.

Walker, Greg, and Mort Walker. "Beetle Bailey." Comic strip. *The Tennessean* [Nashville] 28 Nov. 2006: 4D. Print.

8. FILM

Title. Dir. Director's Name. Distributor, year of release. Medium of publication.

The Princess Bride. Dir. Rob Reiner. MGM/UA, 1987. Videocassette.

The Usual Suspects. Dir. Bryan Singer. Perf. Kevin Spacey, Gabriel Byrne, Chazz Palminteri, Stephen Baldwin, and Benicio del Toro. Polygram, 1995. DVD.

NOTE: You may include other relevant data, such as the names of the writer, performers, and producer, between the director's name and the medium. Fan films also follow this format.

9. INTERVIEW

Name of Person Being Interviewed. If published, "Title" of interview; if unpublished, label Interview and type (e.g., personal or e-mail). Interviewer's Name if pertinent. Appropriate bibliographic information. Medium of Publication, if applicable.

Waits, Tom. Interview with Jon Stewart. *The Daily Show.* Comedy Central. New York. 28 Nov. 2006. Television.

Smith, Kevin. Personal interview. 8–12 Mar. 2012.

Bussee, Michael. Facebook chat interview. 24 Apr. 2013.

10. LECTURE, SPEECH, ADDRESS, OR READING

Speaker's Name. "Title of Presentation." Meeting and Sponsoring Organization if applicable. Location. Date. Medium.

Cofer, Judith Ortiz. "Judith Ortiz Cofer in the Classroom." The Compleat Teacher: Bringing Together Knowledge, Experience, and Research. NCTE 96th Annual Convention.

Opryland Convention Center, Nashville, TN. 18 Nov. 2006. Featured Session.

11. LIBRARY SUBSCRIPTION SERVICE, SUCH AS INFOTRAC COLLEGE EDITION OR LEXISNEXIS: ARTICLE

Author's Name. "Title of Article." *Journal Title* vol. issue (date of publication): pages. Name of Database or other relevant information. Web. Date of access.

Ornstein, Aviva. "MY GOD!: A Feminist Critique of the Excited Utterance Exception to the Hearsay Rule." *California Law Review* 85.1 Jan. 1997: 161–223. InfoTrac. Web. 22 Apr. 2013.

12. LINER NOTES

Author's Name. Title of Material. Description of material. *Album Title.* Manufacturer, date. Medium of Publication.

Cady, Brian. Liner notes. *My Generation.* Decca Records, 1965. Phonograph.

13. MUSIC VIDEOS

Music videos should follow the television format in example 23 and should include performer information along with Music video as Medium of Publication.

Stefani, Gwen. "Hollaback Girl." *Love.Angel.Music.Baby.* Universal, 2004. MTV Hits. 12 Nov. 2006. Music video.

14. NEWSPAPER ARTICLE

Author's Name. "Title of Article." *Newspaper Title* day Month year: pages. Medium of publication.

Caramanica, Jon. "Rap, Both Good and Bad for Business." *New York Times* 8 May 2013: C1. Print.

Lederman, Douglas. "Athletic Merit vs. Academic Merit." *Chronicle of Higher Education* 30 Mar. 1994: A37–38. Print.

Tagliabue, John. "Cleaned Last Judgment Unveiled." *New York Times* 9 Apr. 1994: 13. Print.

15. ONLINE NEWSPAPER OR MAGAZINE

Author's Name. "Title of Article." *Newspaper Title.* Publisher or sponsor of the site, date: Web. Date of access.

Quindlen, Anna. "Getting Rid of the Sex Police." *Newsweek.* Harman Newsweek LLC, 13 Jan. 2003. Web. 28 Mar. 2013.

Caramanica, Jon. "Rap, Both Good and Bad for Business." *New York Times* 8 May 2013. C1. Web. 8 May 2013.

16. ONLINE JOURNAL ARTICLE

Author's Name. "Title of Article." *Title of Journal* vol. issue (year or date): pages. Web. Date of access.

Whithaus, Carl. "Think Different/Think Differently: A Tale of Green Squiggly Lines, or Evaluating Student Writing in Computer-Mediated Environments." *The Writing Instructor* 2.5 (1 Jul. 2002): 42 pages. Web. 21 Apr. 2013.

17. PAINTING, SCULPTURE, OR PHOTOGRAPH

Artist's Name. *Title*. Date of Composition (if available). Medium of Composition. Name of Institution that houses the work or the Individual who owns the work, City.

Leibovitz, Annie. *Nicole Kidman*. 2003. Photograph. National Portrait Gallery, London.

O'Keeffe, Georgia. *Sky Above White Clouds I*. 1962. Oil on canvas. National Gallery of Art, Washington.

NOTE: If the collector is unknown or wishes to be anonymous, use Private Collection in place of the collector's name and city.

18. PERFORMANCE

Title. Performer, Director, other pertinent data. Performance Site including theater (if applicable) and City. date. Performance.

Be a Candle of Hope. Nashville in Harmony, dir. Don Schlosser. First Unitarian Universalist Church, Nashville. 5 Dec. 2006. Performance.

19. RELIGIOUS WORKS

Title of Work. Name of Author or Editor, Title (e.g., gen. ed.) Place of Publication: Publisher, date. Medium of Publication.

Bhagavad-Gita: As It Is. A. C. Bhaktivedanta Swami Prabhupada. Maryborough: McPherson's Printing Group, 1986. Print.

The Holy Bible. Thomas Scofield, gen. ed. Nashville: Thomas Nelson, 1983. Print.

NOTE: You can give the title of the book within the Bible as well as chapter and verse information in your parenthetical citation (e.g., *The Holy Bible* John 3:16 or *Bhagavad-Gita: As It Is* 6.26).

20. REVIEW

Reviewer's Name. "Title of Review." Rev. of *Title of Work*, by Name of Author of work being reviewed (Editor, Director, etc.). *Journal* date: pages. Medium of Publication.

Franklin, Dana Kopp. "*Bend It Like Beckham* Goooooal!" Rev. of *Bend It Like Beckham*, by dir. Gurinder Chadha. *The Rage: All Entertainment* 17 Apr. 2003: 95–96. Print.

21. SOFTWARE OR OTHER NONPERIODICAL PUBLICATION ON CD-ROM (OR DVD)

Author's (or Producer's, Vendor's, etc.) Name. *Title*. Name of Editor, Compiler, etc. Edition, Release, or Version. Publication information (Place, Name, and date). Format (CD-ROM).

Down, Chris, prod. *Ultimate Yahtzee*. Dev. PCA. Beverly: Hasbro Interactive, 1996. CD-ROM.

22. SOUND RECORDING

Artist. "Song Title." *Title of Album*. Performers (when distinct from the artist/composer). Manufacturer, date. Medium of Publication.

Coolio. "Kinda High, Kinda Drunk." *Gangsta's Paradise*. Tommy Boy Music, 1995. CD.

Timberlake, Justin. "Suit & Tie (Explicit)." *Suit & Tie (Explicit)*. RCA Records, 2013. MP3 file.

23. TELEVISION OR RADIO PROGRAM

"Title of Episode or Segment." *Title of Program*. Name of Network. Call Letters, City of the local station (if applicable). Broadcast date. Medium of Reception (e.g., Radio, Television)

"The Blessing Way." *The X-Files*. Fox. WXIA, Atlanta. 19 Jul. 1998. Television.

24. TELEVISION ON DVD

"Title of Episode or Segment." *Title of Program*. Season or edition (if applicable). Name of Network. Distributor, date. Medium of Publication.

"Man of Science, Man of Faith." *Lost*. Season 1. ABC. Buena Vista, 2005. DVD.

NOTE: With television programming, directors and/or performers can be added if relevant.

25. WEBSITE

Author's Name. *Name of Page*. Name of Institution or Organization associated with the website. Date of posting/revision. Web. Date of access.

Irvine, Martin, and Deborah Everhart. *The Labyrinth: Resources for Medieval Studies*. Georgetown University. 1994–2002. Web. 21 Jun. 2001.

NOTE: This same format can be used for blogs and any fan fiction found online.

26. WEBSITE: ARTICLE

Author's Name. "Article Title." *Name of Website*. Name of Institution or Organization associated with the website. Date of posting/revision. Web. Date of access.

Stevenson, Seth. "The Best and Worst Super Bowl Ads." *Slate*. The Washington Post. 2013. Web. 1 May 2013.

SAMPLE WORKS CITED

Here is an example of how a completed Works Cited would look at the end of your essay. The Works Cited is part of the essay and should contain the same header (usually your name and the page number) as the rest of your essay.

Works Cited

Caramanica, Jon. "Rap, Both Good and Bad for Business." *New York Times* 8 May 2013: C1. Print.

Quindlen, Anna. "Getting Rid of the Sex Police." *Newsweek* 13 Jan. 2003. Web. 28 Mar. 2003.

Strauss, William, and Neil Howe. *Millennials and the Pop Culture*. Great Falls: LifeCourse, 2006. Print.

Timberlake, Justin. "Suit & Tie (Explicit)." *Suit & Tie (Explicit)*. RCA Records, 2013. MP3 file.

Yu, Henry. "How Tiger Woods Lost His Stripes: Post-Nationalist American Studies as a History of Race, Migration, and the Commodification of Culture." *Popular Culture: A Reader*. Ed. Raiford Guins and Omayra Zaaragoza Cruz. London: Sage, 2005. 197–209. Print.

APA GUIDELINES

APA style uses a type of cross-referencing that includes in-text, or parenthetical, citations and a References list. In this section, you will find a general overview of APA style rules. For more specific questions, you should consult the most recent edition of the *Publication Manual of the American Psychological Association* or the APA section of your grammar or writing text. Citing correctly is a skill you are expected to have as you write in a variety of courses.

Citing Sources in Your Text

When you make reference to someone else's idea, either through paraphrasing, summarizing, or quoting, you should

- Give the author's name (or the title of the work), the year of publication, and the page (or paragraph) number of the work in a parenthetical citation.
- Provide full citation information for the source in your References section.

Remember that paraphrasing and summarizing involve putting a source's information into your own words and sentence structures, whereas quoting is copying the author's words and structures exactly as written or spoken.

Parenthetical Citations

APA style uses an author–year–page method of citation. This means that the author's last name, year of publication, and the page number(s) from which the quotation was taken should all appear in the text; page numbers for paraphrases and summaries are optional, so check with your instructor. The author's name and publishing year always accompany one another and may appear either in the sentence itself or in parentheses following the quotation or paraphrase. When multiple authors appear in parentheses, an ampersand (&) replaces *and*. The page number(s) always appears in parentheses. The period goes after the closing parentheses. Within the parentheses, the order should be: the author's name, a comma and a space, the year of publication, another comma and space, and the abbreviation "p." (page) followed by a space and the Arabic numeral page number(s). If a citation occurs across multiple pages, you should use "pp." instead and a dash (with no spaces) between the beginning and ending pages—for example (pp. 202–205). Also notice that the quotation mark goes before the parentheses and has no ending punctuation mark within the quotation itself.

EXAMPLE: AUTHOR'S NAME IN TEXT

Yu (2005) claims that Tiger Woods's move from amateur to professional in 1996 "said much about the current situation of race, ethnicity, and capitalism in the United States" (p. 197).

Hague and Lavery (2002) have explained this concept in detail (p. 2).

EXAMPLE: AUTHOR'S NAME IN REFERENCE

"The strange career of Tiger Woods said much about the current situation of race, ethnicity, and capitalism in the United States" (Yu, 2005, p. 197).

This concept has already been explained in detail (Hague & Lavery, 2002, p. 2).

If the work you are referencing has no author, cite in the text the first few words from the References list entry. If the work is an article or chapter, capitalize the first word only (unless the title contains a proper noun or adjective) and do not put it in quotation marks. If it is a book, periodical, brochure, or report, italicize the title and capitalize as you would for the References list.

EXAMPLE: NO AUTHOR GIVEN

In a leaflet distributed at a number of gay pride parades in the '90s, a group of anonymous homosexuals argue that being "queer is not about a right to privacy; it is about the freedom to be public, to just be who we are" (Queers read this, 1990, p. 1).

Note: If the author is specifically given as anonymous, you should use the format (Anonymous, 2002) or (Anonymous, 2002, p. 1).

At times, you may have to use an indirect quotation—a quotation you found in another source that was quoting from the original source. Use "as cited in" to indicate the source.

EXAMPLE: INDIRECT QUOTATION

Eco says that parody "must never be afraid of going too far" (as cited in Hague & Lavery, 2002, p. 1).

Your parenthetical citation should give enough information to identify the source that was used for the material as the source that is listed in your References list. If you have two or more authors with the same last name, use each author's initials in each citation—for example (R. Wells, 2002, p. 354).

Long or Block Quotations

Sometimes, you will want to use long quotations. If your quotation is longer than forty words, omit the quotation marks and start the quotation on a new line. This block quote should be indented one-half inch (five spaces or one tab) from the left margin throughout, should extend to the right margin, and should maintain double spacing. With a block quote, your period will come at the end of the quotation, before the parenthetical citation.

EXAMPLE: BLOCK QUOTE OF PROSE

In "A New Vision of Masculinity," Thompson (1999) calls for a change in the socialization of young boys:

> In his first few years, most of a boy's learning about masculinity comes from the influences of parents, siblings, and images of masculinity such as those found on television. Massive efforts will be needed to make changes here. But at older ages, school curriculum and the school environment provide powerful reinforcing images of traditional masculinity. This reinforcement occurs through a variety of channels, including curriculum content, role modeling, and extracurricular activities, especially competitive sports. (p. 209)

Citing Online Sources

Online sources, particularly websites, often lack specific page numbers. If the author or site has not assigned specific page numbers, do not assign page numbers to online material yourself because page numbers for a website, which are assigned if you print the material, can differ among computers; what appears on page 3 of one printout may appear on page 5 of another. If the creator or author of the source numbers the paragraphs of the source, you can use paragraph numbers in the parenthetical citation as follows: (para. 1) or (¶ 1). If the author does not number the paragraphs, give the heading title and the paragraph of the citation after that heading.

EXAMPLE: AUTHOR IN PARENTHETICAL CITATION

"We miss *Buffy the Vampire Slayer*. We really do. The kicks. The quips. And Willow. Wonderful, wonderful Willow" (Jensen, 2007, ¶ 1).

Adding or Omitting Words in Quotations

If you find it necessary to add a word or words in a quotation, perhaps for explanation or clarification, you should put square brackets around the words to indicate that they are not part of the original text. However, be sure that the words do not change the original meaning of the text.

EXAMPLE: ADDING WORDS TO A QUOTATION

In "Code 2.0," Lawrence Lessig (2006) describes the advent of Second Life: "[It is a] virtual world in the sense that the objects and people are rendered by computers. [It has been] built by its residents [Second Life users] in the sense that Second Life merely provided a platform upon which its residents built the Second Life world" (p. 108).

If you find it necessary to omit a word or words in a quotation, you should use points of ellipsis—three periods in a row with spaces in between—to indicate the deleted words. If information is deleted between sentences, use four periods (the final period of the first sentence and the points of ellipsis).

EXAMPLE: OMITTING WORDS IN A QUOTATION

Lessig (2006) writes, "On any given day, 15 percent of Second Life residents are editing the scripts that make Second Life run. . . . Residents acquired land in that world, and began building structures" (p. 108).

PREPARING YOUR REFERENCES LIST

References should appear at the end of your essay. This list provides readers with the necessary information to locate and read any sources you cite in your text. Each source you use in your essay *must* appear in your References; likewise, each source in your References *must* have been cited in the text of your essay. Remember: Make sure your header (containing the short two- to three-word version of your title and page number) appears on your References page as well as in your essay (top-right corner of each page).

Basic Guidelines for References

- Begin your References on a separate page at the end of your essay. The References page has one-inch margins on all sides.

- This page should have the title References centered at the top (with *no* italics, quotation marks, or underlining).

- Make the first line of each entry flush left with the margin. Subsequent lines in each entry should be indented one-half inch. This pattern is called a *hanging indent*. You can use your word processing software to set up an appropriate hanging indent.

- Maintain double spacing throughout your References with no extra spaces between entries.

- Alphabetize the References by the first major word in each entry (usually the author's last name). Do not use articles for determining alphabetical order.

Basic Guidelines for Citations

- Author's names are inverted (last name first, e.g., Presley, E.) and list only first and middle (if available) initials, not first and middle names. If a work has more than one author, invert all names, follow each with a comma, and precede the final name with "&" (e.g., Lennon, J., & McCartney, P.).

- If you have cited more than one work by the same author, order the works sequentially by year of publication, the earliest first.

- If a cited work does not have a known author, alphabetize by the first significant word in the title of the work. Use Anonymous as an author if, and only if, the work lists the author as Anonymous.

- Capitalize the first word in the titles of essays, books, films, and other works.

- Capitalize all major words in periodical titles, including journals, magazines, newsletters, and newspapers.

- Italicize the titles of books, journals, magazines, newspapers, films, television shows, and album or game titles.

- Do not place quotation marks around the titles of articles or essays in journals, magazines, newspapers, or web pages, or around song titles or episodes of television shows.

- For works with more than one edition, give the edition number and the abbreviation directly after the title of the work—for example, *Feminist frontiers* (5th ed.).

- For periodicals, give the volume number, italicize it (do not include *vol.*), but only give the issue number if each volume starts over with the number 1. Issue numbers should be placed in parentheses directly after the volume number, and are not italicized.

- Give URLs or DOIs (if one has been assigned to the source) for websites and other online sources. You do not need to include retrieval dates unless the content from the source will change over time. Note that URLs are not followed by periods so they won't be mistaken as part of the Internet address. Also note that you should not insert a hyphen in order to break a URL or DOI at the margins of the page.

NOTE: A DOI, or digital document identifier, is assigned to online/digital documents when they have a stable or persistent location. You should include this DOI in your citation if it exists. Only give URLs if the reader can get back to the original source using the URL you have given; cut off lengthy URL addresses at the point where they stop making sense to the reader.

BASIC APA FORMS FOR ALL MEDIA

1. ANTHOLOGY OR COLLECTION

Editor's Name(s), (Ed.). (year). *Title of book*. Place of Publication: Publisher.

Hague, A., & Lavery, D. (Eds.). (2002). *Tele-parody: Predicting/preventing the TV discourse of tomorrow*. London: Wallflower Press.

2. ANTHOLOGY: WORK WITHIN

Author's Name. (year). Title of Work. In Editor's Name(s) (Ed.), *Title of anthology* (page numbers). Place of Publication: Publisher.

Yu, H. (2005). How Tiger Woods lost his stripes: Post-nationalist American studies as a history of race, migration, and the commodification of culture. In R. Guins & O. Z. Cruz (Eds.), *Popular culture: A reader* (pp. 197–209). London: Sage.

3. ARTICLE IN A SCHOLARLY JOURNAL

Author's Name. (year). Title of article. *Journal Title, volume number,* pages.

Robinson, B. (2006). Playing like the boys: Patricia Cornwell writes men. *The Journal of Popular Culture, 39,* pp. 95–108.

4. BOOKS

Author's Name. (year). *Title of book*. Place of Publication: Publisher.

Gonzalves, T. S. (2010). *The day the dancers stayed: Performing in the Filipino/American diaspora*. Philadelphia: Temple UP.

Strauss, W., & Howe, N. (2006). *Millennials and the pop culture*. Great Falls, VA: LifeCourse.

EXAMPLE: TWO BOOKS BY THE SAME AUTHOR

King, S. (1987). *Misery*. New York: Viking.

King, S. (2001). *Dreamcatcher: A novel*. New York: Scribner.

5. CD-ROM ARTICLE

Name. (pub. year). Title. *Publication*, volume, page. Retrieved from Database or CD-ROM Name (CD-ROM Item: item no. if available).

Down, C. (Producer). (2006). Ultimate Yahtzee. *Developer PCA*. Retrieved from Hasbro Interactive (CD-ROM).

6. COMIC, COMIC STRIP, OR ADVERTISEMENT

Name. (Artist or Producer). (date). Comic or comic strip title, if any [medium]. *Publication Title*. page number.

Byrnes, P. (Artist). (2006, November 28) [Cartoon] *The New Yorker*, p. 131.

Walker, G., & Walker, M. (2006, November 28). Beetle Bailey [Comic strip]. *The Tennessean,* p. 4D.

Yves Saint Laurent (Producer). (2007, September). [Advertisement]. *Out*, p. 17.

7. LIBRARY SUBSCRIPTION SERVICE, SUCH AS INFOTRAC COLLEGE EDITION OR LEXISNEXIS: ARTICLE

Author's Name. (pub. year). Title of article. *Journal Title, vol. issue*, pages. Retrieved Date from Name of Database, Location, or URL.

Ornstein, Aviva. (2003). MY GOD!: A feminist critique of the excited utterance exception to the hearsay rule. *California Law Review, 85(1)*, pp. 161–223. Retrieved April 22, 2013 from JStor.

8. Newspaper Article

Author's Name. (full pub. date). Title of article. *Newspaper Title*, pages. Note that if the article appears on discontinuous pages, include all page numbers separated by commas (e.g., F5, F7, F10).

Caramanica, J. (2013, May 8). Rap, both good and bad for business. *New York Times,* p. C1.

Lederman, D. (1994, March 30). Athletic merit vs. academic merit. *The Chronicle of Higher Education*, pp. A37–38.

Tagliabue, J. (1994, April 9). Cleaned last judgment unveiled. *New York Times*, p. 13.

9. Nonprint Media (Including Motion Pictures, Recordings, Television Shows, Radio Broadcasts, Live Speeches, Concerts, Etc.)

Motion Picture

Person or Persons primarily responsible for the product or program. (Person's Title). (year). *Title* [medium]. Location (country of origin): Studio.

Reiner, R. (Director). (1987). *The princess bride* [Motion picture]. Los Angeles: MGM/UA.

Singer, B. (Director). (1995). *The usual suspects* [Motion picture]. New York: Polygram.

Television Broadcast or Series

Name of Producer. (Producer). (Date of broadcast, year for a series). Title of program [Television series]. City where distributor located: Name of Distributor.

Cohen, D. S. (Executive Producer). (1993). *Living single* [Television series]. Burbank, CA: Warner Brothers Burbank Studios.

Single Episode of a Television Program

Writer's Name, & Director's Name. (date of broadcast). Title of episode [Television series episode]. In Producer's Name, *Name of television series*. City where distributor located: Name of Distributor.

Edlund, B. (Writer), & Grabiak, M. (Director). (2002, October 18). Jaynestown [Television series episode]. In J. Whedon (Producer), *Firefly*. Los Angeles: 20th Century Fox Studios.

Radio Broadcast

Name of Originator or Primary Producer. (Date of broadcast). Title of radio program. [Radio broadcast]. City where distributor located: Name of Distributor.

Glass, I. (Host). (2002, December 27). *This American life* [Radio broadcast]. Chicago: WEBZ.

Live Concert or Speech

Name of Artist or Producer. (Date of event). *Title of event* (if any) [Type of event]. Location of event.

Lennox A. (Singer). (2007, October 22). *Annie Lennox songs of mass destruction tour* [Musical concert]. Detroit, MI: Music Hall Center.

Music Recording

Writer's Name. (date of copyright). Title of song [Recorded by if Artist differs from Writer]. On *Title of album* [Medium: CD, record, cassette, etc.]. Location: Label. (Recording date if different from copyright date).

Coolio. (1995). Kinda high, kinda drunk. On *Gangsta's paradise* [CD]. New York: Tommy Boy Music.

Timberlake, J. (2013). Suit & tie (explicit). On *Suit & tie (Explicit)* [MP3 file]. New York: RCA Records.

NOTE: Do not reference in-person interviews in your References list; only cite interviews within the text itself. For television or multimedia interviews, just cite the episode in normal format and then mention in the text who was interviewed.

10. Online Periodical Article

Author's Name. (full pub. date). Title of article. *Newspaper Title*, page numbers (if applicable). Retrieved from URL.

Caramanica, J. (2013, May 8). Rap, both good and bad for business. *New York Times*. Retrieved from http://www.nytimes.com.

Davidson, L. A., & Douglas, K. (1998, December). Digital document identifiers: Promise and problems for scholarly publishing. *Journal of Electronic Publishing*, 4(2). doi: http://dx.doi.org/10.3998/3336451.0004.203.

Quindlen, A. (2003, March 28). Getting rid of the sex police. *Newsweek* [Online serial]. Retrieved from http://www.msnbc.com/news/NW-front_Front.asp.

Whithaus, C. (2002, July 1). Think different/think differently: A tale of green squiggly lines, or evaluating student writing in computer-mediated environments. *The Writing Instructor, 2(5)* [Online serial]. Retrieved from http://www.writinginstructor.com.

NOTE: Give the DOI if available. If not, give the URL of the periodical's home page when the article is available by search, in order to avoid URLs that don't work.

11. REVIEW

Reviewer's Name. (review pub. date). Title of review [Review of the medium *Work title]. Journal, volume*, pages.

Franklin, D. K. (2003, April 17). *Bend it like Beckham* goooooal! [Review of motion picture *Bend it like Beckham*]. *The Rage: All Entertainment,* pp. 95–96.

12. SOFTWARE

Product/Software Name (Version) [Computer software]. (year). Place: Manufacturer.

Macintosh OSX (Version 10.4) [Computer software]. (2006). Cupertino, CA: Apple Computer.

13. WEBSITE

Author's Name. (pub. date). *Name of page.* Retrieved from URL.

Irvine, M., & Everhart, D. (2002). *The labyrinth: Resources for medieval studies.* Retrieved June 21, 2002, from http://www.georgetown.edu/labyrinth/labyrinth-home.html.

NOTE: This same format can be used for blogs and any fan fiction found online.

SAMPLE REFERENCES

Here is an example of how a completed References page would look at the end of your essay. The References page is part of the essay and should contain the same header (a short two- to three-word version of your title and the page number) as the rest of your essay.

Gender and Popular Culture 7

References

Caramanica, J. (2013, May 8). Rap, both good and bad for business. *New York Times*. Retrieved from http://www.nytimes.com.

Cohen, D. S. (Executive Producer). (1993). *Living single* [Television series]. Burbank, CA: Warner Brothers Burbank Studios.

Franklin, D. K. (2003, April 17). *Bend it like Beckham* goooooal! [Review of motion picture *Bend it like Beckham*]. *The Rage: All Entertainment*, 95–96.

Quindlen, A. (2003, March 28). Getting rid of the sex police. *Newsweek* [Online serial]. Retrieved from http://www.msnbc.com/news/NW-front_Front.asp.

Robinson, B. (2006). Playing like the boys: Patricia Cornwell writes men. *The Journal of Popular Culture, 39,* 95–108.

Strauss, W., & Howe, N. (2006). *Millennials and the pop culture*. Great Falls, VA: LifeCourse.

Tagliabue, J. (1994, April 9). Cleaned last judgment unveiled. *New York Times*, p. 13.

6

writing about advertisements

"After earning the highest accolades of the advertising industry—GOT MILK? has not only helped sell millions of gallons of milk, it's become an all-American icon."

—From "Got Milk? Turns 10"

1. Which product played an important role in the film *Men in Black*?

a. Armani suits

b. Ray-Ban sunglasses

c. Smith and Wesson shotgun

d. Play-Doh

2. Match the following product to its catchphrase.

1. LifeCall a. "Can you hear me now?"
2. Burger King b. "I've fallen, and I can't get up!"
3. Dr. Scholl's c. "Are you gellin'?"
4. Verizon d. "Have it your way."

3. The BMW 3Z Roadster was featured in which of the following films?

a. *The Italian Job*

b. *Gone in 60 Seconds*

c. *GoldenEye*

d. *Cars*

4. Which of the following ad campaigns actually hurt sales during its ad period?

a. The Taco Bell chihuahua

b. Microsoft's "Where do you want to go today?"

c. Visa's "It's everywhere you want to be"

d. Lay's potato chips, "Betcha can't eat just one."

5. Name the original product or company being parodied in the adjacent ad.

6. By the time a person is sixty-five years old, she is estimated to have seen approximately how many television commercials?

a. four hundred thousand

b. one million

c. two million

d. one billion

7. What company is being spoofed in the adjacent image of a subvertisement?

Why do you keep bothering me?

© MICHAEL KOVALCHICK

8. Which is the largest group of advertisers?

a. pharmaceutical advertisers

b. automobile manufacturers

c. food marketers

d. financial advertisers (banking, etc.)

9. What brand of candy saw a boost in sales after it was eaten by the alien ET in the film *E.T.*?

a. M & Ms

b. Snickers

c. Reese's Pieces

d. Skittles

10. **Stump Your Instructor:** In small groups, write a question here about advertising and pop culture. Give your instructor five choices for answers.

a.

b.

c.

d.

e.

YOU AND ADVERTISEMENTS

Market researchers and analysts estimate that the average American is bombarded with three to five thousand ads a day (Yankelovich) from a variety of media and sources: television, radio, films, newspapers, magazines, billboards, direct mailings, telemarketers, and Internet banners and pop-ups, as well as flyers on our windshields, bulletin boards, paintings on cars and buses, posters on the sidewalk or the back of a bathroom stall, and ads on T-shirts and cell phones. We find many of these ads entertaining or visually and aurally stimulating; others we find annoying and perhaps manipulative. When taken at face value, advertisements are about selling us a product, a service, a cause, or even a person, especially during election times; however, in reality, most ads are selling much more than that. Many critics, such as Anthony Cortese, claim that advertisers are selling consumers a way of life, a worldview, or a system of values, and that we may not even realize the messages that are really being sold to us. Of course, advertising could also be about art and imagination, especially for the graphic artists, copywriters, music composers, cinematographers, and others who do all of the work that goes into advertisement design and creation.

Advertising is a multibillion-dollar business that underwrites most mass media in the United States. In 2013, a thirty-second commercial during the Super Bowl cost more than $3.8 million (http://www.superbowl-ads .com). Pregame media hype for the two months leading up to the Super Bowl can cost as much as $200,000 plus commercial airtime. Even though Super Bowl advertising is the extreme of television commercials, this price gives a general idea of how much many companies are willing to spend, especially now that these big ads are archived online for viewers. Is it the amount of money spent that makes an ad effective, or are other factors involved? How do these factors affect you as a consumer? What products are you being sold? What cultural ideas are you buying? How can you tell? These are some of the questions you will investigate in this chapter. Your answers to these and other questions you ask about advertisements will give you a starting point for writing about advertisements and their roles in your life and culture as well as the world at large. The reading and writing assignments provided will help you see how others have questioned the messages of advertisements and get you started asking your own probing questions and writing your own answers.

GRAPPLING with Ideas

We encounter advertisements everywhere we turn. In fact, we live in a primarily visual culture where most of us are a walking advertisement for companies.

- How many times a day do you see a company's logo on someone's shirt or jeans?

- Look at what you are wearing: Does a company's logo appear anywhere on your clothing? What about your backpack or purse?

- Are you advertising for any specific company?

WHY WRITE ABOUT ADVERTISEMENTS?

Although we might think we do, we really do not give much thought to advertisements. We believe that we are too smart and independent to be influenced by the ads we see. Postmodern advertising has helped establish this view by making fun of or parodying its own techniques and purposes. Yet, advertising has become one of the most influential texts we encounter. People drive quickly past billboards, use television commercial time to go to the bathroom, or spend only a few seconds glancing over the advertisements before flipping to the next page of a magazine or newspaper. Therefore, advertisers must effectively use those few seconds to grab the viewer's attention. Advertising agencies spend a great deal of time and money tailoring each ad to appeal to a specific target audience and to achieve a specific purpose. Even the simplest and most direct ads can carry subtle and powerful messages for select groups of people. Evaluating and studying advertisements are important activities that will help shape your understanding of the world we live in. Ads can be very powerful and complex to work on the consumers' subconscious. Ads try to persuade consumers through carefully selected words, images, or symbols; therefore, it is important to develop a strong critical eye for the images and sounds you encounter. Writing about advertisements will help you develop this critical stance.

PREPARING TO WRITE ABOUT ADVERTISEMENTS

Advertisements are a pervasive part of our culture; they entertain, they inform, they argue, they sell, and they ask us to think. When you look at or listen to ads for a class or a writing assignment, you will need to view the ads in a way that is probably different from how you normally view them, a way that is a bit more systematic.

As you will discover, there are many different reasons to write about advertisements and many ways to present your writing. Likewise, different methods of experiencing an ad may influence your overall impression of it and the item being sold; consequently, you must ask yourself many different questions about the ad itself as well as your reaction to it. What follows are some different approaches or ideas for you to consider as you dissect an ad.

Examining Advertisements

As you know, advertisements come in a variety of forms, but most share similar elements for you to examine. Radio ads do not have images to look at, but you can still consider all of the pieces that go together to create what you hear. Print ads do not have background music or particular voices for you to hear, but the written text, including images, they present will have a voice or style for you to examine. These questions should get you started analyzing all types of ads, no matter where you encounter them. Use the Got Milk ads at the beginning of this chapter or the Volkswagen ads at the end of the chapter to help you apply the tools that follow; you may also want to use the images in the Coca-Cola case study (see color insert).

Look at the details to determine what the images or people say.

- Who appears in the ad? Is it a famous person or an average person? What effect can a celebrity have on an ad? An average person?

- What are the people's races, ethnicities, genders, classes, abilities, ages, sexualities? How can you tell? What does their presence or absence tell you about the advertisement or advertisers?

- What are their expressions? Body angles? Gestures? Connections to each other and/or the product?

- What props are used? Product images? Models? Puppies? An image of the shampoo bottle or a model with a perfectly styled head of hair? Is the model carrying or holding anything in the ad?

- What is the setting or background of the ad? What can the product placement tell you?

- How does the advertisement speak to you through images? Does the image imply that you, too, can be popular or that this product will get you a date?

GRAPPLING with Ideas

In the 1970s and 1980s, consumer spending dramatically increased; consequently, the spending on advertisements increased exponentially. At the same time, the United States was feeling the effects of social and political movements in the 1960s and 1970s, such as the civil rights movement and the push for women's equality.

- What impact did the civil rights movement have on advertisements in the 1960s and 1970s? What about the women's movement?

- What changes in technology have affected the culture you live in? How has this translated into advertisements?

- What cultural phenomena have led to changes in advertising in your lifetime? How do you feel about these changes?

- What do the images symbolize? What intended and unintended meanings are attached to the symbols?
- What story does the advertisement tell? According to this ad, will your children love you if you bring home this snack? Will your clothes fit better if you eat this kind of cereal?

Look at the placement of text as well as what it says.

- Are there headlines, subheads, written descriptions? What is said? Where are the words placed on the page, screen, or billboard?
- What is the message being communicated? Does it appeal to the viewers' emotions? Sense of logic? Both?
- Is there a double meaning? What is actually said? What is implied? What are you being asked to assume?
- What does the ad not say? What is left out?
- Does the ad use "weasel words" or "equivocation"—words that are intended to mislead or manipulate the reader or viewer? If a product is *new and improved*, what was it before? If this product is *faster*, does the ad tell you what it is faster than? Most cereals are *part* of a healthy breakfast, and most toothpaste brands *help* prevent tooth decay.
- Are there any facts and figures? What do these contribute to the ad and your reading of it?

Look closely at the artistic elements of the ad.

- How do contrasting colors, fonts, and text sizes highlight specific objects and words? What is the effect of these choices?
- What color combination is used? Why? Are there any cultural associations with these colors?
- Does the ad use photographic images or drawn images? What is the effect of this choice?
- If it uses photographs, how does the photo lighting affect the ad's message?

If available, look at marketing factors for the ad.

- What is the source of the ad?
- Who is the target audience of the ad? What is the audience's race or ethnicity? Age range? Gender? Sexuality? Socioeconomic status? Is the ad aimed at a special interest group or subculture?
- What is the date of the ad? Is it a seasonal ad (back to school, Mother's Day, Halloween)? Where is the ad placed? What part of the magazine or newspaper (back cover, inside front cover, next to the "Dear Abby" column)? What businesses are near the billboard? Which Internet sites feature this ad? What television shows run this commercial? What time of day is this commercial run?
- How long have the advertisers been running this ad? Is it part of a bigger campaign? What is its history?

Appealing to Consumers

Advertisements are designed to appeal to our fantasies, needs, or desires. Many critics would say that ads are also creating specific desires and needs or at least the illusion of such. Again, look at the Got Milk ads at the beginning of the chapter, the Volkswagen ads at the end of the chapter, or others in magazines and online. Then consider which of these fantasies, needs, or desires underlie each of the ads.

1. The desire for love, romance, and/or sex: plays on personal attraction, both the desire for others and the need to be desired.

2. The desire for popularity or affiliation: links thousands of products and services to the consumer's desires to be in good company and to be respected; also connects to the bandwagon or everyone-has-it appeal and a desire for prominence.

3. The desire for elegance or luxury, also known as snob appeal: creates feelings of envy and a desire for the best product or name brand.

4. The desire for perfect looks: tells or shows consumers that they are too fat, too thin, too black, too white, too short . . . too imperfect to fit in or be accepted; also referred to as the desire for transfer (that is, use our product and the qualities in our models will transfer to you).

5. The desire to be aggressive: taps the viewer's or reader's feelings of anger.

6. The desire for adventure, high achievement, or escape: focuses on the viewer's ambitions, dreams, wishes, and hopes, often for something new and different.

7. The desire to dominate: appeals to the wish to be powerful and in control.

8. The desire for youth: use our product and you will look and feel younger.

9. The desire for attention: concentrates on the difference in how you are seen now versus how you will be noticed after using the ad's product.

10. The desire for autonomy: focuses on the need to be independent.

11. The desire to nurture: cultivates the caring and compassionate responses of a viewer; this appeal is also tied to the consumer's emotions.

12. The desire for plain folks or a slice of life: uses ordinary people to recommend products.

13. The desire for celebrity or prestige: uses stars and celebrity spokespersons to recommend products.

14. The need to feel safe: appeals to the desire for security; the consumer does not want to be intimidated, menaced, or battered.

15. The need for aesthetic sensations: causes advertisers to make their products visually appealing or arresting.

16. The desire for statistics and scientific facts: piques the consumer's interests through trivia, percentages, scientific studies, or question–answer formats.

17. The desire for humor: appeals to the desire to laugh and enjoy a product.

18. Physiological needs: focuses on the basic requirements of food and shelter.

19. The desire for health: appeals to those who want to be or appear healthy.

20. The desire for convenience: appeals to those who need things quickly or fast.

Subvertising

Subvertising is a method of subverting mainstream ads. It uses well-known ad campaigns, both images and wording, to either speak against the original product or to promote an unrelated value or idea. For example, PETA (People for the Ethical Treatment of Animals) has subverted the Got Milk campaign with its own Got Soy campaign (see opening page of this chapter), and Lactaid brand milk substitute has launched its own Miss Milk? campaign. In addition, you can find Got Jesus and Got MLK campaigns that use the well-known ads to promote their own ideas. Subvertising is often used by social and political movements to gain wider recognition and appeal. Ad parodies can also fall into this category (see examples in the opening quiz).

Consider the various
techniques companies use
to get you to buy their
products.

- Has an ad ever prompted
  you to buy something you
  really did not need?

- When you go to the store
  and are confronted with
  numerous brands of the
  same product, how do you
  decide which one to buy?

- How does the product
  packaging affect you?

- Do advertisements for the
  products ever pop into
  your head? How do you
  feel about that?

Researching and Documenting Advertisements

When writing about advertisements, you will always have to find the specific ad (or ads) you are discussing; this will be your primary source. Besides the ad itself, you may also want to explore the source of the advertisement, such as the magazine, newspaper, website, Facebook page, or billboard location. At times, you may also want to supplement your primary source(s) with secondary or outside sources; reading what others have to say on your topic or primary source may help you write a more balanced and believable review or analysis of an advertisement. (See Chapter 5 for more on research and documentation.)

Areas of research may include the following:

- The history of the product.

- The history of the ad campaign, including budget figures.

- Market figures for the ad and the product being sold.

- Ads for similar and competing products.

- The history or development of techniques used in the ad.

- The evolution of particular types of advertising or approaches to ads.

- The cultures or subcultures represented in the ad.

- How the ad was received by others.

Whether or not you conduct outside research may depend on your assignment and/or your research question. What do you want or need to know to complete your essay about a given ad or advertising campaign? Go back to your initial reading of the ad. What do you need to fill in? How do you want to narrow your focus? As you conduct your research, be open to new ideas and interpretations that may arise but still proceed with some type of plan or questions to be answered. While conducting your research or once you have completed it, you may want to study the advertisement again and look for additional examples to support your argument or test your theories about the ad, its design, or its purpose.

As mentioned previously, your first source is usually the advertisement itself. The availability of commercials and radio spots on the Internet has made it easier to access these types of ads, but you must keep in mind that you may not be viewing the ad as it was intended to be seen, so consider whether or not the format has been changed or distorted in some way. You may also come across ads in a variety of print and online sources, as well as on billboards, sidewalk signs, the sides of buses, flyers on your windshield, and other such random locations.

Places online to check for copies of ads and commercials include the following:

- Commercial Closet Association   http://www.commercialcloset.org
- IFilm   http://www. screenjunkies.com
- Super Bowl Commercials   http://www.superbowl-ads.com
- Television Commercial Database   http://clipland.com/index_tvc.shtml
- YouTube   http://www.youtube.com

You can also search for commercials on websites for particular companies and on many online archives and museums devoted to specific products and services.

Likewise, secondary sources can be found in a variety of places, such as your library's holdings and electronic databases, and through an array of sources, including books, articles, and websites. You may find information about your particular ad, an ad campaign, or a specific genre of ads, such as alcohol or tobacco ads, as well as sources about how to create advertisements or sell products. Consider databases and indexes related specifically to marketing and advertising, as well as those connected to language and rhetoric or perhaps sociology and anthropology, which discuss ads and their impact on our lives and consumer habits.

Although the traditional sources just mentioned are often helpful, with popular culture you sometimes have to look at more contemporary or mainstream sources for additional information. Many of these sources can be found on the Internet, but you will want to evaluate the sources for reliability and trustworthiness. The milk industry will only have good things to say about their Got Milk ad campaign, which has been going strong since 1994, but the PETA group that advocates drinking soy milk instead of dairy has a different take on the campaign. Medical doctors who want to argue with some of the claims of the recent Got Milk ads, especially in regard to losing weight with milk, have yet another point of view about the ad campaign.

When conducting research, remember to record the bibliographic information you will need for your Works Cited page and for your in-text citations. Record information about the advertisements and where they come from as well as any books, articles, and websites you read; you may need to go back to these resources as you write or extend your research. See Chapter 5 for specific guidelines, and see the Works Cited pages at the end of essays in this chapter for citation examples.

KEY questions

Key Questions for an Advertisement Review Essay

- Have you given the reader an overall description of the ad?

- Who is the audience? How can you tell? What assumptions do the advertisers make about the audience?

- Is this a straightforward, political, satirical, or humorous advertisement? How can you tell? What traditions or standards does it rely on to be understood in these terms? For example, is it set up like a David Letterman Top Ten List? Does it use a common slogan such as "four out of five dentists surveyed said . . ."?

- In what ways is the ad designed to manipulate you into buying the product? What emotions and desires does it play upon? What appeals are used?

- Have you begun the review with an attention-grabbing opening? Have you concluded with your final thoughts about the ad being reviewed?

WRITING ABOUT ADVERTISEMENTS

Advertisements can be analyzed and written about in a variety of ways. You may want to look at the images presented, at what the words say, at the colors and arrangements on the page, at where and when the ad appears, at how this ad works with or against other ads for similar products, or at how the product packaging serves as another advertisement. For instance, the Got Milk ads at the start of this chapter, as well as their parodies, are part of the same two campaigns, but the individual ads have specific audiences in mind and, therefore, are arranged in particular ways, including who is and is not in the ad, what the text of the ad says, and how all of it is arranged on the page, as well as where the specific ad appears. Although there are many ways to write about advertisements, this chapter focuses on four of the main assignments given in most composition classes: advertisement reviews, reflection or response essays, analysis essays, and synthesis essays, which can be a combination of any of the preceding types.

Advertisement Reviews or Review Essays

An advertisement review essay is a close examination of an individual ad or a series of ads for one product. This type of essay primarily describes the components of the ad being reviewed, but it might also express an opinion about what is interesting or valuable about the ad. Evaluation is the main focus. You are giving a judgment about the quality and purpose of the ad, backed up with enough information to indicate that your judgment is sound and can be supported by the actual advertisement. These close readings of ads may be found in newspapers, in magazines, and on most news websites discussing new ads and their success, particularly in media and business circles. For a class, your review will most likely be about an advertisement you were either given in class or asked to bring in.

An advertisement review will usually analyze three or four key issues about the ad. Your overall evaluation of the ad can be phrased as the thesis of the essay and may come at the beginning or end of the essay. In the essay, you will often describe the key features and important details of the ad, creating a visual for the reader. You will also identify the audience for the ad and explain how the intended audience is made clear (or not) in the ad. You might

then discuss how the ad is designed to appeal to the audience identified. Finally, you will explain the implicit and explicit messages presented in the ad. During all of these steps, you will want to refer to specific images or text in the ad you are reviewing to support your opinions.

You might also compare the advertisement to other ads for the same product, to ads for competing products, or to other ads by the same company. Take GEICO insurance, for instance. They have launched several different successful campaigns with various themes and spokespersons—the caveman who just wants some respect and whom you can now follow on Twitter; the walking, talking gecko who has more than three hundred thousand likes on Facebook; and Maxwell the GEICO pig whose ringtone you can download from the GEICO website. You could focus on one of these spokespersons, compare them, or even look at them in the news; for example, a number of watch groups have called for the ad in which Maxwell goes on a date to be pulled because they believe it depicts bestiality. This comparative approach will help you show your reader that you are familiar with a wide range of advertisements so that your opinion is taken seriously and credibly.

Reflection or Response Essays

Although reflection or response essays will include some description of the advertisement(s), the main purpose is to use the ad as a starting point for your own reflection or response. The writer usually reflects on his or her own feelings that have arisen through critically watching, investigating, or listening to an advertisement, or the writer can respond to some personal issue or emotion that has arisen during the encounter with an advertisement or a series of ads. This essay will be mostly personal narrative, although it can also include evidence and description from the ad(s) that sparked the personal response. Consider what aspect of the advertisement grabs your attention, sparks your interest in the product, or, perhaps, triggers your anger or disgust. Then consider what you would like to say to your readers about the ad and about your own response. Finally, consider using a concrete thesis statement to explain the purpose of the essay and to keep you on track with your reflection.

Analysis Essays

An analysis essay includes more detailed and extensive descriptions, accompanied by an explanation of their significance, than a review essay does. When you analyze an advertisement, you are defending a view about the ad and how its different elements work or do not work. As with any argumentative paper, you want to offer an idea you have about the advertisement and support it with evidence from the ad itself and possibly outside sources as well. When writing an analysis essay, you will probably want to work from a tentative thesis that explains your overall judgment or argument about the ad. In your essay, you will explain and support this thesis. Similar to the thesis in a review, it offers your opinion, but in addition, it helps other viewers understand the ad: how it functions, why it was created in a certain way, how it affects viewers or listeners, what it means. You can support your thesis with specific evidence and examples from the ad and possibly from outside resources. Remember that analysis requires more than just observations or descriptions; in analysis, you look critically at what the advertisement is doing and present your supported evaluation of this action.

When analyzing advertisements, remember that there may be many valid interpretations for any given ad. For credibility purposes, you need to support your interpretation with specific details about the ad's images, text, colors, and arrangement, as well as its production, placement, and use of appeals. You may also need to support it with research about the ad's cost, impact, designers or producers, and the target audience, especially as it connects to the particular medium used to disseminate the ad. Likewise, you might also consider these factors in similar or competing ads to help determine why the advertisers have taken a particular approach in this ad or series of ads.

Synthesis Essays

The synthesis essay is a mixture of different rhetorical styles and writing purposes. It is a way of combining review with reflection or using personal response to support analysis. For example, you may have come across an ad on a bus or car, like the one pictured here. You may have had a personal response to this ad that will be a good opener for your essay, but this response may have led you to use the analysis questions to really dissect what the ad was doing or why it affected you the way it did. You may have even decided to do some research about the company or the history of ads on

© BILL MOWERY

KEY questions

Key Questions for a Reflection or Response Essay

- Have you clearly indicated how you used the advertisement as a springboard for your thesis?

- Have you expressed your personal response to one aspect of the advertisement(s)?

- Does your introduction direct your audience into your response?

- Does your concluding paragraph include some reflection on both the ad and your response?

- Are your intentions clear in this essay?

Key Questions for an Analysis Essay

- Do you have a clearly stated or implied thesis?

- Do you have a series of reasons supporting the thesis? Are these arranged in a logical and convincing order?

- Are your supporting reasons backed up? Do you provide specific evidence and examples from the ad for each reason you offer?

- Does your introduction orient your reader to the direction of your argument?

- Is your concluding paragraph summative and/or thought provoking without introducing completely new ideas?

buses, including images that show the progression of such ads. When you put all of these rhetorical approaches—personal response, analysis, visual arguments, and research—together, you have created a synthesis essay.

This type of essay may be assigned by your instructor, or you may find that this synthesis of approaches is the best way to answer your research question or support your evaluation. When writing for a class, look over the assignment carefully and speak to your instructor if you are unsure as to whether or not the synthesis essay fits the directions for the assignment. Because the synthesis essay utilizes a variety of rhetorical approaches and allows writers to make decisions based on what seems best for the topic being written about, many instructors and student writers prefer it. When you decide to use a mixture of strategies, be sure to look over the key questions for all of the types of essay strategies you are using in your writing.

ANNOTATED SAMPLE ESSAY

CONSIDERING IDEAS

1. What do you know about the women's movement of the 1970s? Gloria Steinem and *Ms. Magazine*?

2. What kinds of ads would you expect to see in a feminist magazine?

3. How do you think the women's movement affected methods of advertising?

AUTHOR BIO

Cathleen McBride, a mother of three teenage children, returned to Middle Tennessee State University after a twenty-year break to pursue her degree in nursing. For this class essay, McBride focuses on advertising images of women through the years and compares them to the way women are targeted today.

ADVERTISING

Keeping Sexism Alive

Cathleen McBride

I read Gloria Steinem's article "Sex, Lies, and Advertising," in which she describes the difficulties she had in getting advertisers for *Ms. Magazine* in the nineteen seventies and eighties. In reading her description of the challenges she faced, I discovered several disturbing indications of how advertisers see women as consumers and as people. Unfortunately, some of the outdated stereotypes of women used back then are still hanging around today.

Steinem needed to both secure advertising to keep her magazine self-supporting and profitable, and to present products to her readers that fit the overall view of *Ms. Magazine*'s readers as consumers. This was no easy task, as the magazine and its readers were breaking new ground. *Ms. Magazine* was present at the birth of the feminist movement that was changing the views that women had of themselves, and the views the world had of women. As a child during this time, I experienced the conflicting views of the mainstream media and women close to me. My mother explained that feminism meant that women were just as good as men and deserved to be treated equally, such as in getting equal pay for equal work. Television told me that feminists were man-hating bra-burners who wanted to abandon their homes and families to selfishly entertain themselves by stealing good jobs from men, and I can still see traces of this image in popular media today. Women craved more freedom and more choices than simply being "his wife" and "their mother."

When Steinem attempted to redirect the efforts of advertisers to reach her audience that no longer saw themselves as merely housewives, she met both resistance and hostility. Women wanted to see advertising that showed them more than laundry soap and makeup; they needed information on financial products, cars and electronics. Advertisers felt it was silly to market these traditionally "masculine" products to women, and this trend continues. In our modern advertising we see that women need food, cleaning products and shoes, and men want power tools, lawnmowers and electronics. There are, of course, exceptions to these trends, usually just as sexist. For example, women who don't feel powerful or in control are now offered a new solution through advertising. When her son was bullied on the playground, one woman in a recent ad fixed the situation by dragging her to the Hummer dealership where she bought one of the largest vehicles on the planet. Women are now free to compensate for their inadequacies just like men by buying a new car—hardly an empowering suggestion. Another traditionally male market sector, NASCAR teams and sponsors realize women are their fastest-growing fan base, and they have created some rather puzzling ad campaigns as a result. For example, I know that if I am too busy daydreaming about my favorite driver and how cute he is to watch where I am driving, my insurance company will cover the damages when I crash into a big sign and knock it over. Women drivers! When will we ever learn? These examples illustrate how the gender-specific advertising we see today has changed very little from the images of the early seventies. Or is it that these actually are changes in advertising? Are the advertisers finally offering the same level of stupidity to both women and men?

Another illustrative example. Would it help if you knew what brand insurance she was discussing?

Writer acknowledges benefits of the women's movement but then shows how this "benefit" really worked against women.

However, some changes in advertising forced by the women's movement had unexpected consequences. When advertisers finally began to target women who worked outside the home, they were depicted as power-suited executives who delivered gourmet meals and looked like models at all times, creating the unattainable, anti-feminist Superwoman stereotype. It is possible to be a worker and a homemaker and a parent but it isn't possible to do them all perfectly; there simply aren't enough hours in the day, and women everywhere agonize over their inadequacies. Advertisers traditionally used women that were white, blonde, thin and under thirty, bombarding us with images that made the markets for hair color, diet products and wrinkle creams explode. Maybe increased sales of these products were the intended consequences all along.

In her article, Steinem shows us how advertisers control the editorial content of magazines by demanding that their ads should be placed close to certain types of articles, or they will pull the ads that keep the magazine financially solvent. Advertisements for food should accompany recipes, and makeup ads should match fashion "editorials" telling about the newest age-defying foundation and long-lasting lipstick. Women should look pretty, and women's magazines should look pretty and tell women how to look pretty. Television isn't much different, and we see a parade of women who buy pretty clothes and cars and cook pretty food and keep their houses and children clean and pretty. We haven't come very far from the days when June Cleaver did all her housework wearing pearls. A truly insulting ad for Swiffer Carpet Flick shows me that rather than stupidly dragging my full-size vacuum cleaner up the stairs while it's still plugged in, I should buy their small plastic carpet-cleaning device. It's little and cute and you can carry it right up the stairs. Wow! I gotta have that!

Writer connects what the article says about print ads to television ads.

Advertisers basically see the buying public as sheep to be enticed to buy their products, and we should keep this in mind. A commercial I saw recently illustrates this concept perfectly. A herd of sheep is cowering in a pen, and one black sheep walks away from the herd, wriggles under the fence and takes off across a field. Other black sheep soon join him, leading to a growing herd of black sheep parading down the road. They reach a town where we see a sign reading "Welcome Harley Riders," and as the sheep head down Main Street they are joined by hundreds of black sheep, as far as the eye can see, framed on both sides by rows of Harley Davidson motorcycles. I laughed and laughed at this ad and then had to explain myself to the kids; black sheep were once a bad thing but now are a good thing, just like tattoos and Harleys, and they should band together. But when everyone starts doing something, like riding a Harley, is it still cool? At least the ad didn't show bleached blonde black sheep in halter-tops on the backs of the bikes. Times have changed but advertising is still following the same old herd ideas of sexist advertising used in decades past. Whether black or white, mainstream or alternative, male or female, to the advertisers, we are still sheep.

Uses analogy to pull her argument together.

Uses personal response to once again support her opinion and to bring her essay to a close.

Works Cited

Steinem, Gloria. "Sex, Lies, and Advertising." *Gender, Race, and Class in Media: A Text-reader.* 2nd ed. Ed. Gail Dines and Jean M. Humez. Thousand Oaks: Sage, 2002. 223–29. Print.

Source: *"Advertising: Keeping Sexism Alive" by Cathleen McBride. Written for Expository Writing at Middle Tennessee State University with Professor Dianna Baldwin, 2006.*

DECODING THE TEXT

1. What is the author's main idea? How does the author support this idea?

2. Which supporting details do you find the most authoritative?

3. The author compares the general population to a herd of sheep. Is this analogy convincing? Why or why not?

CONNECTING TO YOUR CULTURE

1. Do you think women want more from commercials and print ads?

2. Do you think some commercials are insulting? Or are they just humorous?

3. Have you ever laughed out loud at a commercial? What makes a commercial funny?

4. Is humor a good selling point? Why or why not?

THE READING ZONE

ENGAGING WITH TOPICS

1. What makes you like an ad? Do you want recognizable music? Catchy jingles? Celebrity spokespersons? Artistic images? Do you have a favorite ad?

2. When looking at ads, do you notice how women and men are dressed or undressed? Do you ever wonder what the model has to do with the product or service being sold? Explain your reactions to the use of sex to sell products from cars to tobacco to toothpaste.

3. How are characters like Tony the Tiger or Maxwell the pig used in advertisements? How many commercial characters like Tony can you name? Do you buy the products associated with these characters? Why or why not?

4. Where do you personally encounter the most ads? On the Internet? Television? Magazines? Newspapers? Stadium or subway walls? Have you ever encountered an ad in a place you did not expect? Describe the place and the ad. How did you react to this ad?

5. Do you see people like yourself in the ads you encounter? Do you see people like your friends? Do you ever think about who is not seen in commercials? Do you ever want to be like the people you see in ads? In what ways?

READING SELECTIONS

The readings that follow are organized into three sections: the 1970s and 1980s, the 1990s and 2000s, and the 2010s. This decades organization will be used to organize all content chapters for this textbook and to give a broader picture of what popular culture is and how it affects our daily lives. The readings in each of the sections are not isolated to that decade or section because pop culture is not only what happened at the time but also how the same item or idea is received or remembered later on. Accordingly, in the 1970s and 1980s section, James B. Twitchell discusses Philip Morris's effective ad campaign for Marlboro cigarettes, including how they succeeded despite the 1971 ban on television advertising for cigarettes; Leon F. Wynter, author of *American Skin: Pop Culture, Big Business, and the End of White America,* discusses the movement of black entertainers and athletes into the realm of "pop" and, consequently, the realm of advertising and "coolness"; and Murray L. Bob argues against the late 1980s trend of putting ads in books.

The 1990s and 2000s saw even more diversity in advertising—in both content and location; thus, Beth A. Haller and Sue Ralph are able to discuss the incorporation of people with disabilities and images of disability into mainstream advertisements; Barbara J. Phillips asks you to examine the role of trade characters in advertisements; and Amy Aidman looks at the role of corporate advertising in American schools.

In the 2010s, Joy Parks examines sexism in advertising and questions who is responsible, a discussion sparked by the success of the television show *Mad Men*; Steve Marsh looks at the often unlikely partnerships between advertising executives, certain brands, and indie music groups; and Wilson Rothman discusses the likely success, or not, of running ads on e-readers such as the Kindle. This chapter also includes a visual case study that allows you to examine the role of Coca-Cola and some of their various ad campaigns and logos in today's society.

The readings in this chapter are presented as a way for you to become more versed in investigating and analyzing advertisements as both makers and reflectors of pop culture; however, they are also offered as samples of writing reviews, reflections or responses, analyses, and synthesis essays about advertisements and the advertising industry.

READING SELECTIONS: THE 1970s AND 1980s

CONSIDERING IDEAS

In 1971, the Federal Communications Commission banned television ads about smoking and strengthened regulations concerning the portrayals of cigarette smoking on television programming. The hope was that smoking would decrease. Instead, smoking increased.

1. Why do you think this increase happened?
2. In what other ways has the government, as well as society, attempted to regulate smoking since the early 1970s? Is it working?
3. Do you smoke? How many people do you know who smoke? Why do you or they smoke?
4. Do you think people are enticed by cigarette ads to smoke? Why or why not?

AUTHOR BIO

James B. Twitchell is a professor in both the English and advertising departments of the University of Florida. He often compares advertising to religion and thinks it important for people to study the history of a practice that exerts such influence over our lives. His recent books include Shopping for God: How Shopping Went from In Your Heart to In Your Face *(2007),* Branded Nation: The Marketing of Megachurch, College Inc., and Museumworld *(2004) and* Where Men Hide *(2006). The following essay about the Marlboro Man campaign comes from* Twenty Ads That Shook the World: The Century's Most Groundbreaking Advertising and How It Changed Us All *(2000).*

THE MARLBORO MAN

The Perfect Campaign

James B. Twitchell

Although advertising agencies love giving themselves prizes, there has been no award for the perfect campaign. If there were, Marlboro would win. Suffice it to say that this brand went from selling less than one quarter of one percent of the American market in the early 1950s to being the most popular in the entire world in just twenty years. Every fourth cigarette smoked is a Marlboro. Leo Burnett's brilliant campaign made Marlboro the most valuable brand in the world.

First, let's dispense with the politics of the product. We all know that cigarettes are the most dangerous legal product in the world. They kill more people each year than do guns. And yes, it is dreadful that the myth of independence is used to sell addiction. But never forget as well that it is exactly this danger that animates the Marlboro Man. He came into being just as smoking became problematic and, ironically, as long as anxiety exists, so will he.

And second, cigarettes, like domestic beer and bottled water, build deep affiliations that have absolutely nothing to do with taste. As David Ogilvy said, "Give people a taste of Old Crow and *tell* them it's Old Crow. Then give them another taste of Old Crow, *but tell them it's Jack Daniel's.* Ask them which they prefer. They'll think the two drinks are quite different. *They are tasting images*" (Ogilvy 1985, 87).

In fact, it was the cigarette companies that found this out first. In the 1920s they blindfolded brand-dedicated smokers and put them into dark rooms. Then they gave them Luckies, Pall Malls, Chesterfields, and Camels, as well as European smokes, and asked the smokers to identify "their own brand"—the one they were sure they knew. By now we all know the results. Taste has basically little or nothing to do with why people choose specific brands of cigarettes.

Just as we drink the label, we smoke the advertising. So what's so smokable, so tasty, about this ad?

First, everything fits around the dominant image. The heading and the logo-type fall naturally in place. Product name mediates between visual and verbal. Let's start with the name, *Marlboro*. Like so many cigarette brand names, it is English and elegant and, like its counterpart Winston, deceptively vague. Like the joke about how there's gotta be a pony in there somewhere, there's gotta be prestige in here somewhere. (Oddly enough, Marlboro was first created in Victorian England, then transported to the States as a cigarette for women.) The ersatz PM crest at the apex of the "red roof" chevron on the package hints of a bloodline, and the Latin motto "Veni, Vidi, Vici" (!) conveys ancient warrior strength. Clearly, the power is now both in the pack and in the buckaroo.

The buckaroo is, of course, the eponymous Marlboro Man. He is what we have for royalty, distilled manhood. (Alas, the Winston man barely exists. What little of him there is that is opinionated, urbane, self-assured—and needs to tell you so.) The Marlboro Man needs to tell you nothing. He carries no scepter, no gun. He never even speaks. Doesn't need to. The difference between Marlboro and Winston is the difference between myth and reality. Winston needed to break the rules publicly to be independent ("Winston tastes good *like* a cigarette should"), the Marlboro Man has already been there, done that. Little wonder the Viceroy man ("a thinking man's filter, a smoking man's taste") couldn't even make the cut.

Generating prestige *and* independence is a crucial aspect of cigarette selling. If you are targeting those who are just entering the consumption community, and if the act of consumption is dangerous, then you do not need to stress rebellion—that's a given. What you need to announce is initiation into the pack.

When R. J. Reynolds tested Marlboro on focus groups, they found that it was not rugged machismo that was alluring to young Marlboro smokers, but separation from restraints (the tattoo) *and* a sense of belonging (Marlboro Country). This "secret" RJR report, now available on the World Wide Web, is one reason why the "I'd walk a mile for a Camel" man was subsumed into the more personable, intelligent, and independent "Cool Joe" Camel.

Let's face it, the Camel man was downright stupid. In the most repeated of his ill-fated "walk a mile" ads he is shown carrying a tire (instead of rolling it) across the desert (with no canteen), wearing no shade-providing hat. That he seemingly forgot the spare tire is as stupid as his choosing to smoke. Little wonder Cool Joe pushed him aside. A camel seems intelligent in comparison.

The Marlboro Man's transformation was less traumatic, but no less meaningful. In fact, it is a reversal of the most popular tabloid story of the 1950s. It was to be, as David Ogilvy would say, one of the "riskiest decisions ever made" and one "which fewer advertisers would take." Here's the cultural context on a thumbnail, and what Phillip Morris did about it:

On February 13, 1953, George Jorgensen went to Denmark and returned as Christine. The idea that one could change one's sex was profoundly unsettling to American culture. Once back at home, she uttered the perhaps apocryphal testament to her journey: "Men are wary of me and I'm wary of the ones who aren't."

At almost the same time, another repositioning was occurring. Now, as any modern ten-year-old can tell you, objects have sexual characteristics, too. Philip Morris had a female cigarette, Marlboro, that wouldn't sell. So they sent her up to Chicago to be regendered by Leo Burnett. Miss Marlboro was a "sissy smoke . . . a tea room smoke," Burnett said. Although she had been in and out of production for most of the century, in her most recent incarnation she had a red filter tip (called the "beauty tip," to hide lipstick stains) and a long-running theme: "Mild as May." Men wouldn't touch her, nor would many women.

In December 1954, Burnett took Miss Marlboro out to his gentleman's farm south of Chicago and invited some of his agency cohorts over to brainstorm. Something had to be done to put some hair on her chest, to change her out of pinafores and into cowboy chaps, anything to get her out of the suffocating tea room.

"What is the most masculine figure in America?" Burnett asked. "Cab driver, sailor, marine, pilot, race car driver" came the replies. Then someone simply said, "Cowboy." Bingo! Copywriter Draper Daniels filled in the blank: this smoke "Delivers the Goods on Flavor."

But these admen were not thinking of a real cowboy, not some dirty, spitting, toothless, smelly wrangler. They were city boys who knew cowboys in bronzes and oils by Frederic Remington, or in oils and watercolors by Charles Russell, or in the purple prose of Owen Wister's *The Virginian* or in the pulp of Zane Grey's countless novels. Philip Morris and Leo Burnett now love to tell you that the Marlboro Man was always a "real cowboy." Just don't remind them that almost half of the real cowpunchers were black or Mexican.

No matter, Leo Burnett had just the image in mind. He remembered seeing one C. H. Long, a thirty-nine-year-old foreman at the JA Ranch in the Texas panhandle, a place described as "320,000 acres of nothing much," who had been heroically photographed by Leonard McCombe for a cover of *Life* magazine in 1949. In other words, this Marlboro cowboy was a real/reel cowboy, something like what Matt Dillon, played by James Arness, was on television. A slightly roughed-up, *High Noon* Gary Cooper, a lite-spaghetti Clint Eastwood.

To get to this image, the Leo Burnett Company tried out all manner of windblown wranglers, some professional models, some not. Then, in 1963, just as the health concerns about lung cancer really took hold, they discovered Carl "Big-un" Bradley at the 6666 Ranch in Guthrie, Texas. Carl was the first real cowboy they used, and from then on the Marlboro Men were honest-to-God cowboys, rodeo riders, and stuntmen.

One look at him and you know: no Ralph Lauren jeans, no 401(k) plans, no wine spritzers, nothing with little ducks all over it, just independence, pure and simple. He doesn't concern himself with the Surgeon General. He's his own sheriff. To make sure he stayed that way, all background was airbrushed out. Later he got a grubstake in Marlboro Country.

Even today the Philip Morris Company receives letters from all over the world, mostly at the beginning of the summer, from travelers wishing to know how to get to Marlboro Country.

But there's more to the ad than the free-ranging cowboy. That package with the insignia, built truck-tough as a flip-top *box,* was a badge. With its hearty red, white, and black lettering, the smoker pinned it to his chest on the average of twenty-three times a day. This *vade mecum* of a package was designed by Frank Gianninoto and carefully tested through consumer surveys by Elmo Roper & Associates and the Color Research Institute. Now the *Veni, Vidi, Vici* starts making sense. With this package you are the decorated conqueror. You burn bridges, bust broncos, confront stuff like lung cancer.

Sure, the girlie filter was there for the women (incidentally, the famous Marlboro red came from the lipstick red of the original "beauty filter"), but it was battled by the box, the medallion—the manliness of it all.

Should you still not be convinced, there was always the brand, the literal brand—the tattoo. Remember, this was the 1950s, when tattoos were not a fashion accessory, but an unambiguous sign of antisocial "otherness." But this brand was not on the biceps to signify Charles Atlas manliness; rather it was on the back of the smoking hand, or on the wrist. A strange place for a tattoo, to be sure, but appropriate.

Although research departments may cringe to hear this, the tattoo was not the result of motivational research showing that the image would be super macho. Leo Burnett supposedly thought the tattoo would "say to many men that here is a successful man who used to work with his hands," while "to many women, we believe it will suggest a romantic past."

But there is another story that also may be true. Alas, it doesn't emphasize virility and romance but the bugaboo of interpretation, namely, happenstance. It seems someone at the agency had scribbled on the hand of the *Life* magazine cowboy that there was no copyright clearance for this particular image. The agency sent this image in a paste-up to Philip Morris and then made another version from another cowboy photo to avoid copyright problems. It, too, went to the client. Back came the reaction: "Where's the tattoo on the second cowboy?" Perplexed agency people dug up the original photo and saw the warning scribbled across the wrist (McGuire 1989, 23).

No matter what the story, the tattoo stuck, not because of any massive testing but because everyone knew the branding itself was compelling. You are what you smoke.

When a campaign "works," every part seems compelling. In fact, in great ads, as in great works of art, the sum of the parts is always more than the whole. The visual and verbal rhetoric is so strong that they seem to have always been in place. They seem indestructible. In truth, however, often the greatest act of creativity is knowing when to leave well enough alone. "I have learned that any fool can write a bad ad," Burnett says in one of his pithy *100 Leo's*, "but that it takes a real genius to keep his hands off a good one" (Burnett 1995, 53).

Most of the tinkering with this campaign has been by the government. For instance, many people thought that by removing the Marlboro Man from television in the early 1970s the feds would send him into the sunset. No such luck. You can take down all the billboards and remove him from magazines. "Just a little dab" of this rhetoric "will do ya."

When Philip Morris attempted to introduce brand extension—Marlboro Light—after all the advertising bans were in place, all they did was unsaddle the cowboy and foreground the horse. Now that even mentioning the cigarette by name is becoming taboo, they are mining the original campaign by making Marlboro Country into Marlboro Unlimited and selling lots of logo'd stuff to smokers, calling it Gear Without Limits. By selling annually some 20 million T-shirts, caps, jackets, and other items bearing Marlboro logos, Philip Morris was, for a time, the nation's third-largest mail-order house.

This attempt to get around the fear of legal restrictions on advertising is called "sell-through," and you see it happening with almost all the major cigarette and beer brands. So Smokin' Joe, the super-cool Camel musician, appears on a host of nontobacco products like clothing, beach towels, baseball caps, while at the same time he also appears on the hit list of the FTC as a public nuisance.

And so what is Gear Without Limits for people who want to go to the Land That Knows No Limits? Well, what about products from the Marlboro Country Store like Snake River Fishing Gear ("An outfit made to go where the cold rivers run"), the Marlboro Folding Mountain Bike, a Mountain Lantern in Marlboro red, and the Marlboro Country Cookbook (complete with their green salsa recipe for couch cowpokes). Marlboro has so captured the iconography of cowboydom that they now have ads in mass-circulation magazines consisting *only* of recipes for such grub as Huevos Rancheros, Barkeeper's Burgers, and Whiskey Beef Sandwiches.

My favorite Marlboro ad, however, is an English one in which a Harleyesque motorcycle is set out in the bleak Western plains. The only color in the bleached scene is on the bike's gas tank—Marlboro red. In art lingo, this trope is called *metonymy*.

Metonymy transfers meaning because the host image, the Marlboro cowboy, is imbedded so deep not just in American culture but in world culture that we close the circuit. Ironically, slow learners are helped by the appearance of the warning box telling you that smoking is dangerous! The Marlboro Man may indeed be Dracula to his foes, but he is still the perfect icon of adolescent independence.

Ironically, the greatest danger faced by the Marlboro Man is not from lawmen armed with scientific studies, but from some wise guy MBA in Manhattan who will try to earn his spurs by tinkering with the campaign. This almost happened on April 22, 1993, as Michael Miles, CEO of Philip Morris, thought he could play chicken with the generics who were rustling his customers. Overnight, Miles cut the price of Marlboro by sixty cents a pack.

But the only critter he scared was the stock market, which lopped 23 percent off the price of PM stock in a single day. This day, still called "Marlboro Friday," will live in infamy as it seemed for a moment that other advertisers might follow. The whole point of branding is to make sure the consumer *pays* for the advertising by thinking that the interchangeable product is unique. He knows this when he pays a premium for it. When *Forbes* magazine (February 2, 1987) offered Marlboro smokers their chosen brand in a generic brown box at half the price, only 21 percent were interested. Just as the price of Marlboro is what economists call "inelastic," so is the advertising. Michael Miles lost his job and the company lost $13 billion in shareholder equity, but marketers learned a lesson: you don't fool with Mother Nature or a great campaign.

Works Cited

Burnett, Leo. *100 Leo's: The Wit and Wisdom of Leo Burnett*. Lincolnwood: NTC, 1995. Print.

McGuire, John M. "How the Marlboro Cowboy Acquired His Tattoo." *St. Louis Post-Dispatch 12* Nov. 1989. Print.

Ogilvy, David. *On Advertising*. New York: Vintage, 1985. Print.

DECODING THE TEXT

1. According to Twitchell, how did the Marlboro Man campaign make Marlboro the most popular brand in the world?

2. Twitchell makes a connection between the changing of Marlboro's image and the groundbreaking sex change operation for George "Christine" Jorgensen. Is this comparison believable in the text? Why or why not?

3. Which of the two stories about the Marlboro Man's tattoo do you find most plausible? What are your reasons for this belief?

CONNECTING TO YOUR CULTURE

1. How does the history lesson in this essay connect to you and your views on smoking?

2. How do you think it connects to your peers? Your family?

3. Twitchell says, "even mentioning the cigarette by name is becoming taboo." What is the reason behind this change? How has it affected smokers? Nonsmokers? What other products have been affected in the same way? Do these products have anything in common with cigarettes?

4. What do you think about antismoking ads such as those put out by TheTruth.com? These campaigns may have actually increased smoking; why do you think that is?

CONSIDERING IDEAS

1. Do the people in advertisements look like you and your friends? If yes, In what ways? If no, why not?

2. Are ads more effective if you can see yourself in them? Explain.

3. How could advertisers better represent you?

AUTHOR BIO

Leon E. Wynter, now deceased, was a journalist and radio commentator who created the "Business and Race" column for The Wall Street Journal and published articles in The Washington Post and The New York Times. Wynter was also a commentator on National Public Radio, as well as the author of American Skin: Pop Culture, Big Business and the End of White America. "Marketing in Color" is an excerpt from this 2002 book.

MARKETING IN COLOR

New Niches Flow into the Mainstream

Leon E. Wynter

In the spring of 1999, shortly after securing the freedom of three American soldiers captured by the Yugoslavian Army during the NATO miniwar on Yugoslavia over Kosovo, the Reverend Jesse Jackson paid a call on the headquarters of PepsiCo in the bucolic New York suburb of Purchase. Still basking in the glow of his latest free-lance foreign policy coup, Jackson's mission was to press top executives to throw more corporate-securities-underwriting work toward certain black- and minority-owned firms. With a small entourage in tow, Jackson's very presence in the mostly empty halls of the secluded corporate campus caused a bigger stir than most anybody in the well-starched head office of the perennial number-two cola maker could remember. It remained for one older employee, a black maintenance man, to put the pageantry of the sales call into context.

"This is the most excitement since the day Don King came up here," said Pepsi marketing executive Maurice Cox, quoting the maintenance man's words. Indeed, everyone involved with selling Pepsi seemed to remember the fall 1983 day when the already-legendary, if not infamous, boxing promoter's humongous white stretch limousine, "big—like the kind they have today, only it was back then," parked on the cobblestone path before Pepsi's executive suite. The day Don King brought Pepsi the then-outrageous proposal of a $5 million sponsorship deal for the twenty-three-year-old "soul singer" Michael Jackson and his brothers was memorable enough to merit a chapter, just two years later, in Pepsi president Roger Enrico's 1986 book on the 1980s cola wars.

Many important personages have come to PepsiCo headquarters . . . none of them made the entrance King did. A land yacht of a limo pulled up, and out stepped this man in a white fur coat that had to cost as much as the car. King's pearly gray hair had been freshly electrocuted and was reaching the sky. Around King's neck was a blindingly shiny necklace, on which hung his logo, a crown with "DON" on top, just in case you might forget he is the king.

Such a man did not come quickly through the halls.

"Hi, everybody, I'm Don King," he told one and all.

Enshrining the moment was the least Enrico could do, because his decision to take a deal that only Don King would think of proposing to a *Fortune* 100 firm back then fixed the word *legendary* before the former PepsiCo chairman's name and secured his place in marketing history. It was a meeting that no one doing marketing at Coke's Atlanta headquarters would forget, either. For decades Pepsi had been desperate to gain a marketing edge over Coke. Enrico, who had just become president of the Pepsi-Cola division, was determined to do whatever it took to pull Coke, still the most hallowed American brand name, down to earth. Beyond the theatrics of the messenger, Don King's message was that Michael Jackson was about to shatter previously shatterproof barriers between black entertainers and mainstream popular culture. But even King's bombast failed to anticipate the financial records Jackson would also break along the way on the strength of the *Thriller* album. Released early in 1983, it had already topped the charts with nearly 10 million copies sold by the time King came to Pepsi. *Thriller* went on to quadruple that number and became the biggest-selling album in history. Guinness actually held the presses on the 1984 edition of the *World's Records* book (a first in itself) to include *Thriller* as the top seller of all time, passing Carole King's 1970 *Tapestry,* when the industry-shaking album had still hit only 25 million in sales. The $5 million sponsorship deal Pepsi announced in December 1983 was also a Guinness record; it lasted until Jackson signed a $15 million personal endorsement deal with Pepsi two years later.

The awards, concert attendance, television ratings, and the like connected with Jackson during the mid-1980s, summed up by the term *Michaelmania,* could make up a book by themselves. So could the impact of the "Jackson phenomenon," as it was also called, on the very foundations of media-driven commercial culture. It spawned an orgy of "who is he and who are we as a society" journalistic navel-gazing not seen over a performing act since the Beatles landed in the States in 1964. In one week in March 1984, culture critics at both *Time* magazine and the *Washington Post* vainly exhausted more than six thousand words trying to plumb the connection between the Jackson persona and our collective psyche. Writing right after Jackson took eight out of a possible ten awards at the 1984 Grammys (another record) and searching for meaning, the authors seemed to be drowning in the sea of statistics (1 million albums sold per week for over twenty-four weeks and still counting), in the flood of celebrity swells (Jane Fonda, Elizabeth Taylor, Katharine Hepburn, Brooke Shields, Steven Spielberg) attached to the Jackson tide, and in the wave of historical icon comparisons (Babe Ruth, Al Jolson, Elvis, Howard Hughes, the Beatles).

All they really knew for sure was what the *Post's* Richard Harrington asserted:

The combined evidence of the bottom line, the hard listen and the long view is difficult to resist: Jackson is the biggest thing since the Beatles. He is the hottest single phenomenon since Elvis Presley. He just may be the most popular black singer ever.

And still they missed it.

Harrington was to the point in noting that the breathtakingly styled music of *Thriller* wasn't a breakthrough in itself, and that "Michael Jackson is far more popular than influential (again more like Elvis, rather than the Beatles)." But *Time's* Jay Cocks came closer to the pith of the moment in observing that:

Thriller brought black music back to mainstream radio, from which it had been effectively banished after restrictive "special-format programming" was introduced in the mid-'70s. Listeners could put more carbonation in their pop and cut their heavy-metal diet with a dose of the fleetest soul around. "No doubt about it," says composer-arranger Quincy Jones, who produced *Off the Wall* and *Thriller* with Jackson. "He's taken us right up there where we belong. Black music has [had] to play second fiddle for a long time, but its spirit is the whole motor of pop. Michael has connected with every soul in the world."

But neither analysis detected the fault lines deep in the crust of popular culture that happened to intersect with the frail black performer's mercurial rise. Michael Jackson the earthquake struck where the emerging entertainment-information economy met the mother-seam of color at the core of American popular culture. At the epicenter, on the surface, was the thing called pop.

Pop, as a music-industry (as opposed to musical) category, had always been a euphemism for *white* until Michael unleashed "the power of *Thriller.*" For example, Chuck Berry, for all his classic hit songs and unimpeachable claim to rock and roll's paternity, landed only one number-one pop single in his career, and that was at the end, with the novelty tune "My Dingaling" in 1972. In the 1960s and 1970s, the biggest Motown acts, the Bacharach-David-produced Dionne Warwick hits, and a few black bands like Earth, Wind and Fire garnered black performers their first significant "crossover" spots on the pop charts, but most black acts could aspire only to *Billboard*'s rhythm-and-blues chart. As part of the Jackson Five, Michael Jackson had been one of the exceptions to the industry practices that limited black access to the pop charts. Between 1970 and 1976, the group had landed seven singles in the pop top ten.

Yet for nonwhite performers, even holding precious slots on the pop charts did not a pop star make. Until *Thriller* the unofficial "King" or "Queen of Pop" had always been white, no matter how many records a black artist sold or how much airplay it got.

American pop, as it turned out, is more than an industry chart. True pop icon status, at the very top, is a state of grace that approaches divine right over one's consumer-subjects in the marketplace. It's a cross between being royalty and being in the top management of mainstream affinity, complete with rituals of respect, ceremonies of adoration, and titles. Pop is what Elvis was after he stopped his initial blues shouting and let Colonel Parker make him the perfect (but not too perfect) heartthrob for white teenage girls as the 1950s became the 1960s. He was the "King." Pop is the firm Sinatra controlled before Elvis, and for many Americans over a certain age, he remained the "Chairman" until the day he died. By the time your parents could be seen nodding in agreement with their peers that "I Want to Hold Your Hand" was really classically inspired, it was the Beatles, one of whom (Paul McCartney) was actually knighted by the queen. Pop is the universal white blue-collar factory that Bruce Springsteen ran in the late 1970s and into the 1980s. He was "the Boss."

To be sure, there were titles enough to go around in the marginal kingdoms of R&B and soul and gospel and Latin music: Aretha Franklin—Queen, James Brown—Godfather, Celia Cruz—Queen of Salsa, and so on. Still, no nonwhites needed to apply for mainstream pop music honorifics as the 1970s became the 1980s. Ditto, with a few notable exceptions, pop positions in television, movies, and (significantly) fashion and style. Bill Cosby, Coke's primary general-market pitchman in the 1970s, also sold well for Jell-O and Ford. O. J. Simpson broke entirely new ground for retired black professional athletes with his ubiquitous Hertz commercials. But neither man would be recognized or recognizable as a pop icon until the early 1990s, and not just because they had yet to star in their respective hit television shows. Until Michael Jackson and *Thriller,* marketers simply assumed that no matter how successful a nonwhite performer might be, whiteness was an indispensable requirement for the exaggerated state of mass identification that constitutes "pop stardom."

Then Roger Enrico bet the farm on Michael Jackson and *Thriller*—and won.

As the 1980s began, the business of whiteness-centered pop was, as usual, lurching between cyclical feast and famine. But by the decade's end, the same forces that brought *Thriller*'s eruption would move whiteness from indispensable to merely useful in the business of pop, *permanently,* while raising the influence, the reach, and most important, the aggregate profitability of pop entertainment to unimagined heights. By 1990 America's collective pop culture, bonded to the cutting edge of a revolution in telecommunications and information technology, had assumed the lead role in the world's most powerful global economy. Think about it: In 1980 the business of pop could not have imagined the multidimensional marketing star power of Michael Jackson, Michael Jordan, Whitney Houston, or Eddie Murphy. It hadn't seen the platinum branding of predominantly nonwhite professional basketball, football, and baseball or the "Nikeization" of marketing that attended it. It hadn't even seen a hint of the multibillion-dollar music-fashion-style-literature industry called hip-hop. In other words, in 1980 American commercial popular culture hadn't seen nothing yet.

* * *

Imposing a time frame on such a retrospective analysis is always arbitrary, but I place the first moment during a time-out for a Coke commercial in Super Bowl XIV in January 1980. Today the expense, production, and entertainment values of Super Bowl ads rival those of the game itself, but that Sunday in 1980 marked the unintended debut of the first blockbuster Super Bowl commercial. The unlikely star was a big, fierce black man stooping to kindness toward a little white boy. The one-minute ad, which was immediately acclaimed by media and marketing critics, went on to win numerous awards and remains a fixture on "top commercials of all time" lists to this day. Jack Rooney, a former account executive with Foote, Cone and Belding who later headed marketing for Miller Brewing, echoed the response of every advertising or marketing professional I interviewed when I mentioned the commercial. He said he remembered it "like it happened yesterday." "The big joke in the industry was that something like seventy people claimed responsibility for it," he said.

(Scene: Down the tunnel leading from the football field, Pittsburgh Steeler linebacker Joe "Mean Joe" Greene, battered and bruised, fairly limps toward the locker room. A small white boy with a bottle of Coke follows.)

Boy:	Mr. Greene—Mr. Greene . . . do you—do you need any help?
Greene:	Unh-Unh.
Boy:	I just want you to know—I think—I think—you're the best ever!
Greene:	Yeah, sure.
Boy:	You want my Coke? It's okay—you can have it.
Greene:	No, no.
Boy:	Really—you can have it.
Greene:	(sighs) Okay—thanks.

(Music swells: "A Coke and a smile . . . makes me feel good . . . .")

(Greene downs the Coke in a ten-second-long gulp, then turns toward the locker room. The boy, dejected, starts walking back to the stands.)

Boy:	See ya around.

(Greene turns back.)

Greene:	Hey, kid . . . (tosses his soiled jersey to the boy)
Boy:	Wow! Thanks, Mean Joe!

True, O. J. Simpson had already been the star of a long-running (no pun intended) Hertz campaign for some time when the Joe Greene Coke commercial made its debut. But unlike Simpson's smiling, clean-shaven re-creation of his evasive gridiron maneuvers—in a business suit—"Hey, Kid," as the spot was dubbed by the ad agency that created it, was the first major commercial to harness, if not confront, the fearful stereotypes of black maleness that American political culture had built for centuries and that mass culture had always emasculated or avoided altogether, to make a positive selling point. Here's Joe Greene, a big (six foot four, 260 pounds), belligerent, bearded black warrior-athlete featured in an unguarded (i.e., out of sight of authority) moment of pain and frustration when, presumably, his animal instincts could lash out against an unsuspecting white innocent. No levity or dancing was employed to divert the viewer from the almost primal tension building in each moment until Greene accepts the offering of the Coke. When he throws his head back and opens his throat, and the feel-good music swells, all the power in the scene is focused on the magic in the act of sharing this all-American beverage. As the energy of racial tension in the one-minute drama was gathered and then dispelled, the desired main effect was to move the viewer toward having a Coke. But the more powerful side effects flowed from the momentary cathartic relief of race-related tension. Among them is a benign repression of awareness that the tension had anything to do with Joe Greene's racial persona. Any initial consciousness of the source of the tension is washed away in the wave of joy that follows Greene's jersey into the arms of "the Kid."

Repeated exposure to the ad compounds this repression effect into a long-term deracialization (not the same as deracination) of Joe Greene himself. Perhaps a better term is *humanization.* As the psychological dynamic of cognitive dissonance comes into play over time, the mind finds it uncomfortable to simultaneously hold the specter of Greene as an undifferentiated black brute and the image of the man who shares this special bond of trust and adoration with "the Kid." To reconcile the dissonance, the viewer must embrace one understanding of Greene and abandon the other. Former Coke executive Chuck Morrison joined Coca-Cola's marketing team in 1981, when the Joe Greene ad was still fresh in the beverage industry's mind. As he explained to me when I interviewed him:

> What's interesting about it is it also changed the image of "Mean Joe" Greene. What most people forget is that prior to the commercial Joe Greene was [seen as] one of the dirtiest players in the NFL. Vicious, mean . . . I mean, he wasn't called Mean Joe Greene because his college team was called the Mean Greenes. He was a mean sucker! After the commercial Joe Greene became this curmudgeonly, accepted character—which shows you the power of the Coca-Cola brand.

Or rather, it shows the power of archetypes in popular culture, skillfully manipulated by advertising professionals and massively propagated with the resources of a major multinational marketer. Association with the Coke brand made Greene into a new kind of all-American icon, but only through the exploitation of his images—of the man himself and of his racial persona. Greene, now a coach with the NFL's Arizona Cardinals, says the net effect of the exchange was "liberating." Where once he was seen as unapproachable and depicted in posters in opposing-team cities as "grotesque," the commercial "softened the image and made me more approachable, not just to people who might like football but to young kids, grandmothers, grandfathers, and mothers. To talk not about football but about the commercial, or just to say hello—I enjoyed that very much."

The dynamic elements of "Hey, Kid" the commercial set a pattern that, with ever-evolving variations, could also describe the later mainstreaming of athletes and entertainers of color into commercial pop culture. But at the time, the team at McCann Erickson Worldwide that created the ad were thinking only about selling soda. At first, when interviewed, the commercial's writer, Penny Hawkey, told me the role of race in marketing was the furthest thing from their minds as they set about casting the spot. All they wanted in the athlete was a contrast with "the Kid," and in theory any large, tough, star football player would have done. White quarterbacks naturally headed the list of candidates at the time. The only rules they sought to break were those of then-current soda-jingle conventions; their ambition was to create a one-minute drama. But after thinking it through in hindsight, Hawkey said she realized they ended up casting Greene because they needed the power of race to boost a creative leap.

> The rules we were breaking weren't race but the dull wallpaper jingles. It wasn't that he was black, it was that it was a Coke commercial that had never been done before with dialogue. We said, "Hey, what about dialogue, people's real relationship with this drink," recapturing the moment when a Coke is a normal part of the day.

> Race wasn't a factor . . . it was juxtaposition. The first candidate [we] had in mind was Terry Bradshaw. But he wasn't big enough. . . . I guess, well now that I think about it—*he wasn't black enough.*

Greene, inducted into the NFL Hall of Fame in 1987 for his on-field prowess, has enjoyed his "liberation" from the pre commercial "Mean Joe" image for twenty years. But he told me he never thought much about exactly what prison he was liberated from, or the mechanism by which his freedom was wrought.

> I always said "a large black man and the small white kid—it was the contrast." But I didn't delve into the social ramifications. If you start to dissect them, there's probably some truth [to the notion of racial alchemy in the power of the ad], in that this imposing black man, with a reputation to go along with the size, look, and color, became a person. That's how it affected me personally.

Hawkey, who is now executive creative director with Medicus Communications in New York, said, "We didn't realize we were breaking into new racial territory or opening doors. We didn't realize it would have the impact it did." But the conscious, semiconscious, and unconscious use of racial and ethnic notes to achieve creative and commercial breakthroughs would become a repeated theme as marketers navigated the American dreamscape of color in the 1980s.

Coca-Cola did not create Joe Greene's Hall of Fame success or his style on the football field. And Coke had nothing to do with the racial archetypes that fueled the drama; indeed, its creators were barely conscious of the chemicals they were mixing. But what Coke did do, with its investment of marketing resources, was validate a deeper social trend by giving it expression in commercial popular culture. Baby boomers who came of age during the civil rights movement had been cheering black athletes like Joe Greene on the plantations of our national pastimes for over a decade, without being given permission to idolize them in that most American way: to buy products associated with their names. Coke, however unintentionally, successfully exploited that unvalidated desire to embrace nonwhite hero athletes *in all their nonwhiteness* to sell soda. Four years later, as the NBA was figuring out how to position its product to satisfy and stoke a similar unmet, ineffable desire for something new and exciting, the same unvalidated potential brimmed in popular culture at large.

Maybe it was coincidence, but 1984 just *happened* to be the year that Vanessa Williams broke the color line at the Miss America pageant; that Eddie Murphy starring in *Beverly Hills Cop* virtually tied *Ghostbusters* for the number-one grossing movie ($234 million worldwide, back when a million dollars was a million dollars); and Bill Cosby's *The Cosby Show* debuted as the number-one-rated show on television. And maybe it was a fluke that the artist who was known in 1984 as Prince grossed $58 million that summer playing a black rock star in an interracial romance in *Purple Rain*, while selling out dozens of big-city arena concert dates within hours after the tickets went on sale.

Roger Enrico and Pepsi didn't create Michael Jackson's talent or music, and they certainly didn't create the central place that African-Americans occupy in American pop culture. All Pepsi did, by leading the procession to crown the first black "King of Pop," was to validate what the mass market had already decided. It simply associated brand Pepsi with a fact on the ground that even the music industry hadn't yet recognized, to sell soda. Enrico's moves were all the more radical because, by all accounts, they were unhesitating and virtually unimpeded by deliberation over Michael Jackson's color, which at the time was still unambiguously brown. One result: Pepsi was one of the first major marketers to catch the pop wave beneath a black artist well before it crested, maximizing the return on its investment. It would not be the last.

Enrico acted on his intuition about where the culture was going without regard to race. It hardly seems revolutionary, in retrospect, but it was way-out-of-the-box thinking at the time.

Coke, the Joe Greene commercial notwithstanding, certainly didn't see it. The preeminent soda marketer had three opportunities to get in on the Michael Jackson *Thriller* phenomenon, and it passed each time. The first chance came in the studio in December 1982, right before the album was shipped. Chuck Morrison, then head of Coke's "ethnic" marketing, met with Michael Jackson, Jackson's father and then manager Joe Jackson, and album producer Quincy Jones. Michael really wanted to represent Coke, Morrison told me, and assumed that a preview of the *Thriller* album would seal the deal.

I'll never forget, Michael looked at me and said, "What can I do for you?". . . And I said, "Nothing: The question is what can I do for you? Because I'm gonna sell Coke whether you do it or not." Joe [Jackson] asked for a million dollars, which was unprecedented at the time. I took it back to management at Coke, and they flat said no. They weren't interested in being tied into a personality like Michael. It wasn't that he was black; he just wasn't Cosby to them.

Six months later Jackson electrified a worldwide audience with a now-legendary performance of "Billie Jean" during the television special saluting Motown Records' twenty-fifth anniversary. "Michael gives that performance of a lifetime . . . but they still say no," Morrison recalled. Coke's last chance was the day before Jackson signed with Pepsi. Don King called Morrison "and says, 'Chuck, Michael has said to us take another run at Coke'—but now the price is five million. I go back up, and Coke says no again. The next day he signs the deal with Pepsi."

Coke bottlers "went nuts" the day after it was announced. Marketing chief Sergio Zyman tracked Morrison down in a Los Angeles restaurant, ordered him back to Atlanta, and authorized a $7 million counteroffer, Morrison said, "but the deal was done."

And the rest was history. That summer of 1984 Michael Jackson takes $2.4 billion to the bottom line of Pepsi-Cola. Six share points, just like that, gone. He was absolutely that hot. It was a whole phenomenon; I'd never seen anything like it. It was absolutely brilliant, because it killed two or three birds with one stone. Obviously it was a boon for them with African-Americans, but Michael Jackson was *everybody*. White teenagers loved this boy. Latinos. It was a brilliant stroke, as brilliant as Joe Greene had been for Coke five years before.

Pepsi's success with Jackson opened Coke's eyes to the idea of the browning mainstream. Indeed, in the spring of 1984, singer-songwriter Lionel Richie's single "Hello" topped the pop charts. It was no fluke: six other Richie-penned songs, most sung by Richie (he also gave Kenny Rogers and Diana Ross their biggest hits with "Lady" and "Endless Love," respectively) had reached number one in the previous three years. Suddenly, after Pepsi signed the Jackson deal, Coke could see Lionel Richie as a pop star. It pursued the former Commodores lead singer and was about to sign a deal with Richie's manager, Ken Kragen, Morrison recalled. Then Pepsi found out.

We were supposed to fly to Las Vegas on a Friday to sign the deal. Kragen says Roger Enrico found out, flew to Las Vegas, and put a contract on the table for $8.3 million. But the deal was he had to sign it now, or it's off the table. What do you think Kragen did? Called us and said, "Love you guys—'bye."

The bidding war coincided with *Washington Post* critic Richard Harrington's insightful observation that Richie's success, like Jackson's, represented a quality of cross over for black performers that hadn't been seen before.

In any other year but this one belonging to Michael Jackson, Richie would be the biggest story in the business. At 10 million copies and counting, his *Can't Slow Down* album is living up to its name. He's just begun a forty-city tour expected to gross $12 million. . . . He was the first black entertainer to host a major awards show alone—the recent American Music Awards. Richie's concerts now attract predominantly white audiences, reflecting the appeal he developed in his last few years with the Commodores. . . . Richie is also more popular with white record buyers than black.

Again, it's not that black acts hadn't overcome the record industry barriers to the top of the pop charts before. In fact, as Harrington went on to point out, where some thirty-five songs performed by black acts crossed over to reach number one in the early 1970s, only thirteen had done so in a similar period in the early 1980s. But the categorical difference with Richie, as it would continue to be with Jackson, was that no major marketers competed hammer and tongs to project those black 1970s acts, performers like Stevie Wonder and Barry White, as genuine pop stars. After Richie, Coke went after Tina Turner the same way, for Diet Coke, but lost her to Diet Pepsi. "Pepsi took Lionel *and* Tina; Enrico wanted to keep his foot on Coke's neck," Morrison told me. "That's how we ended up with Whitney Houston."

Houston, in Morrison's recollection, was a "dowdy looking" newcomer with a "mediocre hit" in "Saving All My Love for You" and considerable record industry hype about her musical family pedigree.

We signed her for Diet Coke, and Lintas Advertising glamorized her, put her in this black dress, bought her some hair, and put $22 million worth of general market media behind her. Two months later Whitney Houston was the darling of this country.

Morrison may be overstating the power of Coke's sponsorship at the expense of Houston's considerable talent. Dowdy or not, she had already been featured as a fashion model in the mainstream magazines *Glamour, Seventeen,* and French *Vogue.* But Morrison's larger point rings true. In the age or rather the moment of *Thriller,* major corporate marketers were now willing to do for Whitney Houston what they would not have considered doing for her cousin, the once-incomparable Dionne Warwick, in the 1960s. Early in her run as "Queen of Pop," Whitney Houston was actually packaged as America's sweetheart. She played the role well enough to carry a major movie with it. In *The Bodyguard,* opposite no less a white romantic leading man than the then-red-hot Kevin Costner, Houston played an international pop diva whose appeal far transcends race. It's hard to say whether it was art finally imitating a life like that of Diana Ross or Donna Summer or Tina Turner in the 1970s or merely an extension of the new Houston icon from music videos to feature film. Audiences apparently had little trouble suspending disbelief. Powered in part by her top-selling sound track, the 1992 film took in $411 million worldwide.

* * *

According to [Bill] Katz [president of BBDO New York, the powerful advertising agency], the flow of color into the 1980s cultural mix was so natural, so obviously right and normal that it penetrated beneath the public consciousness of the politics of race. Consciousness is focused on the entertainment experience and then, hopefully, on the product, not on race, which is exactly where marketers want it.

Take when Michael Jackson had his hair burned up. People will say, "I remember this moment in life when the Jackson brothers were dancing for Pepsi-Cola—and Pepsi burned his hair up by mistake." They won't say, "I remember when for the first time ever a black group was in the most popular commercials in America, front-lining for one of the most popular soft drinks." It was secondary that there were five black entertainers. People don't say, "Did you see that commercial with five black people?" What they remember is the commercial, not the phenomenon of a black person in the commercial. That's the beauty of advertising. Because it only works if it entertains you. You remember the "Mean Joe Greene" commercial because it entertained. It had a compelling emotion attached to it.

The peculiar dynamic by which racial identification is almost magically stripped from nonwhite performers and cultural forms as they pass into the mainstream presents an obstacle to finding the larger meaning of all these developments for race and commercial culture. The measure of that obstacle will be taken at length in the conclusion of this book. But there is another nagging question to be raised here and, I hope, to be put to rest. If Ray Charles had already been a living legend for forty years, why did it take so long for marketers and their ad agencies to recognize and exploit it? Why didn't Ray Charles have a national commercial like that in the 1970s? When I asked Katz, he recalled my hypothetical anecdote about what would have happened to the ambitious record executive who, in 1954, set out to put a Little Richard poster on the bedroom wall of every teenage girl in America.

Why no "Uh-huh" in the 1970s?

Because that guy who was gonna haul the record executive of the 1950s in front of Joe McCarthy still influenced society more than he does today. Because society was not prepared to embrace that. It wasn't until society at large was prepared . . . that advertising could take its cue from that [readiness] and portray it.

The first part of Katz's answer is straightforward enough. Corporate American mass media and marketing had been gaining the power and autonomy to ignore the values and biases of the American social and political establishment since the day the first radio station went on the air. If that power and autonomy could be plotted on a graph, said Katz, it would be an upward curve that finally crossed the social and political color line in the 1980s, not the 1970s. If Katz's argument is consistent, the triumph of Madison Avenue over Capitol Hill was primarily enabled by what was real in the culture, not by the size of Pepsi's checkbook or the power of the new technologies it employed. But Katz, and most other observers I interviewed, was utterly at a loss to explain how we as a culture suddenly became ready to accept what we did, when we did. The difference between advertising and the cultural environment in which it operates, said Katz, is that the culture "just happens"—you can't pick out a moment in life where you say, "I remember when I decided it was okay to be multicultural or multiracial." In the end the *how* and *when* is for the sociologists and historians to ponder. All marketers focus on is the fact that 'it' happened, and that 'it' superseded or obliterated any issue of race."

Pepsi said, "I want an entertainer to represent my product. I want to be part of the biggest thing in entertainment since the Beatles. I want . . . the imagery Michael Jackson represents to a new generation of constituents out there. I want the fashion associated with Michael Jackson and his brothers. I want *THAT*. I don't want black; I want that." *At some point, it was no longer that cool was represented by black. It was that cool was cool. And I want cool.*

Source: From American Skin: Pop Culture, Big Business, and the End of White America by *Leon E. Wynter, copyright © 2002 by Leon E. Wynter. Used by permission of Crown Publishers, a division of Random House, Inc. Any third party use of this material, outside of this publication, is prohibited. Interested parties must apply directly to Random House, Inc. for permission.*

DECODING THE TEXT

1. Which celebrities does the author name as groundbreakers in black advertising?

2. What does the author mean when he says Michael Jackson became "pop," and what did it matter that he moved into that particular field?

3. Do you remember any of the commercials or ads mentioned in this essay? If you do, what do you remember most about them?

CONNECTING TO YOUR CULTURE

1. What black celebrities make commercials and pose in ads today?

2. Are these ads part of mainstream advertisements or are they aimed at niche audiences?

3. The author claims that racial identification was stripped from ads in the 1980s. Do you agree with him? Why or why not?

4. The 1979 Mean Joe Green ad mentioned in this essay was recreated in 2012 by Green and comedian Amy Sedaris in order to sell Downy Unstopables fabric freshener. What is the significance of this remake? Does it add to or subtract from the groundbreaking role of the original ad?

CONSIDERING IDEAS

1. How do you define censorship?

2. If authors are pressured to write in certain ways or about particular topics, do you see this as censorship? Why or why not?

3. What role does advertising play in censoring the media?

AUTHOR BIO

Murray L. Bob, *now deceased, was a librarian and author as well as a guest lecturer at the University of Illinois at Urbana-Champaign. He contributed articles to professional journals, national magazines, and newspapers. He also wrote* A Contrarian's Dictionary: 2,000 Damnable Definitions for the Year 2000. *This editorial, "Keep Ads Out of Books," appeared in a 1989 issue of* Library Journal.

KEEP ADS OUT OF BOOKS

Paid Advertisements in Books Will Undermine Our Freest Vehicle of Expression

Murray L. Bob

Whittle Communications recently caused a stir with its proposal to bring commercial television into the classroom—as if kids don't watch enough TV at home! Now Whittle has a new target for exploitation. Its latest venture is books that include advertising.

The company intends to pay several big-name authors $60,000 each to write 100-page hardcover books on timely topics. The books will contain ads throughout and be distributed free to 150,000 "opinion leaders"— just the sort of folks who can't afford to buy books. The company expects eventually to sell the books in stores.

Those of us who grew up thinking of the book as somehow sacred are appalled. Now that books have been used for discreet payoffs by the Speaker of the House and the House Minority Whip, one can't help wondering if bookmaking hasn't suddenly become the exclusive province of bookies.

It may just be a question of what one considers a book. The exudations of Messrs. Wright and Gingrich barely qualify on several scores. And given their 100-page limit, it is hard to resist referring to Whittle's proposed tomes as "half-whits." Unfortunately, not everyone will make such fine distinctions.

PRESSURE ON WRITERS

Whittle's idea raises a number of questions that should be of concern to all book lovers: Will the advertisers try to influence content and style? Will advertising become the chief source of revenue—unlike the present arrangement whereby the reader is king—and affect what is written and how it is written? Self-censorship and pre censorship on the grounds of possible advertisers' reactions are hardly unknown in the mass media.

Video and audio media are notoriously subject to, indeed shaped and reshaped by, advertising pressure. Pressure groups influence advertisers, who influence agencies, who influence networks and/or stations, who influence producers, who influence writers.

Most general magazines carry advertising and seem relatively unpressured. But periodicals, containing a large number of essays on a wide variety of topics, may be better able to defuse, deflect, and resist interference than single-author, single-subject books, subsidized by advertisers. Moreover, the ominous spread in magazines of deceptive "advertorials"—matter in which text and ad are virtually indistinguishable—makes one less sanguine about the prospect of letting advertising jam a foothold in book publishing.

TAMPERING WITH IDEALS

Authors, perhaps romantically, have hitherto been regarded as "free lances." Will they become "hired guns" instead, working for sponsors? Won't their reputation for independence and thus their credibility suffer as a result? One may say that's their problem. But it isn't only their problem. The book, where it is still honorably and independently written, published, and distributed, is the freest vehicle of expression we have—which is why we abhor attempts to bowdlerize it.

Most books are, fortunately, not like the mass media—yet. This is partly a matter of tradition. The history of Western culture is replete with glorious examples of men and women who resisted censorship and suffered imprisonment and other egregious penalties for expressing their ideas in books. Precisely because of their independence from commercial pressures, books make their unique contribution to our civilization: comprehensive, thoughtful, careful, balanced, and unhurried weighing of ideas, free of astriction.

It seems a shame to take a chance on compromising a book in order to make a buck. Ideas are not like other commodities. They are vital to the functioning of a democracy in a way shaving cream is not. And the recipe for keeping ideas vital, yeasty, controversial, and independent shouldn't be as lightly tampered with as shaving cream formulas.

YOU CALL THIS PROGRESS?

It is difficult to see anything progressive about Whittle's gimmick, unless any additional way to make money represents progress. Some contend that ads may reduce the cost of the books. A laudable aim, but surely of less consequence than maintaining their integrity. It remains to be seen whether half-whits will be all that cheap. Since it will cost something to advertise in a little Whittle, companies will certainly pass that cost on to consumers.

There are other ways to restrain book prices. Whatever the publishing industry and regular retailers may say about remaindering, it represents an important way for the public to buy books for less. Whatever publishers say, they do work ever more closely with remainder houses. As for regular retailers, discounting is not exactly unknown, even to them. Paperback originals, such as Saul Bellow's latest book, constitute yet another check on book prices. And if the idea is to get books to people, how about more money for library book budgets?

Ads in books are not a new idea. They have been tried several times before—and have failed. In this case, at least, there are some of us who hope that history will repeat itself.

Source: *"Keep Ads Out of Books" by Murray L. Bob from American Libraries; Jul/Aug 89, Vol. 20, Issue 7, Reprinted by permission.*

DECODING THE TEXT

1. The author mentions the romantic notion of the author as well as the great Western tradition of authorship; he also labels books as sacred. What is he talking about? Does he support this idea in his text?

2. Can you find examples of weasel words in this essay?

CONNECTING TO YOUR CULTURE

1. Bob claims that magazines do not seem to be pressured by their advertisers, whereas video and audio outlets are often controlled by their advertisers. Can you find examples to either support or disprove his two arguments?

2. Do you ever feel pressured to write about certain topics or to avoid topics you would really like to explore? If so, how do you address this pressure?

READING SELECTIONS:
THE 1990s AND 2000s

CONSIDERING IDEAS

Flip through some magazines or some ads online.

1. How are the women portrayed? The men? Is there any difference between the two?

2. What are they wearing? How are they posing? What is in the background?

3. What are they selling? Do the product and the image match in your opinion?

4. How do these ads make you feel about your own appearance or possessions?

AUTHOR BIO

Ted Sherman is a Navy veteran who served in the Philippines and in the Pacific during World War II as well as in Korea. He is a travel writer for travel4seniors.com, travel4people.com, and yahoo.com. He has also worked in advertising, sales promotion, PR, graphic art, photography, travel and humor writing, and speechwriting. Sherman can be reached through Twitter at travel4seniors. The following article was published in the Business and Finance Section of yahoo.com on March 8, 2010.

GENDER STEREOTYPES IN ADVERTISING

Ted Sherman

The slim, sexy young female model, the macho male sports star, the housewife in the kitchen, the mature fatherly authority figure, the cute little girl, the stalwart GI, the dirt-encrusted little boy, the clueless, middle-aged woman driver. Wait just a dang minute! What about that last stereotype? You know, the blue-haired matron whose world consists of hairdressers, lunches with the "girls", dangling jewelry and expensive clothing.

Several years ago, when I was regional ad manager of one of the largest insurance companies, we were all called together to corporate HQ to discuss the company's schedule of upcoming TV ads. Our company had just added auto insurance to its product list, and we were asked to critique its first TV ad touting the new product before the commercial went out to the media.

The ad showed two middle-aged women in a car, gabbing happily together as the one who was driving backed out of her driveway. Suddenly, she knocked over her mailbox, almost hit a kid on a bike and banged into a tree. As the distressed women climbed out of the car, the soothing male voice-over announcer assured them not to worry, because our company's new auto insurance covered the cost of repairs.

When the vice president asked for our opinions about the ad, most of my colleagues nodded the usual approval of blind loyalty, but I piped up to say I objected to the negative stereotype images. I added that I thought it was not ethically right nor good for business to portray middle-aged women as silly caricatures who'd be forgiven for what could have caused a serious accident. Drawing on my experience with insurance ratings and coverages, I said the cost of the repairs for such a stupid accident would probably not be reimbursed.

Needless to say, my uncalled-for opinion didn't earn me any points with our corporate bigwigs, and the ad appeared on TV screens within weeks. Oh, did I mention that our advertising department VP presiding over the meeting was a young woman, a 28-year-old protégé of our company chairman? Talk about gender stereotypes!

Admittedly, there has been much progress in erasing the most blatant gender stereotyping in TV and print ads that prevailed in the early days of advertising. We're seeing less of the stay-at-home, domestic "little wife" character, and more women portrayed in ads as successful in business, law, medicine, real estate, the military, police and other government careers.

With the advent of the home computer and ever-evolving sophisticated computer games, character gender differences are becoming even less pronounced. Today there are just as many super-heroines as there are super-heroes in the ads and in the content of their games. Even the once dominant male voice-overs now share the mike with strong, in-your-face female voices. Move over, Batman, and make room for Robotrixie.

The use of gender stereotypes in advertising has always been an effective marketing device, and there's no indication it will ever change. A company that sells women's clothing, hair dye, or cosmetics isn't likely to use male models, except as moon-eyed background images to the stunning female model closest to the camera.

Portrayal of the stereotypical near-nude female model as a sex image will continue to be featured where they've always been the most effective, in ads for men's products and services. This includes sports, cruise lines, men's hair and sexual prowess restoration medications, casinos, entertainment, and many other areas.

As they say in the TV ad business about stereotyping by gender, age, brains or body weight: "if it ain't broke, it don't need no fixin'."

Source: *http://www.associatedcontent.com/article/2770812/gender_stereotypes_in_advertising_pg2.html?cat=3*

DECODING THE TEXT

1. The author ends with the idea that if it isn't broken, it shouldn't be fixed. Do you think he agrees that advertising patterns should not be changed? What support do you see for your reading of the text?

2. The author begins with a surprising list of images. Does this work to grab your attention? Why or why not? How would you begin this essay?

CONNECTING TO YOUR CULTURE

1. Sherman claims there has been progress in the portrayal of gender stereotypes in advertising, especially since the 1960s and 1970s. Do you agree with him? Why or why not?

2. Could you point to any present-day ads that are built around gender stereotypes? If so, is the ad effective? Why or why not?

3. What other stereotypes are used in advertising? Why?

4. How do ads and images that rely on stereotypes affect you? The general public? How do you know?

CONSIDERING IDEAS

1. Would you feel uncomfortable if most of the ads you saw had images of people with disabilities in them? Why or why not?

2. What if ads only featured minority models or images?

3. What do you know about disability rights and legislation? How does this affect advertising?

AUTHOR BIO

Beth A. Haller is a professor in the Mass Communication Department at Towson University. She has written numerous articles for professional journals as well as coauthored An Introduction to News Reporting: A Beginning Journalist's Guide. Haller has received several writing and reporting awards, including the 2003 National Rehabilitation Association Excellence in Media Award.

Sue Ralph was the program director for the Master of Education in Communications, Education and Technology at the University of Manchester as well as a senior lecturer, from which she is retired. She is currently a visiting professor at the University of Northampton. Her primary areas of research include media and disability, disability and humor, and ethical issues in image-based research. She has contributed many articles to academic journals and edited three books, including Diversity or Anarchy? She also currently serves as the editor for the Journal of Research in Special Educational Needs (JORSEN) and as a consulting editor for the Journal of the International Association in Special Education (JIASE). This article first appeared in Disability Studies Quarterly in 2001.

PROFITABILITY, DIVERSITY, AND DISABILITY IMAGES IN ADVERTISING

Beth A. Haller and Sue Ralph

The disabled consumer is coming of age. Companies in the United States and Great Britain are seeing the profitability of including disabled people in their advertising. But what are the implications of the images produced in these advertisements? Are they moving away from the pity narratives of charity? Are they creating acceptance and integration of disabled people?

* * *

Advocates for disabled people in the US have long known the importance of the "disabled consumer market." Carmen Jones of EKA Marketing (1997) says: "Few companies have enjoyed the profitability that results in targeting the consumer who happens to have a disability. . . . I believe if the business community were educated about the size and potential of the market, then advertising programs with the disabled consumer in mind" would be created (p. 4). In the new millennium, advertisers are realizing that disabled people buy soap, milk, socks, jewelry, makeup, home improvement goods, use travel services, live in houses, and enjoy nice home furnishings. There is some evidence that the disabled consumer is very much more brand loyal than other consumers (Quinn, 1995). For example, the hotel chain Embassy Suites found out that becoming sensitive to the needs of disabled people led to more business. And a study by the National Captioning Institute found that 73 percent of deaf people switched to a brand that had TV ad captioning (Quinn, 1995).

British companies are still more hesitant in including disabled people in their advertisements due to both different advertising methods and societal attitudes. Although print ads are just as frequent in British publications, ads on British television are much less prevalent and more restricted than in the US where about 12 minutes of each half hour of commercial TV are advertisements. In the UK "the total amount of spot advertising in any one day must not exceed an average of nine minutes per hour of broadcasting" (ITC, 1998, p. 1).

However, some companies in both countries were slow to learn what accurate and non stigmatizing advertising images were. For example, in 1990 a Fuji TV ad for film on British television that featured a man with learning disabilities being "improved" by a photograph of him smiling at the end was criticized by disabilities scholar Michael Oliver for its "medical model" approach (Deakin, 1996, Sept. 20, p. 37). The TV ad was interpreted as the Fuji film offering a type of "cosmetic surgery" on the disabled man through the advertisement. Ironically, the ad agency that created the Fuji ad consulted the British charity Mencap, but as Scott-Parker pointed out, "the perceptions and interests of a disability charity are not always synonymous with those of the disabled consumer" (Dourado, 1990, p. 27). Because of early faux pas like this, "disability is still an area in which few advertisers dare to deal" in Great Britain (Deakin, 1996, p. 37).

In both countries, new disability rights legislation—the US Americans with Disabilities Act (ADA) and Work Incentives Improvement Act (WIIA) and the UK Disability Discrimination Act (DDA)—made the business community more aware of disabled consumers and that there are large numbers of them. These legislative acts have also given businesses an understanding that disabled people want to find more and better employment and in turn purchase more consumer goods. Some policy analysts actually called the ADA a mandate for marketers to begin to recognize the formerly invisible disabled market (Stephens and Bergman, 1995). In addition, the WIIA would provide a $1,000 tax credit to help people with severe disabilities cover work-related expenses. President Clinton pushed for the Act with an inclusive society perspective: "As anyone with a disability can tell you, it takes more than a job to enter the work force. Often, it takes successful transportation, specialized technology or personal assistance" (Clinton, 1999).

These types of legislative acts have made the US and the UK more receptive to accommodating disabled people in terms of architecture and communication so more will have the ability to make purchases and become part of each society's "consumer culture." For example, in the US, 48.5 million disabled people who are age 15 and over had an estimated total discretionary income of $175 billion (Prager, 1999, Dec. 15). In the UK, there are 6.5 million disabled people who represent a 33 billion pound market, which will increase (Deakin, 1996).

* * *

CULTURAL MEANING OF DISABILITY IMAGES IN ADVERTISING

Disability studies scholar Harlan Hahn (1987) wrote a seminal article about the role of advertising in culturally defining, or not defining, disabled people. His work creates the framework we will use for analyzing subsequent ads that include disabled people. There is much literature about other societal groups' representation in advertising (Hall, 1997), but we will be focusing specifically on the unique case of advertising's disability images.

Hahn argues generally that advertising's emphasis on beauty and bodily perfection has led to exclusion of disabled people in the images. In addition, the nondisabled audience members' fears of becoming disabled and viewing images of disability meant businesses were hesitant to use disabled people as models.

Apparently the common difficulty of disabled people in gaining acceptance as human beings even permitted the belief that a male seated in a wheelchair was not really a man. Advertising and other forms of mass imagery were not merely designed to the increase sale of commodities; they also comprised a cultural force with an influence that has permeated all aspects of American life. From this perspective, issues of causation, such as whether advertising simply reflected widespread sentiments about disability or whether it contributed to implanting such feelings, become less critical than the assessment of contexts and effects (Hahn, 1987, p. 562).

The context Hahn discusses is disabled people's "inability" to ever fit within a context of beautiful bodies and they are therefore rendered invisible. He points out that advertising promotes a specific "acceptable physical appearance" that then reinforces itself. These advertising images tell society who is acceptable in terms of appearance and that transfers to who is acceptable to employ, associate with, communicate with, and value.

However, Hahn did see signs of hope in changing societal perceptions of disabled people through advertising and other forms of mass communication. He cites many historical examples in which physical appearances/attributes that were once prized were later seen as deviant or unattractive. Bogdan (1988) explained this phenomenon in his study of American freak shows, in which many disabled people were honored as celebrities; however, later people with the same disabilities were institutionalized.

In the modern understanding of diversity as a profitable undertaking for businesses, we argue that the cultural meaning of disability imagery in advertising is changing for the better. As Hahn predicted, some social attitudes are changing and advertising that features disabled people is being associated with profitability, both because of the newfound power of the disabled consumer and general audiences' desire to see "real life" in images. As discussed in the example of the Target advertising campaign, they received several thousand letters of positive feedback and sold products modeled by disabled people at a much higher rate.

Another study done in preparation for the 1996 Atlanta Paralympics illustrated that both households with (49 percent) and without a disabled person (35 percent) valued accurate advertising images of disabled people and were likely to buy products and services that showed sensitivity to disabled people's needs (Dickinson, 1996).

In terms of demographics, disabled people in the US and the UK are now seen as "consumers able to buy." With 6.4 million disabled people in the UK and about 50 million disabled people in the US, businesses are recognizing the vast consumer potential (Precision Marketing, 1997, p. 15). Therefore, the cultural meanings of disability advertising imagery in the UK and the US are capitalistic profitability from a huge consumer base and a thrust to better represent the general diversity of society, which general audiences want. Although there is still discomfort among some nondisabled people in seeing disability imagery, it seems to have much diminished in the US. With equalizing legislation such as the ADA, . . . companies and their advertising agencies are realizing what disability activist and former *Mainstream* magazine publisher Cyndi Jones said in 1992: "Portraying disabled consumers in ads 'is just good business'. . . because most places people go to work or to play have 'one if not a multitude of people who are disabled'" (Goerne, 1992, Sept. 14, p. 33).

However, the UK has only begun to try to convince British businesses with a campaign about the profitability of the disabled consumer in 2000 with the Cheshire Foundation's VisABLE campaign established in May 1999. UK Secretary of State for Education and Employment, David Blunkett, said that VisABLE was "a lead we should all follow" and said government departments would be encouraged to use more disabled people in their advertising (Connect, 1999, p. 5). The campaign was launched to encourage mainstream advertising companies to include more disabled people in their advertising material. The campaign, which coincides with the government initiatives to raise awareness about disability issues and the implementation of the Disability Discrimination Act, was created in conjunction with the National Disability Council (Stirling, 2000).

After an analysis of U.S. advertising practices using disabled people and a National Opinion Poll in the UK, Britain found its citizens open to inclusion of disabled people in advertising. One article in *The Guardian* explained how the VisABLE campaign followed some US companies' lead: "There's concrete evidence from the US of the commercial effectiveness of the enlightened approach," mentioning Target stores' pioneering approach to including disabled people in their print ads from 1990 on (Hilton, 1999, May 30). The opinion poll especially confirmed this trend toward a desire for enlightened advertising with its findings that "80 percent of the general public would welcome more disabled people in advertising. Seventy percent said they would not assume an advert featuring disabled people was directed specifically at disabled people rather than the general public as a whole" (Stirling, 2000, p. 9).

The VisABLE campaign did not ask advertising firms to spend money, but to plan their campaigns to include disabled models. In order to do this businesses needed access to disabled models. Rosemary Hargreaves, press and public relations officer for the Leonard Cheshire Charity for disabled people, which created VisABLE, said, "ad agencies and businesses claim there are no disabled models available, so we set out to challenge this perception by finding a pool of disabled models" (Stirling, 2000, p. 11). A modeling competition was launched as part of the campaign and attracted 500 disabled entrants. The two winners were a deaf woman and a wheelchair-using man, who subsequently appeared in Marks and Spencer's chain store print ads selling women's tights and men's casual wear (*M&S Magazine*, 2000, p. 32, 45). The winners received a modeling contract with VisABLE models, an agency created by Louise Dyson in cooperation with the campaign. The competition is meant to be an annual event and has attracted support from seven leading corporate partners—B&Q, British Telecom, Co-operative Bank, HSBC Hong Kong and Shanghai Banking Corp., Marks and Spencer, McDonald's, and One2One—all of whom have made a commitment to use disabled models in the future.

One company specifically took its own initiative to use the disabled people already in its employ. B&Q, which is a do-it-yourself home improvement chain store, already used its own employees in adverts and for the VisABLE campaign asked its disabled employees to volunteer to be in its ads. The B&Q diversity coordinator explained the policy of using disabled people in this way "is not only good for promoting B&Q as a diverse employer, but is good for raising the profile of all disabled people" (B&Q Talking Shop, 2000, p. 8).

Similar to the US, the VisABLE campaign is helping businesses recognize the power of the disabled consumer market. With 8 million disabled people with an estimated annual spending power of 40 billion pounds, "yet they are an untapped customer source," according to the VisABLE campaign (Stirling, 2000, p. 9). B&Q Diversity Manager Kay Allen points out that in addition to profit reasons and legal reasons such as the Disability Discrimination Act, businesses have "obvious moral reasons. It's absolutely right that companies should cover disability as a diversity issue" (Stirling, 2000, p. 10).

However, not all businesses or advertising agencies have come on board for the VisABLE campaign. Some still associate images of disabled people with charity concerns and inspiration (Ralph and Lees, 2000). Other business people admit that disabled people in advertising is an "alien concept" and that advertisers are not used to taking those kinds of risks ("Tonight," 2000). One advertising firm surveyed said including disabled people in advertising smacks of "tokenism" (Ralph and Lees, 2000).

As mentioned, the positive cultural meanings of profitability and diversity in advertising images do not solve all potential problems with disability imagery. As with all advertising images, the beautiful and least disfigured disabled people are depicted. As mentioned, many early TV ads in the US used primarily deaf people. Good-looking and sports-minded wheelchair users are another important visual category. But this does not truly represent the diversity within the disability community. As a disability publication editor said: "Not every person with a disability is young and beautiful and athletic, just like all women aren't size 10, and all African-Americans don't have degrees from Harvard. . . . I know people with disabilities who aren't pretty. They drool. They scare the average person. So do we do more harm than good showing this cute little girl with CP?" (McLaughlin, 1993, Aug. 22, p. 31).

SOME CURRENT DISABILITY IMAGERY IN ADVERTISING

As mentioned, Target chain stores began a trend by including disabled children and teens in their print ad circulars in 1990. Though hesitant at first, the advertising was a rousing success and the corporate office received 2,000 letters of support early in the campaign.

First, the images are well used because of the way they naturalize disability rather than stigmatize it. In fact, many times it takes several looks at the circulars to actually find the disabled children, whose disabilities are visible, because they are part of scenes of groups of children or a number of images on one page. The way Target uses disabled people in their ads fits squarely within the cultural meaning of diversity in advertising imagery. In fact, in 1994 a circular ad depicted a Latina disabled girl in a wheelchair interacting with a nondisabled Caucasian girls to sell girls pants sets. The ad is even more significant in that it depicts actual interaction between the children, rather than two girls staring at the camera. They are handing something to each other in a kitchen setting. This type of depiction sends several messages: That people of color have disabilities, too, and that interaction between disabled and nondisabled children is quite normal.

In another ad in 1994 for Target, a young blonde woman in a wheelchair is used to advertise women's T-shirts. Although she is alone in the picture and is a typical smiling, blonde model with a peaches and cream complexion, the interesting aspect to this ad is that she is wearing jeans shorts, which show her legs. As a person with a mobility disability her legs are not as muscular as a nondisabled person's might be and this is apparent in the photo. However, the image is not grotesque or disturbing. Once again, it just shows reality and the natural appearance of a wheelchair user's lower body.

In a 1995 Target ad, two teens are featured in an ad for women's cotton T-shirts. They are both smiling, fresh-faced blondes and one is a wheelchair user. The wheelchair is partially obscured by examples of the T-shirt embroidery at the bottom of the photo so only a corner of a wheelchair peeks out. Again, this very subtle approach erases any stigma and makes the wheelchair-using teen the equal of her blonde counterpart in the ad. The nondisabled teen is bent down near to the disabled teen so there is less height difference between the standing and sitting teens.

Finally, Target's ad campaigns realized that wheelchair use is not the only disability or even the most prevalent: In 1995, a circular depicted a boy with a walker in their ad for Power Ranger underwear sets. The walker, however, is placed behind him, possibly so the clothing was not covered in the picture. The boy stands up straight in his walker and is next to a girl modeling Power Ranger underwear for girls. The boy's tanned, smiling appearance is vigorous and healthy and really has little connection to a "medical model" depiction (Clogston, 1990), even with a walker in the scene. Another Target circular in Spanish advertised school uniform wear and featured a young model with a single crutch. She strikes a typical model pose with a sweater slung over her shoulder. She, too, has a healthy appearance and the illustration shows no misshapen extremities. In fact, her only "flaw" is one that normalizes her as a child—she is missing a front tooth. The only possible concern with this image is that it is shot from above her and looks down upon her completely. Finally, a Target promotional flyer on tourist spots in Chicago features a child who appears to be blind interacting with two other children and a large bat at The Field Museum. Again, the interaction among the children and the lack of signification about her blindness normalizes the photo and presents no stigma to the viewer.

* * *

The sporting goods company Nike has used disabled athletes in a number of their advertisements. It should be noted that as media researchers of disability images we are concerned that many ads use disabled athletes which we believe to be an extension of the Supercrip image (Clogston, 1990; Covington, 1989). However, because of Nike's product line, all their advertising images are always of superathletes or athlete "wannabes."

Nike's TV ads have a mixture of the incidental use of disabled models and one featured disabled athlete, Craig Blanchette, who held two world records in wheelchair racing in 1989. The Blanchette spot is called "Cross training with Craig Blanchette" and no scene or mention of his disability is made in the first 27 seconds of the 30-second commercial. He is referred to as a 1988 Olympic bronze medalist. The ad seethes with macho images, first of Blanchette lifting weights, then aggressively playing basketball and tennis. The scenes are intensely athletic, and Blanchette is seen reaching for and making difficult shots. Although he is the focus of the ad, he is not alone. Other male athletic types, both young and old, black and white, are depicted in the background of the weight room, and Blanchette smilingly tosses a basketball to another young man in one scene. Blanchette appears muscular with his massive arms and rugged with his scruffy beard. Only in the last few seconds is it revealed that Blanchette is a wheelchair athlete when the camera pans down and he says: "So I never quit" and turns his back to the camera and races down the track in his sports wheelchair.

Nike officials said it was not relevant to them that Blanchette is a wheelchair-using double amputee. Their VP of marketing explained, "He's a great athlete, which ties to our usual strategy . . . and he's a really motivating guy to be around. The fact that he was handicapped was secondary" (Lipman, 1989, Sept. 7, p. 1). But profitability from disabled athletes or consumers was likely a strong motivation. As a *Wall Street Journal* article says, the Blanchette Nike ad is an example of commercial advertising becoming "increasingly enchanted with the disabled" (Lipman, 1989, Sept. 7, p. 1). Nike also illustrates general inclusiveness in two other TV ads, one of which, "Heritage U.S. Update," has an image of an African American wheelchair racer and concludes with a triumphant white wheelchair user winning a race with "There is no finish line" superimposed in the background. Another Nike ad called "Hope" focuses almost entirely on men and women athletes of color and includes two fast images of wheelchair races and then a concluding image of a wheelchair racer who pulls open his shirt to reveal the "Superman" emblem.

CONCLUSION AND DISCUSSION

This analysis illustrates that companies in the US and the UK are seeing the profitability of including disabled people in their advertising and understanding the benefits of diverse images in advertising. The implication of the images produced in these advertisements is that advertising not only includes disabled people for capitalistic reasons, but realizes these must be accurate images to earn any profit from their use. This means companies have learned, due to their own desire for profits, to move away from the past pity narratives of charity. Our analyses illustrate that corporate America and Britain can create good disability images in advertising that are sensitive and accurate and just represent disability as another slice of life.

However, we recognize that disability images in advertising are not perfect. There is almost total focus on two disabilities: wheelchair use and deafness. For example, McDonald's admitted early in advertising campaigns to taking the path of ease to show disabled people by just including wheelchair users in shots of "hordes of customers" (Dougherty, 1986, p. D26). Ironically, their "easy way out" actually became the best way to depict disability in ads—an incidental use of disability among a variety of people illustrates diversity in a very salient and accurate way. Although the incidence of wheelchair use is actually quite low when compared to other types of disabilities, it is also understood that advertising is a visual medium which needs the equipment cues such as wheelchairs to denote disability as part of the diversity depicted. Disabled screen writer Marc Moss explained that he was initially concerned about how wheelchair users were used in advertising as "proof of corporate soul." However, he does agree "that with varying degrees of finesse, they (advertisers) juggle two points: Their products or services are worthy, and so are people who can't walk" (Moss, 1992, June 19, p. A8).

Of course, as with all advertising, only "pretty people" can become models. This is the area in which many disabled people still have concern about the images of disability in advertising. "It would be nice to have a severely disabled person depicted instead of your superjock 'crip,'" says David Lewis, a quadriplegic who is community relations coordinator for the Center for Independent Living, a non profit support group for the disabled based in Berkeley, California. "Usually disabled people in commercials look like able bodied people in wheelchairs" (Lipman, 1989, Sept. 7, p. 1). However, some disabled people applaud finally being visible in ads or being presented as anything other than a charity case. As one disabled actor said, "the Adonis in a wheelchair is better than the whimpering victim in a corner" (McLaughlin, 1993, Aug. 22, p. 31). Therefore, due to the nature of media effects, we believe that these disability advertising images, even if they tend to focus primarily on beautiful deaf people or wheelchair users, can enhance more acceptance and integration of disabled people into society. Several past studies of the potential for attitude changes toward disabled people through use of media images have confirmed this phenomenon (Farnall & Smith, 1999; Panol & McBride, 1999; Farnall, 1996).

Finally, the better and more prevalent use of disabled people in advertising we believe can be tied to important anti-discrimination legislation in the US and the UK. The ADA kicked off a renewed awareness of disability rights which can be seen in the growing number of disabled people in ads from 1990 on and a better understanding of the disabled consumer market. It can be hoped that the Disability Discrimination Act of 1995 in the UK will lead to the same kind of inclusion of diverse disability in British advertising. The VisABLE campaign is an outgrowth of the consultation around the anti-discrimination legislation.

Historically, this article has documented the changing cultural meanings of disability imagery in advertising. Currently, business concerns see profitability in disability imagery and have found diversity to be good business practice. This is quite a shift from the pre-Rehabilitation Act and pre-ADA days. A National Easter Seals Society executive explained that in the mid-1970s she tried to persuade a Minneapolis company to use a disabled person in a promotional photo: "They were horrified at the idea. . . . They told me they would lose sales, it would scare people—they even used the word disgusting" (Sagon, 1991, Dec. 19, p. B10). By 1992 the same Easter Seals spokesperson praised companies like Kmart when they began a new TV ad campaign using a wheelchair-using actress to portray a customer. "Those of us in the nonprofit world have tried for years to change the way disabled people are perceived," Sandra Gordon of Easter Seals said. "Now it seems the for-profit world is finally lending a hand" (Roberts and Miller, 1992, p. 40).

References

B & Q. (2000, June 8). It all adds up. *B & Q Talking Shop*, p. 116.

Blunkett, D. (1999, Autumn). VisABLE campaign attracts companies and launches modeling competition. *Connect*, 5, p. 5.

Bogdan, R. (1988). *Freak show: Presenting human oddities for amusement and profit.* Chicago: University of Chicago Press.

Clinton, W. J. (1999, January 13). Remarks by the President on disability initiative [White House press release].

Clogston, J. (1990). *Disability coverage in 16 newspapers.* Louisville: The Advocado Press.

Covington. (1989). The stereotypes, the myth, and the media. Washington DC, The news media and disability issues. The news media education national workshop report, pp. 1–2.

Deakin, A. (1996, September 20). Body language. *Marketing Week*, 19(26), p. 37.

Dickinson, R. J. (1996, May 15).The power of the paralympics. *American Demographics*, p. 15.

Dougherty, P. H. (1986, May 14). Advertising: TV spot for deaf viewers. *The New York Times*, p. D26.

Dourado, P. (1990, August 16). Parity not charity. *Marketing*, pp. 26–27.

Farnall, O. (1996). Positive images of the disabled in television advertising: Effects on attitude toward the disabled. Paper presented at the annual meeting of the Association for Education in Journalism and Mass Communication, Anaheim, CA.

Farnall, O., & Smith, K. A. (1999). Reactions to people with disabilities: Personal contact versus viewing of specific media portrayals. *Journalism and Mass Communication Quarterly*, 76(4), pp. 659–672.

Goerne, C. (1992, September 14). Marketing to the disabled: New workplace law stirs interest in largely untapped market. *Marketing News, 26*(19), pp. 1, 32.

Granada Television. (2000). *Tonight* [Television late night news program].

Hahn, H. (1987). Advertising the acceptably employable image: Disability and capitalism. *Policy Studies Journal, 15*(3), pp. 551–570.

Hall, S. (Ed.). (1997). *Representation: Cultural representations and signifying practices.* Milton Keynes: Open University Press.

Hilton, S. (1999, May 30). Snatching defeat from the jaws of a publicity victory. *The Guardian.*

Independent Television Commission. (1998, Autumn). *ITC rules on the amount of scheduling of advertising.* London: ITC.

Jones, C. (1997). Disabled consumers [Letter to the editor]. *American Demographics, 19*(11), p. 4.

Lipman, J. (1989, September 7). Disabled people featured in more ads. *Wall Street Journal,* p. 1.

M&S Magazine. (2000, May/June). Models with a message. p. 115.

McLaughlin, P. (1993, August 22). Roll models. *Philadelphia Inquirer,* p. 31.

Moss, M. J. (1992, June 19). The disabled "discovered." *Wall Street Journal,* p. A8.

Nike. (1989). Craig Blanchette [Television advertisement].

Nike. (1990). Heritage U.S. Update [Television advertisement].

Nike. (1994). Hope [Television advertisement].

Panol, Z., & McBride, M. (1999). Print advertising images of the disabled: Exploring the impact on nondisabled consumer attitudes. Paper presented at the Association for Education in Journalism and Mass Communication annual conference, New Orleans, LA.

Prager, J. H. (1999, December 15). People with disabilities are next Consumer niche—Companies see a market ripe for all-terrain wheelchairs, computers with "sticky keys." *Wall Street Journal,* pp. B1, B2.

Precision Marketing. (1997, May 12). *Life: Disabled people.* pp. 15–16.

Quinn, J. (1995). Able to buy. *Incentive, 169*(9), p. 80.

Ralph, S. M., & Lees, T. (2000). Survey of London advertising agencies. Unpublished.

Roberts, E., & Miller, A. (1992, February 24). This ad's for you. *Newsweek,* p. 40.

Sagon, C. (1991, December 19). Retailers reach to the disabled; Stores see profit in underserved market. *The Washington Post,* p. B10.

Stephens, D. L., & Bergman, K. (1995). The Americans with disabilities act: A man date for marketers. *Journal of Public Policy and Marketing, 14*(1), pp. 164–173.

Stirling, A. (2000). Making disability visible. *Compass, 3,* pp. 8–11.

VisABLE Campaign. (2000). [Video]. Produced by the Co-Operative Bank.

Note: This article from the social sciences uses the APA documentation style.

Source: *Excerpt of article "Profitability, Diversity, and Disability Images in Advertising in the United States and Great Britain," from* Disability Studies Quarterly *by Beth Haller and Sue Ralph, Spring 2001. Reprinted by permission of the Society for Disability Studies.*

DECODING THE TEXT

1. What is the purpose of this essay?

2. According to Haller and Ralph, how has the for-profit advertising industry aided the nonprofit industry in changing the "way disabled people are perceived"?

3. Why do the authors say this image or perception needs to be changed?

4. According to the authors, what businesses have been the most helpful? In what ways?

CONNECTING TO YOUR CULTURE

1. How familiar are you with the advertising campaigns and images mentioned in the text?

2. Can you think of other ads that could now be added to the list?

3. Do you know of disabled groups that are still left out of mainstream advertising? Do you want to see them in ads? Why or why not?

CONSIDERING IDEAS

According to *Advertising Age*, "some of the best-loved ad images of the 20th century have names like Tony, Betty and Ronald. Others, like the Marlboro Man, may not be as beloved, but grew to have tremendous worldwide impact as an instant identifier of Philip Morris Co.'s Marlboro cigarettes." ("Ad Age Advertising Century: Top 10 Icons" *http://adage.com/article/special-report-the-advertising-century/ad-age-advertising-century-top-10-icons/140157/*)

1. How many of these characters can you name?

2. Have you ever bought posters, signs, or clothing with any of these images on them?

AUTHOR BIO

Barbara J. Phillips *is a professor of marketing at the University of Saskatchewan. Her main research interest focuses on the influence of visual images in advertising on consumer response. She has published several journal articles on the topic, and she received the Best Article Award in 2005 from the* Journal of Advertising. *The essay "Defining Trade Characters and Their Role in American Popular Culture" first appeared in* The Journal of Popular Culture *in 1996.*

DEFINING TRADE CHARACTERS AND THEIR ROLE IN AMERICAN POPULAR CULTURE

Barbara J. Phillips

Trade characters have been used as successful advertising tools in the United States for over one hundred years. American popular culture has quietly become inhabited by all sorts of talking animals and dancing products that are used as a communication system by advertisers. In 1982, a research study found that commercials with advertising developed characters who became associated with a brand scored above average in their ability to change brand preference (Stewart and Furse). It appears, then, that society is getting the message. However, although popular with advertisers and consumers, trade characters have been largely ignored in the study of advertising and popular culture. Through a review of the relevant literature, this paper will determine what trade characters are, and how they are employed in modern advertising practice to communicate to consumers in society.

TRADE CHARACTERS: WHAT THEY ARE

Little attention has been given to defining the term "trade character." In a perusal of dozens of advertising textbooks, only a few offer an explicit definition of the term. The rest are silent on the subject, or focus exclusively on what a trade character does as opposed to what a trade character is. Of the authors who define "trade character," several offer vague explanations such as "a character created in association with a product" (Norris). There is little consensus among the remaining definitions; many of the more insightful contradict each other. Therefore, this paper will develop an explicit definition of the term "trade character" that considers four areas of contention: animate versus inanimate characters, non trademarked versus trademarked characters, fictional versus real characters, and trade versus celebrity characters.

ANIMATE VERSUS INANIMATE CHARACTERS

Some of the current definitions of "trade character" are very broad, identifying a trade character as any visual symbol that is associated with a product (Dunn and Barban). By including all visual symbols, these authors classify inanimate objects such as the Prudential rock as trade characters. On the other hand, several definitions specify that a trade character must be an animate being or an animated object (Wright, Warner, and Winter; Mandell) thereby excluding the Prudential rock (unless it is made to sing or dance).

There are two reasons why trade characters should be restricted to animate beings or animated objects. The first is that the word "character," defined by Webster's dictionary to mean "person," implies a living personality. This personality is the focal point of the trade character, whether the character is animate by nature, like Betty Crocker, or animated by design, like Mr. Peanut. The second reason for limiting trade characters to animate beings is to eliminate from the category characterless visual symbols such as corporate logos, and inanimate objects associated with the product through advertising such as oranges for Tropicana orange juice. Neither of these types of visual symbols functions as a trade character. Thus, the first condition used to define a trade character is that it be animate or animated. This includes people, animals, beings (monsters, spacemen, etc.) and animated objects.

NON TRADEMARKED VERSUS TRADEMARKED CHARACTERS

Another contentious issue is the matter of trademarks. Some authors insist that a trade character must necessarily be a legal trademark (Presbrey; Cohen). Other authors disagree (Ulanoff). To resolve this issue, the role of trademarks and trade characters must be briefly addressed.

A trademark is a name, word, or symbol that is protected by law. It is used to identify the source of the product and to guarantee consistency of quality (Morgan). When consumers see the trademark "Coca-Cola" on a bottle, they know who makes it and how it tastes. In comparison, most definitions agree that a trade character is used primarily as a device around which to build promotional programs (Wright, Warner, and Winter; Ulanoff; Mandell; Bohen). Trade characters can appear on product packaging, in advertisements, in sales promotions, or in other related areas.

Although most trade characters are registered trademarks, limiting the definition only to trademarks would eliminate from the category some characters that have been created for promotional use. This is especially true of characters created for advertising campaigns that do not appear on the product package such as the Marlboro cowboy, the Maytag Repairman, and Raid's cartoon bugs. Because these characters are used in the same way as trademarks such as Tony the Tiger or Poppin' Fresh, the Pillsbury Dough Boy, it is difficult to draw a distinction between them. Therefore, another stipulation for the definition of "trade character" is that a trade character does not necessarily have to be a legal trademark. However, it must be used for promotional purposes.

FICTIONAL VERSUS REAL CHARACTERS

Another issue that relates to the role played by the trade character is the inclusion of real life (i.e., non fictional) humans in some definitions (Kleppner; Kaufman). By including real people, the definition of trade character could be stretched to cover celebrity spokespeople such as George Burns and even the "common man" found in testimonial advertising. The individuals in these two much-studied genres of advertising are used in a very different way from trade characters. Their value lies in their credibility as realistic spokespeople. On the other hand, the target audience suspends disbelief when entering the fantasy world of a trade character (Baldwin) such as a vegetable-growing giant or a dancing raisin. In advertising that uses real people, the target audience must identify with (testimonial advertising) or aspire to (celebrity advertising) the spokesperson. This is not the case when using trade characters. Instead, the target audience relates to a trade character as a symbolic representation of the product. For example, the Marlboro cowboy is a white male, yet he is used successfully to advertise to women and minorities. It appears that these groups do not view the character as a real person speaking for the brand (Ramirez). Therefore, another definitional requirement is that trade characters be fictional. Note that although human actors play the parts of such trade characters as the Marlboro cowboy and Mr. Whipple, these characters are still fictional.

TRADE VERSUS CELEBRITY CHARACTERS

Finally, in their work on animation, Callcott and Alvey draw a distinction between "celebrity" and "non-celebrity" spokes-characters. Celebrity characters are those that originated from a source other than advertising (i.e., cartoons, TV, etc.) for purposes distinct from advertising. Examples of celebrity characters include Mickey Mouse and Snoopy. Advertisers frequently license these characters to cash in on a celebrity's current popularity, such as Bart Simpson's endorsement of the Butterfinger chocolate bar. In fact, these characters function as any other celebrity spokesperson (Callcott and Alvey 1) and therefore play a different role than the characters created by the advertising trade, as discussed above. Thus, they should be excluded from the definition of "trade character."

A definition of trade character can be developed by combining the conditions discussed above. *A trade character is a fictional, animate being or animated object that has been created for the promotion of a product, service, or idea.* A trade character does not have to be a legal trademark.

TRADE CHARACTERS: HOW THEY COMMUNICATE

Occasionally, a successful trade character is developed by accident. This was the case in 1904 when the Campbell Kids were added to streetcar advertisements as a visual element that might appeal to women. Campbell's managers professed themselves to be mystified by the Kids' appeal and subsequent success (Scott). It is much more common, however, for advertisers to carefully deliberate over the creation of a trade character and its message. There are three ways that trade characters are used to communicate with consumers: by creating product identification, by promoting a brand personality, and by providing promotional continuity.

PRODUCT IDENTIFICATION

One of the fundamental ways that trade characters communicate with consumers is by creating product identification. A trade character can forge a link between the product, the packaging, and the advertising in the minds of consumers. The use of trade characters for product identification has its roots in the development of trademarks for branded products.

The explosion of trademarks into use as a general marketing tool took place at the beginning of the twentieth century. "In the course of 60 years, from 1860 to 1920, factory-produced merchandise in packages largely replaced locally produced goods sold from bulk containers" (Morgan 9). The product package became the focus of efforts by manufacturers to differentiate their products from the competition. Trademarks were used to help highlight the differences between brands. Even if actual product differences did not exist, consumers who remembered the trademark or the look of the package could still ask for a specific brand by name (Strasser). In this way, the trademark helped the consumer to recognize the brand in a purchase situation.

Manufacturers encouraged trademark recognition by creating promotions that required consumers to cut trademarks from packages and send them to the manufacturer to receive a prize (Strasser). As trade characters were developed for advertising use, many assumed the trade mark's role of product identifier by appearing on the label. For example, the trade character Mr. Clean is displayed on the bottle as a pictorial representation of the brand name. By viewing the trade characters on the product package, consumers may be able to recognize the product even if the brand name has been removed (Wallace). Recent research has shown a strong link between trade characters and the products that they identify. Animated non celebrity (i.e. trade) characters elicited a favorable 71.7 percent correct product recall in respondents (Callcott and Alvey).

The use of trade characters for product identification surpasses the trademark's traditional function of identifying the package. The strength of trade characters lies in their ability to form a bond between the product, the packaging, and the advertising (Kleppner). A successful trade character connects the advertising message to the product so that consumers recall the message when they view the package. The Jolly Green Giant and the Little Green Sprout are examples of trade characters who have achieved a successful product-packaging-advertising link. These characters appear on product labels, in TV and print advertising, and in sales promotions such as coupons and premiums. The two characters tie all of these promotional activities together into a cohesive unit that communicates the message of product quality.

Trade characters do not have to appear on the package to create a strong connection between the advertising message and the brand. When the Marlboro cowboy, who does not appear on the package, was used to advertise cigarettes on television, 95 percent of respondents could identify the sponsor in the first five seconds, as compared to only 16 percent for the average commercial (McMahan). Currently, in some Marlboro print advertisements, the Marlboro cowboy is shown without mentioning the product name (Ramirez). Because of the strong product-advertising link, the trade character is considered sufficient to identify the brand.

PERSONALITY

The trade character's message, however, goes beyond product identification. Trade characters also communicate through their personalities. A trade character's personality can fulfill two functions; it can give meaning to the brand by symbolizing its character, and it can lend emotional appeal to the brand by personifying the product. These two operations, which may be the paramount functions of a trade character, will be discussed below.

Trade characters with distinct personalities were first created during the 1920s. At that time, advertising practitioners uncovered a public desire to be addressed personally by and to receive advice from the media (Marchand). As traditional sources of information such as the family, the church, and the community became less meaningful to consumers, they turned to advertising to enlighten them regarding their role in society. Thus, advertising took on a cultural role that has continued to the present time. Advertising "seeks to render otherwise incomprehensible social situations meaningful, so as to make it possible to act purposively within them" (Sherry 448).

The new trade characters of the 1920s were developed to fill the informational void. These characters were fictional "people" passed off as real personal advisers and confidantes for everything from etiquette to cooking to personal hygiene. The longest-lived of these characters is Betty Crocker, who was invented in 1921 to sign replies to contest questions at General Mills, and stayed to lend her name to their entire product line.

As fictional "personal adviser" trade characters grew in popularity and became commonplace, the next step became personalization of the product itself. "*Printers Ink* praised new techniques of bringing the ingredients of products to life by depicting them as 'little characters with names' and . . . called on copywriters to find the 'face' that lay embedded in every product" (Marchand). Thus, the modern trade character, complete with a distinct personality, was born.

A. Meaning

The first function of the trade character's personality is to give meaning to the brand by symbolizing the brand's character. The trade character does this by transferring its own cultural meaning to what can be an otherwise meaningless product.

Because the manufacturing process is complex and removed from consumers' daily lives, products have lost the cultural meaning that they once possessed (Jhally). All advertising, in general, functions to assign meaning to a product by linking the product to a representation of the culturally constituted world (McCracken). This cultural representation is an image that elicits a cluster of ideas and emotions that are commonly associated with that image. "It is . . . the merchandising of a metaphor which will speak to and be understood by the collective imagination of the culture" (Lohof 442). A consumer connects the image with the product, and thereby transfers the meaning of the image to the product (McCracken). A formerly empty product comes to mean something to a group of consumers. By changing the cultural image that is paired with the product, a product can be made to take on almost any meaning (Kleine and Kernan).

The trade character is one cultural image that advertisers use to elicit meaning. Trade characters express meaning through the communication system known as myth. Myth uses visual symbols to send a message (Barthes) that indirectly addresses human concerns (Levy). Trade characters are archetypes, actors in the myth that embody those factors that matter to individuals and society (Hirschman).

All trade characters use their personalities as symbols to elicit and transfer meaning to the brand. Mr. Peanut is sophisticated, Poppin' Fresh is lovable, and Betty Crocker is reliable. In this way, trade characters establish a desired product image by visually representing the product attributes (Zacher) or the advertising message (Kleppner). An example of the link between the personality of the character and the personality of the product is illustrated by Chester Cheetah, the trade character used to promote Chee-tos cheese puffs. "Chester Cheetah reflects characteristics of Chee-tos puffs themselves. Chee-tos puffs are orange and 'go fast'; Chester Cheetah is orange and 'goes fast.' Chee-tos puffs are cheesy and lovable; Chester Cheetah is cheesy and lovable too" (Wells, Burnett, and Moriarty 450). It is apparent that Chester has been created to embody the attributes of his brand.

However, the creation of a symbolically meaningful trade character is not sufficient to ensure its effectiveness. The consumer must correctly decode the trade character's meaning before it can have an impact (McCracken). Therefore, advertisers must communicate through a vocabulary of readily understood signs so that consumers can correctly interpret the signs' meaning (Morgan and Welton). Trade characters have to express their meanings quickly and effortlessly if they hope to compete in the cluttered media environment. Thus, "the signifiers that will be used most often will be those that are judged to be at once appealing, communicative, normative, proper, and easily-understood in a particular moment" (Scott). The use of these types of signifiers to develop meaningful trade characters will lead to the correct decoding of the trade character's message.

As a result, advertisers frequently use animal trade characters because they are standard mythical symbols of human qualities. For example, "everyone" knows that a bee is industrious, a dove is peaceful, and a fox is cunning (Robin). These stereotypical animal symbols are used to express common hopes, aspirations, and ideals (Neal). Advertisers link these animals to their products because consumers intuitively know what the animals "mean" and can therefore transfer that cultural meaning to the brand.

It is their unambiguous meaning that makes trade characters popular with consumers. The characters are predictable and constant; they always "mean" the same thing. As a result, consumers view them as trustworthy and reliable spokespeople in a constantly changing media environment (Callcott and Alvey).

B. Emotional Appeal

Note that Chester Cheetah is also described as "fun" and "cool" (Wells, Burnett, and Moriarty 450). The second function of a trade character's personality is to give emotional appeal to the brand. A trade character can accomplish this by symbolizing an emotional benefit that is transferred to the product. Also, a trade character lends the warmth of an actual personality to the product (Kleppner) and thereby creates an emotional tie between the consumer and the character (Zacher). This emotional tie is crucial to the persuasive ability of the trade character, especially when the consumer has low involvement with the product category. An advertising executive asks "How do you personalize a message that seems miles away, months apart and mostly relevant to wild animals? Make a bear beg. When Smokey says 'Please,' you feel that he means it" (Nieman A-10).

By association, the character can create an emotional tie between the consumer and the brand, and even between the consumer and the manufacturer. This is because the trade character, through its personality, humanizes the product (Wells, Burnett, and Moriarty) and gives it a conscience (Levy) that makes the product trustworthy. Consumers may not trust Grand Metropolitan, but they trust Poppin' Fresh (PR Newswire). The emotional tie created by the trade character sells the symbolism it represents.

The two functions of the trade character's personality, meaning and emotional appeal, work together to create a successful character. McMahan calls this interplay Visual Image/Personality. It is important that both personality aspects are present, as evidenced by a famous trade character, the Jolly Green Giant. The personality of the Green Giant is full of meaning; he symbolizes nature (Cohen), healthy produce (Zacher), and the size and strength of his company. However, a giant is necessarily large and remote, and perhaps lacks emotional appeal. This could be one reason why, in the 1970s, he received a sidekick, the Little Green Sprout, who is outgoing and enthusiastic (Kapnick). Both characters work together to fulfill the personality functions. The Giant provides meaning and the Sprout provides emotional appeal.

A second example that highlights the importance of synergy between the two personality roles is the extreme care taken by RCA in naming their new trade character, Chipper. RCA's longtime trade character, Nipper, had all but retired by 1990. In his place, RCA created advertisements that attempted to dazzle consumers with technology. However, these ads were found to be confusing and incomprehensible to the target audience. As a result, Nipper was revived as a symbol of tradition and reliability, and a puppy was chosen as a symbol of growth and change. After careful deliberation, the puppy was named Chipper because the name had four associations (Elliott):

1. a computer chip (symbolizing technology),

2. a chip off the old block (symbolizing trust),

3. the definition of "chipper" as "happy and upbeat" (suggesting a positive emotional response), and

4. Chipper rhymes with Nipper (promoting a connection between the two characters).

In choosing this name, RCA ensured that their new trade character's personality would give meaning and emotional appeal to their product line.

The linking together of myth and emotion gives an added advantage to the trade character; it is very difficult for consumers to pronounce a trade character or the claims the character makes "false." Barthes states that myth is a pure ideographic system, that is, it is a system that suggests an idea without specifically naming it. Because trade characters communicate through myth, they represent ideas and attributes that are never explicitly stated, and therefore are less likely to be rejected. For example, the Jolly Green Giant is a symbol of health and nature, but conveys this message without verbalizing it. His message may therefore be accepted without thought. In contrast, an advertisement that proclaims "Our vegetables are healthy and natural" might be met with skepticism and counterargumentation, since canned vegetables can be far from either. Trade characters make puffery palatable (Bald win). By entering into the trade character's fantasy world, the consumer gives the character permission to exaggerate.

This puffery effect is enhanced by the emotion elicited by a trade character. As discussed above, a trade character can symbolize an intangible emotional benefit that is transferred to the product. However, a trade character's offer of fun (Kool-Aid Man), friendship (Ronald McDonald), or excitement (Joe Camel) is not easily quantified or measured. Therefore, these "soft" benefits are free from restrictions and regulations, and can successfully persuade without explicitly promising anything. Through the use of myth and emotion, trade characters are free to suggest product attributes and benefits that could not be expressly stated.

PROMOTIONAL CONTINUITY

The third message that trade characters communicate is promotional continuity. Trade characters can create promotional continuity across advertising campaigns, across brands in a product line, and over time.

A. Advertising Continuity

By appearing in each advertisement, a trade character connects the ads into a meaningful campaign (Bohen). The trade character, in its role of product identifier, signals to the consumer that the ad is for a specific brand. An example of a trade character used for advertising continuity is Little Caesar's Roman. Whether he is the star of the commercial, or appears at the end as a visual tagline, he unites widely dissimilar promotional campaigns by using his presence and his cry of "Pizza! Pizza!" to identify the sponsor.

B. Product Line Continuity

Trade characters can also provide continuity across brands in a product line. The value of using one trade character for several brands is the resulting cumulative publicity; each product connects to and helps to sell the others (Strasser). In addition, each product takes on the attributes symbolized by the character. The Keebler Elves are used in this way. Advertisements show the Elves manufacturing everything in the Keebler line from crackers to cookies to chips. The Elves' magic can link these products together in the minds of consumers and affirm that each is made with Keebler quality.

C. Continuity Over Time

Also, trade characters can provide continuity over time (Wright, Warner, and Winter): Many currently-used trade characters have an impressive longevity: RCA's Nipper was created in 1901, Mr. Peanut in 1916, Snap! Crackle! and Pop! in 1932, and Borden's cow, Elsie, in 1936. Live-action characters can also provide continuity; the Maytag Repairman celebrates his twenty-fifth birthday this year. By using these characters for years or even decades, advertisers build invaluable brand equity (Berger).

There are several advantages to using these characters over many years. Because consumers have prior experience with the trade character, its role as a product identifier is enhanced. Over time, consumers learn to recognize trade characters and the brands that they represent. At first, consumers attributed Eveready's Energizer Bunny to Duracell. However, the longer the commercials ran, the better the consumers became at identifying the sponsor (Liesse). Because consumers already know that a character represents a certain brand, they will be able to easily identify the advertiser when viewing a specific ad.

Another advantage to using a character for many years is that advertisers are able to build on an image that already exists in the mind of the consumer. Once consumers understand a trade character's meaning and link it to the brand, future advertising can focus on reinforcing this connection instead of trying to establish a new one. As a result, the advertising message is usually clear and easily-understood. When consumers see Tony the Tiger in an ad, they know that Tony's message will be that Frosted Flakes are "grrreat."

There is an added advantage for advertisers who use their trade characters for many years—the characters may become the objects of nostalgia. Nostalgia is a positive feeling toward some part of a person's past life (Davis). Because of geographic, occupational, and social mobility, nostalgia for a relatively permanent geographic locale (home) has been replaced by nostalgia for media products rooted in a certain time. This time is usually childhood and adolescence (Davis). Therefore, many consumers have strong emotional ties to trade characters that were advertised in their youth. If these characters are still in use, the comfortable, positive, loyal feelings that consumers have towards them can be transferred to the brand (Horovitz).

There are several reasons why trade characters can be used and reused over time. One reason is that trade characters are created to symbolize relatively permanent product attributes or consumer benefits. The Maytag Repairman represents reliability, and Snuggle, the fabric softener bear, represents softness. As long as these basic benefits remain valuable to the target audience, these characters can continue to embody them. Also, because trade characters are advertising creations, the advertiser has complete control over them. They do not grow old, change their meaning, or demand a raise. The creators of Spot, the 7-Up trade character, state "Every dollar we invest in Spot over the long term comes right back to the 7-Up company because he is ours. And Spot is not going to wind up on the front page of *USA Today* for adultery or drug abuse" (Davis). Finally, trade characters are flexible. They can appear on labels, in advertising, on coupons, on promotions, or "in person." By appearing in different promotional areas, a character's life can be extended. An example is Ronald McDonald, who in addition to appearing in all of the standard promotional areas, will also be used for a nontraditional promotion. He will appear in a video game aimed at reaching the best fast food customers—adolescents (Smith).

D. Limitations of Continuity

There are several limiting factors when using the same trade character for a long time. The character may become dated, may no longer be able to personify the advertising message, or may acquire an undesirable meaning (Cohen). As styles and fashions change, characters can become dated. They can be kept fresh and effective by modernizing them (Berger). Usually, the inner meaning of the character remains the same, but the outward appearance and trappings are changed. For example, Betty Crocker has had her hairstyle and clothing modified many times over the years, and Poppin' Fresh has learned how to rap.

If the advertising message changes, the existing trade character will no longer be able to symbolize its meaning. At that point, the trade character usually has to be retired. Qantas Airways recently abandoned its humorous koala bear trade character for more sophisticated imagery when its focus changed from tourist to business travelers (Porter). In another example, advertisers deemed Smokey Bear unsuitable for use in hard-hitting ads that warned the public about jail terms for setting forest fires. The advertisers wanted to keep Smokey's soft, warm, fuzzy image intact for future soft-sell promotions (United Press International).

As social and political changes take place over time, a benign trade character may acquire an undesirable meaning. This was the case with the Exxon Tiger, who was introduced to convey the concept of smooth, silent power (Rawstone). The character was discontinued in the 1970s because its imagery took on a "wasteful" quality during the austerity of the oil crisis (Levy). However, the tiger was reintroduced in the late 1980s once the oil crisis faded and cultural values shifted again.

The biggest cultural meaning shifts that have affected trade characters are those that stereotype humans, especially minorities. It is important to note that a stereotype is not necessarily negative. All trade characters are based on the skillful manipulation of stereotypes (Morgan and Welton); advertisers use a dove to "mean" peace regardless of a dove's actual behavior in the wild. However, stereotypes have a subtle and persuasive influence that gains power through repetition (Boskin). Once a stereotype of a *group* is imbedded in folklore, it can

A Visual Case Study:
Seeing the World of Coca-Cola

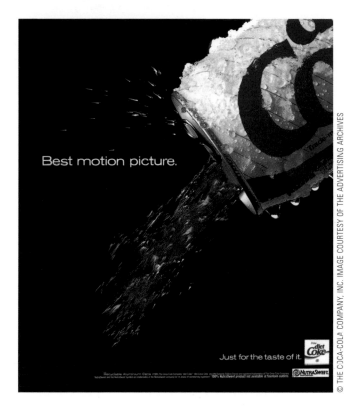

DECODING THE TEXT

1. Which senses does this advertisement appeal to?

2. Can you really experience Coca-Cola like this? Why or why not?

3. What does the NutraSweet label tell you about this ad? What is the purpose behind that label?

CONNECTING TO YOUR CULTURE

1. How does this image make you feel?

2. Why do you think Coca-Cola chose to associate itself with motion pictures? Does this make Coca-Cola more appealing to you? Your friends?

3. Do you remember the campaign "Just for the taste of it"? What was the purpose behind this campaign? What is its appeal? What does it mean to you? To others?

4. Do you drink Coca-Cola at the movies? At other social events? Why or why not?

© DUOMO/CORBIS

DECODING THE TEXT

1. Look at the placement of the Coca-Cola logo at these two sporting events. How does the placement of the ad at the event affect the impact of the ad? What about the size of the ad?

2. Does the ad or the product affect the sport? The players? The fans? The television viewing audience?

3. Who else might be affected by these ads? What networks or groups?

CONNECTING TO YOUR CULTURE

1. What are the connections between Coca-Cola and sports? In what way do both of these connect to you? Your friends?

2. What do these two sports have in common? What are their differences? Who are their audiences? What products do you think are sold at these two sporting events?

3. Have you seen these kinds of ads at sporting events? What events? What did the ads look like? Did these ads have any effect on you? Why or why not?

4. If you were going to create an ad for a sporting event, what sporting event would you choose? What would your ad look like? Where would you place the ad?

DECODING THE TEXT

1. What do you see first when you look at this image? What items or people catch your attention? Why do you think this is?

2. Why are the people's faces cut off? How does this affect your reading of the images?

3. Where do you think this photo was taken? What clues are you reading?

CONNECTING TO YOUR CULTURE

1. Who do you think is responsible for this image? What is the author's/photographer's purpose behind this image?

2. How do the characters in this image compare to those in the sports images across the page? What different images of Coca-Cola do these texts represent?

3. Would Coca-Cola put out an ad with this image? Why or why not? If not, how do you think Coca-Cola would change this image?

DECODING THE TEXT

1. Where do you think this Coca-Cola advertisement ran? Who was the intended audience for this ad? How can you tell?

2. How do the words in the ad work with (or against) the image?

3. What details of this image suggest that it is not from the 2000s? How would this advertisement (with the same audience and purpose you determined above) look today?

CONNECTING TO YOUR CULTURE

1. If the print references to Coke or Coca-Cola were removed from this ad, would you still get the message? Why or why not?

2. What ideas or even ideals do you associate with the image of the flag? Are these the ideas or ideals you associate with Coca-Cola? How do you compare or contrast the two?

DECODING THE TEXT

1. Who might the intended audience for this ad be? Given your idea of the audience, where would you place this ad? Where would it have the most impact?

2. Does the line "a world of refreshment" go with the image? Why or why not?

3. Discuss how the color red works with, or against, the rainbow image.

CONNECTING TO YOUR CULTURE

1. What ideas or ideals do you associate with the rainbow image? Are these the ideas or ideals you associate with Coca-Cola?

2. How does this bottle compare to the flag bottle on the opposite page?

3. Does Coca-Cola represent both of these ideas? Why or why not?

4. Why do you think Coca-Cola chose red as its signature color? What significance does the color red have in your culture?

DECODING THE TEXT

1. What kind of effect do you think was intended by combining Diet Coke and American presidents on Mt. Rushmore? Is the combination effective?

2. What kind of play on language is used in the ad? Is this effective as well?

CONNECTING TO YOUR CULTURE

1. This ad ran in the 1980s. Why might that be important in your analysis of it? Would this ad be effective even today? If yes, why? If no, how might you change the ad to be more effective now?

2. Coca-Cola uses a familiar "monumental" place here with which to associate itself. What are some other places that might be effective for Coca-Cola to use when it wants to market to you? Your friends? How would you design the ad?

3. Coca-Cola, like other companies, also often uses familiar celebrity endorsements, in addition to familiar places. Who are some celebrities you would choose to represent Coca-Cola? Why? How would you design the ad?

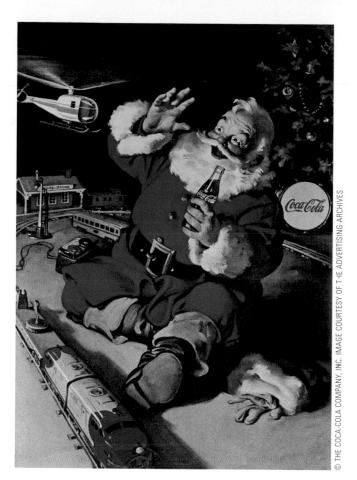

DECODING THE TEXT

1. Describe this image of Santa. How does it compare to other images of Santa?

2. What role has Coca-Cola played in shaping our American image of Santa?

3. What are the other items in this text? What role(s) do they play?

CONNECTING TO YOUR CULTURE

1. Do you consider Santa a celebrity endorsement for Coca-Cola? How does this compare to such endorsers as Bill Cosby, Mean Joe Greene, Jennifer Lopez, or the American Idol judges?

2. Do endorsements make you want to buy a product? Why or why not?

3. Why does Coca-Cola want to be associated with the tradition of Christmas? What other Coca-Cola Christmas ads and images have made a lasting impression on our culture? On you?

4. Does Coca-Cola play a role in your holiday celebrations? If so, describe this role.

5. What do you think about Coca-Cola tying itself to a traditionally Christian holiday?

6. Do you associate Coca-Cola with any other holidays or annual celebrations? Why or why not?

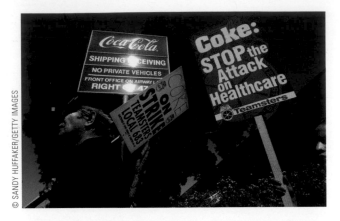

© SANDY HUFFAKER/GETTY IMAGES

DECODING THE TEXT

1. What do you think is the intended message of these visual texts? What is the message that comes through to you personally?

2. Both of these images show collections of objects. How does the arrangement of these objects affect the tone of the image? The message of the image?

3. How does the space or location of these collections affect the message?

4. What do the words within the image tell you literally? Is anything implied through these same words? Why or why not? If so, how?

© KEVIN FLEMING/CORBIS

CONNECTING TO YOUR CULTURE

1. What do these different images say about the effects or influences of Coca-Cola or its place in our culture?

2. Why is collecting Coca-Cola memorabilia such a large business? What draws people to it? Do you know any collectors of Coca-Cola products? Have you ever collected Coca-Cola memorabilia?

3. Do you collect other types of memorabilia? Why or why not?

4. What do you know about labor unions or teamsters? How do you know this information?

5. Have you ever been a part of a strike? What were you protesting?

6. How do these two images fit together? Contrast with each other?

affect an individual's thoughts and actions (Kern-Foxworth). Therefore, if an accepted stereotype of a group is essentially negative, this negative view of the group will be perpetuated. Because of shifting social values, some stereotypical trade characters from the past now convey unacceptable negative meanings to consumers.

Two trade characters who have the dubious distinction of contributing to negative stereotyping of humans are Sambo (and his "brother" Golliwog in the UK) and Aunt Jemima. These two characters were popular and accepted for decades, and since many consumers had no personal experience with blacks, they came to stand for the generic black man and black woman. "The chief problem with stereo-types of ethnic . . . groups is that one character . . . is allowed to stand for a whole diverse collection of human beings" (Kern-Foxworth 56). Unfortunately, the attributes that these characters presented were largely negative (MacGregor). Blacks were presented as childish, comical, subservient, docile, and servile (Boskin; Kern-Foxworth). Over decades of common use, consumers never consciously considered the ramifications of the myth that they were accepting.

Over time, as cultural values changed, society began to examine these trade characters more closely. MacGregor found that the social significance of these symbols had gone far beyond their original intent, and they had become images laden with negative stereotypical cultural meaning. Eventually, the Golliwog came to be perceived as a racist symbol by a substantial portion of British society (MacGregor), and the trade character Sambo faded out of use. In 1968, the Quaker Oats Company scrambled to "update" Aunt Jemima into an acceptable image. She "suddenly lost over 100 pounds, became 40 years younger and her red bandanna was replaced by a headband;" in 1990, she was changed even further, into a "black Betty Crocker" (Kern-Foxworth 63). These major changes in imagery and meaning were necessary to Aunt Jemima's continuance as an acceptable trade character. Thus, it is apparent that shifting cultural values may limit a character's use and effectiveness over time.

Conclusion

In this paper, a trade character has been defined as a fictional, animate being or animated object that has been created for the promotion of a product, service, or idea. Trade characters have become a common element in American popular culture because of their use as advertising tools. In this role, they can communicate in three ways: by creating product identification, by promoting a brand personality, and by providing promotional continuity. It appears, then, that by effectively fulfilling their advertising functions, trade characters have become an easily-understood and accepted communication system between advertisers and consumers. This will ensure that trade characters continue to be an important and enduring part of American popular culture.

Works Cited

Baldwin, Huntley. *Creating Effective TV Commercials.* Chicago: Crain, 1982. Print.

Barthes, Roland. *Mythologies.* New York: Hill, 1957. Print.

Berger, Warren. "A Cult of Personality." *Advertising Age* 1 Jul. 1991: 19-C. Print.

Bohen, William H. *Advertising.* New York: Wiley, 1981. Print.

Boskin, Joseph. "Sambo: The National Jester in the Popular Culture." *Race and Social Difference Selected Readings.* Ed. Paul Baxter and Basil Sansom. New York: Penguin, 1972. Print.

Callcott, Margaret F., and Patricia A. Alvey. "Toons Sell . . . and Sometimes They Don't: An Advertising Spokes-Character Typology and Exploratory Study." *1991 American Academy of Advertising Conference Proceedings.* Ed. Rebecca Holman. Print.

Cohen, Dorothy. *Advertising.* Glenview: Scott, 1988. Print.

Davis, Fred. *Yearning for Yesterday: A Sociology of Nostalgia.* New York: Free, 1979. Print.

Davis, Tim. "What Ever Happened to 'Be a Pepper'?" *Beverage World* Apr. 1989: 26–28. Print.

Dunn, S. Watson, and Arnold Barban. *Advertising Its Role in Modern Marketing.* 6th ed. Hinsdale: Dryden, 1986. Print.

Elliott, Stuart. "RCA Stresses Ease of Use in Electronics Campaign." *The New York Times* 25 Sept. 1991: D8. Print.

Hirschman, Elizabeth C. "Movies as Myths: An Interpretation of Motion Picture Mythology." *Marketing and Semiotics New Directions in the Study of Signs for Sale.* Ed. Jean Umiker-Sebeok. New York: Mouton de Gruyter, 1987. Print.

Horovitz, Bruce. "Famous Logos Brought to Life to Revive Sales." *Los Angeles Times* 7 May 1991: D6. Print.

Jhally, Sut. "Advertising as Religion: The Dialect of Technology and Magic." *Cultural Politics and Contemporary America.* Ed. Ian Angus and Sut Jhally. New York: Routledge, 1989. 217–29. Print.

Kapnick, Sharon. "Commercial Success: These Advertising Figures Have Become American Icons." *Austin American-Statesman* 25 Apr. 1992: D1. Print.

Kaufman, Louis. *Essentials of Advertising.* New York: Harcourt, 1980. Print.

Kern-Foxworth, Marilyn. "Plantation Kitchen to American Icon: Aunt Jemima." *Public Relations Review* 16.3 (1990): 55–67. Print.

Kleine, Robert E., and Jerome B. Kernan. "Contextual Influences on the Meanings Ascribed to Ordinary Consumption Objects." *Journal of Consumer Research* 18 (1991): 311–23. Print.

Kleppner, Otto. *Advertising Procedure.* 5th ed. Englewood Cliffs: Prentice, 1966. Print.

Levy, Robert. "Play It Again, Sam." *Dun's Review* Mar. 1980: 108–11. Print.

Levy, Sidney J. "Interpreting Consumer Mythology: A Structural Approach to Consumer Behavior." *Journal of Marketing* 45 (1981): 49–61. Print.

Liesse, Julie. "Bunny Back to Battle Duracell." *Advertising Age* 17 Sept. 1990: 38. Print.

Lohof, Bruce A. "The Higher Meaning of Marlboro Cigarettes." *Journal of Popular Culture* 3.3 (1969): 443–50. Print.

MacGregor, Robert M. "The Golliwog: Innocent Doll to Symbol of Racism." *Advertising and Popular Culture: Studies in Variety and Versatility.* Ed. Sammy R. Danna. Bowling Green: Bowling Green State U Popular P, 1992. Print.

Marchand, Roland. *Advertising and the American Dream: Making Way For Modernity, 1920–1940.* California: U of California P, 1985. Print.

Mandell, Maurice I. *Advertising.* 3rd ed. Englewood Cliffs: Prentice, 1980. Print.

McCracken, Grant. "Culture and Consumption: A Theoretical Account of the Structure and Movement of the Cultural Meaning of Consumer Goods." *Journal of Consumer Research* 13 (1986): 71–84. Print.

McMahan, Harry Wayne. "Do Your Ads Have VI/P?" *Advertising Age* 14 Jul. 1980: 50. Print.

Morgan, Hal. *Symbols of America.* New York: Viking, 1986. Print.

Morgan, John, and Peter Welton. *See What I Mean? An Introduction to Visual Communication.* London: Edward Arnold, 1986. Print.

Neal, Arthur G. "Animism and Totemism in Popular Culture." *The Journal of Popular Culture* 19.2 (1985): 15–24. Print.

Nieman, John. "As Creatives Rate Them." *Advertising Age* 11 Nov. 1991: A-10. Print.

Norris, James S. *Advertising.* 3rd ed. Reston: Reston, 1984. Print.

Porter, Jeni. "Worldwise Qantas Airline Drops Koala for Mature Int'l Image." *Advertising Age* 21 Oct. 1991: 36. Print.

PR Newswire. "Oh Boy! Pillsbury Doughboy Turns 25!" 20 Sept. 1990. Print.

Presbrey, Frank. *The History and Development of Advertising.* New York: Greenwood, 1929. Print.

Ramirez, Anthony. "Times Change; the Man Rides On." *The New York Times* 8 Mar. 1990: D-1. Print.

Rawstone, Philip. "Marketing and Advertising; The Tiger That Filled Up the Petrol Tank." *The Financial Times* 16 Jun. 1988: 1-12. Print.

Robin, P. Ansell. *Animal Lore in English Literature.* London: John Murray, 1932. Print.

Scott, Linda Marie. *The Rhetoric of the Commercial Cannon.* Unpublished doctoral dissertation. The University of Texas at Austin, 1991. Print.

Sherry, John F., Jr. "Advertising as a Cultural Symbol." *Marketing and Semiotics New Directions in the Study of Signs for Sale.* Ed. Jean Umiker-Sebeok. New York: Mouton de Gruyter, 1987. Print.

Smith, Martin J. "Games Visible Feast for Kids, Companies." *The Chicago Tribune* 19 Apr. 1992: 8. Print.

Stewart, David W., and David H. Furse. *Effective Television Advertising: A Study of 1000 Commercials.* Lexington: Lexington, 1986. Print.

Strasser, Susan. *Satisfaction Guaranteed: The Making of the American Mass Market.* New York: Pantheon, 1989. Print.

Ulanoff, Stanley M. *Advertising in America: An Introduction to Persuasive Communication.* New York: Hastings, 1977. Print.

United Press International. "Keeping Smokey a Softie." 25 Apr. 1985. Print.

Wallace, David. "Myths and Folklore Add More to Labels Than Meets the Eye." *Philadelphia Business Journal* 8.41 (1989): 1. Print.

Wells, William, John Burnett, and Sandra Moriarty. *Advertising Principles and Practice.* Englewood Cliffs: Prentice, 1989. Print.

Wright, John S., Daniel S. Warner, and Willis L. Winter, Jr. *Advertising.* 3rd ed. New York: McGraw, 1971. Print.

Zacher, Robert Vincent. *Advertising Techniques and Management.* Homewood: Irwin, 1967. Print.

Source: *"Defining Trade Characters and Their Role in American Popular Culture" by Barbara J. Phillips from* The Journal of Popular Culture *Spring 1996, Vol. 29, No. 4, pp. 143–158. Reprinted by permission of Wiley-Blackwell Publishing.*

DECODING THE TEXT

1. Phillips uses review and classification to support her general thesis. Identify these rhetorical strategies in the text.

2. Does she use other strategies as well?

3. In your opinion, which of these strategies help her argument? In what ways? In your opinion, do any of her strategies not help her argument? Why?

CONNECTING TO YOUR CULTURE

1. Phillips mentions that one limitation of trade characters is their tendency to become dated. Can you think of any characters in use now that are in need of updating? How would you update the character?

2. If you had to create a new trade character for a product, what product would you pick and what character would you create?

3. What factors will you need to consider as you create your trade character?

CONSIDERING IDEAS

1. What kinds of ads do you encounter on your college campus? What is being sold? To whom? Where are these ads?

2. How are these ads different from those you may have encountered on other campuses, including your high school?

3. Do you think these advertisements affect your education or learning in any way? Is that effect good, bad, or indifferent?

AUTHOR BIO

Amy Aidman teaches film studies at Emory University, where she is also a senior research fellow at the Emory Center on Myth and Ritual in American Life (MARIAL). Aidman is a coauthor of Media and the Make-Believe Worlds of Children: When Harry Potter Meets Pokemon in Disneyland *(2005), which reports on the results of an international study of children's fantasies and their relationship to media. Aidman is also the former director for the Center for Media Education in Washington, D.C. She is currently conducting research on a project at MARIAL entitled "Media as Myth and Ritual in Family Life." Aidman's research interests include childhood and culture, media literacy, family life, and parenting. The following article was published in the December 1995* ERIC *(Education Resources Information Center) Digest.*

ADVERTISING IN THE SCHOOLS

Amy Aidman

Many advertisers view children as a uniquely profitable three-in-one market: as buyers themselves, as influencers of their parents' purchases, and as future adult consumers. Each year, elementary school children have an estimated $15 billion of their own money, of which they spend an estimated $11 billion on such products as toys, clothes, candy, and snacks. Children influence at least $160 billion in parental purchases (McNeal, 1994). As future adults, children are potential consumers for all goods and services. This digest reviews the recent history of advertising to children, spotlights controversial marketing efforts, and focuses attention on the evolving nature of commercial messages directed toward children in the public schools.

Because of the increase in children's spending power in recent decades, advertisers have closely targeted children as consumers (Wartella, 1995). New advertising strategies aimed at children steadily proliferate. The toy-related program or program-length commercial, in which a television program is developed to sell toys, is one that has stirred public attention and debates, as have the 900-number telephone services aimed at children. In the 1980s, children got their own TV networks, radio networks, magazines, newspapers, kids' clothing brands, books, banking, and such high-ticket items as video games and other high-tech products. Other recent advertising tactics include kids' clubs, store displays directed at children, direct mailing to children and their parents, and marketer-sponsored school activities. Linking their products to educational goals, advertisers have reached into the schools by sponsoring such activities as literacy programs, reading projects, anti-drug campaigns, and communication skills training, while rewarding students for good performance with coupons for products and free meals. This spread of advertising in the schools can be seen as part of a historical pattern toward the commercialization of youth (Wartella, 1995).

CHANNEL ONE

Because children spend 20 percent of their time in schools, advertisers have been eager to pursue school-based marketing in many forms. Although traditionally there have been links between business and education in this country (Harty, 1979), commercialism in schools has recently skyrocketed and has spurred public debate. In 1989, controversy arose when Whittle Communications (now Channel One Communications) announced

BOB DAEMMRICH/ALAMY

the test marketing in six school districts of "Channel One" a 12-minute daily news show for students in grades 6 through 12 that included two minutes of age-appropriate ads for products like jeans and soft drinks. In exchange for airing the program each day at the same time for three years, Channel One Communications gives schools a satellite dish, a cable hookup, a television monitor for each classroom, and an agreement to service the equipment for three years. While some state school systems originally said no to "Channel One," the Consumers Union Education Services (CUES) (1995) notes that Channel One Communications reports its program is viewed in 350,000 classrooms. A further concern is that the presence of "Channel One" in classrooms may be evident more in some neighborhoods than in others. For example, one study (Morgan, 1993) found that among those schools showing "Channel One," a disproportionate number are located in areas of high poverty.

Although "Channel One" has attracted a great deal of public attention, in-school advertising takes many other forms as well. According to James McNeal (1990):

> In-school advertising is being talked about more, and in a more critical manner, because of the increasing amounts of it and because of the advent of television advertising in schools. (Criticisms of TV advertising in schools seem to be directed mainly at Whittle . . . because of its intrusive nature and because the firm flaunts its ability to buy its way into schools.) In-school advertising takes an endless number of forms scoreboards and billboards in athletic areas, posters, pamphlets, book covers, lesson plans, films, and vending machines. (p.73)

Although some educators defend the use of commercially produced materials as a way of providing useful supplements to the curriculum or as a way of raising funds and building needed bridges to businesses, other educators oppose it, fearing that market values may, for the most part, take the place of democratic values in the schools. Those who defend the trend argue that commercialism is highly prevalent throughout our society and a bit more advertising in the schools should not adversely affect students. Critics of the trend, however, point to increased pressure on teachers' and administrators' time as they sort through offers from businesses. Many educators do not want to participate in offering up students as a captive audience. According to Molnar (1995), failure to change policies by the end of the century will result in solidifying public education's role in delivering corporate profits.

TYPES OF ADVERTISING

"Captive Kids," a new report by the CUES (1995) summarizes the routes of commercial messages into schools, examines some of those messages, and discusses the meaning of the enormous influx of corporate-produced materials into the schools. The report, which is a follow-up to the earlier report, "Selling America's Kids" (CUES, 1990), divides the examples of in-school commercialism into four categories:

In-School Ads. In-school ads are conspicuous forms of advertising that can be seen on billboards, on school buses, on scoreboards, and in school hallways. In-school ads include ads on book covers and in piped-in radio programming. Advertising is also found in product coupons and in give-aways that are distributed in schools.

Ads in Classroom Materials and Programs. Ads in classroom materials include any commercial messages in magazines or video programming used in school. The ads in "Channel One" fall into this category.

Corporate-Sponsored Educational Materials and Programs. Promotional messages appearing in sponsored educational materials may be more subtle than those in the previous categories. Sponsored educational materials include free or low-cost items which can be used for instruction. These teaching aids may take the form of multimedia teaching kits, videotapes, software, books, posters, reproducible activity sheets, and workbooks. While some of these materials may be ad-free, others may contain advertising for the producer of the item, or they may contain biased information aimed at swaying students toward a company's products or services.

Corporate-Sponsored Contests and Incentive Programs. Contests and incentive programs bring brand names into the schools along with the promise of such rewards as free pizzas, cash, points toward buying educational equipment, or trips and other prizes.

GUIDELINES AND POLICIES

What are appropriate policies for addressing the increasing flow of commercial messages into schools? Those who support the call for guidelines include education groups such as the Association for Supervision and Curriculum Development, the National Parent Teacher Association, and the National Education Association. The Society of Consumer Affairs Professionals in Business (SOCAP) and Consumers International are two consumer interest groups that have formulated guidelines for sponsored materials. These guidelines suggest that education materials should be accurate, objective, clearly written, nondiscriminatory, and noncommercial (Karpatkin & Holmes, 1995, p. 75).

According to Karpatkin and Holmes, the Consumers Union supports the notion of schools as "ad-free zones." The overall goal of collaboration between businesses and schools should be for business leaders, educators, parents, and government officials to work together ". . . to embrace practical, responsible approaches that will protect the educational integrity of our school systems" (Karpatkin & Holmes, 1995, p. 75). In dealing with the issues of in-school commercialism, Karpatkin & Holmes suggest a three-pronged approach that includes:

- Reviewing all sponsored materials and activities and holding them to the same standards as other curriculum items by using the SOCAP or Consumers International guidelines.

- Pursuing noncommercial partnerships with businesses and rejecting the notion that it is ethical to bring advertising into the schools to provide materials or funds to bolster dwindling budgets.

- Beginning the teaching of media literacy in elementary school, to help educate children to be critical readers of advertising, propaganda, and other mass-mediated messages, while helping them gain the skills to be intelligent, aware consumers.

CONCLUSION

With the expanding presence of advertising targeted to younger and younger children, schools have become involved in serving up students as captive audiences to advertisers. It is time to pause and reflect on the appropriateness of various kinds of connections between businesses and schools, and the influence those connections might have on the integrity of education in a democracy. In light of the controversial nature of the issue, as well as the underlying ambivalence toward it, public discussion and workable policies are needed.

For More Information

Consumers Union Education Services (CUES). (1990). *Selling America's Kids: Commercial Pressures on Kids of the 90's.* Yonkers, NY: Author.

Consumers Union Education Services (CUES). (1995). *Captive Kids: Commercial Pressures on Kids at School.* New York: Author. PS 023 660.

Harty, Sheila. (1979). *Hucksters in the Classroom: A review of Industry Propaganda in Schools.* Washington, DC: Center for Study of Responsible Law.

Karpatkin, Rhoda H., and Anita Holmes. (1995). Making Schools Ad-Free Zones. *Educational Leadership* 53(1, Sep): 72–76.

McNeal, James U. (1990). *Kids as Customers.* New York: Lexington Books. McNeal, James U. (1994). Billions at Stake in Growing Kids Market. *Discount Store News* (Feb 7): 4.

Molnar, Alex. (1995). Schooled for Profit. *Educational Leadership* 53(1, Sep): 70–71.

Morgan, Michael. (1993). *Channel One in the Public Schools: Widening the Gaps.* Research report for UNPLUG. ED 366 688.

Wartella, Ellen. (1995). The Commercialization of Youth: Channel One in Context. *Phi Delta Kappan* 76(6, Feb): 448–451. EJ 497 517.

References identified with an ED (ERIC document), EJ (ERIC journal), or PS number are cited in the ERIC database. Most documents are available in ERIC microfiche collections at more than 900 locations worldwide, and can be ordered through EDRS: (800) 443-ERIC. Journal articles are available from the original journal, interlibrary loan services, or article reproduction clearinghouses such as: UnCover (800) 787–7070; UMI (800) 732–0616; or ISI (800) 523–1850.

Source: *Advertising in Schools, by Amy Aidman. Found at* http://www.ericdigests.org/1996-3/advertising.htm

DECODING THE TEXT

1. How can you tell that this essay was written for an academic audience? What features or strategies are used in the essay to indicate this?

2. How effective are Aidman's supporting examples for her argument(s)?

3. What is Aidman's stance on advertising in schools? How can you tell?

4. What kind of publication is *Herizons*? How would this essay change if written for *The Journal of Advertising* or the journal *Gender & Society*?

CONNECTING TO YOUR CULTURE

1. What is your opinion about television in the classroom? What about corporately sponsored programs and materials—such as software, electronics, or textbooks?

2. Aidman advocates "the teaching of media literacy in elementary school, to help educate children to be critical readers of advertising, propaganda, and other mass-mediated messages, while helping them gain the skills to be intelligent, aware consumers." How do you feel about this? Do you see this happening in schools? How is it happening?

3. If you were a high school or college teacher, would you use materials that advertise products in your classroom? Why or why not?

READING SELECTIONS: THE 2010s

CONSIDERING IDEAS

1. Describe an advertisement that you have seen recently in which the product was explicitly marketed to one gender over another.

2. How did you know that this advertisement was meant for one gender and not the other?

3. Does gender-neutral advertising exist? Give an example.

AUTHOR BIO

Joy Parks has been working as a professional writer for more than 30 years. Her articles have appeared in The Boston Globe, *the* Lambda Book Report, Imbibe, Publisher's Weekly, The Globe and Mail, Herizons, Books in Canada, *the* Ottawa Citizen, *and other magazines and newspapers. Parks is also a short story writer, publishing in anthologies from Arsenal Bella Books, Pulp Press, Alyson Books, and Cleis Press. Her short story "Instinct" won the 2007 Gaylactic Spectrum Award for Short Fiction, an award that represents the best in LGBT short fiction in the categories of science fiction, fantasy, or horror. Joy Parks lives in Ottawa, Canada. The following essay was published in the Winter 2009 issue of* Herizons *magazine.*

MAD MEN, MAD WOMEN

Joy Parks

Discussions about women and advertising have been reignited thanks to the level of unapologetic sexism portrayed in the award-winning drama *Mad Men,* a television series about a 1960s advertising agency. But who really was responsible for creating those damaging gender stereotypes in advertising?

It's easy to blame it on the mad men. The first season of the hit AMC TV series received 16 Emmy nominations and was the first basic-cable show to win the coveted award for best drama—plus, it won five others. A period piece depicting the dark side of the lives of senior executives in a New York advertising agency in 1960, *Mad Men* has inspired a retro trend in designer menswear and a fascination with Lucky Strikes and cocktails. It has also unleashed much discussion and debate—online and off—about the show's depiction of the unmitigated sexism in the 1960s workplace.

As TV critic and blogger Aaron Barnhart characterized it, it speaks to a time when "men were men and women were their secretaries."

While there are plenty of complex female characters on the show, the men dominate with their infidelity, overt double standards and unchecked sexual harassment. In addition, the creative team at the fictional Sterling Cooper agency spend much time debating "what women want" and how to sell it them, unleashing a level of misogyny that has pulled scabs off old wounds regarding how women have been portrayed in mainstream advertising.

Feminism—for all of these reasons, and then some—has had a long-standing feud with the advertising industry. While gallons of ink has been spilled on the subject of gender stereotypes in advertising, it was Betty Friedan who fired the first shot, placing much of the blame for women's unhappiness on America's post-war consumer society, and especially on advertisers' exploitation of women.

"It is their millions which blanket the land with persuasive images, flattering the American housewife, diverting her guilt and disguising her growing emptiness. They have done this so successfully, employing the techniques and concepts of modern social science, and transposing them into those deceptively simple, clever, outrageous ads and commercials, that an observer of the American scene today accepts as fact that the great majority of American women have no ambition other than to be housewives. If they are not responsible for sending women home, they are surely responsible for keeping them there."

But were all the ad men really men?

No, says Juliann Sivulka! In her brand new book, *Ad Women: How They Impact What We Need, Want and Buy* (Prometheus), she reveals that the ad men behind much of the advertising feminists labelled as sexist and damaging were often women.

Sivulka takes an in-depth and quite fascinating look at the history of American advertising, from the late 19th century to just a few years ago, linking evolutions in the industry to major societal upheavals in 1880, the 1920s and the 1970s. She uncovers how and why the advertising and marketing communications industry went from a handful of women employees to one in which women far outnumber men.

The trend towards female employees was in direct relation to a new understanding of the marketplace. As women began to be viewed consumers, originally the keepers of the household money and later of their own income, ad agencies and their clients recognized the value of employing women who would, it was believed, better know what would motivate a woman to buy something and, with this insider knowledge, be able to create effective advertising.

In the early 20th century, countless women received a paycheque and a certain amount of career fulfillment through their work in ad agencies—as writers, mainly, but also as media buyers, art directors and home economists who advised manufacturers on new household devices.

One of the most influential of these women was Helen Lansdowne Resor, the daughter of a divorced single mother and the very first copywriter hired at J. Walter Thompson, an agency still regarded as an international expert in gender-related marketing. Resor developed an emotional hard-sell technique that spoke to the consumer's needs rather than the product's features—a revolutionary approach at that time. She wrote in a friendly, advice-driven style and made use of psychology, copy-testing and sampling—elements new to an industry still in its infancy.

Resor also built the women's editorial department to teach other women employees how to create effective advertising for women. Through this group, the J. Walter Thompson agency developed the careers of more women than any other early agency. It hired women for the very quality they were expected to subjugate in order to succeed in most other fields—their outsider perspective as women.

The women who were part of the women's editorial department viewed their work as a feminist activity. Outside of work, they belonged to suffragette leagues, the National Women's party—an early feminist organization founded in 1917 that fought for the passage of a constitutional amendment ensuring women's suffrage—and the League of Women Voters; they published articles, ran magazines and spoke on feminist issues or other related causes. While doing so, they may have led lives that were very different than the housewives they were selling to. They sincerely believed they were helping to make women's lives easier, a belief shared by the women who joined other agencies modelled on J. Walter Thompson's success and who participated in creating the advertising that later feminists would criticize so vehemently.

While the advertising industry in Canada has always been much smaller, Canadians have had their own ad women who went on to contribute to progressive causes. In 1890, journalist Kathleen Blake "Kit" Coleman, along with the editors of the *Daily Mail* and a local merchant, ran a contest to discover the best way to advertise to women. Coleman's famous weekly newspaper column in the *Mail and Empire* featured everything from advice for the lovelorn to her observations on world affairs. She also became the country's first woman war correspondent, reporting on the Franco-American war from Cuba in 1898.

Interestingly, when *Chatelaine* initially hired Doris Anderson in 1951, it was for a marketing position. The former Eaton's copywriter, an ad woman who predates the *Mad Men* milieu, would eventually head Canada's most important women's magazine, leading its evolution from service journalism into a magazine that dealt with public affairs including birth control, abortion and other women's equality issues.

DID THEY OR DIDN'T THEY?

Despite what *Mad Men* would have you believe, in die late 1950s and early 1960s several of the most powerful people in the New York advertising world were women—three of the better known being Mary Wells Lawrence, Shirley Polykoff and Jane Trahey. Wells' agency, Wells, Rich & Greene, was responsible, in 1971, for the justifiably loathed I'm Cheryl, Fly Me ads for the now defunct National Airlines, a campaign often touted as a classic example of sexism in advertising. Polykoff, working for Foote, Cone and Belding, created the long-running Does She or Doesn't She hair colour ads for Clairol. While they now seem dated, condescending and ageist, originally they were meant to encourage women's self-expression.

Of the three, only Trahey demonstrated any feminist sensibility. The owner of Trahey and Co, she rose from a small Chicago in-house agency to eventually become chief of copy at Niemen Marcus in Dallas, then returned to New York to open her own shop. In addition to award-winning ad copy, several books and plays, including the 1962 novel *The Trouble With Angels,* which became a major motion picture, she also penned *Jane Trabey on Women and Power* in 1978. While it, too, seems dated now—since competing with men is considered passé by current feminist standards—this was practical feminism, a how-to book that used humour and insider grit to help women navigate the sexism of the business world. As she wrote in the introduction: "I don't think there's any point in hashing over the sociological, economic, psychological reasons why women don't have any more power in the world than they do. We've been told a hundred times what's keeping us down. What we need are ways to change the situation."

THE NEW WOMEN'S MARKET

While it may be hard to believe, there remain legions of researchers today concerned with the still-elusive women's market. According to Andrea Gardner, author of *The 30-Second Seduction,* the mother market alone has five behavioural groups and marketing experts Carol Osborne and Mary Brown claim there are three different kinds of women baby boomers. Women are still viewed as the primary consumer, and women baby boomers in particular are unique because they are the first generation to have their own incomes in significant numbers. Like previous generations of women, they control household spending, but also have significant personal money. According to experts, women directly or indirectly initiate or influence 80 percent of all consumer spending.

In business, money talks. Advertisers want a financial return on their investment, which means the sheer number of baby boomer women and their significant consumer clout should have the power to force changes in how marketing portrays them. But that isn't happening.

FEWER WOMEN TODAY

With all this information on who women are, what they want and what they have to spend, one would expect advertising directed at them to be less sexist, more diverse and less youth-oriented. But the majority of it isn't. That's because—unlike the earlier part of the past century, when agencies recognized the usefulness of having women craft sales messages for women—most of the decision-makers and creative people in agencies today are men in their 20s and early 30s. In fact, it's getting harder to find women in upper creative positions.

The U.S. Equal Employment Opportunity committee in 2003 noted that women far outnumber men in agencies, at 65.8 percent of jobs. But their status recedes with rank. Women hold 76.7 of clerical positions, 58.2 percent of all professional positions and 47 percent of upper management positions. But on the creative side, where messaging decisions get made, they don't even come close to the early 1920s numbers, or even those of the 1960s *Mad Men* era. Of *Adweek's* 33 top agencies, only four have women as their senior creative director.

In November 2007, the *Globe and Mail,* in an interview with Lorraine Tao and Elspeth Lynn, founding partners of the ad agency Zig, referred to their firm as having a "fun, pop-feminist sensibility." The women had been creative partners at other agencies and their own small Canadian shop was boasting like clients Molson, Ikea, Best Buy, Virgin Mobile and Unilever.

Notably, the duo produced a commercial for Kellogg's Special K cereal that depicted average men deriding aspects of their bodies using classic female scripts. It delivered a strong message about advertising and women's insecurities about body image.

BUYING INTO A BETTER FUTURE

There have been a few ad campaigns in recent years to get it right. Dove's Real Beauty campaign, shot by legendary photographer Annie Leibovitz, featured real women with real rolls, cellulite and wrinkles. The Real Beauty campaign, created by Ogilvy & Mather, also included the YouTube ad Evolution, which used time-lapse photography to demonstrate how ordinary women are made to look perfectly fake for ads. The campaign also saw the company set up a Self-esteem Fund to support programs designed to encourage young girls to develop a healthy body image.

In 2006, the company commissioned a report in nine countries, including Canada, asking nearly 1,500 mature women what was wrong with the advertising directed to them. According to Sharon MacLeod, brand building director for Dove, "75 percent of women over 50 report that anti-aging ads often portray unrealistic images of women over 50. Women are regularly confronted with messages that they should minimize, reduce, eliminate or defy the natural signs of aging."

Ironically, the body-image-positive Dove ads were at the centre of a boycott by the American Family Association for their over-sexualization of women. Leave it to the radical right to turn women's words against them.

Still, Unilever received far more kudos than criticism for Dove's marketing. But will the trend continue? According to media and gender issues expert Jean Kilbourne, author of *Can't Buy My Love: How Advertising Changes the Way We Think and Feel* and producer of the award-winning documentary *Killing Us Softly,* "It all depends on how much soap the ads sell."

WHAT IF WOMEN MATTERED?

What will it take to change how advertisers often portray women? One positive sign is that consumers are complaining. According to the Advertising Standards Council's 2007 annual report, depicting women in a derogatory manner was one of four prime issues cited in the 1,445 complaints the council received, a 40 percent increase compared to 2006. The self-regulating council found that 5.7 percent of the ads cited in 2007 complaints contravened the Canadian Code of Advertising Standards, Those advertisers were asked to amend or withdraw their advertisements.

Women must continue to demand more realistic, more intelligent messages, or simply refuse to buy products by advertisers who create messages that offend them. As Andrea Gardner, author of *The 30-Second Seduction,* writes: "In the end, the ones who have the power to create that shift are today's powerful female consumers, the ones who buy from companies that treasure them."

Source: *Joy Parks.* © Herizons *Magazine, Spring 2009, pp. 22-27. Used by permission.

DECODING THE TEXT

1. What is the purpose of this essay?

2. Do you think the advertisements of the 1960s and 1970s were meant to "encourage women's self-expression"? Why or why not?

3. According to the author, has sexism in ads increased or decreased since the 1960s and 1970s? In what ways?

CONNECTING TO YOUR CULTURE

1. How familiar are you with the television show *Mad Men*?

2. How do advertising agencies market programs or products to you? Are there other classifications or categories that these agencies use?

3. Have you ever bought a product or watched a program despite its sexist advertising? Explain.

4. Have you ever bought a product or watched a program that was marketed to a gender different from your own? Explain.

1. What do you know about indie artists? Do you typically like them? Follow them? Support them?

2. In your opinion, when or how do indie artists become sellouts? Is this a fair description?

3. How might corporate sponsorships frame or shape an artist's work ? Do you think that this framing helps or hinders the artist? In what ways?

AUTHOR BIO

Steve Marsh *is a senior writer at* Delta Sky *magazine, where he profiles stars for feature articles. He is also an Emmy Award–winning senior writer at* Mpls.-St.Paul *magazine, writing features and online arts reviews. The following article was featured in the February 2011 edition of* Delta Sky *magazine.*

I'M WITH THE B®AND

Steve Marsh

After apologizing for taking the stage—"We feel like we're interrupting something," the keyboardist says—Matt and Kim, a punky little two-piece band from Brooklyn, get to work. She's up there with a big smile, clearly taking an ecstatic pleasure in hitting her kick drum as hard as she can while he spits lyrics about walking block after block in New York. Despite Matt and Kim's sweat, only about half of the crowd is into it; the other half is talking among themselves. It's a grand-opening party for Converse's brand-new shoe store in SoHo, and Matt and Kim are being treated as just another amusement, ranking somewhere with the mini lobster rolls and the free vodka cocktails. The guy standing next to me is concentrating on the band, but he notices the crowd's reaction and shrugs. "Ah," he says. "You know how these corporate gigs are."

In fact, this guy knows about these "corporate gigs" more than anybody: He's Rob Stone, the founder of Cornerstone Promotion. Together with co-CEO Jon Cohen, who's also standing with us dutifully paying attention to the band, Stone is responsible for nearly every detail of this corporate gig. Matt and Kim are on Cohen and Stone's fledgling music label, FADER, and Converse is a client of Cornerstone. In fact, their company is the key player in the unique business of matching indie bands or cutting-edge rappers with compatible corporate brands. Cornerstone is the most successful matchmaker between brands and bands in what is, if not a new model for the music industry, at least a vital new nexus where art and commerce can coexist.

In many ways, because of Stone and Cohen, brands and cool bands (the types of bands that, incidentally would've had nothing to do with these types of brands 10 years ago) are, these days, cooler with each other than bands and labels often are. Maybe that's because unlike bands and labels. in our brave new media world, bands and brands actually need each other.

And to be fair to this particular corporate gig, the party is pretty wicked. There are celebrities, such as Gabourey Sidibe, the actress who played Precious, and the Chicago rapper Lupe Fiasco, milling about in the crowd. And Dr. J is backstage somewhere, greeting Converse execs and posing for iPhone pictures. The store itself is also pretty cool: Behind Matt and Kim's heads is a huge black-and-white photograph of James Dean; he's sitting in a canvas director's chair, possibly between takes, wearing glasses and a black sweater and khakis, with his Converse Chuck Taylor lows kicked up on a chair, insouciantly thrust into the foreground.

Earlier, Cohen explained that this store and this party are indicative of the direction Converse is taking its brand. Despite the presence of Dr. J— no doubt a nod to the authenticity of the shoes in a they-actually-used-to-play-in-Chuck-Taylors! way—opening this new SoHo store with a Matt and Kim concert is about embracing downtown. It's about Chucks being the favorite shoe of artists and musicians, who kind of embraced them first (Chucks are cheap and look cool—the two most important factors for any artist). Cohen told me that recently when Dwayne Wade's contract was up, Converse just let him walk away and sign with Nike. "They're concentrating on the strength of their brand now" he says. "The musicians and artists are the ones who support them."

A generation ago, that loop of mutual admiration between brand and musician or artist would've been a short circuit; what's interesting now is how brands such as Converse are interested in giving back. Not content with simply hiring a band for a commercial or even an entire ad campaign, brands are actually investing in the art of recording. Converse, for instance, is the benefactor of the Three Artists One Song series—this summer, they paid for a collaboration between Bethany Cosentino from LA's indie darlings Best Coast, the rapper Kid Cudi and Rostam of Vampire Weekend on an original track, which was then made available as a free digital download. Levi's, another brand that Cornerstone works with, has The Pioneer Sessions, with indie stars such as Dirty Projectors covering Bob Dylan's "I Dreamed I Saw Saint Augustine"—and everything is published and recorded on Levi's dime. Mountain Dew, yet another Cornerstone partner, has Green Label Sound, an actual music label that has released new singles by bands such as Solid Gold and The Cool Kids.

A few hours before the Converse party, I crossed the East River to meet Cornerstone's Stone and Cohen in the indie band mecca: Williamsburg, Brooklyn. They were with Geoff Cotrill, Converse's chief marketing executive, standing in a gutted brick warehouse, a building that formerly served as a dry-cleaning facility. As the three execs sipped hot coffee and cooled their sneaker heels, workers were using a laser level to determine how much concrete would be needed for the new floor. The old warehouse is the next unexpected step in the courtship between brand and bands: by this spring, this building will house The Converse Rubber Tracks Studio, a recording studio run by Converse and Cornerstone.

The men take turns explaining how the place will operate—there will be a "general application process" to select the bands that get to record for free. "Obviously, in a down economy the arts suffer quite a bit," Cohen says. "What we want to do is give young artists from Brooklyn, from Manhattan, from anywhere, the tools to come in and experience how to make music." In a crumbling music business, it's easy to see what the bands get out of it: free studio time, maybe the chance to get some exposure with a free download via Converse.com, maybe some free publicity through Converse's 20 million Facebook friends. But what is big business getting out of it?

"This isn't a play for us to break new bands," explains Cotrill. "Or to be seen as the brand that's trying to be cutting edge. This is literally about providing new artists with a place to record." He really does sound altruistic, a marketing Medici! But c'mon: How will this help sell shoes? After demurring that "the bands selected will have to line up with the Converse brand," Stone explains that Rubber Tracks Studio will function in die same way Nike's training campus functions for its athletes: It's a place for their key "brand users"—the musicians and bands who presumably wear Converse—to meet up and build community. "You're going to have hip-hop artists recording here, alternative rock groups recording here. In the same way Nike's DNA is sports, Converse's DNA is music"

It still feels bizarre to be hanging out in a cold warehouse in Brooklyn that will eventually be a carpeted recording studio with flat screens and a wet bar. It seems like a pretty big investment for some warm fuzzies, smacks a bit of the old anything-goes Silicon Valley days: A solid gold foosball table would have been cheaper than a cush recording studio, right? How did we get here? In a recession how does Cornerstone get a bottom-line-oriented apparel company to splurge so dramatically?

Somehow, a pair of 42-years-olds have the what's-next-obsessed youth-oriented market on lock. Stone and Cohen grew up together in Long Island, and after college, they both worked for record labels. They were both doing marketing and promotion far EMT's SBK label in the early 1990s, and they were responsible for breaking bands such as Blur and Vanilla Ice (Cohen: "I picked him up from the airport when he was the biggest country nobody—a month later be was selling 150,000 records a day"). When they both left SBK, Cohen worked for Columbia-Sony and Stone went to Arista, where he was the liaison to start-up ventures Bad Boy Entertainment and LaFace Records and worked closely with Sean "P. Diddy" Combs. There's a platinum record of Notorious B.I.G.'s *Ready to Die* in Stone's office with an inscription: "TO: Rob Stone, #1 COOL WHITE MAN. . . 4REAL, B.I.G. DA ILLEST! '95"

"We were working for major labels when the record industry was healthy," Cohen says. "But even with all the success at Columbia and Arista, we saw cracks in the foundation. We saw that certain things weren't perfect—the excess, the waste and the impatience. And we would always talk about what if we did this together? What if we started our own label?"

Stone founded Cornerstone in 1996, and Cohen left Columbia shortly thereafter to join him. The plan was to operate as freelance marketing consultants, and eventually to build their own music label. They still worked closely with the labels—with Cohen as the alt-rock guy and "Hip-Hop Rob" as the rap guy, they helped break Beck and Outkast—but they didn't feel like starting their own label was the right move. They were looking at other ways to expand their business when they contacted Sprite in 1998 "I had read an article about Darryl Cobbin" Stone says, "who was running the Sprite brand, and the article had him as brand manager of the year. He took Sprite from nowhere to number two behind Coca-Cola. So I just called him up and said, 'I want to work with you.'" It was Cobbin who turned Stone and Cohen onto a way of doing things differently. "I was talking to him in regular music business terms, and he was giving it back to me in this kind of corporate talk: 'Hey, you have DJs all over the country who can speak to audiences in hip hop and rock; these are conduits to the masses. And if you could help get the word out about brands and products through your network, you would have something special.'"

By applying music-industry techniques to brands, Cornerstone was doing something nobody else was doing. "Even at its healthiest, the music industry had limited resources," Cohen says. "If you think of how Nike will market a product, if you think of how a film will launch, they have multimillion-dollar media budgets. But we knew how to surround the consumer inexpensively. If you think about music, you used radio, you used video. There were the earliest days of the Internet, there was college and field marketing and the streets. There were DJs and mix tapes and all the little tools you create and tours and the way you support touring. There was lifestyle—skate shops, clothing stores, restaurants. There was press. If you took all those touch points, eventually you were going to break the artist. We thought we could do the same thing for brands."

Cornerstone's guru Cobbin is now an executive at Kodak. I called him to ask what sets music apart from other media messaging. He explained that other forms of entertainment and media—television, movies—are typically created by adults for young people. "But music," Cobbin says, "is for youth and is typically created by youth. So it's in. the voice of the constituent that is growing up. Because of that, there is this indelible mark made into the brain, into the memory, of where you were, what you were doing, at the time you heard a particular song. And the reason why it made that indelible mark is because it was created by someone like you or by someone you can relate to." Cobbin goes on: "If your desire is to find a way to credibly connect with that space, I don't believe there's a firm better than Cornerstone in existence."

OK. Makes sense. The only problem is that Stone and Cohen aren't two youths—they're old enough to get the Joe Pesci reference I just made. And we're not too far removed from the era when Kurt Cobain appeared on the cover of *Rolling Stone* wearing his "corporate magazines still suck" t-shirt. A wariness persists—especially within the indie band culture in which Cornerstone operates—about being presented as a capitalist shill. So if the music business is predicated on youth and the aroma of cool, how do Stone and Cohen keep the corporate stink off their company, off the brands they work with and, most importantly off the bands they work with?

I bring up the word *sellout* with Matt and Kim backstage before their corporate gig. It is actually a hard thing to do: They're sweet former art school students who met at Pratt in Brooklyn before playing warehouse parties up and down the coast. They made their first record in their rented practice space before signing with FADER. David Lee Roth wouldn't have to dignify this line of inquiry, I thought, so why should they? But they are actually good sports about it. They appreciate the free shoes from Converse, and with Mountain Dew's help they were able to keep their concerts at $5 a show for their Green Label Sound tour. But, I persist, they play a souped-up version of punk rock; isn't there at least a part of them that wants to, you know, rebel?

Matt admits that his teenage punk band was named Aristocracy. "Spelled with the anarchy symbol?" Kim teases "No," he says. "But, yeah, my 15- to 19-year-old self was more closed-minded about all sorts of things. But when I was 19, I had to admit, "That Destiny's Child song is kind of SICK.""

Basically, Matt and Kim make music for brands because of economic necessity. The music industry is at a point where things are still being handed to potential rock stars, but always with strings attached (even if it's just stigma), so if you want to have a career, you have to choose wisely. "The people who are waiting for a booking agent and a manager and a record label—it's not going to really work out like that," he says. "It happens, but don't bank on somebody coming to sweep you up and take you there. We did everything for ourselves for so many years."

For their part, Stone and Cohen admit that it was a concern, especially in the early days. "Product placement doesn't always look right in the movies," Stone says. "And it doesn't always work with music, either, by any means." They have an ear for this stuff, for what sounds right to their corporate clients and the bands they work with. They have a staff of young people running a label and a magazine. *FADER*, focused on finding cutting-edge acts they can help blow up (Kanye, Drake and the White Stripes all got their first covers from *FADER*). They throw great parties—they thought up FADER Fort, an annual party in Austin at the South by Southwest festival, where broke music fans without festival wristbands can drink free Southern Comfort while watching Kanye rap in a big tent.

Aside from speaking the language of the recording studio and the boardroom and being able to judge what sounds cool and what sounds corny; the essence of Cornerstone's sangfroid might be their cutthroat honesty. While we're discussing how hard it is for bands to make it in the new normal, Stone abruptly cuts us off to say, "That's not the purpose of Cornerstone. We put together campaigns that make sense for brands. We work for record labels, and we work for artists and their managers. But our focus isn't to find a way to make money for artists." Stone's tough love comes off more like a savvy older brother than Stern dad when he says, "Bands will be approached by companies that will have the wrong idea for them, and they have to walk away from it. You have to say no more than you say yes if you're going to be an artist. You have to be true to your music."

Source: *Excerpted from "I'm with the B@and" by Steve Marsh, taken from* Delta Sky, *February 2011. Used by permission of MSP Communications.*

DECODING THE TEXT

1. In your view, is the artist–corporate partnership an effective form of reaching potential consumers?

2. Do you think that these partnerships will become more influential and/or effective as more companies begin to use this form of advertising to reach their consumers? Do you think that artist–corporate partnerships might become more effective than other sources of advertising, such as television or online ads?

3. The author brought up the idea of "Matt and Kim" as being sellouts. Do you think this is an appropriate description of these artists?

4. What was the author's purpose for describing Stone and Cohen's experience in the field of advertising?

5. You'll notice that this essay doesn't have a Works Cited page. What genres and formats have different rules for citations? Why?

CONNECTING TO YOUR CULTURE

1. Have you seen or participated in any corporate-sponsored music events like the events the author mentions (the Green Label Sound tour sponsored by Mountain Dew, the FADER Fort)? Have these events made you more inclined to purchase these brands? Why or why not?

2. What are your favorite music artists; have they collaborated with corporations? If so, in what way?

CONSIDERING IDEAS

1. What technologies do you use in your daily life? How important are they to you?

2. Which of the technologies you use have advertising built in or included in them? Why do you think these ads are built in?

3. What do you think about these ads? Do they affect you in any way?

AUTHOR BIO

Wilson Rothman is the deputy science and technology editor at msnbc.com. Prior to writing at msnbc.com, Rothman worked as a tech correspondent for The New York Times and was a features editor for the blog Gizmodo. This essay first appeared in msnbc.com's Technolog, where Rothman writes about all things tech related.

AMAZON SELLING KINDLE WITH ADS FOR $114

Wilson Rothman

Amazon found a way to shave $25 more dollars off the price of the Wi-Fi Kindle: It's selling ads.

The new edition, which bears the awkward name "Kindle with Special Offers," has two differentiating functions: Delivering Amazon special offers to you, and popping ads up as screensavers where those tranquil etchings used to appear.

The offers are pretty nice. In the first few weeks, Amazon says, "examples" of offers include:

- $10 for $20 Amazon.com Gift Card
- $6 for 6 Audible Books (normally $68)
- $1 for an album in the Amazon MP3 Store (choose from over 1 million albums)
- $10 for $30 of products in the Amazon Denim Shop or Amazon Swim Shop

A full list of the current offers will be accessible from the new Kindle's main menu, says Amazon. The company also says that while the first wave of deals will be for the retailer itself, there will also be deals outside of Amazon in the coming months, once they talk up the program with partners.

Kindle owners are already signed-on-the-dotted-line Amazon customers—that's kinda the whole point of Kindle's e-book system—so these offers make a lot of sense. In fact, people who spent $139 or more on their Kindle may be upset that theirs won't occasionally offer up some instant savings on other Amazon items.

But the ads, well, those may not be so desirable.

As you can see above, they pop up where literary and artistic screensavers currently appear. Launch partners include Visa, Olay, Buick, and Chase. Back in 2005, we all whined about ads showing up on our phones, but when "Angry Birds" was offered to us for free in the Android Market, we downloaded it by the millions, ads and all.

AP PHOTO/MARK LENNIHAN

Still, is the price of our attention a lousy $25? I think there's plausibly a day when Kindles will actually be free—at least with a sizable up-front purchase of e-books, plus recurring ads and offers. But even if that day is far off, why is this product *not* $99? That's the next sweet spot, and it's a shocker that all of the injected marketing couldn't bring the price to that level.

Amazon may not have pushed the price down below $100, but the company is trying to make the ads themselves more palatable to users. It will soon release a Kindle app and website called AdMash that basically lets you vote on ads, using the Hot-or-Not principle where you identify which of two prospective screens looks better. Part of me wants to compliment Amazon for being so considerate in their approach to their advertisees. (Even though it's advertising, the process sounds highly addictive.) But part of me feels like it's asking us to choose the poison that will be dumped into our wells.

So what are your thoughts? Is $25 off, plus the promise of sweet Amazon treats, good enough for you? Or are you holding out for a $99 price tag before you cut off a little piece of your pride?

Source: *Excerpted from "Amazon Selling Kindle with Ads for $114" by Wilson Rothman from Technolog,* http://technolog.msnbc.msn.com/_news/2011/04/11/6453284-amazon-selling-kindle-with-ads-for-114. *Used with permission.*

DECODING THE TEXT

1. What was the author's main point in this essay? What rhetorical strategies did the author use to convey this point?

2. Rothman mentions apps such as Angry Birds, which are free but come with ads, and notes that we download them by the millions. Is this a fair comparison? Why or why not?

CONNECTING TO YOUR CULTURE

1. Do you imagine that, much like Amazon's AdMash site, advertising in the future will be based more on user reviews? Have you seen this development in other technologies you use (Hulu, Google)?

2. What new forms of advertising have you seen recently, much like the Kindle with ads?

3. How does the idea of Kindle ads connect back to Bob's complaint about ads in books? Is it the same? Why or why not?

CONTEMPLATIONS IN THE POP CULTURE ZONE

1. Take a minute to reflect on some current ads for specific women's and men's products. How well do these ads reflect the lives of men and women today? Are there ads that are more gender neutral? How can you tell? How well do any of these ads reflect your life? The demographics of your school or town?

2. *Advertising Age* created the following top ten advertising icons list:

    1. The Marlboro Man—Marlboro cigarettes
    2. Ronald McDonald—McDonald's restaurants
    3. The Green Giant—Green Giant vegetables
    4. Betty Crocker—Betty Crocker food products
    5. The Energizer Bunny—Eveready Energizer batteries
    6. The Pillsbury Dough Boy—assorted Pillsbury foods

7. Aunt Jemima—Aunt Jemima pancake mixes and syrup
8. The Michelin Man—Michelin tires
9. Tony the Tiger—Kellogg's Frosted Flakes
10. Elsie—Borden dairy products

Do you agree with this list? Create your own top ten list for icons or some other characteristic (best music in a commercial, top ten food jingles, top ten ways to sell shampoo).

3. Have you ever tried to sell something (a product, a service, your own skills)? What words and/or graphics did you use? What colors and layout? What image of your product were you trying to convey?

4. Make a list of ads you have seen for recent movies or television shows. How can you tell the intended audience(s) of the ad? Does it match the intended audience(s) of the movie or TV show itself? Why would advertisers advertise to more than one audience? How do they make these decisions? How do they make the ads different for the different audiences?

COLLABORATIONS IN THE POP CULTURE ZONE

1. In a small group, discuss your opinions about the ethical and legal obligations of advertisers—both the ad agencies that create the advertisements and the companies that hire them. Should advertisers have to give the public an accurate and unbiased reflection of themselves? Should advertisers be held responsible if they do not show women and minorities positively? Do advertisers have to be politically correct? If you were to flip through a magazine or glance at the billboards along the highway, would it be a problem if all of the ads only showed young, upper-class, white models?

2. Discuss why some celebrities choose to make commercials only in other countries—for example, Bill Murray's character in the film *Lost in Translation* or Matt LeBlanc's character, Joey, in the TV sitcom *Friends*. Why would they make such a choice? Does this affect the person's status in the United States? Should it? Now that the Internet makes so many of these foreign commercials available to U.S. consumers, do you think some celebrities will change their policies?

3. As a group, select a particular type of product or service: MP3 players, deodorant, beer, insurance. Then look at a variety of different types of magazines and newspapers to find multiple examples of ads for your chosen product. Compare the ads from various sources. Can you guess the audience for the magazine by looking at the ad? What ad characteristics serve as clues (or not)? Are there ads you would change to better address different populations?

4. Product packaging is another form of advertising, even though many may not think about it in that way. As a group, collect packaging for several different brands of the same type of product. What information does the packaging include? How is it set up? Is one package more appealing than another? Why or why not? Does the packaging include a trade character? Celebrity endorsement? Other types of images? What difference do things such as directions or nutrition information make? What about colors and font choices? What types of regulations govern this information?

START WRITING ABOUT ADVERTISEMENTS

Reviews or Review Essays

1. Using an ad in this text or one of your own choosing, write a review of the advertisement. To help you get started, you may want to look at some additional ad reviews in business and marketing magazines as well as texts that take a sociological or interdisciplinary approach. Choose a specific publication to help you begin.

2. Choose an ad that you really like or one that you really dislike. Write a letter or email to the advertising agency that developed the ad; share with the agency executives your review of the advertisement and why you like or dislike the ad. Be sure to give specific details from the ad to support your opinion.

3. Choose a subvertisement created by a social or political agency, such as Adbusters, PETA, or *TheTruth.com*. Review this ad and explain whether or not you think the subvertisement is a good idea and achieves it purpose. What makes the ad work (or not)? Give specific details from the actual ad.

Reflection or Response Essays

1. In "Licensed to Shill," David Browne reports that musicians may be selling out:

   > Last year's [2000] flirty intermingling of pop music and Madison Avenue will go down in the history books, but not for the reasons you think. Yes, it was disconcerting to see Sting shill for Jaguar or 'N Sync have it their way with Burger King; "selling out" now seems a quainter notion than a less-than-$50 concert ticket. But in reality, rock stars have been pitchmen before: In the '80s, Eric Clapton pimped for beer as Michael Jackson moonwalked for soda.

   Do you consider it selling out when musicians sign over their music for radio and television commercials? Have you ever bought an artist's CD because you heard his or her music in an ad? What about when you heard a new artist on a television show or in a movie? Is this the same thing as using a song in a commercial?

2. In her essay about the television show *Mad Men*, Joy Parks notes that the show has inspired a "retro trend in designer menswear." What role do you think film and television play in selling an image of what a properly dressed man or woman looks like? Does this include selling particular designers or brands? Have you ever been influenced to dress a certain way or buy a particular product because of what you saw on the screen? Why? Did the character influence you? The events happening to this character? The time period? How did this advertising affect your life?

3. When you look at print ads or television commercials, do you see yourself and your life represented? If yes, describe an advertisement that represents you and explain how this makes you feel. If no, why not? Are you not looking hard enough, or are the advertisers leaving you out? Why do you think this is happening? What would an ad that represents you look or sound like?

4. Have you ever had a radio jingle stick in your head? What about the jingle appealed to you or made the sound and words stick with you? What would you consider the best jingles you have heard? What made these jingles memorable?

5. As James Twitchell mentions, the Marlboro Man campaign spawned a whole line of Marlboro and cowboy products, including clothes, camping gear, and cookbooks. People have spent a lot of their own money to further advertise the Marlboro name. Coca-Cola has done the same thing with a variety of images and campaigns. What do you think about this pattern or approach to advertising? Do you think it was part of the original marketing plan for Marlboro? Have other brands and companies done the same thing? Do you spend your money to advertise brands for others? If so, what types of products are you advertising? If not, why not?

Analysis Essays

1. Choose a trade character from a single advertisement or an ad campaign and write a profile of that trade character or create its Facebook or Twitter profile. Does your character meet the characteristics delineated by Barbara Phillips? What is the purpose of your trade character? What appeals or needs are being met by this character? Would you change anything about this character?

2. Examine three or four different magazines, and look at the ads targeted specifically to men (for example, cologne or clothing ads) or kids (for example, toys or music). Do these ads show any new trends in the way advertisers attempt to appeal to specific consumers? Discuss any trends that you observe. What do you think is the reason behind these trends?

3. Visit a few of your favorite websites, and notice the web banners. What kinds of products do different types of websites promote? Are there any common features among web banners? Are the banners the same for everyone or targeted toward you and your preferences? How do they know your preferences? How effective must a banner be to sell the intended product or service? How do you define "effective"? How do web banners compare to other types of advertisements? Use specific examples to support your analysis.

4. Choose a product or service that is advertised in multiple ways, perhaps in print and in television commercials. Compare and contrast the two or more types of ads. Some commercials have short versions and long versions for different kinds of advertising spots. What changes do the advertisers have to make when they move from one type or length of advertisement to another? Is one medium or style more effective than another? Why or why not?

5. Create a billboard slogan for yourself. What does the text below your slogan or catchphrase say? What does it look like? What images? What colors? Remember that billboards have to be taken in quickly by viewers as they are driving down the road.

Synthesis Essays

1. Imagine you are part of a citizens' group working to improve the quality of advertising in your community. What kinds of local ads do you see and hear? What recommendations would you make, and what standards would you want to see enforced? Be specific. Illustrate your argument with local ads you find that meet or fall below your expectations.

2. Create a new mascot for a product with which you are familiar. It is your job to convince readers and company executives that your mascot is the best way to sell their product. Your essay will include a visual element as well as a written version of your sales pitch. What form(s) will you choose to introduce your new mascot? Magazine ads, television commercials, radio spots, billboards, web banners, or other forms and venues? Who is the audience for this new mascot? What appeals will you use to sell your new mascot and the product the mascot is supporting?

3. As mentioned previously, *Advertising Age* has created a top ten advertising icons list; they also created lists for the top slogans, jingles, and ad campaigns. Use your own criteria to create a top ten list. Explain your criteria and your top ten choices. If you want, you can create a sort of anti-top ten list in the style of David Letterman. Be sure to use specific examples to illustrate your criteria and your choices. You may want to make this list multimedia and put it on Tumblr or Pinterest.

4. Compile a list of local media outlets that sell advertising space. Contact some of them from a variety of different media, and request their sales information: rate cards, demographics, sample ads or ad guidelines, whatever they have to offer. Then decide on a social issue that is important to you and that you would like to inform others about. Compare the costs and benefits of the various media and discuss which outlet would give you the best value for your advertising money. You may stop here or go to the next step of designing and proposing an ad campaign; do not forget the budget for your campaign.

5. Analyze the ads shown from the various Volkswagen ad campaigns from the last fifty years (pages 186–187). Do the ads appear to be targeting particular audiences? What magazines do you think the various ads appeared in? What television shows ran the commercials the stills are taken from? What appeal is each ad using? Can you distinguish the subvertisements from the advertisements? How can you tell? How do you think Volkswagen responds to the parodies of their ads? Create your own subvertisement for Volkswagen (or some other product).

It's money in the bank...

Volkswagen

Volkswagenwerk GmbH

RABBIT. THE #1 SELLING IMPORT IN JAPAN.

The Japanese obviously know a good thing when they see one. And so more people in Japan are buying Volkswagen Rabbits than any other imported car. Fascinating. But not astonishing.

The Rabbit has more total room than any Japanese car in its class. The Rabbit hops from 0 to 50 mph in 8.3 seconds.

Most Japanese cars don't.

If you're interested in superior handling and maneuverability, you'll get them in a Rabbit, because the Rabbit has front-wheel drive.

Most Japanese cars don't.

If you're interested in economy, a VW Rabbit with a diesel engine got the highest mileage of any car in America for 1978: 53mpg on the highway, 40mpg in the city.

The gasoline Rabbit is no slouch, either, with 38mpg on the highway, 25mpg in the city.

(EPA estimates, with standard transmission. Your own mileage may vary, depending on how and where you drive, your car's condition and optional equipment.)

In short, the Rabbit delivers precisely what thoughtful people anywhere want in a car: performance, room, handling, economy.

So next time you have a yen for a terrific sukiyaki dinner, drive to the restaurant in a Rabbit. And enjoy the best of both worlds.

VOLKSWAGEN DOES IT AGAIN

1980 RABBIT DIESEL NEW YORK TO WASHINGTON ON ONLY 10 GALLONS

AND BACK!

No, we're not kidding. You could actually zip from Lincoln Center all the way to the Lincoln Memorial and back (about 466 miles), on just 10 gallons with a Rabbit Diesel.

Rabbit Diesels are the top two mileage cars in the country. In fact, the 5-speed version gets an EPA estimated 42 mpg, 56 estimated highway. The 4-speed gets an enviable 40 estimated mpg, 52 estimated highway.

(Use "estimated miles per gallon" for comparisons. Your actual mileage may vary with speed, weather and trip length. Highway mileage will probably be less.)

And don't forget, a Rabbit comes with traditional Volkswagen craftsmanship, front-wheel drive, loads of room for people and things, and also happens to be the least expensive Diesel you'll find anywhere.

All that, plus the #1 mileage record in the country.

Add it up, and not only is the Diesel the choicest candidate of the year, the Rabbit is the choicest Diesel.

So the next time you're considering trading Fifth Avenue for Pennsylvania Avenue, consider doing it in a 1980 Rabbit Diesel.

It'll get you something no other car available in the country can get you on only 10 gallons.

Home.

VOLKSWAGEN DOES IT AGAIN

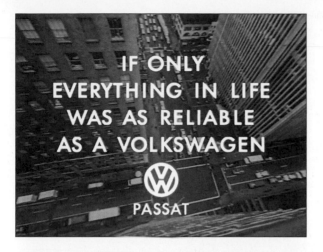

IF ONLY
EVERYTHING IN LIFE
WAS AS RELIABLE
AS A VOLKSWAGEN

PASSAT

Volkswagen recycling

Volkswagen. Wie anders?

The New Beetle Cabriolet.

Less cars, more world. Drivers wanted.

Small but tough. Polo.

7

writing about film

"Life goes by pretty fast. If you don't stop and look around once in a while, you could miss it."

—From *Ferris Bueller's Day Off*

Choose the film or film series that features each quote.

1. "May the force be with you."

a. *Dark Knight* film series
b. *Harry Potter* film series
c. *Star Wars* film series
d. *Twilight* film series

2. "Not to be rude or anything, but this isn't a great time to have a house elf in my bedroom."

a. *The Lord of the Rings: The Two Towers*
b. *The Princess and the Frog*
c. *The Chronicles of Narnia: The Lion, the Witch, and the Wardrobe*
d. *Harry Potter and the Chamber of Secrets*

3. "To infinity, and beyond!"

a. *Independence Day*
b. *Star Trek*
c. *Top Gun*
d. *Toy Story*

4. "You're gonna need a bigger boat . . ."

a. *Titanic*
b. *Poseidon Adventure*
c. *Pirates of the Caribbean: The Curse of the Black Pearl*
d. *Jaws*

5. "There's a storm coming, Mr. Wayne. You and your friends better batten down the hatches, because when it hits, you're all gonna wonder how you ever thought you could live so large and leave so little for the rest of us."

a. *Spiderman*
b. *The Dark Knight Rises*
c. *The Avengers*
d. *Iron Man*

6. "Hey, Cameron. You realize if we played by the rules right now, we'd be in gym?"

a. *Scream*
b. *Pretty in Pink*
c. *Heathers*
d. *Ferris Bueller's Day Off*

7. "I didn't want to have to do this, but you leave me no choice. Here comes the smolder."

a. *Tangled*

b. *Beauty and the Beast*

c. *The Little Mermaid*

d. *The Princess and the Frog*

WALT DISNEY PRODUCTIONS/ALBUM/NEWSCOM

8. "All right, nobody move! I've got a dragon and I'm not afraid to use it!"

a. *Reign of Fire*

b. *Shrek*

c. *Lord of the Rings: The Two Towers*

d. *How to Train Your Dragon*

9. "I had a dream my life would be so different from this hell I'm living!"

a. *Zero Dark Thirty*

b. *Argo*

c. *Les Misérables*

d. *Silver Linings Playbook*

10. **Stump Your Instructor:** In small groups, write a question here with a quotation from a popular film. Give your instructor five choices for answers.

a.

b.

c.

d.

e.

YOU AND FILM

On the surface, films entertain us and allow us to escape from our everyday lives; we can laugh with Zach Galifianakis and cry with Meryl Streep and finish a film with a sense of completion. However, films can do more than just entertain us; they can also represent us and inform us. Sometimes, all we want from a film is mindless entertainment, and sometimes, we use films to provoke us into action. Often, we do not think deeply about the content of a film or the way the film was made, but certain films just beg us to take that step into deep thought, discussion, and action. The readings and writing assignments in this chapter represent the many ways films are part of our lives.

Films are usually made for artistic or monetary reasons or a combination of both. The film industry makes billions of dollars in profits annually from films shown in theaters and even more from DVD sales and marketing tie-ins. It is an unusual film that qualifies as both artistic and as a moneymaker, but this does not stop the engines behind artistic or independent filmmaking. What makes a film artistic? Is it the direction, the cinematography, the costumes, the acting, the content, the marketing? What makes a film a blockbuster? Is it just the money a film makes, or is it the way a film connects in some way to us or our culture? Why do we sometimes distinguish between *films* and *movies*, for example, by calling *Lincoln* a film but *Shrek* a movie? Why are some films more appealing across age groups or genders? Why are some films awarded artistic awards while others become that year's highest grossing films? These are some of the questions you will investigate in this chapter; the answers to these and other questions you create will help you focus on film as a starting point to writing. The readings and writing assignments provided will help you figure out which questions are important to you, and the introductory information in this chapter will help you write about those questions and your own individual answers.

WHY WRITE ABOUT FILM?

Writing about film teaches you to see something familiar in a new and different way. Although some critics argue that writing about individual scenes of a film destroys the beauty of the whole for the viewer, analyzing films allows you to become aware of film elements that you may not have appreciated before. It teaches you to be aware of and look for certain characteristics that you might value in the films that you watch. Sometimes, focusing on film at a deep and critical level can be difficult, but with the availability of DVDs and other types of digital viewing, film has become much easier to study. Many writers find that analyzing film increases and enhances their later film-watching experiences.

PREPARING TO WRITE ABOUT FILM

Films are an important part of our culture, a way to bring people together, to entertain, to inform, and to stimulate critical thinking. However, when you watch films for a class or a writing assignment, you will need to view the films in a way that is probably different from how you normally view them.

Watching and Thinking

As you have already discovered, there are many different reasons to write about film. Likewise, there are many different methods of experiencing a film, all of which may influence your overall impression: Where and when did you see it—big screen, DVD, streaming, stadium seating, art house? How much did it cost you? Who watched the film with you? Why did you see the film? Is the film genre, director, or lead actor or actress one of your favorites?

When you view a film specifically for the purpose of writing about it, you can prepare beforehand. Ask questions about the film: What are people saying about it? What do you already know about the film? How does the film connect to your interests? Consider your expectations going in, especially with regard to technology, budget, genre, intended audience, actor reputation, or director reputation. Take some preliminary notes about what you know and your expectations for the film; you will then have them to compare to your reactions after seeing it.

As you watch the film, question what you see and hear and respond to it. Look and listen for key moments in the film, such as Ferris Bueller singing on the parade float. Also look and listen for key patterns and images, such as the feather slowly drifting down in *Forrest Gump* or the blood going down the drain in *Psycho*. Think about what seems unfamiliar or different within the film.

When possible, it is best to watch the film once for the full effect without taking any notes and then to take notes on subsequent viewings. However, sometimes you cannot watch a film more than once, and you'll have to take notes as you watch. Develop your own form of shorthand or system of abbreviations, so you can take notes without missing parts of the film. It is especially important to note technical aspects of the film you may want to come back to. The first time you watch the musical *Hairspray,* for example, you may jot down the names of the different dances the characters do or at least take down a short description of them so you can go back later and analyze particular camera movements during different dances. You can also annotate or sketch key scenes by taking down short bursts of dialogue or noting character dress for a key scene. What would the ending of *Grease* be without Sandy changing to uncharacteristic clothing? This is an example of something that pops out at you in your first viewing. Shortly after your viewing, fill in your notes. As you elaborate, you will be able to make additional connections to other parts of the film and add examples to key points or patterns.

Many disciplines use film in their instruction and education. Scientists record hours of data for experimental purposes, and musicians use long-format music videos to visually express their sound.

- What role has film played or could it play in your role as a student?

- How about in your current job or in jobs you have had in the past?

- How about in your future occupation?

- When was the film made? Check the closing credits or a film biography.

- Are you familiar with the time period(s) the film represents?

- Where was the film made? Check the closing credits or a film biography.

- What settings or locations are represented in the film?

- Who are the main characters? Secondary characters? Seemingly nonessential characters?

- Are there any scenes, props, or locations that are unfamiliar or unique?

- How does the title relate to the location, storyline, or characters?

- How are the opening credits formatted and revealed to the viewer?

- How does the first scene begin? What is the transition between the credits and this first scene?

- Is this film similar to or different from other films you have watched for class or outside class?

- Did you notice anything about the camera movements? Are there particular scenes that have zoomed in or jumpy images? Are there camera angles that highlight certain characters, locations, or props?

- How does the soundtrack contribute to the film?

- What is the concluding scene or image in the film?

After the film, you can also reflect on what you have seen or heard and on what you have noted. You can even compare these to your previewing notes. As you reflect, think about how your previous viewing experiences affected this viewing, how your belief or value systems affect your viewing, and how your politics affect your viewing. You can also jot down the emotional impact the film has on you; doing this right after you view the film may help you write a more personal response to the film, if you are asked to do so for a class assignment.

As you reflect and make connections in your notes, you can also consider the context of the film itself and do some research: What is the historical background of the film? What were the politics of the time? What were the film regulations of the time? Likewise, consider the film's use or abuse of standard storyline conventions. Again, consider how you experienced the film: Were you reading subtitles or listening to a dubbed audio? Was it on DVD or on your iPod and formatted to fit your screen? Was the theater too hot or cold? Was your neighbor's cell phone ringing throughout the film? Were people talking—to each other, to the characters in the film? Were you disturbed by others text messaging?

Asking questions and reflecting on your viewing experience will help you select and describe relevant details related to key points or elements in the film. Use these details to build your interpretation or analysis of the film. You may also find the need to conduct outside research as you build your argument and support your thesis.

Watching, Analyzing, and Understanding

As you begin to write about film, you might find it helpful to know the language of film production and analysis. In the following sections, you will find brief summaries of the key elements, along with lists of technical terms that you may find useful. Of course, this is not an exhaustive list or description; if you want to know more, see one of the many texts devoted to film criticism and analysis. And, remember, when you write about films, you can focus on the technical aspects or you can focus on how you related to the film. For an analysis essay, knowing the technical terms is important; however, for a personal reflection or response essay, do not get distracted from your own feelings about the film by the technical elements.

CHARACTERS

It is quite common for writers to focus on the development or description of *characters* when writing about film. What would the *Pirates of the Caribbean* film franchise be without Johnny Depp's character, Captain Jack Sparrow? A close reading of a major or minor character can provide many supporting examples for an analysis or synthesis essay or can be the starting point for establishing connections between the character and the writer for a reflection or response essay. Writers often focus on the chronological story of the character's life, referred to as the *arc* of a character or story. In both *Rambo* and *Pretty Woman*, for example, the arc of the character's life has important information about the character's past. How Rambo became a mercenary fighter and how Vivian became a prostitute are key to understanding their characters. Writers who analyze characters deeply usually look at how realistic or stereotypical the character or the character's story is, how the backdrop or clothing or lighting helps define the character, how the character fits in with other characters in the story, and whether the character experiences some kind of change during the progression of the storyline.

WALT DISNEY PRODUCTIONS/THE KOBAL COLLECTION/PICTURE DESK

CINEMATOGRAPHY

Cinematography concerns how the film that viewers see is produced. The cinematographer works with the director and makes decisions about types of lenses, camera positions, and lighting to provide a unique and memorable design for each particular film. The cinematographer also chooses the type of film to be used because different types of film, along with different filming speeds, can affect how the film looks and indicate mood or atmosphere. Consider the film *Pleasantville*, where the focus of the entire film is the juxtaposition of the present day shown in color and the 1950s presented in black and white. Pay attention to the use of light and shadow and the lighting of certain scenes or characters at different times; it is the cinematographer's job to manipulate light and shadow based on how the director wants the scene to look. Also look at how the camera is used. How are close-ups used? Are there scenes when the camera zooms in or zooms out? Are there scenes when camera angles—or points of view—help create the mood or help develop a character? Look for any slight changes that might be deliberate, and investigate what these manipulations might mean.

COMPOSITION

In filmmaking, *composition* refers to the use of space or the shape of an image on film, including how the images are affected by light, how they are positioned in relation to each other and the setting, and how they are positioned in relation to the frame of the film. For example, in any of the *Jurassic Park* or *Transformers* movies, note how the camera backs up and then pans up and up to emphasize size, and in *Little Miss Sunshine*, watch as the camera pulls away from the van each time the family returns to the road after a rest stop. When writing about composition, you may want to look at the screen width or depth of characters, locations, or props. Consider how characters or props are placed in the foreground or background of scenes, and look at how the director angles the camera to highlight characters, locations, or props. You can also consider whether or not you are seeing the whole picture—you are not if the film has been formatted to fit your screen. Movies such as *Avatar* or *Titanic* have multiple characters in many crowd scenes, and if the film has been reformatted for your television, you may not be seeing the entire picture. You may also consider the purpose behind techniques such as split screens and reflected subjects in windows, mirrors, television screens, and so forth. Ask yourself whether or not the arrangement before you on the screen has any special significance: Why is the character always to the left side of the screen? Why are the objects in the foreground out of focus? Why are we watching the character's actions through the window? Why are we looking at the characters from above? In *Rear Window* with its main character in a wheelchair or *Disturbia* with its main character under house arrest, the physical location and position of the character is what guides the entire plot.

CRITICAL OR IDEOLOGICAL APPROACH

When you write an analysis essay, your instructor might introduce a *critical* or *ideological approach* to help you view and dissect a film. For example, she might focus on an approach that utilizes political and social theories, perhaps looking for the postcolonial influence in the latest Bollywood film from India. Film analysis might also utilize historical approaches that consider the social and political climate of the culture and time period presented in a film or the climate of the film as it was produced, such as looking at the presentation of gay characters after the Stonewall riots in 1969. Such a historical perspective might also consider the history or biography of the director, as well as the history of his or her body of work. This biographical method could lead you to auteur criticism, which looks at the director or actor as the author or responsible party of a film and then looks for patterns from a director throughout his or her body of work. When you say that you always enjoy Spike Lee, Judd Apatow, or Meryl Streep films, you are looking at each of these directors or actors as an auteur—you are noting how each embodies his or her own style. Other critical lenses that may be used to examine the content and purpose of a film include psychoanalytic models and theories, feminist and queer theories, and cognitive models. Any of the critical lenses used in other disciplines may be brought to bear on a film and its production. Ask yourself if history has been distorted in some way. Ask yourself how this film was influenced by the politics of the time or what message the director is trying to convey. Ask yourself how minority characters are portrayed in this film. Ask yourself what cinematic and editorial choices were made to conform to the rating codes of the time period.

EDITING

Editing is another key element of film production. A film editor works with the director and producers to add or cut frames or scenes to preserve the storyline and to create the final form of a film. How fast scenes change, how one scene makes its transition into the next, and the use of fade-in or fade-out shots, especially at the beginning and ending of a film, can carry meaning. Look for how your reaction to the entire film or particular scenes is influenced by how the film was edited. Also look for montages, which are scenes built out of many brief shots; montages can signify that an important theme is being emphasized. In *The Breakfast Club*, the fast cutaway scenes in the hallway as the students are trying to get away from the principal give an added urgency to the viewer. Editing can tell you important things about the characters, point of view, theme, symbols, or setting, so be sure to look at how the film is put together. A good way to see the importance of editing is to compare a director's cut of a film to the original offering; *Blade Runner, Apocalypse Now*, and many other films have directors' versions available for you to investigate.

GENRE

Genre, which means "kind" in French, is another important element of film production and film analysis, as it helps viewers identify common patterns. Genre sets up audience expectations and helps audiences believe in what is presented. For instance, in action films, the bad guys are always poor shots while the good guy has almost perfect aim, and viewers usually accept this within the genre of the action film. Genre films usually have familiar or stock characters (the tobacco-chewing cowboy in westerns), filming techniques (the suspenseful music in horror films or nonstop motion in action films), themes (destructive crises or disasters in action films), or settings (historical time periods in dramas). All of these are genre film *conventions*, those recognizable features that each genre exhibits. Genre films can also be subdivided into subgenres; for instance, musical subgenres include comedy musicals (*Hairspray*), dance films (*Step Up Revolution*), concert films (*Woodstock*), and Broadway hits brought to film (*Les Misérables*). Ask yourself if this film is following its generic conventions as *Saw* does—what would *Saw* be without its suspenseful music, its killer brought back to life, or its perceived killer not being the real killer? Or does the film have mixed genres as *Blazing Saddles* does when it combines the conventions of westerns and comedies together? Or does it try to avoid genre conventions or poke fun at them— perhaps commenting on genres themselves, such as in the films *Scream* or *The Cabin in the Woods*? Sometimes, directors and producers use genre to target specific audiences, such as those who like sports or who have an interest in history. Filmmakers often also combine genres to bring a film to a wider audience.

Established genres and subgenres include the films from recent decades as shown in Table 7-1 on the next page.

Table 7-1.

FILM GENRES	SUBGENRES	EXAMPLES
Action/Adventure	Alien Invasion	*Battle: Los Angeles*
	Buddy Cops	*Lethal Weapon*
	Epic Adventure	*300*
	Disaster	*Titanic*
	Revenge	*Kill Bill Vol. I & II*
	Comic Book	*The Avengers*
	Teen Comedy	*Ferris Bueller's Day Off*
Biography	Historical	*The King's Speech*
	Musical	*Ray*
	Sports	*Ali*
Comedy	Mockumentary	*Best in Show*
	Parody	*The Cabin in the Woods*
	Fish-Out-of-Water	*Bad Teacher*
	Group	*Bridesmaids*
Crime/Gangster	Film Noir	*L.A. Confidential*
	Organized Crime	*Scarface*
	Prison	*The Shawshank Redemption*
	Caper	*Tower Heist*
Drama	Coming of Age	*Moonrise Kingdom*
	Social Problem	*Silver Linings Playbook*
	Sports	*The Blind Side*
Epic/Historical	Biblical	*Passion of the Christ*
	Greek	*Spartacus*
	Historical	*War Horse*
	Medieval	*King Arthur*
Horror	Slasher	*Texas Chainsaw Massacre*
	Zombie	*Zombieland*
	Teen Terror	*Friday the 13th*
	Psychological	*Shutter Island*
	Parody	*Scream*
Musical	Comedy Musical	*Hairspray*
	Dance Film	*Footloose*
	Broadway Hit	*Les Misérables*
	Concert Film	*Woodstock*
	Musical Biography	*Walk the Line*
Paranormal	Vampires	*Twilight*
	Werewolves	*An American Werewolf in London*
	Witchcraft	*Beautiful Creatures*
	Ghosts	*Amityville Horror*
Romance	Coming of Age	*Pretty in Pink*
	Historical	*Tristan and Isolde*
	Romantic Comedy	*Crazy, Stupid, Love*
	Star-Crossed	*Romeo and Juliet*
Science Fiction	Alien Encounters	*Cowboys & Aliens*
	Disaster	*The Day After Tomorrow*
	Dystopia	*The Adjustment Bureau*
	Outer Space	*Star Wars*
War	Civil War	*Lincoln*
	Revolutionary War	*The Patriot*
	Aerial Combat	*Top Gun*
	Action Combat	*The Hurt Locker*
Western	Epic Western	*Dances with Wolves*
	Outlaws	*Young Guns*
	Cattle Drive	*City Slickers*
	Spoof Westerns	*Blazing Saddles*

MISE-EN-SCÈNE

Mise-en-scène (meez ahn sen) refers to the items put before the camera, and the way they are placed, as the director prepares for filming. These items include the setting and subjects and the composition of both. Mise-en-scène, also known as production design, is a very important element of film production. Choices made about setting (Hogwarts for the *Harry Potter* franchise), subjects (Bo Derek's braided hair in *10*), and composition (the distance between white and black dancers in *Hairspray*) can make political and/or social comments. Likewise, they can pay tribute to other films or film techniques—even through parody, as in the *Scary Movie* franchise. However, some choices are more economic, as props and costumes can be used to promote businesses, products, and skills. Consider the choices of the Wilson soccer ball in *Cast Away*, the Aston Martin cars in James Bond movies, or Reese's Pieces in *E.T., the Extra-Terrestrial.* Just think of how many times you have seen a film character drinking from a can of Coke or Pepsi. Of course, this capitalistic characteristic of filmmaking can be another area for research and analysis.

GRAPPLING with ideas

We all have our personal favorites when it comes to films or movies. Think about those you have really enjoyed and answer the following questions.

- What is your favorite film genre?

- What are some of your favorite films that make up that genre?

- What is it about these films that you enjoy? Give examples.

SETTING

Setting is where the filmed action occurs and may include a manufactured set in a studio or a natural location. The setting includes the props used for the background and action, the colors of the props and the background, and the arrangement of the props. This setting may be realistic or imaginary and may be digitally enhanced after filming. The setting usually implies time, space, and place and may enhance style, character, mood, and meaning. The setting may even become or be symbolic of a character in the film. Ask yourself whether or not the objects and the props in the setting carry particular meanings or significance: Why does Katniss use a bow and arrow in *The Hunger Games*? Why are the buildings dark with sharp edges in *Inception*? Why is it always raining in *Blade Runner*?

SOUND

Sound also serves numerous functions in a film. It can set the scene, add emotions, serve as background filler, cover for weak acting, create continuity from scene to scene, and direct attention or emphasize climaxes. The soundtrack itself can have four components: spoken words, which include dialogues, monologues, and narration; sound effects, which are sounds made by objects or people—such as the sounds of walking or background sound like the wind blowing; music, which can be instrumental, vocal, or a combination of the two; and silence. Some of these four types of sound can be overlapped or distorted for a special effect that a director is seeking. Additionally, the soundtrack can be created with commercial value in mind, sometimes more than its value to the film. Ask yourself how the sound affects your experience of the film. How would *Beauty and the Beast* be without its songs? How would *The Artist* be without its silent-film star? If possible, watch part of a film without any sound and see how it affects you differently.

Watching, Researching, and Documenting

If you are writing a reflection or response essay, your instructor may not require you to do any outside research. If possible, though, watch the film at least a few times prior to writing your reflection or response. You may, however, want to do some outside research to write a convincing and well-supported review or analysis of a film.

Areas of research may include the following:

- The author's/director's life
- The author's/director's body of work
- The historical background of the movie itself, of the events portrayed in the film, film-production codes at the time, technology at the time the film was made, and so forth
- The culture represented or presented in the film
- How others received the film
- The economic history or budget of the film
- The original source for the screenplay
- The history or development of techniques
- The evolution of particular genres or conventions

Of course, the type of research you will do depends on the questions you want answered, so start there: What do you want or need to know to complete your analysis of a given film or group of films? Go back to your preliminary notes and observations. What do you need to fill in? How do you want to narrow your focus? As you conduct your research, be open to new ideas and interpretations that may arise, but still proceed with some type of plan or questions to answer. Once you have completed your research, you may want to view the film a few more times and look for additional examples to support your claims or test the ideas you have read about and want to incorporate in your analysis.

Your research can lead you to a variety of primary and secondary sources; for more information on using sources in your writing about film, see Chapter 5. Naturally, your first source is the film itself. Films are available in many ways—on DVD, DVR, cable, Netflix, or online—and this has made it easier to access many films, even older films. However you view the film, you need to keep in mind that you may not be viewing the film as it was intended to be seen and that changes in format can distort the quality of the film, including its size, clarity, and color, as well as distorting the soundtrack or even the final cut. Furthermore, you do not get the same experience when you watch a film on a television in your home as you do when you watch it on a large screen in a theater. You can investigate how the film was originally presented, and this may help you find a topic to discuss in your essay. The ability to stop and start films can aid in the close analysis process. Published scripts, and sometimes unpublished scripts if you can find a cooperative production company, can also help with the research process, especially if they contain director notes or interviews and other such extraneous information. Many films on DVD also have commentary from directors, producers, actors, and others associated with the film.

As with any research project, secondary sources can be found in a number of places, usually only limited by what has actually been published and by your imagination. You may find books, articles, and websites about your film, the director, the genre, the techniques used, and other aspects of the film. Make sure you check out your library's holdings as well as the electronic databases available through your school or public libraries, such as Academic OneFile (previously known as InfoTrac), LexisNexis, JSTOR, or the MLA International Bibliography. You may also want to check out the databases and indexes (many only available in print) specifically related to film, such as *The International Film Index, 1895–1990*, or other reference sources such as dictionaries and encyclopedias devoted to film: *The Film Encyclopedia* or *The Complete Film Dictionary*, for example. Use the tables of contents and the indexes in the sources you find to make sure they have relevant information.

As with many pop culture topics, you often have to look outside the traditional sources for additional information. The Internet has numerous worthwhile sites, but be sure to evaluate the site and its purpose before you trust it as a reliable source. Of course, Miramax or Disney will only have good things to say about their latest blockbuster, but a site with an educational or analytical focus will probably give a more balanced review and provide more actual analysis. Some sites to check out, whether for basic facts, reviews, archives, or analysis, include the following:

The American Film Institute	http://www.afi.com
Film Studies—University of Alberta	http://www.humanities.ualberta.ca/english/
Independent Film Channel	http://www.ifc.com
The International Federation of Film Archives	http://www.fiafnet.org
The Internet Movie Database	http://www.imdb.com
Rotten Tomatoes	http://www.rottentomatoes.com
Screensite	http://www.screensite.org
Sundance Film Festival	http://festival.sundance.org

With all primary and secondary sources, remember to always record the citation information you will need for your Works Cited page and for your in-text citations. Record information about the film, any books or articles you read, and any websites you review. You should always know where you found your information and how to get back to it if you need to. See Chapter 5 for specific guidelines, and see the Works Cited at the end of each sample essay for examples of citations for specific sources.

WRITING ABOUT FILM

Film is an artistic medium and can be analyzed in a variety of ways, many of which you have already used to critique other media, such as advertisements or popular music. Writing about film can include a focus on different aspects of the storyline or film process or any of the genres or categories of film, such as student films, blockbusters, independent films, foreign films, documentaries, or animated films. Although there are many types of film writing, four main assignments are given in most composition or film classes: film reviews, reflection or response essays, analysis essays, or synthesis essays, which can be a combination of any of the preceding types.

Film Reviews or Review Essays

In the film review, evaluation is the focus. You are giving a judgment about the quality of the film, backed up with enough information to indicate that your judgment is based on good reasoning. These are the types of articles found in newspapers, in magazines, and on most news websites discussing films that are currently in theaters or newly released on DVD. For a class, your review will most likely be about a film that you watched in class or one that you are required to watch outside class.

Remember that most good films are not perfect, and even the worst films have good points. Some film reviews are balanced and concentrate on both the positives and negatives of the film, whereas other reviews are intentionally slanted toward an overwhelmingly positive or negative point of view. Your overall evaluation of the film can be phrased explicitly as the thesis or argument of the essay. For example, your thesis might look like this: "Although the Disney princess in *Mulan* shares many of the same traits as most other Disney princesses, the film's accurate depiction of Chinese culture makes *Mulan* one of the most impressive Disney animated features ever." However, you can also imply your thesis by providing effective supporting evidence that clearly shows what your main idea or argument is.

Film reviews follow certain conventions. Typically, a brief plot synopsis tells the main conflicts and a little about character development. Do not give a play-by-play of the entire storyline from the film. The essay is usually written in present tense (for example, "*Life of Pi* is one of Ang Lee's finest films" instead of "*Life of Pi* was one of Ang Lee's finest films"), and you do not assume that your reader is extremely familiar with the film. Reviewers hardly ever give away the ending, but if they do, they give a *spoiler alert*, a warning to readers that information that might spoil viewing the film is coming up. You can support your views by mentioning striking aspects of the film, such as impressive sets or costumes, notable visual aspects like color design or music, and acting.

FOX 2000 PICTURES/DUNE ENTERTAINMENT/INGENIOUS MEDIA/ HAISHANG FILMS / THE KOBAL COLLECTION

You can also compare the film to others in the same genre, to ones made by the same filmmaker or starring members of the cast, or to ones that have similar themes. In addition, you can show that you are familiar with a wide range of films so that your opinion is taken seriously and credibly. For instance, if you are reviewing *The Avengers,* you may want to mention other movies made from Marvel comics, especially if those movies depict some of the same characters.

Reflection or Response Essays

Although reflection or response essays will include some description of the film, the main purpose is to use the film as a starting point for your own discussion. The name of this type of essay explains the purpose fairly well. The writer can reflect on his or her own feelings that have arisen through critically watching a film, or the writer can respond to some personal issue or emotion that has arisen during the viewing of the film. Although it is important to use evidence from the film to explain why you are making your specific point, the essay mostly will be personal writing.

Writing a reflection or response essay begins when you decide what aspect of the film sparks your attention. Using this spark, you then decide what you would like to say to your audience. For example, if seeing *Brave* reminds you of challenges you encountered as child, you can use scenes from the film to introduce similar scenes from your life. A solid thesis statement explaining the purpose of the essay will help keep you on track with the film and not on a rant about the issue you are considering.

Analysis Essays

Like the film review, an analysis essay includes descriptions, but these descriptions are more detailed and extensive, and they also include an explanation of their significance. When you analyze a film, you are attempting to defend your view about how the parts of

KEY
questions

Key Qustions for a Film Review Essay

- Have you clearly indicated your judgment of the film's quality?

- Have you provided a brief plot synopsis while avoiding plot summary?

- Have you mentioned specific elements of the film that support your judgment? Have you described these quickly and vividly, using both metaphors and concrete language?

- Have you defined yourself as a credible source? Do you mention that you have seen other films by the same director or actor? Or have you cited secondary sources, if asked to do this type of research?

- Have you qualified your judgment with both positive and negative aspects of the film?

- Have you begun the review with an attention-grabbing opening? Have you concluded it with a memorable sentence or idea?

- Did you write in present tense?

Key Questions for a Reflection or Response Essay

- Have you clearly indicated how you used the film as a springboard for your thesis?

- Have you expressed your personal response to one aspect of the film?

- Did you avoid plot summary?

- Does your introduction direct your audience into your response?

- Does your concluding paragraph include some reflection on both the film and your response?

- Did you write about the film in present tense but use past tense for things that happened in the past?

- Are your intentions clear in the essay?

Key Questions for an Analysis Essay

- Do you have a strong thesis or argument?

- Do you have a series of reasons supporting the thesis? Are these arranged in a logical and convincing order?

- Are your supporting reasons backed up? Do you provide specific evidence and examples from the film for each reason you offer?

- Does your introduction orient your reader to the direction of your argument?

- Does your concluding paragraph reiterate your thesis and provide a vivid ending?

- Did you write in literary present tense?

- Did you avoid plot summary?

the film work (or do not work) together. As with any argumentative paper, you want to offer an idea have about the film and support it with evidence from the film as well as outside sources.

To write an analysis essay, you must first come up with a thesis, whether it is written explicitly in your essay or is implied by what you share in your essay. This is the main idea or argument that your essay will explain and support. Similar to the thesis in the film review, it offers your opinion, but it also helps other viewers understand the film. Typically, in a film analysis, your thesis will say something about why and how a film is made or its meaning. You also must support your thesis throughout the paper with specific evidence and examples from the film and outside resources. Analysis requires more observations about the film than description from within the film. Use details from the film only when they are needed to support your claims, and do not explain every character flaw or storyline point.

When analyzing film, remember that there may be many valid interpretations. You need to support your interpretation with specific scenes, details, or elements from the film. You may also need to support it with research about the director, the context of the film's production, or the history of the film or the film's subject matter.

Synthesis Essays

Sometimes, using personal reflections in a film review essay or using reviews or reflections in an analysis essay can make your writing much more effective. A synthesis essay can be partly one type of writing and partly another; this type of essay can be assigned by your instructor, or you can decide to mix types of writing to create the strongest essay possible. If you are writing for a class, be sure to look over the assignment and speak to the instructor if this type of mixture does not fit strictly into the directions for the assignment. Many instructors and student writers prefer the openness of a synthesized essay, which allows writers to make decisions based on what is needed for point of view, argument, support, or interest. When you choose to use a mixture of strategies, be sure to look over the key questions for the types of essay strategies you are including in your essay.

This introduction to writing about film has included ideas that may be new to you. To process them, read over the sample essay provided to see how the writing and film analysis techniques have been used.

ANNOTATED SAMPLE ESSAY

CONSIDERING IDEAS

1. Do you enjoy sci-fi? Why or why not?

2. If you've seen at least a few sci-fi films, what are some of their characteristics?

3. Do sci-fi films have a built-in audience because of their popularity in many social circles? How could this affect their production? Their budget? Their casting?

4. Are sci-fi audiences stereotypical or stereotyped?

AUTHOR BIO

Chris Driver *is a former staff writer for* Nashvillezine.com *and* Popshot.net. *His writings on film, music, and composition studies have been published in* Magazine Americana: The American Popular Culture Online Magazine, Southern Discourse, *and* COMPbiblio: Leaders and Influences in Composition Theory and Composition *(2007). He wrote the following essay while he was a student at Middle Tennessee State University.*

1968 RESONATES in 2004

2001: A Space Odyssey and the Devolution of the Science Fiction Film

Chris Driver

According to the original trailer for Ridley Scott's *Alien* (1979), "In space, no one can hear you scream." Accepting this logic, one would assume that in space, no one can hear the roaring engines of space cruisers, the percussive blasts of explosions, or the metallic screams of eroding exteriors on too-rapidly descending space ships, but this is not the case in the *Alien* "quadrilogy" of films. Why should series directors Scott, Cameron, Fincher and Jeunet have concerned themselves with details such as these? Why nitpick over continuity or technical details that probably fail to condemn these modern films but nonetheless nudge them farther from the science and closer to the fiction?

Details can often make or break a film, and science fiction directors vof the past two decades have often embraced new technologies while simultaneously adopting a lazy attitude towards realism, content to allow the technology to do all the work and to cover all the details. With his 1968 masterpiece, *2001: A Space Odyssey,* Stanley Kubrick redefined the scope and potential of science fiction film. For several pronounced reasons including Kubrick's meticulous mise-en-scène, his breakthrough approach to the passage of time in space, his use of detailed models, and his incorporation of broad philosophical themes, *2001* remains a powerful, influential work that easily trumps the majority of genre works that have followed it.

> Note how the introduction grabs the attention of the reader. What strategies does Driver use?

> Clearly stated thesis that works as a road map for the rest of the essay.

Note the specific examples from the film.

2001 creates a convincing, detailed, outer-space milieu by comprising every aspect of every shot with stunning visuals, like the sun rising over a vast, empty, prehistoric landscape, a gently rotating space station, gliding along the edge of the earth's glowing atmosphere, or an astronaut's porcelain face, reflecting rainbow colored lights from a blinking control panel. All of these intense visual scenes become unforgettable images, even after a single viewing. Kubrick utilizes a minimum of sound effects, adding to the realism of every scene, but especially to the shots of the astronauts free-floating outside the ship. When Dave ventures out (in his space suit) to retrieve the antenna that HAL has predicted will malfunction, the viewer hears nothing but Dave's rhythmic, internalized breathing, as he floats away—a single swath of bright red in a sea of blackness—along the bone-white, elongated spinal column that is the ship *Discovery*'s bow. The absence of sound effects or even music adds to the dramatic tension and creates a realism that envelops the viewer, and we too feel isolated, vulnerable, and claustrophobic. Kubrick spent a lot of time deciding on every element that makes up every shot, and it shows, but he didn't have the option that some directors have taken advantage of more recently—the option of digitally creating complete environments for their actors, an option which often results in a marked lack of realism. Two examples of this disappointing loss of realism that often accompanies the application of new, computer-based filmmaking technology to science fiction film are the most recent installments of the indefatigable *Star Wars* series. *The Phantom Menace* (1999) and *Attack of The Clones* (2002) rely so heavily on an almost entirely digitized environment (even digitally rendered characters—see the abhorrent, computer-generated Jar Jar) that realism is sacrificed, and the viewer's ability to become lost in a fantastic world is significantly compromised. Admittedly, Kubrick did not have access to the technology that made the recent *Star Wars* films possible, and one wonders what may have happened to the genre if he had. *2001* remains special, largely because of its fantastic, yet precise rendition of a believable space environment.

Focuses on sound effects with specific examples drawn from the film.

Compares *2001: A Space Odyssey* to more modern films a reader might be more familiar with.

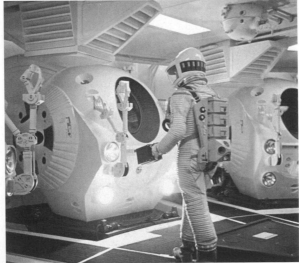

MGM/THE KOBAL COLLECTION

Another aspect of Kubrick's realistic interpretation of outer space that contributes to every viewer's absorption in *2001* is his use of intricately detailed models for all of his space cruiser scenes involving astronauts and motion. The current trend in science fiction film is to create spaceships digitally, relying completely on computer programs to create a flying, spinning, shooting star cruiser that often looks less than convincing. Films featuring this shortcut to effects are numerous; some of them include *Independence Day* (1996), *Wing Commander* (1999) and both recent *Star Wars* films, in which the space ships do not look as detailed or as realistic because of their lack of physical reality. A close look at many of these computer-generated ships reveals a pronounced lack of textural features and depth, a problem typical of a large portion of computer-created spaceships. Witnessing these computer-animated spaceships cruising across the screen has considerably less impact on the viewer, immediately prompting comments about how "fake" everything looks, and when a viewer cannot become absorbed into the fabricated reality of any film, specially a science fiction film, the movies inevitably fail. Each of Kubrick's pods and ships in *2001* are memorable because they are precisely rendered, down to the control panels, lights, buttons and knobs, a level of intricacy reminiscent of the B-52 interiors from *Dr. Strangelove* (1963). His miniatures are so detailed that when the enormous ships cruise by on the big screen, they look like entirely realistic, futuristic landscapes of technology, and disbelief is more than adequately suspended.

Discusses importance of detailed props with specific examples from the film.

Kubrick was never really in much of a hurry, often spending several years preparing for a new project (five years passed between *Dr. Strangelove* and *2001;* twelve years passed between *Full Metal Jacket* and *Eyes Wide Shut*), and his films' chronological progression and editing style are clear reminders of his steady, persistent, yet unhurried approach to filmmaking. Much has been said about Americans and their short attention spans; living in a television culture, the land of Attention Deficit Disorder (ADD) and the soundbyte newscast, we want what we want and we want it now. Kubrick was interested in slowing things down, in capturing an essence; he worked in stark contrast to the frenetic, fractured, rapid-fire editing styles of contemporary science fiction directors like Danny Boyle (*28 Days Later*) and Paul Anderson (*Resident Evil*). In *2001*, during Dr. Floyd's space travels, the details of his journey are meticulously laid out for the viewer. As he flies farther away from earth, we witness his loss of control: as he sleeps, his pen floats aimlessly in the cabin, his arm floating next to it; we watch the stewardess' careful steps in her Velcro shoes, and we note Floyd's "phone call" to his daughter, his examination of the "zero-gravity toilet" instructions, and his careful consumption of what amounts to baby food. Kubrick spares no detail, revealing for the viewer, in long, smooth tracking shots (one of his undeniable trademarks) what it is like to navigate a space station on foot, just how a smaller space ship manages to dock into a larger one, how each person on board station and cruiser meticulously performs his or her duty, and much more. Rather than assaulting the viewer with a montage of editing, Kubrick achieves a thorough, even slow, attentive shoot that focuses on the minutia. Eventually all of these smoothly edited and gently paced scenes clue the viewer in to what space travel must really feel like.

Focuses on Kubrick as auteur.

Refers to cinematography techniques and their effects, supported by specific examples from the film.

A science fiction film that truly makes an impact for generations is one that does more than create an entirely believable visual milieu. As a viewer, being able to dive into a fabricated world and actually accept its reality is a huge step, but it is only the first step required of *legendary* films. These films must be about more than space ships; they must be about ideas—they must force the viewer to think about the human condition. Kubrick did not intend to make a movie about space monsters, dogfights, and laser blasts. His themes incorporate larger philosophical questions, rather than taking an easy road and focusing on the struggle between good and evil (aliens vs. humans, Skywalker vs. Vader, etc.). Kubrick assumes a certain level of intelligence within his audience, and typically chooses not to serve up a didactic moral or ethical allegory on a silver platter. The best science fiction is patently aware of the issues, struggles, and questions that consume a human intellectual. *2001* succeeds because it speculates over human history, ponders the present, and asks questions about the future. What will human kind evolve into, and what characteristics will endure? How much of our fears, jealousies, insecurities, fallibilities, and egos will we impart to our electronic "offspring" (i.e., HAL), and what will the consequences bring? Too many modern science fiction films fail to ask questions like these, and rapidly descend into "good versus evil," slasher, hard-boiled detective, or other predictable genre fare.

> Addresses the theme of the film and the director's intent.

Stanley Kubrick's *2001: A Space Odyssey* will no doubt be analyzed and debated for years to come; this effort has barely scratched its many varied surfaces. Critics and film historians will have no shortage of material to discuss and debate when considering his monumental work. What this author hopes is that *2001*'s legacy will begin to have more of a profound and pronounced effect on the few modern directors who share an attraction to the science fiction genre. It is too late for George Lucas, but perhaps younger directors like Paul Anderson, whose *Alien vs. Predator* is to debut this August, will learn something from a few more looks at a milestone classic like *2001*, realizing that there is so much more to a great science fiction film than computer-generated effects, artificial environments, and scary monsters.

> Conclusion pulls the entire essay together and looks toward the future.

Works Cited

28 Days Later . . . Dir. Danny Boyle. 20th Century Fox, 2002. Film.
2001: A Space Odyssey. Dir. Stanley Kubrick. MGM, 1968. Film.
Alien. Dir. Ridley Scott [original trailer]. 20th Century Fox, 1979. Film.
AVP: Alien Vs. Predator. Dir. Paul W. S. Anderson. 20th Century Fox, 2004. Film.
Dr. Strangelove, Or: How I Learned to Stop Worrying and Love the Bomb.
　　Dir. Stanley Kubrick. Columbia Pictures, 1964. Film.
Eyes Wide Shut. Dir. Stanley Kubrick. Warner Bros, 1999. Film.
Full Metal Jacket. Dir. Stanley Kubrick. Warner Bros, 1987. Film.
Independence Day. Dir. Roland Emmerich. 20th Century Fox, 1996. Film.
Resident Evil. Dir. Paul W. S. Anderson. Sony Pictures Entertainment,
　　2002. Film.
Star Wars: Episode I—The Phantom Menace. Dir. George Lucas. 20th
　　Century Fox, 1999. Film.

Star Wars: Episode II—Attack of The Clones. Dir. George Lucas. 20th Century
   Fox, 2002. Film.
Wing Commander. Dir. Chris Roberts. 20th Century Fox, 1999. Film.

Source: *Reprinted with permission of the author.*

DECODING THE TEXT

1. How does the author connect many sci-fi films into one essay?

2. What is the purpose of using so many films in a relatively short essay?

3. Is this purpose met? How does it strengthen the essay?

4. Does the author consider the elements of a sci-fi film in the essay? How is this addressed?

CONNECTING TO YOUR CULTURE

1. What is the purpose of sci-fi filmmaking?

2. Does this purpose connect to the real world in any way? To your life?

3. How is sci-fi combined with other film genres to appeal to a wider audience? To appeal to you specifically?

THE READING ZONE

ENGAGING WITH TOPICS

1. What makes you want to see a movie? The commercials? Previews of coming attractions? Word of mouth? Social media? Reviews? Big-name stars? Directors? The Academy Awards? Talk show interviews?

2. What are you looking for in a movie? Explain the kind of experience you want, using examples from previous positive or negative viewing experiences.

3. How is music used in film? Do you ever buy soundtrack recordings?

4. Some films are about serious subjects, such as political prisoners (*Argo*), and others are strictly for entertainment (*Bridesmaids*). What serious subjects have been dealt with by films? Make a list of such films. Were some of these films also entertaining? Why or why not?

5. Make a list of your favorite or most-watched films and organize them into categories based on their level of seriousness. How did you decide which ones were more or less serious?

READING SELECTIONS

The readings that follow are organized into three sections: the 1970s and 1980s, the 1990s and 2000s, and the 2010s. The same organization that underpins all the content chapters in this textbook is used in this chapter as well, and the readings in each of the sections are not isolated to that decade or section because pop culture is not only what happened at the time but also how the same item or idea is received or remembered later on. Thus, in the 1970s and 1980s section, we have an essay by Chuthan Ponnampalam on what makes a movie a blockbuster and a David Brennan essay on how the two *Star Wars* trilogies, separated by decades, can be compared. Also in this section, Steve Almond suggests that *Ferris Bueller's Day Off* is one of the most sophisticated teen movies of that era, comparing it to other teen films across the decades.

In the 1990s and 2000s section, Gerald Horne compares Spike Lee's film *Malcolm X* to the true history of Malcolm X, the man. In addition, Peggy Ornstein and Crystal Smith, in their respective works, discuss how pop culture influences both girls and boys as they grow up and see film representations of femininity and masculinity.

The 2010s section includes a case study of four reviews. "Night of the Killer Lamp" is in the list essay format, so the author can categorize and describe how ridiculous some horror movie villains can be, and "Is Marvel Killing the Comic Book Genre?" is in review essay format, so the author can discuss how multiple Marvel comics have been turned into major motion pictures. This section also includes two pieces in the review format: one on the final Harry Potter film and one on *The Cove*, a documentary that shows how far a group of people will go to save dolphins.

The readings here are presented as a way for you to become more versed in investigating film as pop culture; however, they are also offered as samples of writing reviews, reflections or responses, analyses, and synthesis essays about films.

READING SELECTIONS:
THE 1970s AND 1980s

CONSIDERING IDEAS

The *Star Wars* film franchise began in 1977 with what is now called Episode IV.

1. Have you seen this 1977 episode or any of the other films in the series?

2. If you have seen the 1977 episode and the more recent films that make up the first to third episodes, how can you compare the earlier films to the later ones?

3. Do the earlier films seem dated now? Or do you think other aspects of the more recent films are better or worse than the older ones?

4. If you've never seen a *Star Wars* film, what has held you back?

AUTHOR BIO

David Brennan *works as an entrepreneur in Oakland County, Michigan. His interests include reading science fiction and watching films. His favorite books are* Brightness Falls, The End of History and the Last Man, The Rainmaker, *and* Future Shock.

TWO AUDIENCES, TWO SPIRITS

Differences Between the Two *Star Wars* Trilogies

David Brennan

INTRODUCTION

The original *Star Wars* trilogy was explicitly designed to please the common man. The new *Star Wars* trilogy is explicitly designed to please the *Star Wars* fan. Therefore, it is inevitable that the two trilogies have vastly different spirits.

Obi-Wan Kenobi, Yoda, R2-D2, C-3PO . . . all these characters have the same names as they did in the original trilogy, all of them look the same, but somehow they're just not hitting the same notes with the public as they used to. It is the thesis of this study that the different tones of the two *Star Wars* trilogies are the byproduct of intentional, conscious choices George Lucas made in response to changes in the marketplace.

It's important for the thesis of this study that we put a quick end to the transparent lie that George Lucas is guided by some "singular vision" of the *Star Wars* world. He's not. By now the *Star Wars* movies have had so many different versions that the average Kentucky high school graduate couldn't count them all. If *Star Wars* were a man, he'd be going through a bigger identity crisis than Michael Jackson in the middle of a race riot.

The prime victim of George Lucas's ever changing "vision" is the very first movie in the series, *Star Wars: A New Hope*. There have been at least four U.S. versions of this.[1] (But hey, only three of them were "definitive" versions!) The rolodex-list of changes to this poor movie—special effects made and unmade, actors added and dialogue erased—are more than enough evidence to prove that George Lucas has got no definitive "vision." Just to be sure, though, Lucas himself gave an accidental confession when, on the DVD audio commentary for Return of the Jedi, he talks about the unceremonious death of the character Boba Fett: "Had I known he was going to turn into such a popular character, I would've made his death more exciting," Lucas continues, "I contemplated putting in a shot where he [survived his death to please fans of the character.]"

If that's a "singular vision" then Alaska has "a little bit of snow."

It is overwhelmingly clear that the *Star Wars* movies have not been made to suit some mystical vision of George Lucas's. No, both trilogies were made to suit a target audience. The difference in spirit between the old trilogy and the new trilogy is caused by who that target audience is. . . .

THE ORIGINAL TRILOGY

In 1977, when the 20th Century Fox marketing department was deciding how to advertise their summer releases, the paperwork for *Star Wars* probably looked like this:

Movie: *Star Wars*
Target Demographic: EVERYBODY!

Lucas attached the following quote to each copy of his original screenplay for *Star Wars:*[2]

I have wrought my simple plan
If I give one hour of joy

To the boy who's half a man
Or the man who's half a boy

This quote, echoed from Sir Arthur Conan Doyle, laid clear Lucas's ambition to please not just "males between the ages of 18 and 30," not just "children over the age of 6 but under the age of 13." George Lucas wanted to please everybody.

All three movies in the original trilogy—*Star Wars, The Empire Strikes Back,* and *Return of the Jedi*—were designed specifically to please the people of Norman Rockwell's Main Street as well as the people of Greenwich Village's coffee houses. Lucas wanted to bring a smile to gruff lumberjacks but also to gentle poets.

He wanted to please the common man.

Creating a work that is universally appealing is no easy task. So Lucas did what most people in Hollywood do when they're in a bind, he copied somebody else's work.

Lucas modeled *Star Wars* after mythical classics. *The Odyssey, The Legend of King Arthur,* and *Beowulf* have all been acknowledged as source material for *Star Wars.*[3] Lucas was striving to achieve the same populist ends with his story as these myths achieved with theirs, and so he made a conscious effort to have the original trilogy follow in their footsteps. *Star Wars,* therefore, is a second generation fable. You could call it a neomyth.

The first of these three tales for the common man opened on May 25, 1977 and over the course of the next six years George Lucas's *Star Wars* movies were each amongst the most successful of all time. Just as with he was with *The Odyssey* and *Beowulf,* the common man was pleased with *Star Wars* in 1977.

All good things, though, must come to an end, and, the *Star Wars* trilogy's ending did not disappoint. In 1983, the series was brought to a rousing climax with *Return of the Jedi.* George Lucas signed off literally and figuratively in a popular documentary that chronicled the making of the three movies called *From Star Wars to Jedi: The Making of a Saga.* After the credits roll, Lucas is seen giving a military salute as he boards a plane.

"As attractive as the *Star Wars* world is," he says, "sooner or later you have to leave home."[4]

All three parts of the *Star Wars* story—*Star Wars* (1977), *The Empire Strikes Back* (1980), and *The Return of the Jedi* (1983)—were wholly satisfying to the common man, so George Lucas had achieved his goal. It was a story not just enjoyed, but beloved by the common man, and it had ended just wonderfully.

It was all so perfect. . . .

THE NEW TRILOGY

Financial troubles gave birth to a new *Star Wars* trilogy. It turns out that a divorce had dug a fiscal hole for Lucas and he needed to use the beloved *Star Wars* name to climb out of it.[5]

Perhaps it was because he was now beholden to the financial burdens of fatherhood, or perhaps it was because he had grown so attached to wealth that he couldn't dare to lose it, but for some reason George Lucas wasn't going to take any chances with his new trilogy.[6]

George Lucas told the common man to take a hike, because with this new trilogy he had a way to guarantee the financial success he needed. This guarantee was usually a male, usually between the ages of 12 and 24. He usually liked to play video games and he spent oodles of money on pop culture fads. . . .

He was Fanboy, a heavy-spending, pop-culture-junkie who did not even exist when *Star Wars* was released in 1977. Fanboy was such an extravagant spender, in fact, that the people in marketing said that just one of him was worth ten of the common men.

Ironically, for all the control Fanboy would have over the second *Star Wars* trilogy, he hadn't even been a big fan of the first *Star Wars* trilogy until a decade after it had ended.

In 1995, Lucasfilm re-released the *Star Wars* movies with sleek new packaging and "THX Re-mastering 'which supposedly made the decades-old movies looked crisp and modern. The marketing play was a pop culture blitzkrieg and this was how Fanboy first made his presence known to Lucasfilm. It wasn't just the movies that Fanboy threw money at, but comic book tie-ins and action figures and anything and everything else. . . . all for movies that were over ten years old! This formula was such a success in 1995 that it was duplicated again in 1997, this time with a *theatrical* re-release of the movies. . . . ' In a way you've never seen before!"

Fanboy was ecstatic.

Common man, of course, was indifferent to all the hype for these re-releases. Common man had children to feed, loved ones to tend to, and sights to see—so he wasn't interested in buying yet another version of movies he'd already seen in theaters and on video tape. No, common man found all this hype rather silly (and maybe even a little pathetic.)

So Lucasfilm wasn't getting any money from common man. But Fanboy. . . . he wouldn't stop spending! Comic books, video games, toys, Taco Bell, Frito Lay, Pepsi; there was no sense of restraint in Fanboy. In fact, there wasn't much sense in him, *period*. There was just these bizarre, fleeting fads. *"More Boba Fett!"* he cried one minute. *"More computer effects!"* he yelled the next. *"More tude!"* he bellowed soon after! [Note for common man: "tude" is Fanboy-ese for "attitude."]

Of course, mythical tales like *The Odyssey* weren't designed to withstand the trendy scrutinies of Fanboy, nor did they have any pretense of offering their readers an identity. They were designed to entertain the common man, not some niche demographic. Moreover . . . they were just stories.

But again, George Lucas had a different agenda for this new trilogy. For this older, money-driven George Lucas, money talked and everything else walked.

And so, when the first of this new trilogy was released in 1999, it was Fanboy, not common man, who was calling the shots. Watching *The Phantom Menace* and *Attack of the Clones,* you can almost hear Fanboy telling George Lucas what to do. *"Gimme another big slimy creature here. . . . yeah, that's right."* George Lucas nods accommodatingly. *"I want Boba Fett. What, he's dead? Call 'im Jango Fett then, I don't care."*

George Lucas's pandering to Fanboy[7] worked. . . . kind of. While the box office for the new movies were good, somehow they seemed incapable of ever again being *great*.

It is empirically indisputable that the common man has become less and less impressed with the *Star Wars* movies with each passing entry.

BOX OFFICE GROSSES FOR *STAR WARS* MOVIES (Chronologically)

1977, *Star Wars*: 1.2 bil. . . . .(1st out of 5)

1980, *The Empire Strikes Back*: 603 mil. . . . . (2nd out of 5)

1983, *The Return of the Jedi*: 578 mil. . . . . (3rd out of 5)

1999, *The Phantom Menace*: 521 mil. . . . .(4th out of 5)

2002, *Attack of the Clones*: 328 mil. . . . . (5th out of 5)

Note: Figures are adjusted for inflation.
Source: BoxOfficeMojo.com.

Lucasfilm won't even admit that their box office is decaying. Instead, they have more rationalizations than Dean Martin had groupies. They'll say that the box office is declining because the new trilogy is "darker," even though all five of the *Star Wars* movies have gotten the exact same "PG" rating. They'll say that the new movies aren't doing well because they star children or because they're romances, as if *E.T.* and *Titanic* were flops.

If the defenders of the new *Star Wars* movies are correct in their claim that the movies offer some mystical greatness that is invisible to the common man, then certainly educated film critics, with their discerning tastes and trained eyes, would have picked up on these suspiciously elusive qualities and recommended *The Phantom Menace* and *Attack of the Clones* with the same fervor as they did the original trilogy.

They haven't. In fact, the critics' tastes and the taste of the common man mirror each other almost exactly.

PERCENTAGE OF MOVIE CRITICS WHO RECOMMENDED EACH *STAR WARS* MOVIE, (Chronologically)

1977, *Star Wars*: 93%. . . . .(2nd out of 5)

1980, *The Empire Strikes Back*: 98%. . . . .(1st out of 5)

1983, *The Return of the Jedi*: 80%. . . . .(3rd out of 5)

1999, *The Phantom Menace*: 62%. . . . .(5th out of 5)

2002, *Attack of the Clones*: 64%. . . . . (4th out of 5)

Source: RottenTomatoes.com.

The downward spiral is undeniable. A couple more of these and they'll be in *Gigli* territory.

At the end of the day, any objective study will reach the exact same conclusion: the *Star Wars* movie franchise is decaying, slowly but surely.

CONCLUSION

The problem with the second *Star Wars* trilogy was not that it was pandering. As noted above, the original trilogy pandered too.

The problem with the new trilogy is that it is pandering to a fleeting and unstable audience whose tastes change from one week to the next. The first trilogy was built for the human spirit, the second trilogy was built for this very specific niche market that did not even exist when *Star Wars* came out in 1977.

The characters, the settings, the filmmakers: they all have the same names . . . but that does not mean that the spirit of the two trilogies are the same. They aren't.

Notes

1. The four U.S. versions are (deep breath): (1) The original theatrical version without the subtitle "Episode IV, A New Hope," (2) The 1981 re-release version which inserted the aforementioned subtitle as well as some voiceover changes, (3) The 1997 Special Edition version which is different still from . . . . (4) The 2004 DVD version.
2. *George Lucas: The Creative Impulse*. This was the book included with the 1993 laserdisc release of *Star Wars*.
3. Sources stated from the documentary *Empire of Dreams included on the Star Wars* Trilogy DVD set, released in 2004.

4. George Lucas, *From Star Wars to Jedi: The Making of a Saga*, 1983.
5. *The Charlie Rose Show*, 2004. George Lucas says, "[After I finished the original trilogy]. . . . I got a divorce and that sort of set me back quite a ways. . ..one of the reasons to go back to *Star Wars* was it would hopefully make me financially secure enough to where I wouldn't have to go back to studios and beg for money."
6. "There's only one issue for a filmmaker. . . .Will this make its money back so I can make the next one?"—George Lucas as quoted in *Time Magazine*; April 20, 2002
7. "It's harder for them to accept the fact that these are made for adolescents—they're movies for young people they're not movies for 30 year old and 40 year olds."—George Lucas as quoted by Peter Bowes of *BBC News*; May 14, 2002

Source: *"Two Audiences, Two Spirits: Differences between the two Star Wars Trilogies"* by David Brennan. Used with permission.

DECODING THE TEXT

1. How many films are mentioned in the essay?

2. What two groups of films is Brennan comparing? Why does this make for an effective comparison?

3. What is Brennan's main argument? How does he support it? Is his support effective?

CONNECTING TO YOUR CULTURE

1. How does the topic of the essay connect to you and your viewing habits? To your age demographic?

2. Even if you have never seen any of the *Star Wars* films, how can you use this essay as a model of a synthesis essay, one that gives review information, the author's reflection and response, and a comparative analysis of the two trilogies?

CONSIDERING IDEAS

1. Make a list of the movies you saw in the last few summers. What do they have in common?

2. What makes a movie a blockbuster?

3. What are some of the more famous movies in the blockbuster genre?

AUTHOR BIO

Chuthan Ponnampalam *is the managing editor of* The Manitoban, *the official student newspaper of the University of Manitoba, located in Winnipeg, Canada.*

THE SEASON OF THE BLOCKBUSTER

Chuthan Ponnampalam

It's difficult to think of summer without movies coming to mind. Summer blockbusters have become a staple of the warm months—a herald even, that summer has arrived.

As of late, superhero films have been ushering in summer on the silver screen, and before superheroes it was dinosaurs and loveable aliens, with a galaxy far, far away in between. But it was a homicidal shark that began the relationship between summer and blockbusters.

Susan King, a writer for the *Los Angeles Times,* described the birth of this relationship stemming from the film *Jaws.*

"Before the release of the Steven Spielberg-directed thrill ride [...] on June 20, 1975, about a great white shark on a feeding frenzy around fictional Amity Island (Martha's Vineyard), the summer blockbuster didn't really exist," wrote King.

Originally, "blockbuster" was a term coined by the press to describe a powerful bomb that was capable of leveling an entire city block but eventually the term made its way into the entertainment industry and referred to a hit play whose success "busted" other theaters on the block, driving them out of business. The term has since evolved to describe everything from successful films, to bestselling books and video games. Prior to *Jaws,* films such as *Ben-Hur* or *Gone With the Wind,* which did incredibly well at the box office, were described as being spectaculars, super-grossers or super-blockbusters—precursor terms to blockbuster.

After the release of *Jaws* though, blockbuster has come to define a type of film—a genre of film, even—that is not just a success at the box office, but a cultural phenomena and an entertainment event.

Prior to *Jaws,* films usually had a very limited release, only opening in a few major cities at first. *The Godfather* for example, which was considered a critical and commercial success at its release, only opened on six screens initially.

As word of mouth spread about a film and it built momentum, the studio would widen its release. Word of mouth also served as the only marketing for a film. Before *Jaws* came along, marketing and advertising of films was minimal or nonexistent.

Advanced-screenings for *Jaws* were met with a hot reception, which encouraged the executives at Universal Studios to green-light an incredibly wide release. *Jaws* opened to 409 theaters on June 20, 1975.

This pioneer wide release was paired with a marketing campaign that incorporated television spots, which all aided in the genesis of the first-ever blockbuster film.

The film made box office history, becoming the first-ever movie to gross US $100 million, and changed how film studios approach movies—beginning the blockbuster trend.

Thrilled by the success of *Jaws,* film studios all tried to replicate its success by trying to turn films into an event, utilizing marketing and wide releases. Studios also began to plan their entire year around their biggest films, which they called "tent pole films."

Films like *Star Wars, Jurassic Park,* and *E.T.: The Extra-Terrestrial* are all examples of tent pole films, which built on the *Jaws* formula.

Summer blockbuster films have since evolved to include even wider releases and more complex marketing.

The Dark Knight, which shattered record after record, incorporated interactive viral marketing campaigns and opened in 4,366 theaters.

According to Box Office Mojo, an online database of film release information, *The Dark Knight* made over US $158 million during its opening weekend.

Although *Jaws* introduced a new genre in a sense, in the form of blockbuster films, and revolutionized how studios approached not only film but also marketing and release methods, the blockbuster film has also been criticized for pioneering the decline in the quality of films.

Michael Peters, a writer for Suite101.com, discussed this decline: "Since the late '70s, films have desired to entertain, especially in the summer. They have stripped their art house attire and have become 'dumbed-down' escapist filled entertainment (with a tremendous amount of merchandise to boot)."

"To some, the summer is the greatest time for movies. For others, it is a definitely an example of all that is wrong with Hollywood."

Ultimately, though, it is up to the viewer to decide whether a blockbuster is a success or failure—and more importantly, whether the film was worth their time or not. But failure or not, there is no denying that summer is the season of the blockbuster.

Source: *"The Season of the Blockbuster: Homicidal Shark Pioneers Blockbuster Films" by Chuthan Ponnampalam.* The Manitoban/Features. *June 21, 2011. Used by permission.*

DECODING THE TEXT

1. Where does the term *movie blockbuster* come from?

2. Why does the author consider *Jaws* as the beginning of the *blockbuster genre*?

3. What is a *tentpole* film? Why are these important to film studios?

4. The author suggests that blockbusters have led to a decline in quality for summer movies. Do you agree with this? Support your answer with details from the essay or from your own experience.

CONNECTING TO YOUR CULTURE

1. Make a list of the movies you have seen over the past year. How many could be considered blockbusters, and what percentage of all the movies you saw were blockbusters? In calculating this percentage, have you learned anything about your viewing habits?

2. What makes a film quality entertainment for you? And how do you define *quality* for yourself as a movie viewer?

3. Are there any character stereotypes that appear in blockbuster movies that remind you of people you know?

CONSIDERING IDEAS

John Hughes directed many teen movies from the 1980s, such as *Pretty in Pink* and *The Breakfast Club*, which continue to be popular.

1. What teen movies have been made in the last few years?

2. Why do both the classic teen movie and more current versions continue to be popular?

3. How have teen movies changed over the years, or have they changed?

AUTHOR BIO

Steve Almond *is a prolific fiction writer and journalist. He is the author of eight books, including* The New York Times *best seller* Candyfreak: A Journey Through the Chocolate Underbelly of America *(2004) and* Rock and Roll Will Save Your Life *(2010). He currently also reviews books for* The Boston Globe *and* The Los Angeles Times. *His website is* http://www.stevenalmond.com. *"John Hughes Goes Deep" was first published in* The Virginia Quarterly Review (http://www.vqronline.org) *in 2006.*

JOHN HUGHES GOES DEEP

The Unexpected Heaviosity of *Ferris Bueller's Day Off*

Steve Almond

I missed *Ferris Bueller's Day Off* on the first pass, so I never quite understood what all the hubbub was about. And, as generally happens when I miss out on all the hubbub, I took it personally and thus bore a senseless grudge against the film, which I would routinely malign whenever people tried to explain how terrific it was. More often than not, I am really just a very big asshole.

Notwithstanding this, last winter I got sick, so sick I was reduced to raiding my landlord's DVD collection. He had about forty movies, most of which were thrillers of the sort that feature a European secret agent babe who takes her shirt off and a picturesque decapitation. He also had *Ferris Bueller*.

I watched the film in a state of growing astonishment. It was, without a doubt, the most sophisticated teen movie I had ever seen. I wasn't entirely sure it qualified as a teen movie at all. It featured a number of techniques that I recognized from other, later films: direct addresses to the camera, on-screen graphics, the prominent use of background songs to create de facto music videos, the sudden exhilarating blur of fantasy and reality.

More than this, though, Hughes performed an astounding ontological feat. He lured viewers into embracing his film as an escapist farce, then hit them with a pitch-perfect exploration of teen angst. He snuck genuine art past the multiplex censors.

I needn't labor the basic plot—kid fakes being sick, outwits dopey grownups, gallivants around Chicago with pals. Hughes is, like any decent Aristotelian, more concerned with character.

Ferris himself (Matthew Broderick, unbearably young) comes across as a charming manipulator utterly devoted to his own enjoyments. We initially encounter him playing sick on his bed. It is a pathetically stagy performance and he seems mildly disappointed when his doting parents fall for it. We get a few scenes of him mugging for the camera, and the introduction of his inept nemesis, the dean of students, Ed Rooney.

The scene shifts to a sleek, modern home, propped up on stilts and perched at the edge of a bluff. We cut to a dark, sarcophagus-like bedroom, littered with medicine bottles and crumpled Kleenex. A figure lies obscured under a blanket, like a mummy, while an electronic dirge plays in the background.

This is our introduction to Cameron Frye (Alan Ruck), Ferris's best friend. The phone by the bed rings and a hand appears and slowly clicks on the speakerphone. It is Ferris demanding that Cameron come over and spend the day with him. Meaning, essentially, chauffeur him around.

Cameron declines in a froggy voice. He is sick. Ferris repeats his demand and hangs up.

"I'm dying," Cameron whispers. The phone rings again and Ferris mutters, "You're not dying. You just can't think of anything good to do."

We now see Cameron from above. His expression is one of resignation, giving unto despair. And then, fabulously, he begins to sing.

"When Cameron was in Egypt's land . . ."

A rich, somber chorus of voices joins him.

"Let my Cameron go!"

The invocation of the old spiritual is at once strange and revelatory. It has no business, really, in what has been—to this point—smarter-than-average teenybopper fare. But then, neither does Cameron Frye.

Hughes could have simply cast him as a straight man for Ferris. But he does something far more compelling: he renders the pair as a psychological dyad. Ferris is fearless, larger-than-life. He has internalized the unconditional love of his parents and skips through his days in a self-assured reverie. He is what every teenage guy dreams of being: a raging, narcissistic kid who gets away with it. Cameron is an actual teenager: alienated from his parents, painfully insecure, angry, depressed.

It is the tension between these two that drives the action. Ferris dances around the house (accompanied by the theme from *I Dream of Jeannie*). Dad calls from work and Ferris plays him like a Stradivarius. Then he turns to the camera and, with a look of indignation, says: "I'm so disappointed in Cameron. Twenty bucks says he's sitting in his car debating about whether he should go out or not."

Cut to Cameron, at the wheel of a white junker, his long, rubbery face cast in a morbid posture. He sniffs. He stares ahead. He squinches up his eyes and growls, "He'll keep *calling* and *calling* and *calling*. . . ." He puts the key in the ignition, starts the car. He shakes his head and yanks the key out of the ignition. Then, with no warning, he starts to pound the passenger seat. These are vicious blows. "Goddamn it," he screams. The camera backs off to a midrange shot. We hear the car start again and the engine revs and we hear a primal scream at the exact same pitch. Then the car goes dead. "Forget it," Cameron says. "That's it." He flings himself out of the car and stomps back to his empty house. We cut to a close-up of the empty driver's seat. Birds tweet. Suddenly, we hear the crunch of his penny loafers on gravel and a blurry image of Cameron's hockey jersey through the rear window. He is stomping back toward the car. We think: *Ah, he's given in.* Just then he stops and begins jumping up and down and throwing punches at some invisible adversary.

The sequence lasts barely a minute. It is an astonishing piece of physical humor, an emotional ballet worthy of Chaplin. Hell, it's one of the best pieces of acting I've ever seen, period. Because it's not just funny, it's heartbreaking. We are watching a kid utterly crippled by his own conflicted impulses, torn between outrage and obedience.

In a very real sense, he needs someone to take charge. Ferris is more than willing. Within a few minutes, he has kidnapped Cameron, along with the prize Ferrari convertible Cameron's father keeps in the garage. Next, he rescues his dishy girlfriend, Sloane, from school and the trio tear off toward downtown.

Ruck is tall, blue-eyed, big-jawed, movie-star handsome. Broderick looks like a nebbish by comparison. If the film had been made today, and by a lesser director, you can bet your Milk Duds that their roles would be reversed. (Such are the mandates of the beauty gradient.) But Hughes clearly had a feel for his actors. And they so inhabit their roles that you wind up focused on their effect, not their cheekbones.

Hughes has long been hailed as the clown prince of teen angst. Whether it's Molly Ringwald getting felt up by her grandpa (*Sixteen Candles*) or Ally Sheedy teasing her dandruff into a snowfall (*The Breakfast Club*), he knows how to put across the exquisite humiliation of adolescence. Still, most of his films play to formula. *Ferris Bueller* has its share. We know, for instance, that Ferris will prevail over Rooney in the end, and that he will make it home in time to fool his benighted parents.

But the film, as a whole, is a looser, more improvisatory affair. It has a dreamy, superannuated quality. There are all these odd, unexpected moments. A secretary pulls a pencil from her bouffant hairdo. Then a second. And a third. As a teacher drones on about the Smoot-Hawley Tariff Act, Hughes shows us a series of stark close-ups of students. These are actual teens—zits, bad hair, gaping mouths—and their expressions convey actual teen imprisonment: boredom, bewilderment, homicidal intent.

Even a character like Ed Rooney (played with transcendent unction by Jeffrey Jones) is granted his own impregnable sense of logic. He knows Ferris Bueller is making a mockery of his authority, and the educational mission, and that Ferris's popularity makes him the ideal target for Rooney's jihad on truancy. "I did not achieve this position in life," he sneers, "by having some snot-nosed punk leave my cheese out in the wind."

There is no line in the universe that more succinctly conveys the Rooney gestalt.

Or consider what Hughes does with a visit by our heroes to the Art Institute of Chicago. Backed by a soft, symphonic score, he offers us lengthy shots of the most beautiful paintings in the world: Hoppers, Modiglianis, Pollocks. There is no ulterior plot motive; he is simply celebrating the majesty of the work. We see Cameron, Ferris, and his dishy girlfriend Sloane stand before a trio of Picassos, transfixed.

As the music crescendoes, we see Cameron standing before Georges Seurat's pointillist masterpiece, *A Sunday Afternoon on the Island of La Grande Jatte.* We cut to a shot of Ferris and Sloane, the happy couple, necking in the blue light of a stained-glass window, then back to Cameron, alone, staring at the Seurat. Another one of these magical things happens: the camera begins zooming in on the little girl in white at the center of the canvas. We cut back to Cameron, closer now. Then back to the little girl. We see his growing anguish as he realizes that her mouth is wide open, that, in fact, she is wailing.

Okay, good enough: Cameron recognizes himself in the figure of this little girl whose mother is holding her hand but making no effort to comfort her. Got it.

But then Hughes takes us even deeper. He gives us an extreme close-up of Cameron's eyes, then cuts back to the canvas, to the girl's face, then to her mouth, then to the specks of paint that make up her mouth, until we can no longer resolve those specks into an image; they are just splotches of color on coarse fabric. This is the true nature of Cameron's struggle: his anxieties have obliterated his sense of identity.

We then cut, somewhat abruptly, to a German street parade. Cameron is fretting. He needs to get his dad's Ferrari back to the house. Ferris objects. He wants to have more fun. But he also knows that his friend needs to loosen up, to conquer his fear and experience life.

The next time we see Cameron, he and Sloane are hurrying along the parade route. Ferris has ditched them. We cut to a float. Ferris has commandeered a microphone. "This is one of my personal favorites and I want to dedicate it to a young man who doesn't think he's seen anything good today. Cameron Frye, this one's for you." He begins a campy lip-synch of the old torch song, "Danke Schoen." Then he launches into a raucous version of "Twist and Shout." The crowd goes nuts. Ferris has induced mass hysteria in downtown Chicago. This could never happen in real life. It is a Walter Mitty–esque diversion. Which is precisely the point: Ferris has staged this adolescent fantasy of omnipotence expressly for his best friend.

By definition, the adults in a Hughes film are beyond hope of transformation. But it is his central and rescuing belief that teens are capable of change—even the ones who seem to be stock characters. I am thinking here of Jeanie Bueller (Jennifer Grey) who plays the overlooked younger sister and spends most of the film in a snit of sibling rivalry. She is so eager to bust her brother that she winds up in a police station, next to a spaced-out drug suspect (an excellent Charlie Sheen) who slowly chips away at her defenses to reveal the sweet, needy kid living beneath her bitterness.

The prime example, of course, is the relationship between Ferris and Cameron. It is without a doubt the most convincing *therapeutic narrative* in his oeuvre. After all, as much as we may want to suspend our disbelief, is there anyone out there who *really* believes that the Molly Ringwald character in *The Breakfast Club* is going to give Judd Nelson the time of day once they're back in school?

Ferris himself is, for the most part, a fabulous cartoon—half James Bond, half Holden Caulfield. But he understands the very real crisis Cameron is facing and takes it as his role to push his friend into emotional danger.

But Ferris, of course, leads a charmed life. His existentialism comes cheap. For Cameron (as for the rest of us) the experience of pleasure is an ongoing battle against anxiety. Ferris and Sloane can treat the day as just another glorious idyll. For Cameron, it comes to assume the weight of a reckoning.

Toward dusk, he, Ferris, and Sloane return to his house with the precious Ferrari intact. Ferris has a plan: they can run the accrued miles off the car's odometer by jacking the car's rear tires off the ground and running the car in reverse.

As they sit outside the garage, Cameron comes clean about his anxieties. "It's ridiculous," Cameron announces. "Being afraid, worrying about everything, wishing I was dead, all that shit. I'm tired of it." He looks at his friends. "That was the best day of my life," he says. "I'm going to miss you guys next year."

The standard teen film would probably end on his upbeat note. Hughes is just getting started. Cameron heads into the garage to check on the car. Ferris's plan is not working. For a moment, Cameron appears panic-stricken.

Ferris suggests they crack open the glass and adjust the odometer.

But Cameron shakes his head.

"No," he says. "Forget it. Forget it. I gotta take a stand." His tone takes a sudden detour into self-loathing. "I'm bullshit. I put up with everything. My old man pushes me around. I never say anything." He is shouting now. "Well, he's not the problem. I'm the problem. I gotta take a stand. I gotta take a stand against him." As he leans over the hood of the Ferrari, his voice drops to a menacing register: "I am not going to sit on my ass as the events that affect me unfold to determine the course of my life. I gotta take a stand and defend it, right or wrong."

He kicks the car. "I am so sick of his shit! Who do you love? You love the car, you son of a bitch!" He continues to kick at the car: the rear bumper, the trunk, the taillights. These are not gentle little movie kicks. They are charged with a real violence of intent. Thanks to some clever crosscutting, we can see that Cameron has nearly knocked the car off its jack. He is nearly in tears; his entire body is tossed by the savagery. And thus it becomes clear what he's really been afraid of all along: his own murderous rage.

"Shit," Cameron says, "I dented the shit out of it." He laughs, in a manner throttled by regret. Ferris and Sloane—like the viewer—are watching this melt-down in a state of shock. After all, this is supposed to be just a funny little teen movie. But something has happened on the way to the happy ending: a much darker, more authentic psychological event. A catharsis.

"Good," Cameron says finally, in a voice of forced assurance. "My father will come home and see what I did. I can't hide this. He'll have to deal with me. I don't care. I really don't. I'm just tired of being afraid. Hell with it. I can't wait to see the look on the bastard's face."

Cameron sets his foot on the beleaguered rear fender, which, of course, sends the car tumbling off the jack. The rear wheels hit the ground with a skid and the car crashes through a plate glass window and off the bluff.

There is a long, gruesome moment of silence, as the three kids try to grasp the magnitude of what's just happened.

"Whoa," Cameron says. "Oh shiiiit."

Ferris immediately insists on taking the blame. This doesn't feel particularly momentous, given the state Cameron is in. But it does mark a profound transformation in the Bueller weltanschauung. He has risen above his happy-go-lucky solipsism—probably for the first time in his life—and offered to sacrifice himself.

Cameron has undergone an even more radical change. He has developed what my students often refer to, admiringly, as sack.

"No," he says. "I'll take it. I'll take it. I want it. If I didn't want it, I wouldn't have let you take out the car this morning . . . No, I want it. I'm gonna take it. When Morris comes home he and I will just have a little chat. It's cool. No, it's gonna be good, thanks anyway."

I hate trying to convey the power of this scene by setting down the dialogue alone, because Ruck is doing so much as an actor the whole time, with his body, his eyes, his voice. It will seem an audacious comparison, but I was reminded of those long, wrenching soliloquies at the end of *Long Day's Journey into Night*.

I have no idea who won the Oscar for Best Supporting Actor in 1986. It is painful—given the photographic evidence of my wardrobe—for me to even think about that grim era. But I can tell you that Alan Ruck deserved that statue. His performance is what elevates the film, allows it to assume the power of a modern parable.

Look: John Hughes made a lot of good movies. I've seen most of them and laughed in all the right spots and hoped for the right guy to the get the right girl and vice versa and for all the *troubled kids* to find *hope*. I've given myself over to the pleasant surrender of melodrama. But Hughes made only one film I would consider true art, only one that reaches toward the ecstatic power of teendom and, at the same time, exposes the true, piercing woe of that age.

People will tell you they love *Ferris Bueller* because of all the clever lines, the gags. That's what people need to think. They don't want to come out of the closet as drama queens. It's not a kind age for drama queens. The world is too full of absent parents and children gone mean. But the real reason they keep returning to the film is because John Hughes loved those kids enough to lay them bare, and he transmitted that love to us.

Bless him.

Source: *"John Hughes Goes Deep: The Unexpected Heaviosity of* Ferris Bueller's Day Off*"* by Steve Almond, *from* The Virginia Quarterly Review, *Summer 2006, pp. 277–283. Reprinted by permission of the author.*

DECODING THE TEXT

1. How does the author show his appreciation for the film *Ferris Bueller's Day Off* and its director? What is Almond's main argument?

2. What kind of evidence does he use to support his position?

3. Why is Almond writing about this film twenty years after it was made? Could this have been written when the film just came out?

CONNECTING TO YOUR CULTURE

1. Who watches teen films?

2. Why are these types of films often a guilty pleasure, a pleasure that some viewers hide from others?

3. Are there gender differences in how films are made or how they appeal to certain audiences?

READING SELECTIONS:
THE 1990s AND 2000s

CONSIDERING IDEAS

1. Do some web research, and find out about the life of Malcolm X. What kind of man was he? What did he accomplish in his lifetime, and how did he accomplish it?

2. Are biographical films always true, or do they sometimes mislead the audience due to the mythology surrounding a historical figure? Whatever your answer, provide supporting evidence from at least one film you have seen, such as *Walk the Line*, *Ray*, *Lincoln*, *Argo*, *W.*, *Milk*, *Elizabeth: The Golden Age*, *United 93*, or *Ali*.

3. Consider some American myths that are based on historical figures, such as Paul Bunyan, Johnny Appleseed, or Calamity Jane. Take a few minutes and jot down what you know about the person or myth. Then, research that figure's real life. What parts of the myth and the actual facts about the person agree in a consistent way? What parts of the myth and the actual facts about the person do not agree in a consistent way?

AUTHOR BIO

Gerald Horne *is the John J. and Rebecca Moores Chair of History and African-American Studies at the University of Houston. He has a PhD from Columbia University and a JD (Juris Doctor—a law degree) from the University of California, Berkeley. He is a prolific author who has published on W.E.B. DuBois, and he contributes frequently to* Political Affairs *magazine, a monthly online* Marxist *publication. This essay is an excerpt from a full article that appeared in* American Historical Review *in 1993.*

"MYTH" AND THE MAKING OF "MALCOLM X"

Gerald Horne

In common ordinary usage, to engage in myth making suggests falsification, factual inaccuracies, and the like. However, from another vantage point, myths are not necessarily lies, they are explications. These narratives extracted from history perform a symbolic function essential to the culture that produced them. Myths, in this sense, are useful parables and allegories containing lessons for today. They help to explain the world.

That is the good news. The bad news is that myths, at times, can be misleading, not so much for mangling the facts but for neglecting certain facts or distorting the relationship between facts. As we have been reminded repeatedly and accurately, the negative value of myth is reflected in the traditional story of the "Old West." And Hollywood, the anchor of the West, has been a major producer of myths.

What is called the civil rights movement or the post–World War II trajectory of African-American history has developed a certain mythology that Spike Lee's estimable and worthy epic, *Malcolm X,* seeks to replace with an alternative mythology. The traditional myth is centered on Martin Luther King, Jr., with Rosa Parks and the Student Non-Violent Coordinating Committee (SNCC) playing pivotal supporting roles. All of a sudden, in the mid-1950s—during a period, we are told, for some reason otherwise somnolent—Negroes, led by Dr. King and assisted by brilliant attorneys and related law enforcement personnel, not to mention sympathetic white elites, started marching and getting their rights.[1] The U.S. film industry, in *Mississippi Burning, The Long Walk Home,* and other films, has presented a variation of this theme, featuring ever-pious, long-suffering blacks and heroic whites, in a fashion not unlike anti-apartheid epics such as *Cry Freedom* and *A Dry White Season.* During these seasons of racial strife and conflagrations in Los Angeles, such images can be quite soothing and reassuring.

With his usual audacity, Spike Lee has dared to create a competing myth, akin to what Oliver Stone attempted in his alternative myth of Camelot, *JFK. Malcolm X* presents angry, not meek blacks. It suggests that Jim Crow violence and exploitation were eroded not only by smart lawyers and adroit FBI agents but by angry black Muslims and nationalists as well. In this alternative view, the nonviolence and passive resistance of Dr. King is juxtaposed with Malcolm X's language of militant self-defense. The narrative focuses on the many transformations of Malcolm, from terrorized child to hustler to prisoner to narrow nationalist to progressive nationalist.

Neither the King nor the Malcolm myth is an outright falsification (although some of the celluloid versions of the former come perilously close to this shifting border). However, both neglect highly relevant and persuasive evidence because it does not necessarily comport with the contemporary lessons that one is to draw from these myths. For example, in a nation where the Cold War and the Red Scare have been the defining postwar paradigms, the attacks on the civil liberties of black leftists-which were taking place as civil rights for blacks generally were being expanded-are not part of either myth. It is as if W. E. B. Du Bois, Paul Robeson, Ben Davis, Claudia Jones, and William Patterson did not exist. That Spike Lee, a filmmaker, could not transcend in *Malcolm X* limits that have ensnared many historians and activists should not come as a surprise.

* * *

THE MOST SEVERE CRITICS of Malcolm X have to concede that the film does a marvelous job of depicting social and cultural questions. This is all the more striking since Lee has been criticized repeatedly for his drawing of women characters.[2] But even, and perhaps particularly, his staunchest feminist critics (and I am among that group) had to admire the scene featuring Denzel Washington, playing Malcolm Little, sticking his head in the toilet to douse his scalp, which was burning because of a botched effort to straighten his hair. Before the rise of the "black is beautiful" movement, which was anticipated by the post-Mecca Malcolm, this often painful process was devised in part to make the hair of blacks appear more like that of certain whites. As this event occurs, the police burst into his apartment to arrest Malcolm for various crimes. The question of hair, which has been an essential though contradictory component of African-American identity, helps to create a scene that is an instant classic of African-American cinema. Many black men no longer press their hair, although many black women for various reasons find it necessary to do so. Lee's film forces the audience to contemplate these complexities of a gendered racial identity.[3]

This is part of the value of Malcolm X as a historical figure. He is an integral part of the scaffolding that supports a contemporary African-American identity. His fascination with music and dance and night clubs undergirded his bond with blacks. A significant development that is accelerating in Afro-America in the postwar era is cool or hip philosophy. It involves a manner, a language, a mode of dress, and more. It is reflected in Malcolm's well-known fascination with what is called jazz music and that milieu. Quite properly, the figure of Billie Holliday is represented in Lee's film. There is substantial time spent on dance and music, though this is not unusual for Lee, whose father is a noted bassist. Lee also shows how the world of cool and hip can devolve. Malcolm Little's plight—he found it better to hustle, to engage in petty crimes than to work at low-paying jobs where crass exploitation is the watchword-resonates with many contemporary black youth in urban areas.[4]

The problem with this cool or hip philosophy and its present-day descendant, hip-hop, is that the heavily male orientation can shade easily into misogyny or at least insensitivity on gender matters. Again, Spike Lee's flaws in drawing female characters in this film and in his other works are not his alone. It is the inevitable result of a philosophy that arises when the Left is weakened and various forms of narrow nationalism are ascendant.

IN 1993, MALCOLM X STANDS AS AN ICON; many believe that he stands in the pantheon with Martin Luther King, Jr., himself. His figure is so luminescent that he can inspire an alternative myth. A recent poll reported by the black press states that 84 percent of those African-Americans between the ages of fifteen and twenty-four who were queried felt that he was "a hero for black Americans today." However, that same poll found that a substantially smaller percentage of that age cohort knew much about him. This circumstance presents both a situation ripe for myth making and an indictment of how history is taught in this nation. To the extent that accurate and comprehensive knowledge of the past is useful in formulating tactics and strategy for economic betterment, distorted aspects of the Malcolm myths and other myths can be seen as a co-factor in explicating the continuing economic decline among blacks particularly and the U.S. working class generally.[5] It also presents a challenge that the film may not be able to overcome.

Notes

1. Richard Kluger, *Simple Justice: The History of Brown v. Board of Education and Black America's Struggle for Equality* (New York, 1976); David J. Garrow, *Bearing the Cross: Martin Luther King, Jr., and the Southern Christian Leadership Conference* (New York, 1986); Taylor Branch, *Parting the Waters: America in the King Years, 1954–63* (New York, 1988); Clayborne Carson, *In Struggle: SNCC and the Black Awakening of the 1960s* (Cambridge, Mass., 1981); Fred Powledge, *Free at Last? The Civil Rights Movement and the People Who Made It* (New York, 1992); Peter B. Levy, ed., *Let Freedom Ring: A Documentary History of the Modern Civil Rights Movement* (New York, 1992); Carl T. Rowan, *Dream Makers, Dream Breakers: The World of Justice Thurgood Marshall* (Boston, 1993); Kay Mills, *This Little Light of Mine: The Life of Fannie Lou Hamer* (New York, 1993).
2. *Los Angeles Times*, June 23, 1991; Gerald Horne, Review of Spike Lee, Five for Five: The Films of Spike Lee, in *Wide Angle: A Quarterly Journal of Film History, Theory, Criticism and Practice*, 13 (July-October 1991): 140–42.
3. Kobena Mercer, "Black Hair Style Politics," in Russell Ferguson, ed., *Out There: Marginalization and Contemporary Cultures* (Cambridge, Mass., 1990), 247–63; Gwendolyn Brooks, "Helen," in Margaret Busby, ed., *Daughters of Africa: An International Anthology of Words and Writings by Women of African Descent from the Ancient Egyptian to the Present* (New York, 1992), 269–71.
4. Douglas Henry Daniels, "Schooling Malcolm: Malcolm Little and Black Culture during the Golden Age of Jazz," in James Gwynne, ed., *Malcolm X-Justice Seeker* (New York, 1993), 45–58; John Horton, "Time and Cool People," in Thomas Kochman, ed., *Rappin' and Stylin' Out: Communication in Urban Black America* (Urbana, Ill., 1972), 19–31; Richard Majors and Janet Mancini Billson, *Cool Pose: The Dilemmas of Black Manhood in America* (New York, 1992).
5. *Los Angeles Sentinel*, January 7, 1993; City Sun, November 11–17, 1992; Gerald Horne, "Race Backwards: Genes, Violence, Race and Genocide," *Covert Action Quarterly*, 1 (Winter 1992–93): 29–35.

Source: *"Myth" and the Making of "Malcolm X"* by *Gerald Horne.* Published in *The American Historical Review, Vol. 98, No. 2 (Apr., 1993), pp. 440–450*

DECODING THE TEXT

1. What is the thesis of Horne's essay about *Malcolm X*, the film?

2. Who do you think is the intended audience for this essay?

3. What types of supporting evidence does Horne use to support his opinions?

CONNECTING TO YOUR CULTURE

1. How does this essay connect to you and life in the community you live in or the larger community of the United States?

2. Are there myths about your culture or subcultures (for instance, your generation) that are not accurate? What are they, and why do you think they exist?

CONSIDERING IDEAS

1. In general, describe what all Disney animated films have in common. How are their characters, settings, or plotlines similar?

2. How many Disney animated princess films have you seen in your lifetime? List them. If you haven't seen any, what other Disney films have you seen?

3. Describe the general characteristics of a Disney princess. What are some similarities?

AUTHOR BIO

Peggy Orenstein *is a* The New York Times *best-selling author, speaker, and editor. Her* The New York Times *best-selling works include her memoir,* Waiting for Daisy, Flux: Women on Sex, Work, Kids, Love and Life in a Half-Changed World, *and* Schoolgirls: Young Women, Self-Esteem and the Confidence Gap. *She has written articles for* USA Today, Mother Jones, O: The Oprah Magazine, Vogue, Discover, The New Yorker, Salon, Elle, *and* Discover, *and is a contributing writer for* The New York Times Magazine. *She has also been featured on such shows as* The Today Show, Good Morning America, Nightline, *NPR's* Morning Edition *and* Fresh Air *and CBC's* As It Happens. *The following essay is an excerpt from* Cinderella Ate My Daughter: Dispatches from the Front Lines of the New Girlie-Girl Culture, *which was also on* The New York Times *best seller's list.*

ARCHIVES DU 7E ART/PHOTOS 12/ALAMY

"GIRL POWER—NO REALLY" *FROM CINDERELLA ATE MY DAUGHTER*

Dispatches from the Front Lines of the New Girly-Girl Culture

Peggy Orenstein

"*I* didn't like that princess," Daisy said, wrinkling her nose. "She looked funny."

It was two weeks before Christmas 2009, and that could mean only one thing: the annual release of a new animated Disney film. That year, *The Princess and the Frog* premiered amid a blitz of self-congratulatory hype about the studio's First African-American Princess (though the more impressive event will be the introduction of the *Second* or raaybe the *Third* African-American Princess). Américas first black president had been elected just weeks before, the news media enthused, and—as if the two were equivalent—now this! About two-thirds of the audience at our local multiplex had been African American—parents with little girls decked out in gowns and tiaras—which was undeniably striking, even moving. Still, my own response, characteristically, was mixed: sure, it was about time Disney made up for the racism of *Song of the South, The Jungle Book,* and *Bumbo* (and *Aladdin* and *Peter Pan*), but was peddling a café au lait variation of the same old rescue fantasy in a thin-and-pretty package the best way to do that? Was that truly cause for celebration?

"But it's different for black girls," my friend Verna had told me. Verna, who is African American, is mother to a nine-year-old daughter. She is also a law professor specializing in the intersection of race, gender, and class in education law and policy. "There's a saying in our community," she continued, "'We love our sons but we raise our daughters.' Girls learn that you have to *do.* You have to be the worker bee. Princess takes black girls out of that realm. And you know, discounting the baggage of how stultifying being placed on a pedestal can be . . ." She laughed. "If you've never been on it, it looks pretty good."

I took the point, I guess. Certainly, as the mother of a biracial child myself, I identified with the constant scavenger hunt for toys and images that in *some* way resembled my kid. Take the wooden dollhouse I bought for Daisy: its choice of families spanned the skin tone spectrum, but the manufacturer's progressiveness did not extend to miscegenation (or, for that matter, to gay parents). I ended up buying two sets, one white and one Asian, so she could mix and match. It was, at best, an imperfect solution.

Scarcity breeds scrutiny. Given how few black female leads there are in G-rated animation (Anyone? Anyone?), Tiana, fairly or not, was expected to *represent. The Princess and the Frog* was subject to months of speculation before it opened. Outrage bubbled up when the first pass at Tiana's name was revealed: "Maddy," which sounded uncomfortably close to "Mammy." Disney also miscalculated, according to scuttlebutt, by initially making the character a chambermaid for a white woman; in the end, Tiana is a waitress at a restaurant owned by an African-American man. The texture of her hair, the shade of her skin, the fullness of her features, were all debated, as was the suspiciously indeterminate ethnicity of her prince (described as "olive-skinned," he spoke with a Brazilian accent). Disney shrewdly tried to bullet-proof the film by consulting Oprah Winfrey (who also voiced Tiana's mother, Eudora), the NAACP, and an organization called Mocha Moms. Take, *that,* critics! Of course, in the end, Tiana spent most of the film as a (shapely, long-eyelashed) amphibian, which rendered her race more or less moot.

Now here was my daughter, my very own daughter, saying that something about the princess looked off . . . *why?*

"You thought Tiana looked funny?" I asked, trying to keep my voice neutral.

She shook her head impatiently. "No," she said. "Not Tiana. The *princess.*"

"But Tiana *was* the princess," I said.

She shook her head again. "The *princess,*" she repeated, then, after a moment, added, "I liked when she helped the African-American girl, though."

That was when it clicked: Daisy wasn't talking about Tiana; she was talking about Lotte, Tiana's Caucasian friend and foil. *The Princess and the Frog* opened in a flashback: the two of them, as little girls, sitting on the floor of Lotte's icing pink room, while Eudora, a seamstress, read them the story of the princess and the frog. Tiana recoiled as the plot unspooled; Lotte swooned. It was Lotte who had row-upon row of pink princess gowns and a pink canopy bed; Lotte was the one who wished on stars; Lotte had the encyclopedic knowledge of fairy tales; Lotte dreamed of marrying the handsome prince and living happily ever after; Lotte, as an ingénue, swept her hair into a Cinderella' do for the ball. And it was Lotte who, while ultimately good-hearted, was also spoiled, shallow, and ridiculous—oh, and funny-looking; whatever strides Disney has made on race, "ugly" and its stepsibling "fat" still connote stupid or evil in its films. So it was clear—to me, anyway— that the viewer was supposed to dislike, or at least disidentify with, Lotte. But I understood Daisy's confusion: Lotte was also every thing that, up until now, Disney has urged our daughters to be and to buy. How was a little girl to interpret that? How were we parents to interpret it? Was Disney mocking itself? Could the studio actually be uneasy with the frenzy of acquisitiveness it had created? Was it signaling that parents should be more on guard against the very culture it had foisted on us?

Yeah, probably not, but Daisy's mix-up gave me the opening I needed to talk with her (*"with"* being the operative word) about the way the film had presented girls and women, to solicit her own ideas about it. That, in the end, is the best weapon we parents have, short of enrolling our daughters in one of those schools where kids knit all day (or moving to Sweden; marketing to children under twelve there is actually *illegal*—can you believe it?). We have only so much control over the images and products to which they are exposed, and even that will diminish over time. It is strategic, then—absolutely vital—to think through our own values and limits early, to consider what we approve or disapprove of and why.

I can't say what others' personal threshold ought to be: that depends on one's child, one's parenting style, one's judgment, one's own personal experience. It would be disingenuous to claim that Disney Princess diapers or Ty Girlz or *Hannah Montana* or *Twilight* or the latest Shakira video or a Facebook account is inherently harmful. Each is, however, a cog in the round-the-clock, all-pervasive media machine aimed at our daughters—and at us—from womb to tomb; one that, again and again, presents femininity as performance, sexuality as performance, identity as performance, and each of those traits as available for a price. It tells girls that how you look is more important than how you feel. More than that, it tells them that how you look *is* how you feel, as well as who you are. Meanwhile, the notion that we parents are sold, that our children are "growing up faster" than previous generations, that they are more mature and sophisticated in their tastes, more savvy in their consumption, and there is nothing we can (or need) do about it is—what is the technical term again?— oh yes: *a load of crap.* Today's three-year-olds are no better than their predecessors at recognizing when their desires are manipulated by grown-ups. Today's six-year-olds dont get the subtext of their sexy pirate costumes. Today's eight-year-olds dont understand that ads are designed to sell them something. And today's fourteen-year-olds are still desperate for approval from their friends—all 622 of them.

Source: *Pages 179–192 from* Cinderella Ate My Daughter *by Peggy Orenstein. Copyright (c) 2011 by Peggy Orenstein. Reprinted by permission of HarperCollins Publishers.*

DECODING THE TEXT

1. What overall argument does the author make?
2. How strong is her supporting evidence?
3. Does she make you believe or at least seriously consider her argument?

CONNECTING TO YOUR CULTURE

1. What was the first animated film from Disney that you saw? How old were you?
2. Do you think your interpretation of or response to the film would change if you viewed it again?
3. What movies or TV shows did you enjoy as a child? How did those movies or shows depict genders?

CONSIDERING IDEAS

1. Think of some of your favorite films that have young male or female character leads. Create a list of physical, intellectual, and emotional qualities that these lead characters exhibit.
2. Describe the general characteristics of a Disney prince. What are some similarities among them?
3. Out of all the films ever made, which film would you choose to represent your life as an adolescent?

AUTHOR BIO

Crystal Smith writes about social media and marketing. She currently works for nonprofit agencies seeking gender equality and an end to discrimination against women in Canada. In addition, Smith provides pro bono marketing work to the Halton Women's Centre based in Oakville, Ontario. Smith is also the volunteer blog editor for The Pixel Project, a nonprofit organization that works toward ending violence against women using social media, and can be found at www.pixelproject.net. Smith was inspired to write about the impact of popular culture on young boys in The Achilles Effect: What Pop Culture Is Teaching Young Boys About Masculinity after being disappointed with gender portrayals in film while raising her two young sons. The following essay is an excerpt from The Achilles Effect. Her website is www.achilleseffect.com.

THE ACHILLES EFFECT

What Pop Culture Is Teaching Boys About Masculinity

Crystal Smith

While the fathers of male characters occasionally die or leave as well, there is one critical difference: they are replaced. Male friends and mentors abound for a young boy separated from his family, but women are never inserted into the story to take the place of the lost mother.

Consider *Ice Age,* where the male baby enjoys a long sojourn with the all-male cast before being reunited with his father, or *Finding Nemo,* where Nemo interacts with a group consisting almost entirely of males before finding his father. Remy of *Ratatouille* is separated from his father, but finds friendship and his life's purpose with a male chef-in-training who has, coincidentally, recently lost his mother. Like Nemo, Remy reconnects with his father near the end of the film. Exiled penguin Mumble also finds solace in a group of male friends before returning to his colony.

Beyond companionship, many male characters find male mentors to guide them toward their destiny. Male kung fu masters Shifu and Oogway train Po in *Kung Fu Panda.* Brock teaches Ash about catching and training Pokemon. Obi-Wan Kenobi raises Anakin Skywalker to be a Jedi knight. Hiccup in the film *How to Train Your Dragon* has a fractious relationship with his father, but finds something of a mentor in dragon hunting trainer, Gobber. Young cow Otis is seemingly abandoned by his mother in *Barnyard* and then adopted by kind and gentle Ben. Bruce Wayne loses his parents when he is young and is raised by his father's butler Alfred, a man he continues to depend on even after he becomes Batman.

The film *Up* also emphasizes the importance of male influence on boys. As I mentioned in the previous chapter, the parents of male protagonist Russell are divorced. As the movie progresses, the audience learns that Russell's father has virtually disappeared from his life. Following a familiar pattern, Russell finds an older male to replace his missing father and it is this man, Carl, who attends the all-important Wilderness Explorer awards ceremony in place of Russell's father.

Where is Russell's mother? Sitting in the audience, quietly clapping for her son. That she is excluded from the ceremony speaks volumes about how her relationship with her son is to be interpreted. She is the caretaker and the go-to parent, but she is not enough. She must give way to a virtual stranger and allow him to become a second parent to her son.

In pointing out these instances of mother denial (in the words of Silverstein and Rashbaum), I am not discounting the importance of a male role model in a boy's life; I am questioning why, in children's popular culture, a male role model can only come at the expense of the mother.

Of course, mothers are not treated shabbily in all children's entertainment—*Toy Story* and *Happy Feet* both include close mother/son relationships—but, as the examples I have included here demonstrate, it is not at all uncommon to see mothers disposed of or cut out of their sons' lives in some way. That this narrative thread is seen in some of the most popular stories and across all genres in children's film and television—comedy, sci-fi, superhero, and adventure—only underscores how pervasive a theme it is.

To uncover exactly why this theme of mother/son separation appears with such regularity, we need only look at the tenets of traditional masculinity. These masculine imperatives are reflected in popular culture, telling boys that they must be stoic and emotionally detached, they need to present themselves at all times as strong and independent, and they must avoid all things feminine. A break with Mom accomplishes all of these things, leaving fictional boys free to become the real men they are destined to be.

The concept of detachment is especially relevant to boys. As the International Central Institute for Youth and Educational Television (IZI) noted in a 2008 report, children's television places tremendous value on the separation of a boy or man from emotional attachments, traditions, and his background. The break between a son and his mother—carried out by choice or by force—is the ultimate detachment from home and family. It is also presented as a desirable and necessary first step on a boy's journey toward storm, or a wayward youngster who finds himself lost and alone, the message is the same—boys need to be removed from the comforts of home and the sometimes suffocating attentions of Mom in order to become men.

As I noted in the introduction, the imperative to act manly affects boys from a very young age. Dislike of physical affection, feigning toughness, embarrassment about crying—all are ways that young boys try to demonstrate their manhood. This compulsion to act traditionally masculine stems, in part, from the association between feminine behaviour and weakness—an association that is reinforced throughout children's pop culture.

Source: *From* The Achilles Effect: What Pop Culture Is Teaching Young Boys About Masculinity, *by Crystal Smith. Reprinted with permission of the author.*

DECODING THE TEXT

1. What overall argument does the author make?

2. How strong is her supporting evidence?

3. Does she make you believe or at least seriously consider her argument?

CONNECTING TO YOUR CULTURE

1. In what other areas of the popular culture that you enjoy might you encounter stereotyping of genders or gender roles?

2. Think back on the literature that you have read for school. Have any presented particular cultural traditions or backgrounds as so-called normal American?

3. What movies or TV shows do you enjoy now? Can you make a generalization about how these movies or shows depict genders?

READING SELECTIONS:
A CASE STUDY OF REVIEWS
FROM THE 2010s

CONSIDERING IDEAS

1. Where do you go to find information about films you may want to see?

2. How often do you read film reviews?

3. How often do you watch or listen to film reviews rather than read them?

4. What do you think film critics look for in the films that they view?

5. How influential do you think film critics, professional and nonprofessional, are in U.S. culture?

AUTHOR BIO

Each week, the writers of The A.V. Club *issue a slightly slanted pop culture list filled with challenging opinions and fascinating facts. This list essay is an excerpt from the book* Inventory: 16 Films Featuring Manic Pixie Dream Girls, 10 Great Songs Ruined by Saxophone, *and* 100 More Obsessively Specific Pop-Culture Lists, *which combines new lists created especially for the book with a few favorites first seen at* avclub.com *and in the pages of* The A.V. Club's *sister publication,* The Onion.

NIGHT OF THE KILLER LAMP

23 RIDICULOUS HORROR-MOVIE ADVERSARIES

1. Demonically possessed bed (*Death Bed: The Bed That Eats*, 1977)

The title says it all, really. Made for $30,000 over a five-year period—and never officially released until it was dug up for DVD in the early '00s—George Berry's inexplicable surreal-camp-horror film recently earned a mention in Patton Oswalt's comedy album *Werewolves & Lollipops*, in which he suggested *Rape Stove* as a possible sequel. Aside from luring potential nappers and love-makers with the promise of red velvety comfort, the centuries-old "death bed" isn't terribly active, which explains why it's been starving for 10 years in a crumbling estate before amorous young people begin stopping by again. Here's how the devilish contraption works: Victims are disrobed, surrounded by a burbling yellow goo, and sucked into an acid-filled waterbed mattress that dissolves their flesh and bones. Then the bed makes itself, on the off chance that another orgy might develop within the next decade or so. Weirdest touch in a movie full of them: Though the victims are submerged in a kind of acid bath, the sound effect is of someone vigorously chomping on an apple. The bed also snores, leaving viewers to ponder the metaphysical paradox of a bed sleeping on itself.

2. Floor lamp (*Amityville 4: The Evil Escapes*, 1989)

So far, *The Amityville Horror* has spawned a whopping eight sequels, remakes, and spin-offs, but surely none of them is as ridiculous as the cheapie *Amityville 4: The Evil Escapes*, in which Satan stops possessing a house and starts possessing bad household decor. After scaring some particularly flinchy priests, an ugly brass lamp full of evil escapes the much-filmed Amityville and winds up in a California house occupied by recent widow Patty Duke, her three kids, and her mom, Jane Wyatt. (In the process, it gives Wyatt's sister tetanus, in a particularly low-key display of Satanic might.) Even though it has the power to flash ominously, cover itself with flies, somehow stuff the family bird into a toaster oven, and activate a chainsaw and a garbage disposal at inopportune moments, the lamp makes a phenomenally inert villain, and the film's constant attempts to make it frightening border on camp—particularly in the scene where it slowly edges across a room, sneaking up on the unsuspecting Duke. Eventually, after a pitched battle, Duke, Wyatt, and a priest beat the devil—by throwing the lamp out a window.

3. Giant tree (*The Guardian*, 1990)

Here's a solid piece of advice: If you're dealing with an evil tree, stay out of the forest. Not unlike the menace in *Death Bed*, the tree in William Friedkin's *The Guardian* can't really go anywhere, so it mostly relies on sexy nanny Jenny Seagrove to bring it infant sacrifices as part of a tree-worshipping druidic ritual. (For holding up her end of the bargain, the frequently naked Seagrove gets fondled by twigs.) Still, Friedkin and company come up with increasingly ridiculous reasons for potential victims to flee straight into the forest, where they're beheaded by branches, impaled by roots, and swallowed up by a trunk that bleeds the blood of the innocent. Too bad this ancient menace lived to see the birth of its unstoppable modern adversary: The chainsaw.

4. Laundry-folding machine (*The Mangler*, 1995)

The capitalist machine may be oiled by the blood of the workers, but that metaphor was never meant to play as literally as it does in *The Mangler*, a supremely goofy adaptation of a Stephen King short story. Even when working properly, the giant industrial laundry-folding machine at Blue Ribbon Laundry looks like it could take a non-union limb or two. But this one's demonically possessed, fueled by virgin's blood and kept in operation by a Mr. Burns/Dr. Strangelove-like figure (Robert Englund) who convinces safety inspectors to look the other way whenever the body of another sweatshop worker winds up neatly pressed. Like many of the adversaries on this list, the machine is heavy and completely inanimate, but it's surprisingly resourceful, like when it transfers its malevolent powers to an evil icebox. Then again, it needn't be so clever, not when people keep trying to get a closer look by crawling into its hungry maw.

5. Whipped cream (*The Stuff*, 1985)

The B-movie king of great ideas and so-so execution, writer-director Larry Cohen came up with a doozy of a premise for his satirical horror movie *The Stuff*, but the satire was only half-realized, and he seemed to forget about the horror part altogether. Found bubbling up from a snow bank like delicious, delicious oil, "The Stuff" is a whipped-cream-like substance that becomes a taste sensation, a low-calorie, ready-to-eat option for families across America. The one minor caveat? It eats people alive from the inside, turning its hosts into dead-eyed zombies. In concept, Cohen has come up with an ingenious dig at capitalism: the consumer being consumed by consumables. But he has a harder time turning tubs of whipped cream into the Stuff of nightmares.

6. Killer baboon (*Shakma*, 1990)

In theory, a killer baboon driven mad by experimental injections—administered by callous professor Roddy McDowall, no less—sounds like a wicked cool beastie. In practice, said baboon most often takes the form of a limp, furry doll, which its "victims" jerk about while pretending to be mauled. *Shakma*'s few shots of a live baboon going apeshit look suitably unhinged, though more in a comic way than a scary way. As for the cast—a motley collection of TV teens and dimming "stars of the future"—they make better baboon fodder than they do likeable heroes. Absurd or not, it's easier to root for an inanimate fur-suit than for Christopher Atkins.

7. The Fouke Monster (*The Legend Of Boggy Creek*, 1972)

Director Charles B. Pierce takes an unusual approach to the horror genre with *Boggy Creek*, structuring the film like a documentary, full of grainy nature footage and "interviews" with people who survived encounters with the legendary woodland ape-man that some know as Sasquatch, some as Bigfoot, and some—well, the people from Fouke, AR anyway—know as The Fouke Monster. *The Legend Of Boggy Creek* is sleepily episodic, and about as intense as a bloodless G-rated monster movie can be, which means that most of the scares consist of people almost seeing The Fouke Monster before making a pretty wide escape. Whew! That was . . . not that close, really.

8. Goblin army (*Troll 2*, 1990)

There's a good reason there's a documentary in the works about the making of *Troll 2* titled *Best Worst Movie*. This Italian production—originally called *Goblin*, which more accurately describes its bad guys—follows an American family trying to escape a legion of mythical creatures who turn humans into plants, then eat them. Atrocious acting aside, *Troll 2*'s goblins are extra-ridiculous because of their costumes, which resemble potato sacks topped with Halloween masks. Frankly, they're nowhere near as scary as the ghostly grandpa who advises young hero Michael Stephenson to piss all over the family's dinner so they won't undergo "the change." Next to an old man with a pee fetish, a bunch of little people dressed in Dollar Store leftovers barely raises a shriek.

9. Killers from space (*Killers From Space*, 1954)

A trio of space aliens reveals to a nuclear scientist their plans to use America's atomic technology to grow giant mutated animals, destroy all humans, and colonize the Earth. And they'd be a lot easier to take seriously if they didn't make this threat while wearing heavy, hooded black tunics and flashing their ping-pong-ball eyes. If you crossbred Marty Feldman with a Muppet, you'd just about equal the level of menace of the killers from space. (Fun fact: This movie was directed by Billy Wilder's brother. See if you can spot the telltale Wilder sophistication.)

10. Semi-mobile puppets (*Rock 'N' Roll Nightmare*, 1987)

Canadian metal star Jon Mikl Thor scripted and stars in this low-budget, claustrophobic, batshit-insane film about a Canadian metal star who's actually an archangel called The Intercessor. He's itching to fight Satan himself, but for some reason, the Father Of Lies chooses to manifest in the form of disturbingly phallic, one-eyed puppets before showing his true form: a really big, slightly less phallic two-eyed puppet. Or half of one, anyway. The climactic fight scene displays virtually every inch of Thor's body, but only the barely mobile upper half (and feet) of His Satanic Majesty. Hey, even Beelzebub has to make budget.

11. Homicidal vending machine (*Maximum Overdrive*, 1986)

In 1976's *Silent Movie*, Mel Brooks and company hold off bad guys using vending-machine soda as hand grenades. But what if the machine turned evil? That's precisely what happens in this awful Stephen King adaptation, directed by King himself. Under the influence of either a comet tail or alien invaders, all machines suddenly turn homicidal—even a lowly soda machine. It tries to take out an entire Little League team by launching cans from its dispenser. One, naturally, nails a guy in the crotch. All that's missing is someone quipping, "I told you soda was bad for you!"

12. Vampire dogs (*Zoltan: Hound Of Dracula*, 1978)

Pity poor Zoltan. Once he was a peasant's happy dog. Then, after interrupting Dracula mid-bite, he was forever enslaved to the bloodsucking ways of his new master. After a couple centuries, Zoltan resurfaces in 1970s California, intent on terrorizing the family of Dracula's distant relatives, starting with their dogs. A vampire dog isn't the worst idea for a horror-film foe but there's nothing particularly scary about Zoltan, a perfectly pleasant-looking Doberman outfitted with a pair of unconvincing prosthetic fangs (courtesy of a young Stan Winston). Even less scary: Fight scenes in which the actors appear to be fighting off doggie kisses, and a final scene that sets up a sequel involving Zoltan's downright adorable Dracupup offspring.

13. Rapping leprechaun (*Leprechaun In The Hood,* 2000)

By the time *Leprechaun In The Hood* hit undiscriminating video stores in 2000, original star *Leprechaun* star Jennifer Aniston was long gone, the titular diminutive badass had weathered a trip to space in the franchise's fourth entry, and the brain trust behind the series had more or less given up on even trying to be scary. Like *Seed Of Chucky, Leprechaun In The Hood*—which co-stars such paycheck-hungry rap luminaries as Ice-T and Coolio—trades in bad horror for leaden camp as Warwick Davis busts rhymes and menaces a trio of rappers who've come into possession of his magical flute. Yes, magical flute. Cause honestly what's more terrifying than a rapping leprechaun? Oh wait, just about everything. That nevertheless didn't prevent a return trip back to the hood for Davis and the gang in 2002's no doubt grindingly essential *Leprechaun: Back 2 Tha Hood.*

14. Fetus in a bottle (*The Jar,* 1984)

Eraserhead was a cult classic, but it understandably didn't prompt a lot of knockoffs. An exception can be found in the 1984 shocker *The Jar,* a bizarre psychodrama about a hirsute, sullen loner (Gary Wallace) tormented by a mysterious, bottled embryo-like creature that gradually tears his life apart and induces ostensibly frightening hallucinations involving crucifixion and the Vietnam War. Wallace shifts the jar's location around, but he can't outrun its extremely silly, abstract evil. The titular fiend ultimately drives Wallace to kill in what can only be described as the apex of storage-unit-based horror.

15. Tree-monster thingy (*Wendigo,* 2001)

Larry Fessenden makes thinking people's horror movies, which is a nice way of saying his movies are metaphorically rich but not terribly frightening. That certainly holds true of 2001's *Wendigo,* an atmospheric would-be scare fest about a big city family that encounters a half-man, half-deer shape-shifting creature that can transform into anything. Unfortunately, in *Wendigo,* the title beastie transforms into a weird tree creature that's ultimately more silly than scary. Fessenden followed up with this year's *Last Winter,* another metaphor-heavy, scare-light allegory about global warming.

16. Robot monster (*Robot Monster,* 1953)

Often mentioned alongside Ed Wood's *Plan 9 From Outer Space* as a science fiction movie so incompetent that it's charming, *Robot Monster* was made in four days for $16,000 with mainly amateur actors, and it shows. The cheapness and lackluster production design is epitomized by the bizarre appearance of the movie's title villain. Director Phil Tucker cast veteran stuntman and actor George Barrows as Ro-Man the robot monster for one simple reason: Barrows already owned his own gorilla suit. Because that's what a robot looks like, right? A diving helmet was added to give Ro-Man at least some semblance of actually being a mechanical creature, but as *Mystery Science Theater 3000*'s Joel Hodgson quipped, "I've seen Salvador Dali paintings that made more sense than this." Even weirder: Ro-Man talks like Frasier Crane and speaks in sentences that sound like Donald Rumsfeld wrote them: "I cannot. Yet I must. How do you calculate that? At what point on the graph do 'must' and 'cannot' meet? Yet I must. But I cannot."

17. Rug/slug thing (*The Creeping Terror,* 1964)

Unlike Ro-Man, the alien beast in *The Creeping Terror* actually is kind of creepy. And in fact, the same basic concept—an amorphous, amoeba-like creature that eats and eats and eats—was handled well in a similar movie, *The Blob.* What dooms *The Creeping Terror* to laughability is a combination of general filmmaking incompetence and legendary bad luck. The story goes that the filmmakers' original alien costume was either stolen or destroyed only days before filming. The replacement they were forced to build in order to finish the movie is, well, not great. Intended to be a giant slug-like creature, the monster looks like it was sewn together from carpet remnants and tarp. The crewmembers' feet are often clearly visible underneath, and the whole assemblage moves so slowly that the actors playing its victims literally have to stop and wait for it to catch up to them.

18. Octopus-man (*Octaman*, 1971)

Makeup artist Rick Baker has won six Oscars for his work, which includes highly praised creature designs on *An American Werewolf In London* and *Star Wars*. But everyone's gotta start somewhere, and Baker's first movie was inauspicious, to say the least: *Octaman,* a cheapie horror-thriller about a deadly man/octopus hybrid mutant terrorizing a Mexican town. It was written and directed by Harry Essex, who basically rehashed the major ideas from his considerably more successful 1954 screenplay, *Creature From The Black Lagoon.* The monster in *Black Lagoon* is an iconic classic; Octaman is just a guy in a very unconvincing rubber suit. To fake the appearance of eight limbs, Baker simply suspended two extra arm-tentacles by wires attached to the actor's real arms, and attached two pathetic-looking rubber legs to the back of the real legs. Just how bad was the movie? Here's Baker himself, from an interview with the website revolutionsf.com: "The very first film that I did was *Octaman*, with [actress] Pier Angeli. Don't ever watch it. You'll lose all respect for me. I was like, 'I'm making a movie!' It was shot in 10 days. Pier Angeli killed herself immediately after *Octaman* was filmed. Can't blame her."

19. Evil brains (*The Brain From Planet Arous*, 1957)

Earth is invaded by an extraterrestrial evil criminal mastermind—a literal mind. The inhabitants of the planet Arous are brains—giant, disembodied brains with glowing eyes, who can take over human bodies and use them for nefarious criminal purposes, including leering at their host bodies' girlfriends. In practice, though, the brains from planet Arous look more like helium balloons with lightbulbs for eyes.

20. Bulldozer (*Killdozer,* 1974)

Based on a 1944 novella by celebrated science fiction writer Theodore Sturgeon, the TV movie *Killdozer* has one of the weirdest premises—and most awesome titles—of its era. A group of construction workers on a Pacific Island accidentally strike a meteorite with the blade of a bulldozer, releasing a malevolent alien made out of blue light that possesses the earthmover, creating a rampaging, driverless mechanical killer with no apparent need for gas, but plenty of bloodlust. Beyond the premise and title, though, the movie doesn't have much to recommend itself—it's a fairly lackluster made-for-TV blandfest, though it does boast an early credit for future TV star Robert Urich. And it inspired the name of the influential 1990s-era punk band, which counts for something.

21. General proximity to nature (*Frogs,* 1972)

Frogs just aren't very scary. In theory, though, a whole swamp full of poisonous snakes, alligators, spiders, lizards, scorpions, and leeches, with some frogs thrown in as garnish, might be kind of frightening. George McCowan's *Frogs* seems to get this—in spite of the title and the poster depicting a particularly pop-eyed frog with a bloodied human hand poking out of its mouth, the freakin' frogs in *Frogs* never actually kill anyone. They just hang around and try their damnedest to look menacing while cranky billionaire Ray Milland insists his poison-and-pollute anti-nature policies are right and just, no matter how many members of his extended family fall prey to vengeful nature. Unfortunately, their deaths are laughably choreographed, and usually involve shots of victims rolling around screaming in mud or water, interspersed with close-up shots of animals swimming or sitting around peaceably. Some of the better sequences involve death by looking at a zoomed-in shot of a snapping turtle, death by repeatedly grabbing and rolling around on top of an alligator whose mouth is clearly banded shut, and Milland's apparent death by just generally being freaked out by all the frogs in his vicinity. Moral: don't get within 50 feet of nature, or some Spanish moss might fall off a tree and bury you to death while tarantulas watch nearby.

22. Rabbits (*Night Of The Lepus,* 1972)

The trailer for William F. Claxton's *Night Of The Lepus* is all about the mystery: What hideous creature is haunting the night? What's killing all those people? What the heck is the adversary in this film?

Answer: bunnies. Giant carnivorous mutant bunnies. Which look suspiciously like perfectly normal bunnies hopping around in slow motion, with scary roaring and snarling noises superimposed on the soundtrack. Hey, at least they're more ferocious than those frogs.

23. Elevator (*The Lift*, 1983)

Elevators conjure up two very real fears: being trapped in a confined space, and falling hundreds of feet to your death. But making an entire movie (*two* movies, actually, since director Dick Maas remade his original Dutch production as 2001's *The Shaft*, with Naomi Watts) that revolves around a murderously sentient lift takes a certain amount of chutzpah. There's only so much it can do to kill people, though it does somehow develop the ability to empty itself of oxygen to suffocate its passengers, and it gets the drop on an unwitting victim by descending unexpectedly, cutting his head off. Next time, we'll take the stairs.

DECODING THE TEXT

All four of the essays in this case study are reviews that are set up with different reviewing formats. Even so, the review genre is represented clearly by all four.

1. How does the author of this review organize the interpretations of and reactions to the movies featured in the review? Does the format match the content the author is reviewing? Why do you think the list essay format was used?

2. Would you describe this review as positive, negative, or balanced? Why?

3. Does the place where the review was published determine or influence how the author reacted or responded to the films or wrote the review?

4. Did the review make you want to see some or all of the films?

CONNECTING TO YOUR CULTURE

1. What percentage of the films you see each year are horror movies?

2. What is your favorite horror movie? Why?

3. Why do you think the horror-movie genre is so popular in the United States?

AUTHOR BIO

The following essay came from the fansite comicbookmovie.com, a site that utilizes user-generated content. The site came online in 2002 when Hollywood was just beginning to adapt comic books to film form. Currently, comicbookmovie.com is the most active website devoted to the genre, and it focuses on delivering breaking news about current Hollywood projects involving comic book characters.

FILM STILLS/ALAMY

IS MARVEL KILLING THE COMIC BOOK GENRE?

For the past 10 years, Marvel has been putting out CBM after CBM after CBM. Most of these movies have been less than stellar. In fact, most have been quite forgettable. In 2007 alone, Marvel released THREE mediocre and forgettable CBMs: *Ghost Rider*, *Spider-Man 3*, and *Fantastic Four: Rise of the Silver Surfer*. It seemed that people had had enough of getting so many CBMs shoved down their throats. And then *Iron Man* and *The Dark Knight* took everyone by surprise. They changed the entire genre forever. But this past year, it seemed that people again had gotten bored of CBMs. *Kick-Ass* barely managed to make a profit, *Iron Man 2* couldn't even make as much as the first movie, and *Scott Pilgrim* bombed horribly even though it was one of the most acclaimed movies of the year. Maybe movie-goers have had enough? Just look at Marvel's movie schedule: This year alone we're getting *Thor*, *X-Men First Class*, and *Captain America*, next year we're getting a Spider-Man reboot, a Ghost Rider sequel, and a Wolverine movie that no one asked for, and to top it all off, an *Avengers* movie. Not to mention plans to reboot Fantastic Four, Iron Man 3, a Hulk movie with yet another actor playing Banner, and Ant-Man. Believe or not, people might get sick of having so many CBMs shoved down their throats.

Meanwhile, DC have barely released any movies this past decade. But maybe that's part of a bigger plan? Maybe they're waiting for Marvel to run out of characters so they can have the entire market left for themselves? Maybe they want to wait and see how the Avengers does and make a Justice League movie that will pulverize it? Now that the Harry Potter franchise is coming to an end, there's no telling what the future awaits WB/DC.

One thing's for sure, people lately have been craving for originality. Look at Avatar. Yes, it was a rehash of the same story we've heard before a thousand times. But it looked different. People saw it and said "I've never seen anything like this before. The movie went on to gross more than $2 billion at the box office. Look at last year. Movies like *The Social Network*, *Black Swan*, *Inception*, *The Town*, and *The Fighter* were the biggest money makers because they offered movie—goers something new. Something they've never seen before.

In conclusion, maybe Marvel should take a chill pill and relax. They have an eternity to make movies. They don't need to shove 4 movies a year down our throats. They should focus on one, maybe two movies a year at most and make sure they're actually quality movies. It seems that Marvel only care about quantity and profits rather than quality. Besides, I think it's safe to assume that if your movie doesn't have Batman on it, it most likely won't gross over a billion dollars.

Source: *"Is Marvel Killing the Comic Book Genre? Found"* on http://comicbookmovie.com/comics/news/?a=28013.

DECODING THE TEXTS

All four of the essays in this case study are reviews that are set up with different reviewing formats. Even so, the review genre is represented clearly by all four.

1. How does the author of this review organize the interpretations and reactions to the movies being reviewed? Does the format match the content the author is reviewing?

2. Why do you think the author chose to review multiple films, rather than just one?

3. Would you describe this review as positive, negative, or balanced? Why?

4. Does the place where the review was published determine or influence how the author reacted or responded to the film or wrote the review?

5. Did the review make you want to see the films mentioned?

CONNECTING TO YOUR CULTURE

1. Make a list of all the films that are mentioned in this review. How many of them have you seen?

2. What is your favorite super hero(ine) movie? Why?

3. Why do you think the super hero(ine) genre is so popular in the United States?

Drew McWeeny *is a film critic and screenwriter also known by his pseudonym, Moriarty. McWeeny is the former editor of the website* Ain't It Cool News. *Currently, McWeeny writes for* HitFix.com, *where he has a column titled "Motion Captures: Inside Movies and DVD with Drew McWeeny." This essay was published on* HitFix.com *on July 12, 2011.*

FINAL HARRY POTTER FILM WRAPS UP SERIES WITH ELEGANT, EPIC BATTLE TO THE DEATH

Drew McWeeny

Writing about "Harry Potter and the Deathly Hallows Part 2" is going to have to be, by design, writing about the passage of time, the accumulation of experience, and the development of an opinion about not only what JK Rowling accomplished on the page, but what the producers of the series pulled off with the films.

I looked back at my published words about the series. It's not complete, but I reviewed "Chamber Of Secrets," "Prisoner Of Azkaban," "Order Of The Phoenix," "Half-Blood Prince," and the first half of "Deathly Hallows." There's another piece I found as well that was published the week that Rowling released the final book. Quint and I had a long conversation about it on IM, and decided to just cut and paste it as an article that was, more than anything, a chance for the Talkbackers to discuss the book.

My feelings about Rowling as a writer evolved over time, as her work evolved, and my feelings about the books and my feelings about the movies were not always the same. It's strange for me to look back at my predictions about how things would wrap up and see how right I am at times and how wrong I am at others. As you move from review to review, you can sense that I am more and more impressed as they get closer and closer to pulling it off, and I think David Yates has been a key player in how this series worked. I like that he directed the last four films. That's half the series, and I think he's got a lot to be proud of.

This is, after all, one of the most remarkable accomplishments of the last decade of commercial movie making, whether you like them or not. To pull this off, to accomplish all seven of the books, to make them with one cast that grew with the project, ti's something no one's really done before. I've called this the "7 Up" of fantasy filmmaking, and more than ever, that's what it feels like. It's a series about maturing that, by design, did it for real, the storytelling and the cast and the intensity of it all aging up from film to film. Some small steps, some big jumps, but in the end, there's something undeniable going on in the big picture arc of the entire series and it is, simply put, beautiful.

That's a strange description, perhaps, for a big summer blockbuster, but it is an accurate one. There is an eerie beauty to the way this final confrontation between Harry Potter and Lord Voldemort unfolds, and the staging of the Battle For Hogwarts is genuinely epic. And along the way, Yates and screenwriter Steve Kloves, who has been onboard for all but one of the adaptations, have managed to make a movie that satisfies as a conclusion without overplaying that hand. This does not just feel like everyone walking out and taking a bow, an empty victory lap. That would have been easy because Warner already has this one in the bag. The question is not whether this film will or won't make money. It's just a matter of how much. The good news is that they'll deserve it, because they've done something special, and they've done it so well here at the end, where it really matters, that I almost want to accuse them of, yes, magic.

The film opens with the exact same shots that closed the previous film, with Lord Voldemort (Ralph Fiennes) finding the Elder Wand in the tomb of Dumbledore and holding it aloft, and then we cut to

Hogwarts, where Severus Snape (Alan Rickman) stands in a high window, watching the students who are now under his supervision. No dialogue at all. Just a few quick images before the title comes up, and then we're into it. This film assumes you're up to speed, and it quickly ramps up into the first major set piece, an attempt on the Gringott's vault of Bellatrix Lestrange (Helena Bonham Carter). By now, there are tricks and gags that are part of the series, like the use of Polyjuice potion or Harry's Cloak of Invisibility, and it's nice to see how they don't have to stop the movie anymore to explain these things. They just do it and keep moving. And the way the sequence builds, it's apparent how far the "Potter" series has come since the clunky early days of "Sorcerer's Stone." Not only are the effects more polished, which is a given since it's been a full decade, but the world itself is just so firmly defined now, so fleshed out and substantial, and the cast has gotten so good at bringing the details to life, that it's easy now to just get lost in what's happening. You don't feel all the heavy lifting anymore, and as a result, this one races by in a way that feels effortless.

After the Gringott's heist, Harry (Daniel Radcliffe), Hermione (Emma Watson), and Ron (Rupert Grint) need to get back into Hogwarts, and once they do, they need to decide how to handle Lord Voldermort's impending attack. The movie really doesn't do much more than that, story-wise, but it's packed with incident as things accelerate. What keeps the tension so high is the way Voldemort is portrayed here. There's one moment in particular where he walks through the aftermath of a violent encounter, his bare feet on a blood-soaked floor, and just the disconnected disregard for any living thing in his way makes him scary in a way that I wouldn't have thought possible at the start of the series. The very direct goal of finding and destroying the final horcruxes in this film is simple, and the inevitable reveals built into this film have been a long time coming, and they're handled very well. These characters make some major choices in the film, and there are payoffs to things that have been developing over the last seven films. Characters like Luna Lovegood (Evanna Lynch), Ollivander (John Hurt), Griphook (Warwick Davis), Molly Weasley (Julie Walter) and especially Neville Longbottom (Matthew Lewis) all show up here to maximum effect, given their big moments, contributing in vital ways.

The score by Alexandre Desplat is triumphant, and his use of the themes initially established by John Williams is impressive, tying the series together, and Eduardo Serra's photography is perfect for a world teetering on the edge of full-blown magic war. The early Potter films didn't really deliver on indelible images, but as the series has progressed, that's changed, and in this film, there are any number of big iconic sights. What I love is that they're not in the film just to be cool, but are instead important, compelling because of the emotional context, not just because of the light show. The particular mechanics of how the film's conclusion comes together are laid out onscreen in a way that seems to me easy to absorb whether you've read the book or not, handled so that there are many heroes to celebrate when the credits finally roll. The sense of impending menace that is so important to this entry in the series is underlined in scene after scene, whether it's the sight of Dementors hanging in the sky above Hogwarts or a rolling ocean of fire destroying a location that has been key to so many of the films or the gut-punch of two characters, new parents, both dead, but still hand-in-hand, united even in their last moments, and as a result, there is real tension, almost inescapable, always building.

While I personally prefer the "Lord Of The Rings" series overall, I found myself deeply moved by the film's coda, a suggestion that life continues, that there will be continuity in this universe. I'll say this for "Deathly Hallows Part 2," as well . . . it is efficient in its epic sprawl. The film is one of the shorter entries in the series at just over two hours, but it also feels like there's no fat at all on the film. I'm not a big enough fan to know how much they did or didn't cut from the book, but to me, this feels like the proper emotional crescendo to what's come before. One great example of how they got it right is the handling of Snape in the film. Rickman has often been called on to appear in one or two scenes and then exit stage left in these movies, and this time, he plays a crucial role, his real character finally laid bare. Rickman rises to the material and then some, and the whole film benefits from the way he lets Snape's damaged soul reveal itself. His work is so good that it makes me want to go back and watch the earlier films just to see the work he does along the way. I want to see if he's playing all of his stuff on several levels, aware of his secrets but never overplaying them.

Daniel Radcliffe steps up here with the best performance he's given in the series, making heroic choices that justify every prophecy. He is not just the Boy Who Lived now. He is right there, in the heart of the war, fighting, leading, surrounded by friends and family. He is Harry Potter, Gryffindor, or Harry Potter, boyfriend, or Harry Potter, Order of the Phoenix. He is connected to other people, and he is stronger for it. He and Grint and Watson all seem to have finally vanished into the characters, just in time to wrap it all up. Meanwhile, the entire amazing extended supporting cast, a Who's Who of young and old UK-based performers, makes this feel important. I love seeing Maggie Smith play a scene like the one where she activates an important part of the defensive line at Hogwarts, and I think the casting in this series has always said to viewers, "We are taking this seriously, so you should, too." When Dumbledore's brother shows up, it could be anyone. You could have cast Carrot Top at this point just because the price is right, and that would have been that. Instead, it's Ciaran Hinds. He doesn't show up for long, but he makes his presence felt, and that just shows how seriously they take every single role.

I feel very lucky to have watched the "Harry Potter" series unfold in real time over the years. These are going to live on, rewatched for years to come, just like the books, and I look forward to the day I can watch them with my own boys. But for now, I'll just enjoy knowing that I saw a studio pull off something almost impossible yesterday, and I'll marvel at just how poised and confident the entire production seems, how well it all comes together. And when the film finally ends, when those last few images play out, it is more than satisfying. It is triumphant.

Source: *Material taken from HitFix, Inc.* www.HitFix.com.

DECODING THE TEXT

All four of the essays in this case study are reviews that are set up with different reviewing formats. Even so, the review genre is represented clearly by all four.

1. How does the author of this review organize his interpretations and reactions? Does the format match the content the author is reviewing? Why do you think he chose the format that he uses?

2. Would you describe this review as positive, negative, or balanced? Why?

3. Does the place where the review was published determine or influence how the author reacted or responded to the film or wrote the review?

4. In the original online post of this review, the author uses an image at the top of the piece (which is common for the site), a "Related Videos" section that has links to a scene from the film and a trailer for the film, and many live links to his other reviews or other material online about actors and production staff. How do these visual parts of his review help to make the review stronger?

CONNECTING TO YOUR CULTURE

1. How many of the Harry Potter books have you read? And how many of the films have you seen? If you have read the books or seen the films covered in the review, do you think you have an edge on understanding everything the author presents in his review? Why or why not?

2. The Harry Potter books and films are a significant part of our general American culture. Why do you think this series became so popular?

3. How involved were you in participating in the extra activities that surrounded this pop culture phenomenon, such as standing in line for one or more of the books/films or discussing the book/films through social media?

AUTHOR BIO

Rachel Abramowitz *is a former* Los Angeles Times *staff writer and past contributor to several magazines, including* New York Magazine. *Abramowitz is also the author of the 2000 book* Is That a Gun in Your Pocket?: The Truth About Female Power in Hollywood. *Currently, Abramowitz writes television screenplays with her husband, Josh Goldin. The following essay was printed in the August 1, 2009, edition of* L.A. Times.

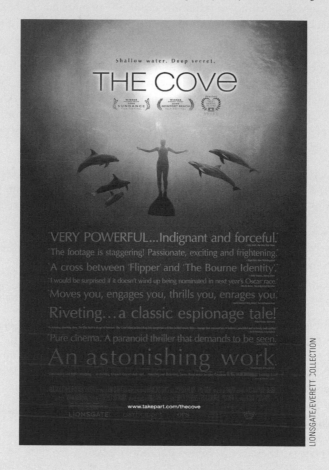

THE COVE *WAS COVERT, DANGEROUS FILMMAKING*

Rachel Abramowitz

How does one expose the secret systematic slaughter of 23,000 dolphins?

It helps to have a billionaire, plus a dedicated activist, a neophyte filmmaker, two of the world's best free-divers, a former avionics specialist from the Canadian Air Force, a logistics whiz trained in transporting pop-music stars around the world, a maritime technician, a military infrared camera for night cinematography, unmanned aerial drones, a blimp and fake rocks specially designed by George Lucas' Industrial Light & Magic to hold secret cameras.

Also required? A willingness to risk arrest, police harassment and potentially much worse.

That was the *Ocean's Eleven*-style team assembled to make this year's Sundance sensation *The Cove*, the unconventional true-life environmental thriller that brings to light the mass killings of dolphins, specifically those exterminated in the Japanese port village of Taiji, just south of Osaka. The footage in the film, which opened in L.A. theaters Friday, is shocking—a tranquilly beautiful Japanese bay turned red with the blood of dolphins, as well as graphic images of fishermen spearing the gentle, highly intelligent sea mammals.

Unlike their larger cetacean brethren whales, dolphins are not protected by the worldwide ban on commercial whaling that has been in effect since the 1980s. Taiji, a bucolic town filled with boats bearing the images of happy dolphins, is, as shown in the film, essentially a dolphin bazaar for marine theme parks hunting for their next attraction, and they are willing to pay $150,000 per dolphin. Unselected dolphins are herded into a heavily protected secret cove where they're slaughtered for food, never mind the fact that, as the film makes clear, dolphin meat is chock-full of mercury—or as one on-screen scientist states: The creatures are essentially swimming toxic waste dumps.

The $2.5-million film, three years in the making, was born of the friendship between National Geographic photographer Louie Psihoyos and Netscape founder Jim Clark, old dive buddies who spent the last 10 years traveling the world searching for the best reefs, which they soon realized were dramatically deteriorating each time they returned.

Psihoyos recalls being in the Galapagos Islands and watching "long-line fisherman fishing in a marine sanctuary" and seeing "bombed out reefs in Indonesia." In response to the devastation, Clark launched the nonprofit environmental group the Oceanic Preservation Society, and Psihoyos began working on what initially was going to be four TV documentaries about the endangered oceans and their species.

Psihoyos started attending mammal conferences and stumbled upon the hero of his documentary, Ric O'Barry, in 2005. The 68-year-old O'Barry, an endearing and obsessed activist, was the original trainer of the five dolphins who played "Flipper" on TV and blames himself for the worldwide popularity of commercial sea parks with their live dolphin acts, a practice he now decries. "A lot of the dolphins in the third world are in people's swimming pools. It's a copycat syndrome," says O'Barry, now a marine mammal specialist for the Earth Island Institute, and leader of the Save Japan Dolphins coalition. "People go to Sea World, and say, 'Wow I can do that.' There're dolphins all over the Caribbean, and Mexico—the whole area is like a dolphin theme park with deplorable conditions. When I see them there, I feel directly responsible. I know the TV series helped to contribute to this mess. There are $2 billion in profits that come from the captive dolphins."

Filmmaking 101

At the time, O'Barry was on his way to Taiji, where he's been going several times a year in an effort to stop the slaughter, often with journalists in tow, and he invited Psihoyos to join him. Seeing the filmic potential in the trip, Psihoyos signed on, although the acclaimed photographer first decided to take a three-day filmmaking course.

"We're all professionals, just not at this," says Psihoyos, with a laugh. "I don't know if this movie could have been made by a professional crew. A professional crew would have turned around and ran. A producer would say 'This is nuts. How long is it going to take? How much is it going to cost?' There were just too many unknowns. The risk of getting hurt or jailed was daily. It didn't take filmmakers to make this film. It took pirates."

Indeed, the film depicts two commando missions into the cove, which is surrounded by razor-wire fences and policed by vigilant fisherman, desperate to keep their business out of the spotlight. There were actually fourteen cloak-and-dagger operations into the protected cove to accumulate enough footage, and a dedicated runner who every day personally and craftily spirited the film out of town. "The reality was a lot scarier than the film shows," Psihoyos says. "We got ran out of town by the police twice." These days, when O'Barry makes his still frequent pilgrimages to Taiji, he always goes in full-blown disguise.

Clark brought in another diver buddy, actor-filmmaker Fisher Stevens ("Short Circuit"), to produce and comb through the nearly 600 hours of film. Stevens in turn brought in other professionals, including editor Geoffrey Richman ("Murderball" and "Sicko") and writer Mark Monroe.

Stevens insisted that Psihoyos actually become the on-screen narrator of the story, providing a charismatic and handsome figure through which to tell the story. "He didn't want to do it at first," recalls Stevens, who eventually convinced him. "The idea was this is not a just a documentary—it's more like a thriller."

Psihoyos says that many of his stories for National Geographic had "an activist bent," but he also had maintained the belief that "a journalist is supposed to be a fly on the wall, he's not supposed to be part of the story. Still I realized if nobody gets active, then nothing would get resolved. I felt it was time to stand up."

Psihoyos and O'Barry hope the film will generate awareness and help bring change to the situation in Taiji. As a country, Japan has also opposed extending the international whaling ban to dolphins. Speaking before the film's commercial release, O'Barry noted, "[The Japanese] don't know this tsunami of bad publicity is coming their way. In Japan, they call it 'giatsu,' which translates into external pressure.... [This] movie is giatsu on a massive scale."

Source: "The Cove *was Covert, Dangerous Filmmaking*" by Rachel Abramowitz. Copyright (c) 2009. Los Angeles Times. *Reprinted with permission.*

DECODING THE TEXTS

All four of the essays in this case study are reviews that are set up with different reviewing formats. Even so, the review genre is represented clearly by all four.

1. How does the author of this review organize her interpretations and reactions? Does the format match the content the author is reviewing? Why do you think she chose the formats that she uses?

2. Would you describe this review as positive, negative, or balanced? Why?

3. Does the place where the review was published determine or influence how the author reacted or responded to the film or wrote the review?

4. Did the review make you want to see the film or learn more about the issue described?

CONNECTING TO YOUR CULTURE

1. What percentage of the films you see each year are documentaries?

2. What is usually the purpose behind making a documentary?

3. Is this purpose something you like to connect with in your film viewing?

4. What is your favorite documentary? Why?

CONTEMPLATIONS IN THE POP CULTURE ZONE

1. Do you prefer fast- or slow-moving films? Chris Driver sees Kubrick's long, slow-moving shots as a positive aspect of the film and film making in general. Do you agree? Driver calls *2001* a classic. Do you think its style or pace has affected or even helped create this film's status? If you have not seen *2001*, focus on a film that uses pacing as a prominent feature, such as *Citizen Kane, Dumb and Dumber,* or *Run, Lola, Run.*

2. The movie industry reaps huge profits each year from blockbusters (movies with big budgets that make even more money). Movies like *Jaws, Star Wars, Jurassic Park, Independence Day,* and *Titanic* have changed the way movies are made nowadays. What have been the positive and negative effects of the blockbuster phenomenon? Are movies better than ever, or have commercial formulas drastically reduced the variety of films released each year?

3. Create a survey about genre preferences at http://www.surveymonkey.com/, and ask your classmates to take the survey. Using the information you gather, what do you notice about the preferred movie genres of your class?

COLLABORATIONS IN THE POP CULTURE ZONE

1. Discuss why movie stars become cultural icons. Think of movie stars from the Hollywood studio era (Bette Davis, Spencer Tracy, Clark Gable, Humphrey Bogart, Marilyn Monroe, Henry Fonda, Judy Garland) and stars of more recent years (Jennifer Lawrence, Bradley Cooper, Scarlett Johansson, Kristen Stewart, Anne Hathaway, Channing Tatum, Jessica Biel, Ryan Reynolds, Ryan Gosling). What do they tell us about American culture? How do they function as symbols? Share your thoughts with your group and/or the class.

2. Form a group and analyze movie ads (in a newspaper, magazine, or website) or movie trailers. Think of various categories that the ads or trailers could be put in according to movie genre or method of composition. Write a description of the traits of each category. Jot down some conclusions about the nature of movie advertising.

3. Form a small group and have each member share the names of the last three films he or she saw. Compare lists. Do you notice any trends concerning the types or genres of films that your group has seen recently?

START WRITING ABOUT FILMS

Reviews or Review Essays

1. Using a film you watched for class or one that you chose on your own, write a film review. Before you get started, though, look at film reviews in different formats and in different publications (for instance, check out reviews for the same film in different magazines or online sites). Choose a specific audience and place of publication before you start writing your film review. Be sure to use a format and vocabulary that would be appropriate for the audience and place of publication.

2. Write two film reviews of the same film, one that is slanted in a positive or negative way and one that is more balanced. Be sure to change the organization, the supporting examples, and the language used as you develop these different reviews of the same film.

3. Choose a film that triggers strong emotions or reactions in some viewers, such as *Precious, Fahrenheit 9/11, The Passion of the Christ, Hard Candy, A Clockwork Orange, Lolita, Borat,* or *Trainspotting.* If you are not familiar with any of these films, check them out at http://www.imdb.com/ before deciding which one to view. Write a review that is specifically geared toward those viewers who normally would not want to see the film. Your review can recommend or not recommend the film for this group.

Reflection or Response Essays

1. In summer 2006, *Entertainment Weekly* ranked what their writers believe are the top ten high school movies of all time (see the list). If you had to choose one high school film to help describe your time in high school, which film

would it be? You can use one of the top ten *EW* films listed or any other film of your choice. Reflect on why the film represents your high school experience, including your thoughts about characters, scenes, storylines, and so on.

The Breakfast Club (1985)	*American Graffiti* (1973)
Fast Times at Ridgemont High (1982)	*Clueless* (1995)
Dazed & Confused (1993)	*Boyz N the Hood* (1991)
Rebel Without a Cause (1955)	*Election* (1999)
Heathers (1989)	*Ferris Bueller's Day Off* (1986)

2. In his essay about *Malcolm X*, Gerald Horne compares the film to the real life of Malcolm X. If you had the chance to write a screenplay of your life, what parts would you be tempted to mythologize, that is, what parts would you want to cut out or change? Why?

3. Many times, we see bits and pieces of ourselves in film characters. Choose a character from a recent film who represents part or all of your own personal character. Reflect on how the film character's presence, language use, actions, or storyline echo your own character. Check with your instructor for instructions about using more than just written text for this essay; if you get the go-ahead, experiment with using visuals from the film and your life to support your reflection.

Analysis Essays

1. Choose a character from a film and write a profile of that character, analyzing his or her qualities. Your general purpose is to inform the audience about this character and his or her role in the movie; however, your opinion will be presented in the details you choose to include. Use the strategies you have learned to explain this character's significance in the film, and consider using visuals such as stills from the film to support this impression.

2. Think about a film you have seen recently and analyze its genre. As a prewriting activity, make a list of particular features of the film that support it being that genre. Keeping the characters, story arc, and setting in mind, write an essay that discusses how the film would need to be modified if it were to be presented in a different genre. For instance, you could take the film *Lincoln* and discuss what changes would need to be made to turn it into a romantic comedy.

3. In this chapter, you read four reviews with different types of reviewing formats, including a list essay, a review essay of multiple films, and two reviews of a film. Choose a recent film that you have seen and find at least five reviews for it, including fan reviews posted online and reviews published in more traditional arenas, such as *The Washington Post* or the *Chicago Tribune*. Analyze the different reviews by looking at the authors' reactions to the film, their use of language, their attention to their audience, and their use of effective supporting examples. Write an essay that divides the reviews you found into different categories (for example, positive vs. negative vs. balanced or list essay vs. review essay vs. review), explain how you divided the reviews, and support your categories by providing specific examples. Check with your instructor about experimenting with text placement and using visuals such as movie stills, charts, or graphs in your paper.

Synthesis Essays

1. In summer 2006, *Entertainment Weekly* chose the top ten films about high school. Create your own top ten list on a theme of your choice and then explain your choices in an essay that provides reasons and examples that support your list.

2. Look at some movie posters, trailers, or advertisements, examining the advertising approaches used to sell movies to audiences. Once you have looked at a few samples and have settled on a few advertising strategies, decide which strategy or strategies work the best on you. Write a synthesis essay that combines review essay and analysis essay approaches to explain which strategies entice you to see a film, how these strategies get your attention, and why they work on you. Consider using film advertisements (posters, movie trailers, and online advertisements) as textual and visual support—for instance, if you analyze movie posters, you can include annotated samples within your essay by using the comment or post-it features in your word processing program.

3. Write an essay in which you consider and explore the reasons that a particular film genre is more popular today with a particular audience. Use review essay strategies to describe the genre and some sample films, and then use analysis essay strategies to discuss why this type of film is popular with the audience you choose. An example of this would be to discuss why horror films (*Friday the 13th, Halloween, The Texas Chainsaw Massacre, Scream, Saw, Hostel*) are more popular among teens than with their parents.

4. View all the films in a film franchise (such as the *Jaws* movies, the *Harry Potter* movies, or the *Twilight* movies). Choose either your favorite or least favorite film from the franchise, and write an essay that supports your choice. Review the film analysis terms presented in the section earlier in this chapter on Watching, Analyzing, and Understanding, and use at least one to analyze the film and support your film choice. Consider using visuals (movie stills, charts, tables, graphs) to support some of the points you make.

5. Hollywood continues to remake films or to create films based on TV shows at an astonishing rate. Investigate films that have been remade in various ways: updating the time period, changing the story ending, converting the story from TV to film, changing gender, or changing race. Argue whether or not remakes are a valuable part of our culture. Check this list for some originals and remakes to get you started on your search.

Original	Remake
The Wolfman (1941)	*The Wolfman* (2010)
Here Comes Mr. Jordan (1941)	*Heaven Can Wait* (1978); *Down to Earth* (2001)
Last Holiday (1950)	*Last Holiday* (2006)
Rear Window (1954)	*Disturbia* (2007)
Ocean's 11 (1960)	*Ocean's 11* (2001)
Psycho (1960)	*Psycho* (1998)
The Parent Trap (1961)	*The Parent Trap* (1998)
Bewitched (1964 TV series begins)	*Bewitched* (2005)
Get Smart (1965 TV series begins)	*Get Smart* (2008)
Dark Shadows (1966 TV series begins)	*Dark Shadows* (2012)
Mission: Impossible (1966 TV series begins)	*Mission Impossible* (1996)
Batman (1966 TV series begins); *Batman* (1989)	*The Dark Knight* (2008)
Guess Who's Coming to Dinner (1967)	*Guess Who* (2005)
Planet of the Apes (1968)	*Dawn of the Planet of the Apes* (2014)
The Muppet Show (1976 TV series begins)	*The Muppets* (2011)
Stepford Wives (1975)	*Stepford Wives* (2004)
Carrie (1976)	*Carrie* (2013)
Charlie's Angels (1976 TV series begins)	*Charlie's Angels* (2000)
Dukes of Hazzard (1979)	*Dukes of Hazzard* (2005)
Fame (1980)	*Fame* (2009)
Footloose (1984)	*Footloose* (2011)
Total Recall (1990)	*Total Recall* (2012)
The X-Files (1993 TV series begins)	*The X-Files* (1998)
Firefly (2002 TV series begins)	*Serenity* (2005)
Spider-Man (2002)	*The Amazing Spider-Man* (2012)

6. The following chart compares films that were nominated for awards and those that became blockbusters in the same year. Write an essay that investigates why award-nominated films do not usually become blockbusters. Be sure to support your argument(s) with specific data or examples. Consider presenting your date by providing visuals such as graphs or charts within your essay.

Award Year	Academy Award–Nominated Films**	Top Grossing Films
2010	127 Hours	Toy Story 3
	Black Swan	Alice in Wonderland
	The Fighter	Iron Man 2
	Inception	The Twilight Saga: Eclipse
	*The King's Speech	Harry Potter and the Deathly Hollows, Part I
	The Kids Are All Right	Inception
	The Social Network	Despicable Me
	Toy Story 3	Shrek Forever After
	True Grit	How to Train Your Dragon
	Winter's Bone	Tangled
2005	*Crash	Star Wars: Episode III—Revenge of the Sith
	Brokeback Mountain	The Chronicles of Narnia: The Lion, the Witch, and the Wardrobe
	Capote	Harry Potter and the Goblet of Fire
	Good Night, and Good Luck	War of the Worlds
	Munich	King Kong
2000	*Gladiator	How the Grinch Stole Christmas
	Chocolat	Cast Away
	Crouching Tiger, Hidden Dragon	Mission: Impossible 2
	Erin Brockovich	Gladiator
	Traffic	What Women Want
1995	*Braveheart	Toy Story
	Apollo 13	Batman Forever
	Babe	Apollo 13
	The Postman	Pocahontas
	Sense and Sensibility	Ace Ventura: When Nature Calls
1990	*Dances with Wolves	Home Alone
	Awakenings	Ghost
	Ghost	Dances with Wolves
	The Godfather, Part III	Pretty Woman
	GoodFellas	Teenage Mutant Ninja Turtles

1985	*Out of Africa	Back to the Future
	The Color Purple	Rambo: First Blood Part 2
	Kiss of the Spider Woman	Rocky IV
	Prizzi's Honor	The Color Purple
	Witness	Out of Africa
1980	*Ordinary People	Star Wars: Episode V—The Empire Strikes Back
	Coal Miner's Daughter	Nine to Five
	The Elephant Man	Stir Crazy
	Raging Bull	Airplane
	Tess	Any Which Way You Can
1975	*One Flew over the Cuckoo's Nest	Jaws
	Barry Lyndon	One Flew Over the Cuckoo's Nest
	Dog Day Afternoon	The Rocky Horror Picture Show
	Jaws	Shampoo
	Nashville	Dog Day Afternoon
1970	*Patton	Love Story
	Airport	Airport
	Five Easy Pieces	M*A*S*H
	Love Story	Patton
	M*A*S*H	The Aristocats

*Winner.

**Starting in 2009, 10 films are nominated for the Best Picture Oscar.

8

writing about social networks

"In light of these events, America is canceled.
Citizens are asked to choose between
Canada and Mexico by 4:00 p.m.
tomorrow."
—From *Saturday Night Live*, Season 26,
Episode 8, "Weekend Update"

1. Who told more than 900 of his religious followers to drink a cherry-flavored, cyanide-laced fruit drink and murdered those who refused in what was considered one of the largest mass suicides in history?

a. David Koresh
b. Marshall Herff Applewhite
c. Jim Jones
d. Jose Luis de Jesus Miranda

GIORGIOMAGINI/ISTOCKPHOTO

2. What percentage of U.S. households play video games?

a. 12 percent
b. 45 percent
c. 67 percent
d. 84 percent

3. Which of the following is not an AIDS activism group?

a. UAA (United Against AIDS)
b. ACT UP (AIDS Coalition to Unleash Power)
c. Audre Lorde Project
d. Broadway Cares/Equity Fights AIDS

4. What percentage of time spent online is spent on social networking sites?

a. 9 percent
b. 22 percent
c. 55 percent
d. 78 percent

5. How many characters is the maximum number allowed in a tweet (on Twitter)?

a. 100 characters
b. 120 characters
c. 140 characters
d. 150 characters

6. Which of the following is not a material commonly used for knitting needles?

a. bamboo
b. bone
c. copper
d. tortoise shell

7. Which of the following is the high school and college sport with more head and spinal injuries than the others?

a. lacrosse
b. soccer
c. football
d. cheerleading

9. What organization has the purpose "to take action to bring women into full participation in the mainstream of American society now, exercising all privileges and responsibilities thereof in truly equal partnership with men"?

a. the Gay and Lesbian Alliance Against Defamation (GLAAD)

b. the National Organization for Women (NOW)

c. the National Women's Studies Association (NWSA)

d. the American Civil Liberties Union (ACLU)

10. **Stump Your Instructor:** In small groups, write a question here about social networking and pop culture. Give your instructor five choices for answers.

a.

b.

c.

d.

e.

DAVID STUART/GETTY IMAGES

8. What is three strikes in a row in bowling called?

a. a knockout

b. a triple crown

c. a turkey

d. a strike out

ANSWERS

1) c. Jim Jones **2)** c. 67 percent **3)** c. Audre Lorde Project **4)** b. 22 percent **5)** c. 140 characters **6)** c. copper **7)** d. cheerleading **8)** c. a turkey **9)** b. the National Organization for Women (NOW) **10)** Your answer

251

"I do solemnly swear (or affirm) that I will faithfully execute the office of President of the United States, and will to the best of my ability, preserve, protect, and defend the Constitution of the United States."

YOU AND SOCIAL NETWORKING

Every four years, with hand on the Bible, the U.S. president repeats this pledge after the chief justice of the Supreme Court. The politician who takes this oath is as much a part of American popular culture as Usher or the actors on *Modern Family*. The character of the U.S. president is even a popular one on television shows and in films, such as Mary McDonnell's President Laura Roslin on *Battlestar Galactica* (in the above photo) or Bill Pullman's President Thomas J. Whitmore in *Independence Day*. Even so, sometimes it is hard to imagine the extensive role that political parties and other cultural groups play in our pop culture. But the truth is we are all members of various groups and organizations that form a vast social network of interests and identities.

You may immediately think of social media sites such as Facebook or Twitter when you hear the term *social networking*, but it is so much more than that. People have been forming groups and clubs and networking far longer than Myspace has been around. Digital resources may have made it easier to network across space and distance, but your local bowling league, the intramural softball teams on your school campus, the fraternities and sororities you rush, the Sunday school class at your local church, the group of friends you play Scrabble with each week are also social networks.

These groups and networks often represent us and even help us form our identities. You are a college student. You are a son or daughter, perhaps a parent or grandparent. You may be a computer science major, a future teacher, or a CEO in training. Perhaps you are working your way through college as a tutor, a waitress, or a computer salesperson. You may be a member of a campus social organization, an intramural sports team, or a religious group. Perhaps you belong to a gym or country club. You might be a Republican, Democrat, Independent, or a member of the Green Party. All of these networks and associations can change the way you view popular culture and the way you are viewed as a potential consumer of pop culture.

Groups and associations often make the news for lobbying the government, filing legislation to promote their issues, or for holding rallies or conferences; however, their role in popular culture is much larger. These organizations often form culture or help it change. For example, Scientology, a religion formed during the last half of the twentieth century, has evolved from a self-help strategy to being known as the religion of celebrities. From members Tom Cruise and John Travolta to its controversial representation on *South Park*, Scientology is both participating in and creating pop culture. Even organizations such as the Popular Culture Association (PCA), whose job is to study the effects and critical implications of pop culture, play a role in validating certain forms of pop culture. For example, at the 2007 PCA conference in Boston, nine panel presentations included a discussion of Stephen King's popular fiction. Of course, King is a popular figure, but networks who study him, as well as his repeated inclusion in the program, will help to maintain or even increase the study of his importance as a writer.

Some networks are bound by space, large areas of literal or figurative geography, and places, more specific locations in a space, so they are also included in this chapter on social networking. Broadly defined, this could include anything as private as your own dorm room or bedroom to public spaces like your favorite store, the Empire State Building, or the state of Texas. The kind of popular culture you experience is often directly related to your environment. For example, in a theater, you will experience films, plays, food, advertisements, and maybe even arcade games. In the Gaslamp Quarter of San Diego, you will experience restaurants, bars, shopping, and art galleries. In a convenience mart, you might see magazine covers, food and cola packaging, lottery ticket sales, and cheap souvenirs. Popular culture can also create environments and the networks connected to them; Disneyland, for example, is a creation of popular culture. If Disney's films and television series were not popular, the theme park would probably not exist and there would not be groups like the Disney Collectors Club or the Disney Movie Club on Facebook.

The essays and writing suggestions in this chapter should encourage you to explore your social networks and what they tell you about your identity and environment. They will also help you to consider economics, class, gender, race, and politics when you think about your own individuality, the groups or subcultures you belong to, and your various daily surroundings.

WHY WRITE ABOUT SOCIAL NETWORKS?

Writing about social networks or networking should help you discover new things about yourself and your environment; however, personal insight is not the only reason to write about these subjects. If you are a member of a group or association, you may choose to write about your organization to promote your agenda, to debate your competitors, or to correct misconceptions. For example, a student who is a member of Greenpeace may choose to write a rationale for membership based on the positive activities of the organization rather than the eco-terrorism for which they are sometimes identified. Or a member of People for the Ethical Treatment of Animals (PETA) may use writing to convince others to boycott fur. You might also research a network that you are not a part of to learn about a different group of people or different interests. Perhaps you could interview someone from your hometown who is a couple of generations older than you about the popular hangouts from his or her teen years.

You may also see groups or networks of which you are a part from a more critical viewpoint by writing about them. This critical perspective may help you reconsider your own attachments and the choices you make in life.

GRAPPLING
with ideas

- Make a list of the ways you are identified by those around you. What labels are assigned to you? Are you an aunt? A Christian? A liberal? A football player? A princess? A snob? A guitar player? A hipster?

- Make a list of as many labels as you can give yourself.

- Now, choose three of these labels to write a detailed description of yourself. Is it accurate?

- Can you adequately describe yourself through these labels?

- What networks do these labels make you a part of?

PREPARING TO WRITE ABOUT SOCIAL NETWORKS

- Where did you hang out in high school? Where did you go in the afternoons?

- Which of your friends had open homes where friends were invited in? Which friends did not? What made a home an open one?

- Where do you hang out now? How do your networks or environments differ from your high-school choices? Are you as comfortable?

- Reflect on and discuss these differing networks and environments.

When you get dressed each morning, you are making a choice, whether conscious or not, about how to present yourself to the world. You know that these choices send messages to those you encounter, whether it is the serious suit needed for your job or a job interview, the flirty top designed to catch someone's attention, or the rainbow jewelry meant to signal a gay or lesbian identity. These markers of present or desired subgroups or networks can be interesting to study and useful to understand. These groups often occupy particular spaces and places, have their own rituals, habits, and codes and may even have their own language. Understanding these networks and places can lend insights to the individuals and groups who inhabit them. But how do you write about these social networks?

One key to writing in this area is to think about the group or network as a type of text that needs to be read critically and analyzed. Networks, groups, and places all carry meanings and messages or signs that can be read, interpreted, and understood, as we do with words on a printed page or screen. For example, you might belong to a network at a gym or workout space, a group of people who come together for exercise. Some may want to build muscle and stamina. Others might want to lose weight. Still others in the group may come because they think it is the popular thing to do. Let's consider the workout space at Curves, a place designed just for women; the bright colors and cartoon drawings of smiling women on the walls send a message that working out will make you happy and carefree. They may also post information about women's health because women are the members of their network. They also have a network or partnership with Avon, so you will see Avon products and ways to order Avon in their workout spaces. As with any text, you will probably need to read it more than once to really understand it. Asking questions of the text, looking for patterns in the text, examining your own biases and stereotypical thinking in connection to the text, and examining what parts of the text interest you or surprise you will all help you understand the text so you can write about it. Conversing with the text will also help; try interviewing members of a group you are fascinated by, visiting a space you want to know more about, traveling to a place of interest, or collecting artifacts that represent a particular network or place. All of the prewriting activities discussed in Chapter 3 can help you write about social networks, but you may also find the following journalistic approach valuable.

- *Who?* Who are the members of this network? Who isn't included? Who hangs out in this space? Who visits this place?

- *What?* What does this group or network do or believe in? What happens in their spaces or places? What draws people to this network?

- *When?* When was this network formed? When does this network gather? When is or was this network popular?

- *Where?* Where does this network or group meet or where is it located?

- *Why?* Why are people drawn to this network or group? Why is this network important to others? Why are people drawn to this network?

- *How?* How does this network or group communicate with or among its members? How is this network connected to a particular culture or way of life?

Asking questions like these should get you started on your journey of exploration and understanding.

Terms to Know

As you explore networks or groups and the spaces and places they occupy, some of the following terms may be useful as you conduct your research or begin your writing.

- **Artifact:** An object, usually of physical substance, that represents or is part of a social network, group of people, or a (sub)culture—such as a Frisbee, a website, or a game piece.

- **Culture:** The defining characteristics of a network or group of people who have connections to each other and share a common language or vocabulary, including behaviors, rules, and rituals—for example, fall rush, with all of its attendant rules and traditions, is part of fraternity and sorority culture.

- **Emic:** A researcher or writer who is an insider, a member of the network under study.

- **Ethnography:** The study of people or cultures, including their networks.

- **Etic:** A researcher or writer who is an outsider, not a member of the network under study.

- **Informant:** A person who shares information about his or her culture with a researcher. May also be known as a research participant or even a coresearcher.

- **Reflexivity:** The process of self-study and reflection that comes about after studying others.

GRAPPLING with ideas

Think of two or three networks, groups, or subcultures of which you are an insider. List the behaviors of each, words or phrases specific to each, rituals or rites of each.

- What do the behaviors tell you about the group? About yourself?

- What about the language? Is it used to keep people out or to bring others in?

- What artifacts represent your group?

Researching and Documenting

Any of the essay types in this textbook can be written without outside research, but often, research will help you expand your topic, support your points, or illustrate to your audience that you are a credible authority on your topic. Research can also help when you are not able to answer your research question on your own.

Areas of research may include the following:

- The history of a network or organization.

- A celebrity's support of or participation in a network.

- The culture represented by a network or group.

- The perception of a particular network in popular culture.

- The economic impact of a network.

- The intended audience for a network.

- The history or evolution of an ideology, scene, or culture associated with a particular network.

- An individual's experience with a particular network or group.

The network, the actual members of a group or association, or the actual activities of a network are your primary, or original, sources; likewise, the actual physical space where a network meets or conducts its business, even if it is virtual, is a primary source, but your research may lead you to a variety of other primary and secondary sources as well. As discussed in Chapters 4 and 5, secondary sources are limited only by what has actually been published and by your imagination. You may find books, articles, and websites from friends, television, or your own library, but make sure you check out your school's holdings as well as the electronic databases available through your school or public libraries, such as InfoTrac College Edition, LexisNexis, or JSTOR. When researching social networks, you should pay special attention to indexes and databases connected to the social sciences, particularly sociology, anthropology, and geography.

You may have to research nontraditional sources for current and relevant information about social networks. In fact, many groups are located, or at least meet, online, or the space you want to investigate may be as diverse as the local park or shopping mall. When using an Internet source, remember to evaluate the site and its purpose before you trust it as a reliable resource. Check out the following sites to get started:

American Institute of Philanthropy	http://www.charitywatch.org
The eBusiness Knowledgebase	http://www.ebizmba.com/
Genealogy.com	http://www.genealogy.com
Google Earth	http://www.earth.google.com
History of Cartography	http://www.maphistory.info
iVillage	http://www.ivillage.com
Lonely Planet	http://www.lonelyplanet.com
Mapquest	http://www.mapquest.com
Project for Public Spaces	http://www.pps.org
Project Vote Smart	http://www.vote-smart.org
Writers Write	http://www.writerswrite.com

When writing about social networks, you may find it useful to conduct your own primary research. For example, to write about a particular network, subculture, or association, you may want to talk to members of the group through interviews or surveys, even comparing the stories of different informants. Likewise, you can observe a group in its meeting space, natural habitat, or other key location to see how members act, the language or words they use, and how they dress or represent themselves. You can also study the documents of a particular network, such as brochures, websites, and letters, for insight into how the group presents itself or interacts with others. As with more traditional research, you will want to keep accurate records of who you talk to, when you talk to them, or when you conduct observations, as well as precise records of what is said.

One tool you may find useful is the double-entry notebook or log. The idea is to take your interview and observation notes on one side or half of the page while leaving space to go back and remark on or respond to your entries on the other side. The first entry represents the language of your informants, notes on your observations, or maps of the places you visit. The second entry represents your personal thoughts about what you have recorded, including questions, your readings of the text, the messages presented by the group, space, or place, your conclusions about what you are seeing and hearing, and your working thesis.

Remember, all sources must be listed on a Works Cited page, so you should write down the information (that is, web addresses, authors' names, where you found the source, and the date of publication) for your in-text citations and the bibliography. Always know where you found your information and

GRAPPLING
with ideas

Think of a network that has lots of rules, perhaps a school or movie theater.

- Who created these rules? What purpose do these rules serve? Are they designed to protect? To control? What happens when someone breaks or trespasses the rules?

- If you were in charge of the network, would you change the rules? If yes, in what ways? If no, why would you keep the rules?

how to get back to it. Also, be sure to record names and dates of interviews for your Works Cited. Chapter 5 provides a reminder of specific guidelines, and the Works Cited pages at the end of chapter readings can provide examples of citations.

WRITING ABOUT SOCIAL NETWORKS

Social networks, the groups they form, the spaces they meet in, and the places they create are very broad fields and can be written about in a variety of ways. You may want to investigate a group on campus you have thought about joining or one you are already a member of; you may even want to review it for your classmates, so they can check it out, too. A network that was important to your family or your favorite hangout in high school may be worth reflecting on or analyzing. You may be interested in finding out about the sports teams in a new city or the amusement park you want to visit on vacation this summer. Your purposes, or your assignment, will lead you to a variety of rhetorical choices that this chapter focuses on: reviews, reflection or response essays, analysis essays, or a combination of these with synthesis essays.

Reviews or Review Essays

A review is a thorough assessment of a particular network or group that often expresses an opinion or evaluation. For example, you might review your school's baseball team and make a prediction about how well they will perform in the upcoming season, or you may want to review the new social media website that just went online. The network that is the subject of your review essay might be completely new or unfamiliar to your reader, so you will want to give some description of the network, including how to locate it online or where it meets in person. Your review may even help your audience decide whether or not to visit a place or join a group. As you are giving a judgment of the network, you will want to provide enough information and examples to support your opinions and illustrate that you are indeed an authority on the subject. Such reviews can be found in local, national, and international magazines and newspapers as well as in brochures and websites. In fact, many publications have columns and regular writers devoted to such reviews, such as the travel section in many magazines, the restaurant review column in your local newspaper, or the online blog devoted to new video games.

A review essay of a social network will usually address three or four important aspects of the topic. Your overall evaluation of the network or group is usually phrased as the thesis of the essay and may come at the beginning or end of the essay, or it may be implied. The network review essay often gives a brief description of the network—the people who make up the group, what brings them together or defines them, what activities the group members sponsor or participate in. When you focus on the space or place of a network, your essay will need to define the space and the purpose it serves, and it may explain how to get to the location (physically or virtually) or what it does; it will probably describe what it looks like and how it operates as well. The space or place review essay will often tie a place to a particular purpose or network—perhaps the audience or potential attendees for the location.

As with anything in life, social networks may have both positive and negative elements, so it is important to present a balanced picture of the topic being reviewed. Balanced reviews are much more believable and make you, as the writer, more credible. Of course, some reviews are slanted in one direction. A group that is trying to recruit

KEY questions

Key Questions for a Social Network Review Essay

- Have you provided a brief summary of the group's purpose or the people who make up the network?

- Have you mentioned specific elements of the network's activities that support your judgment?

- Have you defined yourself as a credible source by writing clearly and giving support for your arguments?

- Have you qualified your judgment with both positive and negative aspects of the network or its activities?

- Have you begun the review with an attention-grabbing opening? Have you concluded it with a final evaluation of the network?

- Did you write in present tense for active networks but in past tense for those that no longer exist?

Key Questions for a Network or Space/Place Review Essay

- Have you clearly indicated your judgment of the environment's quality, comfort, or purpose?

- Have you provided a brief example of your experience in or with the network or environment?

- Have you mentioned specific elements that support your judgment? Have you described these quickly and vividly, using concrete language and metaphors?

- Have you defined yourself as a credible source by writing clearly and giving support for your arguments?

- Have you qualified your judgment with both positive and negative aspects of the network or environment?

- Have you begun the review with an attention-grabbing opening? Have you concluded it with a striking sentence?

- Did you write in present tense for networks or environments that still exist but in past tense for those that no longer exist?

new members is much more likely to present only the good side of the organization. The tourist bureau for a given place is going to present the best possible picture as it works to entice vacationers to visit or asks travel agents to represent it. You might also compare groups or places that share similarities or that are after the same people. You may even write a review that ranks networks or spaces, such as the top ten websites for bloggers or the top twelve zoos in the United States.

Reflection or Response Essays

Thinking about a group you once belonged to or a place you used to visit may bring up thoughts about your own behavior or identity. Considering a network you would like to be a part of may lead you to reflect on what is important to you and how you can achieve your goals. In these instances, thinking about a social network becomes a starting point for your reflection or response essay or a discussion of your own feelings in connection to the text of the network. This reflection or response essay will probably include some reference to specific elements of the network, but you will spend most of your essay relating your own thoughts or responses that have arisen from critically engaging with the network. This essay will often resemble personal or narrative writing.

You can begin your reflection or response essay by considering what aspects of the network make you think, reflect, ask questions, feel pleasure, or get angry. Do you agree with this group's code of conduct or purposes? Does this place bring back good memories or bad ones? Can you relate to the members of this association? Why do you like to hang out in this place? Why do you refuse to enter this space? After thinking about your personal reaction, you can decide what you would like to share with your audience about this network and the best way to share this information. These decisions will then lead you to a working thesis that can guide the rest of your essay and help you connect your reflection or response to the actual network.

Analysis Essays

The analysis essay is more in depth than the review essay and more formal than the reflection or response essay. The analysis essay usually makes a critical judgment about a particular social network or perhaps a series or combination of several networks, groups, or places. It can be more argumentative and perhaps even persuasive—for example, asking the audience to rethink a network, join a group, or vote to protect a place. The analysis essay often includes descriptions of the network or perhaps quotes from informants; these references are frequently extensive and are accompanied by an explanation of their significance. Although this explanation may reflect your personal opinion or interpretation of the network, it may also be supported by evidence from outside sources.

To write an analysis essay, you can start with your thoughts about the network—the idea you want to share with your readers. Then you will use this idea to develop a working thesis that will be either stated or implied in your essay and will guide the points you make as you write. You will want to support this thesis with examples from or about the network, as well as any outside research you have done. Because you are writing about popular networks, you may also include relevant images, screen shots, maps, diagrams, or photos that serve as support; you will also want to explain the significance of these references. With the analysis essay, you should still remember that there may be many valid interpretations, or readings, of the network you are examining. The members of your audience may have had different experiences with the network you are analyzing. You will want to support your own interpretation with specific details about the network and its people, purposes, language, artifacts, or actions.

Synthesis Essays

Sometimes, the best rhetorical approach to your topic is a mixture of approaches. You may discuss your own experiences as a member of a choir when you review the local community chorus. Perhaps your analysis of bowling alleys and the role they play for working-class families will also include a review of the two bowling alleys in town. Perhaps an interview with a group or network informant will lead you to reflect on your own membership in a similar or contrasting group. As you can tell, a synthesis essay combines two or more rhetorical approaches to create the best possible essay for your audience regardless of the topic or argument. If you have been given a specific class assignment, be sure to look closely at the assignment to see if the rhetorical approach has been assigned or if a synthesis essay fits within the parameters of the assignment. You may find it helpful to look over the key questions for each of the types of writing you have decided to use in your essay.

ANNOTATED SAMPLE ESSAY

CONSIDERING IDEAS

1. Should members of a group or organization conform to fit in? Is this part of the price members pay for being a part of the group?

2. What is the meaning behind the old saying "never say never"?

AUTHOR BIO

Dianna Baldwin, associate director of the Writing Center at Michigan State University, is an avid comic book fan/scholar and a Second Life aficionado. Her research interests surround digital writing and range from using tablets in the Writing Center space to how Second Life can facilitate effective consultations. You can contact Dianna at @pooh831 on Twitter. She also blogs at 260days.com. Her work on the Motor Maids has been presented at numerous pop culture and women's studies conferences.

KEY questions

Key Questions for a Reflection or Response Essay

- Have you clearly indicated how you used the network, group, or environment as a springboard for your thesis?

- Have you expressed your personal response to one aspect of the network?

- Did you include minimal summary?

- Does your introduction direct your audience into your response?

- Does your concluding paragraph include some reflection on both the network and your response?

- Are your intentions clear in the essay?

Key Questions for an Analysis Essay

- Do you have a clearly stated or implied thesis that is guiding your analysis?

- Do you have a series of reasons or examples supporting the thesis? Are these arranged in a logical and convincing order?

- Are your supporting reasons backed up? Do you provide specific evidence and examples from the network for each reason you offer?

- Does your introduction orient your reader to the direction of your argument?

- Does your concluding paragraph reiterate your thesis and leave your reader with something to think about in regard to the network you are writing about?

LADIES OF THE WHITE GLOVES

Riding with Pride

Dianna Baldwin

As Zoe sat astride her BMW K1200LTC and watched other Motor Maids pull into position for the upcoming parade, she could feel the sweltering heat of the pavement seeping through the soles of her shoes and sweat began to soak her skull cap underneath her black half helmet. She unfastened it, took it off, and realized that even over the sound of booming motorcycles she could still hear the rumble of thunder in the distance. She glanced to the evening sky and wondered if the nightly thunderstorms would hold off until after the parade was finished.

As she sat there in the discomfort of the heat and motorcycle exhaust fumes, she began to realize that there was a strange sense of pride slowly growing in her that, to be quite honest, had not been expected. It was July the 5th, 2005, the first official day of the annual Motor Maids Inc. convention, and thus far, it had been a hot and humid day in Hagerstown, Maryland. She had ridden over 600 miles through intense heat and humidity as well as dangerous thunderstorms to get there, and she found herself sitting at about mid-point in a parade formation that she had sworn she would never be in. At this position, she knew there was time to sit and reflect on what was about to take place, namely, her first parade with the Motor Maids, and exactly how she had arrived at this point in time.

Zoe had joined the Motor Maids in June of 1999; her first convention was that July. At that time, she declined to participate in the official opening parade, using the excuse that there had been no opportunity to purchase the required uniform. Even now, sitting and waiting for the parade to begin, she cringed at the thought of what she was wearing and what it must look like. The slacks were gray—supposedly, they were to be slate gray but hers were much closer to white than any shade of gray she had ever seen— and her shirt was an official Motor Maid blue shirt complete with her name embroidered on the front; actually, she had borrowed the shirt and it read "Bertha" across the upper left hand side and on the back a rocker stating "Motor Maid North Carolina." She also wore a little white tie that was, quite frankly, beyond description—not resembling a bow tie, nor a regular tie. The ensemble was completed with white gloves and white boots, but she actually wore white Keds. Zoe now recalled that at the first convention several people had offered to lend her a shirt and tie, and she was also told that white tennis shoes could be worn instead of boots. That was what most members wore anyway because getting white boots was tough enough, but white boots with a good nonslick sole for motorcycling was next to impossible and costly. So the group overlooked the use of white sneakers just as

> After giving us some background information that sets the stage for the rest of the essay, Baldwin lets us know that this paper will be a reflection about Zoe's membership in a particular network—The Motor Maids.

Notice this transition that sets up the next paragraph and the next main point of the essay.

they overlooked having the exact correct shade of gray slacks. Of course white gloves could be found with little trouble. Still, Zoe declined their offers, and not without reasons; reasons that as a brand new member she was not quite willing to spout off about at her first convention. She somehow knew that the time for spouting would come soon enough.

And so it did. In January of 2000 came an invitation to attend the annual officers' meeting, where the executive board, all of the district directors, and their assistants came together and discussed what business needed to be brought before the entire membership at the annual convention, allowing only the issues that concern a majority of the members to be on the agenda and weeding out or settling the small stuff. One of the major issues this particular year was the current uniform, which, by all accounts, had really not changed much since the beginning of the club back in the 1940s. Many young members wanted a newer, sharper look, while many of the older ones and some of the younger ones who were traditionalists wanted to keep the current look. They broke off into small groups for discussion. After listening to arguments from both sides in her group, Zoe was asked for her opinion. Well, she thought, they asked; so she frankly, and admittedly, without much finesse, told them, "I will never, as long as I am a Motor Maid, wear this uniform. It is uncomfortable, hot, and quite honestly, ugly. Having come out of the Navy just four years ago," she told this small group, "I will never wear such a uniform, and to be honest, it will have to go through some drastic changes before I would ever consider it." Her comments were not favorably received.

Since we know Zoe is a part of a parade, we can forecast that she is wearing the uniform. There are also some hints about what she's wearing earlier in the essay, but we have to keep reading in order to find out why. In this way, Baldwin keeps the reader's interest.

One of the older members, whom Zoe was not familiar with, attacked her criticism; "Well, then why did you join the Motor Maids?" she demanded.

Zoe thought it over for a couple of minutes and replied, "Because this is the first group of women motorcyclists I have ever met that take riding seriously and that is what I want to be a part of. Many of these other women's groups will allow women to join who do not even own a motorcycle. Not to mention the fact that they seem to rarely ride. I didn't join the Motor Maids for their uniform, but because they know how to ride."

"Well," she stormed back, "if you refuse to wear the uniform you cannot participate in parades or end-of-convention banquets, which means you will not be able to personally receive any awards you might earn and you will miss out on the Motor Maids' biggest social event of the year."

Zoe quietly stared at what had become her adversary and then with a sly grin on her face, and in an attempt to lighten the now tension-ridden atmosphere, she simply said, "I guess I just won't participate then!" One lady laughed out loud but was quickly silenced with a death glare from the all-too-serious woman, and Zoe began to realize just how intense this debate over uniforms really was.

When all of the smaller groups came together to discuss the issues as one large group, the topic of uniforms was definitely the hottest debated subject. The group as a whole could not come to any consensus; therefore, it was decided that the matter would be tabled for another year. In Zoe's opinion, that pretty much sealed her fate as a Motor Maid when it came to conventions. If she couldn't parade and couldn't attend the banquets, why bother going? The important thing was not whether or not she went to conventions, but rather what the Motor Maids were known for: riding. And the Motor Maids in her area were especially good at this, so she shrugged off the disappointment of no uniform changes and went back home knowing that the pleasure of riding with these women and others was really all that mattered.

How is pleasure contrasted with the pride of the title here?

The sound of firing motorcycle engines quickly jerked Zoe back from her stroll down memory lane to the reality that here she sat astride her mammoth motorcycle wearing exactly what she had sworn five years ago to never put on. She shook her head in disbelief and thought to herself, "Never say never!"

With that thought, she donned her helmet, straightened up her bike, retracted the kickstand, and fired the engine. Balty, the name the bike earned when first bought because of its calming ability, like the sound of the ocean, started on the first attempt and purred almost silently when compared to the Harley-Davidsons surrounding her, which sounded more like booming thunder during tornado season. She looked around and realized that there were still bikes falling into formation in the rear, so she put the kickstand back down and contemplated what had occurred after that meeting in 2000.

She had remained true to her promise of never attending a convention, while participating in many of the local rides and events that took place throughout the years. At the yearly January meeting of 2003, which Zoe attended, the officers decided to put together a uniform committee that would be responsible for coming up with a new uniform that the club would vote on at that year's convention in Chico, California. She was excited about some of the suggestions being made, including adopting a NASCAR (National Association of Stock Car Auto Racing) style shirt to be worn with jeans and black boots, but by convention time, the uniform debate had really become heated. Zoe learned from friends who attended this convention that the uniform introduced by the committee was shot down and that the club decided to table the discussion for three years, making the next vote at the convention in 2006. She began to think there was no chance of the current blue and gray ever being replaced.

As she contemplated, she realized that motorcycles were beginning to move in front of her, so she pulled up the kick stand once more, squeezed the clutch, stomped the gear lever into first, and slowly eased on the throttle. As the double lines began to move forward, a dim understanding of why these women would argue so fervently over a uniform that was at the least outdated, and at the most dangerous, began to dawn in Zoe's mind. Brake lights started to flash ahead, and Zoe realized they weren't ready to go, but had simply been tightening up the formation to allow more bikes to line up in the rear.

She placed her bike in neutral and looked around her, really looked around her. There were women of every shape, size, and age surrounding her, but the one thing they all had in common was the way they were dressed. The different shades of gray in the slacks and blue in the shirts didn't really seem to show up so much anymore. Even those who had put on white tube socks over their black boots seemed to fit right in. How could this be? She had just thought, not 30 minutes ago, how out of sync everyone looked with their different variations of a very old uniform. Some women still had shirts they purchased in the 60s when they were made of a heavy polyester material. Zoe silently thanked God that Bertha had bought a shirt that was made of 100% cotton and the gray slacks she had found were actually made of denim. Still, she had to admit that the sense of pride that had begun when she entered the formation was, in part, about this uniform and the way these women looked wearing it.

Baldwin has been building towards this moment from the beginning of the essay. Here Zoe admits that there's pride attached to the uniform. This is the thesis she's been building up to with her reflection and research.

She suddenly became aware that bikes were moving again, and she figured this had to be the real deal this time. She went through the ritual of placing her bike in gear and pulled out when her turn came. The local police had blocked traffic for them, and they slowly made their way from the convention hotel in downtown, Main Street, Hagerstown. Over 100 women motorcyclists were riding in a staggered formation, or side-by-side, at about 30 miles an hour, waving their white-gloved hands at the crowds that were gathering on the streets. Little kids were pointing and waving back while many adults stopped in their tracks to stare: some open-mouthed. Zoe found that the sense of pride that had been growing in small stages suddenly exploded inside of her as she grinned from ear to ear and blared Balty's air horns at the waving kids. She even found herself performing the Motor Maid wave that everyone joked about and she had never fully understood until now.

As the parade continued, Zoe had no more time to reflect on why or how she had gotten to this place; she simply relished the feelings of pride and excitement that she was experiencing. However, once the parade returned to the hotel and she had parked and dismounted Balty, she quietly returned to her room to continue reliving this journey.

Zoe attended that 2003 officers' meeting not because she had any interest in the uniforms, but because she had a new commitment to research and cultural studies. She needed information from these women for one of her projects dealing with the myths surrounding women and motorcycling. Partially from that project, but more from her love and respect of these motorcycle-riding women, she decided to pursue her research on this group in more depth, and as a direct result of that, she had learned that the uniform had always been a popular topic for discussion among these women.

Here Baldwin ties the personal story to the research and sets up another transition for the reader.

Zoe, at first, had little luck in determining exactly when a uniform made an official appearance, but in a 1947 edition of *American Motorcycling* she found a piece on a new uniform that stated, "They are considered by the best fashion designers as being very attractive and practical, being made of good quality gray serge and trimmed with royal blue, the Motor Maid colors" ("The Girl Riders: The New MMA Uniform" 29). Then in a 1948 edition of this magazine, she found a group photo of twenty-seven members, but none were in uniforms. Further research, however, turned up a website called *Motorcycle Goodies* that claimed that the first convention, which was held in Columbus, Ohio in 1944, was when the group decided on a uniform. According to this site "Out of this meeting came the club colors—Royal Blue and Silver Gray—and the Motor Maid emblem in the form of a shield. . . . Initially the uniforms were tailor-made of silver-gray gabardine with royal blue piping. It evolved into a uniform consisting of gray slacks, royal blue over-blouse with white boots and tie" ("Motor Maids History").

In this synthesis essay, Baldwin begins with reflection and a personal narrative Now she is adding in research from outside resources to further illustrate her point about how uniforms contribute to pride in the organization.

She also learned that the Motor Maids earned the nickname "Ladies of the White Gloves" by parading at the Charity Newsies races in the uniform, wearing white gloves as if they were ladies out for an afternoon tea. These gloves soon became a permanent addition. Zoe found evidence of what the 1947 uniform might have looked like in a picture of Dot Robinson, the original president, in a 1950 copy of *American Motorcycling,* but very little of the shirt could be seen.

Zoe then found the evidence she had been looking for in the very next month's edition of the magazine, where she found a group photo of Maids and recognized the uniform that one member was wearing as the current one. The only difference was that the shirt was tucked in, which she had been told by many members was about the only change the uniform had gone through in years: whether to tuck or un-tuck. That this was indeed the current uniform was confirmed by the August edition that same year with a picture of twenty-six Maids, most of whom were in what could be considered the present uniform.

It became obvious to Zoe from the pictures in the magazines that the women were proud of their uniform because they wore it at more events than just conventions and parading. After that group photo in August of 1950, it seemed that Zoe found Maids in uniform in practically every monthly installment. She began to understand what really got her into this Motor Maid uniform she had sworn to never wear; she had thought it was her desire to gain access into the heart and the soul of this group to further her research, when in reality it was her desire to be a part of the pride that these women feel when they don these uniforms and parade for all the world to see and, yes, admire. As Zoe sat and considered all of this, she wondered if the same pride would be felt without a uniform; she somehow doubted it. She had ridden in a huge motorcycle parade for Toys for Tots with Wynonna Judd as the grand marshal and not felt the pride that she had experienced in the Motor Maid parade.

Here Baldwin acknowledges an alternate point of view or argument, but quickly dismisses it with another personal example to the contrary.

It had been a five-year journey getting to where she was, but she was quite glad to have made it, and even though she hadn't changed her mind about the uniform itself—it still needed drastic changes to attract new members into the club—she understood the reason why many of the older members fought so vehemently to keep it as it was.

Zoe wondered if she would feel the same thrill of excitement if she ever paraded again, and her answer soon came. Only six weeks after the Motor Maid convention, she found herself in Sturgis, South Dakota, for Bike Week where the Motor Maids were asked to parade around the race track to kick off the motorcycle races that week. It was a completely different venue than the convention parade, but the same feelings of pride and joy enveloped her as she guided Balty around the dirt track to the cheers of the racing fans. It was then that she realized that regardless of the uniform she would always be proud to wear the Motor Maid blue and gray and be known as one of the "Ladies of the White Gloves."

The closing sentence of the concluding paragraph brings the essay full circle, back to the title that started the piece.

Works Cited

"Motor Maid History." *Motorcycle Goodies.* 5 July 2005. Web. <http://www .motorcyclegoodies.com/>.

"Our Girl Riders: Order Your MMA Uniform." *American Motorcycling* Jan. 1948: 21. Print.

Source: "Ladies of the White Gloves: Riding with Pride" by Dianna Baldwin. Written for presentation at the Popular Culture Association/American Culture Association Conference in San Diego, CA, 2005 and revised for The Pop Culture Zone: Writing Critically About Popular Culture *and 2014.*

DECODING THE TEXT

1. Why does Zoe object to the Motor Maid uniform? What changes her mind?

2. Why does the author use flashbacks?

3. Baldwin uses descriptive details to place the reader at the parade. What did you learn about the parade or the Motor Maids from her descriptions? What images stood out to you as you read the essay?

CONNECTING TO YOUR CULTURE

1. If you were in Zoe's position, would you conform? Why or why not?

2. Have you ever belonged to a group and willingly did something you did not want in order to fit in? What were the consequences of conforming?

3. How do the Motor Maids compare to your perception of bikers?

4. What other women's organizations can you name?

THE READING ZONE

ENGAGING WITH TOPICS

1. Think about what you like to do and where you like to go on the weekends. Do you go to the same places every week? Who goes with you? What do you do there? Why do you like this space or these people? What does this hangout say about you?

2. Where is the last place you went just for fun? The last place you took a vacation? How did you find out about these places? Did you read about them before you went? What did you read? Did you talk to others about them? What did you find out? How did this information affect what you did there or when you went?

3. Where did you grow up? Would you classify the area as rural, urban, suburban, or with some other label? How did this location affect you and the choices you have made? Who were the people around you? What were your schools like? What was the shopping like? The arts? The parks? The sports? Other attractions? What did the members of this community have in common?

4. Do you consider yourself a fan of anyone or anything in particular? A sports team? A television show? A musical group? A particular hobby or pastime? What does it mean to be a fan? How are fans different from general participants or enthusiasts? What behaviors do fans exhibit that others don't?

5. When you go online, where do you spend your time? Do you go online to work or shop, to play games, or to just hang out? Do you have a Myspace or Facebook page? How about Pinterest or Tumblr? Do you like to visit chat rooms or instant message your friends? When you have a research project, do you go to the Internet first? Are there certain sites you visit over and over again? Do you think the Internet has expanded your space or put new limits on it?

READING SELECTIONS

As in previous chapters, the readings that follow are organized into three sections: the 1970s and 1980s, the 1990s and 2000s, and the 2010s. The readings in each of the sections are not isolated to that decade or section because pop culture is not only what happened at the time but also how the same item or idea is received or remembered later on. In the 1970s and 1980s section, you will get a look at the activist network that helped found Earth Day; then William Severini Kowinski takes us to the 1980s' most popular hangout, the mall.

In the 1990s and 2000s, you will have the opportunity to examine black and white sororities on college campuses, as well as a number of different social clubs and community groups that support hobbies such as quilting, scrapbooking, gaming conventions, and Ultimate Frisbee teams. You can also read about the influence of NASCAR and examine who NASCAR fans are.

In the 2010s, you will dive into the digital as you examine the role of gaming in building social networks, consider the practice of religion inside the network of Second Life, and compare Myspace and Facebook.

As mentioned previously, the readings in each of the sections may present information for more than one era because pop culture often carries across time periods and has effects for many years after events have occurred and fads have passed. The readings in this chapter are presented as examples to help you investigate, analyze, and critically respond to pop culture; however, they are also offered as samples of writing reviews, reflections or responses, analyses, and synthesis essays about social networks.

READING SELECTIONS:
THE 1970s AND 1980s

CONSIDERING IDEAS

1. Have you ever participated in an Earth Day celebration? If so, what did you do? If not, why not?

2. Do you recycle soda cans or plastic water bottles? What about paper and cardboard? Other things?

3. Do you think recent "Green" campaigns are enough to change the destruction of our planet? Why or why not?

AUTHOR BIO

The following article was taken from **www.earthday.org**, *a nonprofit organization, the aims of which are to promote the Earth Day movement and to diversify, broaden, and promote the environmental movement.*

EARTH DAY

History of a Movement

Each year, Earth Day—April 22—marks the anniversary of what many consider the birth of the modern environmental movement in 1970.

The height of hippie and flower-child culture in the United States, 1970 brought the death of Jimi Hendrix, the last Beatles album, and Simon & Garfunkel's "Bridge Over Troubled Water." Protest was the order of the day, but saving the planet was not the cause. War raged in Vietnam, and students nationwide increasingly opposed it.

At the time, Americans were slurping leaded gas through massive V8 sedans. Industry belched out smoke and sludge with little fear of legal consequences or bad press. Air pollution was commonly accepted as the smell of prosperity. "Environment" was a word that appeared more often in spelling bees than on the evening news. Although mainstream America remained oblivious to environmental concerns, the stage had been set for change by the publication of Rachel Carson's New York Times bestseller *Silent Spring* in 1962. The book represented a watershed moment for the modern environmental movement, selling more than 500,000 copies in 24 countries and, up until that moment, more than any

other person, Ms. Carson raised public awareness and concern for living organisms, the environment and public health. Earth Day 1970 capitalized on the emerging consciousness, channeling the energy of the anti-war protest movement and putting environmental concerns front and center.

The idea came to Earth Day founder Gaylord Nelson, then a U.S. Senator from Wisconsin, after witnessing the ravages of the 1969 massive oil spill in Santa Barbara, California. Inspired by the student anti-war movement, he realized that if he could infuse that energy with an emerging public consciousness about air and water pollution, it would force environmental protection onto the national political agenda. Senator Nelson announced the idea for a "national teach-in on the environment" to the national media; persuaded Pete McCloskey, a conservation-minded Republican Congressman, to serve as his co-chair; and recruited Denis Hayes as national coordinator. Hayes built a national staff of eighty-five to promote events across the land. As a result, on the 22nd of April, 20 million Americans took to the streets, parks, and auditoriums to demonstrate for a healthy, sustainable environment in massive coast-to-coast rallies. Thousands of colleges and universities organized protests against the deterioration of the environment. Groups that had been fighting against oil spills, polluting factories and power plants, raw sewage, toxic dumps, pesticides, freeways, the loss of wilderness, and the extinction of wildlife suddenly realized they shared common values.

Earth Day 1970 achieved a rare political alignment, enlisting support from Republicans and Democrats, rich and poor, city slickers and farmers, tycoons and labor leaders. The first Earth Day led to the creation of the United States Environmental Protection Agency and the passage of the Clean Air, Clean Water, and Endangered Species Acts. "It was a gamble," Gaylord recalled, "but it worked."

As 1990 approached, a group of environmental leaders asked Denis Hayes to organize another big campaign. This time, Earth Day went global, mobilizing 200 million people in 141 countries and lifting environmental issues onto the world stage. Earth Day 1990 gave a huge boost to recycling efforts worldwide and helped pave the way for the 1992 United Nations Earth Summit in Rio de Janeiro. It also prompted President Bill Clinton to award Senator Nelson the Presidential Medal of Freedom (1995)—the highest honor given to civilians in the United States—for his role as Earth Day founder.

As the millennium approached, Hayes agreed to spearhead another campaign, this time focused on global warming and a push for clean energy. With 5,000 environmental groups in a record 184 countries reaching out to hundreds of millions of people, Earth Day 2000 combined the big-picture feistiness of the first Earth Day with the international grassroots activism of Earth Day 1990. It used the Internet to organize activists, but also featured a talking drum chain that traveled from village to village in Gabon, Africa, and hundreds of thousands of people gathered on the National Mall in Washington, DC. Earth Day 2000 sent world leaders the loud and clear message that citizens around the world wanted quick and decisive action on clean energy.

Much like 1970, Earth Day 2010 came at a time of great challenge for the environmental community. Climate change deniers, well-funded oil lobbyists, reticent politicians, a disinterested public, and a divided environmental community all contributed to a strong narrative that overshadowed the cause of progress and change. In spite of the challenge, for its 40th anniversary, Earth Day Network reestablished Earth Day as a powerful focal point around which people could demonstrate their commitment. Earth Day Network brought 225,000 people to the National Mall for a Climate Rally, amassed 40 million environmental service actions toward its 2012 goal of A Billion Acts of Green®, launched an international, 1-million tree planting with Avatar director James Cameron and tripled its online base to over 900,000 community members.

The fight for a clean environment continues in a climate of increasing urgency, as the ravages of climate change become more manifest every day. We invite you to be a part of Earth Day and help write many more victories and successes into our history. Discover energy you didn't even know you had. Feel it rumble through the grassroots under your feet and the technology at your fingertips. Channel it into building a clean, healthy, diverse world for generations to come.

Source: *Earth Day: History of a Movement*. *Found at* http://www.earthday.org/earth-day-history-movement.

DECODING THE TEXT

1. According to the text, what inspired the first Earth Day in 1970? Why is it still being celebrated now in the 2010s?

2. How did Earth Day change in the 1990s? Was this change positive or negative? In what ways?

3. The article ends with an invitation for you to write your own Earth Day victory. Is this an effective strategy for getting people involved? Why or why not?

CONNECTING TO YOUR CULTURE

1. What kinds of activities happen on Earth Day? Have you ever done any of these on your own or with a group? Why or why not?

2. The article claims that the need to protect the earth becomes more urgent every day and that we see the ravages of climate change every day. What ravages have you experienced? How has it affected your life? Your family? Your hometown or school?

CONSIDERING IDEAS

1. Have you ever taken a seat or stood around in a public space and simply watched the people go by? What did you notice about the people?

2. Did you make fun of any of them? Envy others? Feel sorry for some?

3. Why do so many of us enjoy people watching?

AUTHOR BIO

William Severini Kowinski *works as a freelance writer, covering a variety of topics for magazines such as* Rolling Stone, The New York Times, Smithsonian, Esquire, *and* The San Francisco Chronicle. *His book* The Malling of America *was first published in 1985, and the updated version, entitled* The Malling of America: Travels in the United States of Shopping, *was published in 2002. The 2002 version is listed in the Association for Media Literacy's "A Short List of Essential Resources." The following is an excerpt from the 2002 version of* The Malling of America.

MALLINGERING

William Severini Kowinski

If you had to pick one thing that would typify civilization in the U.S. in the twentieth century, a front-running candidate would be the suburban shopping mall.

—Tom Walker, business editor of the *Atlanta Journal*

On low-clouded nights in Greensburg, Pennsylvania, there are two glowing strips in the sky. The one in the west, which is orange, hovers over Greengate Mall. The one in the east, which is white, is the aureole of Westmoreland Mall. These are the signatures written across the darkness, signing the decree of Greensburg's fate.

On a Friday evening, for instance, the crowded flow of cars on Route 30 edged gently into the off-ramp at Westmoreland Mall. The streams of paired white lights cut into the twilight as the cars wound around the perimeter of the parking lot, heading for separate destinations in the wide expanse of asphalt. In the dim light dispersed from high stanchions, the chuffing and coughing of engines stopping and the last blinks of headlights winking out yielded to the smaller sounds of footsteps and muted voices, as people walked quickly through the cool air and the overwhelming quiet.

Inside the mall it was Michael Jackson Night. He wasn't going to be there, of course, but one of the many Michael Jackson look-alikes fanning out to malls across America was on the center-court stage, with the wet-permed hair, the red-and-black jacket, and the silver glove, duplicating the dance moves from the Jackson videos. A crowd watched from both levels, girls screamed, and a few younger children thought they were seeing the real thing. Meanwhile, the National Record Mart was playing the Jacksons at full volume, Camelot Music displayed the albums and videos, clothing stores had racks of the appropriate fashions, the bookstores had the Jackson bios and picture books, and even a furniture store had a wooden Michael Jackson dummy out front holding a sign that said TRY AND BEAT IT—IT'S A THRILLER.

As I got into the foyer at the main entrance, two teenaged girls who seemed to be leaving did an about-face when they saw two of their friends entering behind me. "God, we've already been here *three hours*," one of them cried. The small court just inside this entrance is where the teenagers first congregate; it's where the swarm gathers, buzzing and swirling with the smell of sweat and hot cologne, the hive in heat. Tonight it was as crowded as a high-school hallway outside the gym at half time of the biggest basketball game of the year.

A little further into the mall itself, two boys were quietly talking about their body-building progress, while one girl sharing a bench with another suddenly shouted emphatically, "I *hate it* when people do that—I *hate it*!" A mixed group of teens in a shifting circle listened to a girl say to a bemused boy, "I *never* said that about her. What did she say about me?"

I made my way past the spectators at the second-level railing around center court who were jostling the card table filled with literature on abortion rights and black women in history, sponsored by the National Organization for Women. Two women were sitting there patiently while people bobbed their heads against the ERA NOW! balloons, trying to get a better look at the dancing clone below.

I stopped at the National Record Mart, where a friend of mine had recently become the store manager. "One kid who works here told me why he likes the mall," Jim said. "It's because no matter what the weather is outside, it's always the same in here. He likes that. He doesn't want to know it's raining—it would depress him."

Hearing this, another teenaged boy who worked there added, "It's better for looking at girls, too. They aren't all bundled up in coats and stuff even in the winter."

I told them that Bobbi (a friend of Jim's and mine who worked in one of Westmoreland's women's clothing shops) told me she was convinced that the glass doors at the mall entrance are purposely tinted dark so it always looks gloomy outside, and customers will decide to stay inside the mall.

The young clerk looked amazed. "We have paranoid friends," Jim explained. On the other hand, it was true that I'd just heard a disc jockey on the radio say, "Outside it's cold and rainy—a great day to spend at the mall." Then he announced the malls where other DJs from his rock music station were hosting promo parties.

I walked toward the other end of the mall, past two older men sitting on a bench in front of the organ store requesting their favorite tunes from the woman playing the display model closest to the doorway, as teenagers passed by, worrying aloud about their popularity. I trotted down the stairs at Kaufmann's department store to my favorite place in Westmoreland Mall. It's just under the stairs, where a bench is built into a planter in a kind of sunken patio, a few steps below the mall court. There is a static lawn-sprinkler fountain sending thin layers of spray into a small pool that reflects elements of surrounding light; the silver rods of the sprinkler parse the red neon from the Radio Shack logo with a diffusion of blue from Command Performance. The bricks around it are tinted an oddly glowing shade of dark red. Green branches of small trees hang over the bench, and above it is a skylight, one of the few sources of natural light in this mall. The place is clearly designed to be a kind of retreat, a cool nook away from the bustle, and people sit there silently, as if no one could see them. It is strange that such a small space could seem so set apart, with an aura of peace and isolation, like a garden. It is the best place in the mall to read, and I was not the only one who sought it out for that purpose.

Farther down the first level a buxom middle-aged couple was walking blandly down the court, wearing identical camouflage battle fatigues, complete with berets. The only difference was that he wore combat boots and she wore running shoes. Two girls were sitting on a bench positioned where they could hear music blaring simultaneously from Camelot record store and through the two-way acoustic suspension speakers on sale at Radio Shack next door: ZZ Top mixing with Paul Simon singing "Still Crazy After All These Years."

There was a Friday-night crowd in the court in front of the three-screen cinema, which at Westmoreland is contained within the mall itself. Kids streamed out of the theater lobby, heading for hamburgers and Cokes at Lums, while the older dating crowd checked the movie times. Westmoreland has two game arcades and more restaurants than Greengate, so entertainment is more of a factor here. That makes Westmoreland the mall of choice for family excursions on the weekend—everyone can go to the movies, either the same film or different ones, with the kids making up the extra time at the video arcades, or their parents with shopping. In fact, a divorced father I knew often brought his daughter here during his weekend visitations. He could take her to a movie, have lunch, and buy whatever guilt-gifts he could afford, without wasting time and energy on driving, parking, and getting in and out of cars and coats.

Westmoreland is the newer of the two malls, slightly larger than Greengate and done in the style prevailing in the late seventies—dimly lit dark-brick tile and wood and nostalgic globe lights, contrasted with gleaming high-tech fixtures and a shiny glass elevator as its centerpiece. Westmoreland also has a strip center out back, with a supermarket, Murphy's Mart, and other stores that supposedly have more of a quick purchase, in-and-out clientele. The enclosed mall is for more leisurely shopping—that, at least, is the theory that now prevails in the mall industry.

Greengate had opened a decade earlier; in the style of an earlier age, it had a supermarket inside it for a long time, and still contains a Murphy's. But Greengate has changed with the times, too. There is a satellite strip center now, and a cluster of buildings out back that houses its cinemas, a bank, offices, a Lady Venus spa, and a V.I.P. nightclub. Because Greengate had been around so long, it had the greater claim to community loyalty, and it plays up that image. Westmoreland was sponsoring more community events than it used to, especially those of a show biz kind, like the Miss Pennsylvania pageants, personal appearances by soap opera stars, and the regional scholastic cheerleading competitions, where junior-high and high-school girls could be rated by university experts on appearance, cheer execution, creativity, and difficulty, and be introduced by a television game-show host. But Greengate was still "the mall" to many people.

Greengate is only a couple of miles down the highway from Westmoreland Mall, on the other side of Greensburg. Inside on this Friday evening, the parade into Greengate began in the fluorescent latitudes of the side-court entrance. Here, every kind of western Pennsylvania citizen that it is possible to assemble or even imagine poured into the mall in their life-costumes: business suits, or overalls and factory-logo baseball caps, frilly blouses and buckskin jackets; in high-heeled shoes, work boots, ballet slippers, and sneakers. The stream clotted briefly outside the video game arcade, where knots of teenagers pattered restlessly, and then divided to flow around a tall birdcage (the aviary) and the indoor picnic area of the food court.

As soon as they hit the mall itself, a brother and sister separated from their parents and took off, racing each other to the same parental disapproval shouted in different pitches. On one bench near the aviary a three-year-old girl in a red jacket, with matching red barrette in her long brown hair, ate a pink ice-cream cone beside her father, who was eating a yellow one and naming for her the birds she pointed to. To the thinly echoed calls of the birds, a young woman strode past, her blond curls touching the shoulders of her sea-green sweater. She was holding hands with a young man in a gray sweatshirt and jeans; in their free hands they were both carrying their coats.

The wrought-iron lawn tables and chairs of the food court were interspersed with sparsely green trees growing out of metal grilles in the lacquered brick floor. At one table a family of three generations huddled around soft drinks from Burger King; at another a middle-aged man with a loud voice argued enthusiastically with two women, pausing to acknowledge greetings from numerous passersby. "How do you know all these people?" one of the women demanded.

Across from the Stuft Potato, a middle-aged man in striped jersey and black cap, reminiscent of French sailors in old movies, talked quietly to a woman in a peach blouse. An old man with crew-cut hair and a huge belly sat on a bench glaring off into the forlorn blankness beyond Thrift Drug. A girl of seventeen or so sat alone at a white table leafing through *Cosmopolitan* magazine, chewing gum, and dreaming dreams. At the next table a young woman, maybe eighteen or twenty, wearing a crisp skirt and vest with her store's ID card on her blouse collar, munched fries and gossiped with co-workers, launched on a career at the mall.

A bearded young maintenance man wheeled his dark-blue cart of brooms, cleaning solutions, and canvas refuse-pouch to an empty white table. His girl friend, wearing a black T-shirt with the insignia of R.E.O. Speedwagon, talked to him between mouthfuls of pizza from the Pizza Place. At the farthest table a circle of old men, all wearing hats, passed around sections of the local newspaper, occasionally commenting on the news of the day, what the President and the Pittsburgh Steelers were up to, and what was interesting in the classifieds. Nearby was a mall perennial, a former teenager whose habitual presence at the mall had turned sullen. Once I heard a shop manager refer to him as The Vulture; he leaned against a planter, ready to pounce.

Jeannie is in her early twenties; she purveys monstrous chocolate chip and pea-nut butter cookies, funnel cakes, and other baked goods at the Cookie Cupboard, one of the small storefronts on the food court. She tries to mitigate the general boredom of standing here all day by keeping an eye on what's going on. "There goes the pharmacist from Thrift, over to the flower shop again," she said. "He's going over there a lot. Looks like the latest mall romance."

But Jeannie's main field of vision covers the clusters of teenagers outside the video game room, and their strategic conferences held near the aviary. She's not too charmed by them, but she remembers it wasn't so long ago that she was among them. "But we didn't stand around like that," she said with evident distaste. "They look terrible." Then she laughed.

"Yeah, I used to come to Greengate once a week, on Friday," Jeannie admitted. "And then I started to come on Saturdays, too. And then I started coming on weeknights—I'd call my girlfriend or she'd call me and we'd say, 'Want to go to the mall?' We even started coming right after school. We did our homework sitting on a bench." She laughed again.

"But I know somebody who had a real romance here," she added. "A girl friend of my sister Delores met her husband here. They met accidentally on purpose. He'd seen her someplace and he wanted to meet her but he didn't want to ask her out. So they arranged to sort of be at the mall at the same time. I think maybe Delores was the one who arranged it. That kind of thing happened a lot. Anyway, she met the guy at Greengate and now she's married to him."

But not everyone was there for fun and romance. "I went back in the supply tunnel with the trash the other night," Jeannie said, "and I turned a corner and there was this couple on the floor. I sort of jumped and said excuse me, and I was getting out of there when I realized that sex wasn't what they were into. They were putting all this stuff they had shoplifted into a big trash bag. It was their stash. I thought about reporting them but they were probably long gone before I even got back out here."

On the other side of the tables and chairs farther up the side court is the place where older people primarily gather at Greengate. They sit at the tables and on the benches there, though some brave the set of benches closer to the games arcade and the kids. There is bus service to Greengate from surrounding towns now, and some is designated for senior citizens. Some older people are here on doctor's orders: the sheltered, comfortable, consistent mall is ideal for walking. There are so many of them, in fact, that Greengate's management has instituted a kind of walker's club for senior citizens, and gives them certificates for the miles they walk. That's become a fairly common practice in malls over the country, and some malls even open their doors a little early to accommodate morning constitutionals.

Greengate's public relations director told me once that the elderly are sometimes frightened by the young, especially when they are rowdy or running. I've heard kids complain about old people being intolerant, but the two groups coexist as those who most regularly use the mall for social purposes. In the outside world, each group is usually confined to its own age-segregated institutions and activities, so the mall is also about the only place these days that the old and the young seem to see each other.

On the corner of the side court is Animal Crackers, a card and gift shop that is one of the minority of independently owned stores in the mall. (Greengate, however, has more of these than most malls.) Inside, a young clerk named Lori was helping a shy father select a stuffed animal for his son. Lori's husband works for a chain of jewelry stores. When he was transferred from their home in Ohio to Westmoreland Mall, Lori found a job at Greengate. "I didn't want to work at the *same* mall," Lori said. "This is close enough." Meanwhile, Mary Gilbert, Animal Crackers' owner, was writing up an order for a gorilla to deliver a dozen blue balloons to a birthday party. Mary will be the gorilla. Kate, Mary's eight-year-old daughter, drifted back from Murphy's, where she had been visiting the parakeets. Near the railing around center court, a grandfather and his grandson consulted a bulletin-board kiosk of tacked-up announcements: craft shows, a quit-smoking class, jazzercise, the Elks festival, the Seton Hill College evening degree program, the St. Vincent College lecture series on "The Future," a ballroom and Latin dancing class, the March of Dimes Wine and Cheese Gala, a community medical seminar, black lung clinics, a Pennsylvania State Police recruiting poster, and a number to call to report UFO or Bigfoot sightings.

At the head of the escalator a tall blonde-haired young man in black velvet jacket and jeans leaned against the railing; it is the traditional spot, held for many years by another long-haired boy until he became embarrassingly older, of the mall regular most likely to be peddling drugs. The uniformed security guard passed him, seemingly oblivious as he mildly walked his beat—the neighborhood cop.

At The Athlete's Foot, a young woman clerk named Marina waved hello. She was not looking forward to the weekend here; her store is in a high-traffic location at the head of the stairs and not far from the corner of side and central courts, so people tend to congregate there. "I just hope it isn't as bad as last weekend," she said. "It was a full moon, and all the crazies were out. Right out in front here, a bunch of young guys locked arms and stood across the aisles and wouldn't let anybody pass. We had to call the police."

Marina stared at the guy at the head of the escalators. "Mall rats," she said. As defined by people who work at the mall, the species known as *mall rat* consists of people who seem to do nothing else but hang out at the mall, all day, every day. Mall employees are also there all the time, not always willingly but at least productively, and therefore in a position to notice and disdain them.

Some mall rats are women, but they are the hardest to spot if they look like regular shoppers, Marina said. Eventually they are seen too often and seen buying too infrequently. They are the mall's kempt equivalent of shopping-bag ladies, except that they must be prosperous and together enough to drive. Most mall rats, however, are young men who may have been regulars as teenagers but somehow never graduated from the mall. One of Greengate's most famous was a former mall maintenance and security employee who lost his job but kept coming back anyway. Another was the aforementioned most-likely-to-be-a dope dealer, who also accumulated a measure of fame for always being accompanied by a very young teenaged girl—always a different one, but always a blonde.

Some mall employees count the teenaged regulars themselves as mall rats, but if these kids at least go to school and spend some money in the mall, they may earn a more decorous designation, like "the mallies." According to Marina's definition, the classic mall rat is unable to hold a job and simply comes to the mall as something to do every day. "I thought maybe you were one," Marina says, "until I saw you taking notes."

On the other side of the second level above central court, two teenaged girls noticed they were being casually followed by two teenaged boys; they stopped to inspect Country Hits of the 70s at the National Record Mart entrance, to let the boys catch up. The boys lost their nerve and walked past. Looking at cassettes inside, Chris, not yet sixteen, was waiting for her boyfriend. They were going to a movie at the Greengate theaters out back. Since they are both too young to drive and the mall is midway between their homes, they are each dropped off here. Their choices are limited to the three movies showing; often they see one they've seen before. I said hello to Chris; she's my niece.

At the foot of the escalator on the first level, two veteran mall salesmen from neighboring stores met at the planter in front of Florsheim shoes and complained about the condition of the greenery. "I told him about those plants," one said. "And you know what he said? They grow that way. Can you believe it? They *get* that way, I told him, but they don't *grow* that way. Those plants are *dead*." In Standard Sportswear, David waited on an attractive young woman who was buying a sweater for her boyfriend's birthday. David told me later that he asked her out and she accepted. He claimed this isn't too unusual.

Meanwhile in center court, customers gathered for the evening's attraction: a Hawaiian dance show, apparently sponsored by the mall's travel agency. Men in checked hunting jackets, women holding blonde babies, old men leaning on canes, and couples holding hands sat on benches and folding chairs in front of the stage to watch a woman playing the ukulele and a younger woman dancing in a modest outfit that seemed to owe as much to mainland pom-pom girls as to island conditions. As the performers sang and danced and talked to the crowd, shoppers kept passing by, some joining the audience for a moment or two. Others were confused about what was going on. "It's *Hawaii*, Ellen," one explained.

The performers asked for volunteers to learn the hula but the only taker was a not entirely self-possessed man in a blue windbreaker who climbed onto the stage and gyrated crazily to the music, grinning at the audience while the performers smiled wan Hawaiian smiles. Meanwhile one of the teenagers watching from above along the second-level railing—a girl wearing a red T-shirt that said SOFT IN THE RIGHT PLACES—did her own dance, a kind of funky hula, for the amusement of her friends. The show ended with the performer's thanks for being invited to "your beautiful mall." The audience applauded, but the reviews by those walking away were mixed. "Not as good as *Love Boat*," one boy said with a shrug.

There is a strong temptation to concentrate on mall weirdness, since there is plenty of it. Besides the mall rats, there are the mall crazies, like the woman with striking blonde hair cut at a severe angle across her luminous forehead who makes continuous circuits of Westmoreland Mall, clinging to the walls; or the middle-aged woman who suddenly stood up on a bench at Greengate, tore off her clothes, and jumped into the fountain. I also heard at Greengate about an elderly woman at a New Jersey mall who showed up every morning with an urn containing the ashes of her husband and father, which she kept all day in a mall locker.

But for the middle-class patrons (including teenagers and the elderly) who make up its majority, the mall has become normal, and by and large they like it. I heard them say why in basically the same terms all over the country, sometimes in response to my questions, sometimes into the cameras and microphones of media doing stories on the mall and my mall trek, or on the phone to radio call-in shows.

"The mall's the greatest thing to bring families together," one woman said. "Father, mother, children—they've got to talk to each other, even if it's at the mall."

"When I have to buy clothes or shoes for my kids in different age brackets, I can come to one place and just go from store to store without fussing with getting the kids in and out," another woman said. "It's just so much more convenient and pleasant."

"I just come to look around and enjoy myself," said a young mother. "To get away from the house, and sometimes the kid."

"The mall is wonderful for senior citizens with no one in their homes and no places to go," said a middle-aged woman. "They can go and see people and be with people. I think that's the greatest thing that's ever happened."

"We meet our old cronies, we go 'round, spend a couple of dollars here and there," said an old man, laughing. "If I have a stroke at home there's nobody there to help me," another man said. "But at the mall, maybe somebody will help me."

"The reason young kids come to the mall is they're too young to do anything else," said a teenaged girl. "Like in seventh and eighth grade we're old enough to be on our own but not old enough to go to like a bar or anywhere, so we walk the mall with our new jeans and our combs in our back pockets and pretend we're hot."

"We come to play video games and pick up girls," a teenaged boy said. "Sometimes the girls pick up the boys but me and my friends aren't that lucky."

"You can sit in the mall and watch all the strange people go by and make comments on them," said another teenager. "Everything's there—the movies and stuff, and all your friends are there."

"I come to the mall to walk around and get some exercise because I have a heart condition," said a middle-aged man. "But also to keep my wife company, so she doesn't spend too much money."

"Usually you meet somebody," said another middle-aged man. "Some days you meet three or four people, some days nobody. Sometimes I meet somebody I haven't seen in ten, fifteen years."

"Walking around," said a young man, holding his girlfriend's hand. "Yeah," she said. "We like to walk around."

That the mall has become not only normal but essential is illustrated in a somewhat crazy way by my favorite Greensburg mall story. It was just a small item in the Police Blotter of the local newspaper, but it said everything. A woman shopper was abducted from Greengate Mall by a young man with a knife, but at a stoplight a few miles away she jumped out of the car and escaped unharmed. Her teenaged assailant fled, but nevertheless he was caught the very next day. This quick triumph of justice was accomplished because the very next day he went back to Greengate Mall and so did the woman he kidnapped. She spotted him, alerted a security guard who called the state police. Since both perpetrator and victim had returned so promptly to the scene of the crime, the police got her identification on the spot, and took the guy away.

But even on a Friday night, for all the fun, romance, craziness, and crime, most of what the mall is about is buying and selling. So through all the entrances the parade continues, as the customers come marching in to the infectious beat of products: the dads shrugged into flannel shirts and down vests, the moms munching yogurt cones, followed by clutches of fiber-filled kids . . . the stringy sophomores in letter jackets and the girls in corduroy gaucho skirts, harness-style boots, and acrylic knit sweater-coats, out on shopping dates . . . the wandering gangs of teenaged girls with identical post-Farrah Fawcett blowy-curl permanents in every imaginable shade . . . the blank-browed men in three-piece suits of polyester or natural blends, their eyes focused somewhere above the crowd . . . the smartly suited businesswomen, their squints ticking off an invisible shopping list, their heels clicking to an internal drummer on the terrazzo tile. . . .

They are all here at the malls, moving brightly through the big bazaar and making the bleep-blip-bleep cash registers sing, and the brap-clack-clack-brraaap money processors burp with satisfaction, ringing up all those electric woks, Coleco Arcade microprocessors, Atari space games, Watta Pizzeria electric pizza-makers, Marie Osmond fashion dolls, tube sox, smoke detectors, leisure slippers, champagne charmeuse tucked-front wing-collar blouses with matching parachute pants, wicker-look bench hampers, microwave popcorn poppers, time/date readout ballpoint pens, black leather bomber jackets, cable knits, sherpa-lined Trailblazers, *Star Wars* digital wristwatches, Barbie Disco radios with special seat for Barbie, handbags "crafted from the finest man-made materials," and ceramic jars of Aramis Muscle Soothing Soak that carry the inscription: "Life is a joy and all things show it/I thought it once but now I know it!"—only $22, soak included.

Source: "Mallingering" from The Malling of America by William Severini Kowinski, pp. 26–37. Copyright © 1985 by William Severini Kowinski. By permission of the author.

DECODING THE TEXT

1. At one point, the author says that the mall has become normal. What does he mean by this? How does he support this idea?

2. Later, he says that the mall has become essential to our way of life. What is he saying about Americans, particularly suburbanites?

3. Kowinski conducted his research in the 1980s. Do you think the mall is still as important today?

CONNECTING TO YOUR CULTURE

1. What attracts you to the mall? How often do you go there? Do you go alone or with family or friends? What do you do when you get there?

2. Today, numerous open shopping centers, rather than enclosed malls, are being built. How do these new centers compare to the malls of the '80s and '90s? Which do you prefer? Why?

READING SELECTIONS:
THE 1990s AND 2000s

CONSIDERING IDEAS

1. What is your perception of sororities and fraternities? What purpose(s) do they serve?

2. Are you a member of a sorority or fraternity? Does your campus even have sororities or fraternities?

3. Should these networks be divided by race or other factors?

AUTHOR BIO

Alexandra Robbins, *public speaker and journalist, has made numerous appearances on various news and talk shows, including* 60 Minutes *and* The Oprah Winfrey Show. *Her written work has appeared in* The New Yorker, Atlantic Monthly, *and* The Washington Post. *She is the author of six acclaimed books about popular culture, including her* The New York Times *Best Seller* The Geeks Shall Inherit the Earth *(2011). The following essay was taken from her book* Pledged: The Secret Life of Sororities *(2004), also a* The New York Times *Best Seller.*

PLEDGED

The Secret Life of Sororities

Alexandra Robbins

Tall, bright, pretty, and outgoing, Melody Twilley is leading me on a tour of the University of Alabama's Sorority Row: two streets full of impressive Greek Revival houses framed by manicured lawns, meticulously pruned shrubbery, and flowers planted in each sorority's colors. Rocking chairs and wrought-iron tables line columned porches straight from a southern grandmother's dreams. The front of the Zeta house is festooned with a large banner proudly proclaiming, "Congrats! ZTA Gini Mollohan lavaliered to BUP Jason Hudson."

Melody and I pass the Tri-Delt house. "Old money," she says, gesturing to the fountain in front of the house, surrounded by brick mosaic and orange flowers, and featuring a sculpture of a cherub. On the sidewalk leading up to the house the Tri-Delt letters are inlaid in metal. We pass the Pi Phi house, where broad windows reflect long Ionic columns tied with yellow ribbons. "New money," Melody points out. She sighs as we continue down Sorority Row. "Ah," she mutters. "Skid Row."

On paper, Melody Twilley is, by anyone's standards, prime sorority material. A graduate of the prestigious Alabama School of Math and Science, Melody won several awards and was chosen to speak at commencement. At the time that she rushed at the University of Alabama, she had a 3.87 GPA and sang first soprano in the campus choir. She was seventeen, having skipped two grades before arriving at college. Her father was known as the largest black landowner in the state.

In the fall of 2000, Melody signed up for fall rush. One of the main reasons she had backed out of going to Rice University at the last minute was that they didn't have sororities. At Alabama, by contrast, sororities practically controlled the student body. The University of Alabama, like many southern schools, runs a segregated rush process: white Greeks rush in the fall for white organizations, while the black Greeks rush in the spring for the black organizations. Melody didn't think anything of joining white rush; she was used to navigating a mostly white community from her time in high school. Many of the more ambitious Alabama students—and a fifth of the campus—join the UA Greek system, which is expected to match them with appropriate future spouses and provide an entree into a powerful state network. Residents who aren't members of the UA Greek system, it has been said, rarely break into the state's political and economic elite. But Melody wasn't motivated by the promise of power and connections. She merely liked the idea of belonging to a sisterhood. It sounded like fun.

So Melody, optimistic and excited, began the year as the only black girl to enter white rush. "I thought I was the greatest. Stupid me. I didn't know they didn't take black people," she explains. The girls seemed nice and Melody looked forward to the social outlet a sorority could offer her. She was especially excited about the Thursday night "swaps," or Greek theme parties—"Pimps and Hos," "Saints and Angels"—in which pledges from sororities and fraternities were matched up. When seven of the sororities invited her back for the second round of rush, she was mildly disappointed that the other eight weren't interested, but didn't think anything more of it.

Only a small group of women were rejected from all fifteen white sororities. Melody was one of them. Over the next year, faculty members and administrators rallied around Melody as a way to encourage the university to desegregate its Greek system and unify its rush process. In the fall of 2001, at the insistent prodding of students, faculty members, and sorority alumnae, Melody rushed again, this time with letters of recommendation from scores of sorority graduates and endorsements from university officials.

"I was glad she was going back through," says Kathleen Cramer, the university's associate vice president for Student Affairs. Cramer, who had been the president of the Kappa Kappa Gamma house when she attended Alabama in the 1970s, gestures in her office with manicured nails and a crisp bob. "I was very optimistic the second time could work. I lined up recommendations, introduced her to alumnae, student, and Panhellenic leaders, and a faculty member and I had a talk with her about rush wardrobe and conversation. We thought we could help her."

Melody wasn't completely willing to believe that she had been rejected the first time around because of her skin color. She still wanted to join a white sorority, and she thought there was a good chance they might take her in. By the third round of rush, only one sorority, Alpha Delta Pi, still had her on its list. Sparkling in an indigo gown, a rhinestone cross necklace and earring set, and smart patent-leather pumps, Melody walked into ADPi, the first house on the corner of Sorority Row. Inside, sisters and rushees were talking one-on-one, mostly about the latest football game. A sister sat Melody down. "There's a rumor going around that you're only going through rush just to prove a point," said the ADPi sister.

Melody was flabbergasted. "You've been through rush—why would anybody go through all of this twice just to prove a point?!" The sister seemed to understand. "I'm here to find sisterhood, fun, and good times, same as everyone else is," Melody continued. "Don't look at me as the black girl going through rush. Look at me as a girl going through rush." They couldn't do it. Once again, every white sorority on campus turned her down.

When I speak about this with Kathleen Cramer, she shakes her head with resignation. "This is a system steeped in tradition, and I think that's part of the problem. Chapters are afraid to go first. I think there's an unarticulated pressure toward sameness, which fosters racism and a homogeneity they'll never see the rest of their lives," she says. In May 2002, Cramer and the Alabama faculty senate sent to each of the twenty-six historically white national sorority presidents a letter requesting help "eliminating barriers to recruitment of diverse members for fraternity and sorority chapters" by deemphasizing the letter of recommendation requirement. Only Tri-Delt responded. (The Tri-Delt president thanked Cramer and said she would work on this issue.) "Most Nationals don't want to talk about it," Cramer tells me. "Nationals have other priorities. These are women who had a very different sorority experience and are struggling with change. They're more worried about the media attention than they are about doing a progressive thing."

The University of Alabama remains the only Greek system in the country never to knowingly admit an African-American. (One sister with a white mother and a black father came forward in 2001 to defend the Greeks, but because she looked like a white girl with a tan, her sorority hadn't known—and she hadn't confessed—her background.) This is a school where many of the alumni, who comprise the largest university alumni association in the world, opposed integration. This is a school where, in the late 1980s—when the campus chapter of Alpha Kappa Alpha, the country's oldest African American sorority, was about to move into what had until then been an all-white Sorority Row—two white students burned a cross on the front lawn of the new house.

"We have one hundred percent illegal segregation here, and the president, vice president, and board of trustees lie about it," says Pat Hermann, a professor at Alabama who has been fighting this issue for twenty years as the liaison to the faculty senate on Greek diversity and the chair of the Student Coalition Against Racism. When I meet with him in his out-of-the-way office on the English department floor, I don't have to prompt him with any questions. He calmly leans forward, eyes flashing through his thin-framed glasses, pale fists clenched in the sleeves of his checked blazer. "There have been a dozen whites in the black system, but there have been and are zero blacks in traditional sororities. This is our third century of total segregation. The administrators would rather support racism and a one hundred percent apartheid policy than take any real steps, steps they claim to be taking."

He points to the current issue of the student daily newspaper, which ran an article about a vice president who had just announced her resignation. "She was one of the very worst vice presidents we ever had. She took no steps. This problem could have been solved in ten minutes, but there is an extreme reluctance to polarize the racist element," he says. "The older Greek alumni are racist and the Panhellenic group here is hard-core racist. They want to make sure there is no desegregation under their watch. They are *not* going to allow a breaking of that line."

Hermann has been an explosive force on the segregation issue on a campus that he says hosts "the most powerful Greek system in America," a system that the sororities control, while the fraternities are "appendages." Hermann has been so vocal that the national office of a white sorority flew in a lawyer from Colorado to discuss cultural diversity with him. "She privately indicated that she supported me, but that her professional obligations required that she represent the other side of the argument." The national president of the sorority, Hermann says, "was very hostile to me simply because we suggested integration. She reacted in a way that, I felt, showed lack of breeding and a cold-hearted commitment to her local chapter's racist policies rather than a civilized, open-minded 'liberal' attitude toward the inevitable integration."

Hermann is disgusted with his university. "I'm pro-Greek, but hard-line racist sororities like all of ours should be disbanded. This is the only social group we allow to discriminate on the basis of race. It's illegal, it's immoral, it's imprudent," he says. This is a school where, Hermann tells me, his tone incredulous, "one of the members of the board of trustees said, 'We're not going to turn our fraternities and sororities into places where just any nigger could get in.'"

"I guess there were too many others saying, 'No, you're not letting that black girl in my sorority,'" Melody tells me now as we continue down Sorority Row. I silently wonder if Hermann ever told her what the trustee said.

"But why would you try again when it seemed those girls didn't want to be your sister?" I ask her.

"That's not what it was," Melody says. "It wasn't that the members didn't want to be my sister. It was pressure from the alumnae saying, 'I don't want a black girl wearing my sorority letters.'"

I give her a skeptical look.

"For the most part I blamed the alumnae, after the second time," she adds. "I can't think that the girls, even after all the pressure, would still not want me. I'm sure it was hard for some of them to agree to turn me down. At least, I would like to think that."

An Alpha Omega Pi sister who works at the library reference desk under Melody's supervision calls out to Melody and crosses the street to greet her. The girls talk about upcoming Formals. "She's a sweet girl," Melody tells me as we walk away. "But we're not allowed to talk about what happened. Rush is a forbidden topic with me. Sorority sisters always change the subject, even my good friends."

I ask her why she didn't consider joining any of the black sororities on campus, one of which expressly told her she'd be welcome. With one exception, the black sororities are housed across campus, far from the venerated Sorority Row. "I didn't know a whole lot about black sororities," Melody says. "And I wouldn't fit in at all. DST, AKA—they'd put me out in two days."

"Why?"

"Because they'd be like, 'You're really a white girl. You're on the wrong row.'"

We watch as, at about ten minutes to the hour, white girls come streaming out of the sorority houses with backpacks and sorority T-shirts, ponytails bouncing as they walk each other to class in small groups. Melody glances at one of the houses, then looks down. "Sometimes I wonder what could have been," she says softly. "It's hardest to see the girls who would have been in my pledge class. Life would have been so much easier if they had just let me in."

* * *

When Melody Twilley found herself without a Greek affiliation, she began researching MSU and dozens of other national multicultural sororities with the aim of founding her own nondiscriminatory multicultural group. At the first open meeting she held on campus for students interested in joining a multicultural society—an entity foreign to the University of Alabama—fifty girls showed up, many of them white. In January 2003, Melody and eight of the girls officially started their own sorority from scratch. For reasons they keep secret, they picked a mascot (the sea horse), colors ("real blue," blush, and silver), a flower (Stargazer Lily), and a jewel (pearl). They came up with a secret group purpose and the letters to stand for it: Alpha Delta Sigma. They wrote rituals, put themselves through an induction ceremony, a pledge period, and initiation, and a sisterhood was born.

Now, as Melody—in jeans, flip-flops, and a T-shirt commemorating a community service event—and I lounge on couches in a student center, coincidentally across from the university's Greek Life Office, she tells me what it's like to be a sister. "We had an ice-cream social Tuesday night, Friday night we had a dinner, and we have to fulfill our community service requirement," she says, "We'll rush in the fall. We're trying to be as close to Panhellenic as possible, but there are some differences."

"Like what?" I ask.

"Well, during Panhellenic rush, [rushees] wait in front of each house and suddenly the doors fling open and the sisters do their 'door songs.'"

"They have door songs?"

"Oh, yes!" Melody puts on a phony wide smile and, in a cheesy little-girl voice, sings and claps the chirpy Phi Mu door song. Then she says, "We can't do door songs because we have no door."

The Panhellenic Association, the university's governing body for the white sororities, has yet to reach out to Alpha Delta Sigma. Melody plans to apply for her group to be accepted as a campus Panhellenic sorority; if Panhellenic rejects ADS, Melody will consider suing them.

A thin white girl passes by and taps Melody. "I'm going to come to one of y'all's things, I promise. It's just finals and everything," she says before moving on.

"Potential New Member," Melody explains to me, her face lit up as she uses one of the terms newly instituted by the national white sororities (it is supposed to replace the word "rushee").

I ask her why it is so important to her to be part of a sorority. "Why not just have friends?"

She tells me that sisters are more than friends. "We want to leave a legacy, perpetuate this. We'll be seniors and then the next year all of us are gone," she says. "I wanted to start a sorority so my future daughter can join it. All the other little girls would get to say, 'My mama was a Tri-Delt,' or 'My auntie was a Pi Phi.'" Melody laughs as she mimics the you-go-girl gesture of snapping in the shape of the letter Z. "My daughter will be able to say, 'My mama *founded* Alpha Delta Sigma.'"

Source: *From the book* Pledged: The Secret Life of Sororities *by Alexandra Robbins. Copyright © 2004 Alexandra Robbins. Reprinted by permission of Hyperion. All rights reserved.*

DECODING THE TEXT

1. Why did Melody Twilley decide to rush white sororities rather than black ones? What was the result of this decision—for her? The white sororities? The black sororities? School administrators?

2. Whose voices does Robbins incorporate into her essay? What role(s) do these people play in the essay; what is their purpose?

CONNECTING TO YOUR CULTURE

1. Is the popular notion that sororities are only concerned with fashion and social events true in your experience? Why or why not?

2. How are sororities presented in popular film? In television shows, like the 2007 show *Greek*? Or the 1978 movie *Animal House*?

3. What is your experience with Greek organizations?

CONSIDERING IDEAS

1. How many NASCAR drivers can you name? How many NASCAR sponsors can you name?

2. Have you ever watched a NASCAR race? If so, describe it. If not, why not?

3. Where have you encountered various NASCAR personalities?

AUTHOR BIO

M. Graham Spann *is an associate professor of sociology at Lees-McRae College. He is interested in issues of community, including the classroom and NASCAR races. The article featured here was first published in* The Journal of Popular Culture *in 2002.*

NASCAR RACING FANS

Cranking Up an Empirical Approach

M. Graham Spann

The death of Dale Earnhardt on the last lap of the 2001 Daytona 500 brought unprecedented media attention to NASCAR fans. Media sources showed fans gathered at racetracks, churches, and other memorial services where they prayed, cried, and talked to each other about what Earnhardt meant to them personally, and to the quality of their lives. Nearly 4,000 people attended a service at the Bristol Motor Speedway in Tennessee, and the Governor of South Carolina declared the week of March 13th, 2001, "Dale Earnhardt Memorial Week." These examples illustrate the connection between NASCAR fans and American popular culture. NASCAR racing fans are some of the most loyal sports enthusiasts and represent a population ready for increased analytical consideration.

Social scientists have paid little attention to fans of automobile racing in the United States. Of particular note is the lack of empirical research on NASCAR fans. On any given weekend from the middle of February to the beginning of November social scientists can find hundreds of thousands of people gathered at automobile race venues across America. The Memorial Day Winston Cup race in Charlotte, North Carolina, for example, typically draws in excess of 180,000 people. NASCAR is an organization that governs a set of rules regarding the technical and engineering components of racing cars; as well as race rules, regulations, logistics, marketing, and general business practices of the sport. NASCAR, founded in 1947, held many of its races in the southern part of the United States, but it is no longer constrained by southern consumers or venues (Fielden). In the past five years, construction of racetracks has taken place in decidedly non-southern places like Chicago, Illinois; Las Vegas, Nevada; Loudon, New Hampshire and Fontana, California. Clearly, people from many different geographic regions now go to the races, making racing one of the most attended cultural and sporting events in America (Howell; Lord).

The search for patterns among groups of people is a basic task of social scientists and this paper suggests a fivefold approach for discovering patterns among NASCAR fans. All sports are embedded in the general patterns of social interaction and organization in society, so the premise here is that NASCAR fans are people participating in collective behaviors that have consequences for individuals (Mills, Nixon & Frey). These consequences may range from unwittingly perpetuating inequality to the development of identity in a (racing) social context. As such, this paper suggests gathering data on (1) the demographic composition of NASCAR fans, especially class, race, and gender; (2) the cultural and sub-cultural phenomena of fans including the role of heroes in fans' lives; (3) fans' sense of community; (4) how fans create their identities around racing norms and values; and finally, (5) the organizational structure of fans. The hope is that scholars of popular culture, sports sociology, and the like will gain some insight into fans of NASCAR racing that will help them set forth a productive research agenda.

DEMOGRAPHIC COMPOSITION

Fans are enthusiastic admirers of a person, organization, or movement (Volger & Schwartz). One popular myth about NASCAR fans is that they are all white, working-class males. Concomitantly, some assume that racism and sexism also flourish among these males given that the confederate flag is a widely displayed symbol at race venues. Social scientists need good information about socially sanctioned exclusivity, intentional or otherwise, among NASCAR fans. We need to critically examine the demographic composition of fans. It is not the case that NASCAR fans are only from one social class position. An increasingly large number of dominant group members from higher classes enjoy the sport. Business executives are now using skyboxes at racetracks to entertain clients, just as they do in professional basketball or football. Furthermore, though income is only one proxy measure of class position, it is worth noting that nearly 13% of NASCAR fans have a household income above $75,000 a year (Simmons Market Research Bureau, Inc.; Performance Research).

Most social scientists agree that it is difficult to separate social class descriptions of Americans from their racial composition. That is to say, racial and ethnic minorities disproportionately occupy status positions near the bottom of the class structure. Clearly, an athletes' race is an organizing feature of most professional sports. Some suggest that overt racism exists when whites occupy more leadership positions and blacks occupy more subordinate positions (Myers). The notion of "stacking" comes to mind here. Loy and McElvogue show how racial segregation in professional sports is positively correlated with the centrality of position. Black athletes are often forced to compete among themselves, rather than with members of other racial groups, for team membership and playing time because they do not typically occupy the most powerful positions (Nixon & Frey).

Wendell Scott is one of the few black drivers in NASCAR's history (Howell), but NASCAR teams currently have limited minority representation. This might partially explain the mostly white fan base. Fans of professional sports typically identify with members of their same racial and ethnic background, but NASCAR, as represented by its top series "The Winston Cup," currently has no drivers from underrepresented groups. Crews who work on the racecars are more racially diverse, but crews typically receive less media and promotional attention than drivers do. Ask any NASCAR fan that you know whom their favorite "right tire changer" is and you will likely get a blank look of confusion. If, however, we compare racing drivers to football quarterbacks and racing crews to football linemen, then the stacking hypothesis is useful.

Nixon points out that when elite sports organizations use exclusive social and economic membership criteria, they reinforce historical segregation patterns. The appeal, then, of certain sports to dominant group members may be a basis for boundary maintenance (Schwalbe, Godwin, Holden, Schrock, Thompson, Wolkomir). The social class of sports fans may vary over time within a nation or community, as well as across nations and communities (McPherson, Curtis & Voy). Collecting data on the demographic composition of NASCAR fans should provide some interesting cross-cultural data because other race organizations in other countries (i.e., Formula 1) may have a more diverse fan base in terms of class, race, and gender.

The gender composition of NASCAR fans could also be included in any demo-graphic investigation. Women drivers have historically been a part of NASCAR racing, but currently only Shawna Robinson is a competitive driver. Messner argues that the propensity for men to be more involved in sports than women is part of our socially constructed cognitive images of what men and women are supposed to be and do. Dominant ideologies of what it means to be a woman or a man typically reflect deeper-seated structural arrangements of society, especially patterns of power, status, and social class. Interestingly, nearly 39 percent of NASCAR fans over 18 are women (Simmons Market Research Bureau, Inc.; Performance Research). Given generally acknowledged differences in socialization practices between females and males, we might partially explain the rather large proportion of female sports fans to changing gender expectations in society (Risman).

About 40 percent of NASCAR fans have attended college (Simmons Market Research Bureau, Inc.; Performance Research), but investigating how level of education affects NASCAR fan participation, their attitudes and beliefs, or other areas of sociological interest has yet to be empirically tested. The same is true for political affiliation. There are, of course, many other demographic variables available for our theoretical propositions, but discovering basic demographics like class, race, gender, education, and political affiliation is a start to an empirical approach of NASCAR racing fans.

CULTURAL AND SUBCULTURAL PHENOMENA

The second empirical approach suggested by this paper is examining NASCAR racing fans from a cultural standpoint. Culture is all human-made products, either material or nonmaterial, associated with a society. Culture is the framework where society's members construct their way of life (Nixon & Frey). Howell chronicles the cultural history of the NASCAR Winston Cup Series and posits that the "regional strength projected by NASCAR racing history—its ties to southern culture and folklore—creates a stereotypical depiction of drivers" (117). These stereotypes are reinforced in movies like *Thunder Road* (1958), *The Last American Hero* (1973), and more recently *Days of Thunder* (1990) starring Tom Cruise. But whether these images help constitute a real-world subculture remains to be discovered.

Is it the case that NASCAR fans constitute a subculture? Doob defines subculture as the "culture of a specific segment of people within a society, differing from the dominant culture in some significant respects, such as in certain norms and values" (66). Two major subcultural patterns may be present among race fans. The first pattern is usually mutually exclusive: fans of General Motors racing cars, fans of Ford racing cars, and fans of Dodge racing cars. Currently, NASCAR teams field Chevrolet, Ford, Pontiac,[1] and Dodge[2] racing cars. This phenomena is of particular cultural and symbolic interest because all of the cars, regardless of make or model, are hand-built, track-specific race cars. Major automobile producers manufacture few of the mechanical parts; rather, fabricators create cars that look like the major automotive brands. Some teams switch brands by simply putting a different body and name on the same chassis. As Berger once said, things "aren't what they seem." Fan loyalty to a particular brand of car may be relevant to the study of NASCAR fans, but we also need to discover if different norms and values exist for fans of the different makes. More importantly, we could discover the boundaries that people maintain which perpetuate the division between fans of the various makes.

Beyond automobile make, the second subcultural pattern among fans is loyalty to, and identification with, a particular driver. This loyalty also takes on symbolic meaning. Readers may have noticed small round window stickers with numbers on people's cars. These numbers correspond to NASCAR drivers' car numbers and are symbolic representations of driver support. For example, the number twenty-eight matches up with the Texaco sponsored Ford of Ricky Rudd and the number twenty-four represents the DuPont sponsored Chevrolet of Jeff Gordon. Most of us have seen sports news reports of Jeff Gordon winning a race, but many drivers have active fan clubs and loyal, lifelong fan followings. Fans of Dale Earnhardt, for example, have already catapulted him to a hero to be worshipped in the folk religion of NASCAR (Lord; Mathisen). As a hero, Earnhardt becomes a symbolic representation of the dominant social myths and values of society (Nixon).

Clearly, sport and culture are interdependent (Luschen). Sport is bound to society and structured by culture. Connecting symbolic patterns is an important part of an empirical approach to NASCAR fans. Social scientists could discover if patterns exist between types of fans and the driver(s) they follow. Are fans willing to support their favorite driver if he/she switches to a different make of car? By looking at fan automotive brand and driver loyalty, we can better identify cultural and subcultural patterns and discover if NASCAR fans really are a subculture.

SENSE OF COMMUNITY

The third empirical approach includes studying fans as members of friendship networks who share a common "sense of community" with other fans (Adams; McMillan and Chavis). Both Tönnies' work on community typologies and Durkheim's insight into social integration (conscience collective) stress the importance of community in human life. Similarly, sense of community ought to be important for NASCAR fans. Sense of community is where people believe their needs can be and are being met by the collective capabilities of the group; feel that they belong; believe that they can exert some control over the group; and have an emotional bond to the group (Sarason; McMillan). Sport spectating is a social activity (Danielson) and if NASCAR fans are a subculture then we should find a higher sense of community among them. Melnick sees sport spectatorship as enhancing people's lives by "helping them experience the pure sociability, quasi-intimate relationships, and sense of belonging that are so indigenous to the stands" (46). Spreitzer and Snyder found that 75% of women and 84% of men viewed sport as a good way of socializing with others. We might then inquire whether sense of community among NASCAR fans exists only at the track or is it pervasive throughout the fan base.

IDENTITY

Studying identity formation among NASCAR racing fans centers on subcultural norms and values. Identity "refers to who or what one is, to the various meanings attached to oneself by self and others" (Cook, Fine, House, 42). Do NASCAR fans build their sense of self around being a "Chevy" or a "Ford" fan? Fans might reinforce such an identity by cheering for a particular brand, rooting for and belonging to fan clubs associated with a particular driver, and finding themselves in social settings where other people have similar identity characteristics. We could look at how racing fans construct a sense of self and how that sense of self affects behavior.

ORGANIZATIONAL STRUCTURES

Finally, social scientists could examine NASCAR auto racing fans from an organizational perspective. We can look at the degree of commitment to racing as a determinant of placement within a hierarchy (Yinger; Fox). Examining the cultural and subcultural beliefs of fans, their commitment to particular automotive brands and drivers, their sense of community, and their identity may give us the social organizational "picture" we need to determine a series of outwardly expanding concentric circles; with the most committed fans occupying the core, inner roles (these will probably be family members and friends who make up the actual teams), and the least involved fans composing the periphery.

CONCLUSION

As Guttmann notes, sport as a social institution includes a number of qualities such as secularism, the ideal of equality of opportunity, specialization of statuses and roles, bureaucracy, quantification of achievement and the keeping of records. By critically examining differences in social class, race, and gender, and by determining cultural and subcultural patterns, we garner insight into the structural foundations of fans' identity, their sense of self, and their sense of community. All of these areas point to the interplay of structural conditions and human action. Why do this? As social science moves into the 21st century, we must study topics people not trained in science can understand. We must continually emphasize the importance of social science and show that the theory and methods of our disciplines can make seemingly ordinary events, like automobile racing, understandable as part of the larger structural and institutional fabric.

Notes
1. Both Chevrolet and Pontiac are GM brand names.
2. Dodge recently re-entered NASCAR racing after a 15-year hiatus.

Works Cited
Adams, Rebecca G. "Inciting Sociological Thought by Studying the Deadhead Community: Engaging Publics in Dialogue." *Social Forces* 77.1 (1998): 1–25. Print.
Berger, Peter. *Invitation to Sociology: A Humanistic Perspective.* Garden City: Doubleday, 1963. Print.
Cook, Karen S., Gary Alan Fine, and James S. House, eds. *Sociological Perspectives on Social Psychology.* Boston: Allyn and Bacon, 1995. Print.
Danielson, M. N. *Home Team: Professional Sports and the American Metropolis.* Princeton: Princeton UP, 1997. Print.

Doob, Christopher Bates. *Sociology: An Introduction.* 5th ed. New York: Harcourt, 1997. Print.

Durkheim, E. *The Division of Labor in Society.* New York: Free P of Glencoe, 1893/1964. Print.

Fielden, Greg. *Forty Years of Stock Car Racing.* Rev. ed. Surfside Beach: Galfield, 1992. Print.

Fox, Kathryn Joan. "Real Punks and Pretenders: The Social Organization of a Counterculture." *Journal of Contemporary Ethnography* 16.3 (1987): 373–88. Print.

Guttmann, Allen. *From Ritual to Record: The Nature of Modern Sports.* New York: Columbia UP, 1978. Print.

Howell, Mark D. *From Moonshine to Madison Avenue: A Cultural History of the NASCAR Winston Cup Series.* Bowling Green: Bowling Green State U Popular P, 1997. Print.

Lord, Lewis. "The Fastest-Growing Sport Loses Its Hero." *U.S. News & World Report* 130.9 (2001): 52. Print.

Loy, John W., and Joseph F. McElvogue. "Racial Segregation in American Sport." *International Review of Sport Sociology* 5 (1970): 5–24. Print.

Luschen, Gunther. "The Interdependence of Sport and Culture." *International Review of Sport Sociology* 2 (1967): 27–41. Print.

Mathisen, James A. "From Civil Religion to Folk Religion: The Case of American Sport." *Sport and Religion.* Ed. Shirl J. Hoffman. Champaign: Human Kinetics, 1992. 17–34. Print.

McMillan, David W. "Sense of Community." *Journal of Community Psychology* 24.4 (1996): 315–25. Print.

McMillan, David W., and David M. Chavis. "Sense of Community: A Definition and Theory." *Journal of Community Psychology* 14 (1986): 6–23. Print.

McPherson, Barry D., James E. Curtis, and John W. Voy. *The Social Significance of Sport.* Champaign: Human Kinetics, 1989. Print.

Melnick, Merrill J. "Searching for Sociability in the Stands: A Theory of Sports Spectating." *Journal of Sport Management* 7 (1993): 44–60. Print.

Messner, Michael A. *Power at Play: Sports and the Problem of Masculinity.* Boston: Beacon, 1992. Print.

Mills, Wright C. *The Sociological Imagination.* New York: Oxford UP, 1959. Print.

Myers, Jim. "Racism Is a Serious Problem in Sports." *Sports in America: Opposing Viewpoints.* San Diego: Greenhaven, 1994. Print.

Nixon, Howard L., and James H. Frey. *A Sociology of Sport.* Belmont: Wadsworth, 1996. Print.

Nixon, Howard L., II. *Sport and the American Dream.* Champaign: Human Kinetics/Leisure Imprint, 1984. Print.

Performance Research. Web. <www.performanceresearch.com>. n.d. Web. n.d.

Risman, Barbara. *Gender Vertigo: American Families in Transition.* New Haven: Yale UP, 1998. Print.

Sarason, Seymour. *The Psychological Sense of Community: Prospects for a Community Psychology.* San Francisco: Jossey-Bass, 1974. Print.

Schwalbe, Michael, Sandra Godwin, Daphne Holden, Douglas Schrock, Shealy Thompson, and Michele Wolkomir. "Generic Processes in the Reproduction of Inequality." *Social Forces* 79.2 (2000): 419–52. Print.

Simmons Market Research Bureau. Web. <www.smrb.com>. n.d. Web. n.d.

Spreitzer, Elmer, and Eldon E. Snyder. "The Psychosocial Functions of Sport as Perceived by the General Population." *International Journal of Physical Education* 11 (1975): 8–13. Print.

Tönnies, F. *Community and Society.* New York: Harper, 1957. Print.

Volger, Conrad C., and Stephen E. Schwartz. *The Sociology of Sport: An Introduction.* Englewood Cliffs: Prentice Hall, 1993. Print.

Yinger, J. Milton. *Countercultures.* New York: Free P, 1982. Print.

Source: *"NASCAR Racing Fans: Cranking Up an Empirical Approach"* by M. Graham Spann from Journal of Popular Culture, *Fall 2002, pp. 352–60.* Reprinted by permission of Wiley-Blackwell Publishing.

DECODING THE TEXT

1. Spann suggests gathering empirical data about NASCAR fans with a fivefold approach. What are the five areas to investigate? Why?

2. How would you suggest social scientists gather these data?

3. Are there other areas of investigation that you would suggest?

CONNECTING TO YOUR CULTURE

1. The author of this essay suggests that we look at sports and sports fans "by critically examining differences in social class, race, and gender." What does he have to say about the social class, race, and gender of NASCAR fans?

2. What sports do you follow? What can you say about the social class, race, and gender of the fans in this sport?

CASE STUDY: HOBBY GROUPS AS SOCIAL NETWORKS

CONSIDERING IDEAS

1. What are your hobbies? What do you like to do in your free time?

2. Have you ever joined a group of other folks who like the same activity? Is it easier to practice your hobby in a group? Why or why not?

3. How much money do you spend on your hobbies? How much time? Do your hobbies ever interfere with school or work? In what ways?

IRA BLOCK/NATIONAL GEOGRAPHIC/GETTY IMAGES

AUTHOR BIO

Amei Wallach *was the chief art critic for* New York Newsday *for more than 22 years and is currently the founding program director for the Art Writing Workshop. She is the author of several essays and articles published in magazines and newspapers across the country, including* The New York Times, The Nation, The Wall Street Journal, Vanity Fair, *and* Smithsonian. *Wallach is also the author of three books, and was the on-air art essayist for the* MacNeil/Lehrer NewsHour. *"Fabric of Their Lives" was published in* Smithsonian *in 2006.*

FABRIC OF THEIR LIVES

Amei Wallach

Annie Mae Young is looking at a photograph of a quilt she pieced together out of strips torn from well-worn cotton shirts and polyester pants. "I was doing this quilt at the time of the civil rights movement," she says, contemplating its jazzy, free-form squares.

Martin Luther King Jr. came to Young's hometown of Gee's Bend, Alabama, around that time. "I came over here to Gee's Bend to tell you, You are somebody," he shouted over a heavy rain late one winter night in 1965. A few days later, Young and many of her friends took off their aprons, laid down their hoes and rode over to the county seat of Camden, where they gathered outside the old jailhouse.

"We were waiting for Martin Luther King, and when he drove up, we were all slappin' and singin'," Young, 78, tells me when I visit Gee's Bend, a small rural community on a peninsula at a deep bend in the Alabama River. Wearing a red turban and an apron bright with pink peaches and yellow grapes, she stands in the doorway of her brick bungalow at the end of a dirt road. Swaying to a rhythm that nearly everyone in town knows from a lifetime of churchgoing, she breaks into song: "We shall overcome, we shall overcome. . . ."

"We were all just happy to see him coming," she says. "Then he stood out there on the ground, and he was talking about how we should wait on a bus to come and we were all going to march. We got loaded on the bus, but we didn't get a chance to do it, 'cause we got put in jail," she says.

Many who marched or registered to vote in rural Alabama in the 1960s lost their jobs. Some even lost their homes. And the residents of Gee's Bend, 60 miles southwest of Montgomery, lost the ferry that connected them to Camden and a direct route to the outside world. "We didn't close the ferry because they were black," Sheriff Lummie Jenkins reportedly said at the time. "We closed it because they forgot they were black."

Six of Young's quilts, together with 64 by other Gee's Bend residents, have been traveling around the United States in an exhibition that has transformed the way many people think about art. Gee's Bend's "eye-poppingly gorgeous" quilts, wrote *New York Times* art critic Michael Kimmelman, "turn out to be some of the most miraculous works of modern art America has produced. Imagine Matisse and Klee (if you think I'm wildly exaggerating, see the show), arising not from rarefied Europe, but from the caramel soil of the rural South." Curator Jane Livingston, who helped organize the exhibition with collector William Arnett and art historians John Beardsley and Alvia Wardlaw, said that the quilts "rank with the finest abstract art of any tradition." After stops in such cities as New York, Washington, D.C., Cleveland, Boston and Atlanta, "The Quilts of Gee's Bend" will end its tour at the Fine Arts Museums of San Francisco's de Young Museum December 31.

The bold drama of the quilt Young was working on in 1965 is also found in a quilt she made out of work clothes 11 years later. The central design of red and orange corduroy in that quilt suggests prison bars, and the faded denim that surrounds it could be a comment on the *American Dream*. But Young had more practical considerations. "When I put the quilt together," she says, "it wasn't big enough, and I had to get some more material and make it bigger, so I had these old jeans to make it bigger."

Collector William Arnett was working on a history of African-American vernacular art in 1998 when he came across a photograph of Young's work-clothes quilt draped over a woodpile. He was so knocked out by its originality, he set out to find it. A couple of phone calls and some creative research later, he and his son Matt tracked Young down to Gee's Bend, then showed up unannounced at her door late one evening. Young had burned some quilts the week before (smoke from burning cotton drives off mosquitoes), and at first she thought the quilt in the photograph had been among them. But the next day, after scouring closets and searching under beds, she found it and offered it to Arnett for free. Arnett, however, insisted on writing her a check for a few thousand dollars for that quilt and several others. (Young took the check straight to the bank.) Soon the word spread through Gee's Bend that there was a crazy white man in town paying good money for raggedy old quilts.

When Arnett showed photos of the quilts made by Young and other Gee's Benders to Peter Marzio, of the Museum of Fine Arts, Houston (MFAH), he was so impressed that he agreed to put on an exhibition. "The Quilts of Gee's Bend" opened there in September 2002.

The exhibition revived what had been a dying art in Gee's Bend. Some of the quilters, who had given in to age and arthritis, are now back quilting again. And many of their children and grandchildren, some of whom had moved away from Gee's Bend, have taken up quilting themselves. With the help of Arnett and the Tinwood Alliance (a nonprofit organization that he and his four sons formed in 2002), fifty local women founded the Gee's Bend Quilters Collective in 2003 to market their quilts, some of which now sell for more than $20,000. (Part goes directly to the maker, the rest goes to the collective for expenses and distribution to the other members.)

Now a second exhibition, "Gee's Bend: The Architecture of the Quilt," has been organized by the MFAH and the Tinwood Alliance. The show, which opened in June, features newly discovered quilts from the 1930s to the 1980s, along with more recent works by established quilters and the younger generation they inspired. The exhibition will travel to seven other venues, including the Indianapolis Museum of Art (October 8–December 31) and the Orlando Museum of Art (January 27–May 13, 2007).

Arlonzia Pettway lives in a neat, recently renovated house off a road plagued with potholes. The road passes by cows and goats grazing outside robin's-egg blue and brown bungalows. "I remember some things, honey," Pettway, 83, told me. (Since my interview with her, Pettway suffered a stroke, from which she is still recovering.) "I came through a hard life. Maybe we weren't bought and sold, but we were still slaves until 20, 30 years ago. The white man would go to everybody's field and say, 'Why you not at work?'" She paused. "What do you think a slave is?"

As a girl, Pettway would watch her grandmother, Sally, and her mother, Missouri, piecing quilts. And she would listen to their stories, many of them about Dinah Miller, who had been brought to the United States in a slave ship in 1859. "My great-grandmother Dinah was sold for a dime," Pettway said. "Her dad, brother and mother were sold to different people, and she didn't see them no more. My great-grandfather was a Cherokee Indian. Dinah was made to sleep with this big Indian like you stud your cow.... You couldn't have no skinny children working on your slave master's farm." In addition to Pettway some twenty other Gee's Bend quiltmakers are Dinah's descendants.

The quilting tradition in Gee's Bend may go back as far as the early 1800s, when the community was the site of a cotton plantation owned by a Joseph Gee. Influenced, perhaps, by the patterned textiles of Africa, the women slaves began piecing strips of cloth together to make bedcovers. Throughout the postbellum years of tenant farming and well into the 20th century, Gee's Bend women made quilts to keep themselves and their children warm in unheated shacks that lacked running water, telephones and electricity. Along the way they developed a distinctive style, noted for its lively improvisations and geometric simplicity.

Gee's Bend men and women grew and picked cotton, peanuts, okra, corn, peas and potatoes. When there was no money to buy seed or fertilizer, they borrowed one or both from Camden businessman E. O. Rentz, at interest rates only those without any choice would pay. Then came the Depression. In 1931 the price of cotton plummeted, from about 40 cents a pound in the early 1920s, to about a nickel. When Rentz died in 1932, his widow foreclosed on some 60 Gee's Bend families. It was late fall, and winter was coming.

"They took everything and left people to die," Pettway said. Her mother was making a quilt out of old clothes when she heard the cries outside. She sewed four wide shirttails into a sack, which the men in the family filled with corn and sweet potatoes and hid in a ditch. When the agent for Rentz's widow came around to seize the family's hens, Pettway's mother threatened him with a hoe. "I'm a good Christian, but I'll chop his damn brains out," she said. The man got in his wagon and left. "He didn't get to my mama that day," Pettway told me.

Pettway remembered that her friends and neighbors foraged for berries, hunted possum and squirrels, and mostly went hungry that winter until a boat with flour and meal sent by the Red Cross arrived in early 1933. The following year, the Federal Emergency Relief Administration provided small loans for seed, fertilizer, tools and livestock. Then, in 1937, the government's Resettlement Administration (later the Farm Security Administration) bought up 10,000 Gee's Bend acres and sold them as tiny farms to local families.

In 1941, when Pettway was in her late teens, her father died. "Mama said, 'I'm going to take his work clothes, shape them into a quilt to remember him, and cover up under it for love.'" There were hardly enough pants legs and shirttails to make up a quilt, but she managed. (That quilt—jostling rectangles of faded gray, white, blue and red—is included in the first exhibition.) A year later, Arlonzia married Bizzell Pettway and moved into one of the new houses built by the government. They had twelve children, but no electricity until 1964 and no running water until 1974. A widow for more than 30 years, Arlonzia still lives in that same house. Her mother, Missouri, who lived until 1981, made a quilt she called "Path Through the Woods" after the 1960s freedom marches. A quilt that Pettway pieced together during that period, "Chinese Coins," is a medley of pinks and purples—a friend had given her purple scraps from a clothing factory in a nearby town.

"At the time I was making that quilt, I was feeling something was going to happen better, and it did," Pettway says. "Last time I counted I had 32 grandchildren and I think between 13 and 14 great-grands. I'm blessed now more than many. I have my home and land. I have a deep-freeze five feet long with chicken wings, neck bones and pork chops."

The first exhibition featured seven quilts by Loretta Pettway, Arlonzia Pettway's first cousin. (One in three of Gee's Bend's 700 residents is named Pettway, after slave owner Mark H. Pettway.) Loretta, 64, says she made her early quilts out of work clothes. "I was about 16 when I learned to quilt from my grandmama," she says. "I just loved it. That's all I wanted to do, quilt. But I had to work farming cotton, corn, peas and potatoes, making syrup, putting up soup in jars. I was working other people's fields too. Saturdays I would hire out; sometimes I would hire out Sundays, too, to give my kids some food. When I finished my chores, I'd sit down and do like I'm doing now, get the clothes together and tear them and piece. And then in summer I would quilt outside under the big oak." She fingers the fabric pieces in her lap. "I thank God that people want me to make quilts," she says. "I feel proud. The Lord lead me and guide me and give me strength to make this quilt with love and peace and happiness so somebody would enjoy it. That makes me feel happy. I'm doing something with my life."

In 1962 the U.S. Congress ordered the construction of a dam and lock on the Alabama River at Miller's Ferry just south of Gee's Bend. The 17,200-acre reservoir created by the dam in the late 1960s flooded much of Gee's Bend's best farming land, forcing many residents to give up farming. "And thank God for that," says Loretta. "Farming wasn't nothing but hard work. And at the end of the year you couldn't get nothing, and the little you got went for cottonseed."

Around that time, a number of Gee's Bend women began making quilts for the Freedom Quilting Bee, founded in 1966 by civil rights worker and Episcopalian priest Francis X. Walter to provide a source of income for the local community. For a while, the bee (which operated for about three decades) sold quilts to such stores as Bloomingdale's, Sears, Saks and Bonwit Teller. But the stores wanted assembly-line quilts, with orderly, familiar patterns and precise stitching—not the individual, often improvised and unexpected patterns and color combinations that characterized the Gee's Bend quilts.

"My quilts looked beautiful to me, because I made what I could make from my head," Loretta told me. "When I start I don't want to stop until I finish, because if I stop, the ideas are going to go one way and my mind another way, so I just try to do it while I have ideas in my mind."

Loretta had been too ill to attend the opening of the first exhibition in Houston. But she wore a bright red jacket and a wrist corsage of roses to the opening of the second show last spring. Going there on the bus, "I didn't close my eyes the whole way," she says. "I was so happy, I had to sightsee." In the new show, her 2003 take on the popular "Housetop" pattern—a variant of the traditional "Log Cabin" design—is an explosion of red polka dots, zany stripes and crooked frames within frames (a dramatic change from the faded colors and somber patterns of her early work-clothes quilts). Two other quilts made by Loretta are among those represented on a series of Gee's Bend stamps issued this past August by the U.S. Postal Service. "I just had scraps of what I could find," she says about her early work. "Now I see my quilts hanging in a museum. Thank God I see my quilts on the wall. I found my way."

Mary Lee Bendolph, 71, speaks in a husky voice and has a hearty, throaty laugh. At the opening of the new exhibition in Houston, she sported large rhinestone earrings and a chic black dress. For some years, kidney disease had slowed her quiltmaking, but the first exhibition, she says, "spunked me to go a little further, to try and make my quilts a little more updated." Her latest quilts fracture her backyard views and other local scenes the way Cubism fragmented the cafés and countryside of France. Her quilts share a gallery with those of her daughter-in-law, Louisiana Pettway Bendolph.

Louisiana now lives in Mobile, Alabama, but she remembers hot, endless days picking cotton as a child in the fields around Gee's Bend. From age 6 to 16, she says, the only time she could go to school was when it rained, and the only play was softball and quiltmaking. Her mother, Rita Mae Pettway, invited her to the opening in Houston of the first quilt show. On the bus ride home, she says, she "had a kind of vision of quilts." She made drawings of what would become the quilts in the new exhibition, in which shapes seem to float and recede as if in three dimensions.

"Quilting helped redirect my life and put it back together," Louisiana says. "I worked at a fast-food place and a sewing factory and when the sewing factory closed, I stayed home, being a housewife. You just want your kids to see you in a different light, as someone they can admire. Well, my children came into this museum, and I saw their faces."

To Louisiana, 46, quiltmaking is history and family. "We think of inheriting as land or something, not things that people teach you," she says. "We came from cotton fields, we came through hard times, and we look back and see what all these people before us have done. They brought us here, and to say thank you is not enough." Now her 11-year-old grand-daughter has taken up quiltmaking; she, however, does her drawings on a computer.

In Gee's Bend not long ago, her great-grandmother Mary Lee Bendolph picked some pecans to make into candy to have on hand for the children when the only store in town is closed, which it often is. Then she soaked her feet. Sitting on her screened-in porch, she smiled. "I'm famous," she said. "And look how old I am." She laughed. "I enjoy it."

Source: *"Fabric of Their Lives" by Amei Wallach from* Smithsonian Magazine, *October 2006, pp. 66–75. Text reprinted with permission of the author.*

DECODING THE TEXT

1. The author gives an example of how cultural opinions of folk art have changed. Now, many crafts, such as quilting, have found their place in museums around the world. What other crafts or leisure activities are still struggling to be accepted as significant to American culture?

2. Would these examples strengthen or weaken the author's thesis? How?

CONNECTING TO YOUR CULTURE

1. Many people use arts and crafts to relax, to express their creativity, and to pass traditions from generation to generation. Do you have any similar traditions in your family?

2. Do your friends have any similar traditions?

3. How do these traditions form networks?

AUTHOR BIO

Felicia Paik *is a former senior editor for* Forbes.com, *a leading Internet media company focused on business and accruing wealth, and she is a former editor of the* Pasadena Star News. *Paik has written for* The Wall Street Journal, The Dow Jones News Service, The New York Times, *and* The Saturday Evening Post, *in which this article was reprinted. "A Cruise for Glue and Scissors" was published in the September/October 2007 issue.*

A CRUISE FOR GLUE AND SCISSORS

Felicia Paik

In the sun-drenched Mexican port of Ensenada, lighthearted passengers from yet another cruise ship bounced down the gangway for a much-anticipated adventure ashore. Decked out in floppy sun hats, smelling of sunscreen and armed with water bottles, they clustered on the pier around waiting tour guides who wore wide, fixed smiles. After 15 hours on the *Monarch of the Seas,* a Royal Caribbean International ship, the travelers had reached their only stop on a three-day cruise from Los Angeles.

Ushered into a squadron of tour buses, they set off for the short ride into town, a living postcard of mom-and-pop stores crammed with dangling piñatas, colorful ceramics, leather belts and silver jewelry. A mariachi band struck its first chord.

Back inside the ship, about forty passengers, all women, had stayed behind. In a cramped conference room lighted by fluorescent bulbs, they sat hunched over folding tables piled full of scissors, adhesive strips, stickers, colorful ribbon, photographs and paper in many shapes and sizes and tints. Intently, they arranged, shaped and glued. Not even a warm sun and the Baja California breezes could beckon them away.

For them, this trip was a scrapbooking cruise, an organized shipboard workshop and getaway for enthusiasts of the increasingly popular hobby of making elaborate albums to preserve memories and tell personal stories.

A survey in 2004 by *Creating Keepsakes,* a magazine about scrapbooking, reported that about 25 percent of American households includes someone who participated in it, supporting a $2.5 billion industry that supplies acid-free paper, durable adhesives, tools and all manner of decorative accessories. Scrapbook stores have opened around the country, Target and Walmart carry scrapbook merchandise, and EK Success, a New Jersey company, says it has a Martha Stewart line of scrapbook products in the works.

Women—and scrapbookers are nearly always women—describe the crafting of their books as a creative outlet, a stress reliever, and a gift to their families. It is also a social activity, fueled by the camaraderie of classes, workshops, conventions and retreats—and now the scrapbook cruise.

Scrapbooking and ships are an unlikely pair, and not only because of the disconnect of huddling over a project while the sea sparkles and deck chairs sit empty. A rocking boat doesn't provide a level working surface; it can be hard even to cut a straight line, some scrapbookers said. Shipboard conference rooms, designed for the laid-back passenger who wants to play hooky, are often poorly lighted and inadequately ventilated for 18-hour work stints.

Yet since their first appearance about six years ago, scrapbook cruises have caught on. Joan Levicoff, vice president of group sales for the Carnival Cruise Line, said her line does more than 20 scrapbooking cruises annually, with groups ranging in size from 30 to 200.

On the *Monarch of the Seas* cruise in 2006, there were about 2,500 passengers, 81 of them scrapbookers (and half of those obsessive enough to skip the offshore excursion), all luxuriating in uninterrupted scrapbook time.

"It's like a drug, being able to scrapbook all night and not have to worry about going home," said Lisa Baldwin, a 39-year-old mother of four who taught scrapbook-technique classes to pay her way onto the cruise.

Deloris Saams-Hoy, 39, who left her husband, children and job behind to join the cruise, had similar sentiments. "I can sleep when I'm at home," she said as she finally headed to her cabin at 4:30 A.M. the first night on board. "I'm determined to get these pages done."

Scrapbook cruises cropped up as part of a trend of theme cruises of various kinds.

"It's a phenomenon that has taken hold across the industry," said Brian Major, a spokesman for the Cruise Lines International Association (CLIA), a trade organization in New York. "Whether it's people interested in Harley-Davidsons, knitting or scrapbooking, there is a trend toward organizing a trip around a common interest."

Theme cruises may have helped the cruise industry's recent growth. Mr. Major's association, whose members are 24 cruise lines responsible for 97 percent of the cruise capacity marketed in North America, reports more than 12 million people in 2006 took a cruise. CLIA predicts one half million more will cruise this year.

According to Ms. Levicoff, scrapbook cruises on Carnival have left from Galveston, Texas, as well as Los Angeles. She said the cruises were usually organized and marketed by a local travel agent, who then approached the cruise line for accommodations and services like reserving conference rooms and providing tables. "We can make arrangements on any of our vessels to do a scrapbook cruise," she said. "And we make an effort to make it a great experience for everyone."

Scrapbooking cruise destinations have included Mexico, Alaska, the Caribbean, Eastern Canada, and the New England states. Debbie Haas, an author of the forthcoming *Chicken Soup for the Scrapbooker's Soul,* led a group on a seven-day cruise to Southampton, England, from New York on the *Queen Mary 2. Creating Keepsakes* sponsored a Mediterranean cruise with stops in Barcelona and Rome.

The scrapbook cruise to Ensenada was organized by Anita Pagliasso-Balamane, a travel agent in San Jose, California, and Picture Passion, a store in nearby Campbell that sells scrapbooking items from rubber stamps to colored staples.

Many of the scrapbookers on the cruise had carried their materials aboard in specially designed scrapbook luggage with brand names like Cropper Hopper and Crop in Style. Beri Anderson, 40, of Elizabeth, Colorado, packed so many materials for the cruise that her baggage was 27 pounds overweight at the Denver International Airport when she set off for Los Angeles. She had to pay a $25 penalty.

"It was definitely my scrapbooking stuff," Mrs. Anderson said. "I brought very few clothes."

During the scrapbooking sessions, the chatty talk often veered away from the hobby itself and into stories of weddings and divorces, bosses and children, triumphs and tragedies—a normal pattern at scrapbooking events.

"Everyone has a story to tell," said Veronica Hugger, a founder of the National Scrapbooking Association in Katy, Texas, near Houston. "Scrapbooking is like writing an autobiography."

And there is always the topic of husbands, who have sometimes been known to have trouble comprehending the scrapbook mania. "Both my husband and 15-year-old son are hard sells," Mrs. Saams-Hoy said.

But she added that she had little guilt about going off alone on the cruise. "My biggest dilemma about leaving," she said, "was that I was going to miss the opening day of my younger son's T-ball and the last day of soccer, because I won't be there to take the pictures."

Pictures that she will need, of course, for future scrapbooks.

DECODING THE TEXT

1. Does the author support her assumption that scrapbooking is primarily for women? Does she need to support this assumption, or did you already agree with that statement before you read the article?

2. What techniques of travel writing does the author use to talk about both the cruise aspect and the scrapbooking aspect of this article? What techniques are different from those in a typical travel article?

CONNECTING TO YOUR CULTURE

1. Do you fit into any specific groups because of your leisure hobbies? Do these groups organize events together? Have meetings? Go on trips?

2. If you answered yes, define your group. What makes you similar to one another? Different from one another? Are you a "demographic"? Could a company market to you?

3. How would a company market to the group of scrapbookers featured in this article?

AUTHOR BIO

Shari Caudron is a former business journalist who became an independent writer. Since then, her work has been published in magazines such as Reader's Digest, The Christian Science Monitor, and Traveler's Tales. She has written two books, What Really Happened (2005) and Who Are You People? A Personal Journey into the Heart of Fanatical Passion in America (2006), which included the following essay on war gamers.

HITLER DID FINE, I CAN DO BETTER

Shari Caudron

"This war will not be over by the next commercial break."

—News announcer during the Gulf War

Ever had one of those dizzying moments, where you find yourself standing among a crowd of people who are so thoroughly alien to you, so thoroughly Not Like You, that it takes every ounce of willpower you possess not to turn and run screaming home to mommy?

Me too.

In fact, I'm having one right now.

It's a sunny summer morning and I've just arrived at the World Boardgaming Championships being held at the Marriott Hunt Valley Inn in a suburb north of Baltimore. When I first heard about the Boardgaming Championships, I began to skip happily around my bedroom. Boardgames? Now *this* was something I could relate to. I envisioned rooms full of pleasant, well-scrubbed people playing Monopoly, Scrabble, Trivial Pursuit, and other games I've been known to play, enjoy, and gloat a little over winning. I was excited by the potential of finding an interest I could relate to; jazzed by the thought that maybe here I'd find my tribe—*my* pigeon racers.

I was also way off the mark.

I'm standing inside the doorway of a hotel ballroom named the Maryland Room. Inside, dozens of people are clustered around banquet tables holding board games, the likes of which I've never seen before. Signs on the tables tell me they're playing "Robo Rally," "VINCI: The Rise & Fall of Civilizations," and something called "Merchant of Venus." I find a description of Merchant of Venus and read: "If you like your grease immortal, your sculpture psychotic, and your genes designer, then this is the game for you."

Huh?

Although I've never heard of games like this, it's not the games themselves that have activated my get-to-safety alarm. It's the participants. They are overwhelmingly male, predominantly white, and most look like they haven't shaven, combed their hair, crunched a fresh vegetable, or experienced a good night's sleep in days. Clad in rumpled and untucked T-shirts, the players look like men who, having escaped the civilizing influence of their wives, have found themselves descending into pits of slovenliness heretofore only dreamed of.

A few minutes ago, I watched a man with curly black hair thrust half a hamburger into his mouth—using the palm of his hand—while trying to discuss something with his tablemates. Unaided by chewing, the compressed burger sat idly inside the man's mouth, straining his left cheek to the bursting point, making conversation all but impossible. I felt sorry for that burger. All cramped up in the dark with nothing to do but wait for further instructions.

Perhaps recognizing the futility of trying to speak with a burger in his mouth, the man then swallowed it—wholly unchewed—in a feat of guttural capacity that could have merited a cover story in a scientific journal.

It's not the first time I've wondered whether hobbies like this are merely an excuse for men to get out of the house.

In fact, since I've been investigating passion, I've found it far easier to find communities of men devoted to singular interests, especially those that involve balls, pucks, bullets, drills, bait, breasts, engines, and bottles of oxygen. But perhaps I'm simply more intrigued by the male-dominated subcultures because they've always seemed so off-limits.

When I was a little girl, I'd spend summers at the family cabin in Northern California, playing on the Eel River with my five male cousins. They were always jokey and dirt-caked and full of stitches, and their fearless vitality thrilled me. I had no brothers and thus no direct daily experience with dirt bikes or dune buggies or playtime that involved imaginary fox holes and machine-gun fire. And I was fascinated by it all. My cousins spent summers backpacking in Yosemite, while my sisters and I worked on our tans.

As a kid, I yearned to sample a bit of that active male world but whenever I'd talk to my mother about, say, riding a motorcycle or scaling a mountain, I got her emergency room lecture. Mom worked in a hospital emergency room throughout my childhood and she knew from nightly experience what a motorcycle and mountain climbing could do to the human body. At one end of the spectrum: cuts. Stitches. Scrapes. Breaks. Burns. Sprains. At the other: death. Skiers landed in the ER. Daredevils landed in the ER. The *Kennedys* landed in the ER. Tame, sensible families like ours did not.

Appealing to my father was useless. He spent his young, active years teaching ballroom dancing at an Arthur Murray studio in San Francisco.

With the world of male passions off-limits, I, of course, craved them all the more. In college, I started camping. I learned to drive a motorcycle. I drank tequila shooters. But somewhere along the line I must have absorbed the message that polite restraint—not unchecked exuberance—was the consummate behavior to strive for. Whenever I forgot that, whenever I got a little stinky and sweaty and *involved,* my mother would reel me back in.

"Honey," she'd say, shaking her head at my silly attempts at tomboy behavior. "Only men and horses sweat."

Reflecting on this, it's no wonder I've been drawn to these secret male worlds with their no-holds-barred behavior. But now, as I look at the board gamers in their rumpled clothing and stale body smells, I believe I may have over-romanticized men and their passions.

And yet . . . I can't seem to pull myself away.

I leave Burger Boy and the Maryland Room behind and enter a hallway where many of the board games being played are on display. I browse their covers.

A game called Battle Cry boasts: "Recreate 15 Epic World War battles. There's just one difference. You are *there!*"

The cover of Cosmic Encounter tells me: "Armed with alien power, you are ready to colonize the galaxy."

Other games include Attila, Air Baron, Acquire, Liberty, Brute Force, Samurai, Attack Sub, Vanished Planet, Squad Leader, Greed, Pay Dirt, and PanzerBlitz.

Given the all-girls family I hail from, I wasn't aware they could build so much testosterone into a board game. The most violent it ever got at our house was when my sisters and I played Feeley Meeley, a game in which players shoved their hands inside holes cut into a cardboard cube and tried to find an object inside, such as a comb or whistle, using only the sense of touch. With four young female hands grasping inside for the same object, we endured our fair share of slapping, jabbing, poking, pulling, threats, tears, and piercing, high-pitched accusations of cheating. I shudder to think what viciousness a game like Air Baron would have unleashed.

Still, looking at the racks of games, I'm mystified by this slash 'n' burn, conquer-and-destroy mentality. Who plays these games anyway? The urge to flee has now given way to curiosity. Asking around for someone to help me, I am connected with Don Greenwood, the convention director.

Greenwood is a large man with a soft belly, oversized glasses, and bushy mustache. He's standing behind a dark wood registration counter, and when I tell him why I'm here, he looks at me and taps his pen on the counter without saying a word. I can't help but think it's because he sees me for what I am: Someone who is acting politely interested in boardgamers, but actually sees herself as a teensy bit superior to them—primarily because feeling supcrior is preferable to feeling left out. If I was Mr. Greenwood, I don't know if I'd talk to me.

His pen continues to tap.

"Okay," he says, finally, "but I have just ten minutes."

He steps from behind the counter and tells a woman standing nearby he'll only be a minute. Unlike other people I've visited with, Don doesn't seem particularly interested in recruiting me.

We begin chatting and he tells me that 1,100 people from around the world have come here to the fifth annual World Boardgaming Championships. This weekend, about 140 games are being played as part of the competition, but hundreds more are being played during open gaming.

"What do the winners receive?" I ask. "Money?"

"There's no prize money. That brings out the daggers."

I wait for Don to tell me what, exactly, they do receive. The silence lengthens.

"So . . . what *do* they play for?"

"Woods."

"Woods?"

"Yeah. Woods. Plaques." Don is no longer tapping his pen, but he might as well be.

"I see," I reply, although of course I don't see anything at all.

Don must sense my discomfort for he takes a deep breath, exhales slowly, and decides that since I'm not going away he might as well answer my questions.

"Okay," he says. "This is how it works."

Don explains that players get points for winning individual events. These points are called laurels. The more competitive the game, the more people who play, the more laurels you get. At the end of a game, the person with the most laurels gets a plaque showing he is the winner of that game. At the end of the convention, the person with the most laurels overall is named the Caesar, the reigning king of the World Boardgaming Championships.

"We do it this way 'cause if there was prize money it would bring out the pros and we'd have to worry about cheating. This way, people play for honor and bragging rights only. This conference is for purists."

I tell Don that I'd expected to encounter more popular board games like Scrabble and Monopoly and maybe—ha-ha—Chutes and Ladders.

Don does not find this amusing.

"There are not party or social games like *you* might be familiar with," he says. "These are niche games. They are highly *involved* games that have *intricate* rules and are heavy on strategy. These games require a *significant* investment of time. They are *not* for the general populace."

Well then.

Don removes his ball cap and scratches his bald head. He has two puffs of curly hair over each ear and smoothes these down before replacing his cap.

I soldier on.

I ask Don why he is attracted to boardgames, and he tells me it's because niche games are tense and exciting, and they allow players to stay involved. In Monopoly, if you get the right real estate, you push everyone else into poverty. In Scrabble, wordsmiths can out-vocabularize their opponents in no time. But niche games allow people to remain emotionally engaged and strategically involved throughout the length of the game. Plus, he adds, they offer a great intellectual challenge.

"Intellectual challenge?" I ask, thinking about the man with the hamburger.

"Absolutely. Many of these games simulate historic, real-world events. I especially like games where you set the parameters so historical events can occur the way you create them."

"So players need some knowledge of history?"

"That's good to have," he agrees, "but math is more important. In fact, most of the people here are extremely well-educated. There are lots of engineers."

I'll be honest. For the last several minutes I've been trying to convince myself that burger-eating boardgamers have nothing to teach me. It's just so foreign here, so *male,* even for my voyeuristic tastes. Plus, the whole gamey gaming environment just makes me want to shower.

But Don's comment about the educational level of participants reels me back in, especially since I had so recently concluded that pigeon racers did what they did because of the lack of intellectual challenge in their jobs. In fact, to date, most of the people I've been with have been predominantly working class. This has made it easy for me to conclude I don't have passions because I've got two master's degrees and thus am simply too educated (she says, head lifted with a misplaced bit of hubris) to bother with them.

But if what Don says is true, fanaticism is not the province of the underemployed, and the people here might have something to teach me after all.

Don looks toward his berth at the registration desk, and I suspect he's about to call time on our conversation. "Um, can I ask one more favor?" I ask.

He exhales again.

I tell him I'm researching passion and would like to talk with some of the most zealous gamers here. "Any suggestions?"

"Head over to the Worthington Room," he says.

"The Worthington Room?"

"Yeah. It's what, Saturday now? The guys in there have been playing the same game since Tuesday."

"The *same* game?"

"You said you wanted passion."

I believe Don Greenwood was telling the truth when he proclaimed niche games were tense and exciting, but I've been standing in the Worthington Room for the last ten minutes and have yet to spot evidence of the action-packed, zip-a-dee-doo-da adventure he referred to.

Inside the room, clusters of men are gathered around large round tables covered by incongruously pink tablecloths. Like the players downstairs, these guys look rumpled and tired, and the room smells like adult male bodies that haven't seen the tiled interior of a shower stall for days. Most are quietly staring at game boards on the tables in front of them. The atmosphere feels heavy, like a room full of students straining to complete their college entrance exams.

A large man with four days' worth of white chin stubble notices me.

"How're you doing?" he asks.

His voice is craggy like that of a lifelong smoker. I walk over to his table, on which sits a game board the size of a hood from a small sedan. He introduces himself.

Steve Voros, he says. Former material control specialist. Ford Motor Company. Now retired. He extends his hand.

I tell Steve that I'm investigating fanatical passion, and he tells me that boy-howdy, have I come to the right place.

"You have to be nuts to play this," he says. "I've been playing for twenty-five years and I'm *still* learning the game."

"*That's* for sure," says the man who's sitting across the table from him.

"Yeah, you wish," Steve replies.

"Are you two playing against each other?" I ask.

"Yeah," Steve says. "We've played four games since Tuesday. We're not like the guys over there." He cocks his head toward the table behind me.

I look over at the table. Steve tells me the men there are playing a World at War, which takes sixty or seventy hours of play time. He's playing its predecessor, Advanced Third Reich, which is not only easier, he says, but also requires a scant twelve hours to complete.

"*Only* twelve?"

"Yeah. We don't go as long, so it doesn't get as tense."

There's that word again. "Tense how?"

"I'll tell you how. You should've been here this morning at about three o'clock. There was a group of guys playing at that table in the corner." He points to a table that now sits vacant. "They'd been playing for about twenty hours straight without sleep when they got into a fight about the rules. One of the guys got so mad he picked up the game and overturned it. You do that, and the game's over."

"Did you see it?"

"Nah, I left about 1 A.M. I just heard the rumors this morning. But I know they're true. You take a bunch of guys who haven't slept, put 'em around a table where the Second World War is going on, and you can expect a few disagreements. Everyone here's pretty smart, so they all think they're right all the time. Just look around."

Steve turns and starts pointing toward the other players in the room. "That guy's a lawyer. That guy's got a Ph.D. in tree hugging. And see that sublime guy over there? He's a neurologist."

I gaze in the direction Steve's pointing but fail to find someone I would characterize as sublime. Still, I'm impressed. Don was right—brainiacs play these games.

Steve turns back to his own table and gestures toward his opponent, a small, slim man with wire-rim glasses. "And this guy here, he knows world leaders."

"Not quite," his opponent says. He has a thick German accent.

We chat, and I learn Steve's opponent is Herbert Gratz from Vienna, Austria. Herbert has attended the World Boardgaming Championships every year since 1991 and, when he's not playing games, he works at the International Monetary Fund at the Central Bank in Vienna. "It sounds impressive, but I'm just a policy advisor to management."

I ask Herbert why he comes to Maryland all the way from Austria every year. "Can't you play these games at home?"

"Oh, no. All the serious conflict-resolution games are published in English," he says. For a small man, he sounds eerily like Arnold Schwarzenegger. "In Germany, you can be legally prosecuted if you publish a game with a swastika on the package. That's why all the games Germans publish are about saving the environment. They all have funny little bunnies skipping through the forest."

Herbert says this with such disdain that I've no need to ask him why he prefers conflict games. Instead, I ask him specifically what it is about Advanced Third Reich that causes him to cross the Atlantic every year to play it for several days on end.

"Because I want to be like the Americans. I want to be like the maniacs that rule the world."

Herbert laughs in a manner that's intended to suggest he's kidding.

"But," he adds, "I also like eating the ribs they serve at the hotel. Of course, in Austria, we have ribs. But they're not as good as the Marriott."

Steve interjects. "You *do* like your ribs."

"I tell you, I do."

Herbert looks around the room at the other players and then turns his attention back to me.

"Okay, seriously," he says. "I started playing this game because I like complicated strategy games. When I was younger, I played chess and bridge. I liked the competition. But now it's not so much about competition. It's about companionship. Like with this guy," he says, pointing to Steve.

I look back and forth between the two men. The unexpected retreat of Herbert's Third Reich swagger takes me by surprise, and I find myself touched by his confession.

"It's true," Steve adds. "We've played together for years."

The two men start bickering over exactly how many years it's been. Five? Four? Six? Watching them, I'm once again struck by the unlikely friendships that form around common interests. How else would a retired autoworker from Detroit come to fraternize with an international money manager from Vienna? Although their interests may be the same, their lives aren't.

"So, tell me," I ask, in an attempt to stop their squabbling, "what is the aim of the game?"

"The victory conditions are not clearly win or lose," Herbert says. "There are shades of winning. You play to lose by only a little. Of course, if the other guy whines ... " he pauses and looks across the table at Steve, "that is also very positive and rewarding."

"Oh, brother," Steve says.

"You said you were on the fourth game?" I ask Steve.

"That's right," he says.

"Have you lost each one?"

"Oh, most certainly."

I leave to let Steve resume his happy losing streak and I walk over to a table where four men are sitting curved over a game board. I stand beside a man wearing a St. Johns ball cap. He's staring intently at the game board and chewing his thumbnail. The other players around the table are conversing. But their conversation is slow, as if their responses are time-delayed because of great distance.

"In my last Euro scenario, the Russians had rockets."

Pause.

"I hate it when they do that."

Pause.

"You going for pizza?"

Pause.

"I *said* are you going for pizza?"

"Nah, I'm gonna hang around here, because it looks like my brother is going to toast Japan."

Pause.

"Yeah. Japan is getting hot."

Pause.

"Will you be hitting me with the bomb?"

Pause.

"I dunno."

As the game proceeds, one of the players sitting close to me attempts to give me a brief, entry-level overview of A World at War. He tells me the game is a World War II strategy game in which two teams—one serving as the Axis powers, the other as the Allies—compete to gain world control. The game is designed to allow players to pursue their own wartime strategies. They build navies to suit their strategic requirements. They deploy armies and air force pools based on projected need. They worry about oil reserves, their nation's economies, and diplomatic alliances with other nation-states. All of these factors have an impact on the war strategies they can eventually put into place, and the options are endless. Japan could choose to invade Australia or India, for example. Germany could develop the atomic bomb. The British position in the Middle East could crumble.

"It sounds complicated," I say, capitalizing on my highly refined journalistic ability to state the obvious.

"Oh, it takes a good ten years to get to proficiency level," he says.

I continue to watch them play and realize that unlike the pigeon racers, these guys have not chosen a passion that utilizes untapped skills and talents. Instead, they are turning up the dial on intellectual strengths they use every day in their professional lives. As lawyers and doctors and academics, they've already developed the ability to synthesize information, think strategically, and create workable strategies. What A World at War appears to do is allow them to fully test these skills in a more intense environment. The fact that they don't have to sleep or shave or shower is merely an added bonus.

During one of the many long pauses, I ask the players how much they've slept over the past four nights and learn they've only broken for three-to-five hours a night—tops.

"And it's not restful sleep, either. You're tossing and turning and thinking about the game. Your adrenaline gets stuck in one mode."

"Yeah. I can't even imagine going back to work on Monday. It'll be like coming back from outer space."

The other players lean forward and appear to grow energized by the discussion of their extreme gaming accomplishments.

"We're like Navy Seals. They train like this too. A whole week without sleep."

"My philosophy is this. If we're gonna do this all week, we're *gonna do this all week.*"

"I totally agree. I had to play all the chits with the wife to come here. Hey . . . wait a minute! Did you bomb him?"

"Naaa."

"Come on. This game is called A World at War, but there's not much fighting going on. It should be called A World at Peace."

This last comment brings their attention back to the game. I watch them for a while seeking clues as to what they're doing. On a nearby chair, I spot the game's rulebook and lean over to pick it up. It's 196 full-sized pages, 8.5 point type, single spaced.

The man with the St. Johns ball cap sees me looking at it. "You ought to talk to the guy who wrote that."

"Who's that?"

"Over there, in the corner." He points to a man wearing a T-shirt from the National Air and Space Museum that features illustrations of World War II bombers. "That's Bruce Harper. He designed the game."

Bruce Harper is a forty-eight-year-old lawyer from Vancouver, British Columbia, who prosecutes tax offenses. He's got pale skin, short reddish hair, and deep purple circles under his eyes. He reminds me of Woody Allen, minus the glasses. He's sitting at the same corner table that was allegedly vacated at three o'clock this morning by the group of angry, overtired players.

In the last fifteen years, Bruce has designed four games: Wrasslin', Advanced Civilization, Advanced Third Reich, and Empire of the Rising Sun. He combined the last two games into A World at War, which—although it officially debuted only four days ago at the World Boardgaming Championships—has been under development for years.

Bruce got into game designing because he understands the importance of rules to a good game and how to write rules that people understand. In 1981, he was playing a game with friends when a question arose about the proper play procedure. He wrote a note to the company making a suggestion about how to improve the rules so as to eliminate such confusion.

"They put my suggestion in the next rule book and before I knew it, I'd become the Q-and-A guy for that particular game," he explains. "You see, for most people rules are sacrosanct. If the rules say that pigs fly, well then, pigs fly. For a game to be successful, the rules have to be clear. You don't want to spend your play time arguing about them."

Bruce speaks the way you'd expect a person who is concerned about the interpretation of rules to speak. He looks me directly in the eye. He prefaces each sentence with long, thoughtful pauses. And although he is eating a Marriott-issue hamburger much like the one compacted earlier by the man downstairs, Bruce takes time to carefully chew every bite before speaking.

"Why are strategy games like A World at War so popular here?"

Chew. Swallow.

"If you read a book about history, say, about World War II, you know how it will end," he explains. "But games like this are interactive. The players themselves decide the outcome based on their own strategic moves. People can say to themselves, 'Hitler did fine up until this point. I can do better.' The challenge of the game is not to recreate actual events, but to respond to different what-if scenarios. For example, what if Japan didn't bomb Pearl Harbor? If all the assumptions are reasonable, and all the rules make sense, then the game proceeds without a problem. But if you get a rule wrong, it can wreck the game."

"Do your skills as a lawyer help you design games?" I know the answer to this, but I have to ask anyway.

Chew. Swallow. Napkin dab.

"Probably. I've learned to write clearly because I understand the problems caused by a lack of clarity. There's an old law from England that's only one page long and has been massively litigated. There's been something like twenty thousand decisions on that one single law. But when a law is clearly written, the need for litigation is diminished. There's far less litigation with a long law than a shorter one because the answer is in the writing. Game designers who don't take time to clarify the rules so that people understand how to follow them, well, to me, that shows an astounding misinterpretation of human nature."

Bruce is clearly not a person I want to be caught jaywalking around.

"What other games do you play?" I ask.

"I haven't played many games besides my own over the last few years. It seems self-indulgent to play when so many people are waiting for my rules." Bruce says this as if the rules he's been working on hold the key to everlasting world peace. Which they might, for all I know.

"So playing games is your passion?"

"Definitely.

"When I'm playing a game like this, I'm totally focused. I'm not thinking about work, or anything else. It's the way I relax. My wife relaxes by reading trashy novels. I relax by coming here. Really, there's no other way I'd rather spend a week than by playing games, acting like an idiot and not sleeping and eating."

Sensing Bruce will have an opinion on the subject, I ask him why it seems there are so many male-dominated subcultures.

"Because guys have to be doing something to get together. Women form social groups easily, but men need an excuse. One guy never calls up another guy and says, 'Hey, let's go have a few beers and talk.'"

"But isn't locking yourself in a hotel for a week pretty obsessive?"

"Obsessive, passionate. Whatever. They both describe the same kind of behavior. I'm proud that I've designed a game that might cause some loner to come out of his house and interact with others. I like to think that I've prevented some crazy guy from heading out onto the street with a rifle.

"I tell you who I feel sorry for," he adds. "I feel sorry for those people who don't have any passions at all. Passion is a great thing in life."

Sheepishly, I say nothing.

"I mean what harm does all this do anyway?" Bruce sweeps his hand from right to left in a room-encompassing gesture. "We're all old friends here, even the people who met just four days ago."

I thank Bruce for his time and walk through the tables to the exit. And as I do, I feel the familiar stab of envy return.

Source: *"Hitler Did Fine, I Can Do Better"* from Who Are You People? A Personal Journey into the Heart of Fanatical Passion in America, *by Shari Caudron, 2006, pp. 93–108. Reprinted by permission of Barricade Books.*

DECODING THE TEXT

1. At the end of the reading, the author states that obsession and passion both lead to the same kind of behavior. How does the author characterize her obsession and passion throughout the text?

2. What details does she give or what language does she use that leads the reader to think of her as obsessed?

CONNECTING TO YOUR CULTURE

1. What is your major obsession or passion? What actions do you take as a result of this passion? How did it develop?

2. Do your friends and family members know about this obsession? Do they share your passion? If not, do they understand your interest?

3. Do you network with others who share this passion? Why or why not?

AUTHOR BIO

Eliza Wapner *works on the design team for* Silver Chips Online. Silver Chips Online *is the independent student newspaper for Montgomery Blair High School in Silver Spring, Maryland. The staff of* Silver Chips Online *and its print partner,* Silver Chips, *has won numerous media awards. This article appeared in* Silver Chips Online *June 7, 2011.*

HOMECOOKED COMPETITION SERVES THE ULTIMATE FRIENDSHIP

Ultimate Frisbee Teaches Blair Students Unconventional and Important Lessons

Eliza Wapner

Sophomore Puck Bregstone leaps to snatch a Frisbee out of the air. As he catches the disc, he lands hard on the ground, accidentally pushing a member from the opposing team down. The time is stopped, not by a referee, but by the players.

Bregstone is part of Blair's Ultimate Frisbee team, Homecooked. Ultimate is a sport that involves throwing and catching a disc, combining aspects of basketball, soccer and football in a fast-paced game of teamwork.

But although the game has a defined set of rules, on the field play is self-officiated, meaning that there are no referees and team members are expected to uphold only the "spirit of the game." The players make all calls and by the standards of this "spirit of the game" philosophy they are required to be fair and uphold the sincerity of the game.

The Washington Area Frisbee Club (WAFC) defines this unique code of conduct as a set of rules that relies on "sportsmanship that places responsibility for fair play on the player." According to WAFC this dedication to the integrity of the game is what really sets Frisbee apart from mainstream sports.

THE TRICKS OF THE TRADE

In Ultimate, the objective is to get the Frisbee in the end zone. After the Frisbee is caught, the player can only move up to three steps before passing the disc to another player. The main strategy of Ultimate is to set up a "stack" or a line of players down the field that helps players reach the end zone to score.

According to the *New York Times,* Ultimate Frisbee was invented by the hippies of the 1960's as an anti-sport that harbored a congenial mind-set; no referees, no previous experience and no intense contact.

In 1979 an organization called USA Ultimate was created to regulate national tournaments and leagues. Since then the sport has continued to grow to include college and high-school students. In fact, in the past year youth Frisbee has taken the US National Governing Body For the Sport of Ultimate (USA Ultimate) by surprise as the number of student members in the organization surpassed the number of adult and college members. The growth in youth Frisbee has seen new leagues and players participating, including the WAFC Washington, D.C. area league that Homecooked plays in.

Three years ago, Kris Gill, former president of WAFC moved to Takoma Park and wanted to get involved with the community by teaching Ultimate. She became the coach of Homecooked and has come every Wednesday since to practice with the team and teach them more advanced skills. Junior co-captain Marcus Clarke praises Gill for her belief in the team. "She's very supportive of the team," he says, "she never puts us down."

This support translates into success. This season, Homecooked stands with a record of two and four. They beat Paint Branch's fairly new team and lost to Sidwell Friend School's established and school funded team.

Gill predicts that as the years go on, the team will continue to improve. She credits this to a strong core of underclassmen team members.

BREAKING THE MOLD

According to Andy Lee, director of manufacturing and communications at USA Ultimate, the sense of responsibility and teamwork is a mind-set that boosts morale, which in turn attracts people to the game. Lee says that this is one of the primary reasons for Ultimate's growing popularity.

"It's one of the underlying principles of Ultimate that teaches sportsmanship, honesty and integrity which appeals to kids and parents," he says. "There is a great life lesson that is taught through the game." According to Gill, this mind-set leads to player's respect towards their own teammates and the players on the opposing team. "You become friends off the field [with your teammates] because of spirit of the game," says Gill.

According to Clarke, even in rough spots the team stands together well and maintains a sense of camaraderie to keep them going strong. During a grueling game against Magruder, Homecooked was losing badly, but they managed to maintain a positive outlook. Sophomore Camille Newell made an inspiring speech, motivating the team to make a four point come back to finish the game Magruder eight and Homecooked four.

According to team member sophomore Devin Rutan, Homecooked Frisbee is based on friendships, making it unique in the school sports arena. "That's what sets us apart from the rest of sports," he says, "[ultimate is] more fun and it's more about companionship of the game and doing something you love."

Source: http://silverchips.mbhs.edu/story/10979

DECODING THE TEXT

1. According to Wapner, how does the spirit of the game reflect its hippie background and set it apart from other organized sports?

2. According to all of the authors in the case study, what is the purpose of social networks based on hobbies? What do participants gain from these networks or groups?

3. Do any of these authors think people take their hobbies or habits to extreme? In what ways? Is this necessarily a bad thing? Why or why not?

4. Where would you expect to find each of these essays? Who are the audiences for each? How do you know?

CONNECTING TO YOUR CULTURE

1. Have you ever made friendships while playing a sport or a game? While completing a crafting project of some type? If so, have those friendships lasted? Why or why not?

2. Have you ever participated in an event or group because you wanted to be around the people in the group? Explain.

3. What is your favorite sport or game? Where did you learn it? With whom?

4. What is your favorite craft project or hobby? Where did you learn it? With whom?

5. What game or hobby would you like to learn? Why?

READING SELECTIONS:
THE 2010s

CONSIDERING IDEAS

1. What games do you enjoy playing? Do you consider yourself a fan of any particular game or online activity?

2. How often do you play games with family and friends versus online or individual games?

3. What does this say about your personality? About the way you spend your free time?

AUTHOR BIO

Jane McGonigal is a game designer, game researcher, author, and the director of Game Research and Development at the Institute for the Future, a Palo Alto, California–based think tank. Her work has been featured in The Economist, Wired, *and* The New York Times, *and on MTV, CNN, and NPR. She has given keynote addresses at TED, South by Southwest Interactive, and the Game Developers Conference, and foresight and strategic advice to companies such as Microsoft, Nintendo, Nike, SAP, Wells Fargo, and Disney. This essay is an excerpt from* Reality Is Broken: Why Games Make Us Better and How They Can Change the World, *McGonigal's 2011 book about gaming.*

STRONGER SOCIAL CONNECTIVITY

Jane McGonigal

More than 5 million people are playing the online word game Lexulous on Facebook. And most of them are playing it with their moms. When the game was released in 2007, it became the first Facebook application to achieve a mass audience, and the familiarity of the gameplay was one of its main attractions. If you know how to play Scrabble, then you already know how to play Lexulous-it's just a slightly modified and unauthorized version of the classic board game, combined with online chat. There's no time limit on turns, and games stay active even when you log out of the social network. Whenever it's your turn, Facebook sends you an alert to your home page, your e-mail, or your mobile phone.

Here's how one Lexulous reviewer sums up its cross-generational appeal: "Everyone in your social network, even your mom, knows how to play Scrabble." No doubt that's why so many of the online rave reviews include the phrase "my mom"—like this one: "I live in Atlanta, and my mom's in Texas. We love to have game night across the miles. Although I am sure she needs a break from me kicking her butt all of the time. (Love you, Mom!)"

I've been reading game reviews for most of my life and I've seen anything close to this many mom references. In fact, it's not that much of a maintain strong, active connections with people we care about but who we don't see or speak to enough in our daily lives.

Eric Weiner, an independent foreign correspondent and author of *The Geography of Bliss,* has covered happiness trends throughout the world. His research has confirmed for him that "our happiness is completely and utterly intertwined with other people: family and friends and neighbors. . . . Happiness is not a noun or verb. It's a conjunction. Connective tissue." Games like Lexulous are intentionally designed to strengthen the connective tissue within our social networks. Each move we make in the game is a conjunction.

We clearly need more social conjunction in our lives. As numerous economists and positive psychologists have observed, globally we make the mistake of becoming less social the richer we become as individuals, and as a society. As Weiner observes: "The greatest source of happiness is other people—and what does money do? It isolates us from other people. It enables us to build walls, literal and figurative, around ourselves. We move from a teeming college dorm to an apartment to a house and, if we're really wealthy, to an estate. We think we're moving up, but really we're walling off ourselves."

Games like Lexulous can help us start chipping away at those walls. Lexulous was the first breakthrough social network game, but since its success, the genre has experienced dramatic growth—particularly on Facebook. In early 2010, a virtual farming game called FarmVille hit an astonishing benchmark: 90 million active players on Facebook, nearly 30 million of whom log in on any given day to harvest their virtual crops and tend to their virtual livestock.

It's an unprecedented scale of participation in a single online game. Roughly one in seventy-five people on the planet is currently playing FarmVille, and one in two hundred people on the planet logs in on any given day to manage and grow their virtual farm. What accounts for this global popularity? FarmVille is the first game to combine the blissful productivity of *World of Warcraft* with the easy gameplay and social connectivity of Lexulous.

Half the fun of FarmVille is earning experience points and gold in order to level up and earn access to better crops and farm equipment, more exotic animals, and a bigger land plot. Every time you log in to the game, you can improve your stats by undertaking a series, point-and-click tasks: plow the soil, buy and plant the seeds, harvest the crops, pet your farm animals. Each crop takes between twelve hours and four days in real time to yield a harvest, so checking in every day or so become a regular habit. You start the game able to harvest just strawberries and soybeans on a humble two-by-six-square plot. Over time, you can work your way up to a "mighty plantation" plot of twenty-two by twenty-two squares, on which you can grow lilies, yellow melons, and coffee—not to mention care for bunny rabbits, pinto horses, and golden chickens.

But the real genius of FarmVille is the social layer on top of this immensely satisfying self-improvement work. The first time you log in to the game, you see a list of your real-life Facebook friends who are already tending their own virtual farms. You can make any or all of them your "neighbors" in the game and visit their farms whenever you want to see how they're doing.

You don't interact directly with these neighbors—instead, like most Lexulous play, FarmVille is an entirely asynchronous experience. While you're tending your own farm, pop-up windows nudge you to play attention to your friends' and families' farms: "Chelsea could use help on her farm. Can you give her a hand?" or "Ralph's crops are looking a little puny. Could you please fertilize them?" Most players spend up to half their time in FarmVille helping others: raking up their leaves, shooing away raccoons, or feeding their chickens. You can also send your neighbors one free gift every day—a virtual avocado tree, a bale of hot pink hay, or a duck, for instance. Meanwhile, whenever you log back in to the game, you'll see a list of neighbors who have helped your farm, and you're likely to find a pile of presents to accept.

The gifts aren't real, of course. The favors don't help you in your everyday life. But the gesture isn't an empty one. Every gift or favor someone bestows upon you helps you achieve your goals in the game. And it's a virtuous circle. Every time you see that someone has helped your farm, you feel the urge to reciprocate. Over time, you build up a rhythm of checking in and helping others in your social network single day.

It's not a good substitute for real interaction, but it helps keep extended friends and family in our daily lives when we might otherwise be too busy to stay connected. Games like Lexulous and FarmVille ensure we'll show up and do our part to nurture our relationships daily, and make a gesture of friendship whenever it's our turn.

Source: *From* Reality Is Broken, *by Jane McGonigal, copyright (c) 2011 by Jane McGonigal. Used by permission of The Penguin Press, a division of Penguin Group (USA) Inc.*

DECODING THE TEXT

1. The author makes mom references in reviews of games like Lexulous. What does this refer to? Why is it important?
2. According to the author, what's the real benefit of giving virtual help or gifts?

CONNECTING TO YOUR CULTURE

1. How many games do you play on platforms such as Facebook or gaming sites such as Pogo? What about apps on your phone or a tablet computer?
2. Do you prefer games you play alone or with others? Why?
3. Do you use the chat feature provided with most of these games?
4. Do you play with people you know or randomly selected strangers on the network? Explain your choices and guiding criteria.

CONSIDERING IDEAS

1. Is organized religion a part of your life? Why or why not? In what ways?
2. Have you ever looked at or logged into Second Life? Have you ever created an SL avatar?
3. What does the term *virtual church* mean to you? What questions does it raise?

AUTHOR BIO

Rachel Wagner *is assistant professor of religion in the department of philosophy and religion at Ithaca College. Wagner has also been included in the edited collection* Halos and Avatars: Playing Games with God *and the* Journal of Religion and Film, *and Wagner has also been interviewed on such popular media channels as NPR and CBC. In 2011, she published* Godwired: Religion, Ritual and Virtual Reality, *a book that explores the intersection between religious studies and virtual reality. This essay is taken from* God in the Details: American Religion in Popular Culture, *an edited collection that explores religious themes in American popular culture.*

OUR LADY OF PERSISTENT LIMINALITY

Virtual Church, Cyberspace, and Second Life

Rachel Wagner

FRIEDRICH STARK/ALAMY

Can someone desecrate a virtual church? Is it possible to commit a "virtual" sin? Who would have thought, a few decades ago, that we'd ask what it means to "really" perform a religious ritual, or whether we need our bodies to do so? But given the recent proliferation of deeply immersive online experiences, these are exactly the questions we now ask. In the online virtual community *Second Life,* for example, one can find a "Catholic" church run by a nonpriest in priest's digital garb, and people attending (and even sleeping through) services; a real-life Buddhist monk spreading the dharma; a replica of a Mayan temple with a real-life donation feature; and recently, a "prim" (a digital representation of a piece of wood, manufactured randomly) that some claim displays a miraculous image of the Virgin Mary. Clearly, there is religion in *Second Life.* But what kind of religion is it?

In 2006, I co-led a team that conducted a series of interviews in *Second Life.*[1] Based on the responses it is clear that, in online environments, distinctions between sacred and profane, virtual and real, play and ritual break down, challenging our sense of what is "here," and what is "there" Boundaries of all kinds—between play and ritual, between virtual reality and material reality, between the physical body and the digital body—are disrupted in online spaces like *Second Life,* raising questions about some of the most pertinent issues at stake in today's discussion of virtual religion. What is happening today may seem strange, new, and fascinating for the study of religion and what it means for people to come together in a collective experience, but it also highlights the notion that religious experience has always been a form of imaginative "play."

Virtual Religions: Churches in *Second Life*

What makes a space sacred? This question seems easier to answer in real life than in virtual space—one either enters a sanctuary or one doesn't. The physical space of a church or synagogue demarcates it as different from the surrounding world. However, in *Second Life,* one can see an erosion of the distraction between sacred and profane space.

Mark Brown is an Anglican priest who was ordained by the Bishop of Wellington, New Zealand, with the charge of "overseeing the virtual ministry instead of one based in a church built of bricks and mortar" (Hamilton 2008). Brown ministers exclusively in *Second Life,* and in his *Christian Mission to a Virtual World,* a missive about ministry in *Second Life,* he offers readers directions about how to download the software, log in, create an avatar (a digital representation of oneself), locate the virtual Anglican Cathedral, and then "teleport" to the Cathedral grounds:

> You would then be welcomed by the service leader and given the liturgy by clicking on a book located on a table near the entrance. You then click on a virtual pew and select "sit." The service leader will then either type the liturgy, or say it for all to hear or offer both . . . When it comes to the sermon the message has been prerecorded and at the appropriate time is streamed into *Second Life.* Following the service people [avatars] congregate around the Cathedral for fellowship and discussion. Wherever you are in the [real] world, if you have a good internet connection and a reasonably powerful computer you can attend church.
>
> (Brown 2008, 6)

Another SL resident called "Alwin Alcott" could be channeling religious theorist Mircea Eliade when he remarks that *Second Life* "can help with understanding the untouchable divine world."[2] Eliade defines the distinction between sacred and profane at "two modes of being in the world, two existential situations assumed by man in the course of hit history" (Eliade 1957, 14). He says that "[r]evelation of a sacred space makes it possible to obtain a fixed point and hence to acquire orientation in the chaos of homogeneity, to 'found the world' and to live in a real sense" (*ibid.,* 23). Despite the impassibility of absolutely identifying sacred and profane in *Second Life,* these categories enable us to examine how users see their own spaces, and how this illuminates the erosion of the distinction between sacred and profane in cyberspace.

In particular, Eliade helps us understand the impulse to build, which the religious person does as a means of staving off chaos, and in apparent imitation of an unchanging sacred realm that is inaccessible in his present life. Entering a space that has not been given order well matches Eliade's description of chaos as "an uncosmicized because unconsecrated space, a mere amorphous extent into which no orientation has yet been projected, and hence in which no structure has yet arisen" (*ibid.,* 1957, 64). In *Second Life,* churches and temples establish for their builders a hierophany—"an irruption of the sacred" that makes an area "qualitatively different" from those around it, and as such "reveals an absolute fixed point, a center" in undifferentiated (chaotic) space (*ibid.,* 26; 21). By building in the profane spaces in *Second Life,* residents "symbolically transform [them] into a cosmos through a ritual repetition of the cosmogony" (*ibid.,* 31). Since, for the religious person, profane space represents absolute nonbeing, this gives a sense of order and predictability to a chaotic realm, and permits for the performance of ritual as it is authenticated by it. It is, for Eliade, a singularly religious act.

However, Krystina Derrickson argues that representation of the sacred in virtual space is not the same thing as the construction of sacred space in real life. Considering the online *hajj,* Derrickson (2008) points out the "ambiguous" nature of sacred space in *Second Life,* where the simulated Mecca "may be considered a form of sacred virtual space," because of the "detailed reconstruction of spiritually-charged physical loci," and the "behavioral regulation encouraged by sim owners in the treatment of those virtual spaces,"[3] For Derrickson, when sacred space is constructed in a virtual context, its sacredness is endowed by intent. The sacredness that any virtual building exhibits is thus contested, reflexively constructed, and subject to simultaneous multiple Interpretations. We can see this in the opinions of *Second Life* resident "Beauman Hargson," who built a virtual replica of a well-known cathedral, and one day discovered a digital penis on its altar. As "Hargson" noted, rather nonchalantly: "one mouse-click and it is deleted so I don't mind too much about that."

Due to then virtual nature, sacred structures in *Second Life,* unlike reallife sacred structures, are infinitely malleable. Digital pollutions are momentary; sanitation is as easy as a click of *the* mouse. The ambiguous quality of "sacredness" in *Second Life* became apparent to me in the spring semester, 2008, when students in one of my classes explored the online *hajj,* and I was uncertain whether one of their avatars should "enter" the digital *hajj* in his Batman costume. Such questions are the hallmark of the contested nature of sacred space in a virtual context.

The ambiguity of the sacred means that certain traditional religious rituals are generally acceptable in *Second Life,* such as lighting Shabbat candles, praying, or meditating However, for those with *bona fide* religious credentials who engage in ritual activity within *Second Life,* there are some limitation to online ritual performance. You can enact an animation to "kneel" while you pray (Hamilton 2008), but you cannot engage in the traditional sacraments. You will find no marriages, baptisms, or eucharists performed in the Anglican Cathedral. The Catholic Church affirms this proscription, and has banned any consideration of virtual eucharists. Rabbi Yosef Y. Kazen argues that the embodied, physical aspect of religious identity is crucial for certain religious practices. Kazen, who manages a number of online resources for Orthodox Jews, claims that rituals such as a bar mitzvah ceremony or a prayer service with a *minyan* (ten adult males) cannot be conducted in a virtual environment. "We don't necessarily see the spiritual reality of what is happening [when we engage in embodied rituals]," he says, "but certain things have to be done with physical people, just as food has to be eaten by physical people" (quoted by Zaleski 1997, 19). Latter-day Saint and Second Lifer "Mo Hax" agrees: "Even though we Mormons take the sacrament (communion) and don't believe in literal transubstantiation, the rite seems out of place in SL, to me at least. . . priestly ordination is done 'by the laying on of hands' Such things require physicality."

Rev. Brown explains that online, the Anglican Church offers only "non-eucharistic services" along with Bible study and discussion groups; that is those things that help to build a sense of community, but which do not require any sense of physicality or verification of religious authority. This sentiment is echoed by New Zealander Anglican theologian BOSCO Peters, who explains his view with implicit references to theological arguments about the relationship between "inner" and "outer" signs of grace:

> Baptism, immersion into the Christian community, the body of Christ, and hence into the nature of God the Holy Trinity may have some internet equivalents—for example, being welcomed into a moderated group. But my own current position would be to shy away from. . . having a virtual baptism of a *Second Life* avatar. Similarly, I would currently steer away from eucharist and other sacraments in the virtual world. Sacraments are outward and visible signs—the virtual world is still very much at the inner and invisible level.
>
> (Peters 2009)

Peters disapproves of performing the sacraments online precisely because he claims they depend upon physicality. The traditional church-administered sacraments, he says, rely upon the "outward" (their physicality). He quips: "Baptism uses water, Eucharist uses bread and wine. We cannot pour a jar of jelly-beans over someone and say they are baptized. We cannot consecrate a bicycle and say this is the Eucharist . . . Hence, we cannot baptize an avatar in the virtual work-as there is no water there, nor is an avatar a person on whom we can confer baptism" (*ibid.).* The efficacy of *Second Life* activities, says Peters, are too "inner" and "invisible," meaning, it seems, that they are too symbolic.

Such claims seem a bit odd when one considers the "inner" and "invisible" activity of the Holy Spirit hoped for by Christians through the performance of the sacraments, and when one observes that the sacraments themselves are "virtual" in that they merely represents something deeper, namely, the work of grace. Mark Brown also insists that his missionary work in *Second Life* is based on the Anglican commitment to an "incarnational mission," an equally problematic assertion for a group that sees physicality as a hallmark of authenticity. It seems that the real problem here is the confusion of what "real" means in a world of increasing representation and replication, and the way that this discussion highlights the "virtual" nature of symbolism already inherent in the most traditional aspects of ritual.

Accompanying the question of physicality is the related question of identity in *Second Life,* which allows people to decide, in some cases, who religiously they would like to be and which religious mask (or masks) they would like to wear. On the one hand, Lisa Hamilton argues that virtual church "offers the safety of anonymity," in that "[n]othing prevents members from creating avatars in the opposite gender, or even ones resembling animals more than humans . . . there are no name tags in the virtual church" (Hamilton 2008). *Second Life* faith communities can invite diverse groups to mingle, as in *Second Life* mosques where Sufi, Salafi, Sunni, and Shia Muslims all congregate, and where, as one Muslim in *Second Life* remarks, "they all talk to each other, which might not be the case in real life, I regret to say" (Crabtree 2007).

On the other hand, questions of identity create new problems in the performance of online rituals. In an interview with "Omega," who read the liturgy and led the mass in *Second Life,* James Wagner Au learned that not all who seem to be priests online really are. As "Omega" explains, he wanted the experience to be "like an actual mass," even though he is not Catholic and even though he is "certainly not a real minister, nor do I do this sort of thing in real life . . . I wanted to bring more real-world things into SL so people could experience them if they couldn't in real life" (Au 2004). At the end of a service conducted by "Omega," a woman asked for a blessing of her unborn child. "Omega" replied that the blessing wouldn't be "legit" or "hold much value" since he was not a "real priest." In classic reflexive posture, the woman claimed "it would count to me."

Sacred (Cyber)Space: The Church of *Second Life*

What if we examine *Second Life* itself as a sacred space, entered into from the profane realm of our own ordinary lives? The computer defines its space (at least with current technology) with a window into which we peer—and into which we are invited to project our selves in some way or another. As Jennifer Cobb puts it, virtual reality is "a place that feels removed from the physical world" (Cobb 1998, 31), just as the sacred space of a church or synagogue "feels removed" from the profane space of the physical world. One enters *Second Life.* One leaves *Second Life.* One shifts one's "appearance" when one enacts one's avatar. One forgoes the ordinary needs of daily life when one enters—there is no eating, no sleeping, and no aging in *Second Life.* Some have even considered the possibility of inhabiting virtual space as a sort of digital heaven, or perhaps, as Cobb describes it, "the Platonic realm incarnate" *(ibid.).*

Passage into *Second Life* involves ritualized behavior set in motion by the log-ins, clicking procedures, and teleporting that allow one to "enter" into the virtual environment. This ritual—what theorist of ritual Victor Turner might have called a rite of passage—is typically the place or time within which a participant crosses from one mode of being into another, typically via a symbolic *limen* or "threshold." According to Turner, rites of passage involve admission into the community at new levels. The initiant "passes through a cultural realm that has few or none of the attributes of the past or coming state," and, once in this stage, stands outside of "the network of classifications" that traditionally organize and confer status. "Liminal entities" are therefore "betwixt and between the positions assigned and arrayed by law, custom, convention, and ceremonial" (Turner 1969, 94–95).

The notion of the threshold resonates well with the boundary where the hardware of the body meets the hardware of the computer that houses a virtual "space," and if there were any place where we might be able to observe the presence of distinctive realms, it would be in the threshold between them. When my avatar first entered *Second Life* in 2006, it appeared on "Orientation Island" which was, at one time, the place where all on avatars were spawned. When one appeared in this digital environment, it exhibited what the *Second Life* developers call the "default avatar look." Everyone's avatar looked exactly the same, with the exception of basic gender patterns. As soon as you learned how to use the controls, however, you could make changes to your avatar's appearance, including its body shape, skin color, and hair and eye color, as well as "attachments" (clothes, objects, etc.). You could also quickly acquire animations, or mini-programs aim that allow specified movements (Rymaszewski *et al.* 2007, 80). Experienced Second Lifers could easily recognize a "newbie" by the quality of ha or bet avatar, and by his or her agility using animations.

The parallels between the rituals performed in *Second Life* and Turner's academic description of rites of passage suggest an important relationship between them. Of the liminal entities engaging in a rite of passage, Turner says "It is as though they are being reduced or ground down to a uniform condition to be fashioned anew and endowed with additional powers to enable them to cope with their new station in life . . . Secular distinctions of rank and status disappear or are homogenized." Turner notes that "as liminal beings they have no status, property, insignia, secular clothing indicating rank or role, position in a kinship system—in short, nothing to distinguish them from their fellow neophytes or initiands." In a rite of passage, "neophyte," says Turner, must "be a *tabula rasa,* blank slate, on which is inscribed new knowledge and wisdom of the group . . . in order to prepare them to cope with their new responsibilities" (Turner 1969, 103). New initiants into *Second Life,* too, are "ground down," in that their real-life selves are shorn away in some respects, leaving only a digital visage that represents them in the "new" world.

Even for those who are long-time Second Lifers, the experience of liminality is refreshed in some ways with each new session, suggesting that the user indeed experiences what Krystina Derrickson (2008) calls "a profound sense of entry." She describes the experience of logging on:

> Once the user enters her password, her avatar begins to materialize, coalescing from a gray mass into a patchwork of flashing colors, and finally into her ultimate form, every time awakening into the sim where she ended her previous session. The sim itself loads, flickering into existence, and bodies begin to appear moving around and beyond her at various distances through she cannot move. There is a sense of immersion in an immaterial but materializing landscape.
>
> *(ibid.)*

This moment of transition, or passage through a ritual portal, has been aptly described by Arnold van Gennep in his more individual look at liminal rites: "the door is the boundary between the foreign and domestic worlds in the case of an ordinary dwelling. between the profane and the sacred worlds in the case of a temple." Therefore, says van Gennep, "to cross the threshold is to unite oneself with a new world" (van Gennep 1996, 532). In the case of *Second Life,* the "door" is the process of logging on: the series of mouse-clicks and intentional digital interactions that constitute the "passage" from one "world" to the next.

Turner's description of the rite of passage extends into the new *Second Life* resident's ongoing orientation into the new world, where the shared nature of the experience is again apparent. Users in new online environments usually must spend some time in what T. L. Taylor calls "newbie zones," where they spend time with other "low-level" players and "learn the initial skills required for the game and the ways to coordinate with other" (Taylor *2006,* 31). Gradually, users "undergo a socialization process" that helps them go beyond initial training and become participants in a "community of practice" *(ibid.,* 32). In *Second Life,* everyone begins with the same status but gradually accumulates animations, customized hair, professionally rendered "skin," and group associations that help them to be recognized as "insiders" or true Second Lifers.

Beyond the point of orientation, *Second Life* is itself a liminal space that affords initiants the freedom to do otherwise unacceptable things, prompting a temporary disruption of social order that helps maintain the *status quo* in real life. In such rituals, liminality temporarily grinds all participants down to the same level, so that the most powerful are subjected to the playful derision of the least powerful, representing what Turner calls *communitas.* Thus we have an explanation for the popularity of an event like the grid-wide winter holiday snowball fight, in which the "Lindens" (the only institutionalized power structure in *Second Life)* are pelted by "everyone else". According to Turner, liminality focuses on the "ritual powers of the weak" (Turner 1969, 102). People are permitted to "revile" the chief-elect "and most fully express [their] resentment, going into as much detail as [they] desire." The chief-elect must simply listen in patience and humility *(ibid.,* 101).

This sense of *communitas* offers some people—those who are typically without power—experiences of temporary potency. Among the topics discussed in connection with video games—and, one could argue,

Second Life—notes Miroslaw Filiciak, are "[e]scapism, getting away from everyday life worries, and deriving satisfaction in doing things that we could never do in the real world" (Filiciak 2003, 99). "Roger Junchke," a self-proclaimed *Second Life* "terrorist," spends his time blowing up virtual churches. The act is excusable, however, since, as "Junchke" claims, "nothing actually gets destroyed in SL so all it really does is lights and smoke." For "Junehke," his actions have a liminal function, in that they are his "benign and petty way of expressing my dislike of Christian fundamentalists."

Not all examples of liminal experimentation—from "naked avatars sitting, on the Koran to a swastika painted on the synagogue" (Ctabtree 2007)—are well received in *Second Life*. According to *Second Life's Community Standards, certain.* areas are designated as appropriate for "offensive" and/or sexual activities and others are not. Upon joining *Second Life*, each resident agrees to a code of conduct that includes a statement about not engaging in "assault" in a "Safe Area"; that is, not "shooting, pushing or shoving another Resident . . . [or] creating or using scripted objects which singularly or persistently target another Resident" (*Second Life* n.d.). According to the authors of *Second Life: The Official Guide*, in the online world you can participate in all the "virtual hedonism" that you want—"having as much virtual sex as possible" or "shooting at other people, possibly while piloting a spaceship" (Rymaszewski *et al.* 2007, 13). You can even purchase animations and identify partners willing to enact virtual rape within *Second Life*, or find avatars who look like children to engage in animated pedophiliac pornographic fantasies. Obviously, the ethical implications of these virtual acts require serious scrutiny. This demands that we take seriously the problem of defining just what kind of "space" *Second Life* is, and who "we" are when we inhabit it.

In *Violence and the Sacred*, Rene Girard argues that societies periodically need a disruption of social order. After establishing his case that society by its very nature is invested with a desire for violence and retribution, Girard argues that, through selecting a sacrificial victim, "society is seeking to deflect upon a relatively indifferent victim, a 'sacrificeable victim,' the violence that would otherwise be vented on its own members." Thus violence is "not denied," but is "diverted to another object, something it can sink its teeth into" (Girard 1977, 4). If this is how things work in *Second Life*, then we can understand the violence in it to be functioning within a broadly religious framework.

One such violent area is the "Death Pit" in *Second Life*. According to Second Lifer Warren Ellis:

A mechanical Death Pit has been constructed on the Potato Farm, a parcel on the north road. A square caged floor. The floor is made out of metal panels. The idea is that people don the Wastelands Combat Head-Up-Display—a piece of software that turns your avatar into a videogame character that can deal and receive damage—pull one of the local, horribly primitive weapons, and slash each other to death in the cage. But the metal panels are tricked out. Some flip under your feet and drop you down a hole. Some pop out, I swear, buzzsaws that are coded to do your avatar damage, complete with squirting-blood animation. If the designer wasn't on *Second Life*, he'd be working at [US military prison] Abu Ghraib. Or for Dr Evil.

(Ellis 2007)

Clearly, the claim that this violence is not "real" contributes to its appeal. The case of the non-player character (NPC) in *Second Life* (and other virtual reality contexts) pushes the question of virtual violence even further. In the Buddhist hells of *Second Life*, one can see crudely-crafted human NPCs perpetually burning, being impaled, and thrown about by huge and loathsome homed creatures. In light of Girard's analysis, it would seem that the NPC victims in the Buddhist hells "can be exposed to violence without fear of reprisal" (Girard 1977, 13) precisely *because* they are permanently liminal, looking like, but not being, fully human. Had these NPCs been programmed with more human-like characteristics or interactive scripts, the problem of liminality in virtual reality would be even more sharply defined.

However, the victims need not be NPCs to fulfill a violent urge in a liminal environment. Girard argues that society is bloodthirsty by nature, and that by offering a sacrifice, people in a given society are appeased, and thus the sacrifice "serves to protect the entire community from its own violence" *(ibid., 8)*. This form of violence, Girard argues, is functional because it is "a form of violence that will put an end once and for all to violence itself" *(ibid., 27)*. The ritualizing of violence, including both actual sacrifice and rituals merely remembering sacrifice, functions for society precisely to "keep violence outside the community" *(ibid., 92)*. The sacrificial ritual, in fact, is "designed to function during periods of relative calm" because it is "not curative, but preventive" *(ibid., 102)*. This may help us to understand the remarks of resident "Thadeus Kalig," who describes a *Second Life* group that was "impailing *[sic]* themselves one night," complete with "blood pools and all." He describes this event as "ritualistic." "Rex Dars" says that the activity in *Second Life* is "a role play and not intended to [be] real." It is "like acting out a screen *[sic]* from a movie." For "Dars," "what happens online is totally sep[a]rate [from real life in most cases] . . . if it [is] play acting and somebody gets 'killed' I see nothing wrong with that."

Game studies theorists Katie Salen and Eric Zimmerman argue that games can "play with meaning" and create a sort of "social contract" within which "forbidden play" can occur. Games can "create social contexts in which, very often, behaviors take place that would be strictly forbidden in society at large." In this "forbidden play" space, the player is "always in danger of [really] overstepping the social boundaries of play, jumping the gun, and breaking the magic circle" (Salen and Zimmerman 2003, 479) Cindy Poremba calls such experiences "brink games." Brink games "use their status as 'only a game' as a strategic gesture." Poremba is interested in those types of "forbidden play" that most intensely play with the boundary between game and reality, games that use the conceit of "it's just a game" with "a knowing wink" (Poremba 2007, 772). "Brink" games exploit the relationship between the real, the virtual, and the taboo, and are exciting precisely because of "the tangible threat of [a] breach" *(ibid., 776)*. Although most *Second Life* users claim that it is not a "game," it does exhibit the qualities of "forbidden play" by inviting its users to find that place where virtuality and reality meet. Of course, none of this answers the question of whether *Second Life* is a place of "play" or a space of shared human community and thus subject to certain standards of decency. The ability to engage in what I call "persistent liminality" means that some people will see their bad behavior as "play" anywhere online, and others will insist that the online world be subject to the same ethical standards as real life.

Not surprisingly, the authors of *Second Life: The Official Guide* explain that in *Second Life,* we can experience powers we might otherwise not: "*Second Life* works as if you were a god in real life. Not an almighty god, perhaps—more like one of those mythological minor gods, who tended to specialize in certain areas, get drunk, have sex, fight, and [most important] cast spells left, right and center . . . And just like a mythological god, you're able to fly, and teleport wherever you like in an instant" (Rymaszewski *et al.* 2007, 7). But just as believers today can imagine Heaven but not enter into it in this life, so those who dwell in the real world can never fully inhabit the "sacred" space of *Second Life*. Game theorists have recognized the yearning induced by virtual reality. Miroslaw Filiciak says that the experience of interacting in virtual reality is characterized by intense desire: "We make the screen a fetish; we desire it, not only do we want to watch the screen but also to 'be seen' on it" (Filiciak 2003, 100). Ken Hillis expresses precisely such a sentiment about virtual reality's ability to induce a sense of longing and transcendence:

There is a widespread belief that space (understood variously as distance, extension, or orientation) constitutes something elemental, and VR [virtual reality] reflects support for a belief that because light illuminates space it may therefore produce space a priori. As a result, VR users may experience desire or even something akin to a moral imperative to enter into virtuality where space and light . . . have become one immaterial "wherein." The ability to experience a sense of entry into the image and illumination enabled by VR's design, coupled with both esoteric and pragmatic desires to view the technology as a "transcendence machine" or subjectivity enhancer, works to collapse distinctions between the conceptions built into virtual environments by their developers and the perceptive faculties of users.

(Hillis 2006, 349)

Although writing before the advent of *Second Life,* Brenda Brasher makes a similar point: "That cyberspace is taken for a materialized instance of eternity may explain in part our passionate obsession with it . . . To the true believers, cyberspace is a temporal heaven. Except, of course, it isn't" (Brasher 2001, 53). The computer functions as a "transcendence machine," inducing in us what Margaret Wertheim calls "a longing for the annihilation of pain, restriction, and even death" (Wertheim 1999, 259), and making our desire to inhabit virtual space strangely akin to our desire for immortality.

Brasher observes in cyberspace what she calls "omnitemporality"—"the religious idea of eternity as perpetual persistence"—and says that cyberspace is "[c]ontinuously accessible and ostensibly disconnected from the cycles of the earth" (Brasher 2001, 52). It is no surprise that cyber-imagination and religious imagination are related:

> [Virtual reality] appeared to its first Western consumers to be a concrete expression or materialization of the monks' concept of eternity . . . It is always present. Whatever exists within it never decays. Whatever is expressed in cyberspace, as long as it remains in cyberspace, is perpetually expressed . . . the quasi-mystical appeal that cyberspace exudes stems from this taste of eternity that it imparts to those who interact with it.
>
> (*ibid.,* 52)

The desire for permanence is also easily seen in virtual memorials of the type Brasher discusses (*ibid.,* 54), and which have also cropped up recently in *Second Life.* Users who wish to mourn the loss (through re-entry into reallife) of a fellow *Second Life* resident can memorialize his or her avatar in *Second Life* with a complete burial and re-usable casket. Of *Memoris,* a virtual graveyard in *Second Life,* blogger Warren Ellis says that, when real-life people die, they are sometimes memorialized in *Second Life* in this new way because message boards, the previous mode of grieving, "makes such losses transient. The community rolls on, and tributes and remembrance get lost in the churn. It is, to say the least, an unusual idea, that in a virtual world a permanent space be erected in memoriam of the people we've lost" (Ellis 2007). An earlier web-page version of a cyber-memorial, *Cyber Heaven,* provokes what Brasher calls "the elusive tang of cyber-eternity" (Brasher 2001, 55), the longing for permanence that is expressed by some in their fascination with virtuality. This permanence remains tantalizingly out of reach in *Second Life.*

But aside from questions about ongoing memorials of the departed, can a soul or self survive the death of the physical body in *Second Life*? SL resident "Harry Bulder" thinks so when he describes the potential for "cybernetic afterlife." Eventually, he says, "people will be able to create what amounts to a 'clone,' of themselves that exists in the network." The virtual clone can "learn what it is like to be 'me' and gradually become indistinguishable . . . but it will not be a mortal being, just a program, and thus without death." For Bulder, the intangible self that enters into *Second Life* could remain there, in digitized form, when the physical body is no longer an acceptable vessel for it. Margaret Wertheim aptly points out that "while the concept of transcending bodily limitation was once seen as *theologically possible,* now it is increasingly conceived as *technologically feasible*" (Wertheim 1999, 263; emphasis in original).

Considering the implications of such theories, Wertheim says that "[t]he idea that the essence of a person can be separated from his or her body and transformed into the ephemeral media of computer code is a clear repudiation of the materialist view that man is made of matter alone" (*ibid.,* 268). This transformation would make *Second Life* a *de facto* nonmaterial heaven, presumably amenable to a postmodern, post-Enlightenment, secular world. Wertheim remarks that cyberspace becomes, in such a view, "a place outside space and time, a place where the body can somehow be reconstituted in all its glory" (*ibid.,* 263). Were cybernetic afterlife to be achieved, the user, or some remnant thereof, would at last fully inhabit the sacred space of virtual reality, and—dare I say—heaven? Wertheim notes that were the "immaterial self" to "survive the death of the body and 'live on' forever beyond physical space and time," we would be "back in the realm of medieval Christian dualism" (*ibid.,* 268). In other words, the "transcendence machine" could enable a final resolution of the liminality of space, place, and person.

Despite its consistent function as a meaningful means of entry into the virtual world, the rite of passage into *Second Life* is not a stable one, and in this way contrasts with many traditional religious rites of passage, especially those that are integral and longstanding parts of a community's life. Early in *Second Life's* development, upon entering the world, one's avatar was spawned looking just like the other avatars of the same gender. More recently, one was led through a series of fluency-building exercises, one of which was a series of challenges to appease the "volcano goddess" while learning how to chat with other users. Today, new avatars are spawned in various "Help Islands" around *Second Life,* and users can define a distinctive avatar before it ever walks in virtual space.

This fluidity is characteristic of the online experience in general; it is "ambiguous"; it resists normal social and cultural classifications; it places us "neither here nor there" but rather "betwixt and between the positions assigned and arrayed by law, custom, convention, and ceremonial" (Turner 1969, 95). In *Second Life,* one doesn't cross over from one state into the other in any kind of permanent way as, say, one might if one were a bar mitzvah or experienced some other coming-of-age rite of passage. Rather, all of *Second Life* invokes a state of persistent liminality and all the complexities that such a notion brings along with it. Such fluidity and persistent liminality also characterize the representation of self in *Second Life.* Sherry Turkle says that when people select avatars in virtual reality, they don't simply "become who they play." Rather, they "play who they are or who they want to be or who they don't want to be" (Turkle 1997, 192). As Elizabeth Reid puts it, in cyberspace identities are self-defined in that "virtual reality is a construct within the mind of a human being" (Reid 1995, 166). The effect of interaction with and through one's avatar can affect one's daily life, since players "sometimes talk about their real selves as a composite of their characters and sometimes talk about their screen personae as means for working on their RL lives" (Turkle 1997, 192). In this respect, virtual environments produce the possibility of "liquid identity" (Filiciak 2003, 92).

Of course, the notion of hybrid identity has always been a part of human experience in drama and in religious ritual. For example, hybridity of identity characterizes Turner's analysis of the function of masks in traditional African ritual. In assessing the role of masks in a ritual for boys' circumcision, Turner found himself uncertain how participants in the ritual viewed the relationship between mask-wearer, ancestor (shade) represented, and the *Mvweng'i* (divine spirit) inhabiting the wearer: "Some informants say that the shade is identified with Mvweng'i, others that shade and masker operate in conjunction. The latter say that the shade rouses Mvweng'i and enlists his aid in afflicting the victim" in the rite of passage (Turner 1969, 17). It is remarkable how the same questions could be applied to one's sense of self in *Second Life:* are you your embodied self, your avatar, the role your avatar is currently playing, or someone else entirely when you are online? Or are you all of these at once?

If the use of avatars in *Second Life* evinces a hybridity of identity, then the same complexity must accompany the deeds enacted by avatars. Indeed, in our interviews residents' opinions about the nature of sin in *Second Life* depended largely upon their views about the relationship between embodied self and avatar. For residents like "Chumov Rapunoch," behavior in *Second Life* is not related to real life at all: "it is less sinning if you do it in SL . . . it's not like real SIN." If people engage in transgressive sexual acts, for example, they "get away with it because there is no harm to anyone . . . even though it is a sin and against the law in RL, people do it in SL, so SL 'downgrades' these actions." For others, it has primarily to do with the intent of the performer. "Rex Dars" told us that "the person mak[es] the decisions [regardless of whether] it's a real-life or *Second Life* body carrying [a sinful action] out . . . but . . . some thing[s] are done [in] a role-play and not intended to be 'real' like acting out a scene in a movie or something . . . it's all subject to interpretation I guess." Intent is also the deciding factor for "Boli Lurri": "If you believe that certain actions are sinful and yet act them out, either in RL or SL, then . . . according to [one's] religion, that person has sinned." So is virtual sin nonexistent because we are not the same as our virtual representations? Or is it "real" sin because we are somehow intrinsically connected to our virtual selves? Can the answer be different for different people (and avatars)?

For other *Second Life* residents, there is a definite continuity between embodied self and avatar, such that acts engaged in within *Second Life* are claimed to be of real-life consequence. *Second Life* resident "Murdoch Moore" told us that "I am still Jewish even when I am in *Second Life* . . . the idea of being someone else in *Second Life* makes me uncomfortable." SL resident "Jonah Song" claims that "*Second Life* is just an extension of RL [real life]. 'Real life' is made up of interactions, the outflowing of people's inner lives. *Second Life* is the same thing." When asked about the notion of the soul, "Song" suggested that the soul can inhabit virtual and real space equally as well: "Just like our physical bodies aren't us, but what our spirits wear to interact in a physical world, we're interacting in a digital world through 'digital bodies.'" The views "Song" expressed about the soul as the seat of moral responsibility allow him to view the relationship between the real world and *Second Life* as morally continuous: "Jesus taught that if you look upon a woman lustfully, you've committed adultery in your heart; or if you harbor murderous thoughts, you've murdered in your heart. We just use our bodies to sin, but it's not our bodies sinning but US. And the same thing is true for a place like the virtual world." For residents like "Song," the self or soul transcends its inhabitation in either digital or physical vessels. One might even say that for "Song," it is the soul that is most real—and that it can, apparently, inhabit our bodies and our avatars simultaneously.

"Horace Max," a Latter-day Saint SL resident, agrees. If we engage in activities in *Second Life,* "the consequences are spiritual." "Max" describes a virtual romantic relationship in which "one friend and I flew around in the sunset, danced and such, but I was plagued with real mortal guilt after that." For "Max," though, the "spirit" resides only in RL: "there isn't a SL spirit." This means that the consequences of activities in *Second Life* can *only* have real-life impact. SL resident "Cloud Meade" concurs: "acting out the things we think—even though it may only be virtual—has [real-life] consequences—ones that can hurt others." "Richard Bartle" makes a similar argument when he advises would-be game designers that virtual worlds "are an extension of real life" because "the interaction between players gives rise to a real-life morality that makes virtual worlds more than the mere games they would otherwise be." Says "Bartle": "it's because *we're* real that virtual worlds must be treated in moral terms as if they were equally real" (Bartle 2003, 589; emphasis in original). In this case, "persistent liminality" calls for a consistent moral framework.

However, one need not believe in God to argue for continuity of meaning between real-life and *Second Life.* Atheist resident "Benji Midway" told us that "SL is no less 'real' than the rest of our lives. The people are 'real' . . . Both my physical body and my avatar's 'body' are actually just a persistent temporal organization of subatomic particles." For "Midway," an avatar is "similarly an extension of [the] body." Because he saw his *Second Life* self as identical to his real-life self, SL resident "Daniel Kendall" eloped virtually with another resident and they were married in-world (that is, within *Second Life).* When asked about the ceremony and its significance, "Kendall" said, "the intent counts. We didn't need the big ceremony. We are married, no matter the physical aspects included . . . [and] it means the same to me as in real-life." When we spoke with "Kendall," he was about to meet his new "wife" in real-life in a few hours. So what are we to make of virtual sin? Unfortunately, there is no simple answer. Different people engage with their avatars in different ways—and how they view the actions of those avatars depends tremendously on the degree of immersion in the lives of their avatars; on the nature of the virtual space they inhabit; and on their view of the relationship between the physical body and the virtual one.

Play, Ritual, and the Virtual: Making Sense of the Sacred

It seems it should be easy to define *Second Life* as either play or ritual—but it isn't. What does it mean to "play" at something, and how does this compare with the performance of a religious ritual? Play and ritual have a long history of imitating one another. Johan Huizinga, a scholar of play and the author of the landmark study *Homo Ludens* (1949)—describes play as "a free standing activity quite consciously outside 'ordinary' life as being 'not serious' but at the same time absorbing the player intensely and utterly" (Huizinga 2006, 107). Huizinga argues that a sacred performance is "played or performed within a playground that is literally 'staked out' . . . A sacred space, a temporarily real world of its own, has been expressly hedged off for it" (*ibid.,* 108). To Huizinga, "[t]he turf, the tennis court, the chess-board and pavement hopscotch cannot formally be distinguished from the temple or the magic circle." We should recognize, he says, "the essential and original identity of play and ritual" so we can "recognize the hallowed spot as a playground" (*ibid.,* 113). This suggests that play and ritual have a lot more in common than we might at first think.

Like the tennis court or the chessboard, *Second Life* is a space apart from everyday life, and can thus be viewed as a form of play. But participation in it also can be viewed as a ritual. To make matters even more complicated, within *Second Life* there are areas that some residents treat as "magic circles" of play, and others that are viewed as arenas for ritual, and how one defines the boundary between them fluctuates widely based on the varying perspectives of the Second Lifers. If we then introduce the boundary between the "virtual" and the "real" into this complex stew, the possibilities for a single ordering paradigm become increasingly unlikely.

Accordingly, T.L. Taylor questions whether identifying such a line between the virtual world and the real world—or between play and nonplay—is even reasonable. For Taylor, the magic circle of play "can hide (and even mystify) the much messier relationship that exists between spheres—especially in the realm of MMOGs [massively multiplayer online games]." If we look at how people have utilized online spaces, he says, "we find people negotiating levels of self-disclosure and performance, multiple forms of embodiment, and the importing of meaningful offline issues and values into online spaces" (Taylor 2006, 152). Calling for "non-dichotomous models," Taylor claims that "the boundary between online and offline life is messy, contested, and constantly under negotiation" (*ibid.,* 153). This "messiness" can be seen in all aspects of theoretical analysis of religion and *Second Life.*

Virtual reality is liminal, fluid, and hybrid, as we are too when we interact with it, making the distinction between religion and media a harder one to draw than we might like. After all, religion and media are both about mediation and communication—how we receive important information, and how its transmission affects reception. Media theorist Stewart Hoover rejects the oversimplified assumption that "the media and religion are separate and competing spheres and that, on some level, they inhabit the roles of 'sacred' (religion) and 'profane' (the media) influences in contemporary life." Instead, what has developed is "a less definite space where those distinctions exist in a state of fluidity and flux" (Hoover 2001, 50). This fluidity is readily evident in what Second Lifers had to tell us in our interviews about five recurring topics: ritual, violence, identity, sin, and the afterlife. These categories cropped up again and again as the ones most important to residents and most pertinent to the discussion of what is really going on with religion in *Second Life.* The notion of persistent liminality is easily recognizable in the contested nature of religious experience in *Second Life.*

It's not just "Orientation Island" or some other initiation activity that produces a liminal state in *Second Life.* Rather, throughout the *Second Life* experience the sacred and profane meet—virtual and real collide—and people are at once here and there, but neither here nor there. *Second Life* seems to offer persistent liminality, the on-demand and consistently ambiguous experience of liminality, characterized by the ambiguities of game/real life, sacred/profane, ritual/play, and self/other. In other words, the dissolution of absolute categories is a hallmark feature of religion in *Second Life.*

So why should we care about *Second Life*? Because it makes us think about what we mean when we talk about sacred space, about ritual, about self and community, and of course about religion. *Second Life* invites what Krystina Derrickson dubs a "Baudrillardian blurring of the RL/SL [real-life/*Second Life*] treatment of space" (Derrickson 2008). In *Second Life,* a place like the online mosque in Mecca is designated as sacred, "and yet it is a contentious designation" (*ibid.*). Does this mean that the distinction between the sacred and the profane has lost significance when applied to *Second Life*? Not necessarily—it seems that what people believe when they enter a virtual context can help us understand what they believe about what happens within it. Remarking on the nature of personal intent in creating meaning in virtual contexts, Lorne Dawson asserts: "All that matter are the experiences that are experimentally generated and manipulated by the skilful understanding and use of words and the temporary worlds they create in the minds of individuals" (Dawson 2005, 25). Even if an easy distinction between the real and the virtual has collapsed in online worlds like *Second Life,* the category of the "sacred" may still have salience for those who utilize it: "In the classic postmodernist mode, the simulation can be substituted for the reality, yet there is not really a complete collapse of the sign and the signified since the focus is still on some seemingly 'authentic' experience" (*ibid.,* 26). In other words, the concept of the "sacred" can help us make sense of how people think about the sacred, even if it cannot point to something about which everyone will easily agree. It seems self-evident that a postmodern, Baudrillardian, reflexive perspective is required—whether we like it or not.

The situation is characteristic of religion-at-large in today's massively-mediated, complex, globalizing, multireligious world. Referring to the construction of religious identity, Wade Clark Roof defines what he calls "reflexive spirituality," seeing in today's world "a situation encouraging a more deliberate, engaging effort on people's part for their own spiritual formation, both inside and outside religious communities" (Roof 1999, 75). This may be the best news yet, since reflexive spirituality is often thinking spirituality, as people decide what to do with the vast menu of options before them. In today's world, "[r]esponsibility falls more upon the individual—like that of the bricoleur—to cobble together a religious world from available images, symbols, moral codes, and doctrines, thereby exercising considerable agency in defining and shaping what is considered to be religiously meaningful" (*ibid.,* 75). In *Second Life,* this "cobbling" may involve some new construction as well, making it possible to consider religious identity in *Second Life* not as deconstructive of identity, but as constructive and deliberate in a way that interaction with less immersive media—and with less virtual bodies—may not be.

Dawson asks if "the exercise of reflexivity, long a hallmark of detached rational thought, is becoming, by radical extension, a new means of legitimating religious practice or even inducing 'authentic' religious experience," so that "the experience of reflexivity is itself being sacralized" (Dawson 2005, 26). This is reflexivity at its most influential—reflexivity alone determines whether or not an individual's use of the internet for online religious experience is "real" or not, and what that means for users. Furthermore, reflexivity itself is subject to the persistent liminality of experience that requires that we decide for ourselves if we are here, there, or somewhere in between. Interacting with *Second Life,* it can be all of the above. Perhaps virtual ritual creates its own justification in the form of self-reflection on its createdness.

Stephen O'Leary seems to be saying something like this when he remarks that "ritual action in cyberspace is constantly faced with evidence of its own quality as constructed, as arbitrary, and as artificial, a game played with no material stakes or consequences" (cited in *ibid.,* 21). But the very notion that construction is a crucial component in interactive new media may cause people to acknowledge more openly the constructed nature of all of religion and to recognize the element of "play" that has always been a part of religious life.

References

Au, James Wagner. 2004. "Where Two or More Are Gathered." *New World Notes* (April 19). http://nwn.blogs .com/nwn/2004/04/where_two_or_mo.html

Bartle, Richard. 2003. *Designing Virtual Worlds.* Indianapolis, IN: New Riders Games.

Brasher, Brenda. 2001. *Give Me That Online Religion.* San Francisco: Jossey-Bass.

Brown, Mark. 2008. "Christian Mission to a Virtual World." *Brownblog* (April). http://brownblog.info/ wp-content/plugins/wp-downloadMonitor/user_uploads/Christian_Mission_to__a_Virtual_W6rId.pdf

Cobb, Jennifer. 1998. *Cybergrace: The Search for God in the Digital World.* New York: Crown Publishers.

Crabtree, Shona. 2007. "Finding Religion in Second Life's Virtual Universe." *Washington Post* (June 16): B09. www.washingtonpost.com/wp-dyn/content/article/2007/06/15/AR2007061501902.html

Dawson, Lorne. 2005. "The Mediation of Religious Experience in Cyberspace." In *Religion and Cyberspace,* ed. Morten T. Højsgaard and Margit Warburg, 15-37. New York: Routledge.

Derrickson, Krystina. 2008. "Second Life and The Sacred: Islamic Space in a Virtual World." www.digitalislam.eu/article. do?articleId= 1877

Eliade, Mircea. 1957. *The Sacred and the Profane: The Nature of Religion.* New York: Harper & Row.

Ellis, Warren. 2007. "The Island of Lost Souls." *Reuters.com* (March 30). http://secondlife.reuters.com/stories/2007/03/30/second-life-sketches-the-island-of-lost-souls

Filiciak, Miroslaw. 2003. "Hyperidentities: Postmodern Identity Patterns in Massively Multiplayer Online Role-Playing Games." In *The Video Game Theory Reader,* ed. Mark J. P. Wolf and Bernard Perron, 87–102. New York: Routledge.

van Gennep, Arnold. 1996. "Territorial Passage and the Classification of Rites." In *Readings in Ritual Studies,* ed. Ronald L. Grimes, 529–36. Upper Saddle River, NJ: Prentice Hall.

Girard, Rene. 1977. *Violence and the Sacred,* trans. Patrick Gregory. Baltimore, MD: Johns Hopkins University Press.

Hamilton, Lisa B. 2008. "Worshipping Online: Is It Really Church?" *Episcopal Life Online* (October 6). www.cuac.org/81834_101368_ENG_HTM.htm

Hillis, Ken. 2006. "Modes of Digital Identification: Virtual Technologies and Webcam Cultures." In *New Media, Old Media: A History and Theory Reader,* ed. W.H.K Chun and T. Keenan, 347–58. New York: Routledge.

Hoover, Stewart M. 2001. "Religion, Media, and the Cultural Center of Gravity." In *Religion and Popular Culture: Studies in the Interaction of Worldviews,* ed. Daniel A. Stout and Judith M. Buddenbaum, 49–60. Ames: Iowa State University Press.

Huizinga, Johan. 1949. *Homo Ludens: A Study of the Play-Element in Culture,* trans. R. F. C. Hull. London: Routledge & Kegan Paul.

———. 2006. "Nature and Significance of Play as a Cultural Phenomenon." In *The Game Design Reader,* ed. Katie Salen and Eric Zimmerman, 96–120. Cambridge, MA: MIT Press.

Peters, Bosco. 2009. "Virtual Eucharist?" *Liturgy* (June 28). www.liturgy.co.nz/blog/virtual-eucharist/1078/comment-page-1

Poremba, Cindy. 2007. "Critical Potential on the Brink of the Magic Circle." *Situated Play: Proceedings of DiGRA [Digital Games Research Association] 2007 Conference* (September): 772–78. www.digra.org/dl/db/07311.42117.pdf

Reid, Elizabeth. 1995. "Virtual Worlds: Culture and Imagination." In *CyberSociety: Computer-Mediated Communication and Community,* ed. Steven G. Jones, 164–83. Thousand Oaks, CA: Sage.

Roof, Wade Clark. 1999. *Spiritual Marketplace: Baby Boomers & the Remaking of American Religion.* Princeton, NJ: Princeton University Press.

Rymaszewski, Michael, Wagner James Au, Mark Wallace, Catherine Winters, Cory Ondrejka, and Benjamin Batstone-Cunningham. 2007. *Second Life: The Official Guide.* San Francisco: Sybex.

Salen, Katie, and Eric Zimmerman. 2003. *Rules of Play: Game Design Fundamentals.* Cambridge, MA: MIT Press.

Second Life. n.d. "Community Standards." http://secondlife.com/corporate/cs.php

Taylor, T. L. 2006. *Play between Worlds: Exploring Online Game Culture.* Cambridge MA: MIT Press.

Turkle, Sherry. 1997. *Life on the Screen: Identity in the Age of the Internet.* New York: Simon & Schuster.

Turner, Victor. 1969. *The Ritual Process: Structure and Anti-Structure.* Chicago: Aldine Publishing Co.

Wertheim, Margaret. 1999. *The Pearly Gates of Cyberspace: A History of Space from Dante to the Internet.* New York: W. W. Norton & Company.

Zaleski, Jeff. 1997. *The Soul of Cyberspace: How New Technology Is Changing Our Spiritual Lives.* San Francisco: Harper Edge.

Notes

1. An earlier version of this paper (with Kim Gregson and Austra Zubkovs) was presented at the national meeting of the Popular Culture Association, Spring 2007. I deeply appreciate the substantial and invaluable assistance offered by Kim and Austra; their work managing the in-world collection of material made the interviews possible. The analysis of the data presented here is entirely my own.

2. An "SL resident" (also referred to here as a Second Lifer) refers to anyone who has created an avatar, passed through the orientation procedures, and become an online member in the world of *Second Life.* Many Second Lifers refer to the virtual world by its initials ("SL"), distinguishing it from the real (or nonvirtual) world, which they often identify simply as "RL." I have changed the usernames of all interviewees in *Second Life* to protect their anonymity. Because all Second Lifers already have a username that masks their true identity, and I met them only via their usernames, I have changed those names to add another level of anonymity within the world of *Second Life.*

3. "Sim" is short for "simulation" and refers to any number of structures made by users in the *Second Life* world. In this case, the sim is the digital replica of Mecca.

Source: *"Our Lady of Persistent Liminality: Virtual Church Cyberspace and Second Life"* by Rachel Wagener in God in the Details: American Religion in Popular Culture, 2nd Ed. Edited by Eric Mazur and Kate McCarthy. pp. 271–290. Copyright Routledge US, 2000. Reproduced by permission of Taylor & Francis Books UK.

DECODING THE TEXT

1. According to Wagner, what questions come up when we start talking about virtual churches and religious ceremonies that happen online?

2. How can Second Life be viewed as sacred space? Do you agree with this definition or view of sacred?

3. How is play a part of all religious life, as described by the author?

4. What citation style is used by Wagner in this essay? Why was this form chosen? How do authors determine which style to use?

CONNECTING TO YOUR CULTURE

1. What spaces or places are sacred to you? Why? Have they always been sacred, or did they become that way over time?

2. What rituals are part of your life? Are they connected to any networks or groups? What are these rituals? How important are they to you? What happens when you miss one?

CONSIDERING IDEAS

1. This essay is about the social networking websites Myspace and Facebook. Which do you use, if any? How or why did you choose?

2. How many hours a day do you spend using social networking websites?

AUTHOR BIO

Steven Levy is a journalist who writes about technology. Levy began writing about the subject in 1981 and joined the staff of Newsweek as a senior editor in 1995. In 2008, Levy joined the staff of Wired Magazine. Levy has written for many other publications throughout the years, including The New York Times, Harper's Weekly, The New York Times Magazine, and Premiere. He is the author of six books, including Hackers, which was named the best sci-tech book written in the last twenty years by PC Magazine, The Perfect Thing, a book about the iPod and its use in the business world, and In the Plex, a book about Google. This essay was published in Newsweek on August 6, 2007.

SOCIAL NETWORKING AND CLASS WARFARE

Steven Levy

For young people, the burning question of our time is "Facebook or Myspace?"

Though there's considerable overlap between the two big social networking services, only one usually becomes the center of a teen's online social life. Most often the choice is made depending on where your friends are. But what determines whether clusters of friends alight on Myspace or Facebook? A controversial answer comes from Berkeley researcher Danah Boyd: it's a matter of social class.

A few weeks ago, Boyd—who has done extensive ethnographic work on online behavior, posted an essay sharing her (admittedly nonscientific) findings after months of interviews, field observations and profile analysis. Generally, she contended, "The goody-two-shoes, jocks, athletes and other 'good' kids are now going to Facebook. These kids tend to come from families who emphasize education and going to college." Myspace is still home for "kids whose parents didn't go to college, who are expected to get a job when they finish high school."

It's also, she says, the preferred digital hangout for outsiders—burnouts, punks, emos, goths, gangstas and minorities.

Boyd does concede that a lot of this may have to do with the fact that Facebook began at Harvard and spread out from the Ivies. But she believes that there's conscious self-identification involved in the choice.

Facebookers are strivers; Myspacers are there in part because they're rejecting the values of preppies, jocks, and tools.

Boyd's essay triggered a firestorm of criticism. Facebook was too cool to comment, turning down my request as abruptly as a cheerleader nixes a nerd's prom invite. But Myspace founders Tom Anderson and Chris DeWolfe were eager to dispel what they considered a wrongheaded take by a researcher they respected. For one thing, the sheer number of Myspace members (many of whom are also Facebook users) makes it hard to talk of a divide: "How are you going to put 70 million people in a box?" asks DeWolfe. (Facebook has 28 million.) He also notes that class has nothing to do with all those who access videos and music on Myspace. (Boyd says she's focusing on which one teens use for their core socializing.) Anderson adds that people go to Myspace for the freedom to design their page the way they want it, while Facebook's more-stringent template enforces a spartan design ethic. Boyd argues that upscalers like Facebook's clean style, while the nonelites prefer the blinglike cacophony that is Myspace. As Boyd writes, "The division around Myspace and Facebook is just another way in which technology is mirroring societal values." If she's right, the Facebook and Myspace debate will be more than a choice of online destination. It will be a hard look into a societal mirror.

DECODING THE TEXT

1. Researcher Dana Boyd claims that the Myspace versus Facebook choice often comes down to social class. She was basing this claim on what type of research?

2. What are the counterarguments to this claim according to Levy?

CONNECTING TO YOUR CULTURE

1. Since this article was written, numerous other social networking sites have been developed online. Which sites do you use? How did you learn about them?

2. Is there any pressure to be on certain networking sites? If so, how? From whom?

3. Do you consider yourself a member of any of the groups mentioned in the essay? Do you think this group is being portrayed positively or negatively in this essay?

CONTEMPLATIONS IN THE POP CULTURE ZONE

1. Have you ever worn a uniform? What was it for? What did it look like? Did it reflect a specific group or a specific place? How did this type of dress affect your mood? Did you feel proud to wear it? Ashamed?

2. Think about your own tattoo or a tattoo of a friend or family member. Describe the tattoo and consider its implications. What does it mean to you? Does it identify a particular culture, group, or network? Why do mainly young Americans get tattoos? Why is tattooing a popular way to memorialize someone's death?

3. Describe the first time you felt a sense of belonging. Perhaps it was with your parents at a family reunion or in a children's worship service. What gave you that feeling? In what circumstances has the feeling been replicated since then?

4. Recently, digital billboards have been placed on busy thoroughfares across the United States; these signs change based on the demographics of your car. What does your car say about you? What would your billboard advertise?

COLLABORATIONS IN THE POP CULTURE ZONE

1. Each group member should identify his or her favorite space and tell the group what makes it so special. What network is it associated with? How is it decorated? Did you choose the décor? As a group, consider why people often identify so closely with their surroundings. Comfort? Familiarity? What does each group member's space say about him or her?

2. To your group, describe a tradition from your hometown. Compare the characteristics of your various traditions. Perhaps you have a local festival, sporting event, or parade that is held annually. What does this event say about your community to your group members?

3. What hats do you wear or have you worn in your life? Each group member should make a list of the figurative hats that he or she wears. How do your lists differ? Does age, gender, race, or sexuality affect your many roles? What about religion, politics, or family?

4. As a group, create a postcard for your composition class to send to a friend you have not talked to in a while. What is on the front? A picture or drawing? A poem or excerpt from an essay? What would you write on the other side to explain your choice? Now, still in your group, create a postcard for your class to send to your parents, grandparents, or guardians. How does the front of the card change? Why does it change?

5. Anonymously, make a list and describe five personal items in your wallet, purse, or school bag using pictures, patterns, brand names, and colors. Then, place these lists at the front of the room. As someone reads from the front of the room, guess who made each list. What assumptions do you make about your peers? About their marketing choices? About their networks?

6. Get together with a group in class, and write a constitution for your class. If a number of you belong to the same network or are members of the same campus or community organization, you could write your constitution for that group. Your constitution can be humorous or serious, but you will need to consider the format of a constitution, the characteristics of the groups, and what you want to share with your members as well as outsiders.

START WRITING ABOUT SOCIAL NETWORKS

Reviews or Review Essays

1. Review the ease of access, safety, and popularity of a local attraction or theme park. You must visit the attraction to complete this essay.

2. Write a review of your favorite restaurant. Describe the ethnicity, the décor, the patrons, and the location. What is the best item on the menu? What would you change about the restaurant if you could? Is the restaurant locally owned or operated? Does this affect your review or patronage?

3. Many organizations sponsor campus events that are open to the student body. Attend one of these events (of which you are not a host), and write an objective review. Briefly describe the hosting organization or association, the purpose of the event, and the success in achieving this purpose. (You may want to read a review of a larger event, such as a Heart Walk for the American Heart Association, as a model.)

4. Review the effect of a devoted fan or fandom network on a television series, song, film, or work of popular literature. Where and how has the fan community built itself? Is there a structure? A name or title for the community? Are there known leaders of this community? What is the intention or purpose of the fan community? Does this fandom network help or hurt the original work, group, or place?

5. Find a virtual space (such as a chat room, an ongoing blog, or an open forum) and review the effectiveness of this space. What is the intended purpose of the space? Is this purpose achieved? Who are the participants in these conversations? Would you recommend this source to a friend or family member?

Reflection or Response Essays

1. Reflect on your idea of love or spirituality by describing one event in your life that reflects the way that you view either. For example, the day of your bar/bat mitzvah might symbolize your personal spirituality, or the night that you got engaged may encompass your feelings about love.

2. Describe the first hour of an experience you had as you entered a new culture, community, association, or group. This example could include your first day in a new school, your first day on the job, or your first day in the freshman dorm.

3. Find a photo of a group you belong to, or used to belong to, then respond to the photo. What does it make you think about or remind you of? What was your role in this group? What did you do with the other members of this group? Are you still a part of this group? Who else is in the group? Does it signify a certain place in popular culture? In your life?

4. Reflect on an experience you have had with an animal, family pet, or animal lover by describing an event in your life when an animal (or animal lover) has played a major role. Describe the experience, and respond to the significance of this animal, or animal lover, in your life.

Analysis Essays

1. Misconceptions about health and disease are often propagated in popular culture. Examine the way that the AIDS epidemic has been exposed or hidden in popular culture. How is it portrayed in the media? Where did you learn facts and details about HIV/AIDS? Research headlines on the subject, and draw your own conclusions.

2. Research the cultural practices of a specific network or community, and analyze the consequences of these practices. You may want to interview a member of the Southern Baptist Convention, Greenpeace, or your city council. What rituals or rites do they practice? When do they meet? What is the significance of their individual roles?

3. Analyze the intended purpose of a controversial association. What do the participants wish to gain through their membership? Is the association effective in achieving its goals? What is the historical background or effectiveness of the association? How is this association or network depicted in popular culture?

4. Discuss prison culture. How are prisons portrayed in film? In song lyrics? On television? Research the history or basis of popular prison myths. What kinds of networks exist within this culture?

Synthesis Essays

1. Review a spot where you have vacationed, and consider the cost to you or to your family. Through your own experience, reflect on the way this locale is advertised. Whom is the local tourism council trying to attract? Does this spot appeal to a certain age, class, or gender? How did it appeal to you or to your family?

2. Choose a specialized word from one of your networks (your academic major, your religious affiliation, your favorite genre of music, your virtual community), and define this word. How is this word used within the network? What does it say about you or your community? Describe this network and its implications in popular culture.

3. In March 2007, the Delta Zeta sorority at DePauw University, called the "Dog House" by other students, was kicked off campus for allegedly evicting twenty-three members who were not considered attractive enough to promote the sorority's exclusive image. Consider other stories like this that you have heard. How are sororities portrayed in popular culture? In the news? On film or television? How are fraternities portrayed? Is their representation different? Why or why not?

4. Several news stories by entertainment journalists have blamed the "Trash Pack" (Britney Spears, Paris Hilton, Lindsay Lohan, Nicole Richie, and so on) for the rise of "prostitots," or young girls—usually tweens—who dress and act promiscuously. Respond to your own choices in music, film, and television as a tween. What appealed to you? Analyze today's tween choices and compare your culture to theirs. What kinds of networks have grown out of this culture?

5. Think about all of the hobbies you have had during your lifetime. What drew you to them? Which ones have lasted? Why do you think some hobbies endure and others exist for just a short time? What is their role in your life? What stories can you tell about your experiences with hobbies and others who practiced the same hobbies?

writing about music

Music creation apps

You name it, you can probably play it on the iPad. That's the genius of the blank slate: All it takes is an app, and your iPad can be just about anything musical, such as a guitar, a keyboard, a drum machine, some sheet music or a beatbox. Heck, if you wanted to, you could replace your recording studio or create an entire rock band with nothing more than an iPad and a suite of apps. And if cranking tunes out of a tablet isn't your thing, there's a host of neat, interactive apps that teach you how to play real instruments.

—Brian X. Chen, *Wired Magazine*

1. Which of the following albums by a female artist made the longest stay on the Billboard 200 chart by any album released in the 2000s?

a. Shakira's *Laundry Service*

b. Christina Aguilera's *Stripped*

c. Taylor Swift's *Taylor Swift*

d. Britney Spears's *Britney*

2. Which of the following artists hit 1 billion YouTube views in 2010?

a. Katy Perry

b. Nicki Minaj

c. Lady Gaga

d. Ke$ha

3. Which group or artist holds the record for the most charting singles of all time on the Billboard Top 100 chart?

a. The Beatles

b. Elvis Presley

c. Michael Jackson

d. Glee

4. The song "We Are the World" was recorded in 1985 to raise money for what charitable fund?

a. Famine in Ethiopia

b. The American Foundation for AIDS Research

c. Comic Relief

d. Sport Aid

5. Which icon of country music boasted, "It takes a lot of money to look this cheap"?

a. Patsy Cline

b. Dolly Parton

c. Reba McIntire

d. Tammy Wynette

6. What was the first major rap single to reach as high as number thirty-six on the *Billboard* charts?

a. "Rapper's Delight," the Sugarhill Gang

b. "The Message," Grandmaster Flash

c. "Walk This Way," Run-DMC/Aerosmith

d. "(You Gotta) Fight for Your Right to Party," the Beastie Boys

HBO/THE KOBAL COLLECTION/PICTURE DESK

7. The Rolling Stones chose their name because of

a. Bob Dylan's "Like a Rolling Stone."

b. *Rolling Stone* magazine.

c. Muddy Waters's "Rollin' Stone."

d. The proverb, "A rolling stone gathers no moss."

KEYSTONE/STEFFEN SCHMIDT/AP IMAGES

8. Which of these is not a disco lyric?

a. "So now go. Walk out the door."

b. "Voulez-vous coucher avec moi ce soir."

c. "You can have a good meal. You can do whatever you feel."

d. "Que sera sera. Whatever will be, will be."

9. The "Beef: It's What's for Dinner" ad campaign uses a score by what composer?

a. Beethoven

b. Gershwin

c. Bach

d. Copland

---

10. **Stump Your Instructor:** In small groups, write a question here about music and pop culture. Give your instructor five choices for answers.

a.

b.

c.

d.

e.

1) c. Taylor Swift's *Taylor Swift* **2)** c. Lady Gaga **3)** d. Glee **4)** a. Famine in Ethiopia **5)** b. Dolly Parton **6)** a. "Rapper's Delight," the Sugarhill Gang **7)** c. Muddy Waters's "Rollin' Stone" **8)** d. "Que sera sera. Whatever will be, will be." **9)** d. Copland **10)** Your answer

GRAPPLING
with Ideas

- Who is your favorite musician or band? How did you hear about him, her, or them? Did a friend introduce them to you? Did you see their video on YouTube, hear them online, catch them on the radio? Or are they a local act?

- Think about how much money a record company or promoter might have spent to get this musician or band to your ears and eyes. How much have you spent on their music, concerts, and merchandise?

GRAPPLING
with Ideas

- What type of popular music is the most foreign to you? Country or bluegrass? Acid jazz or blues? Contemporary folk or indie rock?

- How could you learn more about this type of music? Whom would you talk to or interview? What publications could you read?

- Why haven't you explored this type of music in the past? Why don't you enjoy listening to this type of music now?

YOU AND MUSIC

With the introduction, Ladies and Gentlemen, Rock 'n Roll, and the song "Video Killed the Radio Star" performed by The Buggles on August 1, 1981, MTV debuted as the first television channel devoted to music and music programming. Now, more than thirty years later, the programming of MTV and the many cable channels, such as BET, VH1, GAC, Fuse, and MHD, which promote music and music videos, is less about the actual lyrics and arrangements of popular songs and more about the youth culture that popular music often represents.

Not only is music entertaining and culturally relevant, but it is also a way to express emotion, to gain support for a product, thought, or idea, and some people even use it to help them learn or memorize facts. The readings and writing prompts in this chapter should help you think about the popular music you like and listen to, as well as introduce some music and musicians you may be less familiar with.

Whether you are an avid musician or merely a bystander in the world of popular music, you are constantly bombarded with melodies and lyrics from a variety of sources. The tunes on your iPod, the songs on the radio, the songs you sing in church, the concerts you attend, the soundtrack of your favorite movie or television show, and the jingles on television, the Internet, or radio advertising are all valid examples of popular music. Because pop music is so easily accessible, from downloading songs to streaming new hits online, it is often the focus of writing assignments or classroom activities. The crossover between music and the subjects of other chapters in this text is common and may be useful when you decide to write about pop music.

Music can be a common space for personal, social, and political experiences. Music is (or is not) a reflection of the culture that surrounds it. For example, Bob Dylan's songs from the 1960s give the impression that they reflect the world at that time. His songs are often about protests or are themselves protests. Today, gansta rap also seemingly tells the stories of the disadvantaged. Although songwriters sometimes have social aims that go along with their music, this is not always the case. However, unintended messages still can come from the music itself, whatever the writer's intentions. Because music is a creative endeavor and a direct form of expression, you need to think not only about your personal response to music but also about the means by which music gets to its audience, who the audience is, and the ways in which music is interpreted and used by listeners in a variety of contexts.

Music is produced and created for both financial and artistic reasons. Even music produced solely for artistic reasons usually depends on expensive promotional techniques to become popular. Musicians and bands make money from touring and merchandise sales, whereas record companies make money from CDs, downloadable albums or singles, and selling music for advertising and soundtracks. Artists appear in videos, on awards shows, and even involve themselves in elaborate stunts—such as New Kids on the Block member Donnie Wahlberg setting a carpet on fire at the historic Seelbach Hotel in Louisville, Kentucky, at the height of their early 1990s success—to sell albums and to gain celebrity status. Musicians often cross over to acting, just as actors often promote themselves as musicians.

WHY WRITE ABOUT MUSIC?

Using music as the subject of your writing can help you discover much about yourself, your interests, and your prejudices of classes, cultures, or tastes. Although it is hard to be completely objective about a song, album, or musician whom you already like or listen to, it is important to choose essay topics that you can relate to and learn from. Choosing to write about the music used in a film or commercial to set a mood or develop a theme can also be a learning experience. Becoming a critical listener can deepen your enjoyment of popular music and may even open your ears to music with which you were not previously familiar.

PREPARING TO WRITE ABOUT MUSIC

When listening to music, viewing a music video, or watching an artist perform as part of a writing assignment, you must think critically about the subject. Again, it is important that you take a step back from your own interests and try to see the subject from the perspective of your audience, even if you are using a song or album that you are familiar with.

Listening, Watching, and Thinking

When you listen to music, you are affected by your environment, by those around you, by the quality of the system playing the music, and by your prior experiences with the song, album, artist, or genre. View the video or listen to the song several times to become more familiar with your subject, and try to adjust your situation to remove distractions.

Key Questions for Listening to Music

- How does the title relate to the album or song?

- How does the album, song, or concert start? Are the production credits displayed or revealed?

- How does the packaging affect your interpretation of the music?

- When was the song recorded? The video filmed? The concert staged?

- What is the concluding song on the album? Concluding performance recorded? Concluding shot on the video? Do you think its placement is deliberate?

- Is this song or album similar to or different from others that are in the same genre?

- Is there anything different or special about the production techniques such as connecting loops between tracks, orchestral contributions, or unusual effects?

- How does your prior knowledge affect your experience?

- What cultural beliefs underlie the lyrics of the song or album?

To prepare, ask questions about what you expect. What instruments (if any) do you expect to hear? What do you already know about the artist, song, or album? Who is the intended audience for this album? What initially attracted you to or repelled you from this music? What are people saying about it? Make some notes as you answer these questions so that you can go back and review your initial thoughts.

If possible, take notes about themes, production, and quality as you listen to the music. After you listen to it a few times, reassess the answers to your initial questions. Did anything challenge your original expectations? Look for discrepancies between the preliminary notes you made and the notes you took during the experience. Did you enjoy what you heard? Why or why not?

Now, consider the context of the recording or the performance. Think about historical value (Does it identify a particular time period?), timelessness (Does it mean something different to another generation than it does to you? Will it have meaning or appeal to future generations?), and convention versus invention (What is new? What is traditional to the genre?), as mentioned in Chapter 2. Again, consider your experience. Were you alone or did

GRAPPLING with Ideas

Choose your favorite song, or a song that you are familiar with, and identify the different sections of the song's pattern as listed in the sample.

- Is the song similar to the sample pattern? In what way?

- If it is different, in what way?

- In what way does the song's similarity or difference add to or take away from the quality or value of the song?

you listen over someone else talking? Any part of your environment—from what you are looking at while you listen to a song to the way your speakers are arranged—has the potential to affect your experience.

Remember that details are important when you write about music, so make descriptive notes and answer your questions fully through prewriting activities before you start composing.

Listening, Watching, Analyzing, and Understanding

As with all popular culture, music is a text that can be analyzed; music contains readable elements that contribute to the listener's experience. It is a medium that you are already reading actively (by simply listening to the lyrics or a particular instrument) and passively (by connecting to the sounds and to the tone). As you actively read a song or album, several elements, including the lyrics and the instruments used, should be your focus.

Music has terminology that may be important in writing about the subject. However, it is not necessary for you to be an expert on music theory to write a compelling essay. The following are some basic terms and ideas for you to consider when writing a music essay.

SONG PATTERN

The patterns that follow are a sample only and may not be found in some genres of music such as jazz or classical.

Introduction: The intro, which is usually music or lyrics only, catches the listener's attention with a short refrain or a sample of the song's rhythmic pattern.

Verse: Vocal melody and lyrics. Verses tell the story or develop an idea, as in the chapters of a book or the paragraphs of an essay; usually each verse focuses on a separate but related idea. The verses develop the songwriters' main ideas and prepare the listener for the chorus. For some listeners, the verses give value to a song, or verses may be completely ignored for a catchy chorus.

Prechorus: A vocal and/or melodic foreshadowing of the chorus through tone, melody, or both.

Chorus: The chorus, sometimes called a *hook* or *refrain*, can most easily be described as that part of the song that is most often repeated and, because of this, usually garners the most focus both lyrically and musically. Musically speaking, the chorus is often the most dynamic part of the song.

Bridge: The purpose of the bridge is to break up the monotony of the verse/chorus, verse/chorus musical pattern. A bridge is typically an entirely new melody of music and words or even drums and bass only (sometimes called a *breakdown* or *jam*). The bridge reaches for the highest level of energy in the song, and it often rivals the chorus in its dynamics.

LYRICS

Most songwriters concentrate on expressing a message to listeners, and they often try to connect with the most basic human emotions. Although some lyrics are only meant to entertain, this is not a less important purpose than emotional connection, only different. Lyrics are poetic and can contain some of the same elements that we see when we analyze literature or poetry.

Alliteration: The repetition of sounds at the beginning of words or in stressed syllables, such as the hard "D" sound in the phrase "Dirty deeds, done dirt cheap" by AC/DC.

Meter: The measured arrangement of words and syllables in poetry. One type, ballad meter, is even named after a common syllabic arrangement in hymns and other songs; "Amazing Grace" is an example of this—a line of iambic tetrameter followed by a line of iambic trimeter:

"I once/was lost/but now/I'm found/
Was blind/but now/I see."

Parallelism: The repetition of phrases, sentences, or lines that are similar in meaning or structure, such as the repeated use of the word "low" in the song "Low" by FloRida. The repeated chorus of a song is a form of parallelism.

Rhyme Scheme: The arrangement of rhyming words or syllables in a song or stanza, such as the rhyming of "spoon" and "lagoon" in the lines "protected by a silver spoon" and "by the banks of her own lagoon" in the song "She Came in Through the Bathroom Window" by Sir Paul McCartney.

Stanza: A section of song lyrics composed of two or more lines. A verse is often one or more stanzas.

Structure: The way that a lyric is composed, consisting of line, stanza, and parallelism.

INSTRUMENTATION

The elements of instrumentation can combine to form a cohesive unit—a song or a movement in classical or jazz music. Consider each element individually and as part of the larger song and album to analyze the tone, mood, and purpose of both the lyrics and the music.

Instruments: Musicians use countless instruments, from their own voice to a piano, an electric guitar, drums, violins, harmonicas, and even old washboards. When analyzing the instruments, consider what instruments the band uses, whether or not they use them effectively, and if their use symbolizes anything outside normal use.

Mood: The mood of a song can be shown in many different ways, such as using particular instruments; using a major key, which often implies happiness, or a minor key, which implies sadness; playing different tones; keeping or changing the speed of the rhythm; sharing lyrics; and using or not using countless other elements. Through the mood of the song, listeners hear and feel what the songwriter(s) are attempting to convey.

Electric Versus Acoustic: Electric performances create energy and are perceived as more impersonal, whereas acoustic performances, often referred to as unplugged, may convey a more intimate connection between artist and audience. The artist's use of electric or acoustic instruments may enhance the mood and message of the song or album, and an electric song can seem very different if heard in an acoustic setting.

Live Performance Versus Studio Performance: Many artists choose to record their live performances, complete with the audience cheering in the background, whereas some prefer to record studio performances. The moods that these performances convey can completely change the listener's perception of a song or album.

Technology: Artists have more technological options in music than ever before. Artists are now able to digitally enhance their voices, dub additional tracks over their songs, loop musical interludes throughout the song electronically (such as sampling), or even add a digital audience to a recording. These techniques may also apply to concert performances.

GRAPPLING with Ideas

- The use of technology has been more and less popular over time, but it seems more necessary as the recording industry has discovered that appearance and sex appeal can sell albums. Digital enhancement of a singer's voice also happens in live performances. Is this similar to airbrushing models or actors having plastic surgery?

- Is digital enhancement ethical? Why or why not?

- Name some recent controversies that came from the audience finding out that singers were lip-synching or digitally enhancing their music in some way.

PRODUCTION

Many components exist outside the music itself, including the artist's image, the band name, the album or song name, and the album cover. These external details may add more to a song, album, or performance.

Artist's Image: The way musicians present themselves is crucial to our perception of them and of their music. Hairstyles, clothing, body art, and other deliberate or even accidental choices can influence our perception of the musician and the music.

Album Cover: Packaging can enhance or interfere with the listening experience. The packaging of music might reflect the band's or the record company's purpose, and it has an effect on the way you view music.

Genre: Music can be divided by type, style, form, content, or technique. Some large categories of genres include top forty, pop, rap, hip-hop, alternative, new country, classic rock, dance, R&B, metal, jazz, classical, and gospel. Songs, artists, albums, or performances can often be categorized. Although there is some need by popular radio to classify songs so that they can be marketed, many songs and artists resist this classification. Also, many artists and songs may cross between genres. For example, Taylor Swift has repeatedly been at the top of the country charts and the pop charts at the same time.

How and Where It Is Heard: Whether you hear songs in a car, in a dance club, in an elevator, on a date, on TV, in film, in a doctor's office, or at church, this experience changes your perception of the music.

Concept Album: An album that has one basic theme, tone, mood, or purpose that is consistent throughout. The Beatles' *Sgt. Pepper's Lonely Hearts Club Band* and Pink Floyd's *Dark Side of the Moon* are two popular examples.

VIDEOS/MUSICAL PERFORMANCES

Musical performances can be seen on MTV and subsequent music channels, on formulaic "high school dance" episodes of television shows or teen movies, on music competition shows, at halftime of the Super Bowl, on variety shows such as *Late Night with David Letterman* or *Jimmy Kimmel Live*, and even on comedy series like *Chappelle's Show*. These performances can, again, add to or detract from a musical experience. For more help analyzing videos and live performances, see the chapters on film and television.

GRAPPLING with Ideas

Choose a specific group (for example, young teenage females, Texas cowboys, wealthy blacks).

- Create a list of features that you might want to include for a music video geared toward this specialized audience.

- Write a description or outline of a screenplay for your own music video, being certain to use the features from your list.

- Share your screenplay idea with the class.

Production: Videos and performances are often produced by an entire team of musical and technical artists. Where and how the production was designed and filmed, how much money and time were spent, and where the performance or video will be aired or sold are all important considerations.

Technical and Artistic Features: These features include the language; the video techniques, such as sound, lighting, and camera shots; and the musical techniques, such as tone, rhythm, and presentation used. The actors, extras, or dancers hired may also address the band's or producer's intended audience, mood, and purpose for the song. All of these are technical and artistic choices that a band, producer, or director make before and during the performance or shooting of a video.

Audience: Performances or videos usually target a specific audience. Your social position, race, gender, sexual preferences, background, or academic achievement may play a part in your reception of the performance. Videos and performances may serve a social, economic, or political interest or may address, reinforce, or subvert any beliefs, values, or attitudes. These are important considerations when analyzing a performance/video or an album/song.

Listening, Watching, Researching, and Documenting

If you are writing a reflection or response essay, you may not need to do any outside research, focusing instead on the song, artist, or performance. However, you may need to do some outside research to write a convincing and well-supported review or analysis essay.

Areas of research may include the following:

- The artist's life.
- The artist's or producer's body of work.
- The historical background of the music.
- The culture or cultural ideas represented or presented in the lyrics or video.
- The reception of the song by others.
- The economic history or budget of the album or tour.
- The writer of the song, particularly if different from the performer.
- The history or development of techniques used.
- The evolution of particular genres or conventions.

The research you do will be guided by the questions that you want answered and by the assumed expectations of your audience. See the introduction to each content chapter and Chapter 5 for more information about researching popular culture topics.

For writing about music, your primary text is the song, album, artist, or concert you have chosen to write about, and it may include the album, CD, or DVD packaging. For secondary sources within music, you may use popular publications, such as *Rolling Stone*, *Spin*, or *Magnet*. You might turn to online sources, such as Billboard .com. Academic journals such as *The Journal of Popular Music* are another place to turn for reliable information. Start with the information in your school's library (especially with your school's online databases), but do not be afraid to expand your search to the Internet, a great source for older recordings and all lyrics, and to your own collection of books, magazines, and CDs.

Song lyrics are quoted within your essay in the same style as poetry. See Chapter 5 for more assistance with this.

Some sites to check out, whether for basic facts, reviews, archives, or analyses, include the following:

Billboard Magazine	http://www.billboard.com
The Blues Foundation	http://www.blues.org
Country Music Hall of Fame	http://www.countrymusichalloffame.com
The Grammy Awards	http://www.grammy.com
The History of Rock Music	http://www.historyofrockmusic.com
Lyrics.com	http://www.lyrics.com
The Rock 'n Roll Hall of Fame	http://www.rockhall.com
Rolling Stone Magazine	http://www.rollingstone.com
SoundtrackNet	http://www.soundtrack.net
Yahoo! Music	http://music.yahoo.com

Do not forget to record the citation information you will need for your Works Cited page and for your in-text citations to remember where you found your information and how to get back to it should you need to. See Chapter 5 for specific guidelines and investigate the Works Cited at the end of each sample essay for examples of citations for specific sources.

Key Questions for an Album/Song/ Concert Review or Review Essay

- Have you clearly indicated your judgment of the album's/song's/ concert's quality?

- Have you begun the review with an attention-grabbing opening? Have you concluded it with a striking sentence?

- Did you write in present tense?

- For a song or album, did you mention any background information about the artist, previous recordings, or production? For a concert, did you mention the artist's success?

- Have you provided a brief synopsis of the music and lyrics of a song/ album or the lighting, backup singers, band, dancers, and stage video for a concert?

- Have you defined yourself as a credible source? Have you mentioned specific elements of the album/song/concert that support your judgment?

- Have you described these quickly and vividly, using concrete language and metaphors?

- Have you qualified your judgment with both positive and negative aspects of the song/album/concert?

- If reviewing a song or album, did you discuss the appearance and packaging?

- If reviewing a concert, did you discuss the music that the artist chose (or did not choose) to play or perform? Did you discuss how the artist related to the audience?

- If a song or album, did you discuss the medium? Is it a download or a CD? From a soundtrack? Is the song part of an album? Part of a concept album?

WRITING ABOUT MUSIC

Music as an artistic medium can be written about in many ways; however, this chapter focuses on the four main essay types as discussed in the previous chapters. Whether you focus on the mood that "Jaan Pehechaan Ho" creates in *Ghost World*, Beyoncé's celebrity status after leaving Destiny's Child, or how Guns N' Roses' "Welcome to the Jungle" promotes *Grand Theft Auto: Vice City*, music topics often overlap with other subjects, so look at the suggestions and advice for film, television, gaming, advertising, or celebrity culture in the other content chapters for more advice.

Music Reviews or Review Essays

A listening report on an album or song or a screening report on a concert is usually called a music review. Though descriptive, opinions about quality are often included. An evaluation of some sort is necessary. These judgments about the album, song, or concert are usually written for magazine, newspaper, or website articles and columns. Music review essays differ from music reviews mainly in purpose. A review essay is typically written for a more academic audience and, therefore, may include different kinds of details than a review written for a magazine or blog. However, the strategies for writing a review essay are similar.

For a music review, some objectivity is important. All artistic media have some good and some bad qualities, so try to examine both. When you write a review for a class, your overall evaluation is usually phrased as the thesis or main idea of the essay.

Music reviews differ in the characteristics they possess. For an album or CD review, a writer typically discusses the overall theme of the album, some background of the artist or the album's production, the strongest and/or weakest songs on the album, and perhaps comments on the overall look and design of the album's packaging. Song reviews are much more specific. Although some commentary on the artist or the background of the song's production may be necessary, more detail is significant when discussing the strengths and weaknesses of the song, the lyrics, and the melody. Concert reviews may discuss the music, the sound, the lighting, the songs the artist chose to play or perform (or the songs that they did not play), and the production as a whole. Remember that you could also review a book about a musician, a music writer, or an album; a concert DVD, or YouTube videos or recordings of new, original music.

A review may also compare the song or album to others in the same genre or to others made by the same artist. With concert reviews, it is valid to compare it to others you have attended or watched on DVD. Most importantly, make sure your experience is obvious to the reader so that your opinion is taken seriously.

Reflection or Response Essays

The main purpose of a reflection or response essay is to use music as a jumping-off point for your own discussion. You may reflect on a song that was playing at an important moment in your life or respond to the way an album made you feel the first time you listened to it. Although the essay will mostly be personal, it is still important to use evidence from the song, concert, album, or artist to explain why you are making your specific point.

A reflection or response essay can be written about a song, an album, a band, or a concert that means something to you, that sparks an emotion, or that triggers a memory. Then, think about who your audience is and what you would like him or her to know about this experience. When you are writing about a personal subject, a solid thesis statement may help keep you on topic.

Analysis Essays

There are many reasons to write an analysis of music; most significantly, this type of writing may help you reach a deeper, more critical appreciation of a song, album, or concert experience. To analyze music in an essay, you must first describe what you are analyzing. These descriptive details are important because your purpose is to explain their relation to one another, to the audience, or to you in order to support your main point. Your thesis will explain to your audience what you are analyzing and the major idea you are offering or the judgment you are making about your subject. Also, remember that the key terms from this chapter may give you a vocabulary from which to write about a specific song, album, performance, or video.

When analyzing music, remember that you may be more familiar with the subject than your audience. Identify your audience and do not assume that they listen to the same music that you do or that they agree with your basic assumptions about music. For example, a teenager in 2008 may have a different take on Prince's "1999" than an adult who was a teenager when the song was originally released in 1983.

Key Questions for a Reflection or Response Essay

- Have you clearly indicated how you used the album, song, artist, or concert as a springboard for your thesis?

- Have you expressed your personal response to one aspect of the album, song, artist, or concert?

- Did you focus on reflection (and not lapse into simple summary)?

- Does your introduction direct your audience into your response?

- Does your concluding paragraph include some reflection on both the music and your response?

- Did you write about the song or album in present tense but any past life experiences in past tense?

- Are your intentions clear in the essay?

- Did you explain the significance or effectiveness of your experience?

KEY questions

Key Questions for an Analysis Essay

- Do you have a clearly stated thesis or main point or one that is obvious to the reader?

- Do you have a series of reasons supporting the thesis or main point? Are these arranged in a logical and convincing order?

- Are your supporting reasons backed up? Do you provide specific evidence and examples from the song, album, artist, or concert for each reason you offer?

- Does your introduction orient your reader into the direction of your argument?

- Does your concluding paragraph express the effectiveness or significance of your analysis and provide a vivid ending?

- Did you write in literary present tense if referring to an album or song?

- Did you avoid too much summary?

- Did you consider your audience?

Synthesis Essays

These preceding essay types are not the only ways that you may write about music, and they may often be used in combination. Your needs or those of your audience may be best served by combining the skills used to analyze, respond to, and review an album, song, or concert. Music lends itself to essays that combine review and response or analysis and reflection. Examples of synthesis writing that you may be familiar with include album reviews in *Rolling Stone* that both analyze and review an album or Myspace blogs that review and personally respond as well.

ANNOTATED SAMPLE ESSAY

CONSIDERING IDEAS

1. What songs do you know that are focused on serious issues in society? What are the issues?

2. Do you like these kinds of songs? Why or why not?

AUTHOR BIO

Elizabeth Adams *was a freshman at Michigan State University when she wrote this essay about homeless youth and the song "On the Bus Mall" for her first-year writing course.*

"ON THE BUS MALL":

Homeless Youth Community Affected by Societal Issues

Elizabeth Adams

The Decemberists are known for telling whimsical stories through captivating musical narratives. The main songwriter for the group, Colin Meloy, sets himself apart as a communicator from many writers that support the idea that songs should convey feelings. He feels that songs should be narratives that the listeners can "get lost in." (Carew). In the song, "On the Bus Mall," this angle is clearly displayed through the story of a runaway couple on the streets of Portland. The Bus Mall is a place in between all of the urban areas in Portland that draws a lot of homeless people and crime. The song invites the listener into the story of this young couple that embraces the life of being homeless. It uses grotesque expressions but romanticizes them with the intense love that the life on the streets encouraged. The Decemberists not only engage the listener into the playfulness and the ignorance of teen runaways but also the importance of how environmental factors affect their decisions. Through an analysis of the song, ◄ a research journal and an interview I am able to correlate the societal treatment of the homeless youth and other environmental factors with their deviant behavior.

> The author's thesis not only lets you know her topic, it also sets up a synthesis essay that will be using a variety of types of support and analysis.

Through a playful creation of a fictional story the writer truly takes the listener on a ride through the life of youths on the street. He also ties in important implications that are common among the runaway youth. This story isn't about feeling bad for these homeless teens, it allows one to connect to the characters and truly imagine how these situations could occur. The ignorance in the lyrics exemplifies the paradoxical ideas that can be formed in the minds of the youth. In the song the writer describes the characters as being prostitutes, druggy's and even hustlers in pool halls (The Decemberists). All of these are crimes, but they are embraced because they are seen as a last resort and necessities in the eyes of a sovereign teen on the streets.

Despite all of the horrible activities the characters are involved in, the writer demonstrates how they handle the situations positively in their own eyes. He explains how they got through the pain of being homeless in lines 46-48 of "On the Bus Mall": "As 4 in the morning came on, cold and boring, we huddled close in the bus stop enclosure enfolding. Our hands tightly holding" (The Decemberists). The juvenile belief that love conquers all taints any belief that one needs wealth and structure to be happy in this song. The song is a commentary on these hopeful beliefs and it also displays that teens don't have the capacity to understand the implications these illegal activities present. The folkie voice of the singer provides an invitation for the listener to believe the story and even empathize and embrace this dire situation. A topic that to most seems like a tragedy is depicted as a fantasy in the song. This is accomplished through the engaging voice of the singer and the Victorian and indie literature influences in the lyrics. The dreamy instrumentals created through accordion and bass guitar set the perfect backdrop for this well thought out romanticized narrative.

When writing about music, it is important to write about more than just lyrics. The style of the music and musicians also affects the style and tone of the arguments.

Although this song presents the listener with playfulness and freedom, it also shows the characters being stripped of their youth. The activities that they encounter have an obvious effect on the choices they make and how they encounter further situations. The beginning of the song talks about having to exchange sex for any small source of capital. As the story develops they begin to acquire a more mischievous approach for earning money. Their innocence seems to dwindle based on their actions as the song develops. For example they begin to hustle and learn how to trick others on the streets and they actually think of themselves as "kings among runaways" (The Decemberists).

The author uses lyrics to illustrate her points and support her argument.

This didn't seem to spawn from their initial teen angst but it grew from the difficult environmental influences that they had to adapt to while being homeless. The Decemberists not only engage the listener into the lightheartedness and the ignorance of teen runaways but also the environmental factors that change their actions.

Recently there has been research done on the homeless youth in society and the factors that contribute to their misbehaviors. Interestingly the article, *The Social Construction of Deviant Behavior in Homeless and Runaway Youth: Implications for Practice,* focuses not only on the pathological contributions but also the environmental factors that affect this group's actions. This article brings to the surface that many of the crimes associated with homeless youth are actually just a part of the lived occurrence of being a homeless teen (Miles 1). This research journal mainly focuses on answering two questions, "1. How does the ecological context influence 'deviant' behaviors of homeless youth? 2. How do survival strategies of homeless youth relate to prevailing notions of 'deviance' in society?" (Miles 4). These are very important questions in considering how to treat and even prevent teen homelessness.

Another important aspect of this journal is that these teens have misconceptions on what laws stand for and what they mean. Many homeless are told by police officers different definitions of the ambiguous laws that hold our society's criminal justice system together. Although ignorance is not an excuse, should uneducated teens living on the streets be treated the same as educated teens and/or adults? The laws that directly conflict with the homeless lifestyle are the laws against aggressive panhandling, sitting on sidewalks and urban camping. The increase in these laws against the homeless is due to the increasing homeless population that the country can't support. Also the increase of urbanization and commercial property has caused the homeless to be prohibited in urban areas (Miles 7).

Many police officers use their discretion to arrest the homeless just to get them off the streets, making laws form based on the people they see. Although it is important to keep the community safe from the homeless, it is important to consider that the situations these people are subject to. Especially since homeless teens are often pushed into the homeless lifestyle due to environmental and ecological factors. Subsequently they are pushed into crime due to the conditions of homelessness and their human needs. The flexible laws that push these teens to corrupt areas, like the Bus Mall in Portland, cause them to commit *deviant* behaviors.

> Through this process of adjustment, youth exhibited behaviors which violated societal norms for public behavior. In this way, youth *deviance* reflected more of an adaptive mechanism to oppressive environmental structures in our study, rather than being motivated by an internally driven pathology. *Deviant* behaviors also resulted from social strain related to the adversarial relationship between the youth and members within their community. (Miles 13)

Because this quote from the journal is more than four lines long, it is set apart as a block quote. Notice that the in-text punctuation is slightly different for block quotes.

This article truly brings to the surface some of the important points of The Decemberists song "On the Bus Mall's" plot. The author correlates the crimes committed amongst teen runaways as being situational, just as the writer for the band tells the empathic story of the teens' life on the streets. The song really shows the implications that come from the circumstances and it also shows that the teen's need to adapt to the limited environment that the police allow them to inhabit. Both the article and the song bring up vital points that need to be understood in handling teen runaways. They also display the control that the government has on where the homeless can reside and how this is a fundamental contributor to their misbehaviors.

Fortunately I was connected with a young adult, Sarah Marshall who was a runaway teen for over a year. Over a phone interview I was able to ask some questions about her experience prior, during and after being homeless.

The author uses a mixture of primary and secondary sources to fully understand her topic and the experiences she is writing about.

It was interesting to hear that she was on the honor roll during her freshman year of high school in an urban area in Boston. She also was an athlete and spent much of her spare time dedicated to after school activities. Even though her future seemed promising a rough life at home gave her no choice but to hit the streets. Although she found herself alone in Boston, she established some refuge at a church shelter in the city. This situation seemed better than the streets but she was exposed to a lot of violence among the community in the shelter. She also was constrained by many of the strict rules of the shelter (Marshall).

After a few weeks in the shelter she was put into an all girl half way house where there was equally as much drama among the community. A few weeks after being harassed and threatened by housemates she decided to rebel. She started sneaking out of the house at night with the few friends she was able to make at the house. Although these friends seemed nice at the surface, they were into a lot of partying and street drugs. "I started drinking and taking drugs like marijuana, which led me to harder drugs like cocaine" (Marshall). Then this partying got out of hand and caused her to ditch school and miss curfew. As she began to get in trouble she also started experimenting with guys, especially the ones that sold drugs (Marshall).

All of this seemed pretty overwhelming as I was interviewing her. However after reading about the life of homeless youth it became easier to understand how one could spiral downhill after just a few weeks of adapting to the homeless lifestyle. Sarah had a really difficult time at home which was another contributor to her need to fit in and even revolt. Her mistakes had no relation to her actions prior to being homeless. I asked her how she felt about herself through her deviant behavior. She explained, "I felt like I was so free because I could do whatever I wanted and didn't have to listen to anyone. I didn't even have to follow the strict rules of the house because I outsmarted the patrol nuns." This feeling of freedom is something that I see as a defense mechanism she used to guard against all the abuses and neglect she felt at home and on the streets.

As she began to hang around drug dealers, she continued her exploration of drug abuse and was eventually kicked out of her half way house and school. She lived with one of her boyfriends and was binging on cocaine during all hours of the day with him. Even her first friends from the half way house decided to alienate Sarah because her addiction became too extreme for them. It wasn't until she and her boyfriend began having problems finding the drugs that she began to notice a problem. He started getting abusive to her when he was craving the drugs and she even lashed out at him distraught from mental and physical withdrawals (Marshall).

The acceptance of drug use as a problem influenced her to change her lifestyle. She left her boyfriend and started living at a home in exchange for aiding an elderly woman around the house. Although the elderly woman had a lot of rules regarding curfew and work ethic; Sarah was drawn to the work because it kept her off the streets. She was even able to get another job at a restaurant and take classes to prepare for her GRE. After hearing her life story I was really able to see how difficult that life would be for a homeless teen and even teens struggling with their lives at home. The decision to leave home is a very difficult one; I asked her if she regretted leaving home. "I regret not having a family to rely on, but that was out of my control in the first place. It was safer for me to leave and experience life myself."

Sarah was lucky that she never experienced problems with the police during her time on the streets. I asked her "To what extent did you know what laws you were breaking and how you would be punished?" She told me that although she had some high school education she had no idea how much discretion that the police had over her actions in public. She was especially unsure of the laws that were formed to regulate the homeless community.

Finally I asked her to listen to the song "On the Bus Mall" by the Decemberists. After that I asked her to describe any part of the song that related to her experience.

The author continues to build connections throughout her essay. Here she brings the reader back to the beginning of the essay by asking her interview subject about the song that started this exploration.

She told me that the freedom and cockiness of the characters was something she could relate to. This was because she needed to keep strong on the streets and especially in the half way home and shelter full of angry and competitive homeless teenagers. I then asked if she felt connected to the love that was dominant in the song. She responded, "Anyone I could rely on temporarily I loved at the time, but I was not myself so I don't look back at them with true love" (Marshall).

Ultimately I learned that homelessness among youth is a complex problem. The song presented the implications that can arise and seem normal for a teen trying to survive on the streets. It also brought up harmful limitations that the United States criminal justice system imposes on the homeless. Unfortunately for young teens that are left to live on the streets, the government pushes the homeless into the dangerous areas just outside of urban areas. This led the characters in the song to be trapped in the Bus Mall in Portland. This was presented as a big problem in the research journal which gave me a better understanding of the confines of the Bus Mall. These sources outlined the implications that teens face when deciding to leave a difficult home situation. The interview showed me that even when teens receive help from shelters there is no escaping the violence that is inevitable among the homeless especially when they are confined and hostile.

One thing from the song that still stands as a question in my mind is the strength brought by the bond of people surviving together. The song really mesmerized me with the idyllic love that could be experienced and strengthened through such hardships. The journal displayed only a small hint of this in that the minds of the youth are easily molded by the surroundings and associates. However in the journal this was a downfall in that a lot of negative activities are spread through groups of teens on the streets. This is a paradox in the song, like the many other gruesome issues that are romanticized. The dependence upon acceptance of others and pressures between people is a tough issue. The characters in this song and

Here the author pulls together all of the resources she has used to illuminate her understanding of the song.

even the runaway I interviewed displayed dependence on others, especially a romantic partner.

The indie and folk music genre always interests me and I really enjoy listening to the intellectual and even abstract lyrics. I also acknowledged The Decembrists's music as poetic and witty. After researching the group and their topic I now know that they are influenced by Victorian literature and tell fictional stories to connect to the audience (Carew). To many this fiction may disconnect the audience from the music, but I feel that their method attempts to be personal with the audience. They reach out through fables that relate to everyday people but also involve a lot of imagination and talent in literacy.

Initially I listened to this song and really thought of love as the fundamental meaning. After analyzing the song, a related journal and interviewing a runway, I see the essential meaning of the song as survival. It is a depiction of the crucial adaptation all homeless must face. I always felt that homelessness was a huge issue, but I never related to it before. After analyzing the information I collected, I feel empathetic to the homeless community. This song allows me to see the limited control they have and the challenges that they must face. When I used to live in Chicago and homeless people would ask me for money I felt bad for them. I also believed it was their fault for not fixing the situation or getting a job. I now know that these situations aren't that easy.

Music was always a vessel for me to appease my emotions. Although this remains a function; I've found through analyzing lyrics that music is a way to bring to surface issues. The creative method of music supports the ideas of the artist and relays this information to the public. The songs that we all listen to are as political as they are passionate, and give the artist a way to let society know whatever they choose. It is interesting to me to learn that this song is very humanist and psychologically based because I am a psychology major. My interests relate to the songs I listen to even before I know what they mean, or maybe my interest are due to the music I like. The impact that talented artists have on their listeners is tremendous.

After examining "On the Bus Mall" by the Decemberists, I have a more negative view on the implications that the homeless face. Their actions are caused by governmental discretion and alienation by society. I will no longer allow myself to judge these people for their failure to clean up. I am no longer blind to the mistreatment and abuse of the homeless communities.

The author concludes with what she has learned through the research and writing process, hoping that the reader will have learned some of these same things from her.

This realization has raised my level of suspicion toward the governmental and societal power over the treatment of unpopular groups.

The paper concludes with a Works Cited page, listing all of the resources quoted in the essay. It is missing one resource—do you know what it is?

Works Cited

Carew, Anthony. "The Decemberists Biography—Artist Profile of The Decemberists." *Alternative and Indie Music.* 2011. Web. 11 Mar. 2011.

Marshall, Sarah. Personal Interview. 9 Mar. 2011.

Miles, Bart W., and Scott K. Okamato. "The Social Construction of Deviant Behavior in Homeless and Runaway Youth: Implications for Practice." *Child and Adolescent Social World.* 17 Oct. 2008. Web. 11 Mar. 2011.

Source: *Reprinted with permission from the author.*

DECODING THE TEXT

1. What facts does the author present about homeless communities in this essay?

2. Are you inclined to believe or trust these facts? Why or why not?

3. How does the author connect this analysis to the actual song "On the Bus Mall"?

CONNECTING TO YOUR CULTURE

1. Did you know this song before reading this essay? If not, did you go and listen to it?

2. How does listening to this song affect the reading of the essay?

3. What issue in society would you write about or sing about if you were in a band?

THE READING ZONE

ENGAGING WITH TOPICS

1. Think about the musicians whom you consider icons. Why do you assign them this iconic status? Do popular critics, reviews, and music writers agree with you? Do people outside your generation agree with you?

2. What do you know about the history of rock 'n roll? Research the first number-one rock 'n roll hit on the charts, the first singer classified as rock 'n roll, and the influences on the genre to find out more.

3. Country music has gone through many changes since its early roots in folk and gospel melodies. What similarities can you see in current country or bluegrass hits to the music of its origins?

4. How are women portrayed in rock, R&B, hip-hop, country, and rap music? How do their portrayals differ across genres and across generations?

5. What songs do you like that you would not consider "popular"? Perhaps a Broadway tune or a song you sang in choir? A hymn or a kid's song? What would it take for this music to become more popular? You may want to consider the way rap uses such songs.

READING SELECTIONS

The readings that follow are organized into three sections: the 1970s and 1980s, the 1990s and 2000s, and the 2010s. The familiar decades organization that underpins all content chapters for this textbook is used, and the readings in each of the sections are not isolated to that decade or section because pop culture is not only what happened at the time but also how the same item or idea is received or remembered later on.

The readings here are presented as a way for you to become more versed in investigating music as pop culture; however, they are also offered as samples of writing reviews, responses, analyses, and synthesis essays. In the 1970s and 1980s section, you can examine the rock versus disco debate from the 1970s and then look at the effect MTV and music videos had on music lovers, including the 1980's backlash against graphic lyrics and video content.

In the 1990s and 2000s section, *Billboard* magazine writers analyze the evolution of rap music in television and film. Theodore Matula offers commentary and review on the life of punk legend Joe Strummer, and Kalene Westmoreland addresses women's issues in music with her response to Meredith Brooks's "Bitch" lyrics and to the Lilith Fair. This article is paired with Pink's "Stupid Girls" lyrics for comparison.

In the 2010s section, authors discuss the success of various artists and genres: the legacy of Michael Jackson, the King of Pop; the influence of the television show *Glee,* and the importance of small performance venues for launching new artists.

These readings might inspire you to analyze your own music tastes or to listen to and review an artist, band, or album you are currently unfamiliar with, or they may inspire you to attend a concert or look up some videos online; however, their main purpose is to inspire your response to the vast landscape of popular music over the decades.

READING SELECTIONS:
THE 1970s AND 1980s

CONSIDERING IDEAS

1. What type of music do you listen to? What do you like about it?

2. What connections does your music of choice have to other types of music? What are its influences? Its history? What do you think is the future of this type of music?

AUTHOR BIO

John Rockwell has worked as a music critic, a dance critic, and an editor for the past 30 years. He worked for The New York Times *from 1972 to 2006, moving from classical music critic to pop music critic to chief dance critic. In 2006, he retired from the newspaper to pursue other projects. This historic look at rock and disco music from the 1970s was first published in* The New York Times *in 1990.*

ROCK VS. DISCO

Who Really Won the War?

John Rockwell

Electrified popular music of the last 35 years has suffered its share of attacks from without, the opponents being mainly parents or religious extremists. But it has also been riven by internal polemics, and few of those battles grew fiercer and meaner than the rock-versus-disco wars of the late 1970's.

Disco enthusiasts didn't care much about rock; it provoked indifference more than anything else. But rock fans cared passionately about disco. Mainly white, they acted as if disco, the anthem of homosexuals and urban blacks, was both contemptible and evil. The hysteria reached its apex at the 1979 Comiskey Park record-burning in Chicago, where 20,000 disco albums were consumed in a second-base bonfire to raucous cheers.

Now Rhino Records, those indefatigable anthologizers from Santa Monica, Calif., have issued a spate of disco compilations—two compact disks, "The Disco Years"; a K. C. and the Sunshine Band album, and a best of T. K. Records, "Get Down Tonight." Since Rhino is the hippest of rock historians, the company's involvement signals that disco may no longer be regarded as the epitome of uncool. And with the resurgence of disco-related dance music today, a new generation may be ready to reconsider the disco phenomenon.

In the late 70's, critics condemned disco for being repetitive, commercial, mechanical and trivial—epithets that could be applied to rock-and-roll. As the Rhino compilations emphasize but anyone with ears knew all along, disco and rock are far more similar than dissimilar. Most disco stresses the downbeat in a louder, more unvariegated manner. But both draw from the same black musical roots, and both range far and wide in their musical influences.

Disco could borrow from Caribbean sources, as in the lively, lilting K. C. and the Sunshine Band hits—"I'm Your Boogie Man," "(Shake, Shake, Shake) Shake Your Booty," "That's the Way (I Like It)"—and most of the records from the T. K. studios in Florida. There, Harry Wayne Casey and Richard Finch, the core of the Sunshine Band, wrote and produced many singles for others (above all, the sinuously soulful "Rock Your Baby" for George McCrae). But the influences of rhythm-and-blues, funk and even classical (all those sawing violins and braying horns) are equally evident.

The real reasons for rock fans' denunciations of disco were almost surely racial and social. Disco came, at least at first, from outsider labels like T. K. and outsider cultures like gay, black and Latin. They represented disturbing big-city mores to a heartland that had only recently accepted (and co-opted) rock-and-roll. Disco became popular through channels beyond the usual rock-club/radio-station circuit-urban discotheques, their disk jockeys and fan magazines. Disco disk-burning was the revenge of the white majority against threatening armies at the portals.

Chief among those threats were homosexuals. The late 1970's, before the onslaught of AIDS, marked the apex of gay culture, bursting with an exhilarating, even arrogant confidence in its own strength and future. Disco music, along with an anti-rock cabaret style, was a gay sonic emblem. The Village People were cartoon emissaries to the straight world, but they were really more a marketing ploy, the disco Monkees. A better example was Sylvester, who has since died of AIDS, a brilliant falsetto singer and the best musical product of the San Francisco gay community.

Not all disco was gay. Much of it was crafted by male producers who shaped insinuating instrumental backdrops behind the chirpings, cooings and moanings of nearly anonymous female singers. Sometimes those singers could be fitted into the exaggerated feminine stereotypes doted on by gay culture—dominating (Grace Jones), fashionably airy (Silver Convention) or brassily extroverted (Gloria Gaynor).

Beyond homosexuals, another ground for prejudice against disco was simply misogyny: rock-and-roll in its tougher, more aggressive forms has always been a male preserve. Disco allowed entry to the pop charts for women who might otherwise have been frozen out. The best singer to emerge from disco, Donna Summer, could have succeeded in any style, from rhythm-and-blues to ballads, but disco was the easiest way to make the charts in the 1970's.

Disco was fatally damaged by the payola scandals of the late 70's and, as a dominant yet stigmatized style of the time, was blamed for the downturn in record-company profits. Tastes shifted, in part because the mannerisms of some disco hit makers grew tiresome (those whining Bee Gee harmonies) and partly because promotional enthusiasm flagged. For whatever combination of reasons, disco fell from the Top 40 charts, and rock partisans could congratulate themselves that disco was indeed dead.

But was it? Dance clubs didn't die. From all-purpose dance music—disco in everything but the name—to rap and hip-hop and house, the persistence of a driving rhythmic music, the body liberated against a grid of pulsing metric regularity, lived on.

Of course, many of the songs' intellectual conceits were trivial, weighing in at about one feather on the profundity scale. But music in general and pop music in particular need not always be profound. Aspirations toward seriousness can sound self-conscious and labored. The best disco music—again, one thinks of K. C. and the Sunshine Band—was sexy and fun, and it propelled dancers around the floor with gleeful abandon.

Disco not only gave rise to some truly original producer-artists—Giorgio Moroder in Munich, Nile Rodgers in New York, Mr. Casey in Miami—but also presaged the growing creative role of the producer in pop music. The sophistication of the modern studio, with sampling, digital tape and computerized readouts only the latest wrinkles, now makes the person at the control console the most important force in shaping a pop record.

Disco's mainstream success may have been limited, in fact, because it was so much a studio product, with the resultant difficulty of re-creating in concert the hits of the studio. Had the MTV video revolution been in effect a decade ago, with today's technological possibilities and popular acceptance of lip-synched concerts, disco in its classic form might still be with us.

Perhaps the most misguided complaint against disco was its regular, thumping beat. Little did disco antagonists know, but the era of the rhythm machine and prerecorded, sampled tracks would soon be upon us. Compared to the mechanized regularity (or soothing support) of so many rhythm tracks today, disco sounds downright spontaneous.

Popular music in this century has seen a steady increase in rhythm's claims over melody and harmony. People want to dance, and they have drawn ever more deeply from African and Afro-American traditions, in which rhythm enjoys a primacy unknown in European-derived music. Disco was an important expression of that primacy, part of a succession of overlapping styles that blur together and stretch through today toward the future.

DECODING THE TEXT

1. Despite their competition with each other in the 1970s, Rockwell claims that disco and rock actually have a lot in common. Does he support this statement in a convincing way?

2. Rockwell also claims that the competition is really due to issues of race and sexuality. Is there support for this?

CONNECTING TO YOUR CULTURE

1. How do you feel about the claims of racism and sexism mentioned in this essay? Do you see music being divided along race lines? Gender lines? Sexuality lines?

2. In what other ways are music styles and tastes divided and/or judged?

3. Do you react differently to music recorded and produced in the studio as compared to that recorded live? What difference does it make?

CONSIDERING IDEAS

1. What is the purpose of music videos? Do they promote the music? The artists? Serve their own function?

2. How often do you watch music videos? How do they affect how you feel about the music? Do they help you understand or interpret the lyrics?

AUTHOR BIO

Marsha Kinder *is professor of critical studies in film at the University of Southern California and is best known for her idea of "transmedia," as well as her work on Spanish cinema and children's media. Since 1997 Kinder has directed the Labyrinth Project, an art collective and research initiative on interactive cinema and database narrative at USC's Annenberg Center for Communication. Kinder has published more than ten books and one hundred essays including this one first published in* Film Quarterly *in 1984, soon after the launch of MTV.*

MUSIC VIDEO AND THE SPECTATOR

Television, Ideology and Dream

Marsha Kinder

Music video is a protean form that has proven its magnetic power on MTV, a national 24-hour cable station devoted entirely to this programming on a continuous basis. It is now popping up on other cable stations, frequently appearing between movies the way cartoons and newsreels used to punctuate the spaces between features at movie theaters. It is also breaking into commercial television, where as many as 300 programs across the nation are devoted to music videos during carefully chosen hours.

Music video has even found its way into movies, providing the central creative energy for a subgenre launched by *Flashdance*—films that weave loose narratives around hot dance sequences created by montage and that generate fast-selling videos. The connection with film also proved lucrative in Michael Jackson's *Thriller,* the 14-minute video directed by feature film-maker John Landis (*Animal House, American Werewolf in London, Twilight Zone*). According to *Newsweek* (August 6, 1984), the documentary film *Making Michael Jackson's Thriller,* though it's only a spin-off, has already sold 450,000 cassettes, making it the second-best-selling video in history. *Thriller's* stunning commercial success, extended length and conscious positioning within the horror film genre helped strengthen the link between music video and mainstream film-making. Respected auteurs like Nicholas Roeg, Bob Rafelson, Tobe Hooper and Andy Warhol have entered the field, a trend that challenges the old unidirectional model which assumed *all* directors of commercials and television were fighting their way up from the boob tube to enter the celestial art of Cinema. Now, according to Warhol, "Everyone wants to make music videos!"[1]

What is the significance of this quicksilver phenomenon? Depending on which mass media reports you read, music video is a new means of extending the unique aesthetic possibilities of the avant-garde formerly restricted to independent film-making and video art, a new combination of music and images that redefines audiovisual relations in the mass media, a new means of marketing records and tapes that is saving the pop music industry, or a new source of violent sexist sadomasochistic images infecting the minds of our children.

While all of these perspectives may have validity, the underlying phenomenon that makes them all possible has been ignored: music video seems to be forging new codes of spectator relations, or more accurately, it is making the codes that were already operative in television more transparent. MTV provides a model that highlights through exaggeration the unique aspects of television, particularly those that distinguish the medium from cinema, and that have highly significant implications on two registers—television's relation to ideology and its relation to dream.

In the discussion of music video that follows, there will be no attempt to establish a canon or to create a pantheon of auteurs—projects that are already well under way.[2] I will not be examining the best works that the genre has produced, many of which have never been or are no longer being aired on MTV but are available in video stores and private collections. (Most songs have an even shorter life on MTV than they do on Top 40 radio stations.) Since I will be exploring MTV programming as a model of commercial television, I will limit my discussion to rock video, the station's main staple, though other forms of pop music such as jazz have also entered the field, and I will restrict my examples to those video clips being broadcast at the time I was writing this essay, choosing them almost at random to illustrate what is typical rather than what is most powerful aesthetically.

Presence/Absence of the Visual Image

One of the most compelling aspects of rock video is its power to evoke specific visual images in the mind of the spectator every time one hears the music with which they have been juxtaposed on television. The experience of having watched and listened to a particular video clip on television establishes these connections in the brain circuitry; by repeating the experience very frequently within a short period of time (a situation guaranteed by the repetitive structure of MTV), the spectator strengthens these associations in the brain. Thus later when the spectator hears the song on the radio or in a different context in which the visuals are absent, the presence of the music is likely to draw these images from memory, accompanied by the desire to see them again. This process follows the basic patterns of conditioning well established in the field of cognitive learning.

In rock video it is not merely a matter of whether we hear and see the performer (as we do in live performance at a concert or nightclub). In many rock video clips the visuals do not focus *primarily* on the performer in the act of performing; those that do, risk appearing regressive for they are reverting to conventions used in rock film documentaries from the sixties and seventies like *Monterey Pop* and *Woodstock.* In most rock videos what we do see is a chain of disparate images, which may involve the musical performers, but which stress discontinuities in space and time—a structure that resembles the form of dreams. Though the pulsing kinetic rhythms of the visual montage are invariably accentuated by the musical beat, the continuous flow of the music and lyrics also imposes a unifying identity (sometimes augmented by a narrative component in the lyrics and/or visuals) onto the discontinuous visual track, distinguishing it from the chains of similar images in the video clips that precede and follow this particular musical text.

This structure insures that the visuals will be the primary source of pleasure, for it is the lush visual track that will be withdrawn, withheld or suspended, when the spectator is no longer watching television but *only listening* to the song on the radio or stereo. The reverse situation—the presence of the visuals and the absence of the audio—is not built into the system; it can be achieved only through technical breakdown or through the spectator's intervention (turning off the sound while watching the images). Pioneer plays with this irony in one of its commercials for laser disc players by having blind singer Ray Charles deliver their slogan: "Video for those who really care about audio." This music video structure tends to subordinate the audio component of television by linking it with radio. Although some critics have argued that this linkage enables TV sound to act as a cue that draws the spectator's attention to certain video images, radio still remains the superseded medium which lacks the perceptual richness that television shares with cinema. In all television the visual component is privileged over the audio—a condition which is over-determined by historical, cultural and psychological factors[3] and which is revealed in the very term used for TV spectators, *viewers.*

The complex structure of the visual chain of images in most rock videos makes the reliance on memory and the value of repeated viewings all the more essential. If a person hears the song first before seeing the video clip that combines sound and image, the complexity of the visual form makes it virtually impossible for this listener to predict how the video would look. The situation is very different from the way it was in the sixties or seventies when a rock fan might buy a new album or audio tape by the Stones and then while listening, sit back and imagine how Jagger might look while performing this particular number.[4] It probably would have been even more likely for such a listener to place her- or himself in an imaginary setting and fantasize erotic behavior evoked by the lyrics, or to use the music as a sound track for actual physical acts (sex, dancing, exercise, or what you will). In such instances, the very absence of the live performers (represented only by still images on album covers, which frequently featured suggestive scenes or fetishes instead of the performers) invited the listener to create a waking fantasy. In those days the rock fan was expected to generate his or her own images; the visual component of the fantasies elicited by pop music were not totally prefabricated.

I don't mean to imply that music video is incapable of stimulating viewers to dream up their own chains of images, perhaps in a different style and with new combinations. Yet the remembering of images one has already seen seems an essential first step—a process I have seen prepubescent and teenage viewers transform into a game of Who can remember the most details? This goal of memory retrieval or replication is fostered by some of the performers. When recently interviewed by a video jockey on MTV, Roger Waters assured his fans that those coming to his latest live Concert would not be disappointed when they *heard* "5:05 AM, The Pros and Cons of Hitchhiking," for they would be *seeing* visual effects that equalled those they had seen in the video clip. Most concert promotions currently being aired on MTV stress the extravagance of the visual spectacle as much as the music—spectacle designed to match what is being seen on television.

Music video challenges the listener to play a hip *fort/da* game of Can you recall the absent visuals? Can you return to being a viewer and experiencing the original plenitude of sight and sound? This game is designed to drive all players back to the TV set to compulsively consume those prefabricated fantasy images on MTV (or wherever they can be found), knowing that all popular favorites will be repeated but rarely being able to predict more than a half hour in advance the precise time that any particular clip will be aired. (Didn't the followers of Pavlov and Skinner teach us that inconsistent patterns of reinforcement would intensify and prolong the compulsive repetition of the desired behavior?)

Performance, Narrative and Dreamlike Visuals

Thus far I have been talking as if all music videos had equal visual complexity and were all characterized by one style, neither of which is the case. Yet virtually all rock videos *are* comprised of three distinct components, which are combined with different emphases to create considerable variety within the form. First, the performance of the singer or group identifies the form with the musical genre and with the historic pop tradition of recording live performances on tape or film. Second, a simple or complex narrative carried by the lyrics and/or visual images, and sometimes featuring a guest star, turns the video into a minifilm with specific generic identification (e.g., horror, gangster film, screwball comedy, western, *noir*, melodrama, women's picture), making the visuals easier to remember and providing the spectator with a prefabricated daydream with varying degrees of space left for personal elaborations. Third, a series of incongruous visual images stressing spatial and temporal dislocations makes rock video closely resemble dreams—the primary medium that weaves loose narratives out of chains of incoherent images and that, despite its selective audio component, is predominantly a visual experience. Both performance and narrative work toward coherence, distinguishing the text from other rock video clips; in contrast, the dreamlike visuals work toward decentering and dissolution, revealing the deep structure of all television as an endless chain of images whose configuration into any structural unity or text is only a temporary, illusory byproduct of secondary revision.

The musical performance always dominates the audio, but varies in the degree to which it controls or is even present in the visuals. The narrative element is variable both on the audio and visual registers, sometimes dominating one or both, other times virtually absent except for the tendency of the human brain to read a story into any series of consecutive images, particularly when accompanied by words. The chain of incongruous images is restricted primarily to the visuals, varying in the quantity and pacing of the spatial and temporal dislocations and in the degree to which special effects are employed, but at least minimally present in the form of rapid montage which is featured in virtually all rock videos and also characteristic of commercials. While many commentators have called these dreamlike visuals *surreal,* it is important to distinguish them from the historical surrealism represented in film by Buñuel, a modernist movement which used dream rhetoric as a radical strategy to undermine the power of bourgeois ideology, particularly as it was manifest in the fine arts. In contrast, this postmodernist pop surrealism uses dream images to cultivate a narcissism that promotes our submission to bourgeois consumerism.

Music video has adopted quite consciously the visual conventions of the TV commercial, which has provided many talented directors (like Tim Newman and Bob Giraldi) for the new form. When viewing MTV, it is difficult to distinguish the video clips from the commercials because of close similarities in visual style, background music and short format. The same is true for the MTV news, which usually features three short items promoting commercial ventures, and for the station ID's, which sometimes include brief excerpts from clips of the most famous video stars—all presented in fast montage. These conventions from the commercial have been adopted because of their ability to capture and hold the spectator's attention, which is fundamental to their selling power. Research has shown that this kind of fast-paced visual style holds the attention even of the pre-school viewer, which is one of the reasons why it has been incorporated into kiddie shows like "Sesame Street" and why rock video has such an hypnotic effect on young children. The fast pace of MTV's programming might also be connected with the rise of cocaine as the dominant drug in pop culture in place of acid and grass. In Michael Jackson's Pepsi generation full of Pepper-uppers, Coke is it.

Like all television, the primary function of MTV's rock video is to sell products. While this goal is explicit in the TV commercial and fairly visible on MTV, it is disguised in most conventional programming on commercial television. Nick Browne has argued that while the television program is presented as the primary text and the commercials that temporarily interrupt it as secondary, the opposite is true, for the main function of the program is to provide a suitable environment for the commercial message. The actual television text is "a 'supertext' that consists of the particular program and all the introductory and interstitial materials—chiefly announcements and ads . . ." and "advertising . . . the central mediating discursive institution."[5] MTV exposes the "supertext" by erasing the illusory boundaries within its continuous flow of uniform programming and reveals the central mediating position of advertising by adopting its formal conventions as the dominant stylistic. In fact, *everything* on MTV is a commercial—advertising spots, news, station ID's, interviews, and especially music video clips.

SAMPLE PROGRAMMING ON MTV

Monitored In Los Angeles
Sunday, July 15, 1984, 12 noon–1 pm
* = music videos

12:00   MTV station ID, leading into voice-over of VJ Mark Goodman announcing what clips and news items will be featured in the next half hour.

     *Scorpions: "Still Loving You." Performance ruptured by fragmented visuals and shifts of scene.

12:05   *Bette Midler: "Beast of Burden." Screwball comedy narrative co-starring Mick Jagger, incorporating live performance by Midler, which Jagger eventually joins.

12:10   MTV promotion for stereo hook-up.

     Commercial for Thunderbird cars, with fast montage.

     Commercial for Little Steven album, including shots of live performance and concert schedule (usually included as news items).

     Commercial for Reese's Pieces candy, featuring comic narrative with E.T. lookalike.

     *Don Hartman (performance by the Sorels): "I Can Dream About You." Stage performance by black male singers, the Sorels, is framed by and intercut with romantic narrative about a white couple.

12:15   *The Alan Parsons Project: "Prime Time." Nightmare horror narrative featuring mannequins, some of whom come alive through the magic of special effects. We never see the singer or musicians performing.

12:20   VJ Mark Goodman on screen, comments on clips just aired and then presents the news, including 3 items all promoting commercial ventures:

     Plasmatics singer Wendy O has done her first solo album: VJ presents a brief interview shown on a TV monitor.

     Grace Jones, who made her screen debut in the new Conan film now playing in theaters, will have a new role in the next James Bond movie.

     Judas Priest concert dates.

     Commercial for the new Carpenters Album. The surviving brother talks about his dead sister Karen, who appears in brief excerpts singing their greatest hits.

12:25   *Stray Cats: "Stray Cats Strut." Comic narrative featuring the group performing in an alley, drawing female reactions from a real live puss, two groupies, and an old bitchy neighbor who throws things at them and then switches channels on her TV set but keeps getting their performance or an animated cartoon featuring other stray cats.

     *Elton John: "Sad Songs (Say So Much)." Narrative involving another street performance, but featuring a catalogue of listeners in a variety of contexts hearing those sad songs on radio, TV, stereo, etc., matched by multiple images of Elton performing in a variety of hats and styles.

12:30   MTV station ID

*Ratt: "Round and Round." Narrative that parodies the horror film, featuring an elegant formal dinner where two of the guests are played by Milton Berle. The dinner is disrupted by rock performers in the attic who transform one beautiful guest and the butler, not into vampires or werewolves, but punk groupies.

12:35 *Ultravox: "Vienna." Surreal visual images disguise narrative intrigue, as the lyrics keep telling us "this means nothing to me."

12:40 MTV promotion for appearance of Christine McVie.

Commercial for Mountain Dew soft drinks, with fast montage.

Commercial for Novabeam television, a large screen. "Once you see it, you'll never be able to watch a small screen again."

Commercial for Soft 'n Dri deodorant, featuring a narrative about a young black female newscaster making her TV debut.

MTV station ID

12:45 *Police: "Wrapped Around Your Finger." Performance disrupted by dreamlike visuals involving hundreds of long candles, constant camera movement with deep focus, cross dissolves, dynamic montage, and a flicker effect.

*Rick Springfield: "Don't Walk Away." Romantic narrative with dreamlike visuals that follow the singer to his apartment, where paintings provide settings for a series of inset narratives that tell the same story of a sad parting in a variety of scenes associated with different genres.

12:50 VJ Mark Goodman on screen to promote clips by Sam Hagar and Huey Lewis which will debut on MTV.

Commercial for Chrysler Laser XE—with fast montage.

Commercial for Fabergé body spray—with fast montage.

Commercial for "Electric Dreams," a new movie directed by the man who directed Michael Jackson's "Billy Jean" video (in some of the other commercials for this same movie we are told that it features music by the Culture Club and other MTV video stars).

Commercial for Scope mouthwash, with series of brief narratives.

MTV station ID—featuring brief excerpts from clips of some of the most famous video rock stars like Michael Jackson, Boy George, Billy Idol, etc.

12:55 *Van Halen: "Panama." Performance ruptured by fragmented visuals and brief scenes featuring bizarre or outrageous images, but which still tend to illustrate the lyrics.

1:00 MTV station ID, with voice over of VJ Mark Goodman announcing the clips that will be aired during the next half hour.

Whereas other TV stations usually have to pay for the programs which the commercials interrupt, MTV has no such overhead. No wonder their station ID's are so varied and spectacular; they are practically the only "programs" that MTV produces. This situation highlights the main business of every TV station—not to generate programs, but to deliver viewers (at the lowest cost per thousand) to advertisers who pay both for the commercials and for the time it takes to air them. The music industry is happy to provide the video clips as free programming for MTV because the air time for these thinly disguised commercials is also free. In this sweet business arrangement, as long as the viewers keep watching and buying, both station and advertiser not only profit, but get something for nothing.

All three components of rock video serve consumerist goals. The performance motivates the spectator specifically to buy a particular album on which the featured song is recorded. The name of the group, song, album, and record company appear at the beginning and end of every clip every time it is aired, implying that the spectator should be eager to note this information in order to facilitate the anticipated purchase,[6] More generally, the performance is also selling the performers, whose future commercial ventures (concerts, nightclub dates, and future recordings) the spectator will be expected to support. Both the narrative and dreamlike visuals motivate the spectator specifically to buy, not just the album, but the video itself. If the viewer has no playback equipment, then he or she is motivated to purchase a VCR in order to make the purchase or rental of the video more feasible. The narrative and the visuals also strengthen the viewer's motivation to consume all products affiliated with the performers (other albums, tickets for live performances, T-shirts and toys that display their name or image, soft drinks or other products that carry their endorsement). It is the narrative and dreamlike visuals, with their direct connection to private fantasy, that best define the unique features of rock video, distinguishing it from previous means of marketing pop music and supporting the infrastructure that insures the commercial success of the form.

At this point, it might be useful to examine some specific rock video clips to show the interaction among the three components.

Videos Dominated by Performance

Performance dominates both the sound and image of many video clips, but usually with the intervention of a subordinate narrative or a visual fragmentation that disrupts the temporal and/or spatial unity. In those instances where such disruption is absent or minimal, as in the Pretenders' "It's a Thin Line between Love and Hate," the video seems oldfashioned and tedious. This judgment is supported by the fact that some vintage songs have been released with historic footage of a live concert, granting a place on MTV to dead veterans like Jim Morrison, In such cases, the excitement is generated by the rarity of seeing the "living" record of a great performer who was ahead of his time but will be giving no more live concerts. But for live performers who want to be on the cutting edge, something else is needed.

In White Snake's "Slow 'n Easy," the sensuous, extravagant performance of the singers is periodically interrupted by inserts of a two-lane blacktop and by glimpses of a sexy blonde wearing pearls tightened around her throat. Presumably the "superstitious woman" mentioned in the lyrics, the blonde appears in scenes that take place off stage—as if she is the woman the singer has in mind while performing this song. Yet in some shots she is positioned as a spectator, as if the masochism of her response matches or is evoked by the aggression in the performance. We see a close-up of her throat that reveals the bruises made by the pearls, and a long shot of her sitting in her flashy car deciding whether to pick up the male singer (who stands next to a smashed vehicle on a deserted highway) and then speeding away leaving him stranded in the middle of the road. These suggestive shots and lyrics encourage the spectator to construct a sadomasochistic narrative in which either the man or the woman is bound to be the object of desire and revenge. The crosscutting between the narrative and the performance gradually accelerates in pace, as do the tempo of the music and the cutting rhythm with which the performance is fragmented into close-ups of fetishistic details, an acceleration that renders the song title ironic. Although this video clip is dominated by performance, the fast pace of the montage makes it anything but easy to recall the chain of visual images that accompany the music.

In many videos the performance itself serves as the main narrative event, whose spatial unity is broken by the disjunctive visuals—either through special effects as in "Mental Hopscotch" by the Missing Persons or by shifts in setting as in Nena's "99 Luftballoons." The lyrics in such video clips frequently comment reflexively on the cognitive process that the visual style demands of the spectator (mental hopscotch) or on the direct connection with dreams ("99 dreams I have had, everyone a red balloon"). In "The Heart of Rock 'n Roll" the performance of Huey Lewis and the News is fragmented spatially, as the settings for the singing shift from New York to LA, and to other stops on the tour, and from concert halls, to nightclubs, to the streets; and also temporally, as their performance is situated within the history of rock 'n roll. The inserts of Elvis Presley and other historical precursors that are intercut with present footage of Lewis and the News, are echoed in the contrasting dance styles of different eras as well as in the two historical TV formats of color and black-and-white, between which the visuals constantly alternate. In this video, the self-reflexive visuals narrativize the performance by positioning within it the history of pop music and of television.

Videos Dominated by Narrative

At its most extreme, narrative can dominate both words and images—making the latter illustrate the former and moving the song toward ballad and the visuals toward minifilm, as in the case of Tony Carey's "A Fine, Fine Day." Opening with gritty black-and-white images before shifting to color and relying heavily on flashbacks, this mini-gangster film is presented with low mimetic realism, except for the singing of the narrator (who tells the story of his father released from prison and rubbed out by gangsters all on one fine day) and by the incongruity, at a key dramatic moment, of having the Mafia boss mouth Carey's words—an effect which is comically deflating, to say the least.

Far more typical is the use of a thin narrative line, witty in tone, which provides the basic situation for an erotic fantasy on which the spectator can elaborate according to his/her sexual tastes. The holes in the plot are usually filled by the lush visuals—the exotic settings, costumes, hairstyles and make-up as well as the fast cutting and effects. The narrative line makes these visuals and their sequential arrangement easier to remember, for the order appears to make sense rather than being random. Instead of performing on stage, the singer plays a dramatic role within the story, which includes recitativo or a singing narration.

As a case in point, Van Stephenson presents an explicit masochistic fantasy which transforms a hair stylist into a "Modern Day Delilah." In a witty development of the conceit, the hair-styling equipment becomes elaborate sexual paraphernalia, the beautician herself a feline predator with leonine tresses, and Stephenson the willing Samson. Despite the extravagance of the visuals, they are still limited to illustrating the lyrics. Though it is possible to identify either with Samson or Delilah in this fantasy, it is clearly the male masochist who controls the clip. While watching this video, the spectator is more likely to savor the wit at an emotional distance, storing the images for reprocessing in private fantasies to come.

Eddy Grant's "Romancing the Stone" pits sound against image to design a narrative (the raw material for a romantic daydream) that can be read from multiple points of view. While Grant, a black reggae singer, dominates the sound with his performance, the visuals focus on a white female magazine photographer working on chic shots so that she can afford to fly back to her romance-starved, machete wielding, hip-swinging third world lover in vacation land. Each is a subject of the other's art and fantasies: from his humble shack, he sings to her about how much he misses her; in her urban studio his photograph is displayed like a trophy. He sends her a post card that carries, not only the refrain from his lyrics, but also his moving image carefully packaged and framed. Later it appears in her studio next to his photograph—a moving audiovisual reminder, like a video clip displayed on an Advent, of his talent and appeal and a strong incentive for her to buy a plane ticket as soon as possible (in fact, her paycheck is magically transformed into a ticket by means of a dissolve). Depending on whether one focuses on the music or the photography, The fantasy could be interpreted as a product either of the man or the woman, the black or the white, the colonized Third World which provides the raw talent and lush natural resources or the prosperous colonizer who develops and consumes them. Though at first we only hear him and see her, the visuals intercut between the white woman working in the city (coping with traffic and sexism) and the black man waiting in the tropics—a reversal of traditional sex roles, but a demystification of political-economic realities, particularly in the music industry (where black music is produced, packaged and sold by whiles) and in the movies (where "Romancing the Stone" is the title song of a film that uses the third world as a background for romantic adventures of whites, a typical ploy of Hollywood thrillers). While the surface romance may evoke a daring fantasy of miscegenation and sexual reversals, the underlying politics tell the same old story of commercial exploitation. In this mini-romance, the contrapuntal use of sound and image reveals an ideological subtext; yet by allowing more possibilities for spectator identification, it enhances rather than subverts the marketing strategy of selling reggae to American consumers.

Videos Dominated by Dreamlike Visuals

Those rock videos that are dominated by dreamlike visuals seem to make the richest use of the medium—a judgment widely held by reviewers writing for pop magazines devoted to the art (*Record, Cream, Video, Optical Music,* etc.). Some video clips like Duran Duran's "Reflex," Peter Gabriel's "Shock the Monkey," and Depeche Mode's "Everything Counts" create effects that evoke works by some of the most advanced independent film-makers, such as the rich multilayered imagery of Pat O'Neill. Such connections could presumably cultivate a more receptive audience for independent films, but it's also possible for those avant-garde conventions (that extend backward to Surrealism and Dada) to become co-opted.

The video clips that I find most revealing are those that comment self-reflexively on how rock video works, particularly in its relation to the spectator's private fantasies and dreams. Though we have already noted this tendency in performance-dominated videos like "Mental Hopscotch," "99 Luftballoons" and "The Heart of Rock 'n Roll" and in the narrative-centered "Romancing the Stone," it tends to be developed more fully in clips dominated by visuals and in those that make a balanced use of all three components.

One scene from Duran Duran's "Reflex" is particularly emblematic. We watch an audience watching a movie screen on which appears a giant wave. When it crashes, it breaks free from the screen and invades the audience's space, completely engulfing the spectators. This tidal wave, an archetype from nightmares and anxiety dreams, evokes rock video, whose images carried by the air waves break out of the television set to penetrate the private space of our consciousness and lives.

The process of internalizing media images from movies and television and combining them with private memories to generate new fantasies and dreams is dramatized in Cyndi Lauper's "Time after Time"—a process that is facilitated by repeated exposure, as the song title implies. The clip opens with Cyndi watching a Bette Davis movie on television while her lover sleeps beside her. Certain images from this woman's picture evoke personal associations from the singer's past, which are recombined to form a romantic fantasy that sharply contrasts in visual style and tone with the banal setting of the framing situation.

This same process—involving movies, fantasies and dreams, all mediated through video—is elaborated in Roger Waters's "5:01 AM, The Pros and Cons of Hitchhiking." Opening with movie images from *Shane,* the clip then turns to shots of a woman cruising in a convertible, picking up a handsome blonde hitchhiker. The lyrics reveals that she is an Encino housewife pursuing a romantic fantasy—one that was repressed in *Shane* (where the pioneer housewife never acted on her sexual attraction to the roving gunfighter played by blond Alan Ladd) but liberated in *The Wild One* (a film that is evoked in the clip, not through authentic footage, but through reprocessed lookalike images and whose rolling stone hero, clad in black leather, is associated with Jack Palance, the gunfighter villain whom we see blown away in one of the excerpts from *Shane*). Again, as in "Romancing the Stone," we are presented with a dual point of view—the male singer telling the story and the Encino housewife whose fantasies seem to control the visuals. Yet as the clip progresses, other dreamlike visuals disrupt the narrative—particularly images of a man flying across a cloudy sky. The dual perspective is revealed in the ending when we see a man and a woman asleep in bed, where they have both been reprocessing media images in their respective dreams.

Omnipresence of the Spectator

This self-reflexive attention to the viewing process foregrounds another characteristic of television that is exaggerated on MTV—the omnipresence of the spectator. One video clip that plays with this dimension is "Tell Her About It," where performer Billy Joel is introduced by Ed Sullivan (really an impersonator) for his historic TV debut on "The Toast of the Town" while Rodney Dangerfield (the real comedian in a guest appearance) waits in the wings. The spectator is depicted not only through the live audience in the theater where Joel is singing, but also through diverse TV viewers who watch (or don't watch) his performance in a variety of period contexts, which provide settings for mininarratives eventually involving Joel, whose live presence (like Duran Duran's tidal wave) invades their life space: a neighborhood bar, a family room, a sorority house, a TV studio, and even a Soviet spaceship. In contrast to "The Heart of Rock 'n Roll," here it is the TV spectator rather than the performer whose living continuity with the historic past is dramatized.

Through constant reminders that, at any moment of broadcasting, someone is watching, in television, unlike cinema, the spectator is made to seem omnipresent.[7] This sense is particularly strong in live television, where the omnipresence of the spectator is highlighted as a distinguishing feature of primary value. Live television departs from the basic film-making model (film crew and actors shooting on a closed set) by frequently granting a place for the spectator in the studio or on camera, as we see in game shows and comedy-variety programs like "The Johnny Carson Show" and "Saturday Night Live." The "live" component survives even in the reruns where we viewers are made to feel that we belong to a live audience responding to living legends like John Belushi. As with the historical footage of live concerts on MTV, "live" is redefined; no longer restricted to the recording or transmission, it becomes associated with whatever occupies the present consciousness of the spectator. It's as if by watching television, the spectator gains the divine power of granting life to whoever or whatever appears on screen. The viewer can extend the TV life of Phil Donahue and Joan Collins or kill them off in a season. Of course, it's really the networks and advertisers that decide what's on the screen, but the audience is constantly told that it is their viewing (and buying) habits that control those decisions.

This feeling of the spectator's omnipresence is cultivated even on shows that are taped or filmed. Canned laughter is used on situation comedy series, and viewers are directly addressed in the second person in commercials, on news and sports shows, on children's programs like "Sesame Street" and "Nickelodeon," and by virtually all video jockeys on MTV.

Instead of stressing the changeovers from one VJ to another, which would accentuate them as TV personalities and create the effect of separate programs (as occurs on some music radio stations), MTV makes the transitions subtle. The name of the next VJ is announced along with the upcoming performers and news for the next half hour segment. Sometimes the new VJ is first heard in a voice-over at the end of a station ID before being seen on screen. Other times both VJ's chat together on camera at the end of the connecting station break. Despite the diversity in their age, sex, personality and style, it's as if the main function of these VJ's, who also double as newscasters, is to maintain a continuous live presence that creates the illusion of an on-going dialogue with the audience. On MTV the omnipresence of the VJ helps to strengthen the omnipresence of the spectator.

When an audience is seen, heard or addressed on screen, it signifies for the individual spectator both the object of identification and the Other with whom he or she is temporarily bonded. The TV spectator has a dual role: first, as an individual viewer/listener absorbing images and sounds into one's own consciousness and memory, usually in the privacy of one's own home or bed; and second, as a member of a mass audience or community (McLuhan's "global village") who share common associations, desires and ideological assumptions. In unifying private and public identities, this dual role facilitates the integrated functioning of two complementary actions—both of which are well illustrated in the specific video clips already discussed: (1) the internalizing of TV images into one's own fantasy life, incorporating them into a private reservoir of dream images; (2) the positioning of the spectator in the public marketplace where one becomes an active consumer purchasing products one has been trained by television to desire, thereby contributing to the capitalist economy. Because of advertising's control over television, the private action is made to serve the public goal of internalizing consumerist desires. Nowhere is this co-option more apparent than on MTV.

Presence/Absence of the TV Receiver

Since the TV spectator appears omnipresent, it is the presence or absence of the TV set, the basic receiving apparatus, that is all important. As a receiver, the TV set functions for the spectator in a dual capacity: both as an object of desire and as an object of identification. If you don't have one, you are left out of the community. If you don't have one, your dreams, fantasies and life will be impoverished. If you don't have one, you won't recognize the names and faces of culture heroes that populate mass-circulation magazines like *People* and *Star* and that pop up in conversations. In order to enter the mass culture and its marketing system, you must invest in this basic equipment that promises, not merely temporary admittance to another world, but a dramatic change in you and your world forever. Like buying a Barbie doll, the purchase of a TV set begets other purchases. Once you own and become the basic receiver, you are trained to desire everything it has to offer—as big a screen as possible, color as well as black-and-white, a stereo hook-up, remote control, all of the commercial, PBS and cable stations available, a VCR, and eventually 3-D, high definition and digital television. As in the automotive industry, obsolescence and rapid technological improvement are made to seem inevitable.

Once you possess a TV set, you have unlimited access to the images and sounds it receives. Yet the programming structure with its varied repetitions is designed to create a withholding or suspension that increases your viewing time by intensifying desire. You find yourself waiting for your favorite clip on MTV, waiting for a particular movie to appear on cable or commercial stations, waiting for the particular guest you want to see on the Johnny Carson show, waiting for the sports or weather or whatever news feature will reveal the information you seek, waiting for an instant replay of a dramatic moment in sports, waiting for the reruns of a show that you missed, waiting for the next episode in the soap or miniseries you're faithfully following, waiting for the cable station to reach your neighborhood, or even waiting for your favorite commercial ("Where's the beef?") to explicitly articulate the mechanism of withholding.

When the spectator is not watching television, then he or she, whether out in the world or at home, is still affected by the TV images already internalized. That's when the *fort/da* game really pays off for the sponsoring institution. In the public marketplace, the spectator becomes a consumer looking for the beef—following the cues of point-of-purchase advertising to find and buy the videos, records, T-shirts, soft drinks, and toys promoted on television. In private, the spectator becomes a daydreamer, driving on the freeway listening to songs on the radio or seeing billboards that trigger associations with TV images already programmed into the brain; or by night, a dreamer, reprocessing those TV images into visions of the future. In order to understand the impact that television can have on dreams, it's necessary to know more about the process of dreaming.

Speculations on the Dream Connection

The most compelling dream models that have emerged from recent neurophysiological and psychological studies suggest that dreams are an evolutionary medium that mediates between biological programming and cultural imprinting. More specifically, the Hobson-McCarley Activation-Synthesis model assumes that the rapid firing of giant cells in the primitive brainstem activates the dream by generating signals within the brain; the rhythm, frequency and duration of the dream are biologically determined.[8] The forebrain then selects images from the memory to "fit" the internally generated random signals; this synthetic process (about which little is known) is probably a function of the right-brain hemisphere (that takes a synthetic or gestalt approach rather than an analytic one to problem solving) and also the site for the psychological level of the dream.[9] The images selected from the memory and recombined in new ways carry the cultural imprinting.

This model has significant implications for the study of television and movies since these two mass media play a key role in the imprinting process, supplementing the dreamer's ordinary experience with thousands of prefabricated moving visual images that are directly absorbed into the cultural dreampool and influencing both the form and content of dream texts. Since these two media have appeared fairly recently in the history of western civilization and since certain nations with advanced technology and imperialist tendencies (most predominantly the USA) have specialized in producing texts that could be exported (even via satellite) to other parts of the world, movies and television have the potential to render dreams more similar all over the planet, a tendency that could have far-reaching political and evolutionary implications. (This issue is brilliantly explored on film by Nicholas Roeg in *The Man Who Fell to Earth* and in literature by Manuel Puig in *Betrayed by Rita Hayworth* and *Kiss of Spider Woman,* which is now being made into a movie.)

The strong impact of the media on dreams is based partly on the phenomenological similarities between dreaming and the viewing of the movies and television: the visual primacy of these experiences; their spatial and temporal discontinuity; the double identity of the spectator as passive voyeur and active participant; the physical comfort and partial immobility of the spectator; the abrupt shift to a different physical and psychic state and to the forgetting of most of the images when the lights go on, the tube goes off, or one awakens from the dream; the two-way process of adaptation, involving the use of dreams as a creative source for artists generating movies and videos and the incorporation of media images into the dreams of viewers; the regressive nature of these fictions which arouse pleasure by fulfilling repressed infantile wishes and needs; the guilty feelings evoked by excessive indulgence in these idle pastimes that substitute for constructive work; and the combination of private and communal roles in these experiences which pass for personal pleasures while serving deeper cultural, ideological or evolutionary goals.

While considerable work has been done on dream and film,[10] very little has been written on dream and television.[11] Yet this relationship is particularly important since dreamers start watching the tube from infancy and since television contributes more images to the cultural dreampool than any other medium. While I am in no way denying the important and unique connections between film and dream, I am interested here in exploring the unique similarities between dream and television.

What is particularly fascinating to me and central to my argument is that the main similarities between dream and television which are *not* shared by film are precisely the same characteristics that are exaggerated on MTV: unlimited access, structural discontinuity, decentering, structural reliance on memory retrieval, live transmission and the omnipresence of the spectator. Most of these characteristics have been widely written about by television historians and theorists; what I am interested in briefly suggesting here is their connection with MTV and dreams.

Unlimited Access

While the frequency and length of dreams are biologically determined (a REM period occurs around every 90 minutes and lasts about 20 minutes, making the daily average dreamtime approximately 90 minutes), one can increase the amount of time spent dreaming on any given night by extending the hours of sleep or by taking catnaps throughout the day. The amount of time that can be spent daydreaming is, of course, unlimited.

A similar unlimited access is offered, not by cinema, but by "The tube of plenty," forcing the individual spectator to monitor his or her own time devoted to TV viewing. This temptation is dramatized by the 24-hour availability of rock videos on MTV—a feature that is prominently emphasized in all of the promotional spots for the station.

Structural Discontinuity

All TV viewing is marked by a structural discontinuity caused by frequent interruptions by commercials, station breaks and channel switching. These frequent ruptures are exaggerated on MTV where there is no long program to interrupt, merely a chain of brief segment, all featuring spatial and temporal discontinuity.

Such structural discontinuity evokes a comparison with dreams, which are similarly marked by abrupt scene shifts which Allan Hobson has linked to the bursts of rapid eye movements (REM's) and firings of brain cells that trigger and accompany dreams.

> The rapid eye movements themselves appeared to be generated by the activity of a group of giant cells in the pontine brain stem whose bursting discharge preceded the eye movements during REM sleep. Thus the possibility was raised that specific visual information might actually be generated within the brain. The giant cells not only may drive the eye movements but also may send information into the visual relay nucleus and cortex about the direction and speed of the eye movements. Since this information is highly non-ordered with respect to the external visual world, *scene shifts and dramatic changes in visual dream content might possibly be a function of the generating system* [ital. mine] rather than a censor's attempt to disguise the ideational meaning of 'dream thoughts.'[12]

Both Hobson and Vlada Petrić have compared this structural discontinuity of dreams to cinema: Hobson has charted structural analogies between film devices and dream processes,[13] and Petrić has prescribed the four "most effective cinematic techniques which can enhance the oneiric impact of a film and stimulate the neural activities similar to those occurring during dreaming": "camera movement through space (especially when combined with deep focus"; illogical and paradoxical combinations of objects, characters and settings (while . . . preserving the vivid representation of the photographed world"; "dynamic montage (with concentration on the close-up and subliminal condensation of brief shots"; and "dissolution of spatial and temporal continuity (especially by using 'jump-cuts')."[14] While these techniques can be used to single out certain film styles and auteurs for high praise, they are commonplace in music videos.

Decentering

The structural discontinuity of television creates a constant flow or decentered super-text. Viewers tend to watch television rather than specific programs. This decentering process is carried to an extreme on MTV, where the short commercial is the featured attraction. Though commercially determined, the sequencing of clips has a quality of randomness for the viewer; one sees whatever videos happen to appear on screen while one is watching.

One finds a similar decentering in dreaming, where all dreams on a single night tend to share the same themes, where the dreamer usually remembers specific images of scenes but no clear boundaries around individual dream texts, and where one never knows in advance which dreams or images will appear on the mindscreen. Individual texts of dream and television rarely receive the same degree of artistic status that is ordinarily attributed to film texts—a difference that is more a matter of structural presentation than of artistic merit.

One does not normally find decentering in film. It must be designed as a conscious artistic strategy as in the films of Godard, Makavejev and Alea, usually with the conscious political goal of breaking Hollywood's codes of representation to reveal and oppose the bourgeois ideology they carry. While bourgeois consumerism is also exposed in the decentering processes of television, it is not undermined, but, on the contrary, promoted.

Structural Reliance on Memory Retrieval

The Hobson-McCarley activation-synthesis model posits that while dreaming, the forebrains selects sense images from memory to fit signals about eye movement that are internally generated by the dreamer's own brain and attempts unsuccessfully to render "the series of shots as a continuous narrative."[15] In elaborating on this model, Hobson frequently uses an analogy with film which sometimes becomes strained:

> During walking, the brain is 'taking pictures': images are accepted at a rate of about 10–20 per second. Owing to the operation of the afferent image-efferent signal comparator process and visual blanking, we perceive the visual world as continuous and the visual field remains constant in space. *Our brains shoot, develop, and edit instantaneously* [ital. mine]. The individual images or the fused image (we know not which) are stored in memory (by unknown mechanisms). They can be called up with difficulty and are weakly perceptible in waking fantasy, but are more easily accessible and vividly perceptible in dreams.[16]

In cinema it is impossible "to shoot, develop, and edit instantaneously," but these mental processes are ordinary practice in live video, which suggests that television might provide a better model than cinema for how the human brain processes images during waking hours.

Earlier I argued that one of the most powerful aspects of music video is its programming of viewers to retrieve specific visual images from memory every time they hear a particular song. Although the triggering sounds of the song usually come from external sources like radio or television (unlike the internally generated signals in dreams), the music video fan has been taught to identify with the external receiving apparatus, so some degree of internalization occurs. This process of retrieving the prefabricated video images from memory may help train viewers to retrieve them more readily during REM sleep. In other words, the structural reliance on memory retrieval shared by MTV and dreams may give these music video images a privileged position within the cultural dreampool. The fact that so many rock video artists cultivate the explicit connection with dreams in their song titles and lyrics, in the visual style and images of their video clips, in their narrative themes and situations, and even in the names of some of the groups (like R.E.M., or the Revolving Paint Dream) suggests that they are seeking this position of power.

Live Transmission and the Omnipresent Spectator

As the most solipsistic of forms, the dream takes place inside the spectator, who is by necessity omnipresent. In the live transmission of dreams, the protean dreamer functions, not only as spectator, but also as writer, director, star, supporting players, location, and technical apparatus.

We have already seen how the television viewer is made to feel omnipresent, particularly through conventions associated with live transmission. It is this very quality that fosters the kind of delusional experiences depicted in Martin Scorsese's film *King of Comedy*[17] and in Hubert Selby's novel *Requiem for a Dream* in which isolated viewers lose the boundaries between television images and their private fantasy projections, In a sense these characters cannibalize the world of television, transforming it into a solipsistic medium like dream.

Unlike movies and dreams which suspend one's normal waking experience by functioning as an alternate reality, television and radio, because they are not totally absorbing, only supplement one's ordinary life. TV viewers frequently do something else while watching. If that other activity happens to be daydreaming, a behavior stimulated by many programs and virtually all commercials, then it is easy for the two imaginary realms to be fused.

MTV tries to capture the best of both worlds. Like radio and ordinary television, it can provide a continuous sound track for partying, dancing, sex, or whatever you happen to be doing and brighten up a room with a flashy visual that can be glanced at whenever you get bored . Yet because of the visual intensity of most video clips, it also strives for the all-absorbing attention a spectator normally devotes to films and dreams. It's the omnipresent spectator, constantly addressed in the second person by the MTV VJ's, who decides which mode of viewing to adopt; but the very presence of both options makes it possible to watch the station for longer stretches at a time.

While exercising its powers of manipulation, MTV makes the spectator feel potent and decisive: he or she is the one who chooses which records, videos and products to buy; who picks which styles and behaviors to imitate; who hums the tunes; who memorizes the visuals; who decides when to look and when to listen; who switches the station on or off. Like all television, it trains the spectator to focus on one's personal powers of choice and reception while ignoring the remote sources of transmission—the true Remote Control—whose ideological determinants and manipulative strategies remain mystified.

In this examination of MTV as a model for commercial television, I have focused on the medium's relationship both to ideology and to dream. The observations concerning ideology, for the most part, echo or lend support to arguments of others who have been writing on television. But the speculations on the connection with dreams open new paths that warrant further investigation. Perhaps most essential is the interaction between these two registers—the role of dream in internalizing and reprocessing the ideology transmitted through television, a process that is blatantly dramatized in music video on MTV. In the last sixty years we have witnessed how advertising has colonized the public airwaves, first on radio and then on television. Now, through the medium of music video, commercial interests may be extending their sway over the evolutionary medium of dreams.

NOTES

1. *Record* (July 1984), p. 41.

2. See, for example, "Rock Makers," *Video* (July 1984) by Noë Goldwasser, who writes: "The excitement in pop-music video is being generated by a handful of talented filmmakers working in the video-clip medium. People like Russell Mulcahy, Bob Giraldi, Tim Newman, and Tim Pope crank out clips by the hundreds and send them on their infectious way to MTV, *Night Tracks* and the like. This community of directors amounts to a video new wave which is forging the aesthetic basis of music video in much the same way as the French new wave in film—Godard, Resnais, Truffaut—changed our way of looking at movies 20 years ago. . . . "No one better personifies the music video *auteur* than Tim Pope. . . . He could be called the Jean-Luc Godard of the video age because of his frenetic pace and constantly flowing fountain-head of new visual images. . . . The skinny 28-year old averages about two videos a week in his London studio, and is constantly turning down American groups who come over and throw money at him to make them stars on MTV Stateside." (pp. 81–82)

3. Such causes include the fact that television superseded the audio medium of radio, the neglect of sound and its potentialities both by film-makers and film theorists, and the dominance of vision over all other senses in dreams.

4. One of the few precursors of the new relationship between music and image is the "Memo from T" sequence performed by Mick Jagger in Cammell and Roeg's *Performance* (1970), a visionary rock film that was far ahead of its time.

5. Nick Browne, "The Political Economy of the Television (Super) Text," *Quarterly Review of Film Studies,* 9, 3 (Summer 1984).

6. Unlike credits that appear at the end of a film, these data do not inform the viewer whom to credit for the artistic achievement (for example, the name of the director never appears on the rock video clip); the information is provided solely to increase the likelihood of the sale.

7. Of course, there is also a place for the spectator in cinema, as current work on suture, spectators-in-the-text, and self-reflexiveness have shown; one can even find instances of direct address throughout the history of film. Yet these cinematic practices are not so direct as the on-screen presence of TV studio audiences nor as ubiquitous as the use of direct address on television.

8. J. A. Hobson and R. W. McCarley, "The brain as a dream state generator: An Activation-synthesis hypothesis of the dream process." *American Journal of Psychiatry,* 134 (1977), 1335–1348. Hobson has also presented this model in relation to film studies in "Film and the Physiology of Dreaming Sleep: the Brain as Camera-Projector." *Dreamworks,* I, 1 (Spring 1980), 9–25; and in his reply to Raymond Durgnat's "The Hunting of the Dream Snark", *Dreamworks,* II, 1 (Fall 1981), 83–86; and in "Dream Image and Substrate: Bergman's Films and the Psychology of Sleep," in *Film and Dreams: An Approach to Bergman*, ed. by Vlada Petrić (South Salem, N.Y.: Redgrave Publishing Co., 1981), 75–95.

9. An excellent survey of the issue of involvement of the right brain hemisphere is provided by Bruce Kawin in "Right-Hemisphere Processing in Dreams and Films," *Dreamworks,* II, I (Fall 1981), 13–17.

10. In the psychoanalytic context, the relationship between film and dream has received considerable attention in the line of discourse derived from Lacan and Metz, most prominently in *The Imaginary Signifier*. Still within the psychoanalytic context, but deviating from Metz on important issues are Robert Eberwein's *Film and the Dream Screen* (Princeton Univ. Press, 1984) and Gay Lynn Studlar's *Visual pleasure and the Masochistic Aesthetic: The Von Sternberg/Dietrich Paramount Cycle,* Unpub. dissertation, USC, 1984 (a selection from which will appear in Volume II of *Movies and Methods,* ed. by Bill Nichols, U. of Calif. Press). Vlada Petrić's *Film and Dreams: An Approach to Bergman* is a collection of essays, some of which (including Petrić's work and mine) draw on the neurobiological models. This perspective is also represented in several essays (including ones by Petrić, Hobson, Durgnat, Kawin and me) appearing in *Dreamworks,* an interdisciplinary quarterly on the relation between dream and the arts.

11. The two key works on this topic are Peter H. Wood's "Television as Dream" in *Television: The Critical View,* ed. by Horace Newcomb (New York: Oxford University Press, 1979), 517–535, and "Reality and Television: an Interview with Dr. Edmund Carpenter," *Television Quarterly,* X, 1 (Fall 1972), 42–46. Works that have attempted a three-way comparison usually focus on cinema at the expense of television, arguing that the comparison between film and dream is more interesting (see Raymond Durgnat, "The Hunting of the Dream-Snark," *Dreamworks,* II, I, Fall 1981, 76–82) or more fruitful in generating formal similarities (see Vlada Petrić's "A Theoretical-Historical Survey: Film and Dreams," in *Film and Dreams,* pp. 1–48.)

12. Hobson, "Film and the Physiology of Dreaming Sleep," p. 14.

13. Ibid., 23.

14. Petrić, "A Theoretical-Historical Survey," p. 23.

15. Hobson, ibid., p. 24.

16. Ibid., 23–24.

17. For an excellent analysis of what this film reveals about television, see Beverle Houston's "*king of Comedy*: A Crisis of Substitution," *Framework,* 24 (Spring 1984), 74–92.

DECODING THE TEXT

1. How does the author show that music videos are similar to television shows and films? What kinds of support are used? What support would be used today to make this same argument?

2. Explain the connection of videos to dreams, as claimed by the author.

3. According to the author, what is the connection of videos to advertising?

CONNECTING TO YOUR CULTURE

1. Have you ever disliked a song until you saw the video? How did the video change your opinion?

2. Has it ever happened the opposite way. You liked a song until you saw its video?

3. How often do you look at music videos on television? On your computer? On your phone? Shared through Facebook?

4. Have you ever bought anything (such as an mp3, an outfit, or something else) because of a music video?

CONSIDERING IDEAS

1. Do you think that there should be age restrictions placed on young adults who listen to music? Why or why not?

2. Have you ever been a part of a protest group? What were you protesting? How did you protest?

AUTHOR BIO

Maria Fontenot is professor of mass communications at Texas Tech University; her present work revolves around communication in times of public crisis, such as Hurricane Katrina and the Virginia Tech campus shootings.

Chad Harriss is associate professor of media studies at Alfred University, New York. His research focuses on the procedural drama in pop culture. This essay first appeared in the anthology Media, Culture, and Society in 2010.

DWAYNE NEWTON/PHOTOEDIT

BUILDING A BETTER PIG

A Historical Survey of the PMRC and its Tactics

Maria Fontenot and Chad Harriss

PROLOGUE TO A PARENTAL PIG

In late 1984, Mary Elizabeth 'Tipper' Gore purchased a copy of the soundtrack to Prince's film *Purple Rain* for her oldest daughter, Karenna. As the album played on the family stereo, Gore began to hear things she considered offensive and inappropriate for children. Some of the songs contained graphic descriptions of sexual activities (Nuzum, 2001: 13). For example, the song 'Darling Nikki' opens with the following lines, 'I knew a girl named Nikki. I guess you could say she was a sex fiend. I met her in a hotel lobby masturbating with a magazine' (Prince, 1984: track 5). Content like this enraged Gore to the point that she decided to form a group whose primary purpose was to scrutinize the popular music children listened to and the music videos they watched on television. In April 1985, Gore, wife of then-Senator Albert Gore Jr., a Tennessee Democrat; and Susan Baker, wife of President Ronald Reagan's Treasury Secretary James Baker; and eight other wives of influential Washington politicians from both sides of the aisle decided to do something about these perceived excesses in popular music—hence, the birth of the PMRC (Parents Music Resource Center) (Nuzum, 2001: 14).

By crossing the political aisle, it could be argued that the goals of this organization composed of Washington insiders represented a step to the left for Republicans and a step to the right for Democrats, or at least for those husbands whose wives were involved in this movement. What we mean is that from a conservative perspective this movement carries the threat of an increase in the role, reach, and power of federal government both socially and industrially. However, by asking for voluntary adherence to their suggestions the PMRC was able to avoid making this threat in an overt way, but the implications of resisting compromise were unquestionably there since, as Claude Chastagner (1999) notes, the Recording Industry Association of America (RIAA) had been working at that time to convince Congress to pass a bill (HR 2911 and S 1711, The Audio Home Recording Tax) that would tax blank audiotapes. In short, the industry recognized that a failure to compromise with this group could have consequences that reached beyond this issue (Chastagner, 1999: 7–8).

A BRIEF HISTORY OF PIGS AND THE MEDIA

'Public interest' has a lengthy history in media studies. The incorporation of this phrase into the Radio Act of 1927 and the ensuing decades of definition and redefinition have historically differentiated the First Amendment protections for electronic media as compared to its print counterparts. The appearance of public interest groups (PIGs) provided scholars with clear cultural locales for the various sides of these debates. This article details one such instance by discussing the ways that past regulation, current social concerns and future economic desires collided at the right time, the right place and with the right people. This collision resulted in a mark that we can still see today, but did it really change anything?

In 1984, the PMRC formed to address 'indecency' in popular music. The debate was nothing new, but the organization of 'parents' into a political lobbying group does represent a substantial change in the landscape of this debate. Before progressing into a more detailed analysis of the PMRC's organization and efforts, it seems beneficial to set the stage for this discussion by providing a brief history of broadcast regulation. It may seem illogical to turn to broadcast regulation when the music industry in and of itself is not a broadcast entity, but by recognizing that this industry is ancillary to broadcast and now satellite radio the link becomes more clear-cut. More importantly, early broadcast regulation introduced the concept of public interest into public debates involving media regulation. This introduction arguably provided the foundation for the development of PIGs (an unfortunate or apt acronym depending on the critic's perspective), like the PMRC.

With this in mind, it seems logical to begin these discussions with the basic components and a brief history of the Radio Act of 1927. This Act established the Federal Radio Commission (FRC), which later became the Federal Communication Commission (FCC) (Communications Act of 1934). The purpose of this federal body was to regulate and oversee the operations of radio and later all electronic media. This level of oversight undeniably led to an abridgement of the First Amendment of the United States Constitution. The government argued that this abridgement was necessary for three reasons: public interest, convenience and necessity (Communications Act of 1934).

In 1998, an Advisory Committee on Public Interest met to discuss the impending challenges to this model with the coming of digital television. While tracing the history of broadcast regulation this committee cited scholars Louis Caldwell and William Rowland, and acknowledged that the three reasons listed above were never clearly defined (Advisory Committee on Public Interest Obligations of Digital Broadcasters, 1998). Having said this, the necessity component of this model seems, from the outset, to be the most clearly defined. The committee notes that this component involved the limitations of the electromagnetic spectrum through which broadcast messages are transmitted. Interference occurs when multiple broadcasters attempt to occupy the same space within the spectrum and therefore some form of regulation was necessary in order for any signal to be successfully received. Despite this agreed upon necessity, these powers were later expanded to include cable and satellite media, which do not exhibit this problem to the same degree. Mark Fowler, Ronald Reagan's FCC chairperson, began arguing in the 1980s that spectrum scarcity, and with it the necessity component of this piece of legislation, was no longer a reason to regulate electronic media (Hilmes, 2007: 247–50). Convenience seems simply to refer to the simplification of empowering a known governmental body to make decisions as happens with other 'public utilities'. For the purposes of this article, the borrowing of the fluid phrase 'public interest' as a reason to regulate mass media is the most important component because it has been the most debated and redefined.

In her book *Only Connect* (2007), Hilmes thoroughly discusses the various ways that the FRC defined public interest. Much of her discussion of regulatory history illustrates that the FRC, and later the FCC, often worked in tandem with these media industries to draft the policies and regulations that govern them. The 1998 Advisory Committee stated that the two purposes of broadcast regulation were 'to foster the commercial development of the industry and to ensure that broadcasting serves the educational and informational needs of Americans' (Advisory Committee on Public Interest Obligations of Digital Broadcasters, 1998). The earliest definitions pointed toward public interest as a measure of popularity, or what the public is interested in attending to. In this era, this definition would seem to favor RCA/NBC because of the network-based structure of radio. Networks were able to provide access to more popular talent and more refined programs to larger, mass audiences. However, as Hilmes notes, audience surveys conducted by local newspapers and magazines showed that a measurable number of listeners preferred low-brow, independent content, like Dr John Brinkley's medicine shows that promoted implanting goat glands to treat impotency (Hilmes, 2007: 11–14). After this became apparent, the public-interest-as-popularity definition was summarily discarded and replaced with a definition that more directly favored wealthy corporations. The new definition was based on the investments made by these entities. This definition focused on technological superiority and had an overtly political purpose since the FRC was in the process of trying to reassign radio frequencies to its preferred corporate partners, like RCA/NBC. By basing the definition of public interest on capital investments and technological acquisitions, the wealthiest broadcasters had a distinct advantage and independent broadcasters could be forced on to less reliable and clear frequency allocations. However, even this definition did not force broadcasters like Dr Brinkley off the air. His popularity had earned him substantial profits and he could afford to keep up with the networks' investments. These definitional failures led to a third definition and again shifted the meaning of the phrase.

This time a new definition based on the level of propaganda was created and this opened regulatory doors by allowing the FRC to consider and regulate content by determining whether the content of mediated messages served the larger public good. Public good meant ridding the airwaves of what was considered propaganda, like Dr Brinkley. Ironically, the advertising-based system fostered by the commercial giants did not fit this definition of propaganda. Instead, propaganda was defined as private, selfish interests, like those of trade unions or religious zealots. In short, Hilmes recognizes that the phrase public interest has been defined in various ways over time and that the definition of this phrase is often molded to meet the desired outcome; the way the phrase is defined can be identified as a cultural marker that establishes what elements of society occupy preferred political and cultural positions at a given moment in time (Hilmes, 2007: 63–4). In other words, the definition of public interest has been fluid, mutable and ideologically driven across the regulatory history of the media and the PMRC's attachment to this term is no different. The ways that this group molded our understandings of this phrase to suit their specific ideological ends is identifiable and provides a lens allowing us to understand the culture of the time. Now, it seems prudent to look at the history of PIGs.

PIGs AND POLICY

Of course, any survey with overt historical purposes begins and ends at an arbitrary point and the history of PIGs is no different. As discussed above, the FRC's business was conducted almost exclusively between politicians, or at least political appointees, and members of the broadcast industry. Interest groups were effectively excluded from these early regulatory conversations. It was not until 1966 that the United Church of Christ (UCC) challenged the FCC for the right to present its viewpoints. The UCC is arguably the first media reform PIG to experience any form of success. Once the FCC was forced to open its process to the citizenry at large, the number of interest groups proliferated. Since the 1960s, the number of public interest groups has increased significantly (Cigler and Loomis, 2002: 2). In the 1960s, groups increasingly directed their attention to Washington, DC. Since then, groups seeking influence learned to 'hunt where the ducks are' (Cigler and Loomis, 2002: 10). With this growing number of groups came the rise in single-issue groups, such as the PMRC. But what exactly is a PIG?

Jeffrey Berry (1978) argues, from a political science perspective, that PIGs arise in order to represent their members before government because organized voices are more likely to be heard than individual or unorganized voices. Berry proceeds to analyze two of the early theories that attempt to explain the motivations behind PIG formation. He cites David Truman's idea that PIGs form in response to complex social and cultural disturbances ultimately evolving from *public* interest groups into *political* interest groups. Due to its composition, the PMRC always possessed elements of both since it was a PIG formed primarily by people directly connected to insider politics. Berry contrasts this theory with Robert Salisbury's notions that these groups form in response to organizational failures, where individuals develop relationships in order to forward a common goal that ultimately results in some personal benefit whether that benefit is direct and tangible or indirect and intangible. With respect to benefit, the PMRC is most certainly indicative of the latter, since there is no apparent financial benefit or desire for such benefit for the members of this group. Both theorists that Berry discusses root the formation of PIGs in some identifiable cultural, social, political or economic catalyst and the PMRC does exhibit traits that tie it to both scholars' definitions (Berry, 1978: 380–4). In short, the PMRC did arise in response to an identifiable cultural catalyst and the group exhibits characteristics of a group with overtly political motives. Chastagner refers to the specific cultural catalyst when he writes: 'Its [the PMRC's] purpose was to show the causal link between rock music and social problems such as the increase in rape, teenage suicide or teen pregnancies' (1999: 181). It has often seemed convenient for social activists and scientists to tie societal ills to media offerings, but rarely have any regulatory efforts withstood strict constitutional scrutiny. Because of this, it is preferable to convince an industry to self-regulate, which is precisely what the PMRC attempted to do.

Similar to the political science perspective, economists tend to define interest groups according to objective interests imputed by the researcher. Ken Kollman (1998: 14) uses the term 'interest group' to include any non-party organization that regularly tries to influence government policy. Kollman goes on to define a public interest group as an organization that hunts for a collective good. Of course, any hunt for a collective 'good' is ideologically loaded. This is illustrated by Chastagner's definition of collective identity, which he says is: 'A fictitious, homogeneous community made up of "average people"' (1999: 180). In other words, these groups operate as negotiators within larger cultural discourses that help us understand, as a culture, what *normal* is. Sometimes they work to challenge the dominant views in a culture (e.g. NAACP), but at other times they work to reinforce the dominant positions (e.g. PMRC). Moreover, the notion of the collective good also points to an oversight in the definitions provided by these economists and political scientists. These scholars tend to focus on the group formation aspect of the PIGs while assuming that the definition of the phrase 'public interest' is common sense and static. However, as Hilmes illustrates above this is anything but the case.

PUTTING LIPSTICK ON A PIG

PIGs such as the PMRC, employ many tactics. While those tactics can be generalized easily, the efficacy of these campaigns is more difficult to gauge. In their efforts to influence politics and culture, most groups use a wide variety of lobbying approaches, rather than relying on a single method. The choice of tactics depends on the situation just as much as it depends on the group. Frank Baumgartner and Beth Leech write:

The most effective groups may not be those that are best at a given strategy, but rather those that have the greatest repertoire of strategies available to them and who are most skillful at choosing the right strategy for the issue at hand. (1998: 148)

According to a study by Kay Schlozman and John Tierney (1986), two of the most common tactics used by Washington interest groups are testifying at legislative or agency hearings and direct, face-to-face contacts with legislators or other officials (1986: 151).

Schlozman and Tierney (1986) studied commonly used tactics of Washington interest groups, but their work did not include an account of the efficacy of those tactics. Robert Milbrath (1963) and Jeffrey Berry (1977) not only studied commonly used tactics, but added a measure of efficacy. This measure showed that personal presentations (direct lobbying) and letter writing were cited as the most effective approaches (Berry, 1977: 156). Testifying at hearings, a commonly used tactic, was cited as one of the least effective means. Milbrath's study of lobbyists and 38 Congressional members or their staffs partially echoes Berry's conclusions. Like Berry, Milbrath found that direct personal contact was a highly effective strategy. Contrary to Berry's findings, Milbrath's survey found that testifying at hearings was more effective than letter writing (Milbrath, 1963: 156).

In line with these findings, David Vogel observes:

The public-interest movement simply has no resource that can match the power of capital. Unlike both business and labor, the public-interest movement has nothing that it can withhold from civil society in order to make credible its political demands. Corporations can refuse to invest, and workers can refuse to work. But what can public-interest organizations refuse to do? Public-interest activists have no activity in society outside of their role as pressure groups; they have no source of power independent of the political process. Press conferences, consumer boycotts, and demonstrations are certainly not without impact. But in the long run they cannot match the power to halt or curtail economic production. (1989: 623)

It occurs to us, as media scholars, that these political scientists and economic scholars have underestimated or failed to fully consider the power of the news media and their partner the public relations industry. It seems logical to assume that the level of media coverage that these hearings, conferences, demonstrations, or boycotts receive is an important factor despite being difficult to control or predict. The power of perception is unquestionably a tangible power that these organizations can use to their benefit. Of course, most regulatory hearings and other events do not receive substantial coverage and the public at large is not made aware of the proceedings. However, for the PMRC the hearings resulted from the media attention the movement already had received. Moreover, the big names, like Frank Zappa, who were present at these hearings certainly helped make these hearings more notable and newsworthy. Ultimately, the hearings were undoubtedly effective in creating and maintaining public awareness and widespread debate about the subject of record labeling.

In addition to formal channels of communication, informal channels of communication or group life also play a pivotal role in the democratic process. The social integration provided by group membership and activity helps prepare citizens for their roles in the broader political system (de Tocqueville, 1945 [1835]: 287). One way of participating, as a group or group member, is to engage in outside lobbying. Kollman defines *outside lobbying* as 'attempts by interest group leaders to mobilize citizens outside the policymaking community to contact or pressure public officials inside the policymaking community' (1998: 3). Outside lobbying is applied selectively. Lobbyists and interest group leaders spend many hours and resources crafting careful public campaigns of persuasion. On some policy matters, groups on all sides use outside lobbying widely, while on other issues only groups on one side of the issue use outside lobbying (Kollman, 1998: 4).

Outside lobbying is a common means for elite policy-makers to experience pressure in the form of social involvement. It accomplishes two tasks simultaneously. First, at the elite level it communicates aspects of public opinion to policy-makers. In other words, lobbyists hope to create a perception of popular support (or lack thereof) for a policy-maker's actions or positions. Second, outside lobbying hopes to influence public opinion by changing how selected constituents consider and respond to policy issues. At the center of PIG politics lies the salience of policy issues to constituents. PIG leaders attempt to use their positions to influence the creation and acceptance of policy or self-regulation. Having said that, measuring influence is difficult. The press and general public show a tendency to exaggerate PIG influence. Ironically, as agenda-setting theory has shown, some of the influential power that the press ties to PIGs might be more accurately tied to the press itself. Some scholars conclude that this exaggeration may be related to lack of empirical research on outside lobbying (Kollman, 1998: 6). We might counter by saying that influence is difficult to gauge because this process occurs outside of the public eye using backchannels of communication that are not only difficult to study, but necessarily are meant (for personal and professional reasons) to remain concealed. Put simply, it is more difficult to study private processes than public ones because the uncontrollable variables become nearly impossible to control in a private sphere.

AND NOW BACK TO OUR STORY

Art and literature have been involved with issues of censorship for centuries. However, corresponding to the shift toward conservative politics that defined the 1980s, there seemed to be an increased sensitivity to rock music lyrics. More specifically, these concerns seemed to center on references to sex, drugs and violence. The PMRC organized around these concerns. Alongside the formation of the PMRC, another group of parents and professionals—the Parent Teacher Associations (PTAs) in Cincinnati, Ohio—were also concerned with Prince's lyrics. The Cincinnati groups took the matter to the National PTA convention in 1984. The National PTA adopted a resolution urging the recording industry to place labels on record and cassette covers rating the material pertaining to sex, violence, profanity, and/or vulgarity. As Eric Nuzum (2001: 18) notes, the National PTA also raised the issue of the growing number of teen suicides and attempted to tie these deaths to rock music lyrics.

In late 1984, a 19-year-old Californian named John McCollum committed suicide after listening to the music of Ozzy Osbourne. McCollum's parents filed a lawsuit against Osbourne and CBS records. They believed that the lyrics of a particular song, 'Suicide Solution', encouraged their son to take his life. A similar suicide occurred the following year in Nevada. Two teens made a suicide pact after listening to the music of the rock band, Judas Priest. The teens were also reportedly drinking beer and smoking marijuana. The teens shot themselves, but one of the boys survived. Like Ozzy Osbourne, Judas Priest became embroiled in a lawsuit. The courts ruled in favor of the record labels and the artists. The attorney for the plaintiffs argued that the music and lyrics were dangerous to listeners' health, much like cigarettes. But, unlike cigarettes, whose packages sport warning labels informing consumers of the dangers of smoking, no warning label was given on the album cover (McCabe, 1986: 1). It seemed apparent to many parents that something needed to be done to protect children from the dangers of heavy metal music, but the recording industry refused to implement a ratings system and ignored the National PTA's resolution. Less than a year later, the National PTA found a new ally in its cause—the PMRC (Nuzum, 2001: 18). Together, these two forces garnered enough power to tackle the recording industry.

The PMRC's first order of business was an official letter to the Recording Industry Association of America calling for the industry to develop guidelines for rating music. The letter was signed by the wives of 20 influential Washington businessmen and legislators. At least four of the legislators sat on committees that were scheduled to hear arguments for the Home Audio Recording Act. Through their political and regulatory ties, this group had the built-in advantage of having informal, direct and regular access to policy-makers (Nuzum, 2001: 20). This level of access is arguably what created the most fear within the recording industry. Furthermore, the industry's 'voluntary' acceptance of the PMRC's mandates would most likely not have occurred so readily had the group been comprised of different members. This fact alone makes the PMRC a difficult case for other PIGs to imitate.

Beyond establishing the group's identity and corresponding level of influence, the letter sent to the music industry listed 15 artists who offended the sensibilities of the group, who presumably represent *average* people. The list of offenders was dubbed 'The Filthy Fifteen'. Several on the list were very popular mainstream artists: Motley Crue, Prince, Def Leppard, Twisted Sister, Madonna, Cyndi Lauper and AC/DC (Nuzum, 2001: 21). In the months following that first letter, more than 150 newspaper editorials were written about the PMRC's proposals. The controversy was splashed across the country's newspapers and magazines, but the coverage did not stop with the print media. Reminiscent of Joseph McCarthy's list of communist sympathizers in Hollywood, representatives from the PMRC armed with their list of 'The Filthy Fifteen' made numerous television appearances. They appeared on *Donahue*, *Good Morning America*, *The CBS Morning Show*, *NBC's Today*, *Entertainment Tonight* and the evening news on all three major networks.

According to Nuzum (2001), the PMRC requested six concessions from the recording industry:

(1) Print lyrics on album covers;

(2) Keep explicit covers under the counter;

(3) Establish a ratings system for records similar to that for films;

(4) Establish a ratings system for concerts;

(5) Reassess the contracts of performers who engage in violence and explicit sexual behavior onstage; and

(6) Establish a citizen and record-company media watch that would pressure broadcasters not to air questionable talent. (Nuzum, 2001: 22)

The organization recognized that the more media attention they could generate, the more pressure they could apply to the RIAA to accept its proposal.

Similar to the arguments made during the debates surrounding the Radio Act of 1927, the PMRC repeatedly insisted that their goals were not to limit free expression or censor speech, but instead they wanted to protect listeners and assist parents in making their children's music choices. In short, the free speech debate once again was shifted to a debate about the freedom to listen. Of course the PMRC's proposal was not the first time that the content of music became a cultural worry that resulted in some manner of censorship. In 1940, NBC radio network banned 147 songs by artists such as Duke Ellington and Cole Porter. Ellington's tune, 'The Mooche', was considered too provocative and was blamed for a national rise in incidents of rape, while Porter's 'Love for Sale', was thought to have themes of prostitution. The 1950s also had its share of censorship—censorship that extended from radio into television. On 9 September 1956, *The Ed Sullivan Show* aired Elvis from the waist up. Critics found the performance 'filthy' despite the fact that 80 percent of the available national audience tuned in to see the performance. In 1970, Vice-President Spiro Agnew argued that rock music was brainwashing America's children by convincing them to use drugs. Agnew's speech sparked a crusade to expose drug imagery in rock songs (Dougherty, 1985: 49). Agnew's movement helped to expose 'hidden' messages in music, like the allusion to LSD in The Beatles hit song 'Lucy in the Sky with Diamonds'.

The instances listed above merely provide anecdotal evidence to illustrate a long history of content-based protests involving the music industry and its performers. Despite this history, the 1980s were different. This decade was different in large measure due to a deregulatory environment that gave birth to multiple corporate mergers and acquisitions. In this consolidated environment, the PMRC achieved a new level of success by convincing the largest major retailers to stop selling certain releases. Giant retailers such as Wal-Mart responded to the PMRC's mission with full force. At the urging of the Reverend Jimmy Swaggert, who later had his own moral issues involving prostitutes, Wal-Mart stores across the country started pulling rock music magazines and controversial albums from their shelves. In addition to Walmart, Sears and J.C. Penney announced that they also would stop carrying controversial records and tapes (Nuzum, 2001: 23). This success provided the PMRC with an opportunity to limit access to certain materials without the need to convince a vast and fragmented marketplace that its ideas were acceptable and correct. Having said that, it is also important to understand how and why the PMRC experienced its success.

BUILDING A BETTER PIG

The PMRC formed at a time when the spouses of politicians were active participants in public life. Throughout the 1980s, Nancy Reagan had experienced considerable success in establishing her 'Just Say No' program that encouraged school children to avoid drug use. In England, Diana, Princess of Wales used her position to campaign against the use of landmines around the world.

These women were moving beyond the shadows of their powerful spouses. In short, the 1980s was a complex time because, even though the political climate shifted toward conservatism, there is ample evidence to suggest that, on the heels of the equal rights movement of the 1970s, women were still making noticeable strides toward equality through public participation.

In this climate, the women of the PMRC negotiated directly with industry leaders. Because of the status and connections of PMRC members, the group was able to garner prominent placements in print and electronic media that many other PIGs could only wish for. Editorials were written and the actions of this group were followed by members of the press. We must remember that prominence is a key news value so these prominent people started from an advantageous position and the mainstream media became the group's primary resource for gaining attention and publicity. At the height of this controversy, the PMRC arguably dominated headlines and stories in America's newspapers and magazines. For instance, William Raspberry of the *Washington Post* wrote on 19 June 1985:

They formed the Parents Music Resource Center (655 15th Street NW, Washington, 20005) and managed to swing enough clout to get Stan Gortikov, president of the Recording Industry Association of America, to come down from New York to meet with them. They also persuaded Edward Fritts, president of the

National Association of Broadcaster's, to ask 45 recording companies to supply written lyrics for their albums so that broadcasters can know what they are playing. (Raspberry, 1985: A21)

A couple of months later, another *Post* article mentioned that the PMRC received 'the lion's share' of publicity because of the Congressional and Cabinet- level connections of its members' husbands (Harrington, 1985a: G1). The contradictions of patriarchal dominance and notions of feminist independence were never far from any discussion regarding the PMRC and its cause.

As Raspberry observed, feeling the pressure from the PMRC and its powerful media campaign Gortikov sent a memo urging the RIAA board of directors to consider cooperating with the PMRC. PMRC representatives and Gortikov held a meeting where Gortikov announced that he would try to persuade record companies to be more cooperative. A couple of months later, the RIAA said that its members would cooperate with the PMRC to help develop a system of warning stickers. However, the controversy received so much media coverage that the powers in Washington felt it was necessary to enter the debate. Senator John C. Danforth of Missouri decided to take matters into Congressional hands. In response to the concerns of the PMRC, Danforth announced that the Senate Committee on Commerce, Science, and Transportation would hold a record-labeling hearing on 19 September 1985.

Tipper Gore, whose husband sat on the Senate Committee on Commerce, Science and Transportation, was a feature witness. Susan Baker also testified. Of the 16-member Senate committee, four Senators, besides Al Gore, had wives who were deeply involved in the PMRC. Tipper Gore opened her testimony with the fact the PMRC was asking the recording industry to *voluntarily* label their music. As during the debates surrounding the passage of the Radio Act of 1927, accusations of censorship surrounded the PMRC's labeling campaign. In this environment, Gore, like Herbert Hoover before her, wanted everyone to believe that voluntary labeling was not censorship (Nuzum, 2001: 29). In a letter to the Home section of the *New York Times* Tipper Gore wrote:

I would like to point out, however, that the Parents' Music Resource Center, which I co-founded, is a nonprofit organization, not a lobbying group. It's important to make this distinction because the function of a lobbying group in Washington is to influence Federal legislation. (1988: C11)

The PMRC did not desire government regulation. Instead, they called for a voluntary action. Gore (1988: C11) said that the PMRC was successful in reaching a voluntary agreement with the recording industry that did not involve government regulation or legislation.

Of course, the PMRC did not have to become a typical lobbying group because the threat of regulation was always implicit in its activities. One of the primary lessons provided by the PMRC was that sometimes what you know is not as important as who you know. More importantly though, the PMRC's efforts illustrate the importance of public relations efforts in political and regulatory movements, even though the unusual composition of this group may provide little for other PIGs to emulate. Having said this, the larger lesson of the PMRC is that by achieving its goals through the application of an organized and concerted PR campaign—an indication of the importance of the PR industry in American politics. Moreover, we can recognize the importance of the involvement of media channels in the political process. If the media are used effectively, then seats at the negotiating table can be opened and a more varied set of voices can be heard. Of course, it helps if you know the people who arrange the chairs.

The PMRC's media campaign was so massive that when news of the hearings broke, it quickly became the largest media event in Congressional history up to that time. All major networks, 50 press photographers, and dozens of reporters filled the hearing room to capacity (Nuzum, 2001: 26). The amount of coverage was evident in the print media. The *Washington Post*'s Richard Harrington chronicled the event this way:

On one side was the Parents Music Resource Center, whose members include Susan Baker, wife of Treasury Secretary James Baker, and Tipper Gore. Gore's husband, Sen. Albert Gore (D-Tenn.), sat on the panel hearing testimony. The PMRC is seeking recording industry compliance in warning parents about music that might be considered inappropriate for children.

On the other side were musicians Frank Zappa, John Denver, and Dee Snider, lead singer and songwriter for Twisted Sister, as well as various industry and broadcast representatives. (1985b: B1)

The PMRC had succeeded in melding entertainment with politics to such a degree that the Congressional hearings became must-see TV. In fact, as of this writing Zappa's testimony is still available and frequently viewed on YouTube.

Asking recording artists to involve themselves in this process was another unusual tactic, but again it was one that proved successful for the PMRC. In fact, the PMRC was able to convince some artists that their goals were in their best interests. For example, Mike Love of the Beach Boys donated a $5000 start-up grant. Several musicians made public statements supporting the efforts of the PMRC—Smokey Robinson, Paul McCartney, Harry Connick Jr. and Pat Boone. In short, these were largely artists whose work was 'clean' (Nuzum, 2001: 19). They were persuaded to counter the arguments of those artists who demanded protections of their own and others' artistic freedoms. By doing this, the PMRC was able to show that this debate existed not only outside of the recording industry, but also within it. It was a basic divide-and-conquer strategy.

Finally, after months of wrangling over record labeling and weeks of behind-the-scenes negotiations, the PMRC and the RIAA reached a compromise on 1 November 1985. A voluntary parental advisory sticker emerged. It read, 'Parental Advisory—Explicit Lyrics' (Figure 1). Furthermore, printing potentially offensive lyrics on cassettes, album covers or in liner notes also became commonplace (Harrington, 1985c: H1). The group's membership and the lobbying tactics they adopted yielded some successful results. But how successful were they?

Recall that the PMRC's six objectives were:

(1) Print lyrics on album covers;

(2) Keep explicit covers under the counter;

(3) Establish a ratings system for records similar to that for films;

(4) Establish a ratings system for concerts;

(5) Reassess the contracts of performers who engage in violence and explicit sexual behavior onstage; and

(6) Establish a citizen and record-company media watch that would pressure broadcasters not to air questionable talent. (Nuzum, 2001: 22)

An analysis of them shows that the PMRC may not have been as successful as they were portrayed to be. Although the parental advisory label is a step toward (3), this success is a far cry from a restriction that is universally enforced like the one that exists in the film industry. Moreover, the group's action did not sway the industry in respect to (5). In fact, simultaneous with these discussions, the recording industry was beginning to see the first successes in a genre that would become known as gangsta rap. Wikipedia (n.d.) marks this genre's beginnings in 1984 and notes artists like NWA and Ice-T as early successes. In 1988, NWA's release of 'Straight Outta Compton' seemed to embody almost everything that the PMRC stood against.

The label that the PMRC fought for actually seemed to become a badge of honor for some artists. As often happens, censorship movements actually increase the visibility of their targets. In a *New York Times* article about Ice-T's controversial 1992 song 'Cop Killer', Jon Pareles writes: 'The protests have publicized the song so effectively that the album sold 100,000 copies in a month . . .' (1992: C13). In the end, the successes of the PMRC were limited at best. The group was far more successful in bringing awareness to its cause than they were in bringing about any notable changes in the music industry. The group failed to meet almost every objective that it set for itself. The successes they did experience were modest and largely inconsequential. In fact, the labels that the group fought for may have actually increased the presence of the indecent content that they fought against.

When set against a history of similar protests, it seems apparent that these public debates are cyclical and ongoing. It also seems apparent that campaigns like the PMRC's are rarely successful. If the core audiences do not seek change, then change will not occur. There is much to learn about how PIGs can succeed in the story of the PMRC, but there is also much to learn about a PIG failure. The PMRC targeted the wrong audience and saw itself as a voice of the masses. Unfortunately, this PIG forgot to convince the masses, or least the core audience for these products, that this was the case. Successes in movements like this one are often more symbolic than substantive. Real successes occur when the negotiations take place with society rather than suits.

References

Advisory Committee on Public Interest Obligations of Digital Broadcasters. (1998, December 18). *Charting the digital future: final report of the advisory committee on public interest obligations of digital television broadcasters.* Retrieved from http://govinfo.library.unt.edu/piac/piacreport.pdf

Baumgartner, F. R. & Leech, B. L. (1998). *The importance of groups in politics and in political science.* Princeton, NJ: Princeton University Press.

Berry, J. M. (1977). *Lobbying for the people: The political behavior of public interest groups.* Princeton, NJ: Princeton University Press.

Berry, J. M. (1978). On the origins of public interest groups: A test of two theories. *Polity 10*(3): 379–97.

Chastagner, C. (1999). The parents music resource center: From information to censorship. *Popular Music 81*(2): 179–92.

Cigler, A. J. & Loomis, B. A. (Eds.). (2002). *Interest group politics.* Washington, DC: CQ Press.

Communications Act of 1934 (1934). 47 USC §326.

de Tocqueville, A. (1945 [1835]). *Democracy in America*, trans. G. Lawrence. New York: Doubleday.

Dougherty, S. (1985, September 16). Parents vs. rock. *People Weekly*, p. 23.

Gore, T. (1988, February 25). Not a lobbying group. *The New York Times*, p. C11.

Harrington, R. (1985a, August 29). Discord on record warning. *The Washington Post*, p. G1.

Harrington, R. (1985b, October 20). The Capitol Hill rock war: Emotions run high as musicians confront parents' group at hearing. *The Washington Post*, p. B1.

Harrington, R. (1985c, November 2). Accord on the lyrics labeling firms, parents agree to 2 warning options. *The Washington Post*, p. H1.

Hilmes, M. (2007). *Only connect: A cultural history of broadcasting in the United States*, 2nd ed. Canada: Thomson/Wadsworth.

Kollman, K. (1998). *Outside lobbying: Public opinion and interest group strategies.* Princeton, NJ: Princeton University Press.

McCabe, M. (1986, December 16). Rock band faces trial in teen suicide case. *San Francisco Chronicle*, p. 1.

Milbrath, L. W. (1963). *The Washington lobbyists.* Chicago: Rand McNally.

Nuzum, E. (2001). *Parental advisory: Music censorship in America.* New York: Perennial.

Pareles, J. (1992, July 30). Critics notebook: The disappearance of Ice-T's cop killer. *The New York Times*, p. C13.

Prince (1984). Darling Nikki. On *Purple Rain* [CD]. New York: Warner Brothers Records.

Radio Act of 1927, 44 Stat. 1162 (1927).

Raspberry, W. (1985, June 19). Filth on the air. *The Washington Post*, p. A21.

Schlozman, K. L. & Tierney, J. T. (1986) *Organized Interests and American Democracy.* New York: Harper and Row.

The RS 500 greatest songs of all time. (2004). *Rolling Stone.* Retrieved from http://www.rollingstone.com/news/coverstory/500songs/page/5

Vogel, D. (1989). *Fluctuating fortunes: The political power of business in America.* New York: Basic Books.

Wikipedia (n.d.) Gangsta rap. Retrieved from http://en.wikipedia.org/wiki/Gangsta_rap

Note: The authors of this essay use APA format as their documentation style.

DECODING THE TEXT

1. The authors claim that the PMRC of the 1980s identifies a moment in political history when "past regulation, current social concerns, and future economic desires collided at the right time." How do they show this happening?

2. According to the authors, the PMRC successfully mixed politics with entertainment. How did they do this? Could just anyone have done this or did it matter that the women leading the PMRC had high-profile political husbands? Explain.

CONNECTING TO YOUR CULTURE

1. How often do you buy music that carries a Parental Advisory label? Do you think these labels make any difference in what you purchase?

2. When artists record a CD version of something and then a radio version, how do you compare the two? Do you? Why or why not? How do you decide which one to download?

3. Have you seen the Broadway musical *Rock of Ages* or the recent movie of the same name that draws from the Broadway version? Both of these are satirizing the work of the PMRC. Do you find the play or movie funny? Sad? Effective? Realistic?

READING SELECTIONS:
THE 1990s AND 2000s

CONSIDERING IDEAS

1. Consider the Oscar won by Three Six Mafia for "It's Hard Out Here for a Pimp" in 2006. Has rap reached its pinnacle of popularity and respect?

2. Are there still music enthusiasts who do not embrace rap as a legitimate musical form? Who and why?

AUTHOR BIO

Havelock Nelson *is the coauthor of* Bring the Noise: A Guide to Rap Music and Hip-Hop Culture. *A contributor to* Billboard *magazine and* Entertainment Weekly, *Nelson is a premier journalist in the field of rap criticism.*

Gerrie E. Summers *writes for* Billboard *magazine,* Rapsheet, *and* Rock & Soul. *She also adds to musical conversations through the* Village Voice. *"Rap of the Ages" was published in* Billboard *in 1993.*

RAP OF THE AGES:

Tracking the Highs and Lows of Nearly 20 Years

Havelock Nelson and Gerrie E. Summers

1975

DJ Kool Herc hosts shows at Hevalo in the Bronx, where he spins brief rhythmic sections of records called breaks. The dancers at the nightclub are known as break boys or B-boys.

1978

Disco Fever, "hip-hop's first home," opens in the Bronx.

1979

Brooklyn group the Fatback Band releases "King Tim III (Personality Jock)" on Spring Records. Many in the rap community regard it as the first rap record.

The Sugarhill Gang releases "Rapper's Delight" on Sylvia Robinson's Sugar Hill Records, ushering rap into the commercial age.

The Sugarhill Gang

ANTHONY BARBOZA/GETTY IMAGES

J. B. Ford and former *Billboard* reporter Robert Ford Jr. write and produce Kurtis Blow's "Christmas Rappin'," which gets picked up by a major label, Mercury.

Seminal female rap crew Sequence enters the male-dominated world of recorded rap and drops "Funk Your Head Up" (Sugar Hill).

Mr. Magic's "Rap Attack," which aired on WHBI then WBLS New York, plays an integral part in giving rap exposure outside of clubs; Whodini pays homage to Magic on its track "Mr. Magic's Wand."

Grandmaster Flash & the Furious Five

1980

With "Rapture," Blondie becomes the first mainstream artist to be involved with rap, referring to Grandmaster Flash and Fab 5 Freddy.

Kurtis Blow, the first rapper signed to a major label, Mercury, releases the gold single, "The Breaks."

Kurtis Blow

Afrika Bambaataa and Soul Sonic Force

1982

Trouble Funk's "Drop the Bomb" brings go-go beats to rap.

Tommy Boy establishes itself on the rap map with Afrika Bambaataa & Soul Sonic Force's "Planet Rock," a funky concept built around Kraftwerk-like electro blips.

Grandmaster Flash & the Furious Five puts out "The Message," a landmark reality rap track.

Herbie Hancock collaborates with turntable musician Grandmixer DST and producer Bill Laswell to record "Rockit" (Columbia), perhaps the first summit between a jazzman and a hip-hopper.

1981

In business for six months, Profile releases "Genius Rap," by Dr. Jeckyll (Andre Harrell, now the president of Uptown Enterprises) and Mr. Hyde (Alonzo Brown).

Grandmaster Flash's "Grandmaster Flash on the Wheels of Steel," the first record to capture the excitement of turntable scratching, is released.

Herbie Hancock

LL Cool J

Run-DMC

Malcolm McLaren records "Buffalo Gals" (Island), a track that combines rap with new-wave aesthetics.

Profile Records releases "Sucker MCs" by Run-DMC. This blast of rhythmic minimalism establishes rap's "new school."

1984

Grandmaster Flash & the Furious Five split with Melle Mel, leave Sugar Hill Records and sign with Elektra.

KDAY Los Angeles debuts the first all-rap radio format.

UTFO drops "Roxanne Roxanne," and the 12-inch inspires an unprecedented amount of answer records.

With "Run-DMC," Run-DMC becomes the first rap group to be certified gold.

The Wall Street Journal dubs Def Jam CEO Russell Simmons "the mogul of rap." Today, Simmons' ventures include Rush Management, the Phat Farm clothing line and HBO's *Def Comedy Jam*.

1985

Def Jam forms a landmark distribution pact with Columbia Records. LL Cool J's "Radio" is the first release under the agreement.

Boogie Down Productions releases the classic blueprint for gangsta rap, "Criminal Minded."

On his own label, Schoolly-D releases "PSK What Does It Mean," a seminal hardcore release about a Philadelphia gang.

"Krush Groove," the film starring Run-DMC, the Fat Boys, Kurtis Blow, and others, comes out.

1986

Uptown Records, specializing in R&B-style rap, is launched with a compilation featuring Heavy D. & the Boyz and others.

Run-DMC's "Raising Hell" album, which includes the breakthrough collaboration with Aerosmith, "Walk This Way," is unleashed.

The Beastie Boys' "Licensed to Ill" sells 4 million units.

Scott La Rock, from Boogie Down Productions, is shot to death.

DJ Jazzy Jeff & the Fresh Prince's "Parents Just Don't Understand" is a huge crossover hit.

Four platinum rappers—Run-DMC, the Beastie Boys, Whodini, and LL Cool J—go on tour.

1987

With his Marley Marl-produced single "Raw," Big Daddy Kane becomes hip-hop's man-of-the-moment.

16-year-old MC Lyte makes the first hardcore rap record by a female, "I Cram to Understand U (Sam)."

Public Enemy debuts with "Yo! Bum Rush the Show," an album that emphasizes Afrocentric music.

1988

Ruthless Records drops Eazy E's "Eazy Duz It" and, more importantly, NWA's "Straight Outta Compton," two recordings at the leading edge of West Coast gangsta rap.

De La Soul's "3 Feet High & Rising" is released by Tommy Boy, ushering in "the D.A.I.S.Y. age."

Public Enemy

It opened the door for alternative acts like PM Dawn, Mo Phi Mo, Arrested Development, etc.

Kitted-up Jumps become urban America's new status symbol.

Public Enemy's masterful "It Takes A Nation of Millions To Hold Us Back" comes out.

Rick Rubin leaves his post at Def Jam and forms Def American.

Source: *"Rap Of The Ages: Tracking the Highs and Lows of Nearly 20 Years" from* Billboard *magazine, 1993, pp. 34-38 by Nelson Havelock. Reprinted by permission of* Billboard *magazine via* Wright's Media.

DECODING THE TEXT

1. How do the visuals contribute to the timeline of rap "highs and lows"?

2. What do they signify about the progressing culture of rap music and of the rap industry?

CONNECTING TO YOUR CULTURE

1. What songs or albums have defined the highs and lows of your musical life?

2. Describe the first song you remember and the year you heard it; continue your path through high school or into college. You might include pictures and share this with friends or family.

CONSIDERING IDEAS

1. Music halls of fame often have regulations for eligibility; for example, artists become eligible for induction into the Rock 'n Roll Hall of Fame twenty-five years after the release of their first single. Many musicians have not lived to see their induction into the Rock Hall. Is this fair?

2. What eligibility requirements would you recommend?

AUTHOR BIO

Theodore Matula *is an assistant professor of composition and rhetoric at the University of San Francisco's College of Arts and Sciences. He has published in* Communication Studies *and* Popular Music and Society, *where this obituary for Joe Strummer was printed in 2003.*

JOE STRUMMER:

1952–2002

Theodore Matula

Joe Strummer's death this past December was not a rock and roll death; there was no suicide, no blaze of glory, no drug overdose, no airplane missing in a snowstorm over the heartland. The punk legend (whose real name was John Mellor) apparently collapsed in his Somerset home after walking the dog. His wife, Linda, was unable to revive him.

Strummer's death produced a relatively mild response in the media and popular culture world, including a few memoirs in places like the *New York Times* and *Rolling Stone,* and a tribute performance at the Grammys, where Bruce Springsteen, Elvis Costello, and Dave Grohl performed the Clash song "London Calling." (Unaccompanied by any explanation or context, other than Strummer's image at the conclusion of the "year of deaths in the music world" segment, the performance prompted *Chicago Tribune* music critic Greg Kot to ask how any of the musicians responsible for the song's "slaughter"—aside from fellow Brit, Costello—had anything to do with Strummer.) The underwhelming response to Strummer's death should not lead social critics and scholars of popular music to overlook the significance of Strummer's career, though. Strummer's career is noteworthy not only to those who appreciate the Clash's strident political lyrics, but also to those interested in music's ability to articulate social critique, and to those intrigued by the amazing range of musical innovation sparked by punk. Strummer's contributions both to the music world and to the pursuit of social change continued up to his death, and his influence surpasses his involvement with the Clash.

Strummer—and, in a larger sense, the band he fronted, the Clash—shows how problematic and contradictory the standard myths of punk can be—particularly those associated with the idea of punk as an authentic voice of social rebellion. While the Sex Pistols were promoting a mindless anarchic punk—the ascendancy of a new and particularly shocking breed of rock and roll "bad boys"—the Clash was producing Marxist-inflected social critique on albums like *Give 'em Enough Rope* and *Sandinista* and cranking out great anthems with titles like "I'm So Bored with the USA" and "White Riot," all of which made them a frequent object of attention and affection, heroes among left-leaning academics and popular music fans. Yet, they labored for Columbia Records, filling the coffers of large corporations even as they complained about the corporate control of music on songs like "Complete Control," "Hitsville, UK," and "Capital Radio One." Their songs were also used to sell blue jeans and automobiles, showing how easily coopted punk could be even as it was celebrated for its capacity to articulate social rebellion through violation of the norms of taste and decency, and by breaking expectations of genre. The Clash is a symbol of rock music as a politics of resistance as well as perfect proof that anything—even explicitly anticapitalist revolutionary messages—can be readily coopted in the service of consumerism and the interests of powerful corporations. In fact, their oft-repeated slogan—"the only band that matters"—is the product of the marketing efforts of Columbia Records. ("Ha, you think it's funny," sings Strummer on one Clash song, "turning rebellion into money?")

Strummer himself also confounds the myths of punk: in particular, the social realist assumptions visited by music critics and popular culture academics who connect the authenticity of punk to its putative origins in the "the street." Strummer has often been considered one of the most influential political spokesmen from the "punk street." (The myth is that he removed Mick Jones from the band in the wake of decidedly nonpolitical hit singles like "Train in Vain" and "Should I Stay or Should I Go?".) Yet, John Mellor was born the son of a diplomat and worked as a prefect in an upper-class school. In an interview shortly before his death, he chafed at being called the "voice of his generation" and often claimed, even while being involved in Rock against Racism and recording songs whose lyrics skewered Thatcherite policies and the British caste system, that he was apolitical.

Despite this seeming political ambivalence, Strummer's career shows us how punk, even if easily coopted and reanimated in the service of capitalism, can shape the way its listeners approach political realities of everyday life. Punk finds the "cracks and fissures" in capitalism and oppressive social relations (even if it sometimes spackles them over with its own variety of sexism and domination), encapsulating a moment, or a grievance, or a fault and amplifying it and turning our rage towards it. My own experience serves as testimony: I began listening to the Clash as an undergrad in the 1980s, and their music played no small role in transforming my adolescent critique of freedom into a more coherent view that focused on the inequities of social class and political power. If punk is easily appropriated by capitalist forces, it is also sometimes effective in articulating a critique of capitalism with a protreptic energy capable of positioning its audience in struggles over justice and social change.

But aside from its debatable role as an instrument of political and social change, punk has had an undisputed effect on the evolution of popular music esthetics. The Clash was a big part of this influence—for example, introducing dub, reggae, and world music to three-chord rock in the late 1970s. Strummer continues this fusion on two albums released in the last four years. If you haven't been paying attention, then you may not have noticed that, after a decade-long hiatus, Strummer returned to recording in 1999, fronting a new band, the Mescaleroes, who released two thoroughly satisfying records—*Rock Art and the X-Ray Style* (1999) and *Global a-go-go* (2001)—that blend worldly folk with dance grooves, punkish vocalist and straight-up rock. This kind of hybrid style can easily come off as cliché or careless cultural appropriation, but Strummer and the Mescaleroes use it to make the world sound like both a smaller place and a bigger place than most would consider it.

This convergence of the local and the global—the recognition that people's struggles are *the people's struggles,* even if they are articulated in different ways in different contexts—seems to be the most prevalent theme on these two records, both politically and musically. In this way, these records tell us something about the significance of hybridity and intertextuality in contemporary popular music. Like the Clash before them (as well as Rancid, Ani DiFranco, the Mekons, and others), the Mescaleroes blend these musics not only to make a new sound, but to make a politics of connection imaginable.

The most obvious case is on one of the best songs from these recent efforts, "Bhindi Bhaghee," in which Strummer recounts an actual event in which a "kiwi" (New Zealander) accosted him, looking for "mushy peas." Strummer tells him that they "haven't really got any around here" and then launches into a catalog of the local delicacies this stranger may find in his "humble neighborhood," a list that ranges from "dal" to "humus" to "rocksoul okra" to "exotic avocados and toxic empenadas." Later, when the stranger asks him what the music in his band is like, Strummer struggles to find an answer. He stammers over several bars: "Umm . . . umm . . . . It's sort of like . . . and it's got a bit of . . ." and finally, with African guitars, flutes, a synthesized beat, and a Wurlitzer organ flailing away behind him, he finds his words: "ragga, bhangra, two-step tanga, mini-cab radio, music on the go!/umm, surfbeat, backbeat, frontbeat, backseat, there's a bunch of players and they're really letting go!/We got brit pop, hip hop, rockabilly lindy hop, gaelic heavy metal fans fighting in the road."

Combined with the more overtly political offerings on these records, the overall effect is one in which music constitutes a common forum that celebrates "the people" by revealing how implicated we are in each other's struggles. If punk could never establish a politics of freedom and equality because it imagined and practiced these values through a radical individualism, Strummer and the Mescaleros come a little closer by linking these values to interdependence and a dialogic awareness that is wrapped into the music itself.

In a divisive political climate marked by a lack of responsiveness to the marginalized and the critics of powerful interests, where an imperial United States moves unilaterally on the world, Strummer's music summons a space that feels tonic. This message doesn't belong to any one generation, and he may not be the voice of his generation, but his is a voice that will be sorely missed.

Source: *"Joe Strummer, 1952-2002" by Theodore Matula from* Popular Music and Society, *2003 (Taylor & Francis), pp. 523-528. Reprinted by permission of Taylor & Francis Group (http://www.informaworld.com) via Copyright Clearance Center.*

DECODING THE TEXT

1. How biased or unbiased is the author of this tribute about the significance of Strummer's musical contributions?

2. What details in the article support your interpretation?

CONNECTING TO YOUR CULTURE

1. An obituary is often a review of someone's life, giving specific details and general evaluations. Are obituaries important in American popular culture?

2. Write an obituary for your favorite living musician. What details do you already know? What would you have to research?

CASE STUDY: PERSONAL EMPOWERMENT AND POLITICAL ACTIVISM IN MUSIC

CONSIDERING IDEAS

1. Name as many female music groups and bands as you can think of throughout the history of popular music. Do you think there are fewer bands made up of female musicians? If so, why?

2. Are females more likely to be solo acts? If so, why?

AUTHOR BIO

Kalene Westmoreland is an instructor of English at the University of Alabama. She enjoys watching, writing about, and researching many areas of popular culture, including Buffy the Vampire Slayer. "'Bitch' and Lilith Fair" was published in Popular Music and Society in 2001.

"BITCH" AND LILITH FAIR:

Resisting Anger, Celebrating Contradictions

Kalene Westmoreland

Feminism has moved away from a struggle for equality toward an engagement with difference, an assertion that girls can have the best of both worlds (that they, for example, can be both violently angry and vampily glamorous). [Third wave] feminism owes much to the struggles of second wave, yet it differs in many ways, especially in the way it is defined by contradiction.
—Klein 207–08

I'm a bitch, I'm a lover, I'm a child, I'm a mother, I'm a sinner, I'm a saint, I do not feel ashamed . . .
—Meredith Brooks, "Bitch"

"Bitch," a top ten hit song by singer/songwriter/guitarist Meredith Brooks, illustrates the inherent contradictions of third-wave feminism while it celebrates emotion and anger from a feminist perspective. "Bitch" draws on feminism, music, and anger; as an anthem for the commodified commemoration of women through Lilith Fair, the song reclaims femininity by celebrating traditional feminine qualities and tenets. Lilith Fair, a rock music festival that toured the nation from 1997 until 1999, drew on musical variety, feminist carnival, and political consciousness to critical and popular acclaim. Lilith Fair and "Bitch" represent a restrained, moderate anger, which highlights a "celebratory" message; the song and festival can be read as responses to the Riot Grrrl movement, which relied on visceral anger to reject rigid gender roles. Responding to the Riot Grrrl movement's use of anger, "Bitch" and Lilith Fair promote more tempered feminist solutions and praxis—solutions voiced in "Bitch" and manifest throughout Lilith Fair.

"Bitch" and Lilith Fair promote a feminist message by revising the less mainstream feminist message of Riot Grrrls. The Riot Grrrl movement appropriated the term "girl" (among others, such as "bitch," "whore," and "slut") in order to critique and challenge patriarchal definitions of women. Similarly, by reclaiming the connotations of the word "bitch," Brooks uses a sexist term to criticize sexism. Brooks expands the list of possibilities for women while subversively alerting listeners to complex gender issues by embracing and appropriating the negative connotations of the word. In a similar manner, Lilith Fair promotes Brooks and other female artists; it operates as a proactive medium for feminism to reach and affect masses, a necessary goal in a postfeminist era when many young women either passively accept or blindly reject the advances made by their foremothers. As progressive representations of feminism's developing third wave, "Bitch" and Lilith Fair neither completely accept nor reject second-wave feminism. Instead, much like third-wave feminism, the focus and goals of Lilith Fair and "Bitch" are multifaceted and multistrategic, fusing useful and diverse feminisms together. Leslie Heywood and Jennifer Drake, editors of *Third Wave Agenda: Being Feminist, Doing Feminism*, explain third wave feminism and its inherent reliance on contradiction: "Because our lives have been shaped by struggles between various feminisms as well as by cultural backlash against feminism and activism, we argue that contradiction . . . marks the strategies and desires of third wave feminists" (2). Heywood and Drake carefully position third-wave feminism as the alternative to conservative postfeminism, which pits second- and third-wave's tenets ("victim feminism" vs. "power feminism," respectively) against one another, in favor of the "power feminism" of third-wave which "serves as a corrective to a hopelessly outmoded 'victim feminism' (2). For Heywood and Drake, however, the "second and third waves of feminism are neither incompatible nor opposed" (2). Instead, they define third-wave feminism "as a movement that contains elements of second wave critique of beauty culture, sexual abuse, and power structures while it also acknowledges and makes use of the pleasure, danger, and defining power of those structures" (3).

Unlike postfeminism, third-wave feminism treats personal empowerment and political activism equally and interdependently; Lilith Fair, for example, has the potential to turn a personal experience, such as attending a concert, into an opportunity for activism through its emphasis on feminist charities and activity booths. Fans may peruse the political booths and wonder about the political structures that have prevented such a commercially successful, female-rostered show before. Further, "Bitch" and Lilith Fair focus on the woman writer—a strategy of second-wave feminism—in their use of the singer-songwriter by featuring performers like Brooks. In this new formulation, third-wave feminism tends to fuse "the confessional mode of earlier popular feminisms with the more analytic mode that has predominated the academy" (Heywood and Drake 2). Nowhere does third-wave feminism more explicitly perform this fusion than in the confessional singer-songwriter tradition.

Brooks and her Lilith Fair cohorts belong to what Simon Reynolds and Joy Press, authors of *The Sex Revolts*, call a tradition of confessional singer-songwriters, which distinguishes them from other categories, such as "tough rock chicks."[1] However, through its variety of musical acts, Lilith Fair's musical diversity seems to fuse the myriad categories which Reynolds and Press explore, such as "tomboys," "tough rock chicks," and "confessional singer-songwriters," among others. Taken together, the artists of Lilith Fair exemplify third-wave feminist praxis as they use the "personal" to achieve a political end—to enlighten audiences into engagement with some form of feminist activism. Lilith Fair and "Bitch" answer questions of structural and aesthetic rebellion that Reynolds and Press pose, such as when they ask, "Is it better to sacrifice aesthetic power for the sake of political explicitness, or to opt for purity of artistic expression, at the expense of being understood?" (384). Though diversity is key to Lilith Fair's appeal and success, and contradiction is fundamental to "Bitch," these two examples of third-wave praxis offer a negotiation of the seemingly oppositional choices which Reynolds and

Press question, a negotiation which diminishes the distance between the artists—both as individuals and, as in Lilith Fair, a collective of voices, "presenting a strong, unified front . . . or exploring their inner turmoil" (355). The categories which Reynolds and Press discuss are easily deconstructed, yet their description of confessional artists is pertinent to examining the messages of Lilith Fair and "Bitch" (233–34). "Bitch" and Lilith Fair exhibit a "soul-baring" which "turns suffering into an affirmation: a kind of strength through vulnerability. For a particular breed of female singer songwriters, personal candor and political concern are different sides of the same coin . . . they believe wrongs can be righted in both private and public realms, if only the truth can be uttered—if the tissue of the lies is torn apart and an 'authentic' reality revealed" (249).

This "strength through vulnerability" can be seen in the lyrics of "Bitch." If we view the contradictions embedded in the collective feminine voice as feminist stories, we will encounter more than a text or song. Instead we will encounter what Patricinio Schweickart refers to as a "'subjectified object': the 'heart and mind' of another woman . . . who comes into close contact with an interiority—a power, a creativity, a suffering, a vision—that is not identical with her own . . . To understand a literary work, then, is to let the individual who wrote it reveal [herself] to us in us" (212–13). "Bitch" exemplifies interiority as Brooks reveals herself through her lyrics: she catalogues traditional concepts of womanhood—lover, child, mother, goddess—embraces each temporarily, and finally, rejects them by embracing and redefining a negative stereotype of femininity, the bitch.[2]

"Bitch" offers listeners a reflexive discourse, in part due to Brooks's voice and image as artist/woman. "Bitch" not only transcends semantic realignment through its lyrics; the tone of the song—gutsy, guitar-driven, and passionately discontent—enables Brooks to assert her femininity as well. Brooks's version of femininity appeals to listeners through her lyrics, authoritative guitar playing, and assertive voice. As Brooks vacillates between contradictory labels and definitions, framing her rant against patriarchal limitations with a confessional tone, she creates a believable voice and compelling subjectivity. Brooks's song fulfills the call of critics like Neil Nehring, who states that "emotion . . . supplies a missing link . . . between tactile vocality and meaning" (133). This theory of reflexivity and authentic subjectivity is closely related to Schweickart's concept of interiority. Through her explicit emotional connection with audience, Brooks also fulfills Schweickart's call for an exploration of symbolic self-definition; "Bitch" explores a "symbolic self-definition" for both Brooks and her female listeners. Thus, rock music and feminist theories work in concert in "Bitch," altering the definition of what it means to be a "bitch," to play feminist rock music, and to be considered a success in a patriarchal industry.

Although Brooks's "Bitch" and other songs, such as Missy Elliott's "She's a Bitch," have improved the image of women-in-rock, feminist advancement within the patriarchal rock industry is still slow. In the introduction to *Angry Women in Rock,* Andrea Juno states "We are currently at an interesting stage in the history of rock with the recent influx of women entering as a steady and unstoppable force. Perhaps, like a Trojan horse or a mutating virus, they can't help but change the status quo in, as yet, unknown ways" (5). Juno wrote this in 1996, one year before "Bitch" was released and spread a message of appropriation, one year before Lilith Fair was conceived and spawned its message of feminist rebirth and community. While Juno's skepticism was warranted in 1996, her ideas must now be reassessed in light of "Bitch" and Lilith Fair. The success of "Bitch," along with the success of Lilith Fair, solidifies what once seemed only a trend, the importance of female performers. Andy Steiner, a reporter for *Ms.*, notes the sweeping change in the music industry in an article that reveals Lilith Fair's importance, "The Last Days of Lilith":

Just three years ago, it was common practice for radio DJs to refuse to play two songs by women artists back to back. Too many girl singers kill the buzz, the theory went. You need to throw a guy in the mix or the estrogen will pollute the air. . . . Then, suddenly, everything changed. Lilith Fair [drew] large crowds at each stop that first summer and [made] a strong and sassy statement about the commercial power of women artists. The message spread to other corners of the industry and, poof, the format changed to all Lilith, all the time. The Grammys became a regular girlfest, radio stations put more women in their lineups, and sales of recordings by Lilithians hit record highs. For women in music (and their fans), things never looked better. (61)

Although "things never looked better" in 1999, as Steiner reflected on Lilith Fair's cumulative effects, Juno's suspicion of rock's patriarchy is still warranted. While Steiner's analysis of the current status of women-in-rock is accurate and invigorating, Juno's preemptive warnings about complacency are appropriate, especially since Lilith Fair, the most important feminist vehicle in recent years, has drawn to a close.

"Bitch" exemplifies the progressive feminist message Lilith Fair promotes, in part because it celebrates personal empowerment.[3] Through her song's lyrics, Brooks contradicts a masculine perspective by compromising with her discontent male companion, who is exasperated with Brooks's contradictory nature; by social standards, this complex construction of femininity justifies the term "bitch." Schweickart incorporates Judith Fetterly's analysis of "immasculation" to explore the complex process of disqualifying a male point of view in terms which are applicable to Brooks's song:

> notwithstanding the prevalence of the castrating bitch stereotype, the cultural reality is not the emasculation of men by women, but the *immasculation* of women by men. As readers and teachers and scholars, women are taught to think as men, to identify with a male point of view, and to accept as normal and legitimate a male system of values, one of whose central principles is misogyny. (205)

The process of overcoming immasculation is complex and difficult, yet images of immasculation as a process in "Bitch" highlight anger as a healthy emotion.

Significantly, Brooks does not rail at the male character in the song; rather, we hear her character overcoming immasculation by alternately soothing and challenging him to embrace her self-definition as a "bitch." She begins the song with temperate understanding: "I hate the world today/You're so good to me /I know but I can't change/tried to tell you/ but you look at me like maybe/I'm an angel underneath /Innocent and sweet/ Yesterday I cried/Must have been relieved to see/The softer side/I can understand how you'd be so confused/I don't envy you/I'm a little bit of everything all rolled into one." As the first verse builds toward the anthemic chorus ("I'm a bitch, I'm a lover/I'm a child, I'm a mother/ I'm a sinner, I'm a saint/I do not feel ashamed/I'm your hell, I'm your dream/I'm nothing in between/You know you wouldn't want it any other way"), Brooks identifies and categorizes feminine traits that play into typically masculine perspectives, such as using the term "bitch" to refer to any assertive woman.

Thus, the speaker in the song overcomes immasculation while simultaneously overtly and subversively exploring confining gender roles. Using a generic male partner, one who is intimidated and confused by the speaker's complexity, Brooks challenges patriarchal assumptions about women: "So take me as I am/This may mean you'll have to be a stronger man/Rest assured that when I start to make you nervous/ And I'm going to extremes/Tomorrow I will change and today won't mean a thing." The process of immasculation nears its end in "Bitch" as the chorus is repeated and then altered to allow for a celebration of self and reclamation of the term: "I'm a bitch, I'm a tease/I'm a goddess on my knees . . . I've been numb, I'm revived/Can't say I'm not alive/You know I wouldn't want it any other way." This final catalogue of terms is paradoxical: the speaker equates "bitch" with being a "goddess," which suggests ultimate power, yet she is also on her knees. The speaker challenges what it means to be a bitch, concluding for herself and her audience that she must embrace all connotations of the term. "Bitch" provides a space where residual anger about the difficult process of overcoming immasculation is explored as a celebration.

Brooks's image as artist/woman is central to her message of empowerment and appropriation; Brooks successfully creates dialectic between listeners and creators of feminist music. For example, Brooks creates two positions as writer and speaks to two audiences. On the surface, Brooks sings to her lover ostensibly about her multifaceted nature; however, in the chorus, she catalogues and reclaims the larger paradoxes of femininity. Her assertions extend beyond the context of the lover who serves as the tentative audience of her song; instead, to her larger audience—demographically similar to Lilith Fair's audience, which was composed largely of women who might identify themselves as third-wave feminists—she makes strong claims about the inner struggle of self-definition and acceptance as a feminist. "Bitch" emphasizes feelings and ideology harmonizing in a feminist resistance and challenges postmodern, cynical listeners to embrace feminist rock. Brooks's song performs a tolerant feminist position as articulated by Nehring: "'Just because someone is not resisting in the same way you are'—because he or she values feelings over your ideology, for instance—does not mean they are not resisting" (171).

In addition to Brooks's feminist voice and image, her resistance is informed by her status as guitarist. Resistance and interiority in feminist music is informed by musicianship and production; we must understand more than the lyrics of these critical and popular reassessments of feminism by letting the writer, as Schweickart invites us to do, reveal herself to us in us. Brooks achieved this intimate revelation in the first stage of the songwriting process by cowriting the song with a female friend, Shelly Peiken, who Brooks thanks in the cover of her album: "for making me laugh my ass off and pushing the edge with me . . . you bitch." In this vein of recognizing and celebrating the process of songwriting and production, Brooks proudly identifies herself first as a guitarist. Brooks's online bio at www.Meredith Brooks.com notes that

> She can stand tall when noting that she played every lick of guitar on Blurring the Edges, including glass slide, some e-bow, wah-wah, and a canny layering of vintage and high-tech Stones-inspired rhythms. "If I had listed a guy as a guitarist in the liner notes, everyone would've thought that he played all the cool stuff. So I decided to do it all myself just to prove that I could. Now I want all those 13 year olds—especially the girls who don't have role models—to look at me with confidence and say 'I can do that,' and go pick up a guitar. When I was growing up, I didn't have many female guitarists to look up to." (paragraph 6)

Brooks defines herself as a guitarist, reveling in a form of artistic and feminist resistance unavailable to singer/songwriters. For a female artist to identify herself primarily with her instrument and secondly through her voice is a critical difference between artists like Brooks, many of whom have not been heard since the heyday of the Riot Grrrl movement, and performers like Alanis Morissette, who constitute the majority of female representation in music today. Gillian Gaar notes the reluctant progress of female guitarists in *She's a Rebel: The History of Women in Rock and Roll*. She points out that the "non-traditional" role of female lead or solo guitarist was always deemed unusual because of its rarity, but it was assumed (by many in the 1970s) that "as more women became rock musicians the idea of women-in-rock would lose its validity . . . [but] women are still by and large defined in that order—as women first, and rock performers second" (xi–xii).

Although her guitar-playing is a central part of her feminism, Brooks's voice is also crucial to the song's ability to incite communication with its listeners. She says, "I really believe in the beauty of scratch tracks. The lead vocal and guitars on 'Bitch' are scratches—the vocal was recorded as I was playing a Martin acoustic, live to tape. Of course, we later set up to record the 'real' vocals, but we never could beat the rawness of it and innocence of those scratch tracks. They were just 'it'" (Molenda 24). Although Brooks is not by any means the only solo female guitarist performing today, her voice and message in "Bitch," when combined with her solo guitarist status, are parts of what Nehring sees as an "important achievement" in feminist music. "For women to play and sing through the same forms dominated by men is inherently a form of resistance, refusing to accept the definition of woman as the male's subordinate "Other" (164).

Brooks's capacity to become a role model for her audience is part of her feminist achievement. In a topic thread entitled "Role Model" on the official Meredith Brooks website, which Brooks herself moderates, a young fan named Laura, posting as "grace," states that Brooks is a role model for her, specifically because "I never really had many women guitarists to look up to until blurring the edges [with the single for "Bitch"] came out. When I heard that I realized that it was possible to be a female guitarist and to play rocking music" (Grace, paragraph 2). Not only does Brooks appropriate the term "bitch," she also reclaims for herself and for audience members such as Laura the instrument which signifies "male power and virtuosity, the legitimate expression of phallic sexuality, perversity . . . and violence" (Nehring 164).

The success of "Bitch" as an accessible rejection of the "castrating bitch stereotype" shows how second-wave theories of feminist reader response apply to third-wave feminist rock, how the "dialectic of reading" becomes a dialectic of listening and resistance (Schweickart 213). Brooks's audience encounters the subjectified object through her image and through the inversion of the word bitch, a dichotomously personal and generic term, one which all women at one point fear and must come to terms with before they can invert its larger cultural meaning. In "Appropriating the Bitch," Jim Roderick discusses the distinction between the patriarchal, oppressive meaning of the word and the empowered, subversive meaning which Brooks is illustrating: "'Bitch' [is] someone who doesn't support the patriarchal-ruled relationship. . . . [There is a] power of being a bitch, [or] a woman who subverts the patriarchy, leaves and stays away from the physical, mental, emotional, and spiritual oppression of patriarchy" (2). Brooks's appropriation of "bitch" is a step in changing or eradicating its subjugating meaning, but it is also a continuance of the more radical appropriation which the Riot Grrrl movement began. Nehring assesses this process:

> Any sensate, honest male knows full well that supposedly wild-eyed radical feminists are absolutely right about our culture: Women are on constant display, everywhere, as semen receptacles. The "gaze," when it comes to women, is real; Riot Grrrls write BITCH, RAPE, SLUT and WHORE on their bodies because that's what a lot of men *already* see there. Beyond actual physical assault, though, as well as pornography and the whole sex industry, the problem is how "normal" guys have learned to look at women—as well as how *not* to hear them, a problem women in punk rock are obviously working on. (153)

Brooks's emphasis on temperance may be crucial to understanding a more persuasive feminism that Riot Grrrls reject. "Bitch" may not be a revolutionary statement but Brooks can perhaps reach more male listeners as well as female. Brooks says that "men completely get [the song's meaning] and are so relieved that somebody's saying it; all they want us to do is admit that we can be irrational and illogical sometimes, and then it's their job to put up with it" (Willman 65). Indeed, male listeners, whether in passive consumption or as active fans, must engage the term in new ways, both in general attitudes toward women and in the context of personal relationships with them.

Brooks's message in "Bitch" moves towards balancing aggression and compassion in the context of a "healthy" relationship wherein gender differences are capable of being understood and affirmed by both partners; more importantly, the message defies the patriarchal systems which still dominate self-formation and socialization. This dual message, which focuses on public and personal self-formation, is common in confessional feminist rock music. The liberating nature of Brooks's song becomes a subversive strategy for listeners, who identify with multiple readings of the song, allowing potential essentializing to become more personally suited to individual listeners. What Schweickart sees as interiority is obvious in the community of Brooks's listeners and fans, who have contributed to the "Meanings" portion of "Meredith Brooks Mania," a website devoted to her music. Although only a few examples are available on the "meanings" page, and few of them are credited to anyone in particular (though there are perhaps more female contributors than male), the messages are nonetheless important for reading the song as an open dialectic. The collection begins with one listener responding somewhat naïvely: "This is such a cheerful song. It starts from a depressing place 'I hate the world today' and carries the listener to a very happy state 'I wouldn't want it any other way!' It's hard to still be depressed by the time the song ends" ("Meanings" paragraph 1). Recognizing the uplifting nature of the song is an important contribution to its meaning—for this listener, female solidarity is achieved through an emotional connection to the performer and the optimistic mood the song creates.

The website offers more aggressive, critical feminist responses, exemplifying how reader response criticism applies to a third-wave feminist song. One listener suggests that an open community is implied in the song's meaning, commenting that "'Bitch' is not just a song, it's a revelation. After listening to this song, it got me to thinking; I'm many different people inside. I'm sure you can relate" ("Meanings" paragraph 4). Another listener, seeking adaptation from the inherently emotional and personal text of the song, comments on the song's effect on feminism and popular culture. Her comment reinforces Brooks's artistic and feminist intent: "Meredith is trying to perform 'semantic realignment' to change the world's perception of the word 'bitch.' Instead of condemning the less pleasant parts of ourselves, let's honour each of those many parts instead"

("Meanings" paragraph 3). Inverting the definition of "bitch," along with viewing the scope of the song as moving beyond the narrative between the two primary audiences of lover and solitary listener, shows that Brooks's fans are aware of her optimistic brand of feminism.

Comparing Brooks's use of "bitch" to a more recent appropriation reveals a compelling praxis of the song's celebration of contradiction. While "Bitch" uses emotion, ideology, and guitar-driven assertiveness to form resistance, Missy Elliott, one of the most successful female rap artists, approaches appropriation of "bitch" through overt philosophies about female aggression and power. Like Brooks, Elliott resists patriarchal ideology through her appropriation of the term "bitch." Just as Brooks appropriates the signifier of "male power and virtuosity," by proudly playing the guitar, Elliott's role as producer reclaims the term's meaning in a positive manner (Nehring 164). Whereas Brooks emphasizes emotional and psychological healing through appropriating "bitch," Elliott emphasizes practical perspectives of being a "bitch," relating her experiences in the music industry to women's life experiences. Elliott has released the single "She's a Bitch" from her sophomore effort, *Da Real World,* and she frequently discusses the term in interviews. In an interview with *Ms.,* Elliott proclaims, "I think sometimes you have to be a bitch in this business to get where you want to go. Sometimes you have to put your foot down because it is a male-dominated field. If you don't, people will walk all over you. I think bitch is a strong word. I feel like I'm a bitch in power" (McDonnell 82). Although Elliott's opinions on a feminist reclamation of the term are pertinent, her ethics of production prove her stance. Devoting more time to production than performance (Elliott was a featured performer on 1998's Lilith Fair tour), she has "traded fame for power" in the industry. She says that she "became a bitch in power because when I walked in, I asked for what I wanted. At the end of the day, if this is the way I want, this is the way I'm going to have it" (84).

Elliott's blunt, unequivocal assertion of power shows another side to the "bitch" persona, presenting a practical image for audiences. While Brooks's song is confessional and soul baring and achieves "a kind of strength through vulnerability," Elliott's efforts belong to what Reynolds and Press have called the "tough rock chick category" (249). Her inclusion on the Lilith Fair tour in 1998 added to the variety of performances and the depth of the tour's feminist message. Elliott's credentials as producer/rapper, combined with her aggressive attitude, enable her to resist the term as a negative description of feminist success. In fact, it is Elliott's overtly aggressive attitude as rapper and producer that distinguishes her effort to reclaim "bitch." Although Brooks and Elliott achieve appropriation of "bitch" differently, they successfully reclaim the term while using celebratory messages to create a daring, aggressive feminist stance.

The potential to create more aggressive feminisms is borne out in Lilith Fair, the ongoing tour which started in 1997. If "Bitch" is anthem, Lilith Fair is praxis of the tenets of the song's embedded contradictions which help define femininity and third-wave feminism. Just as "Bitch" may be heard as appropriation which is more accessible to a larger audience than its Riot Grrrl predecessors may be, Lilith Fair, too, adapts Riot Grrrl anger and transforms the carnival to affect its audience on progressive feminist issues and identity. Lilith Fair embodies and has the potential to rectify the anxiety over feminist identity, the "I'm not a feminist, but . . ." syndrome—or turning it around to "I am a feminist, but . . ."—because it celebrates women's roles without anger, though it does not deny the "energy" which emotion may invoke.

Lilith Fair and Brooks's use of "bitch" created anger within feminist circles. Founder Sarah McLachlan found herself embroiled in a less than harmonious feminist discourse with critics who charged she was bringing female artists together with little concern for their talent or their musical diversity. *Ms.* berated McLachlan "for her reluctance to use the word 'feminist'" because of its negative connotations; in order to accomplish her goal, she later explained, she felt it necessary to say that Lilith Fair wasn't about "chopping anyone's dick off" (Childerhose 71). She later responded "I'm sure *Ms.* was upset by what I had said . . . but if I took every opportunity to spout feminism then, sadly, men would be terrified of the tour. And in order for Lilith to achieve our goals, we couldn't have it be marginalized" (71). While McLachlan takes "the ghettoization of women" and subverts it—"turning it in to something positive"—as spokesperson she must contend with the remnants of the anger associated with feminism, as well as reassess her own understanding of feminism. Andy Steiner interviewed McLachlan for *Ms.* during Lilith Fair's third and final tour: "'Yes, I'm a feminist . . . Lilith doesn't have anything to do with men in a negative sense. It's about bringing women up'"(83).

McLachlan has since become more comfortable with her role as feminist leader; Steiner describes her response—she says "'yes, I'm a feminist,' with some exasperation"—in the same terms as Buffy Childerhose in *From Lilith to Lilith Fair* (Steiner 83). Childerhose concentrates on the press coverage these issues received and McLachlan's exasperated reactions to popular (mis)readings of feminism:

> She's quick to point out that she's never denied being a feminist. "Absolutely, I'm a feminist," she says. "And I don't hate men. I know that it's ridiculous that I have to say those things in the same breath, and I don't want to have to. Yet," she explains, "many people still equate feminism with man-hating. I tried to diffuse that thinking because I don't think that's what feminism is. But," she concedes, "I can't escape what many people still believe it to be." (71)

While she didn't "spout" feminism to the press, McLachlan and fair organizers made feminism accessible, at least, in any given venue on any particular date, through its music, the alley of informative, political booths, and the celebratory atmosphere; thus, Lilith Fair alters (but does not contrast) the type of celebration which Riot Grrrl concerts offered. Nehring cites Angela McRobbie as he develops his argument that Riot Grrrls are a reincarnation of punk's spirited political resistance and anarchy, but her words apply to Lilith Fair's less vitriolic conception and celebration:

> . . . especially from a feminist point of view stressing the importance of feelings in them-selves, "perhaps [politics] is not what we should be looking for in any case." What it may be more realistic to look for, suggests Angela McRobbie, "are cultural forms and expressions which seem to suggest new or emergent 'structures of feeling,'" especially among young women. In exploring "a greater degree of fluidity about what femininity means," the Riot Grrrls, for example, are significant for trying to change how feeling itself is valued, especially anger—no longer something to be ashamed of and repressed but to celebrate. (xxviii)

Anger may not be one of the many emotions which the Lilith Fair experience invokes—in fact, Lilith Fair is often lauded specifically because it offers a contrast to the testosterone-driven festivals it competes with—but anger is nonetheless a muted source in its genesis.

The festival is the brainchild of Sarah McLachlan, a Canadian singer/songwriter whose music is ethereal and sentimentally cathartic. The idea for Lilith Fair began for her as an alternative to "alternative" music; McLachlan's vision for a feminist music fair rejected the andro-centric music that derived from mainstream pop and the reactive feminism of the Riot Grrrl movement. She writes in the foreword of *From Lilith to Lilith Fair,* acknowledging her indebtedness to her angry predecessors: "The fact that there have been women's festivals happening all over North America for years, even though my knowledge of them was sadly limited, helped to create a space where my idea could be heard, accepted and brought into mainstream" (xii). Lollapalooza, an alternative music national tour that generated and reflected early '90s music trends, offered variety, but it lacked adequate female presence. When McLachlan approached her manager several years ago about possibly headlining with Paula Cole, the promoters railed against the idea, telling her simply to forget it, but "Sarah angrily pushed for an explanation. 'Nobody wants to pay to see two women in one night,' they declared" (Childerhose 19).

The blatant sexism of the patriarchal record industry, which included radio programmers who refused to add more than one female act during a week and would not play women artists back to back, angered McLachlan. The industry exploits complacency among female performers, who typically do not push for more airtime and publicity, yet female artists dominate the charts. This hegemonic paradox frustrated McLachlan into action as she began to formulate the idea for an all-women tour and music festival. The tour began with trial dates in late 1996; those dates proved to McLachlan that the patriarchal system of musical promotion was hopelessly inaccurate and unjust and could easily be toppled, at least within the context of her tour and her attempts at mainstream feminism. Plans for a full-scale, 35-date tour were soon under way. By the time the tour wrapped up, Lilith Fair was the most successful tour of the summer.

McLachlan's decision to use the Lilith myth to promote the tour exemplifies how "Bitch" and Lilith Fair consistently rewrite traditional feminine stereotypes and stories. These revisions exclude the negative connotations of anger and denigrating terms while they simultaneously celebrate femininity and feminism. In the foreword of *From Lilith to Lilith Fair,* McLachlan pieces together the Lilith myth, the story of Adam's first wife who refused to be subservient to him; after Adam refused to keep her as his wife, she began birthing hundreds of the devil's spawn daily. The angels who were sent to find her warned her that "if she didn't return, God would kill one hundred of her children a day (not very PC of him—funny how God never got a bad rap about that . . .). Despite the dire consequences, Lilith never went back to a subservient life with Adam" (xiii). In her revision of the story, McLachlan chooses the "parts that can guide us in our lives" and discards the elements that displease her. McLachlan's version, which informs the masses of Lilith Fair attendees, ignores the parts of the story that vilify her or call her a demon, because these alterations are "surely only the rantings of terrified men who were trying to keep other women from getting any silly ideas" (xiii).

The National Liberty Journal, a product of Jerry Falwell Ministries, illustrates the alarm felt among conservatives as McLachlan revises the Lilith story. A recent article in the *NLJ,* entitled "Parents Alert," warns that "to alter the content of the Bible in even the smallest way results in man attempting to create God in his image. This is the false hope of Lilith who has been concocted in order to create politically-correct image of equality" (Smith paragraph 12). "Parents Alert" adamantly opposes Lilith Fair, despite its positive message and concerns: "Christian parents are advised to consider the Lilith legend should their children become interested in the concerts . . . [while] Lilith Fair does donate a portion of earnings to the worthy Breast Cancer Fund . . . it also supports Planned Parenthood" (paragraph 17). McLachlan's feminist revision of the myth reforms and appropriates negative connotations, just as "Bitch" does for the opprobrious term it revises. Through this revision, along with the celebratory atmosphere of Lilith Fair, Schweickart's theory of interiority moves beyond feminist literary theory and into a more tangible realm of a live audience.

Lilith Fair's tempered version of feminism does not emphasize anger. We must question whether this lack of emphasis suppresses the full range of emotion possible and if such cathartic moments that attendees speak of are complete. Neil Nehring makes a strong case for the need for anger in feminist music and the Riot Grrrl movement. Reacting against innumerable recent self-help manuals which teach consumers how to suppress anger, Nehring suggests through his study of emotion that "the problem with psychotherapy that stresses catharsis is its notion that feelings require discharge not to seek their social causes but because they're unhealthy symptoms of individual dysfunction that reason must gain control over, to have done with them" (111). By seeing Lilith Fair as a medium for a feminist message, a medium that exists along the same continuum as Riot Grrrls, I am not suggesting that the full range of human emotion must be present in order for the fair's goals to be achieved. However, I suggest Lilith Fair presents an opportunity for the audience to undergo a simultaneous personal and social catharsis. As Buffy Childerhose recounts her initial Lilith Fair experience, she seems to be describing undergoing a mystical catharsis as she realizes what she has previously missed as a feminist and music lover: "When the crowd joined in to help the women of Lilith sing 'Closer to Fine' with the Indigo Girls, all the distance created by rock venues and star systems became a dim memory. I actually felt like I was a part of what was happening on the stage and in the crowd. People throughout the stadium exchanged genuine smiles with on another" (Childerhose 2). Lilith Fair empowers attendees by participating in social causes and charities as it convenes in each city on the tour, donating to community shelters and empowering attendees with knowledge of various feminist and humanist causes. The tempered anger plays a role in catharsis, but anger does not necessarily have to enter into the equation as Nehring's analysis of anger suggests and requires. Instead, the catharsis from complacency and apathy towards empowerment and interiority can be channeled through the "love and respect" McLachlan aims for (Childerhose 70).

A moderate feminist message is an effective strategy for a top ten hit and a music festival; the celebration of femininity which "Bitch" and Lilith Fair have stimulated challenges traditional ideas of women in rock. Neil Nehring states "the best female artists are fully aware at all times that they are parodying conventions of female representation and the processes by which various media propagate them. (Whether the audience gets the joke, of course, is always a sticking point" [170].) "Bitch" and Lilith Fair encourage the audience to get the joke because they reveal progressive feminist strategies that ironically employ anger and female solidarity to promote women in rock; both engage with difference and contradiction, offering listeners possibilities for self-acceptance and social change. Brooks's and Lilith Fair's use of "Bitch" draws the audience's attention to stereotypes of femininity, and in so doing, exemplifies third-wave feminism's positive effect on rock.

Notes

1. Press and Reynolds offer categories to describe threads of feminist music history, yet acknowledge that artists often overlap these strategies (233).
2. While vulnerability is an inherent factor in the concept of interiority, as well as in "Bitch" and Lilith Fair, it does not equate to the "victim feminism" which helped to define second-wave feminism. See Leslie Heywood and Jennifer Drake's analysis and rejection of conservative postfeminism in *Third Wave Agenda: Being Feminist, Doing Feminism,* 2–3.
3. Many of Brooks's listeners have expressed their appreciation for the personal empowerment that "Bitch" promotes. See the following websites for message boards and fan input: http://www.musicfanclubs.org/meredithbrooks/mblinks .html, http://www.hollywoodandvine.com/meredithbrooks/, where fans can read posts from Meredith Brooks and post their thoughts on her message board, and http://www.angelfire.com/ca2/umbx2/stories.html, where fans have posted personal stories about "Bitch" and Brooks.

Works Cited

Brooks, Meredith. "Bitch." *Blurring the Edges.* Los Angeles, 1997. CD.

Childerhose, Buffy. *From Lilith to Lilith Fair.* New York: St. Martin's Griffin, 1998. Print.

"Fan Stories." *A Site Dedicated to Meredith Brooks: Prepare to be Mesmerized.* Web. 27 Apr. 2000. <http:// www.angelfire.com/ca2/umbx/index.html>.

Gaar, Gillian. *She's a Rebel: The History of Women in Rock and Roll.* Seattle: Seal, 1992. Print.

Grace. "Role Model." *Hollywood and Vine Bulletin Boards: Meredith Mondays.* Web. 14 Apr. 2000. <http:// www2.hollywoodandvine.com/UBB/Forum9/HTML/000050.html>.

Heywood, Leslie, and Jennifer Drake. "Introduction." *Third Wave Agenda: Being Feminist, Doing Feminism.* Minneapolis: U of Minnesota P, 1997. 1–20. Print.

Juno, Andrea. *Angry Women in Rock.* New York: Juno, 1996. Print.

Klein, Melissa. "Duality and Redefinition: Young Feminism and the Alternative Music Community." *Third Wave Agenda: Being Feminist, Doing Feminism.* Ed. Leslie Heywood and Jennifer Drake. Minneapolis: U of Minnesota P, 1997. 207–25. Print.

McDonnell, Evelyn. "Missy in Action." *Ms.* June–July 1999: 82+. Print.

"Meanings." *Meredith Brooks Mania.* Web. 27 Feb. 1999. <http://www.musicfanclubs.org/meredithbrooks/ bitscub.html>.

Molenda, Michael. "Songcraft: Meredith Brooks." *Guitar Player* June 1998: 24. Print.

Nehring, Neil. *Popular Music, Gender, and Postmodernism: Anger Is an Energy.* Thousand Oaks, CA: Sage, 1997. Print.

Press, Joy, and Simon Reynolds. *The Sex Revolts: Gender, Rebellion, and Rock 'n Roll.* Cambridge, MA: Harvard UP, 1995. Print.

Roderick, Jim. "Appropriating the Bitch." Paper. Louisiana State University, 1996. Print.

Schweickart, Patricinio. "Reading Ourselves: Toward a Feminist Theory of Reading." *Contemporary Literary Criticism,* 4th ed. Ed. Robert Con Davis and Ronald Schliefer. New York: Longman, 1998. 197–219. Print.

Smith, J. M. "Parents Alert: Secrets of the Lilith Fair." Web. <http://www.liberty. edu/chancellor/June1999/lilith.htm>.

Steiner, Andy. "The Last Days of Lilith." *Ms.* June–July 1999: 60+. Print.

"Up Close and Personal." *Pollyanne* 2 May 1999. Web. <http://www.meredithbrooks.com/upclose/bio.html>.

Willman, Chris. "Meredith, She Rolls Along." *Entertainment Weekly* 13 June 1997: 65. Print.

Source: "'Bitch' and Lilith Fair: Resisting Anger, Celebrating Contradictions" by Kalene Westmoreland from Popular Music and Society, 2001 (Routledge), pp. 205-220. Reprinted by permission of Taylor & Francis Ltd. (http://www.tandf.co.uk/journalsRoutledge) via Copyright Clearance Center.

AUTHOR BIO

Pink, singer-songwriter, musician, actress and activist, released her first album in 2000. Since then she has released five more albums, won three Grammy Awards, two Brit Awards, and five MTV Video Music Awards, in addition to having eighteen Top 20 Hits on the Billboard charts and three number-one hits on the Billboard Hot 100. In 2009, Billboard magazine named Pink the number-one pop musician of the decade, and in 2012 VH1 named Pink number ten on their list of the Hundred Greatest Women in Music. The video for "Stupid Girls" won the MTV Video Music Award for Best Pop Video in 2006.

STUPID GIRLS

Pink

Stupid girl, stupid girls, stupid girls
Maybe if I act like that, that guy will call me back
Porno Paparazzi girl, I don't wanna be a stupid girl

Go to Fred Segal, you'll find them there
Laughing loud so all the little people stare
Looking for a daddy to pay for the champagne
(Drop a name)
What happened to the dreams of a girl president
She's dancing in the video next to 50 Cent
They travel in packs of two or three
With their itsy bitsy doggies and their teeny-weeny tees
Where, oh where, have the smart people gone?
Oh where, oh where could they be?

Maybe if I act like that, that guy will call me back
Porno Paparazzi girl, I don't wanna be a stupid girl
Baby if I act like that, flipping my blond hair back
Push up my bra like that, I don't wanna be a stupid girl

(Break it down now)
Disease's growing, it's epidemic
I'm scared that there ain't a cure
The world believes it and I'm going crazy
I cannot take any more
I'm so glad that I'll never fit in
That will never be me
Outcasts and girls with ambition
That's what I wanna see
Disasters all around
World despaired
Their only concern
Will they **** up my hair

Maybe if I act like that, that guy will call me back
Porno Paparazzi girl, I don't wanna be a stupid girl
Baby if I act like that, flipping my blond hair back
Push up my bra like that, I don't wanna be a stupid girl

[Interlude]
Oh my god you guys, I totally had more than 300 calories
That was so not sexy, no
Good one, can I borrow that?
[Vomits]
I WILL BE SKINNY

(Do ya thing, do ya thing, do ya thing)
(I like this, like this, like this)
Pretty will you **** me girl, silly as a lucky girl
Pull my head and suck it girl, stupid girl!
Pretty would you **** me girl, silly as a lucky girl
Pull my head and suck it girl, stupid girl!

Baby if I act like that, flipping my blond hair back
Push up my bra like that, stupid girl!

Maybe if I act like that, that guy will call me back
Porno Paparazzi girl, I don't wanna be a stupid girl

Baby if I act like that, flipping my blond hair back

Push up my bra like that, I don't wanna be a stupid girl

DECODING THE TEXT

1. Does Westmoreland's use of only one song's lyrics, by a singer who is often considered a one-hit wonder, affect her argument?

2. Would the inclusion of lyrics by other artists, such as Pink's "Stupid Girls" have helped or hurt her main thesis?

3. Who or what is Pink criticizing in "Stupid Girls"? What alternative to this stupidity does she envision?

4. Do you think Pink's lyrics indicate a feminist stance? Why or why not? Is it the same type of resistance and feminism Westmoreland, or Brooks, espouses? Why or why not?

CONNECTING TO YOUR CULTURE

1. Think of your favorite female songwriter. Is she seen as a feminist or are her song lyrics viewed in this light? Is this a fair assumption to make?

2. Now, consider your favorite male artist. Are any such assumptions made about him? About male songwriters in general?

CONSIDERING IDEAS

1. Have you ever listened to any of Michael Jackson's music? What? When?

2. What is your impression of Jackson's music and his legacy?

3. Do you think that the media represent famous people (musicians, movie stars, athletes) fairly or unfairly? Explain.

AUTHOR BIO

Todd Leopold works as the entertainment producer for CNN.com. "Michael Jackson, A Man Apart" was published on CNN.com on June 25, 2009.

MICHAEL JACKSON, A MAN APART

The King of Pop Leaves Behind a Legacy of Music and Style That Changed Entertainment

Todd Leopold

He was lauded and ridiculed. He broke down barriers and built them around himself. He soared to heights unimaginable with his music, and he made the ignominious front page of gutter tabloids worldwide.

For Michael Jackson, the spotlight was always present, and the rest of the world followed.

With "Billie Jean" and "Beat It"—the latter with Eddie Van Halen's scorching guitar solo—he was almost single-handedly responsible for getting videos by African-American artists on MTV and helped revitalize the moribund Top 40 format in the early 1980s.

"Michael Jackson made culture accept a person of color way before Tiger Woods, way before Oprah Winfrey, way before Barack Obama," said the Rev. Al Sharpton, a friend. "Michael did with music what they later did in sports, and in politics and in television. No controversy will erase the historic impact." In Depth: Michael Jackson special report

"Thriller," a 14-minute video extravaganza directed by John Landis, paved the way for the elaborate music videos to follow—including Jackson's "Scream," recorded with sister Janet in 1995, which cost a reported $7 million and may be the most expensive video ever.

His incredible dance talent, a modern twist on the Motown moves he witnessed as a child, led to a heightened focus on choreography in pop music videos and stage shows.

His 1982 album "Thriller" smashed records. It was No. 1 for 37 weeks and, at its peak, sold a million copies a week. To date, it has sold nearly 50 million copies worldwide. The achievement set a high bar for Jackson; when his 1995 greatest-hits CD, "HIStory," sold 7 million copies, it was considered a relative failure.

Jackson was also a fashion icon, his heavily zippered leather jackets a de rigueur 1980s fashion accessory, his single, spangled glove beyond compare.

On the down side, Jackson also led in making pop stars the subject of the paparazzi and tabloids in a way, perhaps, equaled only by such icons as Frank Sinatra, Elvis Presley and the pre-"Sgt. Pepper" Beatles. Rumors abounded, from his pets to his sleeping habits to his cosmetic surgery, all fodder for the press. After stories arose of possible child molestation, he never got back in the media's good graces; he was treated as a traveling circus.

From the time he was a child, it was obvious Michael Jackson was something special. In 1966, when he was 8, he joined his brothers in the band his father put together and started singing lead with brother Jermaine.

Though Motown Records was the top label of the 1960s, inventing what it called "the Sound of Young America," by 1969—when Jackson and his brothers in the Jackson 5 first hit the charts—the label was finding itself out of step with the psychedelic and hard-soul sounds of the times.

Enter the quintet from Gary, Indiana.

Motown signed the group in 1968 and poured its all into the Jackson 5's first single, "I Want You Back"— the writing and production team were credited as "The Corporation"—and Jackson's imploring, dramatic vocal rocked America. The song hit No. 1 in January 1970, and was followed by three more No. 1s in quick succession.

Thanks to their squeaky-clean image, the Jackson 5 became teen idols, unusual for a group of African-American youngsters. Michael Jackson's face appeared on the covers of teen magazines; the band even became the subject of an animated Saturday-morning TV show, another first for an African-American group.

But it was in the 1980s, when Jackson became a worldwide phenomenon, that his impact really began to be felt.

He was much imitated, from his hair to his clothes to his dance moves. The music was superbly crafted pop, produced by Quincy Jones and often written by Jackson himself. Even rock critics approved; the album "Thriller" earned an A from the picky Robert Christgau, among others.

There came a moment, around that time, when pop music went into a Jackson era. "Thriller" had nine songs; seven of them became singles. Jackson teamed with Lionel Richie to write the fundraising song "We Are the World"; it was his presence, as much as that of Richie, Bruce Springsteen and Stevie Wonder, that propelled the song to No. 1.

Jackson reteamed with his brothers for an album, "Destiny," and accompanying tour. It was the hottest tour of the year, despite complaints about sales practices. (Partly because of the controversy, Jackson announced publicly he was donating all his money from the tour to charity.)

He was a role model. At the peak of his fame, there were reports of a humbly dressed Jackson ringing doorbells as part of his Jehovah's Witness faith.

Though Jackson's image eventually became sullied by the molestation allegations and stories of eccentricity, there was never any doubt about his entertainment legacy. "Thriller" and "Bad" are still among the top sellers of all time. His fluid dance moves and stage presence set standards that rising stars—often compared to Jackson—struggle to equal.

"Of all the thousands of entertainers I have worked with, Michael was the most outstanding. Many have tried and will try to copy him, but his talent will never be matched. He was truly one-of-a-kind," said Dick Clark, who would know.

And then there's the music, from the early, explosive joy of the Jackson 5 hits to the elegant ballads, down-and-dirty grooves and ecstatic dance hits of his solo years. "The Love You Save," "Billie Jean," "Beat It," "Bad"—they are pop music boiled down to its best essence, with a good beat, an engrossing melody and even, sometimes, a message of love and fellowship.

It's enough to take a listener to the moon.

DECODING THE TEXT

1. The author says at the end of the essay "though Jackson's image eventually became sullied by the molestation allegations and stories of eccentricity, there was never any doubt about his entertainment legacy." What strategies does the author use to connect these two representations of Jackson throughout the essay?

2. How effective are these strategies? Explain.

3. What other writing strategies might you suggest?

4. Does the author have any bias toward Jackson? Explain.

CONNECTING TO YOUR CULTURE

1. In what medium was this essay published? How do you know? What are some defining characteristics?

2. In your opinion, is this essay credible? Why or why not?

3. Consider a musician whom you think has been unfairly represented by the media. What are the assumptions made about her or him? Explain.

CONSIDERING IDEAS

1. Do you think that the media has the power to remove stereotypes from popular culture?

2. What influence has the media had on stereotypes in the past, both positively and negatively?

AUTHOR BIO

Alexandra Pecci is a freelance writer specializing in lifestyle, travel, history, and health writing. Her work has appeared in The Washington Post, Eagle Tribune, Cape Ann Summer Guide, The Andover's Magazine, Taste of the Seacoast Magazine, and Babble. "The Power of Glee" appeared in the Eagle Tribune on December 19, 2010.

THE POWER OF GLEE

Singing Groups Gaining Popularity Thanks to Fox T.V. Series

Alexandra Pecci

"Can you play an F for us?"

Eleven high school students are gathered around a piano in a music studio on a cold Saturday morning at Brooks School in North Andover. They're part of the school's a cappella ensemble, and are learning an arrangement of "Have Yourself a Merry Little Christmas."

"Do you guys like 'Glee'?"
"Yeah, we love 'Glee,'" they enthuse.
"Is it realistic?"
"No way," they shout, amid peals of hysterical laughter.

There are no football players beating up the chorus kids here. Although, as in "Glee," one of the Brooks football players, Ara Bilazarian, is a chorus kid. There are also no elaborate, Broadway-quality sets, no musical numbers that come together spontaneously, and no heavy relationship drama. Instead, there are early Saturday morning rehearsals, working over and over again through difficult harmonies, and kids who seem to be brimming with confidence.

Still, singing in the chorus still carries with it a slightly "dorky" stigma, and the kids say "Glee," the Fox comedy/drama that focuses on a high school glee club in Ohio, has helped change that perception.

"I think it made music seem cooler," said Ani Bilazarian, Ara's younger sister. Their a cappella director, Brooks' head of music Claudia Keller, agreed.

"I think more people are listening to a cappella because of 'Glee,'" she said. "Maybe it's made singing more acceptable."

Mark Mercer, director of vocal music for Andover schools, said he's seen an uptick in participation in chorus over the past year, especially among boys, and he credits at least some of that to the popularity of "Glee."

"I honestly think it's really done the middle school well, because we had a ton of boys join this year," he said.

"Last year, we had 38 boys total between the middle schools and high school. And I teach in three middle schools and one high school. This year, we have over 100 boys enrolled."

The trend extends beyond the Merrimack Valley. Nationally, 42.6 million Americans are members of choirs, according to a 2009 study by the nonprofit group Chorus America—nearly double the number reported in 2003. More than 10 million choir singers are children.

"It seems like (choir) people overall are enthusiastic to finally have a presence in mainstream media," said Jan-Marie Peterson, spokeswoman for Chorus America, a national group that promotes choruses.

Mercer echoes, too, the fact that "Glee" has made singing and music more acceptable. "I think 'Glee' definitely has brought to the forefront that singing is OK," he said.

Mercer and Keller said the students they teach also draw inspiration from the music "Glee" uses on the show, including pop songs like Lady Gaga's "Bad Romance" and Madonna's "Vogue." Keller said sometimes the students will come in raving about the great arrangement they heard on "Glee" the night before, and the class will listen to it online.

Valerie J. Becker, artistic director of the Treble Chorus of New England, said the students in her chorus appreciate the pop music on the show, even if they stick to performing more classical pieces.

"The kids talk about it all the time," she said. "They love it because it's a little bit of drama but it's also a lot of music."

But groups at both Andover and Brooks schools incorporate pop music into their performances. For example, Mercer's show choir set this year consists of "Eye of the Tiger" by Survivor, "Strut" by Adam Lambert, "You Found Me" by the Fray, and "Mercy" by Duffy.

"I think the thing about 'Glee' that has really turned me on is I love how they do their mash-ups because it takes songs new and old and it fits them in unique ways that are pretty fun," Mercer said.

Mercer also loves that "Glee" has introduced an all-boys group called the Warblers onto the show, since it's something he hopes to do in Andover someday. Until then, choirs can continue to ride the wave of "Glee's" popularity and help young people understand that it's not dorky to be a singer.

"I definitely think it's brought something to the table that says singing is cool," Mercer said.

Source: *http://www.eagletribune.com/lifestyle/x1666505910/The-power-of-Glee-Singing-groups-gaining-popularity-thanks-to-Fox-TV-show*

DECODING THE TEXT

1. According to the text, in 2009, 42.6 million Americans belonged to a choir, almost twice the number who were in a choir in 2003. The author appears to attribute this number to television shows such as *Glee*. Do you think that this number is attributable only to *Glee*? Might there be other factors which contribute to this increase?

2. The author also indicates that there has been an increase in boys' participation in choirs because of Glee. Might this be attributable to Glee, or to other social and cultural factors? Explain.

CONNECTING TO YOUR CULTURE

1. What effect does the media have on the social standing of the group, sport, hobby or activity in which you are involved? Have you ever been stigmatized or applauded for your participation in this activity by the media?

2. What effect has the media had on your views regarding choirs? The arts in general?

3. Reflect on how television has influenced your views on social issues in general. For example, how have television shows influenced the way you think about social class? Gender? Race? Sexuality?

4. Do you watch *Glee*? If so, have your perspectives on choirs, singing, and the like changed?

CONSIDERING IDEAS

1. How popular is country music among your group of friends? Explain.

2. If you listen to country music, who is your favorite musician or group? Why? If you don't listen to country music, why not?

AUTHOR BIO

Mark Crawford writes for *CMA Close Up News Service/Country Music Association. This article was published on* musicnewsnashville .com *on April 19, 2011.*

STREET SURVIVAL

Success Strategies for Country Music Venues

Mark Crawford

Finding a lively bar with Country talent in Nashville is about as easy as flagging a taxi in Manhattan. And thanks to tenacious entrepreneurs around the United States, fans far from Music City are finding it easier than ever to hear top talent and enjoy a true "Country club" experience.

It's not easy to break into markets not known as hotbeds for the genre. For those who do succeed, though, the critical step often involves consistent messaging to fans and booking talent with name recognition or some airplay at radio. One of the best ways to do this is to develop great relationships with local Country radio—not just for advertising, but also for bringing in new bands, organizing benefits and events and brainstorming about how to deliver more for the local Country consumer.

"Our business-building strategy starts with radio and ultimately ends there," said Ed Warm, co-owner of Joe's Bar, which opened in 1997 and has offered Country Music exclusively in Chicago since 2003. "We have an incredible relationship with one of the best Country radio stations in the nation, WUSN. They believe in us, and we've formed a partnership with them that is second to none and goes beyond just music. We team up as often as we can for charitable causes, concert series and other community events."

"Over the last five years, we have done lots of advertising with WYCD in Detroit," added Joe Hellebuyck, co-owner of Coyote Joe's, located 20 miles north of Motor City along the Clinton River and a Country haven since it reopened after repairing flood damage in 2004. "When a new band is on the road, premiering a new song and looking for places to play, they'll do interviews on WYCD and then perform at Coyote Joe's."

The trickiest part of booking talent is timing. Because of their size, typically from 1,200 to 2,000 in capacity, these venues can't afford to pay top national touring acts. Instead, they focus on new or developing talent from Nashville. "We try to predict when new artists will be peaking before they go national and bring them in then," said Scott Durland, owner of the Grizzly Rose, open since 1989 in Denver. "For example, we had Taylor Swift for two nights at $10 per ticket. We also booked Lady Antebellum before they took off nationally."

But how do you forecast who will be hot and when? By staying in touch with Nashville's recording industry. "I've learned so much about our booking from the record labels," said Warm. "The record companies are so far ahead of the curve with getting the word out on their artists, and they rarely miss on their eye for talent. I listen to what they have to say."

Cowboys Dancehall provides live Country entertainment and dancing at two locations in Dallas and one in San Antonio. "The key to booking national entertainment is to bring in top Country stars at a price that maintains volume sales," said Danny Perez, Marketing Director, Cowboys Dancehall. "The expense incurred for name entertainment is offset by the ticket price. The seating capacity of each venue allows Cowboys to book name entertainment at ticket prices that customers can afford. Each venue attempts to book at least one major act per month."

"Acts must be well known nationally and be at a price point that our customers can afford," Durland agreed. "Customers are very price-sensitive. You can't overpay for acts; at $30 or higher, we would lose business."

The key, then, is to deliver what customers want, budget to bring in a good national act as least once a month and focus on performers who charge affordable rates because they're on the way up—or, as the Grizzly Rose often does, artists who don't dominate the charts as often anymore or tour as much but still have powerful name recognition and legions of longtime, devoted fans.

Local and regional bands can also be part of the formula. For example, each Cowboys location features house bands that play behind rising new singers who may not be able to travel with a full band on the road. "These house bands rotate between the venues, helping to maintain enthusiastic performances and high customer interest," said Perez.

These points are the meat of the business. The meal is complete when you add a robust Internet presence. Cowboys Dancehall and the Grizzly Rose are among many Country venues that invite customers to become members and form a community online that will carry over into meeting at the club.

The final ingredient is the premises itself. Coyote Joe's fans can count on DJs between live shows, nonstop videos on 36-inch big-screen TVs and a ladies night three times a week that includes free mechanical bull rides—all key parts of Hellebuyck's strategy to present a total package of music, entertainment and pricing.

This type of planning can offer real and potential fans a uniquely personal experience of the music while also broadening exposure for fresh talent and maintaining steady work for veteran performers. "We were told by a lot of 'experts' we couldn't do live Country Music in Chicago. We'd do this for six months or a year and then we'd be out," said Warm, whose club embraced the Country format in 2003. "Well, even during the recession, we've booked bands all the time, kept marketing and advertising budgets the same and fought to keep ticket prices down. We stayed consistent, and that's why we're still here: The industry and fans saw that we were committed to Country."

Source: *"Street Survival: Success Strategies for Country Music Venues" by Mark Crawford,* CMA Close Up *March 21, 2011.*

DECODING THE TEXT

1. The author notes, "The key to booking national entertainment is to bring in top Country stars at a price that maintains volume sales." Have you ever felt that you paid too much or too little for a music concert? Why or why not?

2. Relationships with radio stations as well as an Internet presence are two key factors to building success according to the author. How do these work for up-and-coming artists?

CONNECTING TO YOUR CULTURE

1. Do you think that certain genres of music thrive more easily in certain geographical locations? Why or why not? Explain.

2. How many concerts have you attended in the last year? In your lifetime? Explain.

3. What elements of country music (or other music genres) do you like the most? What elements do you like the least? Explain.

CONTEMPLATIONS IN THE POP CULTURE ZONE

1. Rewrite the lyrics to your favorite song as a parody. Think of examples by "Weird Al" Yankovic or the cast of *Saturday Night Live.*

2. Look at the cover of an album or CD you have never heard before and describe the cover in detail. Then, draw some conclusions about the artist and/or songs on the album. What does the artwork tell you?

3. Make a list of the top five songs that relate to your major area of study. For example, for a science list you might include "The Planets" by Gustav Holst, "Sounds of Science" by the Beastie Boys, and "Love Potion No. 9" by The Clovers. What can these songs add to your field? Do they detract from the reality of the field?

COLLABORATIONS IN THE POP CULTURE ZONE

1. Develop a soundtrack for your writing class. What music would start out each class, play while you freewrite, or serenade you as you leave the room?

2. In a group, make a list of as many American Top Forty songs as you can think of from the past three months. This can be presented as a countdown as in the past by Casey Kasem and more recently by Ryan Seacrest on

radio stations across the country and online. If students from another country or planet were to hear these songs only, what judgments would they make about the United States and its culture?

3. Collaborate with a classmate to convince each other to listen to an album, song, or artist he or she is otherwise unfamiliar with. Find out from your partner what details are important in the music he or she enjoys and listens to. Make a list of these details and answer his or her questions about your song or artist. How do your lists differ? Can his or her questions be answered for your artist, and vice versa, or do your details work more appropriately for the music choices you have already made?

START WRITING ABOUT MUSIC

Reviews or Review Essays

1. Review one of your favorite songs or albums from high school. When writing your overall evaluation, think back on the reasons that you liked the song then and on the way your opinions have changed over time.

2. Consider your favorite film or TV show. How does the soundtrack add to or detract from the action? Describe and evaluate the soundtrack and its contributions, while also considering why producers chose the music. For an example, look at the following list of songs from the *Forrest Gump* soundtrack; the soundtrack contained more than fifty musical selections and became a big contributor to the buzz around the film.

   "Hound Dog," performed by Elvis Presley

   "Pomp and Circumstance," written by Sir Edward Elgar

   "Blowin' in the Wind," written by Bob Dylan

   "Fortunate Son," performed by Creedence Clearwater Revival

   "Respect," performed by Aretha Franklin

   "All Along the Watchtower," performed by The Jimi Hendrix Experience

   "California Dreamin'," performed by The Mamas and the Papas

   "Hello, I Love You," written and performed by The Doors

   "Mrs. Robinson," written and performed by Simon & Garfunkel

   "On the Road Again," written and performed by Willie Nelson

3. Read an article or book on your favorite musician. Then, review its assessment of him or her. What was the author's thesis? Remember to include your opinion of the author's writing style, purpose, and effectiveness.

Reflection or Response Essays

1. *American Idol* winner and country singer Carrie Underwood credits several 1980s' hair bands among her biggest musical influences. Can you see this influence in her music? Her performance style? Her "look"? How has the music you listen to impacted your culture, fashion, activities, friends, and so on? Reflect on your musical choices and their influence on your life.

2. Tell the story of the first song you remember. Who was singing it? Where were you when you heard it? How do you feel when you hear the song now? Was it an appropriate song for someone your age? Try to remember the feeling the song gave you as a child, too.

3. What song do you listen to when you are angry? Hurt? Sad? Happy? When you want to celebrate? What makes these songs perfect for your many moods? Reflect on the characteristics of these songs that allow you to revel in your own emotions.

4. In the soundtrack of your life, which song is the most significant and why? Address a letter to someone important to you and explain the meaning of this song.

Analysis Essays

1. Write an essay in which you analyze what type of music appeals to the different generations of your family or a friend's family. Try not to overgeneralize but to learn what appeals to your parents, grandparents, children, or even older brothers and sisters and why.

2. Analyze the advantages and disadvantages of downloading music. Does it affect the music industry? Does it affect your finances, time, or convenience or those of your friends? Is paying for downloads the solution to piracy problems?

3. At what age should children or teenagers be allowed to listen to anything they choose? Should a thirteen-year-old listen to Marilyn Manson or a ten-year-old listen to the band Judas Priest? Remember to consider a child's psychological development in your research and writing.

4. Programs such as *American Idol*, *The X Factor*, and *The Voice* have launched numerous careers, but not always those of the winners. How do you account for the success of those who may have been voted off or knocked out in the early rounds? Or the success of the runner-up as opposed to the winner? What role do these shows play in producing talented musicians (and actors and models)?

Synthesis Essays

1. Compare the way that sexuality is treated in two different genres. Is rap music really more offensive to women than rock music? Or than 1920s' jazz? This may include both the review of and response to two or more songs or artists.

2. In a season fourteen episode of *The Simpsons*, "How I Spent My Strummer Vacation," Elvis Costello's glasses are accidentally knocked off, and he cries, "My image!" How does the appearance of your favorite musician affect his or her image or audience? What does he or she normally wear? How would you describe his or her style? Review the effectiveness of this person's public image and analyze the importance of image on the marketing, production, and consumption of his or her music. You might think about performers who repeatedly remake their image such as Lady Gaga or Madonna.

3. Write lyrics to describe the most significant aspect of one friend or family member's life. Then, use the chosen aspect to define his or her importance to you.

10

writing about television

"Television is an invention that permits you to be entertained in your living room by people you wouldn't have in your home."

—From David Frost, as quoted in *A Companion to Television*

An image from the A&E television show Hoarders

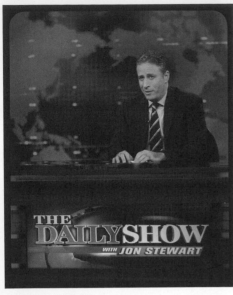

JASON DECROW/AP PHOTO

Match the catchphrase with the television show.

1. "Did I do that?"

2. "How you doin'?"

3. "Make it work!"

4. "If it weren't for you meddling kids!"

5. "Live long and prosper."

6. "Oh my God! They killed Kenny!"

a. *Star Trek*

b. *Project Runway*

c. *Friends*

d. *South Park*

e. *Glee*

f. *Scooby Doo*

7. "The tribe has spoken."

8. "Here it is—your moment of Zen."

9. "Who lives in a pineapple under the sea?"

10. "And that's how Sue sees it."

g. *Spongebob Squarepants*

h. *Family Matters*

i. *The Daily Show with Jon Stewart*

j. *Survivor*

11. **Stump Your Instructor:** In small groups, write a question here with a catchphrase from a television show. Give your instructor five choices for answers.

a.

b.

c.

d.

e.

PHOTOS 12/ALAMY

YOU AND TELEVISION

Television influences us every day of our lives whether we acknowledge it or not. The most recent census shows that Americans now own 2.4 televisions per household, and a 2012 Nielsen research report shows that the average American spends more than thirty-four hours a week watching television, plus another three to six hours watching programs on DVDs or DVRs. You can now even easily carry your television shows with you on cell phones, iPods, Kindle Fires, and wireless computers. Television entertains and engages us just as much as it invades and shapes many aspects of our culture and world. It influences elections, it provides access to worldwide events, and it never sleeps. And because of this accessibility, even though some may not own or watch television, they still cannot completely avoid the influences of television, whether it is on themselves, their family and friends, or the culture at large.

WHY WRITE ABOUT TELEVISION?

Reading and then writing about television help us investigate exactly how television plays a role in our lives. For some, television does not play any role or a minor role at best, but for others, television is a major part of everyday experiences. Even if you do not watch much television yourself, how television may or may not affect the lives and cultures of those around you is very important. Television is around us all the time, whether it is in the room and turned on or not. One of the most interesting aspects of writing about television is keying into exactly how influenced you and the people around you are by it. We often hear how watching television can negatively impact the lives of children or teenagers. However, there are also positive impacts, as reported by Daniel J. Anderson in his 2004 *Newsday* article, in which he relates that, regardless of parents' educational level, family size, or preschool intelligence, how viewing *Sesame Street* helped students attain higher high school grades than book reading and how watching *Mister Rogers' Neighborhood* predicted the increase of student creative activity in areas such as art, music, and creative writing. Television can also affect our clothing and hairstyles, as many styles worn by television characters are imitated across various populations. Do you remember the "Rachel" haircut taken from *Friends*? Conversations are punctuated with words made popular by television characters or news anchors, as in "mind-meld" from *Star Trek*, "d-oh" from *Simpsons*, and "yadda-yadda-yadda" from *Seinfeld*.

PREPARING TO WRITE ABOUT TELEVISION

Most of us have spent a considerable amount of our time as children and adults watching television. For some of us, television has been a babysitter, a companion, or our only source for entertainment and news. Depending on your relationship with television, you may have to watch it differently when you are planning to write about it. Some of the strategies given in previous chapters may help you, especially the strategies used in Chapter 7.

Watching and Thinking

You will probably want to watch a television show differently from the way you have before, focusing on the parts that you will use as supporting examples in your writing. Whenever you write a review or a reflection, you will focus

- How does the title relate to the television show?
- How does the show start? How are the opening credits displayed or revealed?
- When was the television show created? How long has it been on?
- Where was the television show created?
- What type of show is it?
- What kinds of characters inhabit the world of the show?
- Did you notice anything about the camera movements? Were they jumpy? Close up? Slowly fading in or out?
- What is the concluding image of the television show?
- Is this television show similar to or different from other television shows?

KEY questions

Key Questions after Preliminary Viewing

- How did the television show match or not match your previewing expectations?
- How did this episode or show compare with others in the same series or other series?
- What is the historical background of the show?
- How does your own belief or value system affect how you experienced the show?
- How do your political beliefs or the beliefs of those close to you or the politics of the time period of the show affect your viewing?

on those parts of a show that trigger your reaction to it. When you analyze a character or a scene, you will need to watch parts of a show multiple times to take your analysis to a deeper level. And if you want to combine some reflection and analysis into a synthesis essay, you will most likely combine the strategies for writing these types of essays. For instance, if you are asked to analyze the change in family comedies across the past few decades, your analysis could focus on your personal reaction to how characters such as Archie Bunker from *All in the Family,* Dr. Huxtable from *The Cosby Show,* Homer Simpson from *The Simpsons,* and Jay Pritchett from *Modern Family* react when their children get into trouble. This personal reaction could also focus on how your own father treated you and how these television characters relate to what happened in your home.

Because there are many reasons why you watch television, your particular reason for watching may relate directly to how you react. Why did you view this show? Were you required to watch? Did you have to pay to watch—pay-per-view, cable movie channel, iPod, DVD rental? Did you watch by yourself? How and why you watched may influence your overall impression of a show or a character or an assignment, and you should take this into consideration as you begin to think critically about what you are watching.

Just as with any other topic that you may analyze, when you watch television specifically for the purpose of writing about it, you may want to prepare yourself by using some of the key questions that follow. Take notes. Question what you see and hear. Watch for key characters or moments. And be prepared to watch more than once.

If you are watching a television show because you have a writing assignment, try to watch the show straight through at first without taking notes or doing anything that is out of the ordinary for your regular viewing. Then, go back and watch the episode again and take notes on technical aspects, key characters or scenes, or things you want to focus on and return to. If that is not possible, try to use an effective shorthand system for note taking so the flow of the show is not interrupted. After you have viewed the show each time, try to fill in your notes by elaborating with examples, noting key points that you want to research a bit more, or connecting to other shows or characters or episodes from your own life.

After viewing the show, ask yourself these additional questions to expand your critical thinking and writing options. Answering these questions about your viewing experience will help you figure out what you want to write about and also help you find the details needed to support your argument(s) or conclusion(s).

Watching, Analyzing, and Understanding

For technical analysis, writing about television is similar to writing about film; refer back to Chapter 7, for ways to focus on and write about characters, cinematography, composition, critical approaches, genre, mise-en-scène, setting, and sound. One of the first ways you can begin to analyze television shows is by trying to categorize the show into a television genre.

TELEVISION GENRES	1970s	1980s	1990s	2000s	2010s
Action/Adventure	Kung Fu	Hart to Hart	Baywatch	24	Justified
Animated	The Flintstones	The Simpsons	Daria	The Boondocks	Family Man
Anthology	Night Gallery	Mystery!	Red Shoe Diaries	Masters of Horror	Masterpiece Classic
Cartoons	The Pink Panther Show	She-Ra: Princess of Power	Pokemon	SpongeBob SquarePants	Phineas and Ferb
Children's	The Muppet Show	Sesame Street	Barney & Friends	The Wiggles	Dora the Explorer
Cop/Detective	Starsky and Hutch	Cagney & Lacey	NYPD Blue	Monk	Elementary
Courtroom Drama	The Bold Ones: The Lawyers	L.A. Law	Judging Amy	Boston Legal	The Good Wife
Crime Drama	Mannix	The Equalizer	Oz	The Sopranos	Sons of Anarchy
Drama	Dallas	China Beach	Northern Exposure	Desperate Housewives	Mad Men
Family Drama	The Waltons	Father Murphy	Seventh Heaven	Brothers & Sisters	Parenthood
Family Sitcom	Good Times	The Cosby Show	Roseanne	The George Lopez Show	Modern Family
Game Show	Family Feud	Hollywood Squares	Who Wants to Be a Millionaire?	Deal or No Deal	Pyramid
Horror/ Supernatural	The Addams Family	Friday the 13th	Angel	Lost	The Walking Dead
Hospital Drama	Marcus Welby, M.D.	St. Elsewhere	Chicago Hope	Grey's Anatomy	House
Miniseries	Roots	North and South	Stephen King's The Stand	Band of Brothers	American Horror Story
News	60 Minutes	20/20	The O'Reilly Factor	The Daily Show	Last Word
Procedurals	Police Story	Murder, She Wrote	Law & Order	CSI	NCIS:LA
Reality	An American Family	That's Incredible	The Real World	Laguna Beach: The Real Orange County	Snooki & JWoww
Reality/ Competition	The Dating Game	Dance Fever	America's Funniest Home Videos	American Idol	The Voice
Sci-Fi/Fantasy	Wonder Woman	Beauty and the Beast	Highlander	Heroes	Doctor Who
Sitcom	Maude	The Cosby Show	Friends	The Office	New Girl
Soap Opera	All My Children	Knots Landing	Melrose Place	Passions	Nashville
Sports	Sports Challenge	SportsCenter	NFL Monday Night Football	Cold Pizza	60 Minutes of Sports
Talk	The Phil Donahue Show	The Oprah Winfrey Show	The Arsenio Hall Show	Ellen: The Ellen Degeneres Show	Late Night with Jimmy Fallon
Teen	Welcome Back, Kotter	Fame	My So-Called Life	The O.C.	Pretty Little Liars
Television Movie	My Sweet Charlie	The Day After	If These Walls Could Talk	Broken Trail	Jesse Stone: Benefit of the Doubt
Variety	The Richard Pryor Show	Saturday Night Live	In Living Color	Chappelle's Show	America's Got Talent

TELEVISION GENRES. Due to television's similarities with film, you will find that many genres, including subgenres, may exist across various categories, such as drama, comedy, and action. Television has also developed a specialty that is unique to this medium—the series. Established genres and subgenres include the following television programs and series from recent decades.

Some very popular television genres are shown on American television, including the following general types.

HULTON ARCHIVE/GETTY IMAGES

CHILDREN'S TELEVISION. Feeling too grown-up to write about children's television? You may want to reconsider because children's programs offer a seemingly endless supply of challenging topics. How does television fulfill its mission as America's number-one babysitter? How many children's television networks or channels are there? Don't forget to count all the different branches of a children's network, such as the multiple cable channels owned by the Nickelodeon or Disney networks. What patterns can you detect concerning gender roles, race relations, and environmental issues? What products are advertised in the commercial breaks? What are the possible effects on the adults of tomorrow—as voters, consumers, and critical thinkers? Children's television shows, such as *Good Luck Charlie, Phineas and Ferb,* and *Young Justice,* can provide excellent essay topics.

COMEDY SHOWS. Presenting real life in a humorous, often satirical way, comedy shows frequently mock everyday life and everyday people. Consider the sketch comedy in *Saturday Night Live,* sitcoms such as *Big Bang Theory,* animated characters such as those in *The Simpsons* or *Family Guy,* or even cable networks such as Comedy Central dedicated to showing comedy shows day and night. Comedy shows usually address a number of important issues, such as gender, race, sexuality, and class. The exploration of these shows can tell you and your audience many things about U.S. society.

DOCUMENTARIES AND REALITY TELEVISION. The documentary is more than an educational supplement for school. Most documentaries teach us about issues we otherwise might never encounter: foreign cultures, unfamiliar customs, wild and strange animals, and natural disasters. Television documentaries are available in many forms and venues, such as those seen on *Frontline, NOVA,* and the Documentary and History Channels on cable. Reality television shows, such as *Survivor* or *American Idol,* are often placed in the documentary category as well, but rarely are any shows considered as credible as most television documentaries. Many questions raised about these shows are of an ethical nature and are well worth developing in an essay. How real are reality television shows? Do contestants forfeit their right to privacy when they participate? How do technology and computer animation influence the reality of documentaries—for example, shows about extinct species? What is the appeal in watching people like the Kardashian family?

DRAMA. Drama, especially in series format, is probably one of the most dominant genres on television. Its subgenres are plentiful and popular. You will notice that dramas can be presented as either serial shows (*Once Upon a Time* or *Parenthood*) or shows that open a story or multiple stories and close them within one episode (*CSI* or *Castle*). Television dramas and film dramas have much in common and can be analyzed in similar ways on the technical, artistic, and story levels. Some sample drama subgenres are given here.

- Action Series (*Nikita*)
- Hospital Drama (*House*)

- Miniseries (*Band of Brothers*)
- Police Series (*CSI*)
- Postmodern Drama (*Lost*)
- Science Fiction (*Doctor Who*)
- Teen Series (*The Vampire Diaries*)
- Western (*Justified*)

NEWS.   We may not like to think of it, but in reality, news shows and programs have become a profitable business just like any other to the point that twenty-four-hour news channels proliferate across the airwaves. In this context, the question of objectivity might strike you as the most intriguing. How does the competition among different channels influence the presentation of the news? Investigating how a major news story is covered by *NBC Nightly News with Brian Williams* as compared to how that same story is covered by *The O'Reilly Factor* or even *The Daily Show with Jon Stewart* can make an exciting essay topic. What are the different political agendas of broadcasting stations, and what effect does that have on their coverage? What has become of journalistic integrity? What are the differences between news coverage in the United States and, for example, in a European country?

POPULAR ENTERTAINMENT.   The category of popular entertainment shows includes a number of shows that, like all other programs, strive to entertain the viewer, but its concept does not follow any of the genres mentioned so far. The most obvious difference is probably the absence of actors, although not necessarily of acting. Examples include game shows, such as *Jeopardy!*; talk shows hosted by people like Jimmy Fallon and Chelsea Handler; and also sports and music broadcasts, such as those on ESPN and MTV. These productions usually appeal to an audience's unrefined or even crude tastes, and analyzing this supposedly uncultured audience alone provides a rich subject. In fact, it is quite easy to find each of these types of popular entertainment shows because most of them have their own channel on cable.

SOAP OPERAS.   The soap opera is a typical television genre that began on radio. Its short, half-hour to one-hour format is ideal to promote a number of products in commercial breaks and make even busy people feel that they can squeeze soap operas into their full day. The audience's fascination with this genre is a topic as intriguing to analyze as the programs themselves. People sometimes even plan their work or school days around their favorite soap or catch up on a week's worth of shows by watching SoapNet or the Soap City channel on cable or satellite. Soap opera characters and shows can become very popular. In fact, one of the highest-rated shows in soap opera, or even television, history was the wedding of Luke and Laura on *General Hospital* on November 16, 1981, with 30 million viewers tuning in. Nighttime dramas can also be soap operas with shows such as *Nashville* or *Parenthood* having many of the same qualities as a daytime soap. With daytime soaps dwindling on network television, some of them, such as *One Life to Live* and *All My Children*, have moved online for daily viewing through sites such as Hulu or iTunes.

Watching, Researching, and Documenting

You may not need to do any outside research for a response or reflection essay about a television show because this type of writing usually uses your own life as its central focus, but you may need to investigate the television show itself to help you provide the content that sets up the response or reflection. If you are writing a review or an analysis of a television show, you may need to do even more outside research to create an effective and well-supported essay.

Areas of research may include the following:

- The writer's or director's life.
- The writer's or director's body of work.

- In general, what is your favorite television genre?

- What are some of your favorite television shows that make up that genre?

- What is it about these television shows that you enjoy? Give examples.

- Do these shows play at a certain time of day or on particular channels? Do you always watch HBO or HGTV? Perhaps you usually watch late-night talk shows or early morning game shows?

- The backgrounds of the cast.

- The historical background of the television episode or show itself, the events portrayed in the program, television production codes at the time, technology at the time the television show was made, and so on.

- The culture represented or presented in the television show.

- How the television show is or was received by others.

- The economic history or budget of the television show.

- The original source for the script.

- The history or development of filming or televising techniques.

- The evolution of particular genres or recognized storyline or character conventions.

Since this type of research hinges on what you want answered, one of the best places to start is with a list of questions. Create your own list, try to answer as many questions as you can, and then start your outside research. Check out Chapter 5, it suggests helpful strategies and sources for you to use. For research on television, in particular, you may find reference sources helpful. Look for dictionaries and encyclopedias devoted to television, such as *The Television Encyclopedia* or *The Complete Television Dictionary*. Look for online sources as well, but be sure to look for reliable and balanced information. Most networks and television shows now have websites, and many shows also have fan fiction sites. Some of the more reliable online sources are listed here.

Academy of Television Arts and Sciences	http://www.emmys.tv/
The American Television Institute	http://www.earlytelevision.org/ati.html
Brilliant but Cancelled	http://www.brilliantbutcancelled.com/
FanFiction.net	http://www.fanfiction.net/tv/
FlowTV: A Critical Forum on Television and Media Culture	http://flowtv.org
The International Federation of Television Archives	http://www.fiatifta.org/cont/index.aspx
The Internet Movie Database	http://www.imdb.com
Museum of Broadcast Communications	http://www.museum.tv/museumsection.php
Rotten Tomatoes	http://www.rottentomatoes.com/
Screensite	http://www.screensite.org

WRITING ABOUT TELEVISION

Writing about television in a composition class offers many opportunities to investigate your reactions and the reactions of those around you to television and how it shapes us and our culture. You and your peers may want to talk or write about your reactions or responses to particular shows you watch together or to shows that interest only you. Since most students have different viewing schedules or interests, the wealth of topics is never ending.

Writing about television can be much like writing about film or literature because it shares many similarities with these other types of media. However, since television is available to a much greater number of people than film or literature, your knowledge of how television shapes your world may be even more developed. Just as with film or literature, some critics would argue that picking apart characters, scenes, or language may destroy the beauty of the whole for the viewer. However, analyzing television programs or television in general can help you become more aware of the elements that make up the whole. It might allow you to appreciate aspects of television that you may never have appreciated before or push you to clearly see how television affects our culture in many ways.

BOB D'AMICO/ABC/PHOTOFEST

You may want to investigate the structure of *Modern Family* or the music of *Nashville.* Your investigation could focus on how these make you reflect on your own life or interests or how these technical aspects compare with other television shows. If you are more interested in social and cultural phenomena, television is ideal for investigating its positive or negative influences on you or your culture, whether that culture is the culture of a professional community as seen on *Bones* or the culture of an ethnic background as focused on *The Cleveland Show.* Whatever way you choose to use television in your writing, the wealth of channels, agendas, voices, and programming is what makes television an exciting medium for critical thinking and writing.

Just like film, television is considered an artistic medium and can usually be interpreted or analyzed in many ways. Though there are many options to choose from when you are writing about television, four main types of assignments are common: television reviews or review essays, reflection or response essays, analysis essays, and synthesis essays.

Television Reviews or Review Essays

Just as with film, a review of a television episode, show, or genre is basically a screening report; however, it is not just a synopsis of the plot of the show or the series. Some kind of evaluative opinion is

KEY questions

Key Questions for a Television Review Essay

- Have you clearly indicated your judgment of the television show's quality?

- Have you provided a brief plot synopsis while avoiding plot summary?

- Have you begun the review with an attention-grabbing opening? Have you concluded it with a striking sentence?

- Did you write in literary present tense?

- Have you mentioned specific elements of the television show that support your judgment? Have you described these quickly and vividly, using concrete language and metaphors?

- Have you defined yourself as a credible source by writing clearly and giving support for your arguments?

- Have you qualified your judgment with both positive and negative aspects of the television show?

Key Questions for a Reflection or Response Essay

- Have you clearly indicated how you used the television show as a springboard for your thesis?

- Have you expressed your personal response to one aspect of the television show?

- Did you avoid plot summary?

- Does your introduction direct your audience into your response?

- Does your concluding paragraph include some reflection on both the television show and your response?

- Did you write about the television show in literary present tense but any past life experiences in past tense?

- Are your writing intentions clear?

expected, along with description that supports your judgments or opinions. These are the types of essays normally found in journals such as *The Journal of Popular Film and Television,* in magazines such as *Entertainment Weekly,* and on online review sites such as Salon or Rotten Tomatoes. Just as with film reviews, television reviews usually follow particular conventions. Your overall evaluation can be an explicit thesis or argument in the essay, such as in this thesis: "Although *Ugly Betty* focuses on a main character who is Latina, the show continues to perpetuate cultural stereotypes." However, instead of giving an explicit thesis or argument at the beginning of their review, some review writers build up their description of different aspects of what they are reviewing and then lead their readers to the final evaluation at the end of the essay.

Reflection or Response Essays

Remember that reflection or response essays usually include some description of the television show as a way to begin your discussion. However, this description should not be overwhelming or the only information given to the reader. Be sure not to just present a description of the story itself. Reflection or response essays are quite personal in nature, so be sure that you reflect on your own personal feelings or ideas that came about due to watching the show. The show should ignite something personal that you are excited or impelled to share with your audience. For instance, writers watching an episode of *Survivor* might discuss how one participant's lies to the other castaways reminded them of how they were lied to by a friend at one time.

Analysis Essays

When you write an analysis essay about a television episode or series, you are giving a strong opinion or an argument about an idea you have about the television show. You want to come across to the reader as an expert, providing a strong argument and supporting this argument with evidence from the show. Analyzing a television show usually means that you are focused on one or more particular aspects of the show's structure(s), meaning(s), or effect(s). For instance, you could write about how the structure of *The Simpsons* often follows the same structure as a nonanimated comedy. Or you could delve into the meanings behind certain key elements of scenery in *The Walking Dead* or *Doctor Who* or investigate the effects that violence on television has on elementary schoolchildren. You are trying to convince the reader that your understanding of the show is true, and you do this by using specific and effective evidence either from the show or from the viewers. Remember, you are not just describing; you are arguing that your analysis is true, so when you use descriptive information, be sure it supports your argument rather than just shares an interesting part of the show. Strong supportive detail can include specific descriptions of scenes or specific details about characters or locations, outside research about the writer or director and the choices he or she makes, or the context or culture that surrounds the show.

Synthesis Essays

As a genre, synthesis essays do just what the title implies—they synthesize other approaches into one essay or take a broad view across multiple shows or time periods. Although a review usually involves stating whether or not you liked a show, it might be made stronger by using some analysis, or an analysis might be more effective with some personal reflection in it. The essay writing described here is not given to restrict you but to help guide you when asked to write specific types of assignments. However, the type of assignment you are given or choose to write will help you determine whether you need to break out of just one type of essay writing. If you choose to write using a combination of strategies, be sure to check with your instructor and then look over the key questions for the types of writing you are including.

ANNOTATED SAMPLE ESSAY

CONSIDERING IDEAS

Make a list of at least ten television shows that depict the lives of teenagers.

1. How realistic are these shows?

2. Is it necessary for teen comedies and dramas on television to be realistic for the shows to become hits?

AUTHOR BIO

To help you process ideas for writing about television, Andrew Coomes's essay comparing Dawson's Creek *with* My So-Called Life *is included here. Coomes could have written a review of either show or a personal response that focused on how one or the other show affected or changed his life. However, he chose to write an analysis essay that uses outside sources to support his arguments and conclusions. Note where he supports his ideas and how he incorporates outside sources into his prose.*

Andrew Coomes *wrote this essay as a student at Middle Tennessee State University. He is now a high school English teacher whose writing interests include film and television studies. His essay "Timing Is Everything" was published in* Dear Angela: Remembering My So-Called Life *(2007). Coomes's book chapter entitled "Inspiring Writing: Using Film in the Composition Classroom" is included in the 2011 book entitled* Movies, Music and More: Advancing Popular Culture in the Writing Classroom.

KEY questions

Key Questions for an Analysis Essay

- Do you have an implied or explicit thesis?

- Do you have a series of reasons to support the thesis? Are these arranged in logical and convincing order?

- Are your supporting reasons backed up? Do you provide specific evidence and examples from the television show for each reason you offer?

- Does your introduction orient your reader into the direction of your argument?

- Does your concluding paragraph provide a vivid ending?

- Did you write in literary present tense?

- Did you avoid plot summary?

TIMING IS EVERYTHING

The Success of *Dawson's Creek* and the Failure of *My So-Called Life*

Andrew Coomes

Note how Coomes highlights or blueprints the types of relationships that are the focus of the rest of the essay.

Created and written by Kevin Williamson, the first season of *Dawson's Creek* (WB, 1998–2003) bears an uncanny resemblance to Winnie Holzman's *My So-Called Life,* which ran for only one year on ABC (1994–1995). Although *My So-Called Life* and *Dawson's Creek* deal with many of the same issues, the former was ahead of its time, and the latter is more self-aware and gives the issues more life and panache. The two shows have nearly identical characters, plots, and soundtracks, but viewer interest (or lack thereof) caused *My So-Called Life* to be cancelled and *Dawson's Creek* to thrive. *My So-Called Life* and the first season of *Dawson's Creek* both portray the lives of high school sophomores and their relationships—friendly, romantic, and family. In his 1994 review of *My So-Called Life,* James Martin states, "Perhaps the best part of the show is the dead-on portrait of high school life, with its moments of learning and love as well as boredom and lunacy. In this arena, *My So-Called Life* is as clever as any mainstream film satire of high school" (24). The same words could have been used to describe *Dawson's Creek* just four years later.

Both shows revolve around a central character, Angela Chase (Claire Danes) in *My So-Called Life* and Dawson Leery (James Van Der Beek) in *Dawson's Creek.* Angela's viewpoint is constantly revealed though her voice-over narration; however, because there is no voice-over in *Dawson's Creek,* we learn about Dawson's through his conversations with his best friend Joey Potter (Katie Holmes) and his actions. In Michael Krantz's article "The Bard of Gen-Y: Hot-wired into Today's Teens, Kevin Williamson is Giving Hollywood Something to Scream About," Van Der Beek asserts, "[Williamson's] characters are incredibly honest. They say things teenagers are thinking but don't necessarily say, especially about sexuality" (106). While Angela's honesty is in her mind, which audiences are privy to through her voice-over, Dawson's honesty is revealed to the audience (and the characters surrounding him) through his speech and actions.

In addition to the similar main characters, Angela's parents and Dawson's parents also share similar characteristics. Graham and Patty Chase (Tom Irwin and Bess Armstrong) are essential elements of *My So-Called Life,* partly because they help attract adult viewers, but mostly due to the influential role of parents in a teenager's life. Mitch and Gail Leery (John Wesley Shipp and Mary-Margaret Humes) have the same purpose in *Dawson's Creek,* serving as role models, albeit not always the best role models. The pilot episodes of both series unveil a marital affair when

Note the use of a transition to another point of comparison.

Angela sees her father talking to another woman late at night, and Joey sees Dawson's mother kissing another man late at night. While Graham calls off his affair in the second episode, "Dancing in the Dark," the temptation of another affair appears with Hallie Lowenthal (Lisa Waltz) in the "Self-Esteem" episode. The threat and temptation of an affair is constantly present, but Graham never actually cheats on Patty. *Dawson's Creek*, on the other hand, is more aggressive with the affair subplot, devoting much more time and excitement to the affair. Gail actually does cheat on Mitch with her co-worker Bob Collinsworth (Ric Reitz), and Mitch eventually finds out about it in the "Hurricane" episode. The remainder of the first season shows Dawson trying to cope with his parents' possible divorce and Mitch and Gail struggling to keep a 20-year marriage alive.

The relationships of the younger characters in both series are just as complex and complicated as the adults'. Love triangles and unreciprocated love are key elements in both *Life* and *Dawson's*. Although Angela is oblivious to the fact, her friend Brian (Devon Gummersall) wants to be much more than friends, but she is too infatuated with Jordan Catalano (Jared Leto) to notice. Likewise, Joey is in love with Dawson, but he is in love with Jen Lindley (Michelle Williams). In the "Betrayal" episode, Angela is enraged when her friend Rayanne Graff (A. J. Langer) sleeps with Jordan just as Dawson is upset when his friend Pacey Whitter (Joshua Jackson) kisses Jen in the "Detention" episode. The betrayal of the central characters' best friends causes ripples in the friends' relationships and the love interests' relationships as well. Because Pacey only kisses Jen as part of a game of Truth or Dare, Dawson is quick to forgive his friend, but Angela is not as forgiving. Rayanne is not playing a game, and having sex with Jordan completely demolishes her friendship with Angela. In the last episode of *My So-Called Life*, "In Dreams Begin Responsibilities," Brian confesses his love to Angela, but she leaves with Jordan before she can respond. If a second season had followed "In Dreams Begin Responsibilities," this cliffhanger may have been resolved, or at least developed further. Unfortunately, ABC cancelled the series due to poor ratings, leaving its audience with no sense of closure. *Dawson's Creek* ends its first season with the "Decisions" episode in which Joey, like Brian, confesses her love to the main character. *Dawson's Creek* goes a step beyond *My So-Called Life* when Dawson tells Joey that he shares her feelings and kisses her, providing some closure to the season.

Life and *Dawson's* also shared a love for music. In her essay on "The Teen Series," Rachel Moseley observes that, "At the imaginative center of the teen drama, as in soap, are place, character and relationships, and emotional drama is often heightened through the use of close-up and (generally romantic pop) scoring (for example, *My So-Called Life* and *Dawson's Creek*)" (41–42). The soundtracks from both shows often comment on the actions taking place during a scene. For example, in the pilot episode of *My So-Called Life*, Angela cries because she sees her father talking to

Coomes includes names of characters, actors, and episodes, and he also gives full descriptions of all of these to give support to his claims.

Coomes connects two types of pop culture media here.

his female co-worker in the middle of the night, and R.E.M.'s "Everybody Hurts" begins to play. Likewise, in the pilot episode of *Dawson's Creek*, The Pretenders' "I'll Stand By You" is playing as Dawson confesses to Joey that their friendship will last through the tough adolescent years. The correlating songs and scenes continue as both series progress. In "The Zit" episode of *My So-Called Life,* Enigma's "Return to Innocence" plays as Angela watches young girls with their mothers and ponders the significance of beauty and appearances of women in society. The song reflects the idea that children don't think about outward appearances, and Angela's desire to return to this innocence of childhood is signified in her words, "People are so strange and complicated that they're actually beautiful—possibly even me." In the "Dance" episode of *Dawson's Creek*, Jann Arden's "You Don't Know Me" plays as Joey watches Dawson dance outside with Jen. The significance of the song is twofold: Dawson is falling in love with Jen, but he doesn't yet know Jen's history of sex, drugs, and alcohol in New York; and Joey is falling in love with Dawson, but he doesn't yet know her true feelings for him. Throughout many of the episodes of both *My So-Called Life* and *Dawson's Creek,* the music follows along with story, and the songs' lyrics help relate the significance of images on screen.

Both shows also have controversial gay teenage characters, Rickie Vasquez (Wilson Cruz) on *Life* and *Dawson's* Jack McPhee (Kerr Smith). Frank DeCaro addresses these similarities in his article "In With the Out Crowd," noting that *My So-Called Life* was criticized for its focus on the gay community, but *Dawson's Creek* and other teen dramas on The WB made the exploration of the gay lifestyle more acceptable (44). Kevin Williamson states in "Outings on the Creek" that he "didn't want to make it an open-and-shut one-episode situation. I wanted to explore the complexities of a young boy coming to terms with his homosexuality, very much the way I did in a small town" (Epstein 46). Both Rickie and Jack openly express their homosexuality and have male love interests that are discussed overtly as well.

Coomes uses secondary sources to support his own ideas.

Both *My So-Called Life* and the first season of *Dawson's Creek* explore the reality of gay teachers as well. Mr. Katimpski (Jeff Perry), the drama teacher in *My So-Called Life*, connects with Rickie and even offers him a place to stay when Rickie becomes homeless in the "Resolutions" episode. In the days before *Will and Grace* (NBC, 1998–2006), *Queer as Folk* (Showtime, 2000–2005), and *Queer Eye for the Straight Guy* (Bravo, 2003–present), Mr. Katimpski and Rickie were two of the very few gay characters on television, and they offered realistic portrayals of gay men. They both have a lot to lose if people found out they are gay: Mr. Katimpski stands to lose his job, and Rickie always risks being beaten, as he often is. Likewise, Mr. Gold (Mitchell Laurance), the film teacher in *Dawson's Creek*, hides his homosexuality in the first season of *Dawson's Creek* until the aptly named episode "Discovery." Rickie and Mr. Katimpski helped pave the way for Jack, Mr. Gold, and the number of other gay television characters that have appeared since *My So-Called Life.*

Note that Coomes does not give a list of similarities and then a list of differences. He fleshes out the previous paragraphs of similarities and then starts to wonder why and how these two shows met such different receptions.

With so many similarities between the two series, why did one thrive and the other get cancelled? The main reason *Dawson's Creek* succeeded and *My So-Called Life* failed was not their respective homosexual characters as the previous paragraph may suggest; it was the number of people watching the shows. *Dawson's Creek* was able to attract more viewers partially because of its popularity on a new television netlet, The WB. In Bruce Fretts's article "High School Confidential: *Dawson's Creek*," Joshua Jackson explains that by airing on The WB, "we can avoid *My So-Called Life*-itis", (36) which, of course, is the medical condition of a short-lived television series. Another reason for *Dawson's Creek*'s success was its audience's acceptance and desire to see the world, both the good and bad parts, from the viewpoint of a 15-year-old. *My So-Called Life,* though still offering the same realistic viewpoint of a 15-year-old, was simply not able to keep an audience. In "Please Remember, *Dawson's Creek* is Fiction," Ken Parish Perkins says, "For *Life* to have succeeded then—and for any series dealing honestly with teenagers to gain an audience now—there must be an acceptance of their interpretation of the world as a scary, sometimes depressing place" (219). *Dawson's Creek,* just three years after *My So-Called Life,* was able to accomplish this feat, giving a realistic portrayal of teen life and doing so for an audience that was finally willing to accept the bad with the good.

My So-Called Life was merely three or four years ahead of its time. Dealing with so many of the same issues, plots, and character types, the main difference between *My So-Called Life* and *Dawson's Creek* was the years they were released and the television networks on which they debuted. Unlike *My So-Called Life, Dawson's Creek* had other television series to help pave the way to make its content more acceptable to viewers. *Buffy the Vampire Slayer* (1997–2003) and *Felicity* (1998–2002), both on The WB, and even *My So-Called Life* itself set the stage for *Dawson's Creek*. In his 1995 review of *My So-Called Life,* Ken Tucker declares,

Coomes starts to reach his conclusions here about why *My So-Called Life* did not meet the same reception as *Dawson's Creek*. Note how the similarities of the shows have been presented first and in much more length than his conclusions. Why doesn't this weaken the essay?

There was nothing else like this on the air last season—no show at once so serious and so entertaining, so insightful yet so much fun. Had the series continued for another season, who knows what sort of dramatic miracles lead actress Claire Danes might have performed as Angela, what twists there might have been in the marriage between Patty and Graham? (50)

We are left with even more questions after *My So-Called Life*'s finale: "What happens when the central character actually falls in love with the best friend who has secretly desired her the entire season?" and "Does a marriage last after it has battled the infidelity of one of the spouses?" *My So-Called Life* could not provide the answers, but *Dawson's Creek* had the narrative time, the will, and the audience and could address similar questions.

Another reason for *Dawson's Creek*'s first season success was its postmodern self-awareness as a teen drama, an ability Williamson had already exhibited in blatantly self-aware horror films *Scream* (1996) and *I Know What You Did Last Summer* (1997). *Dawson's Creek* and *My So-Called Life* were both teen dramas, but *Dawson's Creek* overtly recognizes itself as a teen drama through its writing, characters, and plotlines. Between *My So-Called Life*'s cancellation and *Dawson's Creek*'s debut, this self-awareness became an acceptable style. In the "Dance" episode, Dawson asks Joey at the end of a drama-filled night, "What did we learn from tonight's *90210* evening?" Referencing Aaron Spelling's teen drama from the 1990s, Dawson draws attention to his own actions and experiences resembling a television teen drama. "My So-Called Soap: The Creator of *Scream* Goes 90210; Scary" describes the cast of *Dawson's Creek*: "Improbably self-aware"; "this hyperverbal Party of Four all speak in the same jaded mix of pop-culture referencing and therapyspeak" (68). Dawson and Joey even go so far as to discuss cliffhangers of television shows in the final episode of the first season. In their introduction to *Teen TV: Genre, Consumption and Identity*, Glyn Davis and Kay Dickinson describe scenes like this flawlessly:

Witty, knowing and slightly mawkish, such dialogue highlights key elements of the texture of *Dawson's Creek*: a use of language which is too sophisticated for the ages of the characters; frequent intertextual references; recourse to a sense of community based on generation; a blunt, somewhat melodramatic use of emotion and aphoristic psychological reasoning; and a prominent pop music soundtrack. (1)

While the lack of self-awareness was probably not part of the reason *My So-Called Life* was cancelled, the postmodern characteristic quickly became an essential element of contemporary television in the late 1990s, contributing to *Dawson's Creek*'s success.

Holzman's *My So-Called Life* and Williamson's *Dawson's Creek* were both milestones in teenage television dramas, providing opportunities for the genre to flourish. However, timing and ratings were the downfall of *My So-Called Life* and, eventually, *Dawson's Creek*. Surviving six seasons, *Dawson's Creek* was cancelled due to poor ratings. In "*Dawson's Creek*: 'Quality Teen TV' and 'Mainstream Cult'?," Matt Hills defines the series as quality television because of its "status both textually (via its representations of relationships and character reflexivity) and intertextually (by aligning itself with Williamson's other, high-profile work in teen horror cinema)" (54). Though *My So-Called Life* did not have the same "high-profiled" connection with Holzman's work, the series easily falls into the same textual and cult TV categories that Hills describes as evidence of quality television. Additionally, in their introduction to *Quality Popular Television*, Mark Jancovich and James Lyons state that "contemporary television has witnessed the emergence of 'must see TV', shows that are not simply part of a habitual flow of television programming but, either through design or audience response, have become 'essential viewing'" (2). Again, both *Dawson's Creek* and *My So-Called Life,* through their design as eminent teenage television dramas, fit Jancovich and Lyons' description of quality television.

A secondary conclusion is reached here—both shows were quality television. Why is this an effective conclusion to the entire essay? Why do you think Coomes chose to include this rather than just listing similarities and differences of the two shows?

Although *My So-Called Life* was short-lived and *Dawson's Creek* eventually died as well, both series are the epitome of quality television and provide viewers with insightful comments on the reality of adolescence.

Works Cited

Davis, Glyn, and Kay Dickinson, eds. *Teen TV: Genre, Consumption and Identity*. London: British Film Institute, 2004. Print.

Dawson's Creek: The Complete First Season. Perf. James Van Der Beek, Michelle Williams, Joshua Jackson, and Katie Holmes. 1998. Columbia Tristar, 2003. DVD.

DeCaro, Frank. "In with the Out Crowd." *TV Guide* 1 May 1999: 44–46. Print.

Epstein, Jeffrey. "Outings on the Creek." *The Advocate* 16 Mar. 1999: 46. Print.

Fretts, Bruce. "High School Confidential: *Dawson's Creek*." *Entertainment Weekly* 9 Jan. 1998: 34–37. Print.

Hills, Matt. "*Dawson's Creek:* 'Quality Teen TV' and 'Mainstream Cult'?" *Teen TV: Genre, Consumption and Identity*. Eds. Glyn Davis and Kay Dickinson. London: British Film Institute, 2004. 54–67. Print.

Jancovich, Mark, and James Lyons, eds. *Quality Popular Television*. London: British Film Institute, 2003. Print.

Krantz, Michael. "The Bard of Gen-Y: Hot-Wired into Today's Teens, Kevin Williamson Is Giving Hollywood Something to Scream About." *Time* 15 Dec. 1997: 105–106. Print.

Martin, James. "My So-Called Life." *America* 17 Sep. 1994: 24. Print.

Moseley, Rachel. "The Teen Series." *The Television Genre Book*. Ed. Glen Creeber. London: BFI, 2001. 41–43. Print

My So-Called Life: The Complete Series. Perf. Claire Danes, Bess Armstrong, Wilson Cruz, Jared Leto, and Devon Gummersall. 1994–95. BMG, 2002. DVD.

"My So-Called Soap: The Creator of *Scream* Goes 90210; Scary." *Newsweek* 19 Jan. 1998: 68. Print.

Perkins, Ken Parish. "Please Remember, Dawson's Creek Is Fiction." *Knight Ridder/Tribune News Service* 19 Feb. 1998: 219. *InfoTrac*. James E. Walker Library, Murfreesboro. Web. 3 May 2003.

Tucker, Ken. "*My So-Called* Death." *Entertainment Weekly* 16 June 1995: 50–51. Print.

Source: *From* Dear Angela: Remembering My So-Called Life, *edited by Michelle Byers and David Lavery. Reprinted with permission from Lexington Books.*

DECODING THE TEXT

1. How many similarities does Coomes use to compare the two teen dramas?

2. If Coomes had to drop one of the similarities, which one do you think should be deleted? Why?

3. What is the disease Coomes calls *My So-Called Life*-itis?

4. What are some of the questions viewers were left with when *My So-Called Life* was cancelled?

CONNECTING TO YOUR CULTURE

Both of the teen dramas Coomes discusses in this essay play heavily in syndication, especially on channels owned by Nickelodeon.

1. How familiar are you with these shows?

2. Does Coomes's essay make you want to watch them?

3. Teen dramas supposedly represent the lives of real teens. Based on Coomes's description and what you've seen of these two shows, do they represent the life of the average teen? Of you as a teen?

4. What teen dramas are playing on television this season?

5. Do they represent your life as a teen? Why or why not?

THE READING ZONE

ENGAGING WITH TOPICS

1. In what ways does television enrich your life? Negatively impact your life?

2. What are some of the stereotypical characters that are depicted in television dramas, comedies, or reality shows? Why do you think that writers and producers continue to create television shows that include such stereotypical or stock characters?

3. If you had to choose the top three television shows that you have ever seen, what would they be? Why would you choose these three and leave others off your list?

4. Every once in a while, television characters break stereotypical boundaries on television. Consider Miranda Bailey on *Grey's Anatomy*, Kurt Hummel on *Glee*, or Hurley from *Lost*—all of these characters were new to television, breaking stereotypical boundaries. Why do characters such as these become so popular with the viewing audience, and why does it take television programs so long to introduce these types of nonstereotyped characters?

5. Are there certain groups that are constantly portrayed on television in a negative manner? What are these groups? Why do writers or producers bring these characters to television?

6. Is your culture—whatever culture or subcultures you belong to—portrayed accurately on television or even portrayed at all?

READING SELECTIONS

Using the decades approach, the readings about television are divided into three sections: the 1970s and 1980s, the 1990s and 2000s, and the 2010s. Essays are placed into these sections based on many factors, including when the essay was written and what the author is writing about, and they are presented here as thought-provoking samples of popular culture writing. In the 1970s and 1980s section, five writers review *Roots,* a 1977 miniseries that dramatized the life of Alex Haley—author of the book by the same name—and his family line. The miniseries celebrated its thirtieth anniversary in 2007 with a newly packaged DVD set, making these reviews relevant once again. This section also includes a review by Michael D. Ayers of the best *Saturday Night Live* musical performances and an obituary essay about the death of the VHS tape.

Next, in the 1990s and 2000s section, Ariel Crocket and Greg Braxton discuss the intermingling of reality shows and minority characters on television, and Mark I. Pinsky proposes that cartoons can teach many things, including faith. Also in this section, we provide a case study on how homosexuality is represented on television, including a satiric essay from *The Onion,* an *Entertainment Weekly* essay on (lack of) tolerance and what Mark Harris calls the "Official Entertainment Remorse Machine," and also an analysis essay from *Entertainment Weekly* on the representation of gay teens on television.

The 2010s section begins with Joanne Ostrow's essay on how television watchers are now using a variety of technology to watch their favorite television programs. This section continues with an intriguing look by Carina Chocano into how hoarders are represented on television. And the section concludes with a visual essay by Andrew Shears, showing how a visual can stand alone as text.

READING SELECTIONS:
THE 1970s AND 1980s

CONSIDERING IDEAS

Roots was a thirteen-hour miniseries broadcast in 1977 and watched by millions.

1. How familiar are you with this miniseries and its theme?

2. Check online for information on how popular this miniseries was in its first showing. Why do you think it resonated with Americans in the 1970s?

3. How much do you know about African American history and culture?

AUTHOR BIO

Since 1969, The Black Scholar *has become one of the leading journals of black cultural and political thought. After ABC broadcast the thirteen-hour miniseries* Roots *in 1977, the editors at* The Black Scholar, *in keeping with their interest in publishing topics of concern to the African American community, asked a number of "black intellectuals, media workers and scholars" to comment on their reactions to* Roots *in a special edition of* The Black Scholar Forum. *Five of those reviews and responses follow.*

ABC PHOTO ARCHIVES/ABC/GETTY IMAGES

THE BLACK SCHOLAR FORUM

A Symposium on *Roots*

(*Roots* marked such a major event in the history of television and its treatment of the black experience, that the impact has seriously been examined by many who viewed *Roots*. The success and controversy of the television production and the book *Roots* has taken many forms.

One notable development is that Alex Haley is suing his publisher, Doubleday & Co., for allegedly failing to sell or promote the book properly. In other developments, the National Book Awards gave *Roots* a special citation of merit, and most recently, the authenticity of the African section of *Roots* has been questioned by British journalist Mark Ottaway of the *London Times*.

Particular concern has been raised by the black community over the extent to which the recent television sequence of 13 hours broadcast by ABC-TV during the last week of January 1977 accurately reflects the plot, characters or intentions of Alex Haley's epic treatment of the black experience. *The Black Scholar* asked a number of black intellectuals, media workers and scholars to comment on the television production of *Roots*. We have published their responses in this symposium. We welcome remarks, ideas and criticism from our readers.)

Source: *"The Black Scholar Forum: A Symposium on Roots" by Robert Staples, p. 37, 1977. Reprinted by permission of* The Black Scholar.

AUTHOR BIO

Robert Staples *is a former professor at the University of California, San Francisco, where he taught sociology. He is the author of* The Black Woman in America: Sex, Marriage and the Family *(1973),* Black Masculinity: The Black Male's Role in American Society *(1982),* The Urban Plantation *(1987), and* The World of Black Singles: Changing Patterns in Male/Female Relations *(1981). Staples is also a coauthor of* Black Families at the Crossroads: Challenges and Prospects *(2004) and, most recently, the author of* Exploring Black Sexuality *(2006). Staples has also contributed more than 100 articles and reviews to sociology journals and various magazines.*

ROOTS

Melodrama of the Black Experience

Robert Staples

It is not easy to sort out one's feelings about the television production of *Roots*. On the one hand it is tempting to succumb to the flattery bestowed upon blacks by the national attention paid to a television show in which we are the major, and in most cases positive, protagonists. As a scholar and critic it would be equally convenient for me to conclude that it gave the black masses a feeling of pride and militancy and hence, its overall impact was beneficial to our cause. Upon further reflection I find it hard to settle for just those conclusions.

Unlike some critics I will not dwell upon any unique racial motives behind the showing of *Roots* at this juncture in our history. I assume that as is true of most television productions they made this one for profit without regard for any higher value. The fact that the television show did not conform strictly to the book is no different than other TV or movie adaptations of books or plays. That it was not historically accurate is again a typical way that the mass media takes liberties with historical and contemporary facts. In essence *Roots* was a typical television melodrama played out in a prosaic fashion which attracted the attention of the American public due to a combination of socio-psychological factors.

For whites it confirmed their view of blacks as victims of an institution which none of them created or feel responsible for. It imbedded in the public consciousness a view of black problems as deriving chiefly from historical forces which in turn have fashioned an incapacity of Afro-Americans to adjust to the imperatives of Euro-American culture. The blacks who witnessed the television show may have a greater, if inaccurate, awareness of their past. But, the tragic consequence of *Roots* for many blacks is that it has chained them to a fictional past without explaining where and why they are today. *Roots* told us little about how our use as human capital shored up a fledgling industrial order in the South nor did it explain our use as a scapegoat for all of America's problems.

To wit, *Roots* set in motion blacks trying to find out who and where their ancestors are while we do not know where in the pecking order our children will be. Its markedly apolitical character did not describe how the modern political state continues to exploit us with its oppressive machinery in order to maintain this society's equilibrium. In short, *Roots* was like the proverbial Chinese dinner: we feel satisfied when eating it but are still hungry a few hours later. Someday we may be diners at the freedom table but the television production of *Roots* was nothing more than an ephemeral episode in a saga that is still being played out.

Source: *"The Black Scholar Forum: A Symposium on Roots" by Robert Staples, p. 37, 1977. Reprinted by permission of* The Black Scholar.

AUTHOR BIO

Clyde Taylor *is a former professor in Africana studies at New York University and at NYU's Gallatin School of Individualized Study. His publications include* Vietnam and Black America *(1973) and* The Mask of Art: Breaking the Aesthetic Contract—Film and Literature *(1998).*

ROOTS

A Modern Minstrel Show

Clyde Taylor

The serious questions black people have to direct to the TV version of *Roots*, or any dramatic presentation, begin with authorship and direction. Can it be *black* drama (drama *for* black people) when neither author nor director is black? *Roots* on television fails this test on all counts except for one hour directed by Gilbert Moses.

In the white artistic control behind ABC's televising of *Roots* lies a clue to one very important possible motive behind the production (not forgetting other possibilities, like money, mind-manipulation, etc.). The motives of white artists in dealing with black reality are usually couched, more deeply than we generally realize, in the obscure, complex, self-serving impulses of minstrelsy. *Roots* televised was yet another offering of black images in animation, enacting the perception of white creative controllers as to what it must be like to be black in America.

We should not be deflected from recognizing the minstrel motive by the comparatively high quality of the production or the scraps of good intentions displayed. The historical fact is that many of the original minstrel shows contained liberal, even anti-slavery, sentiments. The recent dramatization of *Minstrel Man* was excellent in many ways and surpassed some episodes of *Roots* in skill and subtlety. (Some of the worst aspects of *Roots* on TV came in sequences not in the book, that degenerated into the "they-went-thataway" modes of *Gunsmoke*.) But artistic skill and liberal sentiments are misleading barometers when assessing the impact of the varieties of minstrelism.

If *Roots* on video has elevated the creative possibilities of television, that fact is in harmony with American cultural history, which owes (but seldom pays for) some of its greatest leaps to either the presence of black creativity or to the curious impetus that the black presence has on white American imagination. ABC's television spectacular should be seen in continuity with the phenomenally successful nineteenth century minstrel shows and also with the enormous influence that *Shuffle Along*, a *black* musical, had on subsequent American musical comedy.

In cases like *Roots*, what must be weighed is the *total* gain or loss, not just the artistic. Harriet Beecher Stowe's *Uncle Tom's Cabin* may have helped to end slavery, but we are right to remember the later mythic and cultural damage its images of black people effected, too. If, in the area of politics, the ultimate measure is freedom, in esthetics the comparable measure must be total truth. Sterling Brown says "they take two steps forward, then one step back" of the white productions that, in my opinion, *Roots* is heir to. And as Malcolm pointed out,

Why should we be grateful to a man who pulls his knife *half-way* out of our backs?

Source: *"The Black Scholar Forum: A Symposium on Roots"* by Clyde Taylor, pp. 37–38, 1977. Reprinted by permission of The Black Scholar.

AUTHOR BIO

Chinweizu is a Nigerian poet, critic, and journalist. In the 1970s, he was an associate professor at San Jose State University. He is the author of many works, including the historical study The West and the Rest of Us: White Predators, Black Slaves and the African Elite *(1975)* and Energy Crisis and Other Poems *(1978).*

ROOTS

Urban Renewal of the American Dream

Chinweizu

That *Roots-TV* was produced and massively promoted is not difficult to understand when it is seen as supplying one of the finishing touches to the imperial reformation which the American establishment undertook, seriously, but with all deliberate speed, after the Korean no-win war. Having racially integrated various parts of American society, the liberal establishment had to buttress its exercise in internal decolonization and neo-colonization of Afro-America with a reshaped popular memory of American history. Since the history of Afro-America could no longer be profitably slandered and distorted, or treated as problematic, unique, and apart, there developed a need to integrate the American saga of those who were brought with the American saga of those who came, making them mere variants of the quintessential American saga in pursuit of the American Dream. Therefore, a suitably rehabilitated portrait of slavery had to be inserted into the national historical memory. Given this clue to the question, why now?, still, why the choice of *Roots* for this role? But what would have been the alternatives?

Haley's *Roots* is unquestionably a saga of vast scope, and about indomitable human spirit. But still, *Chicken George was no Nat Turner.* Given its objectives, what sort of story would the establishment pick up and project? One which would compel a more radical or a less radical questioning of the system? Imagine a film, *Nat Turner*, made with even so mild a treatment as that in the movie *Spartacus*. Would any network pick it up and risk having all those young and impressionable all-American kids who rooted for Chicken George root instead for Nat Turner? But, leaders of slave revolts aside, where were the field hands in *Roots-TV*? As a brief review in *Rumble* points out: "Anyone who knows anything about the nature of slavery in this country knows . . . (that *Roots-TV*) was understated. This is not to say that Haley's book is anything but authentic. But only to point out that the life of the field hand was much more severe than what we saw in the production."

Now, put yourself in the position of the establishment's manipulators of the national memory. If you were concerned with grounding a program of neo-colonial racial integration upon a shared national memory of slavery, and were on the lookout for the best possible material, and along came a highly researched historical saga about an Afro-American family which survived and made good, a saga that most Afro-Americans, as survivors of slavery and as a people fed up with Jim Crow travesties, could identify with, but nevertheless a saga which, by the particular historical circumstances it faithfully treats, does not provide as radical a criticism of slavery as some others might do, would you not snap it up and give it maximum exposure? I would say that an establishment would have to be, not asleep, but rather too busy surrendering its power in order for it to pass up such a grand opportunity.

On the matter of its content and impact, clearly, the view from *Roots-TV* is not the whole picture of Afro-American enslavement. Muted and inauthentic as it may be in comparison to Haley's *Roots*, still, as a saga of survival, *Roots-TV* is significant for, and fundamentally representative of, Afro-America today. (After all, did the Nat Turners bequeath progeny to the Bicentennial? Not very likely.) At the very least, it ought to retire from the minds of its viewers the old stereotypes invented to serve segregation; it ought to indelibly stamp upon the popular American mind the historical fact that the USA is much more the rightful patrimony of Afro-America than it is that of any immigrant groups who arrived after the Civil War. It ought to drive it home that the oppression and degradation which Kunta Kinte's family, and all Afro-American families, survived were not due to biology, but were social, and entirely man-made. It ought also to impress upon all blacks that, besides family cohesiveness, their survival required contributions from the entire spectrum of the enslaved population, from those who died in revolts, whether on slave ship or on plantations, as well as from those who would be considered Toms. The importance of, and lessons from such contributions, should never be minimized, for group-survival is a many-sided business.

It should, however, still be stressed that this partial rehabilitation of Afro-American history was not done for the primary benefit of Afro-America, but rather for the present purposes of the Euro-American establishment. One should not allow oneself to be conned into gratitude. After all, what they have done through *Roots-TV* is to help Haley to rectify in the national mind some of the distortions they had deliberately concocted and enforced for centuries. To reinforce and supplement the positive impact of *Roots* and of *Roots-TV*, Afro-America needs to produce more corrective books and films on Afro-American history. Otherwise, when the establishment turns desperately and unabashedly fascist, under pressures from the disintegration of its global empire, the positive impressions from *Roots-TV* will be eroded and replaced, with little, if any, difficulty. Besides, *Roots-TV* should not be allowed to become another example of the one-star tokenism system. Shall the networks be allowed to wait another century before they correctly present other periods of Afro-American history, such as Reconstruction, the Great Betraying Compromise of 1877, the Afro-American experience in the labor unions, in the ghettos, etc., and so put *Roots-TV* in its larger historical context? What about a film of *Invisible Man*, for instance? Or of Malcolm X, or even Nat Turner, each done from the point of view of others besides the winners? After all, the networks cannot claim anymore that there is no audience for authentic Afro-Americana!

Source: *"The Black Scholar Forum: A Symposium on Roots" by Chinweizu, pp. 38–39, 1977. Reprinted by permission of* The Black Scholar.

AUTHOR BIO

Charles (Chuck) Stone has been a journalist, a novelist, a political speechwriter, and a professor. He was a columnist and the senior editor for The Philadelphia Daily News *from 1972 to 1991, and he was nominated twice for the Pulitzer Prize. Stone taught journalism at the University of Delaware and then became the Walter Spearman Professor at the University of North Carolina at Chapel Hill, from which he retired in 2005. His books include* Black Political Power in America *(1968),* King Strut *(1970), and the children's book* Squizzy the Black Squirrel *(2003).*

ROOTS

An Electronic Orgy in White Guilt

Chuck Stone

It was an electronic orgy in white guilt successfully hustled by white TV literary minstrels.

With incredulous docility, some 80 million Americans sat transfixed in their separate but equal sanctuaries for the final two-hour episode of the eight-part black historical soap opera, *Roots*, trying to winnow the screen's message from conflicting images in color of black good and white bad.

But images are not carved in the Gibraltars of antiquity. Ideas are. For its literary gracefulness, *Roots*, the book, will stand in solitary preeminence, distinguished by its narrative sweep, historical detail and eloquent craftsmanship. Alex Haley is the Thucydides of our day, interpreting the Black Diaspora as majestically as the Greek historian catalogued the Peloponnesian War.

He labored hard for his people. From the Afro-Caribbean island of Jamaica, my Afro-American friend, Haley, wrote me on June 4, 1974, that "the book aspires to be the symbol saga of all of us of African ancestry." The griot from Tennessee succeeded, painstakingly unraveling the umbilical cord that had stretched a tortured distance from Africa to America.

But *Roots*, the television drama, was aimed at a white market. Television executives rarely produce shows aimed solely or primarily at blacks, even if 24 million blacks watch TV 21 percent more than whites. Nor are blacks hired to do anything more than entertain.

One of the cruel paradoxes of the TV show, *Roots*, was the lily-white cast of writers. "We were not involved in the production or the writing," said Robert Hooks, one of America's most together black actors.

Given those exclusions, why, then, would a major network set aside eight consecutive nights budgeted at $6 million to document this electrifying black experience?

For the same reasons, we would like to conclude, Harriet Beecher Stowe wrote *Uncle Tom's Cabin*. And that's what the television version of *Roots* was   an electronic *Uncle Tom's Cabin*. But an essential difference distinguishes the two artistic expressions.

Uncle Tom's Cabin, which sold an incredible 300,000 copies (the bestseller of its day in 1851), was written to sell the American people on the emancipation of black slaves by raising the public conscience. ABC-TV's *Roots*, which was watched by one-third of all Americans, was produced to sell advertising for the enrichment of white TV executives by raising network ratings. There was an added dividend. A convenient one-shot expiation of white guilt accumulated over 200 years.

The one-third of all Americans who were mesmerized by this epochal event—and despite its flaws, the television showing of *Roots* was one of the great emotional experiences of all time—was probably the same percentage which clung to the evening news on August 28, 1963, and heard the beloved prophet, Rev. Martin Luther King Jr., "go tell it on the mountain."

The combined outpouring of black and white humanity for the "March on Washington" capped by King's soul-wrenching exhortation seemed a natural watershed for black economic and educational empowerment.

Instead, the "March" disemboweled the civil rights movement. Blacks did eke out some symbolically spectacular political gains, but the economic condition of blacks has actually worsened disproportionally since then.

The televised *Roots* has fertilized similar expectations of racial progress. Many black and white social critics are convinced this remarkable black soap opera will somehow modulate the racist conscience of America. Will it? Will we move from a second post-Reconstruction retrogression toward *Plessy vs. Ferguson* to a progressive "era of *Roots*"?

I doubt it. Television is a therapeutic catharsis, not a social engineer. Fashion—not faith—is its food. There will be no new jobs created, slums rebuilt, criminal justice made more fair, white police assassinations of blacks prevented, or ghetto schools transformed merely because *Roots* was shown on television.

What the televised *Roots* did accomplish, however, was to give many blacks who had not known who they were—or who had not read the book, *Roots*—an ennobling sense of their pastness. At last, they could unshackle a subliminal Tarzan mentality and boldly bind a blessed tie of American Negroness to African antiquity.

For whites, *Roots* was another fascinating, but powerful, evening of entertainment. Many were shocked, appalled, even angered, by this accurate depiction of their tawdry past. In that the televised *Roots* seared many white consciences for the first time, the drama achieved a magnificent landmark in entertainment, and, I'm almost tempted to add, educational history. Yet, so far it's still business as usual as television networks—not only ABC-TV, but CBS-TV and NBC-TV—continue to merchandise a vast wasteland of Negro minstrels.

In the cold sobriety of several weeks later, was the televised *Roots* faithful to the quintessence of the black experience? Moderately so. Even an all-white stable of TV writers can not emasculate that much black history.

But there's a basis for comparison. *This Far by Faith* is an hour-long television documentary on the black church, conceived by a black advertising executive and narrated by Brock Peters, one of our black artistic luminaries.

Sensitively written, it explores emotional nuances that only an inhabitant in the black ethos could describe. Near the end of the film, Peters embraces the enormity of the black church's liberating ethic as defined by a triad of black prophets. First, he mentions Adam Clayton Powell and Malcolm X (what white writer could deal with that?).

Then, the film cuts to a church window pane and we hear once again those heart-throbbing cadences of the black Baptist preacher . . . "I have a dream today . . . Free at last, free at last, thank God a-mighty, I'm free at last."

Peters pauses, looks aside and murmurs with gentle reverence: "The voice of the griot."

That one exquisitely poignant moment which chills my spine even now as I now recapitulate it was what ABC-TV's white writers spend eight episodes of *Roots* trying to say.

Source: *"The Black Scholar Forum: A Symposium on Roots"* by Chuck Stone, pp. 39–41, 1977. Reprinted by permission of The Black Scholar.

AUTHOR BIO

Robert Chrisman *founded* The Black Scholar: Journal of Black Studies and Research *in 1969. He has also published two collections of poetry:* Children of Empire *(1981) and* Minor Casualties *(1993). He formerly served as a visiting professor at the University of California, Berkeley, and he was the chair of the Black Studies Department of the University of Nebraska at Omaha until 2005.*

ROOTS

Rebirth of the Slave Mentality

Robert Chrisman

Like many black viewers of the epic film *Roots,* I watched the series with mixed emotions—anger, disgust, exhilaration, and, in the main, extraordinary identification with the fate of Kunta Kinte and his family. Superbly acted, the first three sections of the *Roots* film provided a view of the despicable slave trade and the subsequent brutalization of black people in the United States that burned like a blowtorch.

But despite its artistry, its candor, *Roots'* end effect upon me was irritation, bemusement, frustration, not for what it said, but for all the things it did not say.

Perhaps that frustration has its basis in the final lessons of the *Roots* film, which seem to be "survival by any means necessary." In the case of Kunta Kinte and his descendants, this meant submission to floggings, rape, murder, the destruction of the family, and the brutality of forced labor. A mood of resignation to any kind of calamity pervades the *Roots* film and whatever the atrocity be (the breaking of Kunta, the cutting off of his foot, the heart-rending sale of Kunta's daughter Kizzy) the response of the blacks is muffled outrage, canny calculation, and voluntary debasement of themselves to soften the inevitable blow from their white oppressors.

Tomming is first presented as a tactic used by the slaves to assuage the guilt, fear, and suspicion of whites, but as *Roots* unfolds, it becomes the way of life for black peoples, their primary response to critical situations. While tomming is a basic strategy for survival, it is not a strategy for liberation. Had blacks during slavery been interested only in survival, the slave system would have lasted much longer than it did.

But blacks did not comply, they resisted. The varied and active resistance of black slaves took the form of arson, theft, sabotage, and over 130 documented slave rebellions, including Nat Turner's uprising; further, the successful Haitian revolution and *Amistad* rebellion helped make the slavery system costly, dangerous, and untenable. The vigorous activity of the black underground railroad subverted the security of the plantation system; and the heroic resistance organized in the Northern states by escaped slaves like Frederick Douglass, Harriet Tubman, Sojourner Truth, and free men like Martin Delaney, David Walker, and Henry Highland Garnet clearly establish active black resistance to enslavement.

While *Roots* was primarily the story of a particular family, it is nonetheless regrettable that it bypasses these larger social dimensions, that it does not firmly establish the fact that many black and white people were actively engaged in a struggle to destroy the slave system, for a complex of reasons.

Even the immediate social dimensions of black life are lacking in *Roots.* Rarely do we see the community of blacks at work, church, or other collective activity. Rather, the focus, indeed the obsession, of the series is events that disrupt, torment, and test the integrity of the *Roots* family—rape, mutilation, sale, miscegenation. Even manumission becomes a calamity.

In this respect, *Roots* is a soap opera, for the main thematic concern of that genre is the disruption of domestic life through a series of crises and confrontations and problems besetting the principal characters. Soap opera excludes social, political, and economic realities; its universe is the family home; its concerns are infidelity, incest, romance, rape, abortion, and bastardy. So it is with *Roots.* Though this film spans a period of great political activity from 1750 through the late 1860s, it is anchored in the feral passions of the plantation, the dialectic of the house on the hill and the shack in the back.

Roots' mixture of helpless blacks and brutal whites recalls *Uncle Tom's Cabin* which, after its success as an abolitionist novel, became the most successful, longest running play in U.S. history, being performed continuously in various ways from the 1860s on into the early twentieth century. It is an ironic possibility that after emancipation *Uncle Tom's Cabin* served to entrench those racist stereotypes that had sustained the vanquished institution of slavery—that of the meek, frightened and submissive slave, and in this fashion had a reactionary as well as a progressive propaganda function.

Because *Roots* is a confession, and one volunteered by the criminal, the nature of the crime is necessarily distorted. The whites in *Roots* are savage, sadistic, and brutal with an intensity that, consciously intended or not, has the effect of intimidation upon the contemporary audience. While *Roots* is most graphic in displaying the sexual activity that occurred between white males and black females ("I always did like a lively nigger gal," says Chuck Connors at one point), no mention whatever is made of sexual activity between black males and white females. Yet the obsession with relations between black males and white females was a cornerstone of white terrorism against blacks, the ideological linchpin of the night rider. In addition to this dishonesty *Roots* also exposes the need whites have to view blacks as superior to themselves and at the same time impotent and relegated to quiet survival, to being a source of wisdom and solace to benighted white men and women in the tradition of the hundreds of patient, understanding and enduring blacks that populate the white American mind.

The 1960s demonstrated that black people had not only survived slavery but transcended its deleterious effects in the continuing drive for complete equality and freedom from racism, and the 1970s continue to enrich the black consciousness with new perspectives and understandings being gained from the struggle in Southern Africa, the Watergate revelation, the Cointelpro scandals.

But *Roots's* image of hapless blacks is a regression to a less heroic, less dignified, black image than that we saw and projected during the 1960s.

Much of our struggle during that period was to destroy the slave mentality so graphically resurrected in the *Roots* film.

That struggle still continues.

Source: *"The Black Scholar Forum: A Symposium on Roots." "Roots: Rebirth of the Slave Mentality" by Robert Chrisman from* The Black Scholar, *1977, pp. 41–42. Reprinted by permission.*

DECODING THE TEXTS

1. Based on the authors' reviews of *Roots*, why was it not only a successful miniseries but also a controversial one? Give specific examples.

2. The multiple reviewers in *The Black Scholar* presented different viewpoints about the same miniseries, but all of the reviews shared a common thread. What was that common thread? Why do the authors choose different aspects of the miniseries and African American history or culture to support their points of view?

3. Why does Chinweizu call *Roots* a "partial rehabilitation of Afro-American history"?

4. In his review of *Roots*, Robert Chrisman calls the miniseries a soap opera and considers this its biggest fault. What support does he provide for this claim?

CONNECTING TO YOUR CULTURE

Roots portrays a time that many in the United States know nothing about or have forgotten. In fact, until the thirtieth anniversary of the miniseries, many people had forgotten the miniseries as well.

1. Are there times in your life—within your culture or subculture—that others know nothing about? Is this due to ignorance or deliberate forgetfulness or some other cause?

2. Even though they share a common overall thread, the five reviewers share different views and perspectives about the same miniseries. Describe a recent television show (episode or series) that inspired differing perspectives among you and your friends or family. Where did the differences lie?

3. Both Coomes in the earlier annotated sample essay and the *Roots* reviewers say that the television programs in question do not necessarily depict the cultures—teen culture or early African American culture—accurately. When have you felt like you have been depicted in a way that does not accurately reflect who you are or what your culture is?

CONSIDERING IDEAS

1. If you have watched *Saturday Night Live (SNL)*, what is your favorite episode? Does your choice have something to do with the host or the musical guest(s)?

2. Whether you have watched *SNL* or not, which musical performers do you think best represent your culture and should be invited to the show?

AUTHOR BIO

Michael D. Ayers is currently an arts and entertainment journalist and editor at MTVI live.com. He regularly writes for New York Magazine, The Village Voice, Vanity Fair, and Reuters, and has also been published in The Washington Post, ABCNews.com, The Chicago Sun-Times, Billboard, and The Boston Globe. Before becoming a full time journalist, Ayers taught college courses in sociology and culture. This piece was originally posted on aoltv.com.

SNL MUSICAL GUESTS

Best *Saturday Night Live* Performance Videos

Michael D. Ayers

Since its debut in 1975, *Saturday Night Live* has been synonymous with bringing pop music to the late-night, weekend masses. Now in its 35th season on NBC, *SNL* has indeed become the holy grail for musicians.

Over the years, many memorable performances have graced the *SNL* stage. In this list, we select the 7 best. Some were energetic, some were raw and emotive, some were quirky and fun.

But mostly, they were all daring for broadcast television at the time.

SINEAD O'CONNOR (OCTOBER 3, 1992)

Love it or hate it, Irish singer Sinead O'Connor churned out one of the most—if not the most—historic performance on *SNL*. Doing an acapella version of Bob Marley's 'War,' she replaced a few of the lyrics with accusations of the Catholic Church's involvement in sexual abuse cases. At the very end of the song, O'Connor matched the lyric "evil" with a photo of Pope John Paul II, and promptly tore it up. [**Watch the Video on YouTube.**]

NIRVANA (JANUARY 11, 1992)

The seminal grunge band Nirvana made their *SNL* debut with 'Smells Like Teen Spirit' on the same day that their CD, 'Nevermind,' reached number one on the Billboard charts. The performance ushers in that raw, hard rock sound that was missing on this show for most of the '80s. At the same time, this performance effectively served as the introduction of Nirvana to mainstream America. [**Watch the Video on YouTube.**]

PAUL SIMON AND GEORGE HARRISON (NOVEMBER 20, 1976)

In this classic performance, two of pop music's most accomplished songwriters teamed up for sparse, acoustic renditions of each other's tunes. Simon backed Harrison on 'Here Comes The Sun,' and Harrison returned the favor on Simon's 'Homeward Bound,' giving it a slightly bluesy feel towards the end. Simon was hosting the show that night, but it was the pairing of these two songs—back to back, no less—that was one of the series' first musical gems.

ELVIS COSTELLO AND THE BEASTIE BOYS (SEPTEMBER 26, 1999)

For its 25th anniversary special, *Saturday Night Live* booked the Beastie Boys to perform their anthemic hit, 'Sabotage.' But after only a few bars in, their set was literally sabotaged by Elvis Costello, who ordered the band to launch into his own song, 'Radio, Radio.' The performance not only paired two pop giants; it also parodied Costello's infamous *SNL* debut in 1977, in which he abruptly switched from 'Less Than Zero' to 'Radio, Radio,' much to the dismay of his record label and Lorne Michaels.

THE BLUES BROTHERS (NOVEMBER 11, 1978)

Originating from an *SNL* sketch starring Dan Aykroyd and John Belushi, the Blues Brothers morphed into their own band. And in 1978, these soul revivalists churned out a high-energy, explosive performance of 'Soul Man,' which solidified them as not just parodies, but musicians that could be taken seriously. While their authenticity is probably something still up for debate, there's no denying that these two had some serious dance moves. [**Watch the Video on YouTube.**]

FRANK ZAPPA (DECEMBER 11, 1976)

It's hard to imagine someone like Frank Zappa gracing the *SNL* stages these days. But the '70s, well, that was a different story. In this performance of 'I'm The Slime,' his head was superimposed in the kick drum, while lyrics were taught to the audience on a blackboard. This is one of the creepiest, silliest and campiest performances in *SNL* history. But at the same time, it kept true to Zappa's very anti-establishment outlooks. [**Watch the Video on YouTube.**]

ARCADE FIRE (FEBRUARY 24, 2007)

There's nothing like a good, Who-esque guitar smash—and that's exactly what the Arcade Fire did on their first *SNL* performance. As the song 'Intervention' was winding down, Win Butler took the time to remove his acoustic and sent the splinters flying. While it's a slightly redundant concept, it still made for quite an entrance, giving the song an exclamation point that is hard to come by on late night TV these days. [**Watch the Video on Internet DJ.**]

Source: *SNL* Musical Guests: Best *Saturday Night Live* Music Performance Videos, by Michael D. Ayers. Posted November 6, 2009. Found at http://www.aoltv.com/2009/11/06/snl-musical-guests-best-saturday-night-live-performance-video/ © 2012 AOL Inc. Used with permission.

DECODING THE TEXT

1. Why does Michael Ayers choose the seven musical performances for his list of best performances? What supporting evidence does he give?

2. After viewing the seven performances on www.youtube.com, do you agree or disagree with his choices?

3. In the original piece posted on aoltv.com, Ayers includes three visual supports to the written text: an image of Sinead O'Connor tearing up a picture of the Pope, a video clip of Paul Simon and George Harrison, and a video clip of Elvis Costello and the Beastie Boys. Why do you think he chose to use these three particular visuals and no others?

CONNECTING TO YOUR CULTURE

1. After viewing the seven performances on www.youtube.com, find three more musical performances from *Saturday Night Live* that you can add to the list, so the list includes performances that represent your generation.

2. Which performances do you (and your group, if in a small group) believe should stay on the list, and which should be taken off? Why?

3. Choose a venue for musical video performances, such as MTV, VH1, or CMT, and create your own list of best performances. What is it about your list that represents you, your culture, or your generation?

CONSIDERING IDEAS

1. Were you part of the generation that watched movies on videotape? If so, when and why did you switch to DVDs?

2. The majority of (VHS and) DVD rental stores have vanished. Why do you think that is?

AUTHOR BIO

James Hebert is the theater critic for The San Diego Union-Tribune, *writing about the arts for this newspaper since 1997. He has an MA from Columbia University and has won more than twenty journalism awards, including the national arts writing prize from the Society for Features Journalism for his profile of Twyla Tharp, the choreographer.*

TECHNOLOGY'S FAST-FORWARD FINALLY ERASES VHS

James Hebert

Never mind that your VCR has been flashing "12:00" since the Reagan administration. This time, for the venerable VHS video format, the clock really has struck midnight.

The demise of VHS, age 30, became official with the major studios' recent announcement that they've stopped releasing movies on videocassette. The lone exceptions: kids' flicks featuring the likes of Barney.

A dinosaur. Perfect.

Variety, the Hollywood trade paper, saluted the format's trudge into oblivion with a snarky obit, noting that VHS "died of loneliness" and that it's "survived by a child, DVD, and by TiVo, VOD and DirecTV."

The passing of VHS is not exactly a news flash. Most video shops have long since erased tapes from their shelves. And good luck stuffing a cassette into one of those little red Netflix envelopes.

But the familiar, boxy tapes have been around so long—and endured such extended death throes—that it can be hard to remember what a craze VHS and its doomed archrival, Betamax, touched off when they dropped on pop culture.

Rewind your mind to a time when the simple ability to freeze a TV image seemed like some mystical video voodoo; when taping programs for later viewing was such a rush that users filled shelves with instantly ignored compilations of "Knight Rider"; when whole weekends were planned around acquiring a first-day copy of "Sixteen Candles" or "Flashdance."

The heady sense of control over the entertainment experience that the VCR offered—such a revelation then—is what ignited the home-video revolution. And it's what continues to drive pop-tech breakthroughs of today, from the endless extras and options on DVDs to the portability of video iPods to the bottomless promise of downloadable everything.

"For many, many people, video was—in its time—the new medium," says Deirdre Boyle, associate professor at The New School for General Studies in New York and author of "Subject to Change: Guerrilla Television Revisited," which chronicles the earliest days of video.

"And it had all the promises of democratic, egalitarian access that we now think about when we talk about the World Wide Web, the digital revolution."

Mark Palgy was so taken by the retro wonder of the pre-TiVo Era that he named his Louisville, Ky.-based band after a pressing question of the time: VHS or Beta?

It also struck him that the phrase gets at the transience of pop culture, since it's a question no one asks anymore, now that VHS and Beta are both relics.

"The thing about just having a movie in your house was really cool," says Palgy, who was born the same year as VHS. "Before that, I guess you just caught a movie on TV, or you had to go see a movie at the theater.

"Now, they don't even keep a movie in the theater longer than two weeks before it's out on DVD."

"BIG, CLUNKY AND EXPENSIVE"

"Watch what you want, when you want it," chirped the jingle for Video Library, a pioneering rental chain that launched in 1979 and grew to 43 stores before Blockbuster bought it out in 1988.

The slogan promised something so novel that figuring out how to follow the advice proved confounding for some first users.

"When I started, that whole first year we could not advertise 'VCR,' because nobody knew what that was," recalls Barry Rosenblatt, Video Library's founder. "We had to call them 'videocassette recorders.'

"And there was rarely a day that somebody didn't rent a cassette, call us up later and ask where to put (the tape) in their TV. It happened time after time."

Rosenblatt would gently advise the perplexed that they needed to have a VCR first.

Those initial machines, he recalls, were "big, clunky and expensive," and most early buyers wanted them for recording TV shows—what we now like to call time-shifting—since prerecorded movies barely existed.

His first shop opened with about 30 mainstream features, and about 90 adult titles—an indication of how strongly the adult-video segment drove the adoption of VCRs.

Adult movies also would play a pivotal role in the famous "tape wars" of the 1980s, a phenomenon that's being replayed today in the market battle between the rival Blu-ray and HD-DVD disc formats.

Sony launched Beta a year before JVC debuted VHS, and seemed to have the inside track, partly because its image quality was considered superior. For a while, rental stores carried copies of movies in both formats.

But when the adult business turned to almost exclusive VHS distribution, Beta faded quickly.

Guy Hanford, who co-owns the independent Kensington Video in San Diego, says his store still has a stock of about 800 Beta movies, which he sells for maybe 50 cents apiece to the occasional customer with a functioning Beta VCR.

Kensington Video, a neighborhood landmark that opened in 1986 and has long specialized in hard-to-find movies, is one of the few around town that still carries videocassettes.

As big outfits like Blockbuster have gone all-DVD, Hanford says he's actually seen business pick up for the store's VHS tapes.

"It's been a boon," says Hanford, who notes that the shop's 30,000 VHS titles represent about 25% of its rental business.

"It started about two years ago, when Blockbuster started abdicating videos completely. They got rid of videos that are impossible to find on DVD."

For the business in general, though, shedding VHS seems a sensible move. The Consumer Electronics Association, an industry trade group, estimates that only 310,000 VCRs will sell in the United States this year.

That's less than half the number that sold in 1980, when just 1% of Americans owned VCRs. (The figure grew to 95% in 2000, but has been dropping since.)

And in 1980, the average price for a VCR was $771. Today, it's plunged to just $52.

A single movie cost way more than that in VHS's heyday. Hanford remembers 1986's "Platoon" as being the first to break the $100 price barrier. Rosenblatt says a typical retail price was $79.95; those cost him $60 apiece wholesale, which made it hard to keep enough rental copies of popular movies on the shelves.

BE KIND, REWIND

It'd be hard to find anyone who's nostalgic about the prices and the scarcity and the long lines that were common at video shops in the 1980s.

But like any cultural movement, VHS leaves its own peculiar folklore as it recedes.

Who can forget that pesky 50-cent charge for failing to rewind one's rental movie? (Which spawned a cottage business in little gizmos that did nothing but rewind tapes.)

Shops lived and died on their reputation for enforcing the rule. Kensington Video never instituted it, but the failure to rewind "did drive us nuts."

Not a problem with DVD—although Hanford maintains he has more damage issues with discs than VHS tapes, because DVDs are mishandled and easily scratched.

Then there was the tracking control, which turned a fuzzy picture into a slightly less fuzzy picture—if you could make it work. ("We still have people who haven't figured out what their tracking control is for," Hanford says.)

There was the little tab that had to be pulled out so as not to accidentally tape over the home video of Johnny's bar mitzvah. And VCR Plus, which addressed confusion over how to program a VCR by introducing an entirely new breed of confusion over keying in long strings of numbers.

And while a VHS tape is a pretty stout device, it has a significant weakness: If one part of the cassette is played repeatedly, the picture starts to drop out, and the tape can even break.

Funny, Hanford could generally guess which parts of certain movies would be affected when they came in for repair.

"'Splash'—Daryl Hannah's heinie," he observes, referring to a scene in which Hannah's mermaid character becomes an unclad human. "Definitely Phoebe Cates' topless scene in 'Fast Times at Ridgemont High.' And 'Animal House'—John Belushi looking through the girl's window."

When pop-punk band FenixTX recorded an ode titled "Phoebe Cates" in 2001, it included the lyrics:

"I've been in love since the day I saw 'Fast Times'. It's on permanent rewind and can you guess my favorite part?"

Even with its glitches, one of the most powerful aspects of VHS was that it simplified and standardized the video medium like nothing before.

"From the standpoint of recording, it was a lot more foolproof," Boyle says. "Idiot-proof, in a sense. Also, it made it a much more stable platform for distribution."

"The cassette standard was very, very important because it made things more predictable."

At VHS' peak, video stores were so ubiquitous that even small towns could have five shops within a quarter-mile of each other, as tiny Ramona, Calif., did in 1985. Some 700 million movies were rented nationwide that year.

Rosenblatt remembers the mania around some of the biggest releases.

"'Star Wars,' definitely," he says. "We'd have special events, bring someone in costume as Darth Vader. People would line up like crazy."

"That would attract almost as many people as when we'd bring in Playboy's Playmate of the Year"—another promo gambit the company employed.

Boyle remembers the shops as being an integral part of a town or neighborhood's social scene.

"Soccer moms or singles on a Saturday night, browsing for videos and hooking up," is the picture she has in her mind.

"I'm certainly having a difficult time watching the video stores going out of business all around me," Boyle says. "It's not just the stores; it's the whole access to the culture.

"It was a place you could hang out. A lot of my students in the past would work their way through school at places like that," some of them becoming filmmakers eventually.

"I'm old-fashioned in wanting a social context," she adds. "And I think that's one of the things that does get lost. Not just the technology of VHS—but that sort of hitching post."

Rosenblatt, who has come out of retirement to start an audiobook-rental business, isn't sure the VHS craze can ever be duplicated. But he looks back upon it with both satisfaction and some amazement.

"It was quite a business," says Rosenblatt. "I feel proud I was involved in something that became so big.

"Now, when you say 'VCR,' people know what you're talking about."

SIDEBAR

VHS Timeline

1975: The Sony Betamax goes on sale in the United States. The LV-1901 console, consisting of a VCR and a 19-inch television set, retails for $2,495.

1976: The Japanese electronics company JVC's "Video Home System" (originally called "Vertical Helical Scan")—or VHS—debuts at a price of $1,000.

1977: RCA begins selling the first VHS-based VCR in the United States.

1978: Magnavox releases its Magnavision videodisc player, along with "DiscoVision" movies on disks. The player sells for $695, while the 12-inch disks are $15.95.

1980: Household penetration of VCRs reaches 1%, on sales of 805,000 machines. The figure would reach 6% two years later, and about 30% by 1985.

1984: After years of "format wars," VHS achieves clear victory over Beta; 80% of VCRs manufactured are in the VHS format. The previous year, VHS machines already had outsold Betas 3-to-1.

1985: Walt Disney releases the first direct-to-video title, "Love Leads the Way" (on both VHS and Beta).

1993: Sony stops offering Betamax products in the United States.

1995: "The Lion King" debuts on tape, and becomes the top-selling home video of all time. It's the high-water mark for VHS.

1997: Digital Versatile Disc—or DVD—is introduced.

1999: "The Matrix" hits 1 million in sales—the first DVD to do so.

2002: DVD—now the fastest-growing consumer-electronics product in history—surpasses VHS in sales, with 65% of the total video market.

2006: Hollywood studios announce they will no longer release new movies on VHS.

Source: http://www.signonsandiego.com/uniontrib/20070401/news_lz1a01vhs.html

DECODING THE TEXT

1. Look through Hebert's essay and make a list of words and phrases he uses to describe VHS tapes. What do his choices of language bring to the essay?

2. *Variety*, a Hollywood trade paper, published an obituary for the VHS, saying that it had "died of loneliness" and was "survived by a child, DVD, and by TiVo, VOD, and DirecTV." Which medium for watching television shows do you think will be the next to "die"? Why?

CONNECTING TO YOUR CULTURE

1. Make a list of the ways in which you watch television shows. What media do you use? How often do you use each one? Share your list with others in the class, and then figure out what is notably different in how people watch television. Explain why you think there is such a difference.

2. Hebert describes the VHS craze as something that may never be repeated again. Think about some recent innovations, choose one, and then discuss how its popularity compares to the VHS popularity Hebert describes.

3. Consider the question "VHS or Beta?" One of Hebert's sources—Mark Palgy—discusses how this question represents the transience of pop culture. Create a list of pop culture elements or innovations that you believe will be obsolete in ten years, and share your list with your classmates. Discuss why pop culture is so transient.

READING SELECTIONS:
THE 1990s AND 2000s

CONSIDERING IDEAS

1. What are some of the most popular comedy or drama shows today that feature African-American characters?

2. Are you a fan of reality shows? If so, which ones? If not, why don't you enjoy them?

AUTHOR BIO

Ariel Crocket *is a staff writer at* hellobeautiful.com, *a website that is described as "the premiere site for the Black woman who seeks total control of her life."*

IS THE BLACK TELEVISION SERIES DEAD?

Ariel Crocket

Ahh, the 90's, one of the best decades in the history of the Black television series. "Martin," "The Fresh Prince Of Bel-Air," "Living Single," "The Jamie Foxx Show," "Moesha," "The Wayans Bros," "The Cosby Show" and "The Parkers"–all shows that will forever be timeless in Black TV. I can watch reruns of these shows over and over again and even know what will happen next and still laugh hysterically, cry when someone gets married, and laugh again.

Fast forward to the present and you can barely get a second season out of these watered down, slapstick style comedy TV series' like "House of Payne," VH1's "Single Ladies" and BET's "Let's Stay Together." I would never even think of buying a DVD series of ANY season of these shows. Why not? Well, these are not necessarily shows that you can watch rerun after rerun and not get annoyed by much less remember they existed six years from now.

Like your parents boasted about shows like "Good Times," "Sanford & Son," and "The Jeffersons" to us, we'll skip right on over the host of black TV shows post-new millennium and go back to the hilarious black comedies of the 90's and tell our children about it. As of late I've been noticing a pattern taking shape within Black television, and that is that ratings seem to always be an excuse behind a show getting pulled. Which makes me wonder, if nobody is watching black sitcoms anymore then what are they watching, because TV is definitely still being watched.

The other day a very influential black woman spoke briefly on the state of black television and it really made me wonder. Then I realized it, I've been trained. I can't speak for the readers out there but I realized that I've been trained to like what (before just a few years ago), I swore I'd never fall victim to: and that is my love for "real-life" drama or "reality TV." The television industry has trained me to become transfixed with seeing pointless drama instead of the scripted, yet positive images and lifestyles that in my own reality would take much hard work to attain. The industry figured out what myself as well as many other reality TV lovers "desired to see" before we even realized it–which is the highly-scripted and well-rehearsed drink-throwing, hair-shifting, "Who Gon' Check Me Boo"-style drama on TV every week. What I didn't know was that the public (if you don't like reality TV, you can quietly exclude yourself from this group) has become obsessed with the idea of "real-life" drama, which is exactly why you have reality shows like "Basketball Wives," and "Real Housewives of Atlanta" and shows that we think are reality are the total opposite.

Not only that, but we actually watch and create celebrities out of reality TV 'stars' as opposed to watching well-trained actors and then we complain when these TV series' dissipate due to low ratings. I realized that the problem is much less the commentary and content of these shows and more so the people and the TV industry giving the people what they want. Ultimately what I'm saying is that, with the many different black TV shows that has came and went over the course of the last 10 years, I can count on 1 hand the amount of shows that have made a lasting impression.

Many people complain and say that we have no black TV shows yet divert their time to reality television. Evolution is definitely a great way to promote change and growth but do you think reality TV has enough longevity to permanently take over for the Black Television series? Is the Black Television Series dead? And if so can it be revived, if so what would it take to make these shows more memorable and widely accepted?

Source: *http://hellobeautiful.com/hellobeautiful-original/arielcrockett/is-the-black-television-series-dead/*

DECODING THE TEXT

1. Why does Crocket believe that the 1990s was one of the best decades in the history of black television series?

2. What does Crocket say has helped lead to the demise of good black television series?

3. Who ultimately does Crocket blame for the demise of all good television?

CONNECTING TO YOUR CULTURE

1. Do some web research and find out what the top five reality series are right now. Do these reality shows actually depict the reality of people's lives? Why or why not?

2. At the end of her essay, Crocket asks whether reality television has enough longevity to take over the black television series completely. What's your response to her question?

3. At the end of her essay, Crocket also asks what it would take to make black television series more memorable and widely accepted. What's your response to her question?

CONSIDERING IDEAS

1. Why do you think reality shows are so popular?

2. With so many reality shows on television, the production of other types of shows has decreased. Is this a positive or negative result? Why?

AUTHOR BIO

Greg Braxton is a staff writer for the Los Angeles Times *and has also appeared in interviews about his articles on NPR.*

THE GREATER REALITY OF MINORITIES ON TV

*While scripted shows still largely reflect a white male society,
the faces we see on reality shows are more diverse.*

Greg Braxton

The much-maligned world of reality television is winning praise these days for "keeping it real" in an unexpectedly relevant way—reflecting a more diverse America than its more highbrow cousins in scripted prime-time shows.

Despite decades of public pressure on the major networks to diversify, the lead characters in all but a few of prime-time scripted shows this season are still white—and usually young and affluent. In contrast, reality programs consistently feature a much broader range of people when it comes to race, age, class and sexual orientation.

For example, CBS' "The Amazing Race" includes an Asian American brother-and-sister team and two African American sisters in its 14th season, which premiered Sunday. Three African Americans are in the current cast of CBS' "Survivor." Four African Americans and two Tongan Americans have been featured on the current season of NBC's "The Biggest Loser."

By contrast, a report released last year by the National Assn. for the Advancement of Colored People, titled "Out of Focus—Out of Sync," accused the networks of perpetuating a view of the nation that recalls "America's segregated past." The 40-page report charged that non-whites are underrepresented in almost every aspect of the television industry—except for reality programming.

That's no accident, according to reality TV producers and creators.

"We're looking to create shows that everyday people can relate to, and for that you really need a true representation of the population," said Dave Broome, executive producer of NBC's "The Biggest Loser."

"A couple of seasons ago, there was an over-the-top character who was white that we could have cast, but we sacrificed that for a Latino. That's how important that is."

The culture mix is driven by more than just political correctness. Although reality shows aren't directly in the business of bringing racial and ethnic enlightenment to America, they are in business.

For shows that thrive on conflict and drama, a collection of cast members from varied backgrounds often serves that goal. Unresolved issues surrounding race, class and sexual orientation can either quietly fuel tension on programs or generate outright emotional explosions.

"I don't believe the makers of unscripted programs are necessarily all pro-social," said Jonathan Murray of Bunim-Murray Productions, whose shows include MTV's reality veteran "The Real World." "A lot of times it comes down to the fact that diversity just makes those shows better."

Of course, being involved in reality TV is not always an uplifting experience. Participants are subject to humiliation on the air (and, occasionally, eternal infamy on YouTube). The more outrageous the show's concept, the more likely contestants are to be ridiculed or even scorned. But at least unscripted television is an equal-opportunity offender.

Though the issue of race is often secondary to unscripted series' story lines, it does at times directly fuel the drama. William "Mega" Collins, an outspoken African American houseguest on the first edition of CBS' "Big Brother," was the first evicted from the show after he angrily confronted his predominantly white fellow participants about race. CBS' "Survivor" in 2006 sparked a furor when the series initially divided tribes along racial and ethnic lines.

Just as the military and professional sports—two arenas not heralded for their liberal thought—became the unlikely vessels for breaking racial barriers decades ago, reality programming may be a similarly transformational force in bringing greater diversity to television today.

Source: *"The Greater Reality of Minorities on TV" by Greg Braxton. Copyright © 2009. Los Angeles Times. Reprinted with permission.*

DECODING THE TEXT

1. Why does Braxton say that reality shows represent the real population of the United States better than other types of shows?

2. Why does Braxton say it is better business for television to provide a variety of cultures in the casting of shows?

3. Braxton compares reality shows with scripted comedies and dramas. Who does he say is better at casting? Why?

CONNECTING TO YOUR CULTURE

1. Create a list of your favorite television shows. What communities or cultures are represented in these shows? What communities or cultures are missing?

2. Out of all the reality shows on television, which represents your culture the best? Why?

CONSIDERING IDEAS

1. How do religion and entertainment coexist on television?

2. How does religion influence television?

3. How does television influence religion?

AUTHOR BIO

Mark I. Pinsky is a former journalist who writes about issues of faith, media, and popular culture. In addition to his contributions to Christianity Today, The Columbia Journalism Review, *and* The New York Times, *he is the author of* The Gospel According to The Simpsons: The Spiritual Life of America's Most Animated Family *(2001) and* The Gospel According to Disney: Faith, Trust and Pixie Dust *(2004). "Cartoons (Seriously) Can Teach Us About Faith" was published in* USA Today *on November 27, 2006.*

CARTOONS (SERIOUSLY) CAN TEACH US ABOUT FAITH

Mark I. Pinsky

Do television's Homer and Bart Simpson have anything to teach us about eternal questions such as how God wants us to worship him, or whether there is one true faith? What does the controversial cable cartoon show *South Park* have to say about the nature of the soul, or how the founders of the world's great religions might get along with each other in the hereafter? Nowhere on the small screen are these weighty issues dealt with on a more regular basis than in edgy, animated comedies.

For some reason, many who might shun such serious topics when presented by religious and educational leaders will listen to debates about theology if they are presented in the context of a cartoon. Over the years, *The Simpsons* has broken long-running TV taboos by including religious plots, themes and characters. My survey of nearly 300 episodes confirms at least one academic study that religion is a staple of the show's plots, jokes and images. Like most Americans (but unlike most live characters on TV), the Simpsons say grace at meals, attend church regularly, read the Bible and pray aloud. For almost 20 years, the show's gifted, highly literate writers, producers and directors have drawn on the divine in ways that animate sincere faith and belief—without caricaturing them.

These days, apart from Billy Graham or Jerry Falwell, America's best-known evangelical is probably Ned Flanders, the Simpsons' goodhearted next-door neighbor. Christians on college campuses have adopted the affectionate, if overdrawn, character as a mascot. As early as 1996, Gerry Bowler, professor of history at the University of Manitoba, called Flanders "television's most effective mortal (i.e., non-angelic) exponent of a Christian life well-lived." *The Simpsons* has been the subject of more than a score of academic papers, including some at Christian colleges and universities, and for good reason.

"The satiric *Simpsons* program takes religion's place in society seriously enough to do it the honor of making fun of it," Bowler wrote in one of the earliest papers. Evangelist and long-time fan Tony Campolo writes that the show "can easily be mistaken for an assault that ridicules middle-class Christianity. It is not! What the show is really depicting through the antics of the Simpsons is the character of some of the people who are in our churches, and the ways they choose to live out their faith. . . . As an evangelical Christian, I find that *The Simpsons* provides me with a mirror that reflects my own religious life."

BART, LISA AND THE SOUL

In one episode dealing with moral dilemmas, bad boy Bart sells his soul to his friend for $5. His sister Lisa is appalled. "How could you do that?" she asks. "Your soul is the most valuable part of you. . . . Whether or not the soul is physically real, Bart, it's the symbol of everything fine inside us. . . . Bart, your soul is the only part of you that lasts forever." In his DVD commentary on this episode, *Simpsons* creator Matt Groening observes, "I love these religious shows, these spiritual shows," which often critique organized religion while honoring sincere faith, "because they please both the Christians and the atheists. Each has their own belief or non-belief system."

Increasingly, *The Simpsons* is not alone in integrating religion and entertainment. Other shows have walked through this door Groening has opened (or kicked in), including *Futurama, King of the Hill, Family Guy, American Dad* and, yes, even Comedy Central's *South Park*. Together, these shows reach millions of viewers—mostly teens and young adults—and millions more through DVD sales and fan websites. Some fans of these shows might spend more time watching them than they do attending weekly religious services.

While the post-*Simpsons* shows deal with faith less frequently, and with considerably less respect, the grappling can be deep, even on a series as nasty, naughty and nihilistic as *South Park*. In one episode, Eric Cartman, the show's pint-size, potty-mouthed villain, cries out to God in despair. After his friends decide to ignore him, Cartman believes he has died and become a living ghost. "How can my own God forsake me?" he asks. Cartman concludes his spirit is trapped on earth, blocked from going to heaven because of his unforgiven sins. So the venal and cynical fourth-grader goes to everyone he has offended in life to ask for forgiveness, and to atone for his sins.

South Park is that part of TV Land where the profane regularly head butts the sacred, a show that has stirred up controversy over episodes about Scientology and Islam. But another episode, devoted to the history and modern practice of Mormonism, was recently the subject of an academic paper and a panel in Salt Lake City. No doubt many Mormons were outraged by the episode's snarky portrayal of their religion—at least if they heard about it, if not saw it. But those attending the symposium on religion and popular culture, sponsored by the liberal Sunstone Education Foundation, were serious and appreciative of the treatment their faith received.

Why this growing interest in religion in cartoons? Why are young viewers willing to accept it and take it seriously? And is this a good thing? As someone who spends a lot of time in houses of worship, where young people are often scarce, I think it is.

ENCOURAGING DIALOGUE

Some critics may dismiss the discussion of religion in cartoons. But when people, especially young people, sit in a sanctuary pew or a lecture hall to hear someone discuss religion, a veil of skepticism often descends over their minds, filtering what follows. Yet when they are at home or in their dorm rooms, on their couches, watching an animated comedy, their minds tend to remain more open. While few viewers are likely to be spiritually transformed by watching these shows, they can be exposed to aspects of faith, and to critical issues of religion they know nothing about, in a non-threatening way. Serious dialogue can grow out of silly situations.

As hapless Homer Simpson puts it, "It's funny 'cause it's true."

Source: *"Cartoons (Seriously) Can Teach Us About Faith" by Mark Pinsky, p. 21 from* USA Today, *November 27, 2006. Reprinted by permission of Mark Pinsky.*

DECODING THE TEXT

1. Are you surprised that Ned Flanders from *The Simpsons* is cited by Pinsky as one of the best-known evangelical Christians on television? Why or why not?

2. Do you agree or disagree with Pinsky's main argument?

3. What details does Pinsky use to support his argument?

4. Pinsky discusses the connection of the sacred to the profane. What subjects do you consider sacred? Where do you draw the line in how these subjects can be presented?

CONNECTING TO YOUR CULTURE

1. Pinsky believes that serious dialogue can come out of silly situations, including the silly situations that occur on animated shows. Do you agree or disagree? Why?

2. Is there something in your life or the lives of those close to you that might be resolved or at least discussed if the first attempt at discussion was part of a silly situation?

3. Is humor good medicine for serious thoughts or problems? Why or why not?

20TH CENTURY FOX TELEVISION/PHOTOS 12/ALAMY

A CASE STUDY: GAY CULTURE AND TELEVISION FROM THE 1990s AND 2000s

CONSIDERING IDEAS

1. After doing some web research, describe some situations in which particular television characters or television shows have been boycotted or censored by groups. What were the boycotts about? What action did the boycotting group want the television network or studio to take? Do you think that television boycotts are effective?

2. Do you believe that gay characters on television shows represent an accurate view of gay culture? What is gay culture anyway? Is there such a culture?

3. What power do words have? Are there words that people might use to describe you but that you find uncomfortable or offensive? If you were called these words, how would you feel? What would you do?

FRANRIC/FOTOLIA LLC

AUTHOR BIO

The Onion *is a widely read national print publication and website* (http://www.theonion.com) *that offers a satirical take on traditional news outlets. It was founded in 1988 by two students at* the *University of Wisconsin–Madison.* *"Letter D Pulls Sponsorship from* Sesame Street*" was posted on December 7, 1997.*

LETTER D PULLS SPONSORSHIP FROM SESAME STREET

The Onion

A spokesperson for the letter D announced Monday that the consonant is withdrawing sponsorship from *Sesame Street* following a Children's Television Workshop announcement that a homosexual muppet will soon join the show's cast.

"The letter D is proud to have brought you many wonderful *Sesame Street* episodes throughout the program's 28-year history," said Patricia Willis, public relations director for D. "But the letter D does not condone the sort of morally questionable lifestyles that *Sesame Street* is advocating with the introduction of this new character. It can no longer in good conscience associate itself with the show."

Willis said D's withdrawal is effective immediately, and applies to both capital and lower-case versions of the letter.

The gay muppet, "Roger," will be introduced on *Sesame Street* Dec. 23, CTW director Leslie Charren said. Thus far, no other sponsors have pulled out, though the number seven has requested an advance tape of the episode before it makes a decision.

Many public-television insiders believe D's withdrawal was motivated by a desire not to alienate religious conservatives, a section of the population that employs the letter frequently.

"D is for, among other things, demagoguery, dogma and doctrine, words crucial to right-wing groups like the Christian Coalition," said Yale University political-science professor J. Wright Franklin. "It is likely that D felt it could ill afford to offend such a large segment of its users."

While a long-term replacement for D has not yet been secured by *Sesame Street*, the number three will temporarily fill in for it in a number of the show's animated shorts. Other pieces will simply skip from C to E, with vocalists stretching out C into two syllables to match the rhythm of the alphabet song.

Sesame Street is stung by the sudden departure of its longtime supporter. Speaking to reporters, cast member Cookie Monster said: "Me disappointed letter D choose to end relationship with *Sesame Street* due to pressure from extremely vocal minority. We accused of endorsing deviant lifestyle. Me say homosexuality natural, not immoral. Diversity and enrichment. That's good enough for me."

AUTHOR BIO

Mark Harris *is a writer and former executive editor of* Entertainment Weekly, *where he has published many articles on film, television, books, and music. "Sorry Situation" first appeared on* http://www.ew.com *on January 25, 2007.*

SORRY SITUATION

Mark Harris

For a while, Isaiah Washington was actually going to get away with it. I'm talking about how things felt before the Official Entertainment Remorse Machine kicked in—the denial, then the half-baked small apology, then the more impressive, bigger, "I'm scared" apology (the one that goes, "I have sinned, I must look deep inside myself and deal with my issues, I shall summon leaders of the offended community to meet with me") with a side order of official corporate rebuke, presumably followed by regret-soaked on-air interviews and a group hug. For three months, all the evidence suggested that everyone—Washington, *Grey's Anatomy* creator Shonda Rhimes, Touchstone TV, and ABC—had decided it was no big deal for an actor to refer to a gay colleague as a "faggot" on the set and that if everyone just averted their eyes, the word would become a tiny speed bump that a show could bounce over without looking back.

Forgive my skepticism, but I'm not a huge fan of apologies that come only after an evident threat to one's livelihood; I have difficulty believing that they spring spontaneously from a troubled soul. After all, it wasn't until Washington used the word again (during his "denial" at a press session after the Golden Globes), and two of his castmates called him on it, that a public outcry forced the issue. After Mel Gibson's Driving While Anti-Semitic bust, he was probably still looking for a post-mug-shot clean shirt when acts of contrition started flying out of his publicist's fax machine. And Michael Richards still had his own racist slurs ringing in his ears when he threw himself on the mercy of David Letterman. So why did it take a producer, a show, a network, and a corporation such an unconscionably long time to locate their sense of the right thing to do?

If I sound grudging about Washington's apology, it's not because I don't believe him (I suppose time will tell if he's sincere). It's because now that he's started the Machine, everyone is reading from the same script, and we already know how this trite old plot plays out. Pop culture (and that includes all of us who are pop culture consumers) has become addicted to a cycle of misbehavior followed by regret followed by a warm wallow in forgiveness in which we agree to pretend that saying you're sorry undoes whatever was done. And anyone who isn't willing to play that game gets labeled a bad sport or a sore winner.

So, at the risk of sounding uncharitable, let me hold off on accepting that apology for a moment. Considering that everyone in a position to do something about it was content to let the word *faggot* hang in the air all winter, I'm sure they'll indulge me if I mention a few regrets of my own. I'm sorry that the first time this happened, Shonda Rhimes, whose commitment to on-air diversity is evident (even if the evidence stops short of including an actual gay staffer at Seattle Grace), thought it was okay to write this off as a private affair rather than immediately let the many offended fans of her show know how hateful she thought that epithet was. I'm sorry that T. R. Knight, the target of Washington's slur who came out following the incident, didn't have the instant, unqualified, and loudly public (because that matters) support of every one of his colleagues. I'm sorry that the overall non-reaction to Washington's behavior helped to reinforce a perception that some quarters of the African-American community tolerate homophobia, a stereotype that is only going to divide us more unless both groups fight it at every turn. I'm sorry that it took ABC half the TV season to remind itself of its corporate responsibility. I'm sorry that not a single sponsor of *Grey's Anatomy* had the guts to speak up, even last week. I'm sorry that we in the gay community didn't make a lot more noise about this a lot sooner. I'm sorry that so many actors choose—and it is, whatever they tell themselves, a self-serving choice—to stay in the closet, since the more out actors there are, the less okay homophobia in entertainment becomes. I'm sorry that there aren't more gay characters on television: I don't want quotas or tokens, but I do think that shows like *Grey's Anatomy* and *Lost* and *Heroes*, which pride themselves on the variety of their ensembles, could expand their vision to better reflect their world, since series ranging from *The Office* to *The Wire* have shown that it's not so hard. Most of all, I'm sorry that the rerun ritual that Washington's apology invites us to watch is likely to obscure all this.

Anyone who calls a colleague a faggot and manages not to get fired should count himself lucky. But Washington's use of the word didn't break anything that wasn't already broken, and his apology won't fix it any more than his dismissal. For all the progress that has been made fighting homophobia, and for all the ways in which the entertainment industry has led that fight, we clearly have miles to go. The problem is a lot bigger than Isaiah Washington, and the solution doesn't come gift-wrapped in the words "I'm sorry."

AUTHOR BIO

Jennifer Armstrong *writes about pop culture and spent nearly a decade writing for* Entertainment Weekly, *where she was a senior writer covering TV and women in entertainment. She is the author of* Why? Because We Still Like You, *a history of the original* The Mickey Mouse Club *and is currently working on a book about* The Mary Tyler Moore Show, *to be published by Simon & Schuster. Her writing has been featured in* Glamour, *the* Chicago Sun-Times, Match.com, Salon.com, Details.com, *and* Budget Travel, *and her essays have appeared in the anthologies* What Women Think About Contemporary Weddings, Bewilderment, Altared: Bridezillas, Big Love, Breakups, *and* Coffee at Luke's: An Unauthorized Gilmore Girls Gabfest. *She has provided pop culture commentary for ABC, VH1, A & E, and CNN. She also cofounded and continues to run* SexyFeminist.com. *"Gay Teens on TV" was published on* EW.com *on September 1, 2011.*

GAY TEENS ON TV

Led by a poignant anti-bullying arc on "Glee," gay teens
are finally having their stories told all over television. EW takes
an in-depth look at how producers and networks are making up
for years of on-air silence and providing inspiration for real-life
youth (and parents) still searching for answers.

Jennifer Armstrong

When Rickie Vasquez came out to his family on a 1994 episode of *My So-Called Life*, he ended up bruised, bloodied, and living in an abandoned warehouse full of homeless teens, afraid to tell even his closest friends why his uncle had kicked him out of the house just before Christmas. He didn't even utter the word "gay" on screen until the season finale, which became the show's final episode—and that was only to console a girl he'd rejected.

No wonder Rickie felt the need to keep his sexual orientation painfully tucked away—he was completely alone when it came to gay teens on television. He was the first on a prime-time network show, and he'd be the only one for another five lonely years. In fact, there would be just a handful more in the next 10 years. "It was cathartic in some ways and painful in others," says the man who played him, Wilson Cruz, now 37, whose real life inspired many of Rickie's story lines. "The biggest part was the acknowledgment of our existence and our pain, which we hadn't seen at all on television before that."

If only Rickie could see *Glee*'s Kurt Hummel now. The breakout character (played by Chris Colfer) on TV's most buzzed-about network show has won an Emmy nomination, a Golden Globe, and viewers' hearts with an at times poignant, but often, well, gleeful depiction of a modern gay teen. It took Kurt only four episodes to say the words "I'm gay" to his dad, to which his father shrugged and said, "If that's who you are, there's nothing I can do about it. And I love you just as much." He sealed it with a hug, and a new kind of gay hero was born: one who's loved as much for his boa wearing as he is for fending off bullies and forming a touching stepbrotherly bond with his former crush.

Kurt, incidentally, spent his Christmas episode duetting on a wildly flirtatious version of "Baby, It's Cold Outside" with his new dreamy male idol, Blaine (Darren Criss). "That was by far the gayest thing that has ever been on TV, period," Colfer says. "Forget *AbFab,* forget *Beautiful People* and *Will & Grace.*" The song became the most downloaded track off the Glee Christmas album—and ubiquitous on the radio during the holidays. "I was proud of that," *Glee* co-creator Ryan Murphy says. "I think it pushed the envelope a bit."

Unlike Rickie, Kurt and Blaine are far from alone in their boundary pushing this TV season. Gay characters have gone from one-time guest stars, whispered tragedies, and silly sidekicks to not just an accepted but an expected part of teen-centric television. The change reflects real teens' lives: The percentage of schools with gay-straight alliance clubs is up from 25 percent in 2001 to 45 percent today, indicating the increasingly visible role that gay kids are playing in the high school landscape. With the average coming-out age now 16 (down from 19–23 in the '80s), according to the National Gay and Lesbian Task Force, it only makes sense for teens on TV to tackle the issue. "With our millennial audience, it's what they expect to see," says ABC Family exec VP of programming Kate Juergens. "Don't Ask Don't Tell was such a vestige of an older generation."

Speaking of which, the trend reflects not only demographic shifts but also the social and political climate. It was telling that when Colfer took home a Golden Globe on Jan. 16 for his moving portrayal of a bullied teen, his tear-jerking acceptance speech ended with these words of encouragement to fans: "To all the amazing kids who watch our show . . . who are constantly told 'No' . . . by bullies at school that they can't be who they are . . . well, screw that, kids." Despite the uptick in gay characters like Kurt—and out teens in general—it's a message that's still sorely needed in a world that doesn't always reflect the same kind of happy-ending acceptance TV is almost obliged to depict. Nine out of 10 lesbian, gay, bisexual, and transgender students have been harassed because of their sexuality, according to the Gay, Lesbian, and Straight Education Network (GLSEN). And while Kurt is lucky to have supportive friends, there are many real teens out there feeling as if they have nowhere to go and no one to talk to—and the results have been devastating. A spate of teen suicides (at least six in September) linked to brutal bullying incidents prompted the U.S. Department of Education to draft anti-bullying guidelines for schools—and reinforced the need for empathetic portrayals of high schoolers on TV. The celebrity-studded It Gets Better campaign (in which everyone from Barack Obama to Kim Kardashian recorded video messages of hope and support) surely helped some struggling gay teens, but TV shows that form long-lasting relationships with their audiences can resonate even more. "I think young gay people look at [Kurt and Blaine] both as role models," says Murphy, "and it means something to see their lives perhaps for the first time reflected on screen."

Jason Galisatus, a 17-year-old student ambassador for GLSEN, would be the first to agree with Murphy. "I think that Kurt will become a historical figure in LGBT history," says Galisatus. "My friends talk about the episode where he came out to his dad. We all talk about how amazing that is and how crazy it must be to live in a conservative, Midwestern community and be able to be open about your sexuality. That's very inspiring to all of us, and we can say, 'Well, hey, if Kurt can do it, why can't we?' Frequently, even if it is just a show, it does give us hope that coming out is not always a horrible thing to do." And a little hope can often go a long way. The Trevor Project, which runs a toll-free suicide hotline for gay youth or those questioning their sexuality, has been receiving numerous calls from teens who have been moved to pick up the phone after watching relatable TV characters such as Kurt. "There are conversations that happen with counselors that point to characters on TV," says Trevor Project executive director Charles Robbins. "Obviously, Glee is dealing with a very spot-on issue with Kurt's character. Since September, our call volume has increased, and that coincides with the Glee story lines and all the news media coverage of gay bullying."

But these story lines are not designed to speak solely to kids; the relationship between Kurt and his father can also serve as a lesson for parents. A 2009 study from the Family Acceptance Project at San Francisco State University found that LGBT teens rejected by their families were eight times more likely to commit suicide, which makes series that feature accepting parents—and the consequences of peer rejection—all the more critical. "It role-models to parents that the right answer is to love your kid," says Gay & Lesbian Alliance Against Defamation (GLAAD) president Jarrett Barrios. "The greatest fears in coming out come from how your family and your peer group are going to respond. This increasing number of story lines makes it impossible to assume that there are no gay people around you. It makes it uncool to be a bully."

Audiences are learning such lessons with greater frequency this season than any other in TV history. More than two dozen gay teens currently populate the airwaves on cable and network shows in regular and recurring roles, from The CW's *90210* to Showtime's *Shameless*, from MTV's *Skins* to ABC *Family's Pretty Little Liars*. "Just having an LGBT teen presence is a huge change over the last few years," says JB Beeson, deputy executive director of the National Youth Advocacy Coalition. Notes Barrios, "It's important for [gay teens] to know they're not alone, which is what it felt like 30 or 40 years ago."

Teen-skewing networks are leading the way in showing even more facets of gay life. Both ABC Family and MTV have been cited at the top of GLAAD's annual Network Responsibility Index. *Glee*, however, has taken the message to a mass-audience network on a top-rated show—while also giving viewers a character they love.

"I'd be disingenuous if I didn't say at times we were wondering if this was where the audience wants to go," Fox Entertainment president Kevin Reilly admits. "But I've been really heartened to see that they love Kurt."

Networks haven't always been so willing to take such chances on young gay characters. The year of 1994 felt like a watershed: First MTV smashed barriers with the inclusion of 22-year-old gay man Pedro Zamora in the third season of its hit series The *Real World*; then Rickie's plotline played out poignantly on *My So-Called Life*. "It wasn't even a problem with the network," says *My So-Called Life* creator Winnie Holzman (who also included a gay teen character this past summer on ABC Family's *Huge*). "The thing I got the most pushback about was in the pilot, when he puts eyeliner on in the girls' bathroom. I remember I mentioned *The Crying Game*, which had just come out, and Michael Jackson wearing eyeliner [to convince the network]. So they went with it."

It looked like a sign of progress. But with *My So-Called Life*'s cancellation after just one season, major networks weren't exactly rushing to tackle teen drama in any way, much less address the plight of gay teens. Instead, grown-up shows tiptoed into prominent gay depictions in the late '90s—with Ellen DeGeneres's coming-out episode on her sitcom *Ellen* in 1997, followed by the comic spin on adult gay life portrayed on *Will & Grace* starting in 1998—and LGBT teens were left by the wayside.

There wouldn't be another gay teen in prime time until 1999, as youth-targeted programming found a home on The WB and slowly began leading the way in telling coming-out stories that reflected the *Will & Grace* effect. On the network's signature hit *Dawson's Creek*, Jack McPhee (Kerr Smith), a football player and love interest of Joey Potter (Katie Holmes), came out, even kissing a guy on screen, beating *Will & Grace* to the first romantic male kiss ever on American network TV. It was an arc creator Kevin Williamson says the fledgling network cheered from the beginning, thanks to its sensitive handling. "What I was proud of is I felt it was very emotional," Williamson says. "And everyone accepted him. In terms of changing the face of the television landscape, I feel like we did what we could in our own little way."

The WB welcomed another gay character the following year with Alyson Hannigan's Willow Rosenberg on *Buffy the Vampire Slayer*. But once again, such trailblazing did not bear immediate fruit: Aside from a gay brother here or a "confused" guest star there, major networks continued to keep their teen characters locked safely in closets. As Beeson says, "It would always be one character on one episode and never be discussed again. Like one girl would decide she wanted to try a lesbian kiss or something." The latter, in particular, has often done as much harm as good to the cause: "The good part is that characters are showing sexual fluidity on TV," Beeson says. "But on the other hand, it kind of sensationalizes and demeans lesbian relationships. It makes them seem like just a phase."

Fans of soapy Fox drama *The O.C.* will certainly recall Marissa Cooper's (Mischa Barton) "phase," when in 2005 she traded in making angsty eyes at hunky Ryan Atwood (Ben McKenzie) for making out with punky new girl Alex (Olivia Wilde). The arc ran a mere six episodes—something exec producer Stephanie Savage blames, in part, on a jittery network. "We could've had more support in terms of making that a long-term story line," says Savage, now an exec producer on *Gossip Girl*. "There were definitely some questions about how long we were doing this story. And we did have to do some editing to make kisses shorter and pull back on some physicality of the characters."

Savage is not the only producer to note past network resistance. While The WB received kudos for *Dawson's Creek* and *Buffy*, Murphy says he had trouble selling even peripheral gay-themed story lines to the network for his cult favorite *Popular* (1999–2001), which included a character with a lesbian mom and an episode about gay bashing. "I remember I did have trouble, and [the network] would say things like 'Could you make it a little less gay?'" Murphy says. "Being that I was a gay person, I thought that was weird."

Today's wave of TV-industry acceptance began on the outskirts of teen-oriented cable—namely, on the relentlessly pioneering Degrassi, a Canadian drama that airs on TeenNick (formerly The N) in the States. Since 2003, Degrassi has been responsible for no less than eight prominent lesbian, gay, bisexual, or, yes, transgender characters in its ever-rotating cast. These days, football player Riley (Argiris Karras) is coming out, while

Adam (played by Jordan Todosey, a 15-year-old girl) is struggling to explain to friends that he's female-to-male transgender. "This is something that comes with the times," co-creator Linda Schuyler says. "People are realizing that the lines of sexuality are not just drawn between gay guys and lesbian girls, but there is a sliding scale of sexuality, and that's something new. We thought, 'We gotta start portraying these characters.'"

With Degrassi leading the charge, times have certainly changed—in a way that seems to have more staying power than previous advances. Momentum has built to an unprecedented variety of three-dimensional characters over the past few years that is just beginning to reflect the many real faces of gay teenage America: some effeminate, some not; some closeted, some unapologetic; some accepted, some marginalized; and many with more going for them as characters than just their sexual orientation. Finally, gay teens are coming close to being depicted on screen with a diversity that can match heterosexuals of the same age.

Thanks to *Glee* and its 14.1 million viewers, gay teen characters are now reaching more eyes than ever, as Kurt's run-in with bullying has dominated the first half of the musical's second season. It's also led to the addition of wildly popular mentor/love interest Blaine. "They're kind of like the Joanie and Chachi of our generation," Colfer says. True enough, audiences are pulling for the couple just as they have for such iconically sweet teen pairings of the past. "When we made the announcement that Kurt was getting a boyfriend, people went bats—, they were so excited," Colfer adds. "And then you add Darren, who is incredibly talented, and people are just jumping up and down." For Criss, the real sign of progress is that the pairing has caused no controversy whatsoever. No protests. No outcry. No loss of corporate sponsors. (In fact, General Motors will be sponsoring *Glee*'s post-Super Bowl extravaganza on Feb. 6.) Even their suggestive yuletide duet caused far less commotion than, say, some of their *Glee* costars posing provocatively (and heterosexually) in *GQ* magazine. "It's become less and less about the obvious frame of it, the young teen gay couple on the popular network show," says Criss. "It's more about just a favorite character having a love interest, which is awesome."

While the networks have come a long way recently, many in the industry feel there is still work to be done in portraying young gay characters and the often overlooked slights they face on a daily basis. "Even if it's not someone being antigay against a person," GLAAD's Barrios says, "the language we use—'That's so gay'—is still hurtful." And though gay characters have become a staple on dramas, particularly on teen networks, they're entirely absent from mainstream sitcoms and tween networks like Disney Channel and Nickelodeon. When asked about its lack of gay teen characters, Disney Channel responded with the following statement: "We recognize our responsibility to present age-appropriate programming for millions of kids age 6–14 around the world, and we aim to tell great stories with an array of relatable characters and themes that address the needs and aspirations of our young viewers, augment Disney Channel's themes of communication and optimism, and fulfill our brand promise to encourage kids to 'express yourself,' 'believe in yourself,' and 'celebrate your family.'"

Even on the dramas where gay teens are prominent, "I'd like to see even more empowered characters," the National Youth Advocacy Coalition's Beeson says. "It's so often about characters struggling to come out or struggling with their identity. But there actually are young people who are out and have a lot going for them, instead of being bullied all the time or their parents not accepting them." Adds Barrios, "There are still barriers to be broken, like the barrier Degrassi broke with regard to the first trans teen. That shows us that even with all this progress, there are still plenty of new issues to be found in there."

The good news: Young gay characters are on a momentous roll, after years of stops and starts. In fact, prime time's original gay teen, Wilson Cruz, who works with GLSEN, believes we're finally on track—if awfully slow in getting there. "I think we've now reached the natural progression of what should've happened right after *My So-Called Life*," he says. "Do we have farther to go? Absolutely. But better late than never."

DECODING THE TEXTS

1. *The Onion* is a very well-known satirical online newspaper around college campuses, and this "Letter D" piece is an excellent example of satire or parody. What makes this piece satirical or a parody? Is there a special tone, organization, or structure that makes this piece work?

2. What does Harris mean when he uses the term "Official Entertainment Remorse Machine" to describe how celebrities handle significant lapses in their behavior? What other instances of the Official Entertainment Remorse Machine have you seen recently?

3. According to Armstrong and her sources, why is Kurt Hummel from *Glee* a historical figure in LGBT history?

4. How would you describe the tone of the three essays that make up this case study? How does tone relate to how you read the essays?

CONNECTING TO YOUR CULTURE

1. Are there any characters in your real life who are underrepresented on television? If so, why do you think television studios do not find it necessary to depict these characters on the screen?

2. Think of the people who are your closest friends. For what reason would they want to boycott something or someone? Would you agree with the boycott? Would you take an active or inactive part? Why?

3. Harris talks about the lack of true remorse that celebrities have when they have lapses in their behavior; however, the idea of the remorse machine can also be transferred into our own noncelebrity lives as well. How have you or someone close to you acted when you, he, or she was remorseful for bad behavior? Is there a certain script or set of conventions you follow with your family? With your friends? With your peers at school or colleagues at work?

READING SELECTIONS:
THE 2010s

CONSIDERING IDEAS

1. How do you watch your favorite television series? Do you watch it as it is broadcast on a network? Or do you watch it later on a DVR or cable On Demand? Or do you use a medium other than a television to watch it, such as Hulu or Netflix on a laptop or iPad?

2. If you watch television shows other than on a television, why do you use the other medium? Is it to save time? Is it to skip commercials?

AUTHOR BIO

Joanne Ostrow is a television critic for The Denver Post, *where she has a column titled "Ostrow Off the Record." Her all-time favorite television series are* My So-Called Life, The Wire, The Simpsons, Mad Men, Freaks & Geeks, *and* The Sopranos. *She can be reached through Twitter at ostrowDP or through email at jostrow@denverpost.com. "Dropping TV Service" was published on* denverpost.com *on June 9, 2011.*

DROPPING TV SERVICE IN FAVOR OF WATCHING WEB CONTENT GAINS POPULARITY

Joanne Ostrow

If you have more patience than money, you may want to cut the cord.

If you have the technical know-how to find your favorite movies and TV shows somewhere other than on your television set, it may be time to cut the cord.

And if you are philosophically opposed to sitting through commercials, it just may be time to get out those scissors.

Cord-cutting—quitting cable or satellite TV in favor of online video sources—has become a popular move for people who want more control over their television watching.

Believers say it's the dawn of a new era of more personalized entertainment choices; skeptics say it's more about saving money in a down economy. Naysayers say the hype outstrips the facts—TV remains extremely popular.

But this is no hype: In 2010, approximately 1 million U.S. households cut the cord. By the end of this year, 2.07 million households are expected to have dropped cable during the past four years, according to the Convergence Consulting Group, a company that reports to the entertainment industry.

More people are turning to free Internet video sites such as YouTube (now 2 billion views a day and counting) and Hulu, or to subscription services like Netflix, which streams video instantly to computer screens and can be rigged to play on large flat-screen TVs.

Rather than pay upward of $75 a month for cable, they spend $7.99 a month for Netflix and Hulu, or 99 cents to $2.99 per selection on iTunes or Amazon. And the online services are making their move to capture these wandering customers: Netflix is producing original content; YouTube just began offering a made-for-Internet movie.

Some cord-cutting is attributable simply to challenged incomes: "Cord cutting is concentrated at the low end of the market, and is much more frequently a return to free broadcast TV than it is to Internet video," says a recent report from another consultant, Bernstein Research.

But at the higher end of the market, folks are increasingly buying gizmos that deliver online content to the big screen. A number have popped up in recent years, though they can be pricey: GoogleTV is $300. Apple TV is $99. Roku is $100.

According to the latest Nielsen Co. report, time spent viewing video on computers at home and work increased by 45 percent over the previous year.

"Premium full-length content is where the viewers are heading," Nielsen concluded.

That's likely why Google thought it was worth $1.65 billion to buy YouTube recently.

"I HAVEN'T LOOKED BACK!"

Is it a phase, or the end of television as we know it?
The buzz favors those who've cut the cord and are happy to talk about it.

"I cut cable from my apartment in 2009 and haven't looked back!" Sara Buettner of Broomfield said in an e-mail. "I watch whole seasons of shows on Netflix or watch current episodes on Hulu. It's like I'm behind the times with everyone else though—I'm the last to know about viral videos, celebrity scandals, risque ads or anything else 'exciting' that happens in pop culture."

Luckily, she said, she couldn't care less. The budget-conscious are raving too.

"I pay less than $17 a month for television entertainment; it's like someone trying to sell me a car when I have an EcoPass. I get every bit of telly that I need, and I've got the patience to wait for it. That said, I do watch one show as new episodes are released—'Glee'—but I watch it on Fox's website," said April Gosling of Denver.

What are people watching on their computers? Television.

According to eMarketer, more than one-third of online adults in the U.S., or nearly 60 million people, routinely watch full-length television shows online.

While television remains by far the most popular device for viewing content (Consumer Electronics Association research finds nine in 10 households view content on a TV), half of U.S. households are also watching on computers. Further down the list are car video, cellphones-smartphones and MP3 players.

A PERSONAL DECISION

Still, there are good reasons to keep the cord intact, and that makes the decision on how to watch TV a very personal one. Sports programming and certain popular cable shows, such as "MythBusters" or award-winning HBO series, won't show up on the Internet for months after they play on their primary outlet. Local news, local chat and infomercial offerings—none of that is handy online.

"We watch the majority of our TV using Netflix, Hulu and borrowing DVDs from the Denver Public Library," said Thomas Spahr. "I really enjoy the change because we are far less likely to turn on the television to veg out."

But he acknowledges a trade-off.

"The one thing I do miss is watching the Rockies, but radio works just fine, and there are plenty of great bars around my home in the Highlands.

"It's a very small sacrifice to make in favor of the extra $1,100-ish a year I will have in my pocket once I break up with Comcast."

And what about social bonding? Cutting the cord can mean abandoning the social aspect of TV viewing, the connections made in watercooler discussions of current programs.

Though that can be a good thing too. "We cut off our cable almost four years ago because we had the TV on way too much, and our then- infant son was becoming too attracted to it," wrote Julie Peasley of Denver. "We now allow our almost 5- year-old to watch TV, but it's still Netflix or DVDs rented from the library."

MADE-FOR-WEB CONTENT

As a younger generation forsakes the cord, newer technology companies see a chance to meet and keep them on the Web.

Internet businesses are flirting with becoming programmers too.

"Girl Walks Into a Bar" is the first motion picture (with big-name stars) produced solely for Internet distribution—playing, for free, on YouTube.

Due in 2012 is "House of Cards," starring Kevin Spacey, Netflix's entry into the content-producing field. The aim is to be more than a pipeline into people's homes; Netflix also wants a piece of what's flowing through the pipe.

The latest push in this direction: Google is investing $100 million to create programming that will air on 20 new channels on YouTube. The content will be low-cost and Web-only. The YouTube goal is a kind of content that lives somewhere between cat-flushing-toilet videos and network TV shows; that is, low-cost programming that avoids the rough-edges of user-generated content but isn't a pricey, polished TV show.

Will the cord-cutters ultimately reshape the business? Clearly, we're in a time of turmoil and experimentation in the techno sphere of our lives.

For now, connected devices seem to require more effort and know-how than the old "vegging-out" experience of the tube. And, for the majority of viewers, that may be the determining factor.

Source: *"Dropping TV Service in Favor of Watching Web Content Gains Popularity" by Joanne Ostrow. Copyright* The Denver Post. *Used with permission.*

DECODING THE TEXT

1. What are some of the reasons Ostrow suggests you should "cut the cord" to your television and watch your shows on another medium?

2. Ostrow gives a quotation from one of her sources who says that she is missing out on pop culture because she has cut the cord to her television. What is she missing? And would this be a good enough argument for you to continue watching television shows on a television set?

3. What are some of the reasons Ostrow gives for not cutting the cord to your television yet? Do you agree with these reasons? Why or why not?

CONNECTING TO YOUR CULTURE

1. How often do you watch programs on your television? Compare your answer with your classmates' answers.

2. If you're not watching shows on your television, what type of medium and technology do you use instead?

3. If you only watch programs on your television, what has stopped you from moving your viewing to other media or technology?

CONSIDERING IDEAS

1. Do you know anyone who holds onto their memories by holding onto a lot of stuff?

2. How much stuff do you keep in your house to remind you of people or events from your life? Where do you store it? How often do you look at it?

3. Have you ever seen *Hoarders* or *Hoarding: Buried Alive*? If not, view a few episodes or clips of episodes on Hulu, Amazon, or YouTube, and discuss with your classmates what your reaction is to these shows.

AUTHOR BIO

Carina Chocano is a freelance writer whose work has frequently appeared in Salon, The New York Times Magazine, The New York Times, The New Yorker, The New Republic, The Daily, *and* New York. *Chocano is also a former* Los Angeles Times *film and TV critic and a former TV critic for* Entertainment Weekly. *She can be reached through Twitter at Carina_Chocano. This essay was published in* The New York Times Magazine *on June 17, 2011.*

UNDERNEATH EVERY HOARDER IS A NORMAL PERSON WAITING TO BE DUG OUT

Carina Chocano

In 1947, Erich Fromm, a humanist, psychoanalyst and philosopher, developed a theory of character that divided people into five "orientations," mostly determined by their relationship to stuff. He characterized four of these—the receptive, exploitive, hoarding and marketing orientations—as part of the "having" mode, which is focused on consuming, obtaining and possessing. (The fifth orientation was "productive," which focuses on experience and human connection.) Fromm specifically linked the hoarding orientation to the Protestant work ethic and the American merchant middle class and argued that this orientation is characterized by, among other things, being "constipated and squinty."

You have to wonder what Fromm would make of A&E's "Hoarders" or TLC's "Hoarding: Buried Alive" or Animal Planet's "Confessions: Animal Hoarding" or any of the other reality shows on which discreet cameras follow psychologists, professional organizers and specialized cleaning crews into the terrifying homes of people possessed by an uncontrollable need to buy, collect or keep every old magazine, novelty bunny purse, errant pen cap, fast-food wrapper, thrift-store find, broken lamp, stray cat, marked-down sweat pants, newspaper clipping, commemorative snow globe and/or petrified dog turd that has ever crossed their threshold.

The compulsion on display wouldn't have been totally alien to Fromm, because 1947 also happened to be the year the Collyer brothers, those legendary proto-hoarders, were found dead in their Harlem brownstone, buried under 120 tons of waste. But the public fascination with the Collyers' story was predicated at least in part on the fact that their predicament was exotic and rare. Even the most jaded 1947 tabloid reader would no doubt be shocked to learn that one day there would be enough hoarders living among us to keep three or more reality shows in original episodes week after week.

It would have been just as unthinkable to them, no doubt, as the idea that one day our economy would not only consume more than it produced but also rely on consumption and credit to drive it; that the resultant debt, combined with a government-sanctioned stint of willful blindness, would bring us to the brink of world financial collapse; and in the dark, queasy, anxious aftermath of all of this, that television shows about compulsive hoarders would suddenly place a stranglehold on our collective fascination. This, it seems, would have been harder to predict.

It's the self-imposed squalor that draws you in at first—the abject horror of it. Piles of trash so high you can touch the ceiling from their summits. Desiccated rat carcasses buried under years' worth of newspapers. Rooms filled with enough handbags, shoes and clothes to stock a good-size store. Inaccessible beds, stoves and refrigerators. Fetid bathrooms. What kind of person lives like this?

Initially, at least, we watch these shows for the same reasons we troll Web sites like Awful Plastic Surgery— to marvel at the human capacity for self-destruction, which can be so creative, so wildly inventive, so blind. But the popularity of hoarding shows—and the rip-offs, spinoffs and homages they've inspired ("Storage Wars," in which treasure hunters bid on the unknown contents of abandoned storage containers, for instance, and "Extreme Couponing," which is basically "Hoarders" for neat freaks)—suggests that there's something else here that hooks us: the idea that our relationship to our stuff has the potential to distort and derail us.

This fear has always been with us. Plato and Aristotle wrote about hoarding money. Dante chastised hoarders; Dickens mocked them. The Maysles brothers abandoned their documentary about Jackie Kennedy upon meeting her flamboyant, reclusive cousins Big Edie Bouvier and Little Edie Beale. The filmmakers understood that the Beales, with their feral cats and their ancient playbills, were infinitely more interesting than the self-possessed Jackie, who famously displayed such mastery over her stuff, marshaling it in service of her image.

It's a philosophical question, of course. To resolve the constant tension between the spiritual and the material would be to learn how to live. You have to be soulless not to grapple with it once in a while, especially in a society like ours, where after an unthinkable national tragedy, our leaders instruct us to shop.

For a while, starting around the beginning of the aughts, the same networks that now take us into the homes of people who treasure their expired tuna cans more than they do their children specialized instead in a certain type of shopping and makeover show. The format rarely varied. Various style "experts" would go into the homes and closets of "regular people" and judge their contents. The participants would stand by, sometimes sadly, sometimes defensively, and allow themselves to be shamed into facing what bad shoppers they were, what subpar consumers, how they failed to stay on trend or dress appropriately for their age, rank or station. Participants were shamed into hauling the contents of those closets and living rooms out to trash bins and then treated to shopping sprees in which, say, $1,000 had to be spent in 15 minutes or else be forfeited. Somehow, the dissonance between the mindless shopping frenzy and the thoughtful remaking of the image— how could years of buying the wrong thing be helped by racing through a discount store throwing whatever you could grab into your cart?—was never addressed. The goal is to fill the space.

"Hoarders" made its premiere in August 2009 (its fourth season starts this week) and "Hoarding: Buried Alive" followed not long after. Whether consciously or not, these shows present the other side of excessive materialism. The gleeful shopper barreling through the racks at Marshalls or Macy's, using her newfound "skills" to acquire a better wardrobe, has been replaced by the sheepish weirdo who spends six hours a day at her favorite consignment store and hasn't seen her floor in a decade. Either way, a void is suggested.

The show "Hoarders" reportedly started out on a lighter note, more along the lines of Style's "Clean House," with its sassy host and its fun-times garage sales. It evolved into the reality horror show it is today when it became clear to producers what they were dealing with—namely, the mentally ill. So the networks reoriented the shows to focus on the rescue. They come not to gawk at the hoarders but to help them. They explain that the looming piles of junk are merely the physical manifestation of psychic clutter. It's this promise of healing that makes it O.K. to embark on a horrifying tour into the helplessness of others: the promise that underneath every hoarder is a normal person waiting to be dug out.

Throughout history, compulsive hoarding has been regarded as a sin, an unsavory character trait (a form of miserliness), a sociological consequence of capitalism, an instinctual nesting behavior and a form of obsessive-compulsive disorder driven by anxiety. It wasn't until the beginning of the 20th century that psychologists began to see the drive to acquire as an integral part of identity formation. (Jean-Paul Sartre also believed that the self does not distinguish between what is "me" and what is "mine"), and it wasn't until the 1990s that studies on compulsive hoarding were conducted. The first unexpected finding for the psychologist Randy Frost and Gail Steketee, dean of the School of Social Work at Boston University, was that the problem was much more prevalent than was thought. Their research lead to the classification of compulsive hoarding as its own syndrome (a disorder disorder!), now on its way to a likely inclusion in the pantheon of contemporary mental infirmities, the DSM-V.

It's now known that hoarders have trouble with impulse control. Like compulsive gamblers, they are driven by what Frost calls the allure of opportunity. There's a romance in trash that fits with this lottery or prospecting mentality. You see it at work in "Storage Wars," as people bid on unknown objects. A kind of magical thinking takes hold. The bidders aren't looking for anything in particular. They're not dealers of antiques or art or rare toys who are hunting for specialized treasures. They're not applying their expertise in mysterious curios. What appeals is the idea that something—anything—of value lurks beneath the surface, a surface that looks to everybody else like a giant pile of junk.

Frost and Steketee also found that hoarders were not driven by anxiety to acquire or collect items but by positive emotions. Anxiety enters the picture only when they try to throw anything away. Hoarders see things in things that other people don't. They find value, comfort, solace, a buffer against loss, accumulated history in their stuff. Things become externalized parts of themselves—their memory, their plans, their feelings. To discard objects intended for future use (a project, a plan, a projection) feels like dashing hopes, losing opportunities, squandering potential. They can't let go of anything. They are at a literal impasse. We judge them, but we're like them too. A New York playwright recently staged a piece about his real-life decision to abandon his career in the theater that involved giving away all his theater books to the audience. One reviewer complained that he felt as if he'd been asked to witness a suicide.

There's something particularly disturbing, especially for city dwellers who live in small spaces, about seeing all this square footage filled to the ceiling with trash. With their creepy music and their sudden reveals and their own sensational lexicon, hoarding shows represent the "home"—the ultimate fetish object of the first part of the millennium—as a nightmare space in which people are literally crushed or crowded out by their stuff. The junk in the house is referred to as "the hoard." A packed house is "hoarded out."

It's the flip side of the American dream, and there's something particularly depraved about it: the terror of pointless excess, the middle-class home as trap. Or if what gets you is information overload, there's a connection to that as well. Hoarding, often co-morbid with A.D.H.D., can be a symptom of an inability to process information. You get the picture. Hoarding shows are themselves hoarded out with metaphors for our all of our modern predicaments. Watching the televised hoarders gingerly scale the hostile terrain of their modest rooms, with the precipitous heights and narrow passes, like a dazed herd of wayward Alpine goats, it's hard not to get anxious and apocalyptic about materialism and junk culture. Maybe that's a good thing. Maybe the shows' popularity hints at a collective longing to sort it all out; at a feeling that there's something underneath it all that's worth digging out and holding on to; at a lingering hope that the experts will be along any minute now to coax us gently into letting go.

DECODING THE TEXT

1. What does Chocano say draws viewers into shows about hoarders?

2. Chocano uses insights and quotations from psychologists in her essay. What do these professional describe as being some of the reasons for hoarding?

3. How and why does Chocano relate hoarding to the American Dream?

CONNECTING TO YOUR CULTURE

1. After you watch a few episodes of one of television's hoarding shows, create a list of qualities that the hoarders have in common. Do you have any of those qualities? How about anyone in your family or any of your friends?

2. Hoarders can be classified in a variety of ways, including those who hoard particular items, those who do not clean, or those who over-organize. After you view some episodes on hoarding or do some research, create a system that classifies different types of hoarding. Share your classification system with your classmates.

CONSIDERING IDEAS

1. Name some television programs that are filmed in your area of the country or depict your area of the country. Do they give accurate representations of what you see around you?

2. If you were to create a television program about your city or state, what would you call it? What characters would have to be part of the program? Where exactly would it be set?

AUTHOR BIO

Andrew Shears *is an assistant professor of geography at the University of Wisconsin-Fox Valley. His work has been published in* International Interactions, Antipode, The Journal of Emergency Management, *and* Seeds of Change *magazine. His artwork was also featured in the textbook* Laboratory Exercises in Applied Physical Geography and Earth Science. *Shears blogs at* www.andrewshears.com/blog.

FIFTY STATES, FIFTY TELEVISION SERIES

Andrew Shears

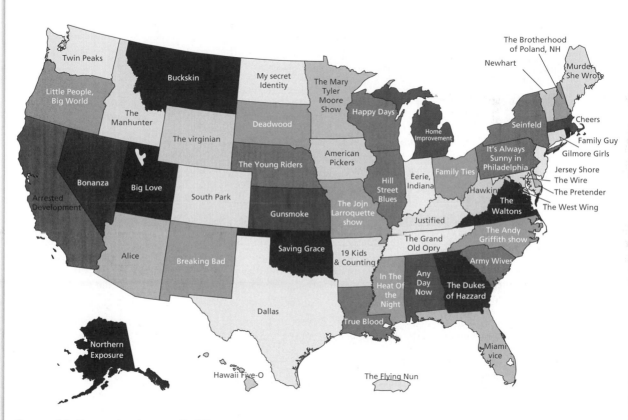

Source: http://www.andrewshears.com/?p=209

DECODING THE TEXT

1. When Shears first published this map visual on his website, he included some commentary for each of the state/television program match-ups he made, basically rationalizing why he chose one program over others. Since that commentary is not provided here, is the visual enough to be an effective text?

2. In his description of this visual essay, Shears calls it a "remixed version" of his original map because he made changes based on feedback he received from his readers. If you were to make one change to the map, what would it be? Why?

CONNECTING TO YOUR CULTURE

1. Check which television program Shears matched with the state you live in, and do some web research on the show. Do you think his choice is an effective representation of the state you live in?

2. Create a similar U.S. map, but place on the map film or book titles that represent your state. Share your map with your classmates, and discuss the different choices made.

CONTEMPLATIONS IN THE POP CULTURE ZONE

1. What exactly do you like about watching television? Consider the television shows that appeal to you the most and compare them to the ones that you do not enjoy. Make a list of reasons you like the shows you do, considering the following topics: the visuals that television provides in comparison to other information forms, the content that television focuses on, the availability of television compared to other media, and the format of television shows themselves, along with their commercials.

2. When we open a magazine or book to read, we have certain expectations about the format, the organization, and the content. What kind of expectations do you have when you turn on a television show (choose one type of show) and read/watch it?

3. Consider all the different ways you watch television. Compare your viewing with your classmates or within a small group. If you had to describe the average viewing methods of an average college student, what would be your guess? Why?

4. Some shows on networks such as PBS or the History Channel are obviously educational, but in what other ways can television be educational? Consider the different genres and subgenres.

COLLABORATIONS IN THE POP CULTURE ZONE

1. Television is not only entertainment, but it is also big business. To keep making money, networks need to keep their viewers, especially during commercial breaks. Are there different types of commercials on regular networks (ABC, CBS, NBC, FOX) than on cable networks (Lifetime, USA, TNT, TBS, FX)? Why or why not? What other ways do television networks use to advertise products?

2. Many television series now offer website content for their shows. Some shows, such as *Conan*, offer special content online that regular viewers who do not go to the website miss out on, and other shows, such as *New Girl* or *So You Think You Can Dance*, provide second screen viewing, with which you can interact in a variety of ways with the show as it is being broadcast. Investigate some of these shows and categorize the type of information that networks are offering online. Whom are they trying to attract with this type of information? Are they successful?

3. Choose a particular time of day and flip through all the channels offered on your network or cable system. Note what programs are playing on each channel and how many of the programs are of interest to you. Compare your lists with others in the class, and answer these questions and others that your group might have.

   • Can you always find something that you want to watch on television? Why or why not?

   • What types of shows are more prevalent at the time of day you chose for flipping through the channels? Why do you think this is so?

   • How much of a difference in availability does having cable make?

4. What is the first television viewing that you can remember? What kind of show was it? How old were you? Has that show influenced your life in any way? Why or why not?

START WRITING ABOUT TELEVISION

Reviews or Review Essays

1. Choose two shows that you believe are completely different in at least one way, and write a review essay that compares and contrasts the two shows. For example, you can compare *The Daily Show with Jon Stewart* and *The Colbert Report*. Consider the content, the audience, the actors or leads, the direction, and the time period of the shows as you structure and expand your essay. Refer to the review essays in both the television and film chapters as models.

2. Choose one of your least favorite television series and take a fresh look at it by pretending to be someone who likes the series. Write a review of the series, taking care to stay within this new persona throughout the essay.

3. Write a review that focuses on how a particular television series bends stereotypical depictions of a particular American subculture (for instance, skateboarders, gay teens, African Americans, pregnant teens, white middle-class working women, intelligent high school students). Refer to the reviews included in both the television and film chapters as models.

4. Watch an awards show (such as the Academy Award, the Golden Globes, the Emmys, the People's Choice Awards), and write a review of the show. Be sure to focus your review so that it is obvious whether you thought it was or was not worth watching, using detailed examples from the show to support your opinions.

Response or Reflection Essays

1. Reflect on which television series depicts or represents you and your life the best. Write an essay that explains how and why this series defines or describes you.

2. Ask your friends and family what they believe the most controversial show(s) are on television. Choose one of these shows and write an essay about why a television viewer might be bothered by the show(s). Give details from the series or particular episodes to support your argument(s). Then, discuss whether the show bothers you or not and why.

3. What is your (least) favorite television series of all time? In an essay, reflect on why this is your (least) favorite, explaining how this program is different from all the other ones you have watched in your lifetime.

4. Review the visual essay in the shape of a U.S. map by Andrew Shears at the end of the chapter. Write an essay in which you agree or disagree that the television show listed for the state you live in actually represents you and your state.

Analysis Essays

1. Videotape or audiotape a five-minute conversation on a sitcom (such as *Modern Family* or *New Girl*) and a five-minute conversation from a type of drama (such as a family drama like *Parenthood* or a mystery/thriller show like any of the *CSI* series). Write out the conversations fully and then look for ways the language on the sitcom differs from the language on the drama. In an essay, analyze the differences and propose an argument about how writers and audiences view these types of programs differently because of the language used.

2. Some television programs incite deep emotions, sometimes to the point where groups or organizations will initiate boycotts. Research an instance of television boycotting and either analyze why the boycott was organized or argue that the boycott was necessary or unnecessary. You can begin your search for boycotts by doing a simple web search using the phrase "television show boycott."

3. Animated television shows often include overblown or stereotypical characters. Choose one animated television character, explain how the character is defined through his or her actions and words, and decide whether the depiction of the character is stereotypical. Consider using images of the character as supporting evidence for your argument.

4. In the following quotation, writer Carl Sagan encapsulates a conundrum that is commonly discussed with regard to violence on television. Do you think that violence on television makes children more violent? Investigate some outside sources and write a nonbiased essay on the different sides of this complicated issue. Consider using visual support within your essay, such as images, graphs, and charts.

> There is a report that says that kids who watch violent TV programs tend to be more violent when they grow up. But did the TV cause the violence, or do violent children preferentially enjoy watching violent programs? (Sagan 203)

Synthesis Essays

1. Just like with films, popular television shows rarely win awards (see the list below). What is it about these popular television shows that those who vote for Emmy Awards are unwilling to notice or reward? Reflect on which type of show—popular or award winning—you watch more often and discuss why this is true.

EMMY

Outstanding Comedy Series

2010	Modern Family
2005	Everybody Loves Raymond
2000	Will & Grace
1995	Frasier
1990	Murphy Brown
1985	The Cosby Show
1980	Taxi
1975	M*A*S*H
1970	My World and Welcome to It

Outstanding Drama Series

2010	Mad Men
2005	Lost
2000	The West Wing
1995	NYPD Blue
1990	L.A. Law
1985	Cagney & Lacey
1980	Lou Grant
1975	Masterpiece Theatre: Upstairs, Downstairs
1970	Marcus Welby, M.D.

Nielsen: Highest Average Rating No. 1

2010	American Idol
2005	American Idol
2000	Who Wants to Be a Millionaire?
1995	Seinfeld
1990	Roseanne
1985	Dynasty
1980	60 Minutes
1975	All in the Family
1970	Rowan and Martin's Laugh-In

Source: © Cengage Learning.

2. *Cocooning* was a term coined in the 1980s for staying at home and watching television instead of going out to see movies or doing some other activity outside the house. Do you consider yourself someone who cocoons at times? If so, describe how you cocoon, when you do it, and why. Investigate the cocooning practices of your family, friends, peers, and colleagues by developing a survey with questions that will help you define cocooning and explain the practices that can be associated with it. You can create your own survey at http://www.surveymonkey.com/. Be sure to include the data you collect in some way in your essay, whether in your introduction, conclusion, or to support arguments in the body of the essay.

3. Write an essay in which you consider and explore the reasons one genre (for instance, children's television, comedy shows, or soap operas) is so popular among college students or another group of viewers.

4. Create a visual essay that uses bracketology, which is based on the final-four system used in sports (see Figure 10.1). Fill in your favorite sixteen TV shows in a particular genre (note that the brackets in Figure 10.1 represent the creator's idea of the best comedy of all time), narrow them down to eight, narrow them down to four, narrow them down to two, and then narrow them down to one, explaining each step of your narrowing process in your essay. This essay requires you to reflect on your reactions and analyze a specific theme or item across many television programs. You can then compare your winner with others in class. Here are some ideas for topics (some adapted from *The Enlightened Bracketologist: The Final Four of Everything*, edited by Mark Reiter and Richard Sandomir):

Bloodiest, smartest, or scariest horror scene ever shown on television
Best one-liners on a television comedy
Smartest presidential character ever depicted on a television show
Most stereotypical character ever
Television shows that make you cry the most
Best new word given to the English language by a television show

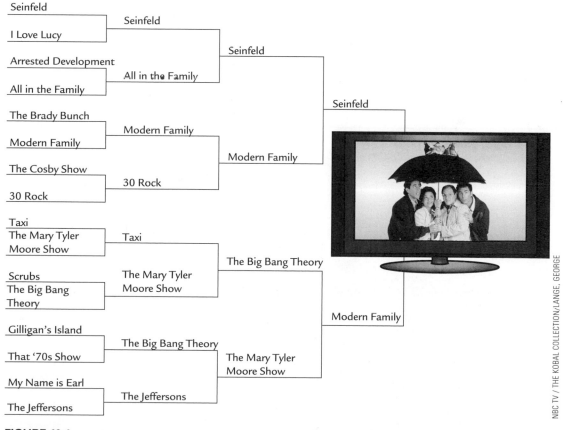

FIGURE 10.1

FOR FURTHER READING

CHAPTER 1

Ashby, LeRoy. *With Amusement for All: A History of Popular Culture since 1830*. Reprint ed. Lexington: Kentucky UP, 2012. Print.

Gravett, Paul. *Graphic Novels: Everything You Need to Know*. New York: Collins Design, 2005. Print.

Grazian, David. *Mix It Up: Popular Culture, Mass Media, and Society*. New York: Norton, 2010. Print.

Jenkins, Henry, ed. *Hop on Pop: The Politics and Pleasures of Popular Culture*. Durham: Duke UP, 2002. Print.

Johnson, Steven. *Everything Bad Is Good for You: How Today's Popular Culture Is Actually Making Us Smarter*. New York: Riverhead Trade, 2006. Print.

Mirzoeff, Nicholas. *An Introduction to Visual Culture*. New York: Routledge, 2000. Print.

Storey, John. *Cultural Theory and Popular Culture: An Introduction*. Athens: U of Georgia P, 2009. Print.

CHAPTER 2

Belton, John, ed. *Movies and Mass Culture*. New Brunswick: Rutgers UP, 1996. Print.

Bright, Brenda Jo, and Liza Bakewell, eds. *Looking High and Low: Art and Cultural Identity*. Tucson: U of Arizona P, 1995. Print.

Browne, Ray B., ed. *Mission Underway: The History of the Popular Culture Association/American Culture Association and the Popular Culture Movement, 1967–2001*. Bowling Green: PCA/APA, 2002. Print.

Davis, Debra. *The Oprah Winfrey Show: Reflections on an American Legacy*. New York: Abrams, 2011. Print.

Fiske, John. *Television Culture*. London: Routledge, 1987. Print.

Freccero, Carla. *Popular Culture: An Introduction*. New York: NYUP, 1999. Print.

Giroux, Henry A. *Disturbing Pleasures: Learning Popular Culture*. New York: Routledge, 1994. Print.

Hebdige, Dick. *Subculture: The Meaning of Style*. London: Routledge, 1981. Print.

Johnson, Stephen. *Everything Bad Is Good for You: How Today's Popular Culture Is Actually Making us Smarter*. New York: Riverhead Trade, 2006. Print.

Sellnow, Deborah D. *The Rhetorical Power of Popular Culture: Considering Mediated Texts*. Thousand Oaks: Sage, 2009. Print.

Storey, John. *An Introduction to Cultural Theory and Popular Culture*. Athens: U of Georgia P, 1998. Print.

———. *Inventing Popular Culture*. Malden: Blackwell, 2003. Print.

CHAPTER 3

Glenn, Cheryl, and Loretta Gray. *The Writer's Harbrace Handbook*. 5th ed. Boston: Wadsworth, 2012. Print.

King, Stephen. *On Writing*. New York: Pocket Books, 2002. Print.

Lamott, Anne. *Bird by Bird: Some Instructions on Writing and Life*. New York: Anchor Books, 1995. Print.

Strunk, William, Jr., E. B. White, and Roger Angell. *The Elements of Style*. 4th ed. Boston: Allyn and Bacon, 1999. Print.

Truss, Lynne. *Eats, Shoots and Leaves: The Zero Tolerance Approach to Punctuation*. New York: Gotham Books, 2006. Print.

Zinsser, William K. *On Writing Well: The Classic Guide to Writing Nonfiction*. New York: Collins, 2006. Print.

CHAPTER 4

Adler, Mortimer J. *How to Read a Book*. New York: Touchstone, 1972. Print.

Buckner, Aimee. *Notebook Connections: Strategies for the Reader's Notebook*. Portland: Stenhouse, 2009. Print.

Frank, Marjorie. *Graphic Organizers for Any Subject: Any Level*. Nashville: Incentive, 2007. Print.

Hennings, Dorothy Grant. *Reading with Meaning: Strategies for College Reading*. New York: Longman, 2004. Print.

Kress, Gunther, and Theo van Leeuwen. *Reading Images: The Grammar of Visual Design*. New York: Routledge, 2006. Print.

Langan, John. *Ten Steps to Improving College Reading Skills*. Philadelphia: Townsend, 2008. Print.

Smith, Brenda D. *The Reader's Handbook: Reading Strategies for College and Everyday Life*. New York: Longman, 2009. Print.

CHAPTER 5

Bogle, Donald. *Blacks in American Films and Television: An Encyclopedia*. New York: Garland, 1988. Print.

Boorstin, Daniel. *The Image: A Guide to Pseudo-Events in America*. 1961. New York: Vintage, 1992. Print.

Cawelti, John. *Adventure, Mystery, and Romance: Formula Stories as Art and Popular Culture*. Chicago: U of Chicago P, 1976. Print.

Cultural Studies Central. Web. <http://www.culturalstudies.net/index.html>.

Dunne, Michael. *Metapop: Self-Referentiality in Contemporary American Popular Culture*. Jackson: UP of Mississippi, 1992. Print.

Ewen, Stuart. *All Consuming Images: The Politics of Style in Contemporary Culture*. New York: Basin, 1988. Print.

Fiske, John. *Understanding Popular Culture*. Boston: Unwin Hyman, 1989. Print.

Gabler, Neal. *Life: The Movie: How Entertainment Conquered Reality*. New York: Knopf, 1998. Print.

Gibaldi, Joseph. *MLA Handbook for Writers of Research Papers*. 7th ed. New York: Mod. Lang. Assoc., 2009. Print.

Hague, Angela, and David Lavery, eds. *Teleparody: Predicting/Preventing the TV Discourse of Tomorrow*. New York: Wallflower Press, 2002. Print.

Harris, Joseph, Jay Rosen, and Gary Calpas. *Media Journal: Reading and Writing about Popular Culture*. 2nd ed. New York: Longman, 1998. Print.

Hebdige, Dick. *Subculture: The Meaning of Style*. New York: Routledge, 1979. Print.

Jenkins, Henry. *Textual Poachers: Television Fans and Participatory Culture*. New York: Routledge, 1992. Print.

Johnson, Steven. *Everything Bad Is Good for You: How Today's Popular Culture Is Actually Making Us Smarter*. New York: Penguin, 2005. Print.

Kaplan, E. Ann. *Rocking around the Clock: Music Television, Postmodernism, and Consumer Culture*. New York: Methuen, 1987. Print.

Marc, David. *Comic Visions: Television Comedy and American Culture*. Malden: Blackwell, 1997. Print.

McLuhan, Marshall, and Quentin Fiore. *The Medium Is the Message: An Inventory of Effects*. 1967. New York: Genko, 2005. Print.

Modleski, Tania. *Loving with a Vengeance: Mass-Produced Fantasies for Women*. Hamden: Shoestring, 1982. Print.

———. *Studies in Entertainment: Critical Approaches to Mass Culture*. Bloomington: Indiana UP, 1986. Print.

Mukerju, Chandra, and Michael Schudson, eds. *Rethinking Popular Culture: Contemporary Perspectives in Cultural Studies*. Berkeley: U of California P, 1991. Print.

Nye, Russell. *The Unembarrassed Muse: The Popular Arts in America*. New York: Dial Press, 1970. Print.

Publication Manual of the American Psychological Association. 6th ed. Washington: APA, 2009. Print.

Radner, Hilary. *Shopping Around: Feminine Culture and the Pursuit of Pleasure*. New York: Routledge, 1995. Print.

Research Channel. Web. <http://www.researchchannel.org>.

Simon, Richard Keller. *Trash Culture: Popular Culture and the Great Tradition*. Berkeley: U of California P, 1999. Print.

Stark, Steven D. *Glued to the Set: The 60 Television Shows and Events That Made Us Who We Are Today.* New York: Free, 1997. Print.

University of Chicago Press. *Chicago Manual of Style.* 16th ed. Chicago: U of Chicago P, 2010. Print.

Wolf, Naomi. *The Beauty Myth: How Images of Beauty Are Used against Women.* New York: Anchor, 1992. Print.

CHAPTER 6

Adbusters. Web. <http://www.adbusters.org>.

Advertising Age. Web. <http://www.adage.com>.

The Advertising Age Encyclopedia of Advertising. Ed. John McDonough and Karen Egolf. New York: Routledge, 2002. Print.

Cortese, Anthony J. *Provocateur: Images of Women and Minorities in Advertising.* 3rd ed. Lanham: Rowman, 2007. Print.

Cronin, Anne M. *Advertising Myths: The Strange Half-lives of Images and Commodities.* London: Routledge, 2004. Print.

Encyclopedia of Major Marketing Campaigns. Ed. Thomas Riggs. Detroit: Gale, 2000. Print.

Encyclopedia of Major Marketing Campaigns. Vol. 2. Ed. Thomas Riggs. Detroit: Gale, 2006. Print.

Freccero, Carla. *Popular Culture: An Introduction.* New York: NYUP, 1999. Print.

Gender, Race, and Class in Media: A Critical Reader. 3rd ed. Ed. Gail Dines and Jean M. Humez. Thousand Oaks: SAGE, 2010. Print.

Kilbourne, Jean. *Killing Us Softly.* 1, 2, and 3. Northampton Media Educ., 1979, 1987, 2000. Video Series.

Mierau, Christina. *Accept No Substitutes: The History of American Advertising.* Minneapolis: Lerner, 2000. Print.

Sports, Culture and Advertising: Identities, Commodities and the Politics of Representation. Ed. Steven Jackson. New York: Routledge, 2004. Print.

Twitchell, James B. *Twenty Ads That Shook the World: The Century's Most Groundbreaking Advertising and How It Changed Us All.* New York: Three Rivers, 2000. Print.

Zeisler, Andi. *Feminism and Pop Culture: Seal Studies.* Berkeley: Seal, 2008. Print.

CHAPTER 7

Cavallero, Jonathan J. "Gangsters, Fessos, Tricksters, and Sopranos: The Historical Roots of Italian American Stereotype Anxiety." *JPF&T: Journal of Popular Film and Television* 32 (2004): 50–63. Print.

Clover, Carol J. *Men, Women, and Chain Saws: Gender in the Modern Horror Film.* Princeton: Princeton UP, 1992. Print.

Corrigan, Timothy. *Short Guide to Writing about Film.* New York: Longman, 2011. Print.

Dick, Bernard F. *Anatomy of Film.* 5th ed. Boston: Bedford/St. Martin's, 2005. Print.

Documentary Films. Web. <http://www.documentaryfilms.net>.

Ebert, Roger. *The Great Movies.* New York: Three Rivers, 2003. Print.

Jenkins, Henry. *Confessions of an Aca-Fan: The Official Weblog of Henry Jenkins.* Web. <http://www.henryjenkins.org>.

———. *Convergence Culture: Where Old and New Media Collide.* New York: NYUP, 2006. Print.

Kaveney, Roz. *Teen Dreams: Reading Teen Films and Television from 'Heathers' to 'Veronica Mars'.* London: Tauris, 2006. Print.

Lee, Spike. *Spike Lee's Gotta Have It: Inside Guerrilla Filmmaking.* New York: Fireside, 1988. Print.

Maltin, Leonard. *The Disney Films.* 4th ed. New York: Disney, 2000. Print.

———. *Leonard Maltin's 151 Best Movies You've Never Seen.* New York: Harper, 2010. Print.

Moscowitz, John E. *Critical Approaches to Writing about Film.* 2nd ed. Boston: Pearson, 2006. Print.

Variety. Web. <http://www.variety.com>.

CHAPTER 8

Baldwin, Dianna, and Julia Achterberg, eds. *Women and Second Life: Essays on Virtual Identity, Work, and Play*. Jefferson: McFarland, 2013. Print.

Browning, Dominique, ed. *House of Worship: Sacred Spaces in America*. New York: Assouline, 2006. Print.

Calmes, Anne M., ed. *Community Association Leadership: A Guide for Volunteers*. Alexandria: CAI, 1997. Print.

Caudron, Shari. *Who Are You People? A Personal Journey into the Heart of Fanatical Passion in America*. Fort Lee: Barricade, 2006. Print.

Gray, Jonathan, and Cornel Sandvoss. *Fandom: Identities and Communities in a Mediated World*. New York: NYUP, 2007. Print.

Hills, Matthew. *Fan Cultures*. London: Routledge, 2002. Print.

Jenkins, Henry. *Fans, Bloggers, and Gamers: Media Consumers in a Digital Age*. New York: NYUP, 2006. Print.

Low, Setha M., and Denise Lawrence-Zuaniga. *The Anthropology of Space and Place: Locating Culture*. Boston: Blackwell, 2003. Print.

McGonigal, Jane. *Reality Is Broken: Why Games Make Us Better and How They Can Change the World*. New York: Penguin, 2011. Print.

Scott, John G. *Social Network Analysis*. London, Sage, 2012. Print.

Zachary, Lois J. *Creating a Mentoring Culture: An Organization's Guide*. San Francisco: Jossey, 2005. Print.

CHAPTER 9

Azerrad, Michael. *Our Band Could Be Your Life: Scenes from the American Indie Underground 1981–1991*. London: Little, 2001. Print.

Blecha, Peter. *Taboo Tunes: A History of Banned Bands and Censored Songs*. Montclair: Backbeat, 2004. Print.

Escott, Collin. *Good Rockin' Tonight: Sun Records and the Birth of Rock 'n' Roll*. New York: St. Martin's, 1992. Print.

Jackson, Blair. *Garcia: An American Life*. Boston: Penguin, 2000. Print.

MacDonald, Ian. *Revolution in the Head: The Beatles' Records and the Sixties*. New York: Holt, 1995. Print.

Marks, Craig, and Rob Tannenbaum. *I Want My MTV: The Uncensored Story of the Music Video Revolution*. New York: Dutton, 2011. Print.

McNeil, Legs. *Please Kill Me: The Uncensored Oral History of Punk*. London: Grove, 2006. Print.

Palmer, Robert. *Deep Blues: A Musical and Cultural History of the Mississippi Delta*. New York: Penguin, 1982. Print.

Smith, Richard D. *Can't You Hear Me Callin': The Life of Bill Monroe, Father of Bluegrass*. London: Little, 2000. Print.

Werner, Craig. *A Change Is Gonna Come: Music, Race, and the Soul of America*. New York: Penguin, 1999. Print.

CHAPTER 10

Allen, Robert C., and Annette Hill, eds. *The Television Studies Reader*. London: Routledge, 2004. Print.

Castlemon, Harry, and Walter J. Padrazik. *Watching TV: Six Decades of American Television*. Syracuse Syracuse UP, 2010. Print.

Edgerton, Gary R., and Brian G. Rose, eds. *Thinking Outside the Box: A Contemporary Television Genre Reader*. Lexington: UP of Kentucky, 2005. Print.

Fiske, John. *Television Culture*. London: Methuen, 1987. Print.

Jenkins, Henry. *Textual Poachers: Television Fans and Participatory Culture*. New York: Routledge, 1992. Print.

Joyrich, Lynne. *Re-Viewing Reception: Television, Gender, and Postmodern Culture*. Bloomington: Indiana UP, 1996. Print.

McNeil, Alex. *Total Television: The Comprehensive Guide to Programming from 1948 to the Present.* 4th ed. New York: Penguin, 1996. Print.

Miller, Toby, ed. *Television Studies.* London: BFI, 2002. Print.

Modleski, Tania. *Loving with a Vengeance: Mass Produced Fantasies for Women.* Hamden: Archon, 1982. Print.

The Museum of Broadcast Communications. Web. <http://www.museum.tv>.

Simon, Ron, Robert J. Thompson, Louise Spence, and Jane Feuer. *Worlds Without End: The Art and History of the Soap Opera.* New York: Abrams, 1997. Print.

Spigel, Lynn. *Make Room for TV: Television and the Family Ideal in Postwar America.* Chicago: U of Chicago P, 1992. Print.

INDEX